TURNER AT PETWORTH

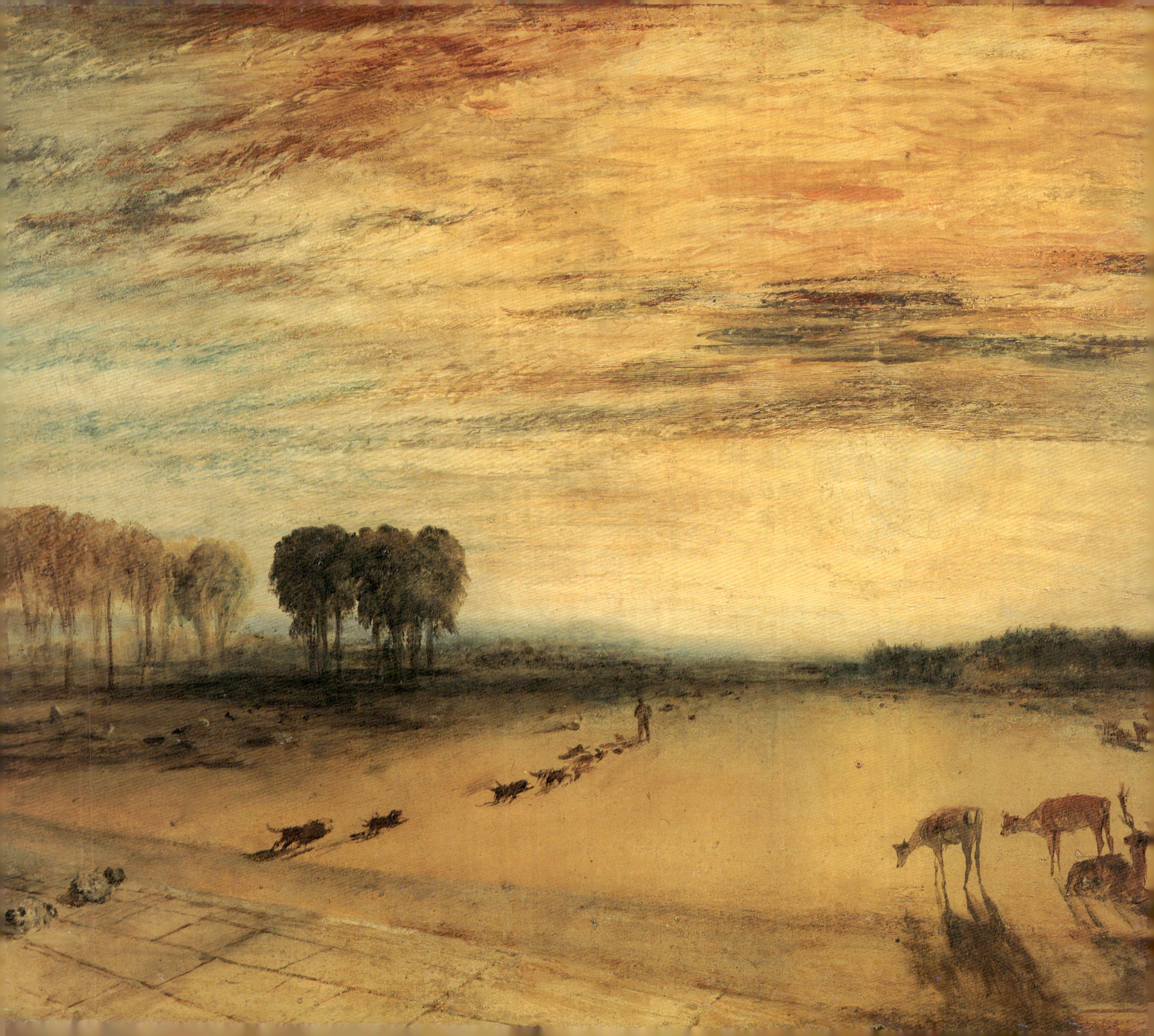

Turner at Petworth

PAINTER & PATRON

Martin Butlin   Mollie Luther   Ian Warrell

The Tate Gallery

frontispiece
Petworth Park: Tillington Church in the Distance 1827 (detail)

ISBN 1 85437 004 9 (cloth)
Published by order of the Trustees 1989

Designed by Caroline Johnston
Published by Tate Gallery Publications,
Millbank, London SW1P 4RG
Typeset by Gloucester Typesetting Services in
'Monotype' Bulmer 11pt 2pt leaded
Printed in Great Britain by Westerham Press Ltd on 150gsm Parilux
and 150gsm Cartridge specially made by Stoneywood Paper Mill

The production of this book has been supported by
UBS Phillips & Drew

Contents

Preface

This book celebrates the new collaboration between the National Trust and the Tate Gallery over the world-famous collection of Turner's paintings at Petworth and his association with that house and the patronage of the third Earl of Egremont. In 1984 the ownership of the Turners at Petworth was transferred from H.M. Treasury to the Tate Gallery; the pictures however remain at Petworth House as part of the Egremont Collection, administered by the National Trust.

In this book we have brought these works together with the oil paintings associated with Petworth now in the Turner Collection housed in the Clore Gallery at the Tate Gallery in London, and also, published for the first time in their entirety, the full series of gouaches on blue paper of scenes at or associated with Petworth. Recent scholarship has shown that certain works previously associated with Petworth are in fact scenes at East Cowes Castle, the home of the architect John Nash on the Isle of Wight, and the attribution of certain other works as between the two houses is still uncertain. For this reason our selection of works to be illustrated here is a catholic one and includes a number of works that definitely or potentially should rather be associated with East Cowes Castle.

This publication grows from the work of three colleagues at the Tate Gallery. I should like to thank Martin Butlin, Mollie Luther and Ian Warrell for the research which they have undertaken and all those whose contributions are acknowledged in detail elsewhere. The Tate Gallery is especially grateful for the encouragement and cooperation which it has received over this publication from Lord Egremont and the National Trust, while the book itself could not have been produced without the generous sponsorship of UBS Phillips & Drew.

Nicholas Serota *Director*

Acknowledgements

The first chapter of this book is by Mollie Luther, who also assembled most of the written material on which the main text of this book is based. Chapter 4, the two appendices and the notes on the plates, together with most of the new research that has gone into the book, is the work of Ian Warrell. Chapters 2, 3, 5 and 6 are by myself. In addition we have all consulted with each other and made suggestions on each other's contributions.

The main text, chapters 1 to 6, is largely a summary of accepted knowledge based on secondary sources, though we hope that we have introduced a few new ideas. For this reason footnotes have been kept to a minimum. Certain abbreviations allow quick reference to the main sources (see p.11) but on the whole we have drawn without specific references on the publications about Petworth and Turner listed in the Bibliography. However, certain specific references, particularly to recent publications, are given. The two appendices by Ian Warrell break new ground and publish a large amount of new material. The original sources are therefore fully documented in the footnotes.

There are a number of general acknowledgements we would like to make. The ground-work on Turner's drawings and gouaches of Petworth was provided, in the case of works in the Turner Bequest, by A.J. Finberg in his *Complete Inventory of the Drawings in the Turner Bequest* of 1909, and for works outside the Bequest by Andrew Wilton in the catalogue of watercolours that appears in his *Life and Work of J.M.W. Turner* of 1979. Full catalogue entries on the oil paintings related to Petworth are provided in Martin Butlin and Evelyn Joll, *The Paintings of J.M.W. Turner*, revised edition, 1984; the entries on the works at Petworth are by Evelyn Joll.

However, our knowledge of Turner's work at Petworth has been radically up-dated by two important articles by Patrick Youngblood, first his general survey of artistic activity at Petworth and the gouaches showing the interior, published in ' "That House of Art": Turner at Petworth', *Turner Studies*, vol. 2 no. 2, winter 1983, and secondly his recognition that certain works formerly thought to show scenes at Petworth are in fact based on Turner's visits to East Cowes Castle, published in the article 'Three Mis-Identified Works by J.M.W. Turner', *Burlington Magazine*, vol. CXXV, 1983. An important identification of a hitherto unidentified painting with Petworth has been made by Sarah Reid in her article on ' "A Vaulted Hall" *c.* 1835 by J.M.W. Turner: its setting identified' in the *Burlington Magazine*, vol. CXXIX, 1987.

It is on these foundations that the new material published here for the first time has been based, and we must also acknowledge the most helpful advice of our colleagues Robin Hamlyn, Ann Chumbley, Julia Clarkson and Andrew Wilton, and also of Ann Forsdyke and Stephen Tate. Alison McCann, assistant archivist of the West Sussex Record Office, has read our text and given us the greatest help.

We must also acknowledge the assistance that we have received from the National Trust, in particular Gervase Jackson-Stops, Alastair Laing and Christopher Rowell. Norman Thomas and the staff at Petworth have been most helpful in organising the photography of works there under the supervision of Alec Cobbe. We must thank John Webb for his energy and skill in taking new colour transparencies of many of the works at Petworth. Christopher Gatiss of the Courtauld Institute, Ian Dejardin of the Royal Academy and Sue Valentine of Agnew's have been most helpful in supplying further photographs. The enthusiasm of John Parfitt of the Westerham Press has ensured an ideal degree of cooperation over the printing of this book and we must also thank Caroline Johnston for her sensitive design, and Jane O'Mahony and Lindsey Candy for typing and constantly re-typing much of the text.

Martin Butlin *Keeper of the Historic British Collection*
September 1988

Explanations and Abbreviations

The full names and titles of all publications referred to in the notes or text are given in the Bibliography on p. 287. In the case of references given in the text the following abbreviations are used:

'BJ 18', etc, refers to the catalogue numbers in Martin Butlin and Evelyn Joll, *The Paintings of J. M. W. Turner*, revised edition 1984

'R 10', refers to the catalogue numbers in A. J. Finberg, *Turner's Liber Studiorum with a New Catalogue Raisonné*, 1924, which retains the numbering of W. G. Rawlinson, *Turner's Liber Studiorum*, 1876 and 1906

'TB XC–6', etc, refers to the numbering in A. J. Finberg, *A Complete Inventory of the Drawings in the Turner Bequest*, 1909

'W 592', etc., refers to the catalogue numbers in Andrew Wilton, *The Life and Work of J. M. W. Turner*, 1979

References to the diaries of Joseph Farington, kept from 1793 until his death in 1821, and now in the Royal Library, Windsor, can be traced, using the dates given, in the recent complete edition published by Yale University Press from 1978 onwards.

Where Turner exhibited a picture in his own lifetime the title given is that in the first printed catalogue, if one can be traced. Idiosyncrasies of spelling or punctuation are followed without comment. The abbreviation 'RA' refers to the Summer Exhibitions held at the Royal Academy in London, and those to Turner's gallery to the artist's own gallery in Queen Anne Street.

A reference to a 'fig.' number means that the illustration falls within the text pages, to a 'plate' number means that the illustration is one of the series at the end of the book. A credit in the caption to an illustration to 'Petworth House' means that the work concerned is the property of the Tate Gallery but remains at Petworth House; those credited 'National Trust, Petworth House' are the property of H.M. Treasury in the care of the National Trust at Petworth House, while those credited to 'Lord Egremont, Petworth House' remain his property. Pictures credited to 'Tate Gallery' are in the Clore Gallery for the Turner Collection at the Tate Gallery, London.

Measurements are given in millimetres followed by inches in brackets; height precedes width.

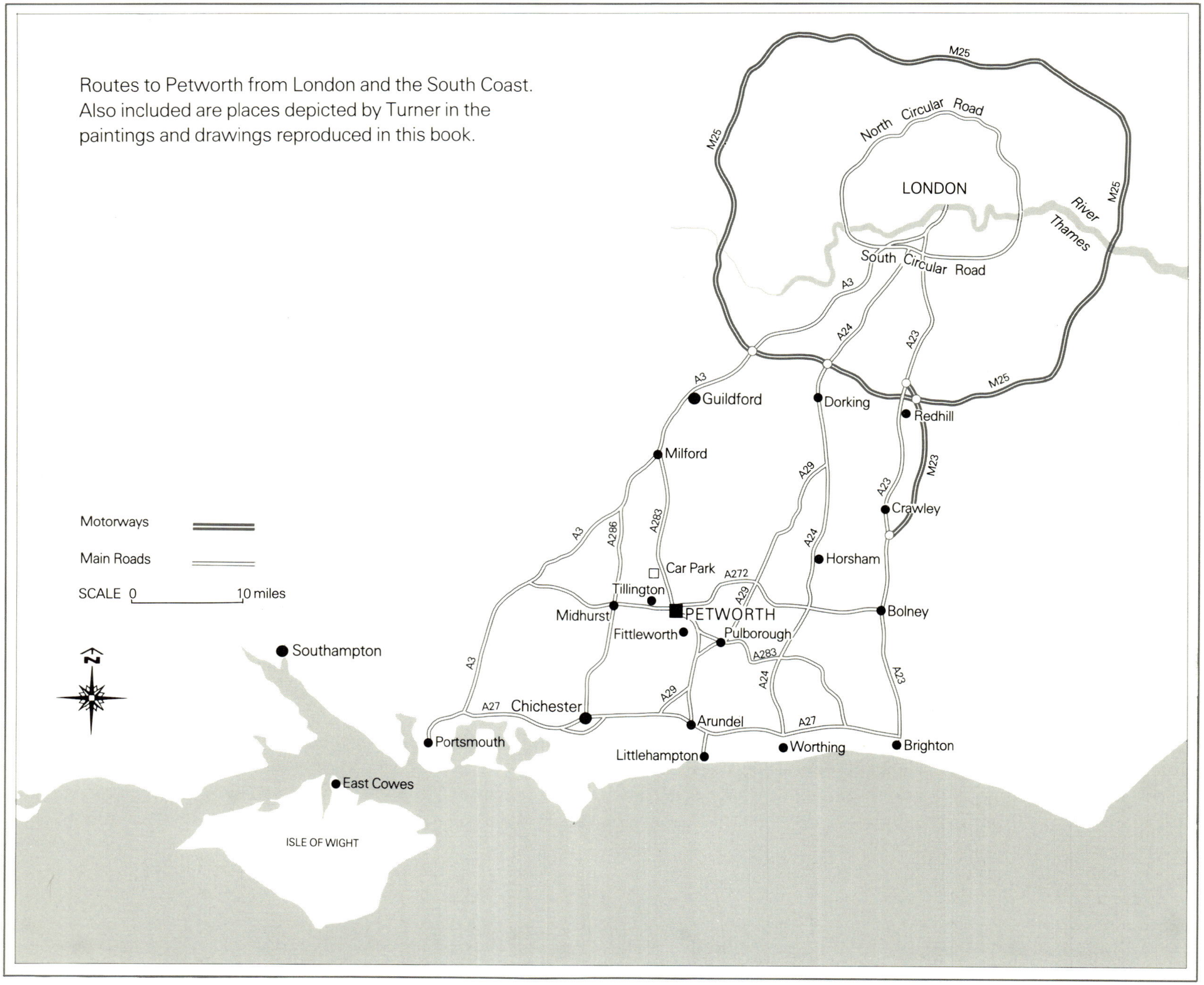

fig. 1 Map of the District

CHAPTER 1

Petworth: the house, its times and its people

> . . . one day I found the Petworth sketches in the Tate Gallery, and watched the life of a great country house with Turner's vision. There was the park, the lake, and there were people waiting for dinner, playing the piano . . . Then last spring . . . I saw the reality; sat where Turner had painted, saw the very points of view, and lingered in rooms where hung some of the scores of scintillating canvases that make the Petworth gallery the equal of any national collection.

Christopher Hussey, writing in 1925 following a visit to Petworth in preparation for a series of articles for *Country Life*,[1] captures the feelings of so many visitors to Petworth over the years. Since the opening of the Clore Gallery for the Turner Collection in April 1987 a room has been devoted to the paintings relating to Petworth and East Cowes, but no admirer of Turner should miss the opportunity to visit Petworth and see for himself the great house and magnificent park, landscaped by 'Capability' Brown in the 1750s, which inspired these works, and also the paintings by Turner to be found there.

Petworth was important to Turner in several ways. Firstly, the third Earl of Egremont, who was a leading collector of contemporary British art in the first half of the nineteenth century, assembled at Petworth what is now the largest group of paintings by Turner outside the Tate Gallery. His early patronage, together with that of other aristocrats (William Beckford of Fonthill, the Duke of Bridgewater, the Earl of Harewood and Sir John Leicester, later Lord de Tabley), must have helped to establish Turner's reputation, and his choice of paintings is interesting to us not only as a reflection of his own personal taste but as an indication of what was fashionable at the time. Secondly, in addition to the works that he had himself acquired, Lord Egremont had inherited a fine collection of Old Master paintings, which is one of the few great country-house collections to have survived virtually intact to this day. As Martin Butlin demonstrates in chapter 3, these pictures were to exercise a profound influence on Turner. Thirdly, after the death of his close friend and patron Walter Fawkes of Farnley Hall in 1825 and the death in 1829 of his father to whom he was very attached, Petworth became for Turner almost a second home. His response to the atmosphere of the exceptional household there and to the magnificent interior of the house and the park is recorded in a series of over a hundred drawings on blue paper, reproduced here in their entirety for the first time (plates 1–135). These were not commissioned works – Lord Egremont did not collect watercolours – so they were made presumably purely for Turner's own pleasure and, to quote the late Kenneth Clark, 'They are not only enchanting in themselves, they are the best introduction to Turner'.[2]

Ideally, the first view of Petworth House should be from the lake (fig. 2) and the visitor from London is recommended to stop in the first car park on the Northchapel Road and walk across the park. After about twenty minutes the house and lake suddenly appear, still looking (despite the tragic loss of trees in the hurricane of October 1987) remarkably as they did in 1809 when the third Earl of Egremont commissioned from Turner the portrait of his country seat, sub-titled by the artist 'Dewy Morning' (fig. 35). Turner did not of course set up his easel in the park, as he mischievously shows Canaletto doing in one of his Venetian views ('Bridge of Sighs, Ducal Palace and Custom-House, Venice: Canaletti Painting', BJ 349); he made a pencil sketch on the spot (fig. 3) and then worked on the painting in his studio.

A picture at Belvoir Castle (fig. 4) shows the west front of Petworth House as it looked in about 1700. At that time the main entrance was on this side of the house, directly into the Marble Hall. Today this entrance is no longer used and the public may enter the house via

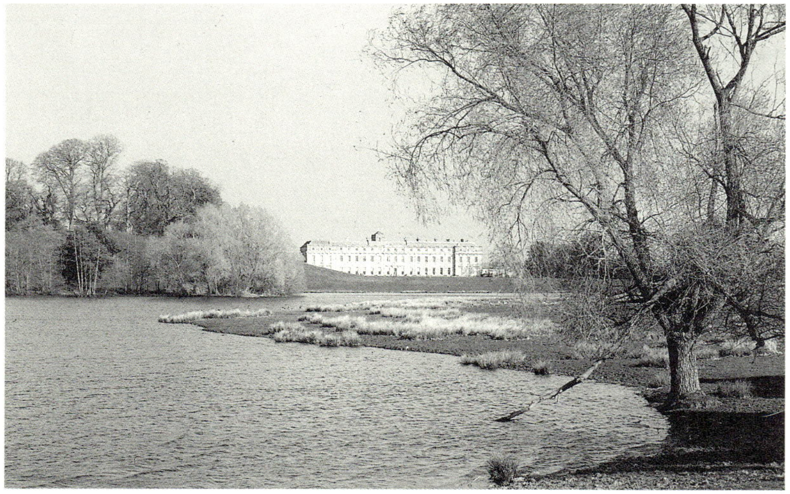

fig. 2 Petworth House from the Lake (photo: National Trust Photographic Library)

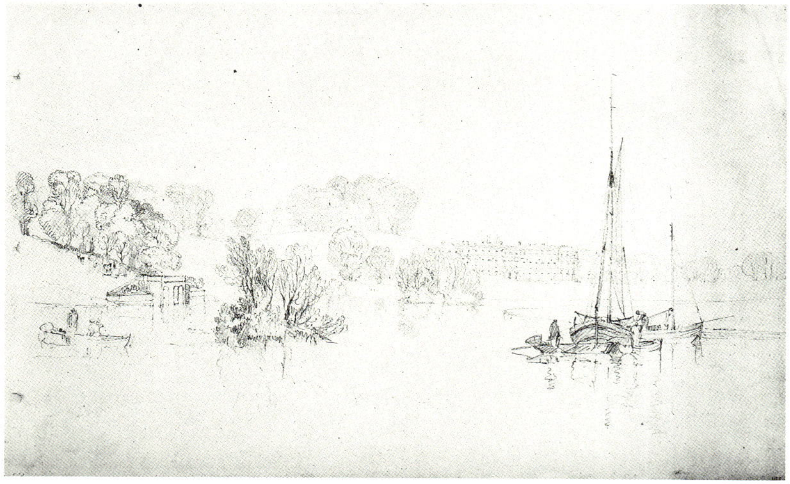

fig. 3 *Sketch for 'Petworth, Sussex, the Seat of the Earl of Egremont: Dewy Morning'*, ('Petworth' sketchbook, TB CIX, p. 4), 1809, Pencil 225 × 370 ($8\frac{7}{8} \times 14\frac{1}{2}$), Tate Gallery

Church Lodge, which is beside St Mary's Church in the centre of the town. The church, incidentally, appears in a recently identified early drawing by Turner (fig. 127) which can be dated with reasonable confidence to 1792–94, thus proving that Turner had visited Petworth some years earlier than hitherto had been supposed. After walking through a series of long passages, the visitor arrives at the east front of the main house, to be confronted by a bewildering array of architectural styles[3] which present a striking contrast to the imposing façade of the west front. To the right of the public entrance is the oldest part of the house, the thirteenth-century chapel, and immediately above its pointed east window is the Old Library with its distinctive fan-light window. In the 1820s and 30s this room was used by Turner and other artists as a studio and the window features prominently in one of his best-known drawings (plate 49).

There are fine views of the park from the public rooms on the ground floor on the west side. However, on a sunny day, before touring the house, it is pleasant to walk round the outside of the North Gallery and enter the park through the gate in the low wrought-iron railings. On the terrace outside the Marble Hall, one can stand on exactly the spot that Turner chose as his view-point in two of the panoramic landscapes of the park of *c.* 1828–30 (figs. 75 and 76). The earlier version, in which Lord Egremont's dogs rush across the park to greet him as he returns to his chair after an evening stroll (frontispiece), is especially evocative. In reality, of course, the sunset is seldom as dramatic as this and one is reminded of the occasion on which somebody is supposed to have said to Turner 'Yes, but, you know, I never see sunsets as you paint them' and to have received the retort 'No, but wouldn't you like to!'[4]

Petworth is unusual among great English country houses in its proximity to the town. Seen from the east on the A 272 from Billingshurst, the house with its high boundary walls coming right down into the main street appears to dominate the town and surrounding countryside like a medieval fortress. The site on which Petworth House now stands was, in fact, once a Percy castle, enlarged from an existing manor house after a licence to crenellate was granted in 1309. The Percys, an immensely rich and powerful family with vast possessions in the North of England, had acquired the Petworth estate in 1150 but it was not until the 1570s, after the eighth Earl had been released from the Tower on condition that he lived in the South of England, that Petworth became the chief seat of the family. These were turbulent times and his

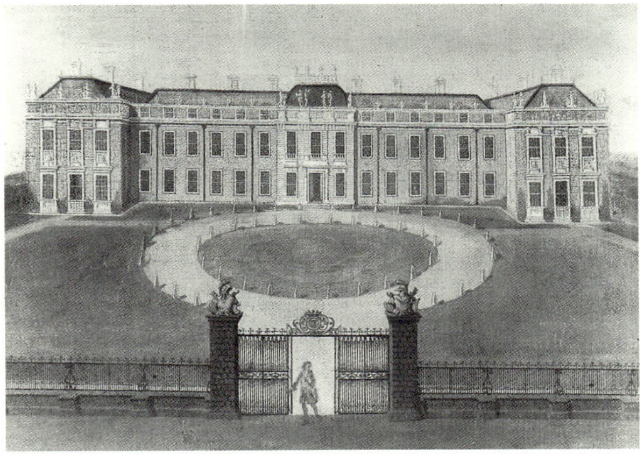

fig. 4 George London: *The West Front of Petworth House*, *c.* 1700, 1194 × 2134 (47 × 84), The Duke of Rutland, Belvoir Castle

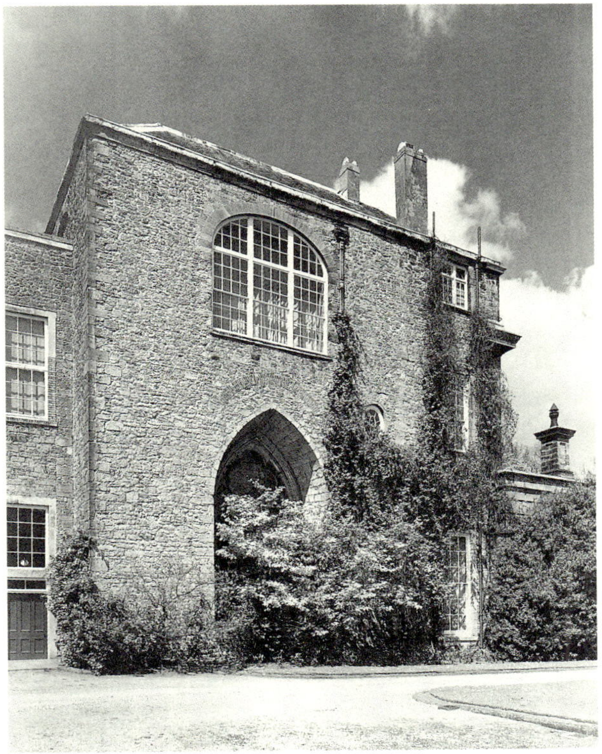

fig. 5 Petworth House: the exterior of the chapel (photo: A.F. Kersting)

son Henry (known as 'the Wizard Earl' on account of his scientific interests) was also imprisoned in the Tower, on suspicion of complicity in the Gunpowder Plot of 1605. A picture by Turner (fig. 94) shows his daughters, Lucy, Countess of Carlisle and Dorothy Percy visiting him in prison; the figures are taken from portraits by Van Dyck (figs. 54, 55 and 56).

It was Algernon, tenth Earl of Northumberland, a distinguished connoisseur, who was responsible for acquiring most of the magnificent paintings by Van Dyck still at Petworth, including the posthumous portrait of his father. The portrait of the Countess of Bedford (fig. 56) is particularly fine and has been described by Sir Oliver Millar as 'The most beautiful of the female portraits painted by Van Dyck for Northumberland and in every way one of Van Dyck's most magical portraits'.[5] The tenth Earl also bought several paintings by Titian, including 'The Vendramin Family' now in the National Gallery.

He died in 1668 and his son Joscelyn survived him by only two years, leaving a daughter Elizabeth who inherited the vast Percy estates. After being given in marriage twice before her sixteenth birthday, in 1682 she was finally married to Charles Seymour, sixth Duke of Somerset. Known as the 'Proud Duke', he must have been an impossible man to live with – he is said 'to have insisted on his children always standing in his presence, and to have cut the inheritance of one of his daughters when he fell asleep and woke to find her seated'[6] – but he put his young wife's fortune to good use and embarked on the rebuilding of Petworth House. His architect, perhaps the Frenchman Daniel Marot,[7] was responsible for the imposing west façade, which originally, as can be seen in the picture at Belvoir, was not quite as featureless as it is today.

The 'Proud Duke' seems to have been more interested in rebuilding the house than in collecting pictures but he was responsible for the addition of one superb picture to the collection, 'Jacob with Laban and his Daughters' (fig. 52), painted for Signor Cardelli in Rome in 1655, which was one of the first works by Claude to enter an English collection. Portraits of the Duke and Duchess of Somerset hang in the Carved Room surrounded by cascades of flowers and fruit in Grinling Gibbons's inimitable style.

The 'Proud Duke' died in 1748, to be followed two years later by his son Algernon, leaving no direct male heir. The estate was divided between his son-in-law Sir Hugh Smithson (later Duke of Northumberland) who inherited the Percy lands and Charles Wyndham (later second Earl of Egremont) who inherited the Petworth estates.

This was the great age of landscape gardening and in 1751 'Capability' Brown was invited to Petworth to put forward a plan for transforming the grounds into a more 'natural' landscape. The result, his masterpiece, and one of the finest examples of eighteenth-century landscape gardening to have survived in its original form, was later to inspire some of Turner's most beautiful paintings and drawings. Late in life the second Earl became interested in classical sculpture: many of the works now on display were bought for him in Rome but they remained unpacked on his death in 1763 and were later arranged by his son in the specially built North Gallery.

George O'Brien Wyndham, third Earl of Egremont, Turner's friend and patron, inherited Petworth at the age of twelve. After being educated at Westminster School, he embarked on the customary Grand Tour of Europe, following it up with a shorter trip some two years later. He showed perhaps his first sign of eccentricity in concentrating not as was usual on the landscape and antiquities of Italy but rather on Northern Europe, Dresden, Berlin, Prague, Vienna, Frankfurt and Paris, and, on the later trip, Paris and Venice, the last a much less frequent goal of pilgrimage than Rome. As well as his interest in the arts and racing – he won the Derby and the Oaks five times each, all but one with horses he had bred himself – Lord Egremont was more than usually involved in local affairs, particularly agricultural reform (see pp. 105–23), and was Lord-Lieutenant of Sussex from 1819 to 1835.

As a dashing and extremely wealthy young man, he must have been much in demand in London society. In 1774 Mrs Delany described him as 'a pretty man, has a vast fortune, and is very generous, and not addicted to the vices of the times'.[8] In 1780 he became engaged to Lady Maria Waldegrave, but the marriage never took place and he chose instead to live with Elizabeth Iliffe, commonly known as Mrs Wyndham. Their first child was born in 1787 but they were not actually married until 1801, legitimising their children but losing the title. Mrs Wyndham seems to have shared Lord Egremont's interest in the arts. According to Farington, writing on 18 December 1798, 'She professed to have great delight in painting and devotes much of her time to it'. Farington also noted 'She seldom comes to town, not oftener than once a year, but thinks she shall come in the Spring to see the Orleans collection which I mentioned to her'.

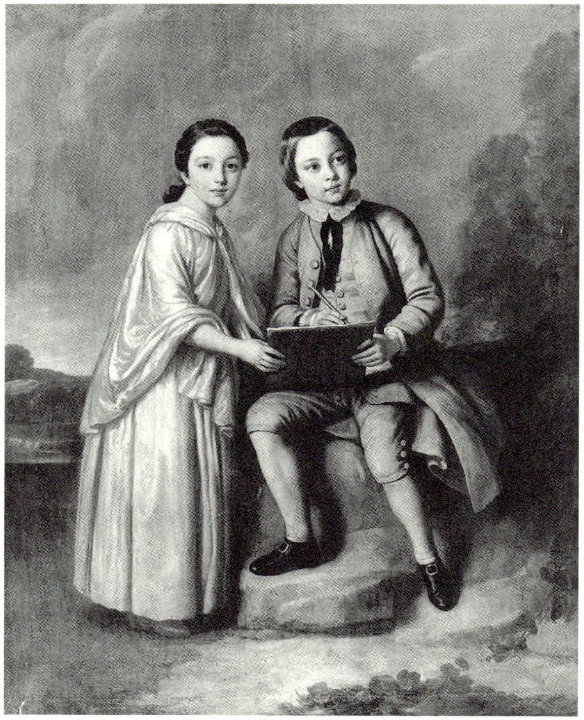

fig. 6 William Hoare: *George Wyndham, later third Earl of Egremont and his sister Elizabeth, later Countess of Carnarvon, as Children*, c. 1762, Oil on canvas 1473 × 1194 (58 × 47), Lord Egremont, Petworth House

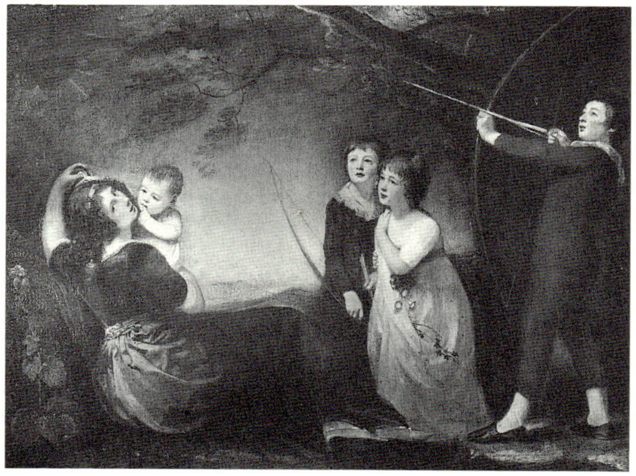

fig. 7 George Romney: *The Egremont Family*, 1795, Oil on canvas 1689 × 2286 (66½ × 90), Lord Egremont, Petworth House

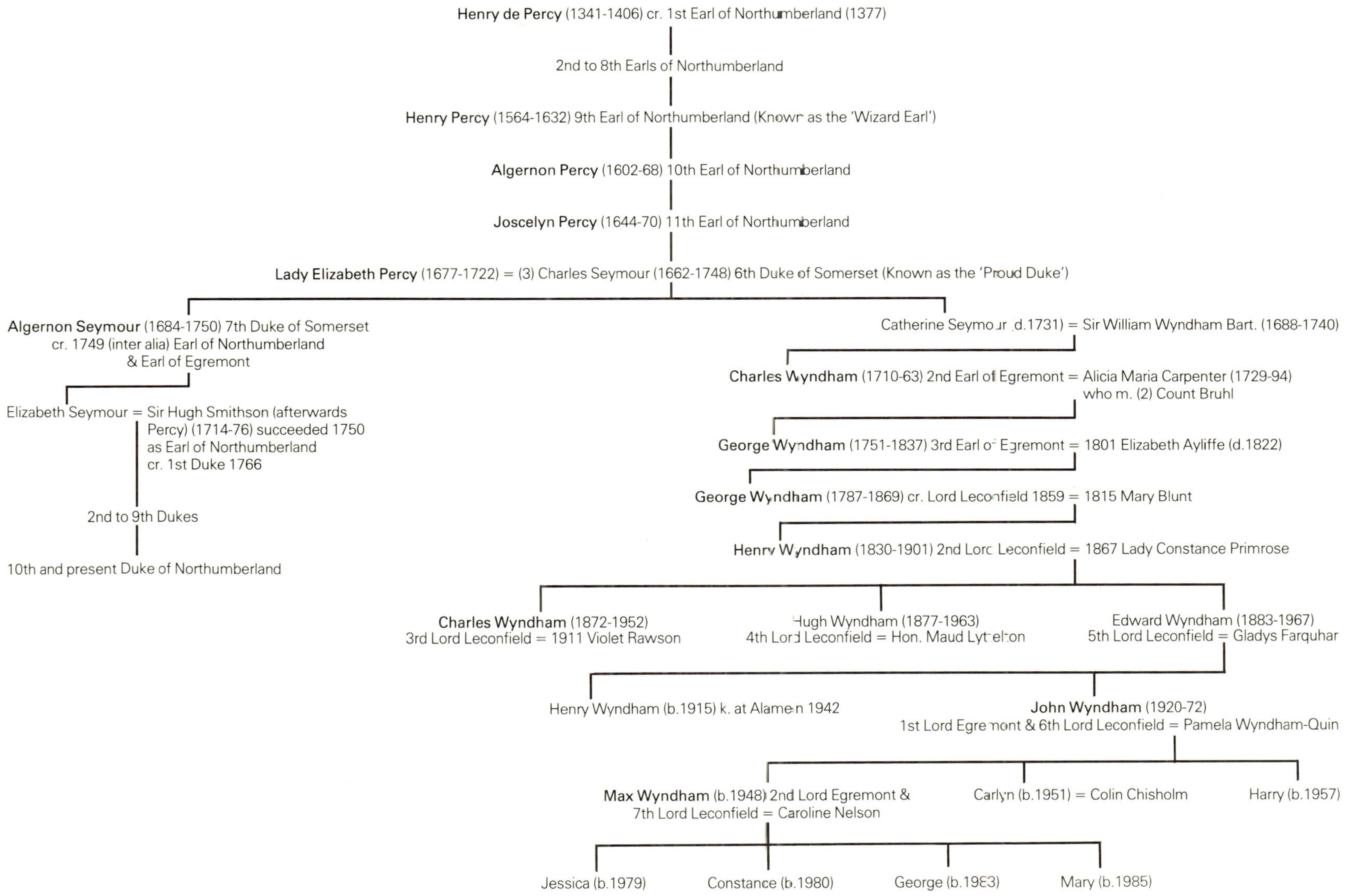

Owners of Petworth appear in bold type

fig.8 The Owners of Petworth (reproduced by kind permission of the National Trust)

In 1803 the Egremonts separated and Lady Egremont left Petworth. Although Egremont House in Piccadilly had been sold in 1794, Lord Egremont continued regularly to visit London where he kept a house in Grosvenor Place. He did not marry again but he seems to have had other mistresses and other children, notably Elizabeth Fox who bore him four children in the 1790s. Later, in 1813, Lord Blessington reported that 'Nothing will convince Lady Spenser that Lord Egremont has not forty-three Children, who all live in the House with him and their respective Mothers; [and] that the latter are usually kept in the background but when any quarrels arise, which few days pass without, each mother takes part with her Progeny, bursts into the drawing room, fights with each other, Lord E., his children, and, I believe, the Company, and makes scenes worthy of Billingsgate or a Madhouse'.[9]

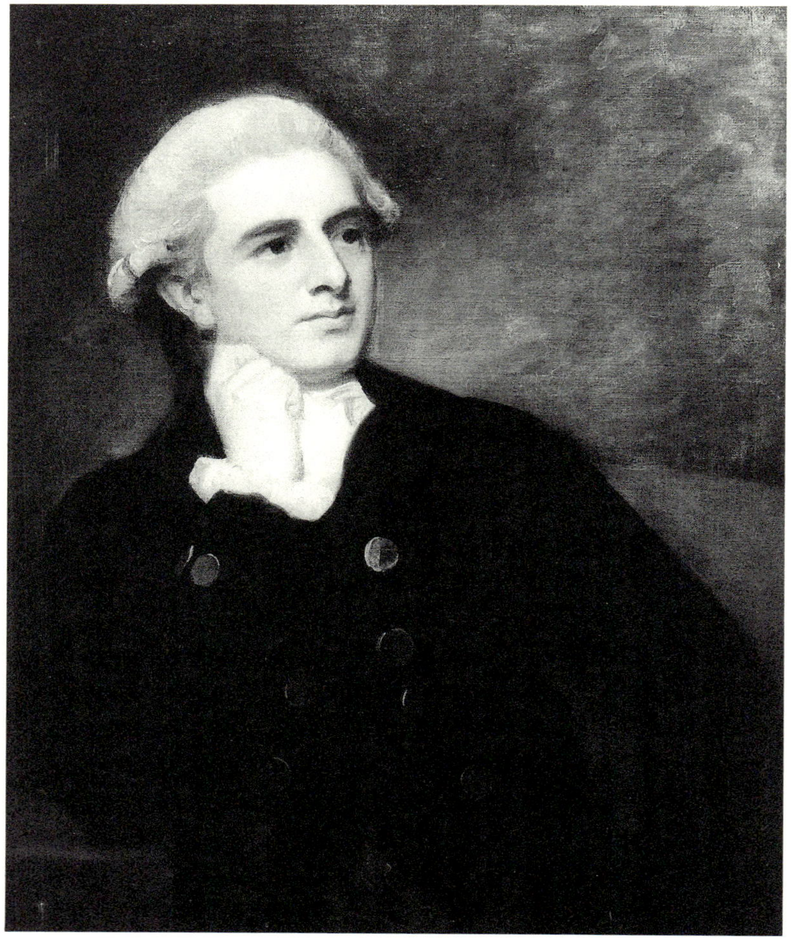

fig. 9 George Romney: *George Wyndham, third Earl of Egremont*, ?1795, Oil on canvas 762 × 635 (30 × 25), Private collection (photo: Thos Agnew & Sons Ltd)

Turner began exhibiting at the Royal Academy at a very early age, in 1790, and it was probably at one of the annual exhibitions that Lord Egremont first saw his work. Although the earliest Turner in the Petworth Collection, 'The Egremont Seapiece' (fig. 16), was exhibited at the Royal Academy in 1802, the exact date of its purchase has yet to be established. However, Lord Egremont certainly visited London several times that summer[10] and, given his interest in contemporary art, it seems likely that he would have attended this exhibition. Of the early Turners at Petworth, only 'Dewy Morning' (fig. 35) and 'Cockermouth Castle' (fig. 36, another Egremont property in Cumberland originally part of the Percy estates) were commissioned; the others, discussed in detail in chapter 2, were mostly bought at Royal Academy exhibitions or from Turner's own gallery. There seems to be no firm evidence to suggest that at this stage Turner's relationship with Lord Egremont was other than a conventional one between artist and patron.

Lord Egremont's taste in pictures seems to have been more conventional than his private life. Like Turner himself, he was very much a product of the eighteenth century who would probably have been educated on the principle that 'Whate'er Lorrain light-touched with softening hue'[11] should be admired. Certainly he appears to have preferred such tranquil Claudean scenes as the views on the Thames, which he bought between 1805 and 1810, to Turner's more dramatic works of these years. He could, for instance, have bought the great 'Snow Storm: Hannibal and his Army Crossing the Alps' at the Royal Academy in 1812, but he acquired instead 'Hulks on the Tamar' (fig. 38) and 'Teignmouth' (fig. 37) which were exhibited at Turner's own gallery in the same year.

It is difficult to appreciate today what an impact the collection of Old Masters at Petworth must have made on Turner as a young man, but his response to the Altieri Claude ('Landscape with the Father of Psyche Sacrificing to Apollo', now at Anglesey Abbey), which he saw in London in 1799, was recorded by Farington in his diary on 7 May: 'Turner said He was both pleased and unhappy when He viewed it, – it seemed to be beyond the power of imitation.' Although he grew up in the Covent Garden district of London, not far from Trafalgar

Square, there was then no National Gallery to visit. The first public gallery to open was that at Dulwich in 1811. A picture in that collection, Watteau's 'Les Plaisirs du Bal', can be seen in the background of Turner's 'Watteau Study by Fresnoy's Rules' of 1831 (fig. 93). The National Gallery opened in 1824 (though it did not move to the present building until 1838). In Turner's day there were few illustrated art books and his major sources of information would have been the paintings he saw in the houses of aristocratic patrons like Lord Egremont and in the sale rooms, and engravings.

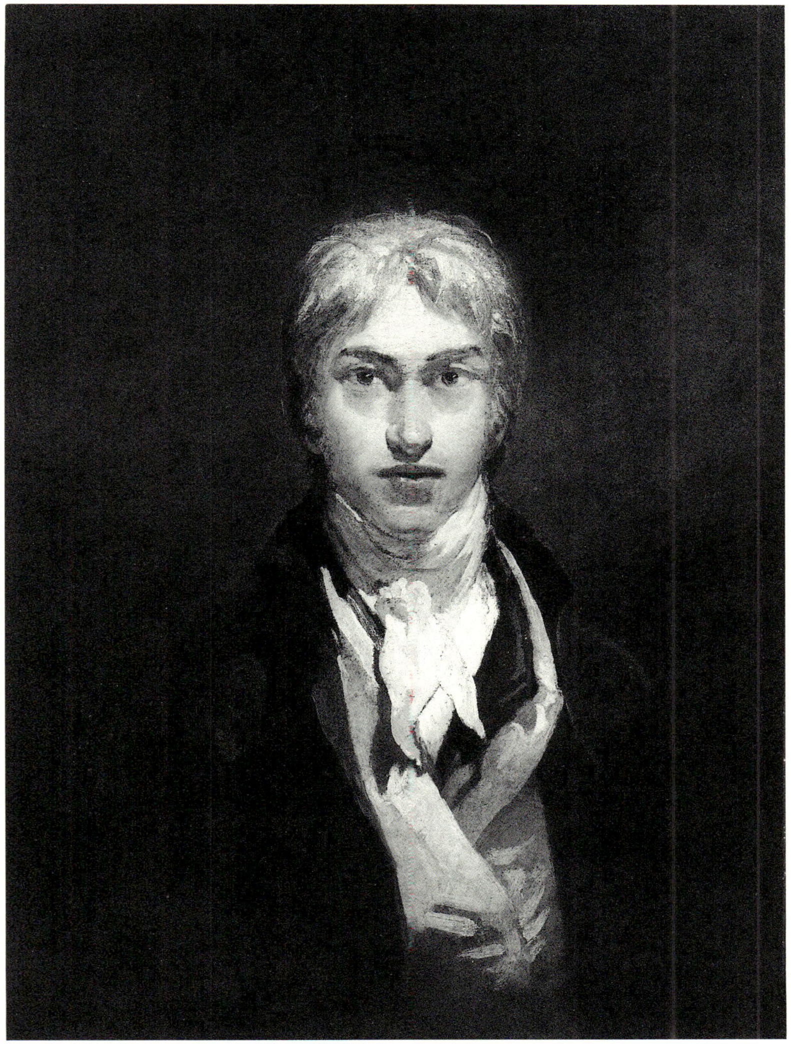

fig. 10 J.M.W. Turner: *Self-Portrait*, (BJ 25), *c.* 1798, Oil on canvas
745 × 585 (29¼ × 23), Tate Gallery

In 1814 Turner entered 'Apullia in Search of Appullus' (fig. 53), which is a near copy of the Petworth Claude, for one of the British Institution's annual premiums (see p. 48). The long break that occurred in Lord Egremont's patronage of Turner between 1812 and the late 1820s has never been satisfactorily explained and it has sometimes been suggested that this incident offended Lord Egremont. Although this seems at variance with all that is known of Lord Egremont's character, it is true that he acquired no further paintings by Turner for over ten years, although he continued collecting works by other artists.

The decade 1815–1825 was, in any event, a busy one for Turner. After Napoleon's final defeat at Waterloo he began to travel widely on the Continent, visiting Belgium, Germany and Holland in 1817, before making the long-awaited visit to Italy in 1819. Like so many other Anglo-Saxons, he was overwhelmed by the clear light and bright colours of Italy, especially of Venice. The experience of Italy was to have far-reaching effects on his art and by the time, probably shortly before his second visit to Rome in 1828, he received another commission from Lord Egremont, to paint four long landscapes to hang beneath seventeenth-century portraits in the Carved Room at Petworth, Turner had evolved his own distinctive style.

From the mid 1820s, Turner began to spend a lot of time at Petworth. He worked on the landscapes in the Old Library, at least in part, locking the door against all but Lord Egremont. 'Chantrey [the eminent sculptor, later Sir Francis] was there at the time, and determined to see what Turner was doing; he imitated Lord Egremont's peculiar step, and the two distinct raps on the door by which his Lordship was accustomed to announce himself: and the key being immediately turned, he slipped into the room before the artist could shut him out, which joke was mutually enjoyed by the two attached friends'.[12]

By this time the household at Petworth had become even more eccentric and in 1823 Henry Edward Fox noted that 'The want of comforts, of regularity, and still more the total absence of cleanliness, made it, splendid and beautiful as it is, far from being agreeable . . . People of all descriptions, without any connection or acquaintance with each other, are gathered together and huddled up at the dinner table'.[13] It was this aspect of liberty hall that, on the other hand, attracted artists. Benjamin Robert Haydon, for instance, invited to stay in November 1826, shortly after his release from the Fleet Prison, was placed 'in one of the most magnificent bed rooms I ever saw' and described Lord Egremont as 'literally like the Sun. The very flies at Petworth seem to know there is room for their existence, that the windows are theirs. The dogs, the horses, the cows, the deer & pigs, the Peasantry & the Servants, the guests & the family, the children & the Parents, all share alike his bounty & opulence & luxuries.'[14]

Many other artists and their families were entertained at Petworth. The American artist C.R. Leslie was a frequent visitor and there is a delightful story of Turner making a paper boat for one of his sons to sail on the lake.[15] Leslie had almost as close an attachment to Petworth as Turner himself and, like Turner, recorded some of the rooms including, in a picture now in the Tate Gallery (fig. 11), the Carved Room, which must have been painted shortly before the installation of Turner's landscapes.[16] Evidence that at least two of the landscapes were installed by August 1828 is provided by a letter from Thomas Creevey to Miss Ord[17] which also contains a splendid description of a dinner party at Petworth:

> ... We formed in a very excellent habitable library and drawing room united, our party being nearly domestic – us five, Ld. Egremont and Misses Wyndham, Mr. King and Mrs. who was one of the Misses Wyndham, and a Brother of his, the eldest male Wyndham, Lord Charles Somerset, and his daughter, Mrs. Wyndham, Lady Emily Marsham ... a Chaplain and another young lady ...
>
> The dinner was of the first order, turtle, venison, moor game, &c. without stint. The servants, too, very numerous tho' most of them advanced in years and tottered, and comical in their looks. The wax candles too were sufficiently numerous to light us all up well tho' we were at one end of a room sixty feet long, the wainscoat of which was Gibbons' carving in wood ...

Other visitors of note included John Constable, who was introduced by Leslie to Lord Egremont. After worrying unduly about whether he should write to Lord Egremont announcing his exact time of arrival or not,[18] Constable eventually visited Petworth in September 1834. A coach was put at his disposal and he made a number of drawings of the

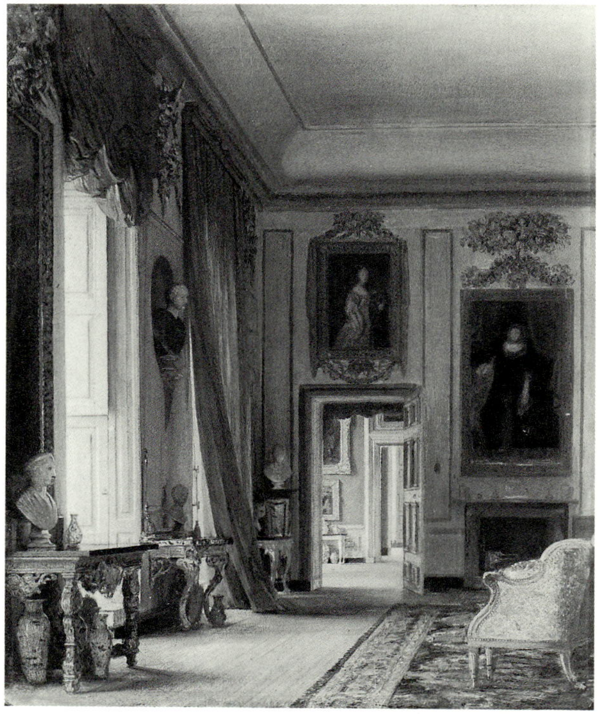

fig. 11 C.R. Leslie: *The Carved Room, Petworth House*, c. 1826, Oil on millboard 352 × 300 (14 × 22), Tate Gallery

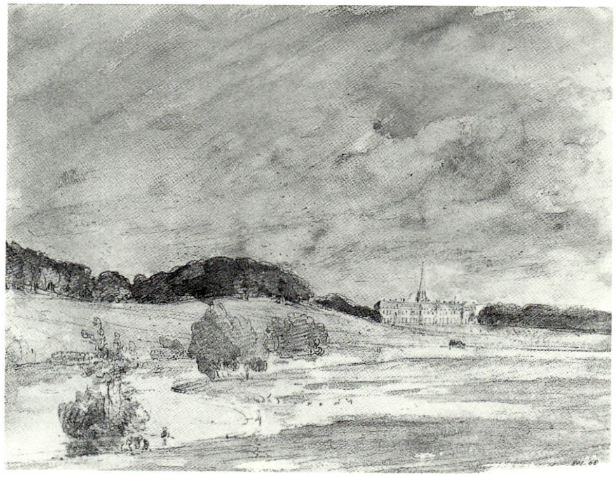

fig. 12 John Constable: *Petworth House from the Park*, 1834, Pencil and watercolour 207 × 272 (8⅛ × 10¾), Victoria and Albert Museum

Sussex countryside, including one of Petworth House from the Park (fig. 12).[19] There is however no painting by Constable at Petworth today. Constable himself suggested that Lord Egremont failed to buy any of his paintings because 'landscape affords him no interest whatever'[20] but this is obviously not correct. Quite apart from his patronage of Turner, Lord Egremont acquired several fine landscapes by earlier artists, including works by Gainsborough (fig. 40) and Wilson.

One of the most attractive aspects of Lord Egremont's patronage was his benevolence. He commissioned not only landscapes from successful painters like Turner and family portraits from Thomas Phillips (fig. 13) but contemporary sculpture as well. Flaxman's colossal 'St Michael Overcoming Satan' (fig. 14) looms in two of Turner's most atmospheric drawings of the North Gallery (plates 43 and 44) and Carew's statue of one of Lord Egremont's dogs can still be seen on the lake. He was particularly generous to Carew, commissioning a large number of statues, and was heard to remark 'When I am gone he will be a beggar',[21] a prophecy to be fulfilled when the ungrateful Carew, after unwisely bringing a law suit against Lord Egremont's executors, was declared a bankrupt.

Lord Egremont's agricultural interests are discussed later in this book. These were years of agricultural depression and he had started a tradition of giving a feast for his tenants and the poor of the district on his birthday, 18 December. In May 1835, because of his illness the previous December, the feast took the form of a fête in the park. Greville describes the elderly Lord Egremont 'rejoicing in the diffusion of happiness'[22] and the event is also recorded in Witherington's picture of 1836 (fig. 15). 4,000 people were invited but some 6,000 turned up and were fed. 'Gentlemen from the neighbourhood carved for them, and waiters were provided from among the peasantry'. There were marquees and a band of music but the provisions, despite the fine weather, remained wintry: 'plum puddings and loaves were piled like cannon balls, and innumerable joints of boiled and roast beef were spread out, while hot joints were prepared in the kitchen, and sent forth as soon as the firing of guns announced the hour of the feast'. In the evening the park gates were thrown open and, for an assembly of 10,000 people, there was a great display of fireworks.

In 'Fête in Petworth Park' Witherington depicts Lord Egremont as a sprightly figure riding among his guests but he was at the time already in his eighties and died a few years later on 11 November 1837. The

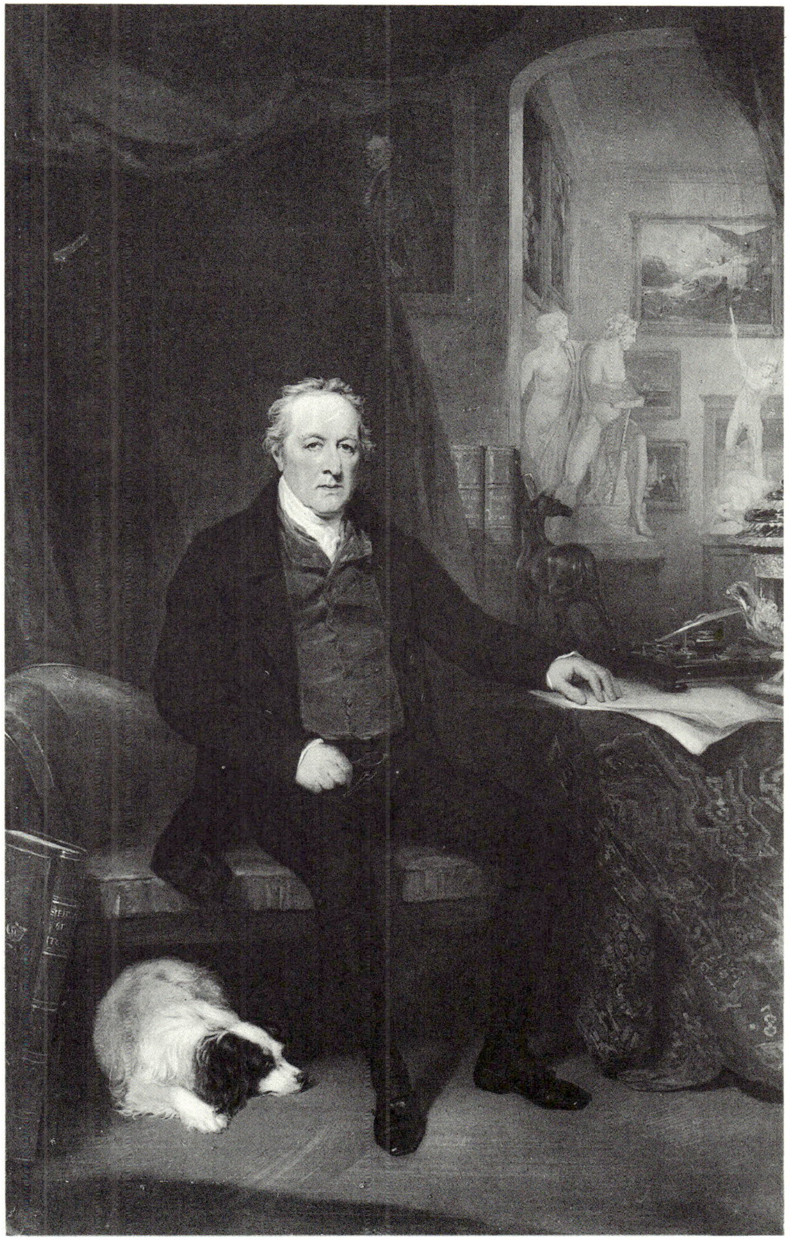

fig. 13 Thomas Phillips: *George O'Brien Wyndham, third Earl of Egremont*, *c.* 1811, Oil on canvas 1867 × 1550 ($73\frac{1}{2}$ × 61), The National Trust, Petworth House

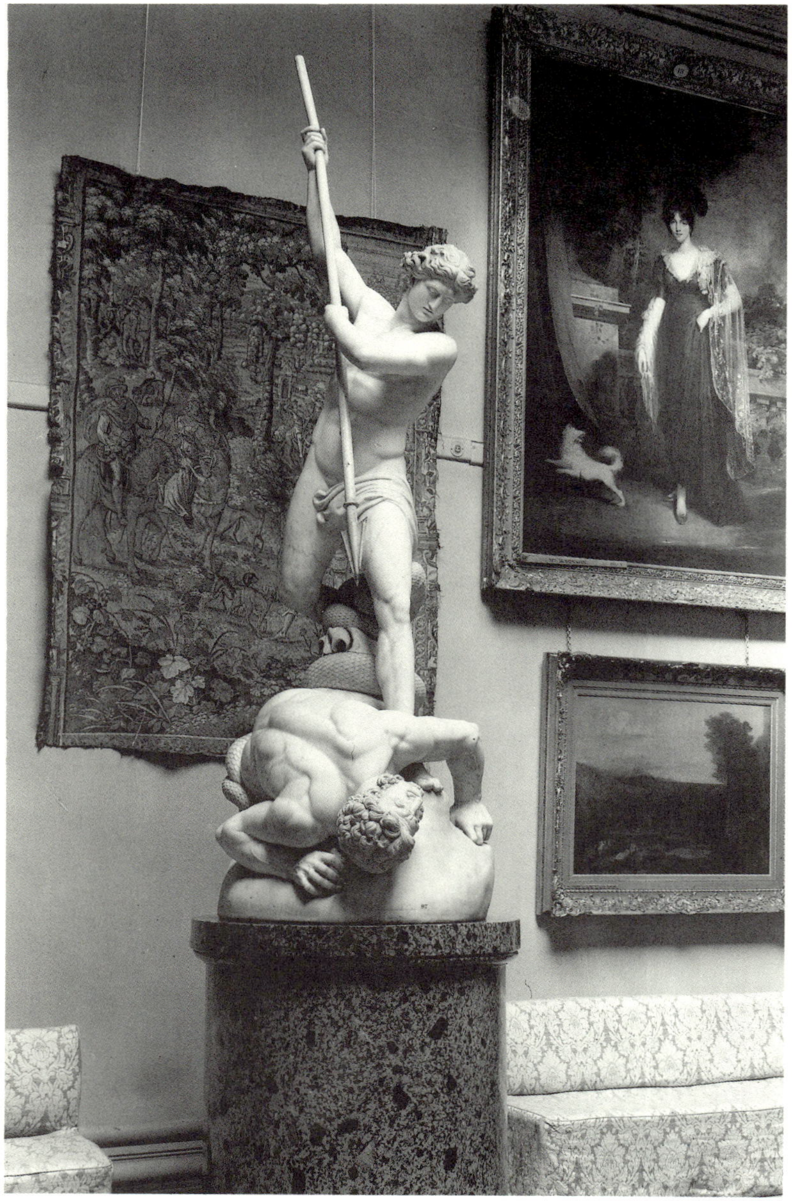

fig. 14 John Flaxman: *St Michael Overcoming Satan*, 1826, height 3353 (132), The National Trust, Petworth House

funeral, although private, was more like a state occasion and is reputed to have been witnessed by, perhaps, 6,000 people.[23] Turner of course was there and other artists included Edward Carew, C.R. Leslie and Thomas Phillips. After the death of Sir Thomas Lawrence in 1830 Turner had recorded his impression of the funeral in a watercolour exhibited at the Royal Academy but his very personal tribute to the passing of his greatest patron is almost certainly the beautiful and mysterious oil 'Interior at Petworth' (fig. 99).

Lord Egremont's death marked the end of the Golden Age of Petworth. Born into one of the great land-owning families of England in the middle of the eighteenth century, he had lived to see the accession of Queen Victoria. So far as we know Turner never visited Petworth again. His later works, though including innumerable masterpieces in both oil and watercolour, rarely demonstrate (with the notable exception of his depictions of Venice) that special affinity and sense of place that give his portrayals of Petworth and its social life their peculiar power and fascination for the public.

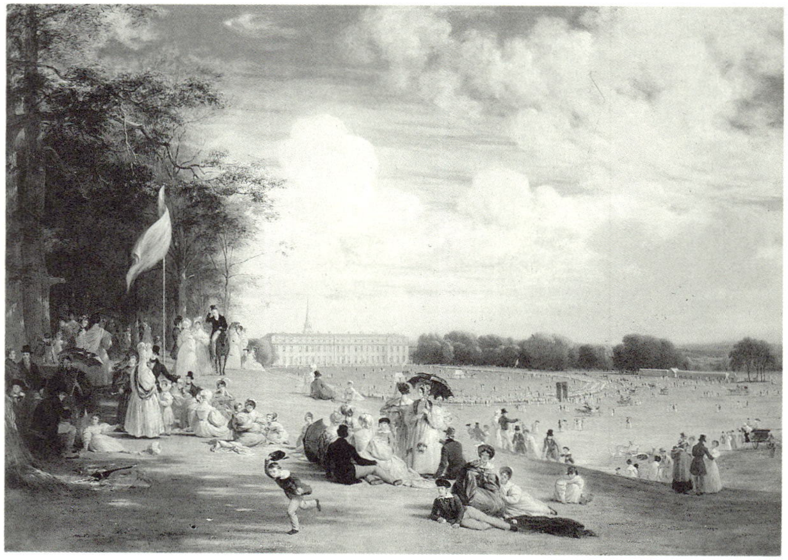

fig. 15 William Frederick Witherington: *Fête in Petworth Park, 1835*, 1836, Oil on canvas 838 × 1207 ($33 \times 47\frac{1}{2}$), The National Trust, Petworth House

Notes

1 Hussey 1925, p. 974. Christopher Hussey's articles on Petworth still remain one of the most entertaining and comprehensive accounts of Petworth House and its history.
2 Clark 1970, p. 12.
3 Readers interested in the architecture of Petworth House are referred to Jackson-Stops 1977 (1).
4 Hussey 1925 p. 974.
5 Oliver Millar, *Van Dyck in England*, exhibition catalogue, National Portrait Gallery, 1982–83, p. 83.
6 National Trust Guide 1988, p. 58.
7 See Jackson-Stops 1973 and 1977 (1), pp. 326–29, and Gervase Jackson-Stops, 'William and Mary and the Country House', *National Trust Magazine*, no. 54, Summer 1988, p. 14.
8 Letter from Mrs Delany to Bernard Granville dated 31 December 1774 in *Dictionary of National Biography*, Vol. XXI 1909, p. 1159.
9 Lindsay 1966, p. 172.
10 Information kindly supplied by Mrs Alison McCann of the West Sussex Record Office from H. A. Wyndham's notebook in the Petworth Archives. This records that Lord Egremont attended the House of Lords on 31 May and again on 28 June when Parliament was dissolved. Since it is reasonable to assume that he came up to London for the start of the London season he may well have visited the exhibition in its early weeks.
11 James Thomson, 'The Castle of Indolence', xxxviii, *James Thomson Poetical Works*, 1965, p. 265.
12 George Jones' manuscript, *Recollections of Sir Francis Chantrey*, 1849 (reprinted in Finberg 1961, p. 325).
13 *The Journal of the Hon. Henry Edward Fox*, 25 October 1823. Edited by the Earl of Ilchester, 1923, pp. 183–85.
14 Haydon, 15 November 1826.
15 Robert C. Leslie, *A Waterbiography*, 1894, p. 57.
16 For a detailed discussion of this picture, see Hamlyn 1984.
17 Creevey 1948, pp. 291–92.
18 Beckett, III, pp. 114–15.
19 For other drawings made while Constable was staying at Petworth, see Reynolds 1984 under 1834.
20 Beckett, VI, p. 171.
21 Kenworthy-Browne 1977, p. 373.
22 Greville 1888, III, pp. 86–88.
23 A detailed account of the funeral procession, taken from the *Brighton Patriot*, 28 November 1837, was reprinted in Youngblood, *Turner Studies* 1983, p. 31.

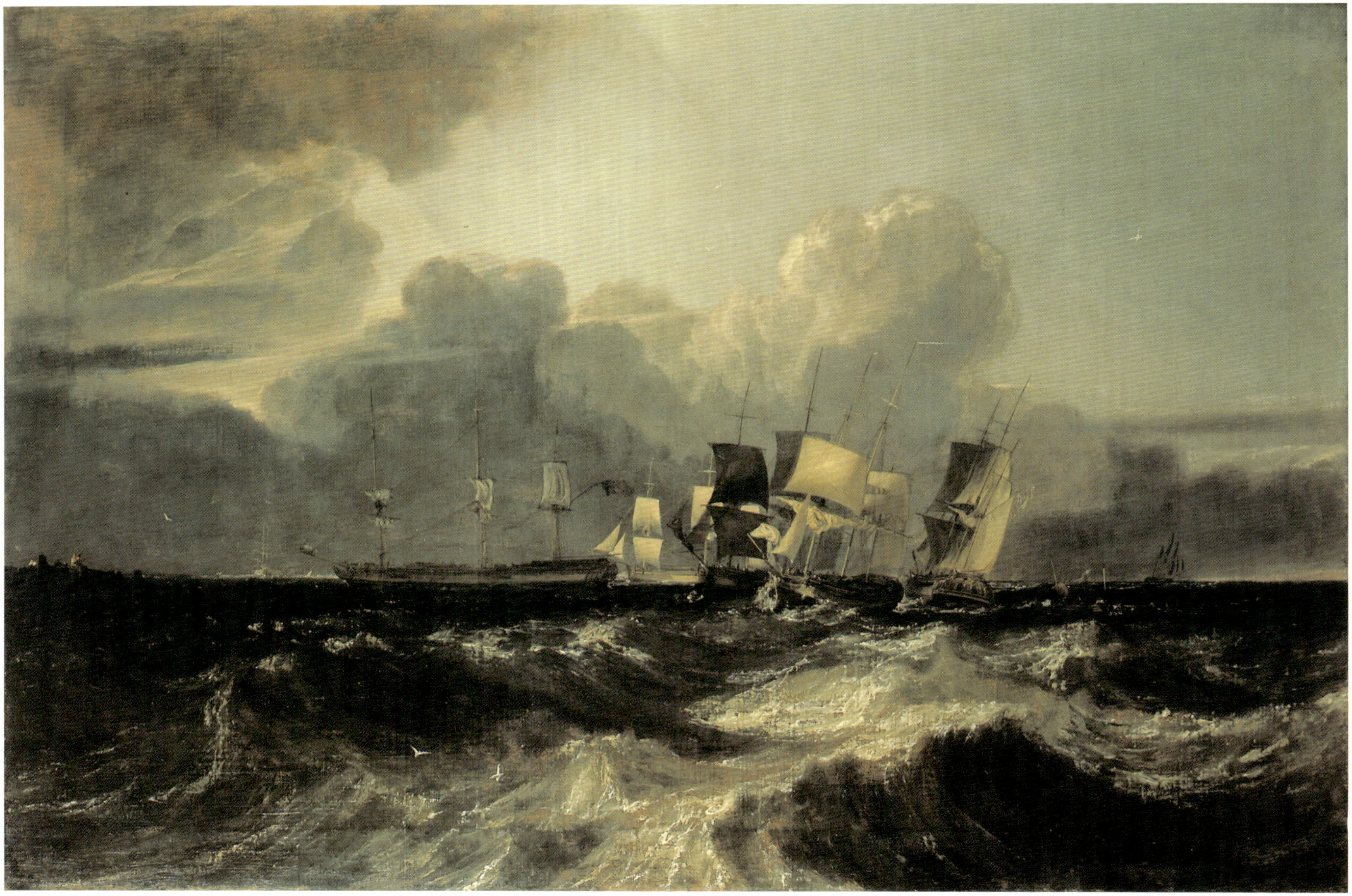

fig. 16 *Ships Bearing up for Anchorage* (*'The Egremont Seapiece'*) (BJ 18), R.A. 1802, Oil on canvas 1220 × 1830 (48 × 72½), Petworth House

CHAPTER 2

The Early Paintings by Turner at Petworth

Lord Egremont's first purchases of works by Turner, all oil paintings, cover the years 1802 until 1812.[1] These were Turner's heroic years in which he strove to justify his election in February 1802, at the youngest possible age, as a full member of the Royal Academy. Year after year the exhibitions at the Academy, or occasionally at the British Institution or Turner's own gallery, were dominated by paintings by Turner that revealed his ambition to exceed all his predecessors in the fields both of landscape and seascape; these were usually large in scale and were always bolder in treatment than any work by his contemporaries. In 1802, at the Royal Academy, he exhibited 'Ships Bearing up for Anchorage' (fig. 16; BJ 18) and 'The Tenth Plague of Egypt' (BJ 17), a development of the 'The Fifth Plague of Egypt' (BJ 13) of 1800. In 1803 he exhibited 'The Festival upon the Opening of the Vintage of Macon' (fig. 39; BJ 47), the two paintings of 'Bonneville, Savoy' (BJ 46 and 50), and 'Holy Family' (BJ 49), and in 1804 'Boats carrying out Anchors and Cables to Dutch Men of War' (BJ 52). In 1805 Turner did not exhibit at the Royal Academy, largely for reasons of art politics, but exhibited 'The Shipwreck' (BJ 54) and probably 'The Deluge' (BJ 55) in his own recently constructed gallery adjacent to his London house. In 1806 he showed 'Fall of the Rhine at Schaffhausen' (BJ 61) at the Royal Academy and, at the newly formed British Institution, 'The Goddess of Discord choosing the Apple of Contention in the Garden of the Hesperides' (BJ 57). In 1808 he showed 'Spithead: Boat's Crew Recovering an Anchor' (BJ 80) at his own gallery, and again at the Royal Academy the next year. In 1809 he showed 'Thomson's Æolian Harp' (BJ 86) at his own gallery and the following year, in the same location, 'The Fall of an Avalanche in the Grisons' (BJ 109). In 1811 he showed at the Royal Academy 'Mercury and Herse' (BJ 114) and 'Apollo and Python' (BJ 115). This series of ambitious works culminated in 'Snow Storm: Hannibal and his Army Crossing the Alps' (BJ 126), exhibited at the Royal Academy in 1812. Out of all these large-scale works, deliberately designed by Turner to display his range and power, only the first was bought by Lord Egremont (fig. 16). All the rest of Lord Egremont's purchases, whether landscapes or seascapes, were domestic in scale and calm in mood. A number were views on the Thames, and there was one pastoral classical subject, two coastal seapieces including one of the Thames Estuary, and two pictures of sites directly associated with Lord Egremont's estates. The two latest pictures in this group, one if not both of which were exhibited at Turner's gallery in 1812, show a widening of range in so far as subject matter is concerned, being scenes on the coast of Devon, but developing to an extreme degree of refinement the delicate, atmospheric style preferred by Lord Egremont to Turner's more robust works of this period.

Lord Egremont's taste at this time is in strong contrast to that of his nearest rival among Turner's patrons, Sir John Leicester, Bart., later Lord de Tabley, whose range was much wider, including not only similarly atmospheric studies of his own house and on the Thames but including also genre, as in 'A Country Blacksmith' (BJ 68), and two large dramatic pictures depicting the force of nature, 'Shipwreck' and 'Fall of the Rhine at Schaffhausen'. When Lord Leicester's collection was sold in 1827 it is noticeable that Lord Egremont bought a work by Turner that echoed the taste of his earlier acquisitions, 'Tabley, Cheshire, the Seat of Sir J.F. Leicester.: Calm Morning' (fig. 34), a work particularly close to the view of Petworth of a year later.

Unfortunately the dates at which Lord Egremont acquired his pictures are not always known, what evidence there is being indirect. However, although it is not clear whether he bought 'Ships Bearing up for Anchorage' (BJ 18) actually at the Royal Academy in 1802, it is certain that he owned it by 1805 when Turner annotated a drawing for the picture in the 'Calais Pier' sketchbook with the words 'Ld. Egremont's p['picture']'. This means that it was definitely the first Turner to be acquired by Lord Egremont, 'Narcissus and Echo', exhibited at the Royal Academy in 1804, being known to have been still in Turner's possession in 1810; Lord Egremont's other works all date from 1805 or later.

'Ships Bearing up for Anchorage', also known as the 'Egremont Sea-piece', is one of the great early seapieces by Turner, and was described in the *Daily Advertiser and Oracle* as 'a most forcible and judicious performance, well drawn and admirably coloured'. The foreground is dominated by large, boldly painted waves which overpower in their scale the dangerously juxtaposed ships in the middle distance. The drama of the ships' anxious search for anchorage is underlined by the dramatic sky and also by the unusual width, in relation to the height, of the canvas; when the composition was adapted for the print published as part of Turner's *Liber Studiorum* (R 10) in 1808 the composition was condensed into a more usual format. However, in comparison with Turner's other paintings of stormy seas of these years, 'Ships Bearing up for Anchorage' is noticeably more disciplined, with a strong emphasis on horizontals and with many of the major forms lying parallel to the surface. Perhaps it was this discipline, based on Turner's study of the paintings of Poussin and Claude, that particularly attracted Lord Egremont. Certainly his next three purchases, in chronological order of execution, shared this strict classical discipline of composition.

'Narcissus and Echo' (fig. 25; BJ 53), although exhibited at the Royal Academy in 1804, was, as we have seen, not acquired by Lord Egremont until considerably later. In Turner's 'Finance' sketchbook of about 1810 it is included in a list of unsold pictures and it may well have been sold to Lord Egremont at about this time, possibly at a reduced price; there is some evidence that it belonged to Lord Egremont by 1819. Here the composition, and the subject, is again indebted to the work of a French painter of the seventeenth century, Gaspar Dughet Poussin rather than Nicholas Poussin. The scene is set in the classical, Mediterranean world that Turner had not yet visited, and the composition is again disciplined by horizontals and verticals. The Royal Academy catalogue included a quotation from Addison's translation of Ovid's *Metamorphoses*. Echo, condemned on account of her loquacity to speechlessness save for the echoing of another's words, is pining away for love of Narcissus:

> 'Ah! Youth beloved in vain!' Narcissus cries;
> 'Ah! Youth beloved in vain!' the nymph replies.
> 'Farewell!' says he. The parting sound scarce fell
> From his faint lips, but she reply'd 'Farewell!'

The painting, a delicately expressed example of Arcadian melancholy, is the only classical subject by Turner at Petworth.

The group of views on the Thames shows the gradual loosening of Turner's style and handling that seems to have resulted from his short-lived practice of making oil sketches out of doors, many from a boat. These sketches, all at the Tate Gallery, fall into two groups. The first (e.g. fig. 18; BJ 160–76), on canvas and in all but one case in Turner's usual roughly three-foot by four-foot format, are normally dated *c.* 1806–7; some are related to drawings in the 'Thames from Reading to Walton' sketchbook of *c.* 1806 or to finished oil paintings exhibited in the years 1808–1810. They include views on the Thames estuary as well as on the river itself. Besides these pictures on canvas there is another group of smaller sketches painted on mahogany veneer (e.g. fig. 19; BJ 177–94), probably executed at much the same time, *c.* 1807.

The earlier of the finished oils of Thames subjects at Petworth seem to precede these oil sketches. The first, 'Windsor Castle from the Thames' (fig. 26; BJ 149), is signed 'IMW Turner RA ISLEWORTH' and there is a watercolour study for the picture in the 'Studies for Pictures: Isleworth' sketchbook which can be dated to 1804–5 (TB XC-29V); Turner was definitely living in Sion Ferry House at Isleworth by May 1805. Turner first opened his own gallery in 1804 and annually thereafter but no catalogues have been traced for his early exhibitions so it is not possible to say what pictures he exhibited. However it is known that he would not allow copies to be made in his gallery and the existence of a free copy by Rowlandson, presumably done from memory, of 'Windsor Castle from the Thames' (in the Yale Center for British Art, New Haven) suggests that this picture was exhibited there, probably in 1805.[2] Again it is unknown when Lord Egremont acquired the picture.

The composition is Turner at his most classical and controlled, strongly indebted to Nicholas Poussin in the way the main forms, even including the clouds, lie parallel to the picture surface; in this it is close to 'Ships Bearing up for Anchorage' and to the two Bonneville land-

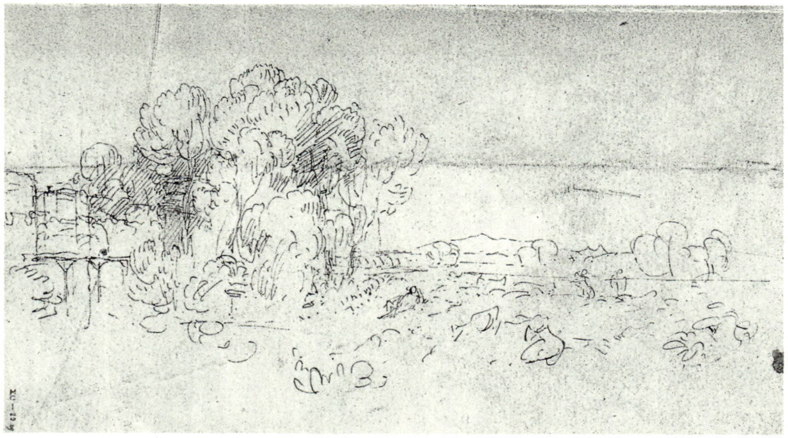

fig. 17 *Sketch for 'The Thames at Weybridge'* ('Studies for Pictures: Isleworth' sketchbook, TB XC, p. 29 recto), *c.* 1804–5, Pen and ink 257×148 ($10\frac{1}{8} \times 5\frac{13}{16}$), Tate Gallery

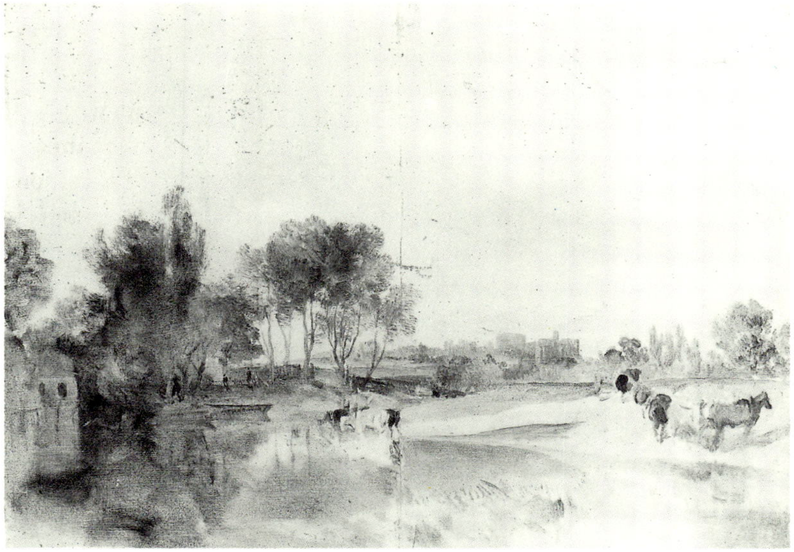

fig. 18 *A Thames Backwater with Windsor Castle in the Distance* (BJ 163), *c.* 1806–7, Oil on canvas 865×1210 ($34\frac{1}{8} \times 47\frac{5}{8}$), Tate Gallery

scapes exhibited at the Royal Academy in 1803. The colouring too is cool and classical, particularly in the sky. Nevertheless, but typical of many of Turner's depictions of scenes in England, the activities of the girls with their sheep and the boatmen on the Thames bring a feeling of everyday life to the scene and push the ostensible subject, the royal castle at Windsor, into the background.

The same classical elements are found in 'The Thames at Weybridge' (fig. 27; BJ 204) which until recently was dated rather later in the decade but is so close in its formal characteristics, relatively dark and subdued colouring and handling to 'Windsor Castle from the Thames' that it too must date from *c.* 1805–6. Again there are sketches for the composition in the 'Studies for Pictures: Isleworth' sketchbook (TB XC–6, 9, 29, 31). In this case the classical element is stressed by the fragment of classical entablature in the foreground and the glimpse of a temple among the trees in the middle distance; these features give the picture the feeling of a capriccio rather than an actual view on the Thames. When the composition was engraved for the *Liber Studiorum* (R 68) in 1819 it was entitled with the more general, alternative name for the Thames, 'Isis', and it was not until the 1850s that the picture was recorded with the present title. In fact it forms a perfect pendant to 'Narcissus and Echo'. In one of the sketches in the 'Studies for Pictures: Isleworth' sketchbook (fig. 17; TB XC–29) the composition is even closer in that instead of the peacock now shown perching on the entablature there is a reclining figure akin to those in the other picture.

A considerable relaxation in formal composition and a closer approach to nature can be seen in 'The Thames near Windsor' (fig. 28; BJ 64). It has been suggested that this is one of the pictures seen by Benjamin West in Turner's gallery in 1807 and described by him to Farington as 'Views on the Thames, crude blotches, nothing could be more vicious'; that Turner did include Thames views in his exhibition in 1807 (for which again no catalogue has been traced) is suggested by John Landseer's review of Turner's exhibition the next year which, as we shall see, helps to identify some of the later pictures at Petworth. In any case, although the painting shows a scene of everyday activity as in 'Windsor Castle from the Thames', the forms are looser, the sky and receding river more freely handled, and there is generally more air in the composition than in either that picture or 'The Thames at Weybridge'. The freer handling and more relaxed style seem to reflect Turner's work sketching on the Thames (e.g. fig. 18; BJ 163).

A further relaxation can be seen in 'The Thames at Eton' (fig. 29; BJ 71) which was described by John Landseer, as 'Eton College', in his long review of the exhibition in Turner's gallery in 1808 in the *Review of Publications of Art*.[3] Lord Egremont is known to have bought 'The Forest of Bere' from this exhibition and it may well be that he also, later on during its course, bought this painting together with 'The Confluence of the Thames and the Medway' and 'Margate'; however there is no definite evidence for this. There is a freshness of observation in 'The Thames at Eton' that again seems to reflect Turner's days spent making oil sketches on the river (e.g. fig. 19; BJ 181). The composition is less formal than that of 'The Thames near Windsor', and there is more atmosphere and depth in the trees; the distant chapel is more impressionistically painted than the castle in 'Windsor Castle from the Thames'. The informality of the painting is furthered by its being of a smaller size.

Leaving aside for the moment other works in the 1808 exhibition, the series of views on the Thames now at Petworth concludes with 'Near the Thames' Lock, Windsor' (fig. 30; BJ 88), exhibited in Turner's gallery in 1809, a year for which we at last have a copy of the catalogue. The general principles of composition are much the same as in 'The Thames at Eton', with the activity of the figures displayed across the foreground and with buildings shown atmospherically beyond the trees in the distance; Turner has, however, returned to his more usual three-foot by four-foot format. In 1808 John Landseer had not altogether surprisingly related the title 'The Thames at Eton' to Thomas Gray's *Ode on a Distant Prospect of Eton College*; in 1809 Turner actually quoted from Gray in his catalogue:

> Say, Father Thames, for thou hast seen
> Full many a sprightly race,
> Disporting on thy margin green,
> The paths of pleasure trace,
> Who foremost now delight to cleave
> With pliant arms thy glassy wave.

Once again, it is not known precisely when Lord Egremont acquired this picture. Two days after the opening of the exhibition, on 26 April 1809, Sir Thomas Lawrence wrote to a Mr Penrice of Yarmouth suggesting that he might buy the work, presumably still unsold at this time. The comments of the future President of the Royal Academy show his appreciation of the younger artist: 'The subject is "A Scene near Windsor", with young Etonians introduced . . . If the expression can apply to landscape it is full of sentiment, and certainly of genius . . . it is in his [Turner's] peculiar manner, but *that* at its best; no Flemish finishing, but having in it fine principles of art, the essentials of beauty, and (as far as the subject admits it) even of grandeur'.

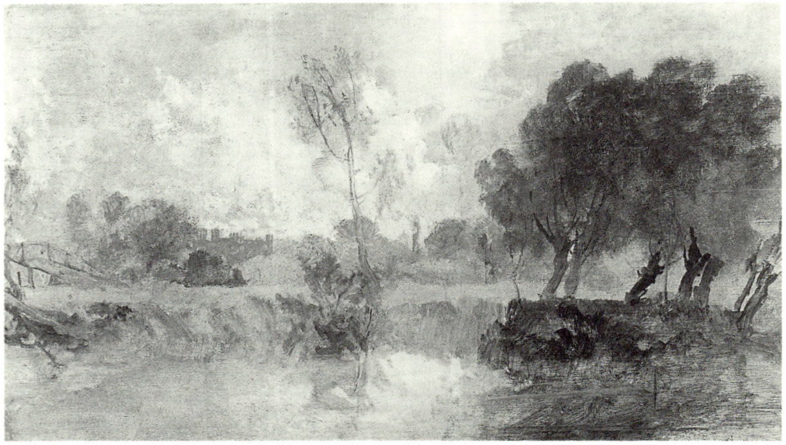

fig. 19 *Eton from the River* (BJ 181), *c.* 1807, Oil on mahogany veneer 370 × 665 (14¼ × 26⅛), Tate Gallery

As far as is known none of the pictures discussed so far were definitely commissioned by the Earl of Egremont and some, as we have seen, were purchased some years after they were painted. In the case of 'The Forest of Bere' (fig. 31; BJ 77), exhibited in Turner's gallery in 1808, the artist may deliberately have been seeking Lord Egremont's patronage. As is demonstrated in Appendix 1, Lord Egremont was deeply concerned in the various activities on his estates, and it may well have been that Turner was trying to exploit this interest. However, there is no evidence that Lord Egremont owned the Forest of Bere or even parts of the Forest of Bere as has been suggested in the past. Indeed, the fact that as early as 1835, in H. Phillips' catalogue of the Petworth Collection, this picture had lost its original title and was referred to as 'Evening. A Pond Surrounded by Willows. Sunset. Cattle drinking. Men stripping Osiers' suggests that there was no special identification of the Forest of Bere with Lord Egremont's interests.

In any case, Lord Egremont did buy the painting shortly after the opening of the exhibition, as was noted in the *Examiner* on 8 May 1808. John Landseer, in his review, praised the picture for 'the rich and harmonious union of its parts . . . Though it is nothing as a subject, it is everything as a picture'. Clearly any special significance in the subject was a secret between Turner and Lord Egremont. Landseer goes on to relate the painting, 'for making a few cattle and a setting sun the subject of an admirable picture', to the work of Cuyp, who 'would be humbled, we conceive, by a too near approach to this picture of Turner'. However, even stronger seems to be the influence of two other artists less usually associated with Turner, Rubens and Gainsborough; this is apparent particularly in the warm interweaving of foliage and the light of the setting sun.

The two seascapes from Turner's 1808 exhibition now at Petworth are distinct in style from each other; indeed it is possible that 'The Confluence of the Thames and the Medway' (fig. 32; BJ 75) may date from some years earlier. In his review of the 1808 exhibition John Landseer stated that 'The greater number of the pictures at present exhibited are views on the Thames . . . including the pictures of Thames scenery which Mr Turner has formerly exhibited', and it is perhaps not stretching this hint too far to suggest that the Thames Estuary scene could also have been 'formerly exhibited'. The crispness and solidity of the clouds, and the 'prevailing freshness, and cool and silvery tone' remarked upon by John Landseer of this picture, are closer to 'Windsor Castle from the Thames' than to works of later years, and the density of the waves and the clustering together of the ships are closer to 'Ships Bearing up for Anchorage' than to Turner's other Thames estuary paintings exhibited in his gallery in 1808, 'Purfleet and the Essex Shore' (fig. 20; BJ 74) and 'Sheerness as seen from the Nore' (BJ 76). Similarly, the delicately but incisively suggested forms of the distant port of Sheerness on the horizon recall Turner's device in 'Ships Bearing up for Anchorage' of drawing the eye to the horizon with a sharply defined line of light; again, the comparable depiction of Sheerness, 'as seen from the Nore' in the other exhibit of 1808, is much more atmospherically and diffusely painted. There is a watercolour showing a hoy crossing and partly masking a man of war like that in the right half of 'The Confluence of the Thames and the Medway' in the 'Hesperides (1)' sketchbook (TB XCIII–41), which also includes sketches for the painting of that title exhibited in 1805; this also supports a rather earlier date. A drawing of fishing boats in the 'River and Margate' sketchbook (TB XCIX–32) of *c.* 1807 may however also be related.

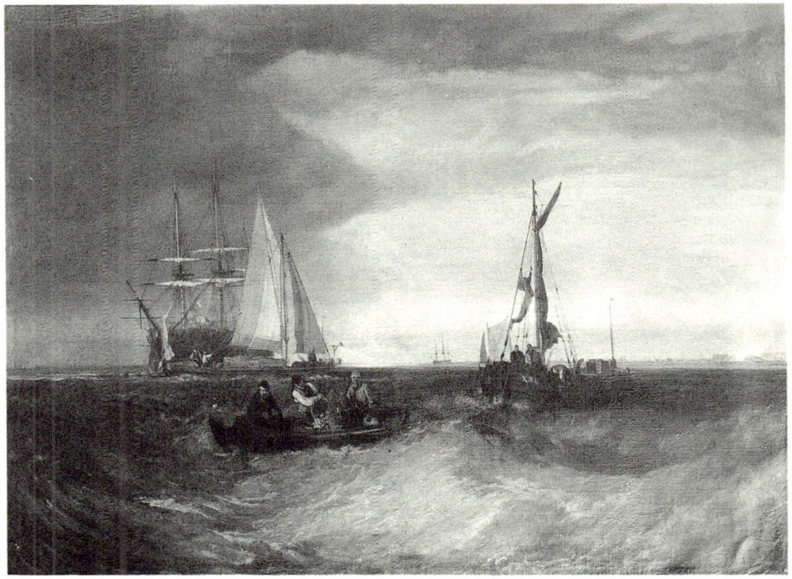

fig. 20 *Purfleet and the Essex Shore as seen from the Long Reach* (BJ 74), Turner's gallery 1808, Oil on canvas 915 × 1220 (36 × 48), Private Collection, Belgium

'Margate' (fig. 33; BJ 78), the other seapiece at Petworth included in Turner's exhibition in 1808, is much more atmospheric and unified in treatment, lacking the sharp distinction of forms of 'The Confluence of the Thames and the Medway'. John Landseer, in his review, noted the particular features of this painting: 'The town of Margate itself in a morning mist from which the pier is emerging . . . The detail of the town and cliffs, being lost at the early hour which is represented, in the mistiness of the morning, and only the bolder forms being discernable', and 'The mill and brewery on the summit of the cliff behind which the sun is rising', which 'from their general forms alone being visible, become objects of great interest in the landscape – appearing like magnificent temples'. This new interest in an all-embracing atmospheric unity seems to reflect the rapid development of Turner's style that accompanied his making of oil sketches in the open air both on the river and on the Thames estuary in about 1806–7, as for example

'Shipping at the Mouth of the Thames' (BJ 175), and the closer view of 'Margate, setting Sun' (fig. 21; BJ 174).

The next painting at Petworth in order of execution, exhibited in 1809, the same year as 'Near the Thames' Lock, Windsor' but at the Royal Academy rather than in Turner's own gallery, is 'Tabley, Cheshire, the Seat of Sir J. F. Leicester, Bart.: Calm Morning' (fig. 34; BJ 99). This did not however become part of the collection of Lord Egremont until 1827, having been painted for Sir John Leicester together with its companion, 'Tabley, the Seat of Sir J. F. Leicester, Bart.: Windy Day' (fig. 22; BJ 98); on the death of Sir John Leicester, later Lord de Tabley, the second painting remained in the collection of his heirs while 'Calm Morning' was sold with other pictures on 7 July 1827 and was bought by the third Earl of Egremont. The composition of both pictures is basically the same, only the weather conditions being different. Turner painted a small oil sketch of the composition in the 'Tabley' sketchbook, used when Turner was actually staying at Tabley in the summer of 1808 (BJ 208). This has been cut out and folded as if for dispatch through the post, and may have been sent to Sir John Leicester for approval. What is interesting is that the large water tower, which forms such a prominent, if not disturbing, feature in both the larger oil paintings, is absent from the sketch; presumably it was Sir John Leicester himself who insisted on its being included.

Despite the presence of the tower the two paintings were well received by the critics. The *Repository of Arts* wrote that 'the views of Sir John Leicester's seat, which in any other hand would be mere topography, touched by his magic pencil have assumed a highly poetical character. It is on occasions like this that the superiority of this man's mind displays itself; and in comparison with the production of his hands, not only all the painters of the present-day but all the boasted names to which collectors bow sink into nothing'. The critic of the *Morning Herald*, referring to 'Calm Morning', wrote 'In this felicitous imitation of a calm morning, the Artist has evidently taken Cuyp for his study; and it is but just to aver, that he has preserved the aerial perspective better than any other Artist within our remembrance, at least in this country. There is such *repose* in the whole composition, each part harmonizes with its adjunct object so happily, that a troubled spirit might dwell upon this picture in contemplation, until the nervous system were reattuned by quietude, receiving an imperceptible anodyne through the operations of sympathy'.

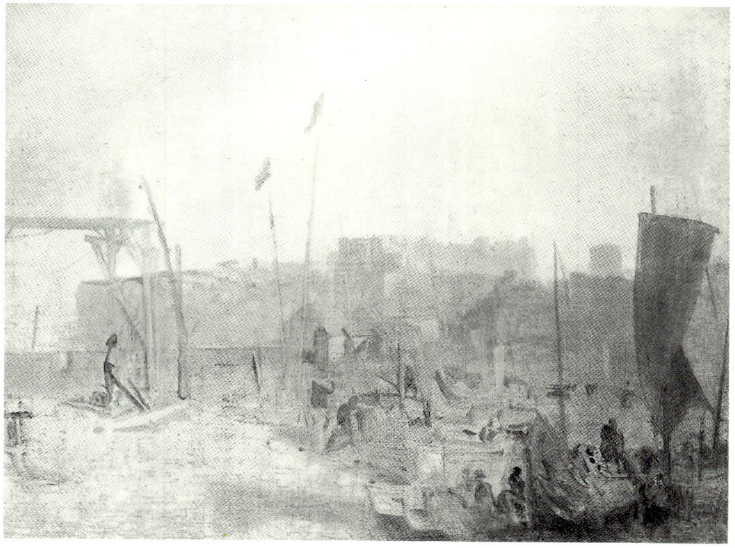

fig. 21 *Margate, Setting Sun* (BJ 174), *c.* 1806–7, Oil on canvas 855 × 1160 (33¾ × 45⅝), Tate Gallery

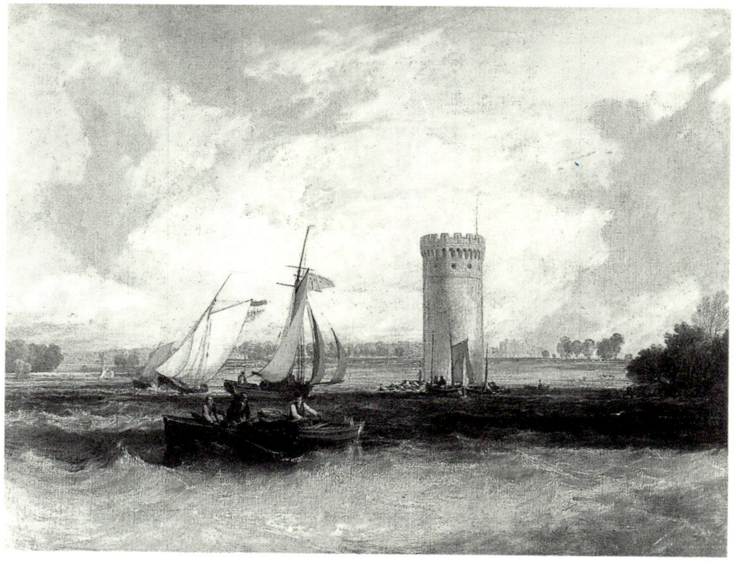

fig. 22 *Tabley, Cheshire, the Seat of Sir J. F. Leicester, Bart.: Windy Day* (BJ 98), R.A. 1809, Oil on canvas 915 × 1205 (36 × 47½), The Victoria University of Manchester (on long loan to the Whitworth Art Gallery, Manchester)

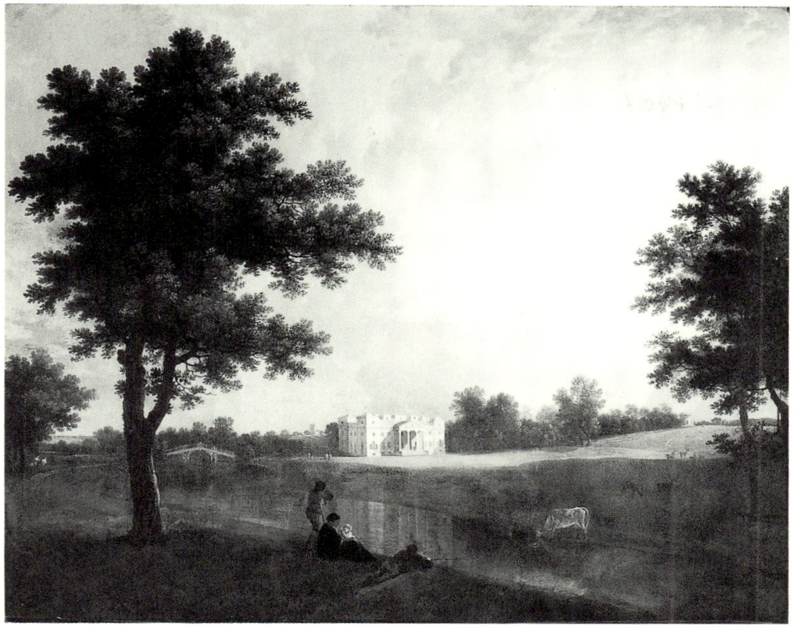

fig. 23 Richard Wilson: *Croome Court*, 1758, Oil on canvas 1220 × 1675 (48 × 66), Reproduced by permission of the Croome Estate Trustees

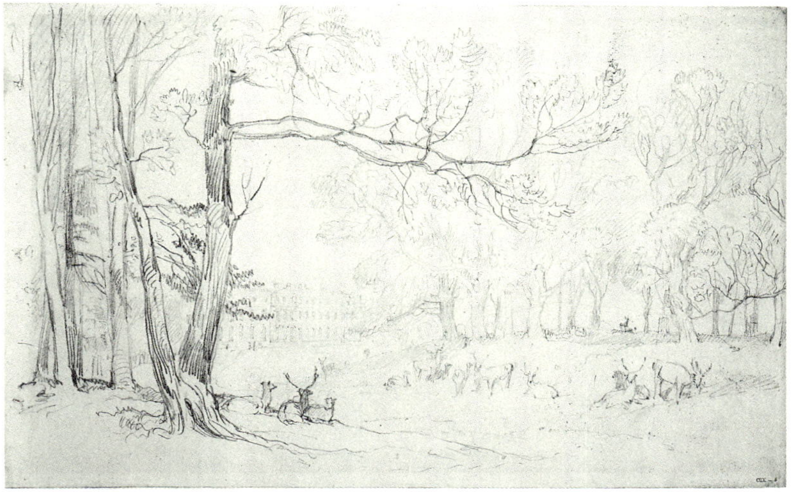

fig. 24 *Sketch for 'Petworth, Sussex . . . Dewy Morning'* ('Petworth' sketchbook, TB CIX, p. 5), 1809, Pencil 225 × 370 ($8\frac{7}{8} \times 14\frac{1}{2}$), Tate Gallery

It was in fact the success of the two Tabley pictures at the Royal Academy in 1809 that led, among other commissions, to that by Lord Egremont for two pictures exhibited the following year, 'Petworth, Sussex, the Seat of the Earl of Egremont: Dewy Morning' (fig. 35; BJ 113), shown at the Royal Academy, and 'Cockermouth Castle', shown in Turner's own gallery. 'Petworth . . . Dewy Morning', like the Tabley paintings, continues the tradition of the country house portrait, with the house set far back in its setting, established by Richard Wilson with such paintings as 'Croome Court' of 1758–9 (fig. 23). Here there is no obtrusive water tower but Turner seems, almost perversely, to have tucked the end of the house away behind the slope on the left and given prominence to the boat house in the left foreground; just so did he tend to relegate Windsor Castle to the background in his various pictures of that subject. Nevertheless, his skilful design means that the house, though distant, is the focal point of the picture, picked out as it is by the spire of Petworth church behind. There are two related drawings in the 'Petworth' sketchbook (figs. 3 and 24; TB CIX–4 and 5), in use in the summer of 1809.

This seems to have been one of Turner's first exhibited oil paintings in which he employed a white ground, thus lightening and heightening the tonality of the painting and bringing it closer to the luminosity of a watercolour – Turner was of course a long-established master of the use of watercolour washes over white paper. The novelty of effect was noted by the critic of *La Belle Assemblée*, who affected to doubt that the picture was by Turner had it not been 'for the information in the catalogue'. He added 'it was manifestly Mr. Turner's design to express the peculiar hue and pellucidness of objects seen through a medium of air, in other words to express the clearness of atmosphere. To effect this purpose it was necessary to select those dark material objects which serve as a foil to aerial light and to produce atmosphere by their contrast. Mr. Turner has neglected to use these necessary foils and has thus made a confusion between aerial light and the appropriate gloom of objects. Failing in this forcible opposition, without which a painter can never express atmosphere, the appearance of the picture is that of a mere flimsy daubing without substance or distinction, without either shape or colour. A man of Mr. Turner's experience should have understood better the principles of his art'. However, this criticism was countered by the praise of other critics. The review in the *Public Ledger and Daily Advertiser* reads: 'The chief excellence of this picture is the execution of the water, and the dewy vapour that floats through the vallies; the latter effect is most happily expressed and, apparently, by a very simple process, that of a kind of light scumbling and glazing . . .'. The *British Press* considered it 'Another most beautiful landscape, in which the water is pre-eminent, for the excellence with which it is finished. In clearness and brilliancy, we have never seen it excelled'. The transformation of Turner's early style was now complete.

Lord Egremont's other commission, 'Cockermouth Castle' (fig. 36; BJ 108), shows another property in his possession, the castle formerly in the possession of the Earls of Northumberland but which had passed in 1750, with the Egremont title and indeed Petworth House, to Sir Charles Wyndham, father of the third Earl. Again there are drawings for the picture in the 'Petworth' sketchbook (TB CIX–14, 24) and also, in the case of the second painting, a sketchier drawing in the 'Cockermouth' sketchbook (TB CX–16). The two paintings were not, however, designed as a pair, 'Cockermouth Castle' being considerably smaller, in fact matching the format of 'The Thames at Eton' of 1808 with which it still hangs as a pendant, despite the lack of any personal association of Eton with Lord Egremont (he was in fact educated at Westminster). In 'Cockermouth Castle' Turner reverses his usual procedure and makes the castle the largest element in the composition, pushed back behind low-lying trees but still dominating the work by sheer bulk and dwarfing the signs of local activity.

The last two paintings from this phase of Turner's connection with Petworth are 'Teignmouth' (fig. 37; BJ 120) and 'Hulks on the Tamar' (fig. 38; BJ 119), both estuary scenes from the south-west of England and both, potentially at least it has to be said in view of their disturbing condition, among the most poetic works of this period. Following his visit to Devon and Cornwall in 1811, Turner exhibited five oils based on sketches made on that tour at his gallery in 1812. 'Teignmouth' was one of them and 'Hulks on the Tamar' may well have been the otherwise lost painting of 'The River Plym' (BJ 118) also in that exhibition; the mouths of the rivers Tamar and Plym enter the sea within two miles of each other either side of Plymouth and such a confusion could easily have arisen, not least in Turner's own mind given similar confusions on his part.[4] According to C. H. Collins Baker, in his *Catalogue of the Petworth Collection* of 1920, both works were inscribed with dates by Turner, 'Teignmouth' in 1812 and 'Hulks on the Tamar' in 1811, but in both cases Turner's signature is worn and there are illegible traces at best of any possible date. Both pictures demonstrate Turner's power by this time to use a specific landscape to evoke mood in the fullest Romantic manner. The spindly masts in 'Hulks on the Tamar' and even more the skeleton of the derelict ship on the right of 'Teignmouth' cut against the idyllic sky to searing effect. With their relatively high key and their overall suffusion with light they look forward to the group of Petworth landscapes of the late 1820s.

The overall impression of the early oil paintings by Turner at Petworth, and of Lord Egremont's taste as reflected in them, is of the poetic landscape, sometimes tinged with classical allusions, that Turner categorised in his *Liber Studiorum* as 'P' or 'EP', 'Pastoral' or 'Elevated Pastoral'.[5] Similarly, the marines, with the exception of the earliest, 'Ships Bearing up for Anchorage', are of much the same mood. Lord Egremont's taste then, if not as adventurous as that of Sir John Leicester's, was consistent and leads one to appreciate what is perhaps a less generally recognised aspect of Turner's range of achievement. The ever growing refinement and subtlety of means is something to marvel at, particularly when one places it besides the rhetorical splendour of much of the work that Turner was doing at the same time.

Notes

1 Turner's oil-paintings are fully catalogued in Martin Butlin and Evelyn Joll, *The Paintings of J. M. W. Turner*, revised edition 1984; the catalogue numbers are referred to here in the abbreviated form 'BJ 18', etc. This publication should be referred to for full information about exhibitions, literature, contemporary reviews, sketches and so on. All the Turners at Petworth were catalogued by Evelyn Joll; minor revisions to BJ 77, 99 and 204 were made by Martin Butlin in *The Tate Gallery: Illustrated Catalogue of Acquisitions 1982–84*, 1986, pp. 69 and 72.

2 See Wilton 1987, p. 71, pl. 99: Turner's oil is repr. as pl. 97, and the watercolour sketch in the 'Studies for Pictures: Isleworth' sketchbook as pl. 98.

3 This review is discussed and fully transcribed by Luke Herrmann, 'John Landseer on Turner: Reviews of Exhibitions in 1808, 1839 and 1840 (Part 1)', *Turner Studies*, vol. vii, no. 1, Summer 1987, pp. 26–33.

4 Two examples will suffice: Turner's Royal Academy exhibit of 1802 entitled 'The Fifth Plague of Egypt' (BJ 13) in fact shows the Seventh Plague; 'Venice, from the Porch of Madonna della Salute' (BJ 362), shown at the Royal Academy in 1835, in fact actually shows the church with its portico on the right.

5 For the various categories of landscape as set out by Turner in his *Liber Studiorum* see Alexander J. Finberg, *The History of Turner's Liber Studiorum with a New Catalogue Raisonné*, 1924, pp. xxxvii–xlii, and, for the latest discussion on the contested identification of 'E. P.', Gage 1987, p. 139.

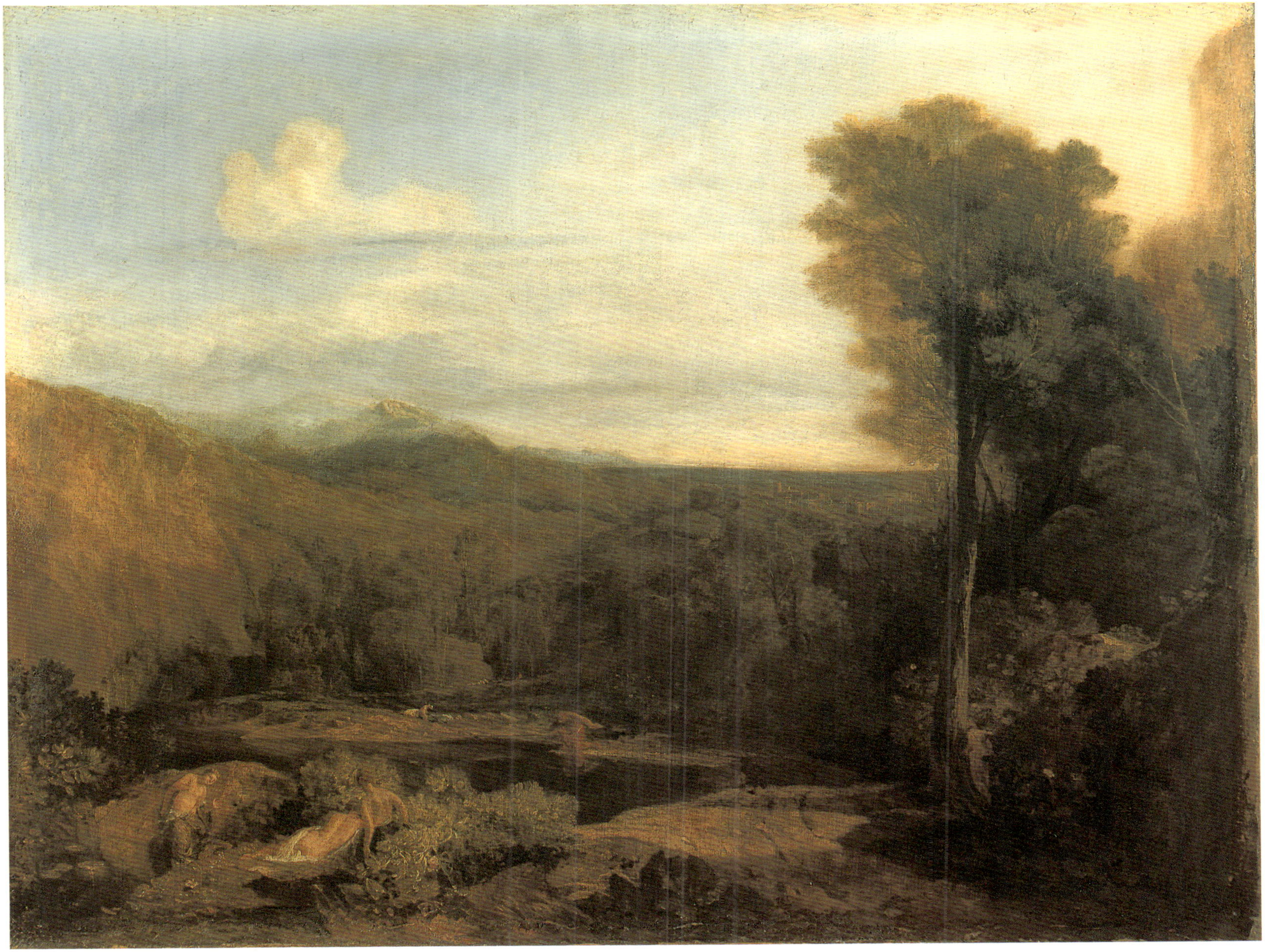

fig. 25 *Narcissus and Echo* (BJ 53), R.A. 1804, Oil on canvas 865 × 1170 (34 × 46), Petworth House

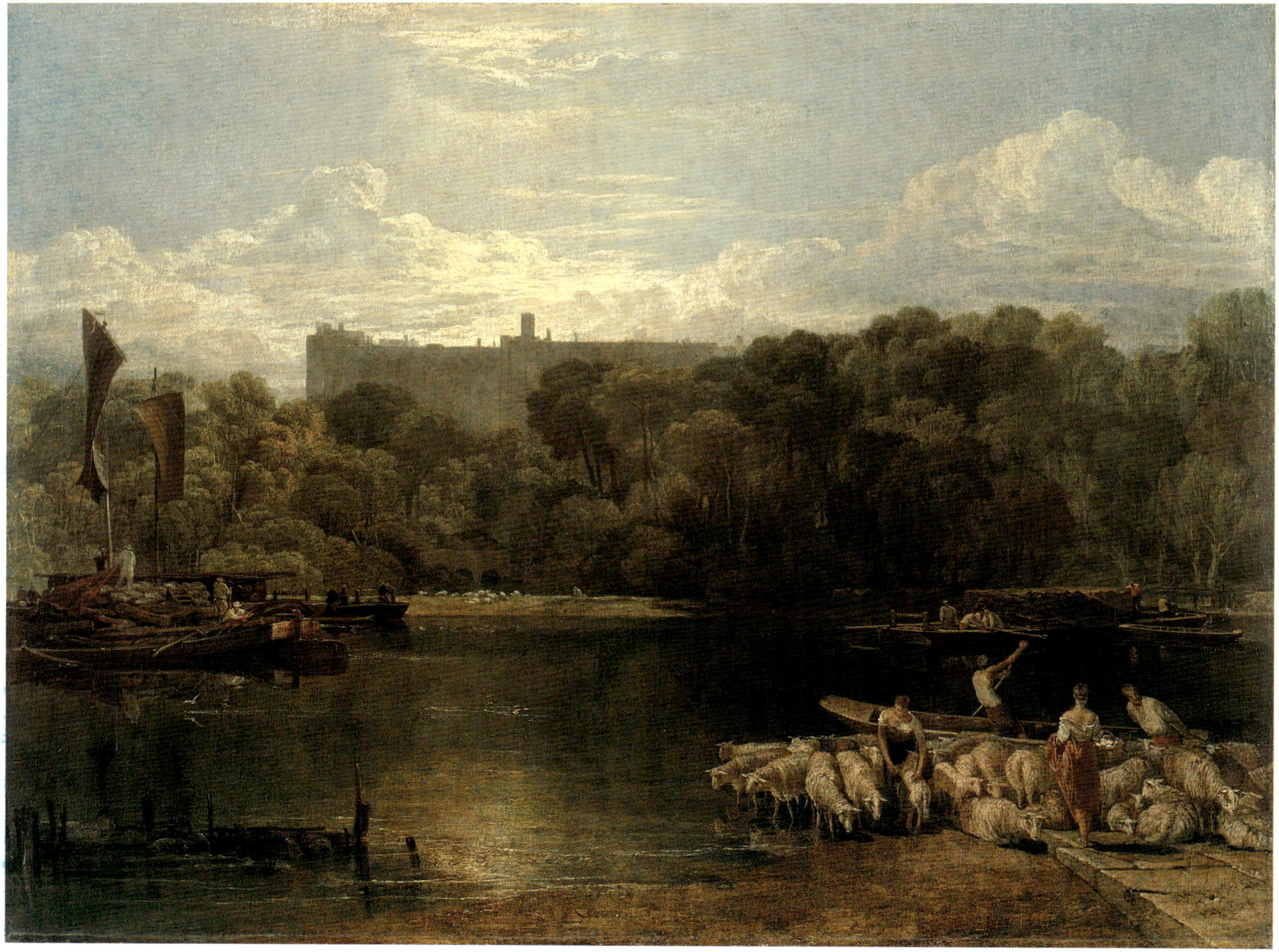

fig. 26 *Windsor Castle from the Thames* (BJ 149), *c.* 1805, Oil on canvas
910 × 1220 ($35\frac{3}{4}$ × 48), Petworth House

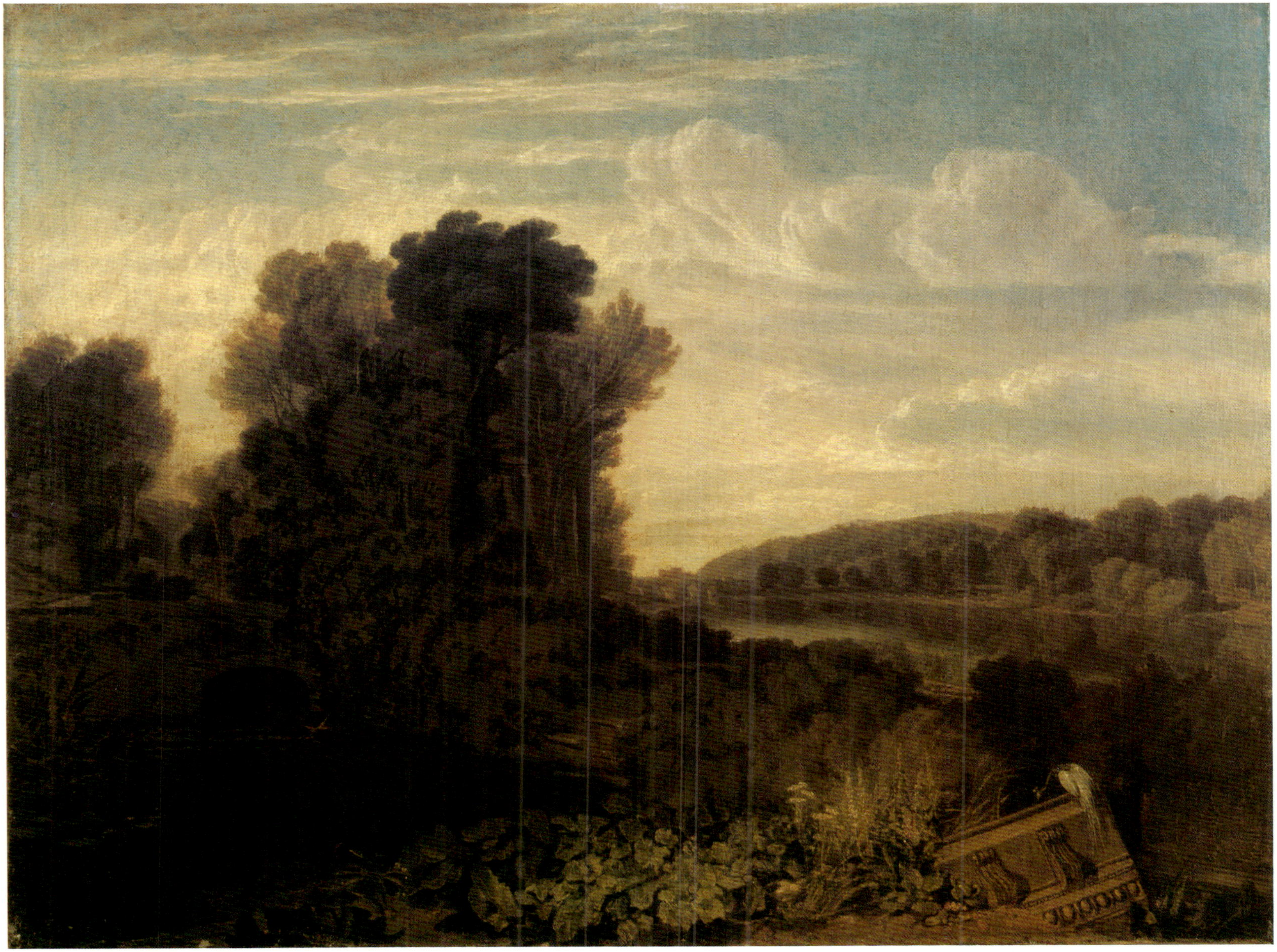

fig. 27 *The Thames at Weybridge* (BJ 204), *c.* 1805–6, Oil on canvas
890 × 1195 (35 × 47), Petworth House

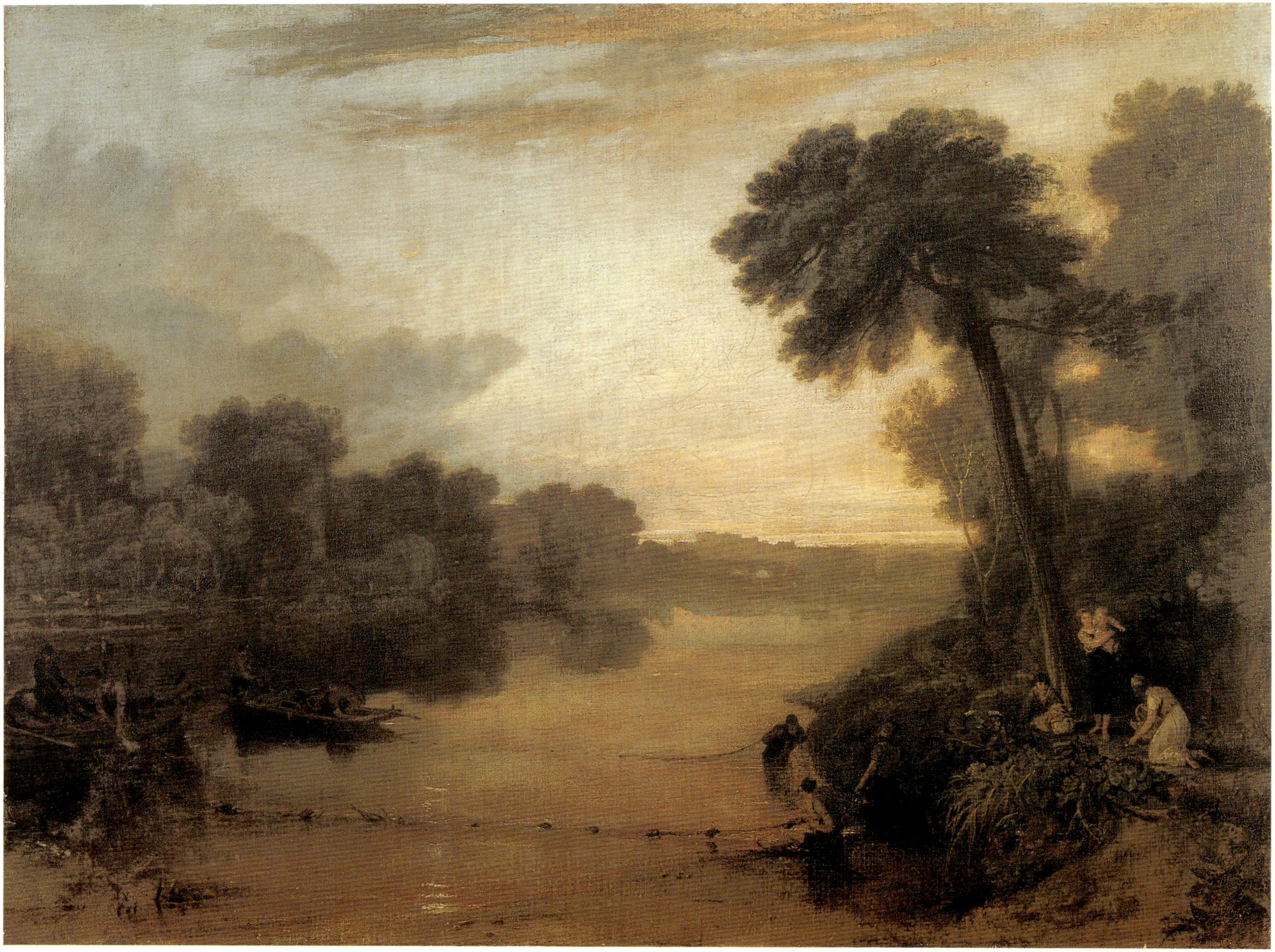

fig. 28 *The Thames near Windsor* (BJ 64), ? Turner's gallery 1807, Oil on canvas
890 × 1195 (35 × 47), Petworth House

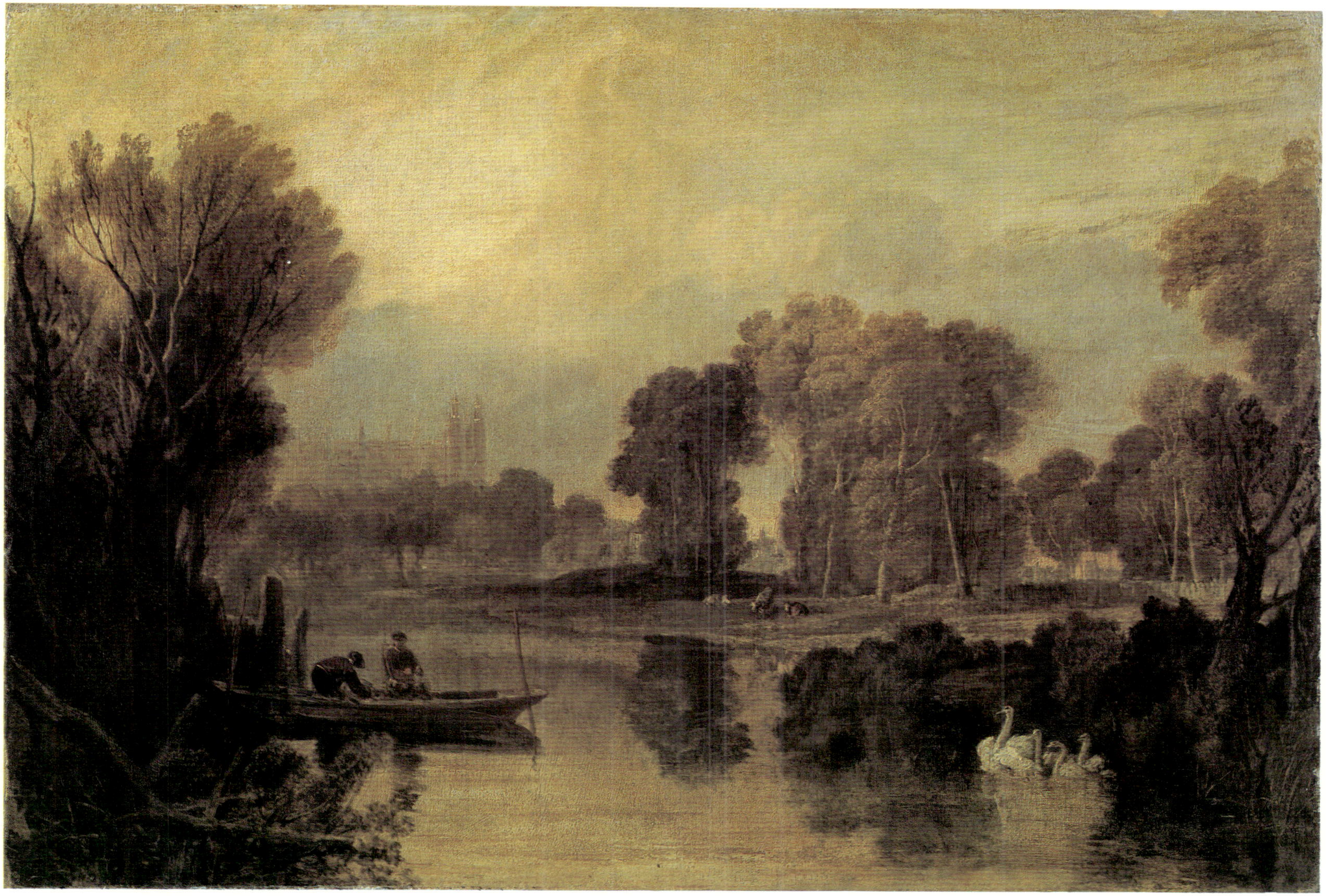

fig. 29 *The Thames at Eton* (BJ 71), Turner's gallery 1808, Oil on canvas
595 × 900 ($23\frac{1}{2} \times 35\frac{1}{2}$), Petworth House

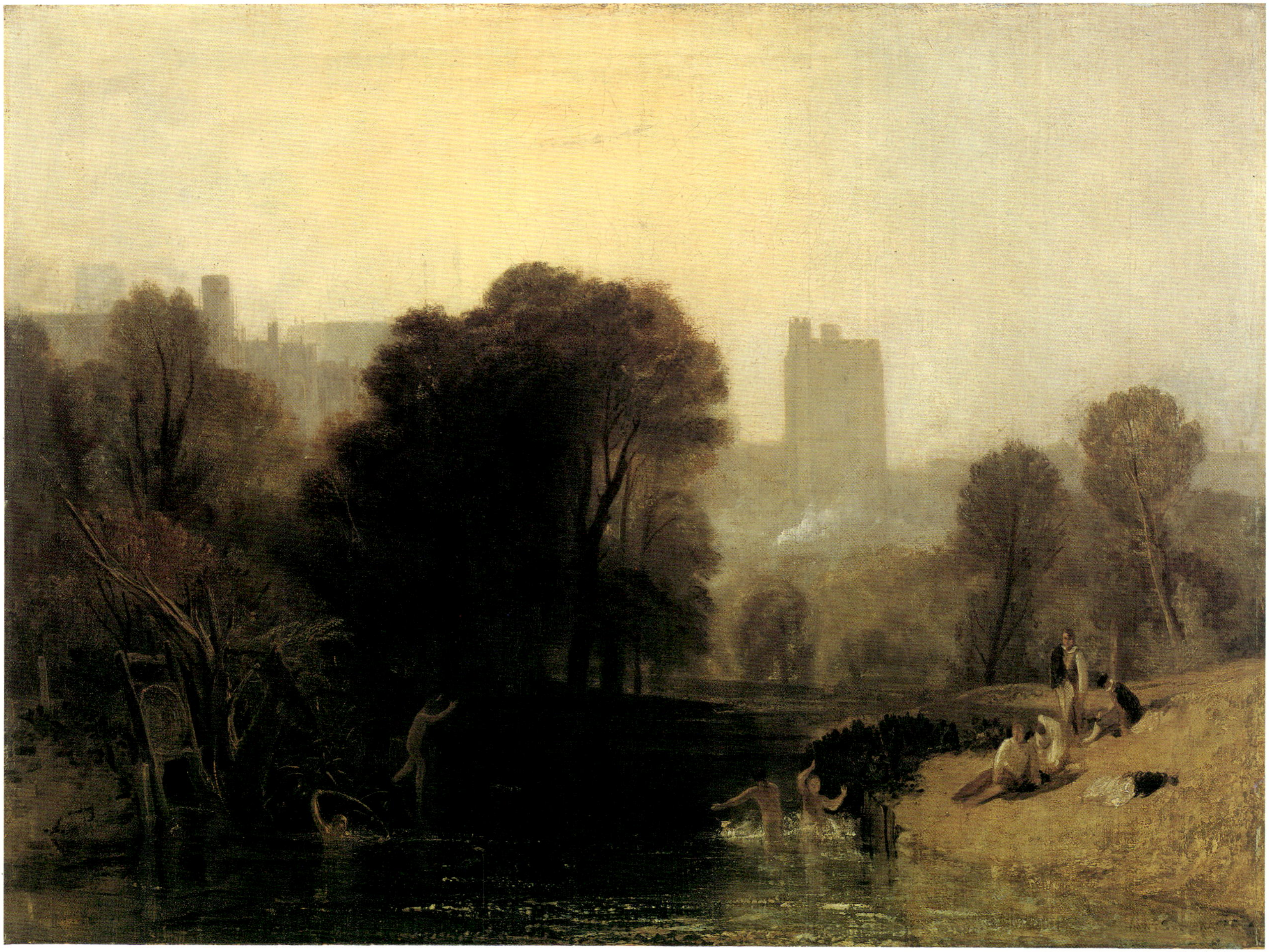

fig. 30 *Near the Thames' Lock, Windsor* (BJ 88), Turner's gallery 1809, Oil on canvas
890 × 1180 (35 × 46½), Petworth House

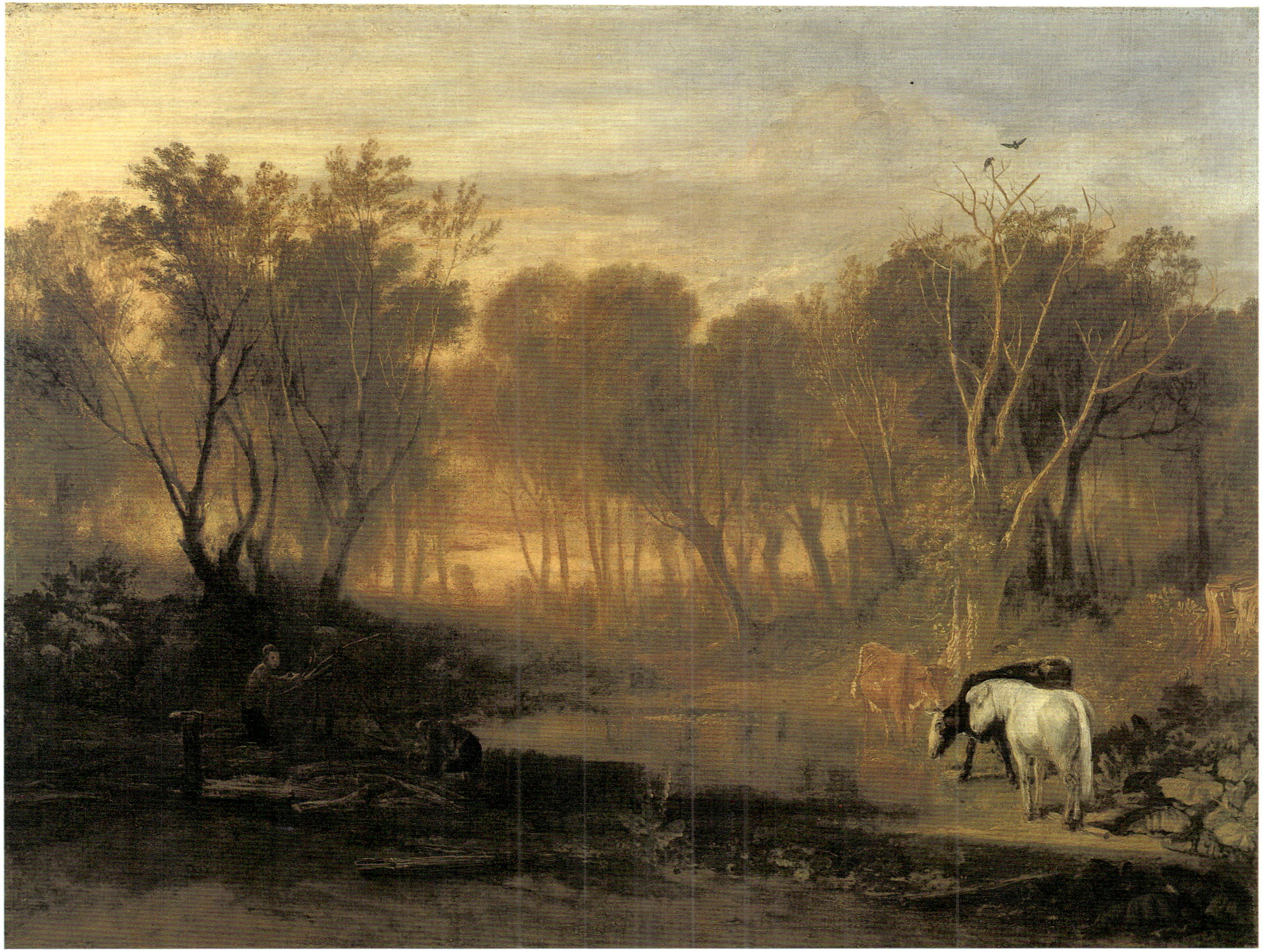

fig. 31 *The Forest of Bere* (BJ 77), Turner's gallery 1808, Oil on canvas
890 × 1195 (35 × 47), Petworth House

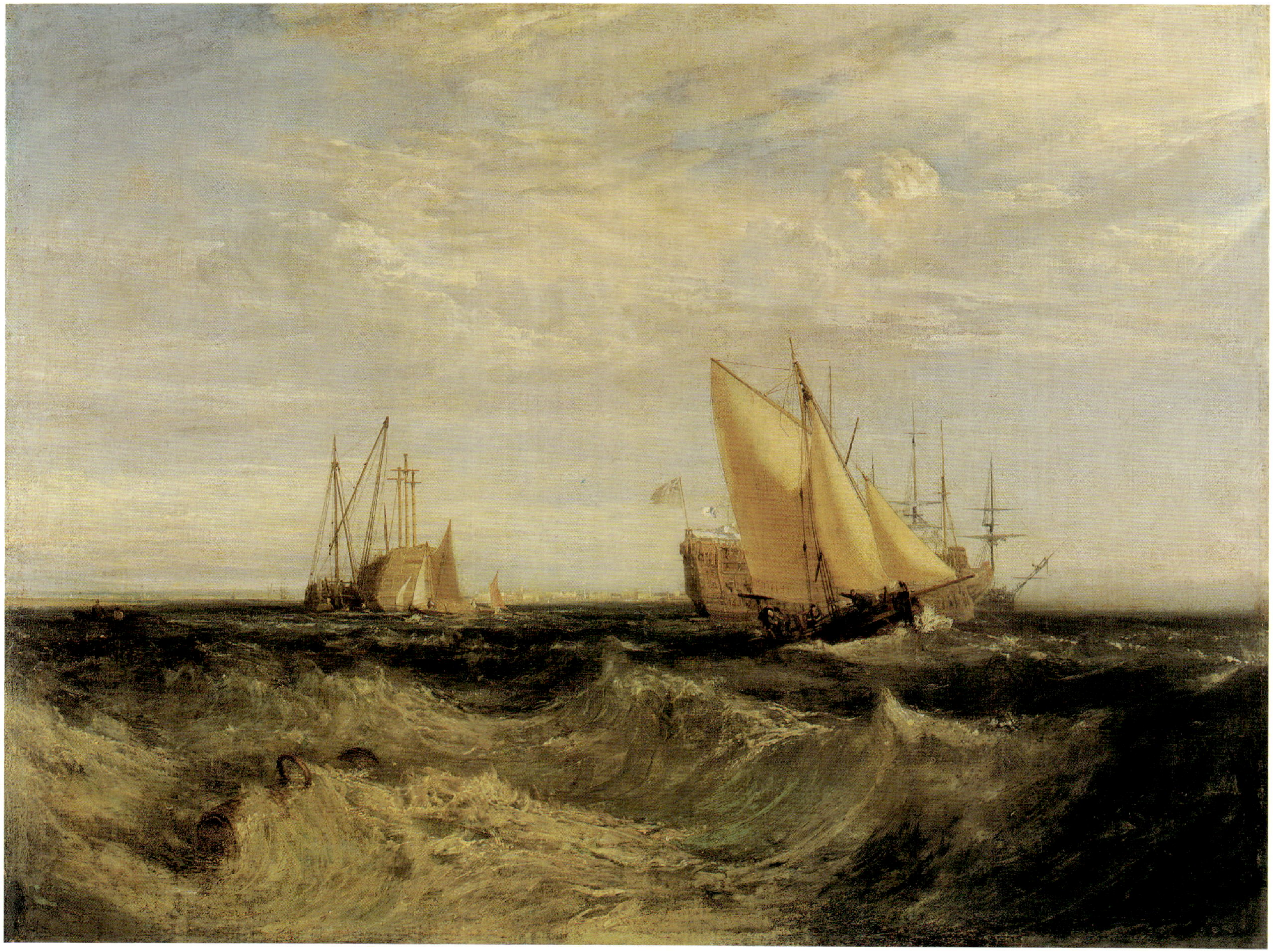

fig. 32 *The Confluence of the Thames and the Medway* (BJ 75), Turner's gallery 1808, Oil on canvas 910 × 1220 ($35\frac{7}{8}$ × 48), Petworth House

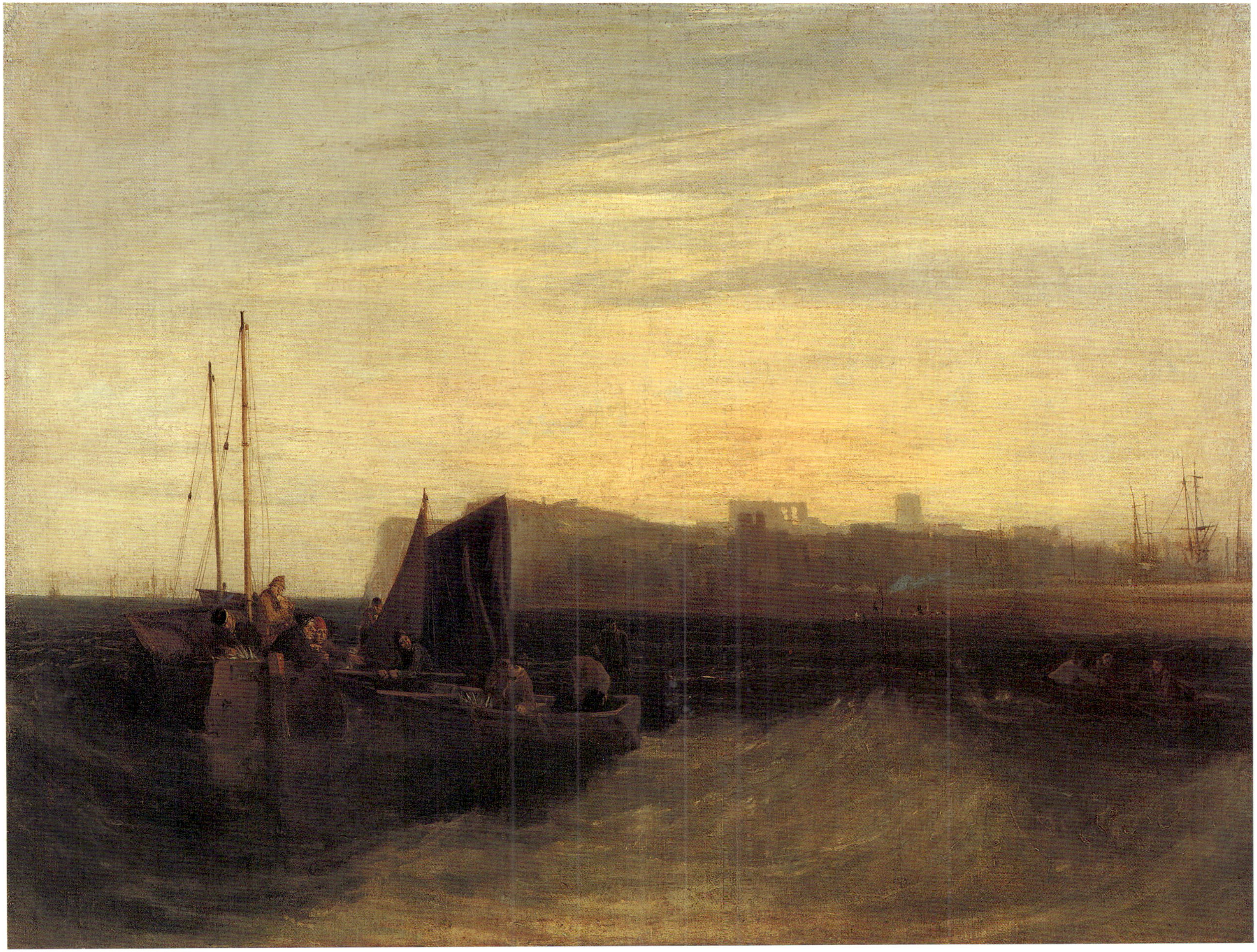

fig. 33 *Margate* (BJ 78), Turner's gallery 1808, Oil on canvas 900 × 1205 ($35\frac{1}{2} \times 47\frac{1}{2}$), Petworth House

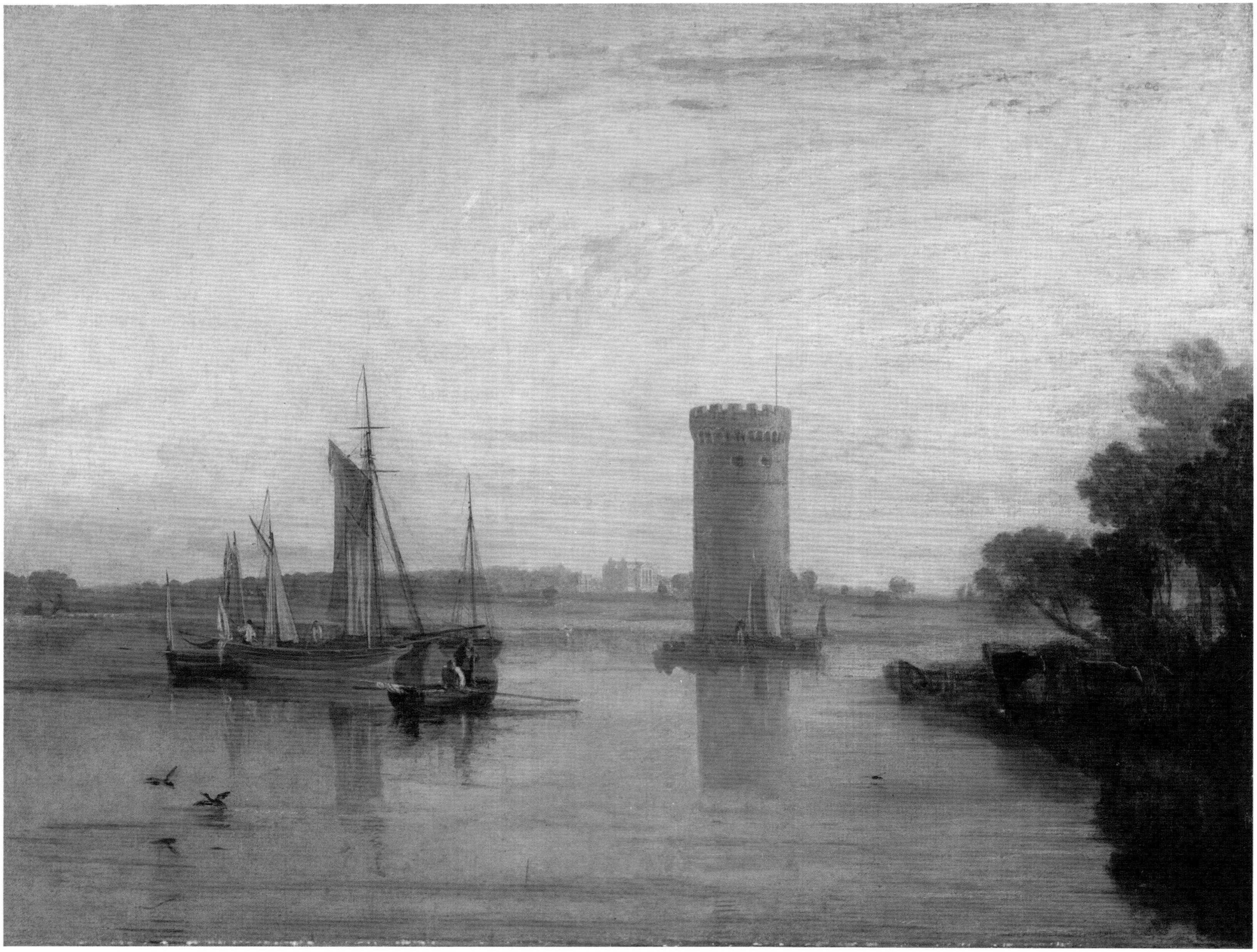

fig. 34 *Tabley, Cheshire, the Seat of Sir J.F. Leicester, Bart.: Calm Morning* (BJ 99), R.A. 1809, Oil on canvas 910 × 1215 ($35\frac{7}{8} \times 47\frac{3}{4}$), Petworth House

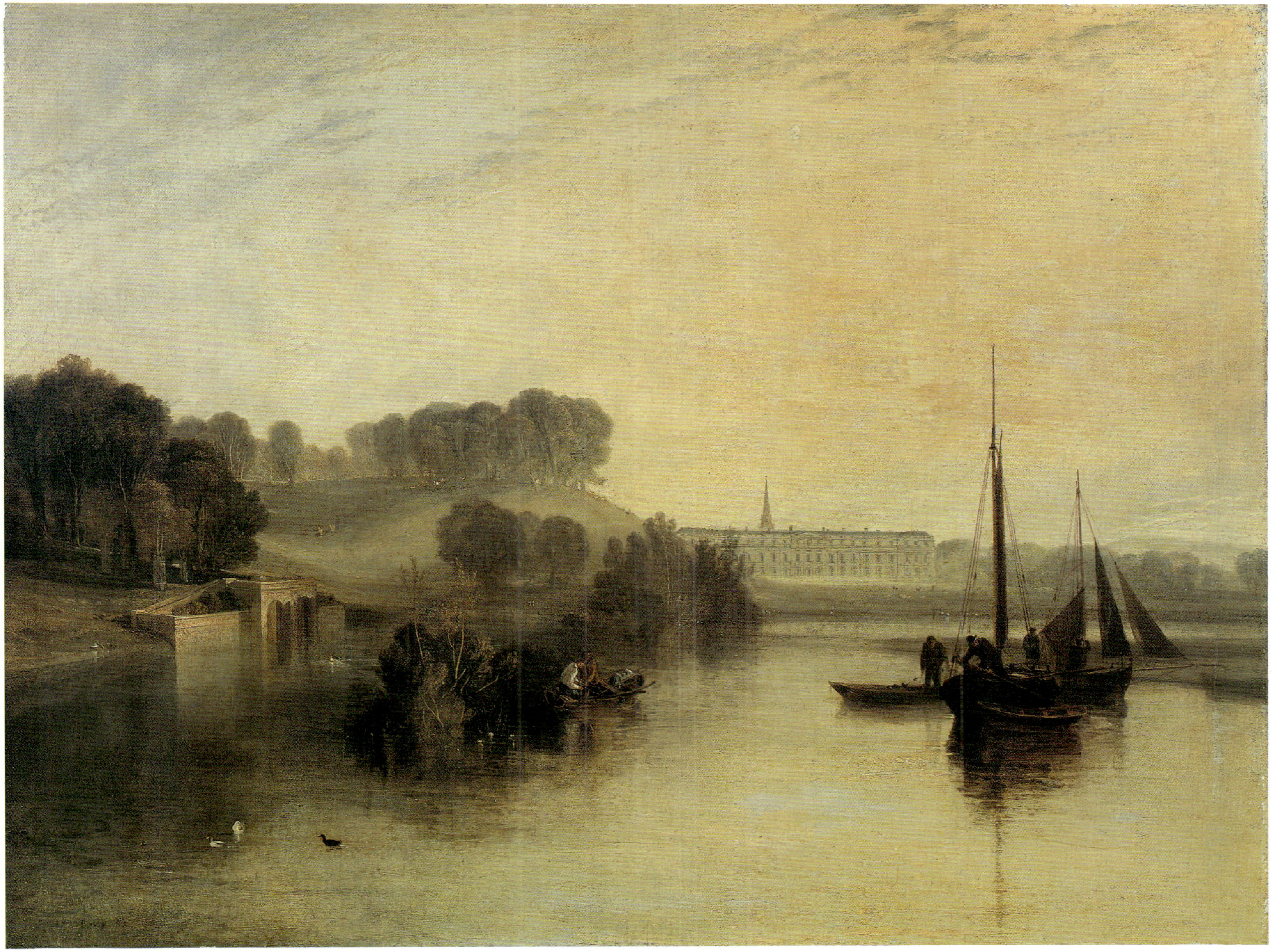

fig. 35 *Petworth, Sussex, the Seat of the Earl of Egremont: Dewy Morning* (BJ 113), R.A. 1810, Oil on canvas 915 × 1205 (36 × 47½"), Petworth House

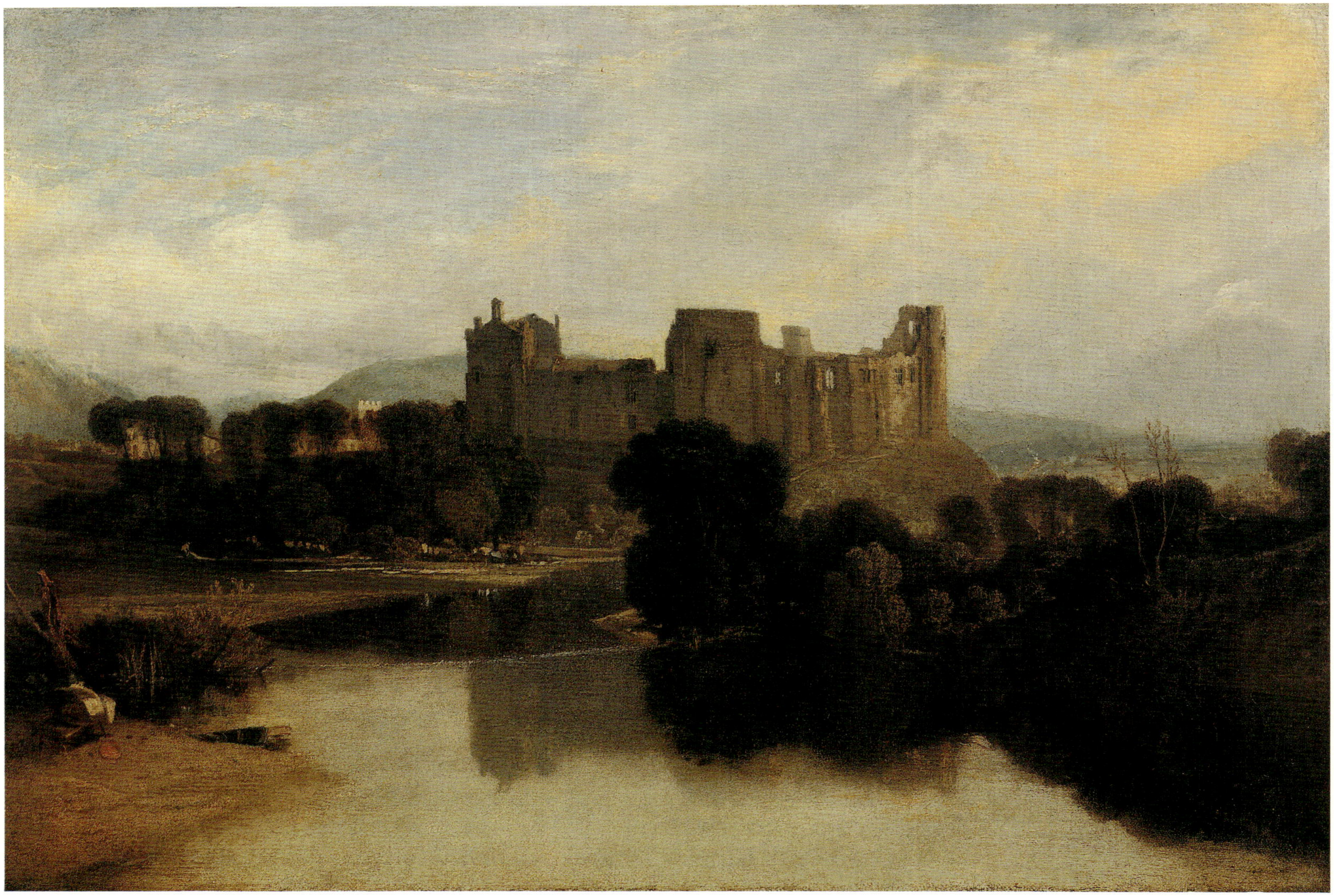

fig. 36 *Cockermouth Castle* (BJ 108), Turner's gallery 1810, Oil on canvas
605 × 905 ($23\frac{3}{4} \times 35\frac{5}{8}$), Petworth House

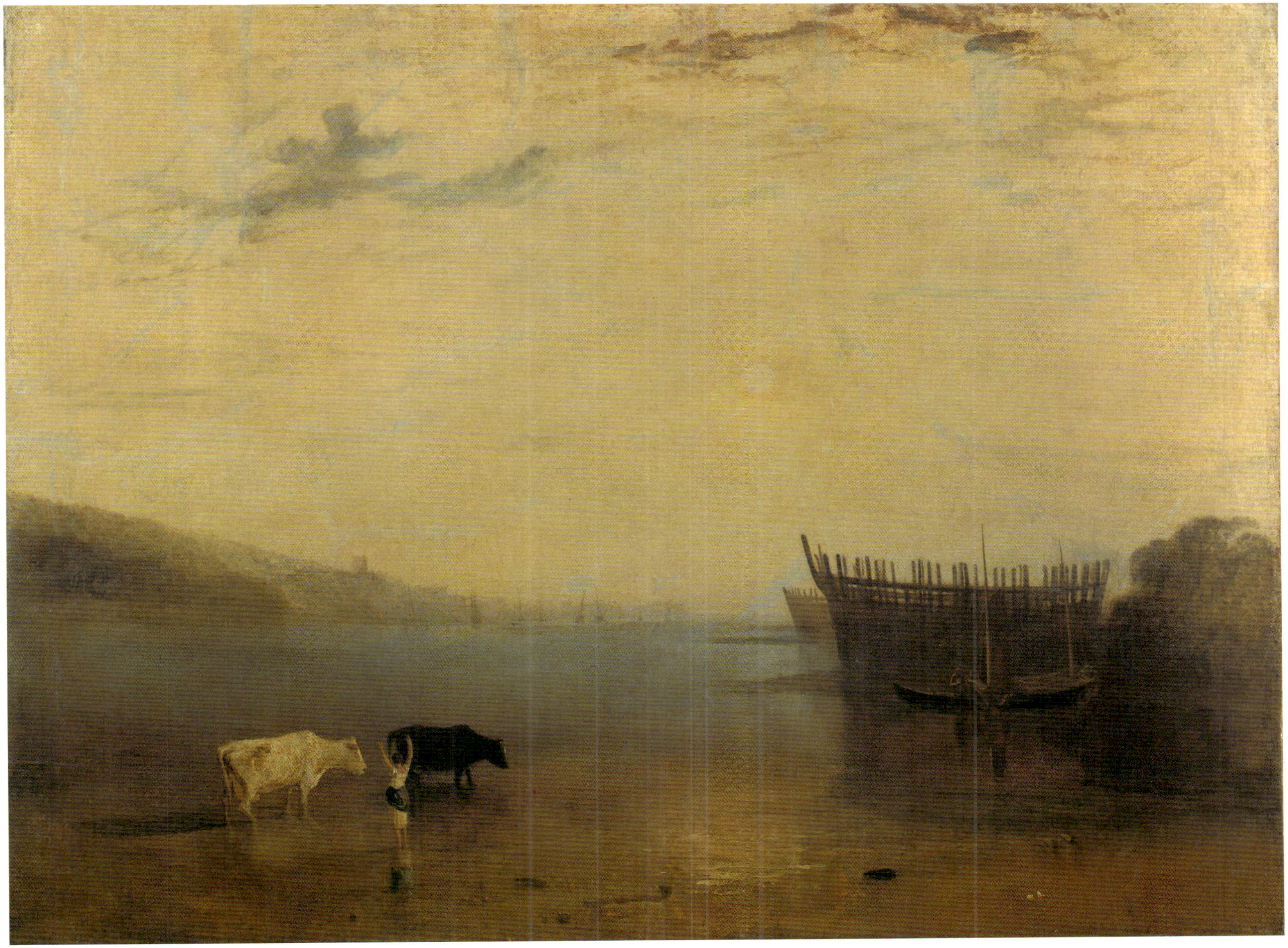

fig. 37 *Teignmouth* (BJ 120), Turner's gallery 1812, Oil on canvas
900 × 1205 (35½ × 47½), Petworth House

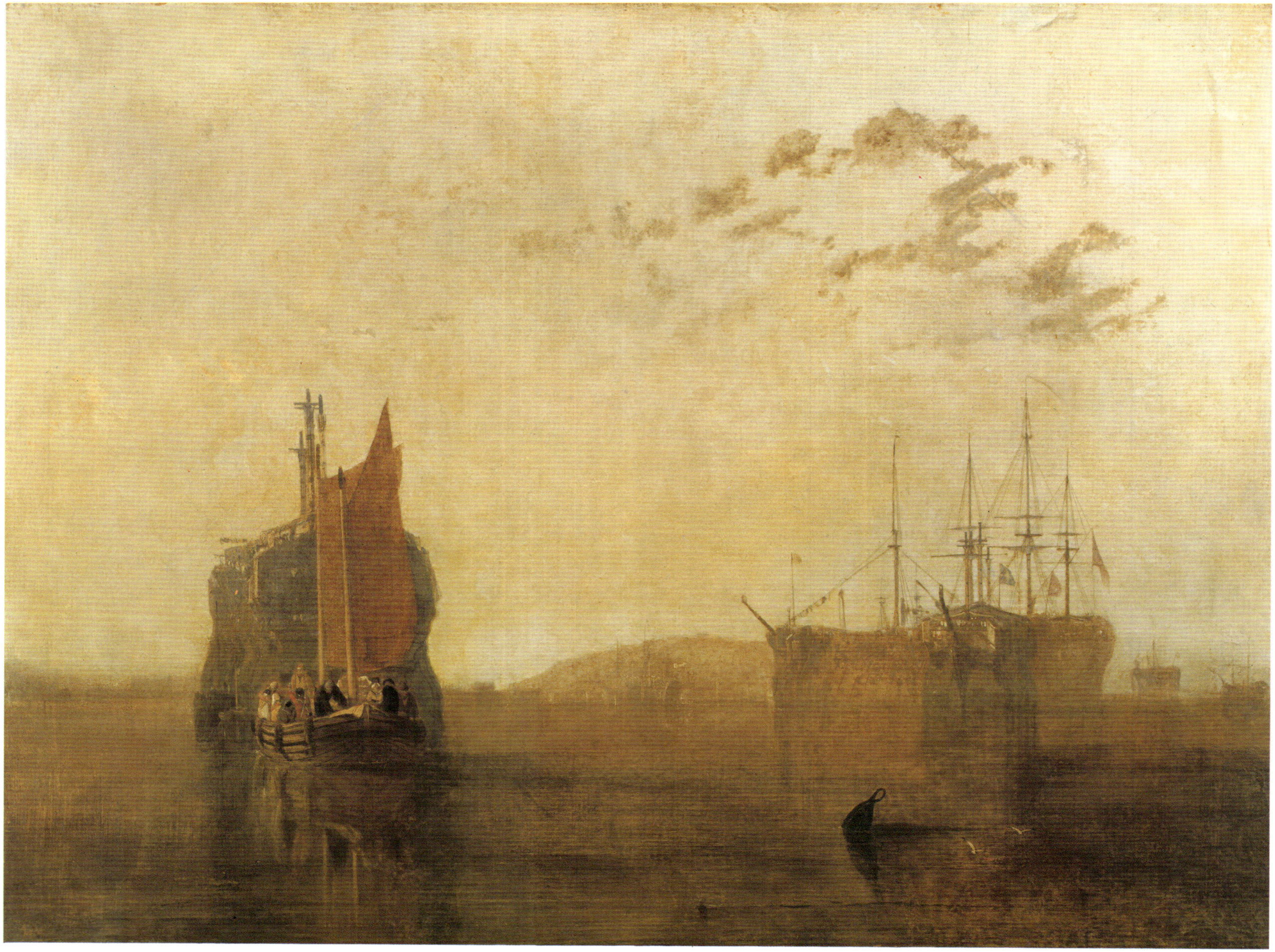

fig. 38 *Hulks on the Tamar* (*or 'The River Plym'?*) (BJ 119), ? Turner's gallery 1812,
Oil on canvas 900 × 1205 ($35\frac{1}{2} \times 47\frac{1}{2}$), Petworth House

CHAPTER 3

Turner and the Petworth Collection

Unlike most of the collections of art which Turner could have seen in England, that at Petworth has remained more-or-less intact, and in its original home, to this day.[1] Those works by Turner that were purchased by the third Earl of Egremont are, of course, still there, though they are now cared for by the Tate Gallery. Of the two most important dispersals of works from the collection, the first took place before Turner's real association with Petworth began. This was in 1794, when, after the sale of Egremont House in Piccadilly, most of the works of art there were transferred to Petworth and there was a weeding-out sale of 141 lots at Christie's. These were mainly of seventeenth-century Italian and Dutch paintings but as nothing fetched more than £20 it is unlikely, even allowing for the relative value of money at the time, that anything of real importance was sold. In 1927 however fourteen important paintings were sold, including works by Bronzino, Chardin, Frans Hals, Holbein, four Rembrandts and a Watteau. These works would have been known to Turner and, as we shall see, some influenced his own paintings. Finally, since the handing over of the main part of the collection to the nation in 1957, a few minor works have been sold from among those remaining in the possession of the family.

Most of the Old Master paintings at Petworth were acquired by the second Earl of Egremont in the middle of the eighteenth century, though Claude's 'Jacob with Laban and his Daughters' was bought by the second Earl's grandfather, the sixth Duke of Somerset (known as 'the Proud Duke'). As well as the artists already mentioned, the collection of Old Masters included works by Gaspar Poussin, Jacob Ruisdael, Salomon Rysdael, Hobbema, Cuyp, Bassano, Sassoferato and Canaletto. The great collection of works by Van Dyck included a number of family portraits, part of a large collection of portraits which had gradually built up, as was typical in English country houses, from the early seventeenth century onwards.

The third Earl's contribution was largely to create a collection of contemporary or recent works by British artists, including Turner. These included further family portraits but also works in all genres, with particularly large representations of Beechey and Thomas Phillips. Other artists included James Barry, George Clint, Thomas and William Daniell, Copley Fielding, Fuseli, Gainsborough, John Glover, Francis Grant, Hilton, Hodges, Hoppner, George Jones, C.R. Leslie, Northcote, Romney, Reynolds, Smirke, Wilkie and Richard Wilson.

In general the collections, both of Old Masters and of British paintings, represented contemporary tastes, though there were some slightly unusual earlier works by or at least attributed to Van Eyck, Elsheimer, Corneille de Lyon and Le Nain among the Old Masters, and William Blake among the contemporary British artists. However, the first two of the three works by Blake now at Petworth seem in fact to have been acquired by the Countess of Egremont after her separation from the third Earl in 1803; the third, possibly commissioned by the Earl, was only acquired after the artist's death.[2]

Lord Egremont's practice of holding open house for artists at Petworth made his collection particularly accessible. As early as 1798 the gem-engraver Nathaniel Marchant reported to the diarist Joseph Farington that he saw in the Great Hall at Petworth 'several of the pictures of Vandyke standing and Collins the Miniature painter, Philips [sic] the Portrait painter and a clergyman from Cambridge copying them. This was liberally allowed them to do by Lord Egremont'. Some of the sculptures in Lord Egremont's collection were actually finished in the North Gallery (which was indeed sometimes referred to as 'the Studio') and elsewhere, and of course Turner's own use of the Old Library as a studio is well-known. Other artists also used the Old Library and there is evidence that they were able to take pictures and *objets d'art* from elsewhere in the house into this room or elsewhere for study. In 1834

Constable wrote to C.R. Leslie that 'The Gainsborough was down when I was at Petworth. I placed it as it suited me – & I now, even now think of it with tears in my eyes'.[3] In the same year, on 5 September, Leslie wrote to Constable that 'The Gainsborough which you truly feel is still on the ground, and there is a very fine Wilson which perhaps you did not see. There is a gem of a Bassan[o] also, which came from London since you were here, and which Lord Egremont allows me to have in my room'.[4] An inventory compiled by H.W. Phillips,[5] the son of Thomas Phillips, in 1835 lists works then in the Old Library, including two Fuselis, the three Blakes, a group of Hoppner portraits, three Gaspar Poussins, and the Washington Allston 'Jacob's Dream' that is shown in one of Turner's gouaches (plate 46). It is not surprising, therefore, that the collection at Petworth had a particularly strong influence on Turner, as on the other artists who worked there.

As well as supplementing the range of art, both past and present, that Turner would have known from visiting other houses and from sales and exhibitions in London, including those of works from the Orleans collection in the 1790s, to say nothing of the pictures he saw at the Louvre in Paris in 1802, certain specific influences on his own paintings from works in the Petworth collection can be seen. The most persistent is that of Claude's 'Jacob with Laban and his Daughters' (fig. 52), a typical, if unusually large, panoramic view based on the Roman Campagna that inspired a whole series of Turner's paintings. The first was 'The Festival upon the Opening of the Vintage of Macon' (fig. 39; BJ 47), exhibited at the Royal Academy in 1803, though in this case Turner's knowledge of the Claude was probably based on the engraving made after the original painting by Woollett in 1783.

In 1814 occurred the somewhat strange affair concerning Turner's painting 'Apullia in Search of Appullus' (with the sub-title 'Vide [for 'see'] Ovid') (fig. 53; BJ 128). The various puzzling aspects of this episode have been clarified by Kathleen Nicholson.[6] During these years the British Institution awarded two or three premiums annually for paintings 'in Historical or Poetical Composition' together with one for 'the best Landscape'. In 1807 the regulations stipulated that these should be 'proper in point of Subject and Manner to be a companion' to an Old Master, preferably one by Claude or Poussin, though this no longer applied in 1814. These prizes were intended to encourage young artists, and no full Royal Academician had competed since 1810. Nevertheless, Turner submitted 'Apullia in Search of Appullus' but he seems deliberately to have sent it too late to qualify, on 15 January rather than on or before 4 January; he did not even apologise for his lateness. He thus managed to avoid having his painting formally judged, and it seems that his act was a deliberate challenge to the British Institution on account of its conservative tastes, particularly as embodied in its two main supporters, Sir George Beaumont and Richard Payne Knight.

An anonymous letter in the *Examiner* for 13 February pointed out that the picture was 'not an original composition, being really a direct copy of Lord Egremont's Claude', and indeed Turner's work is very close to 'Jacob with Laban and his Daughters'. The group of figures has been enlarged from four to six, to fit the new subject, and the architectural forms and a few other details differ, but all the main elements of the composition are the same. Moreover Claude had painted a 'Landscape with the Apulian Shepherd'[7] in 1656, a picture that belonged to another of the patrons of the British Institution, the Marquess of Stafford, thus involving another element in Turner's tease; Turner would have known this picture, in the Bridgewater House collection, from having painted his 'Dutch Boats in a Gale' (BJ 14) as a companion to Willem Van de Velde the younger's 'A Rising Gale' when it was in the possession of Lord Stafford's uncle the Duke of Bridgewater in 1801.

In Turner's painting the way that the central nymph looks out at the spectator as if in mockery may well be deliberate: the Apulian shepherd was transformed into a wild olive tree with bitter berries as a punishment for having mimicked a group of nymphs, and Turner may have chosen the subject to mock the British Institution for encouraging the mimicking or imitation of works by Claude. Further, Sir George Beaumont had attacked Turner for debasing Claude's style, and Turner, in his various modifications, may have been deliberately pointing out how he could improve on his model. By adding a tower to the bridge in the near distance, and a further bridge and river in the far distance, he added to Claude's formal devices in leading the eye into the distance, and at the same time he brought a greater unity to the painting by eliminating minor details and casting an atmospheric play of light and shade over the whole picture. William Hazlitt, writing in the *Morning Chronicle* for 5 February 1814, saw the dependence of Turner's pictures upon Claude as an advantage: 'All the taste and all the imagination being borrowed, his powers of eye, hand and memory, are equal to anything', but he found the figures even worse than Claude's. As if to ram his point home, Turner exhibited a completely transformed vision

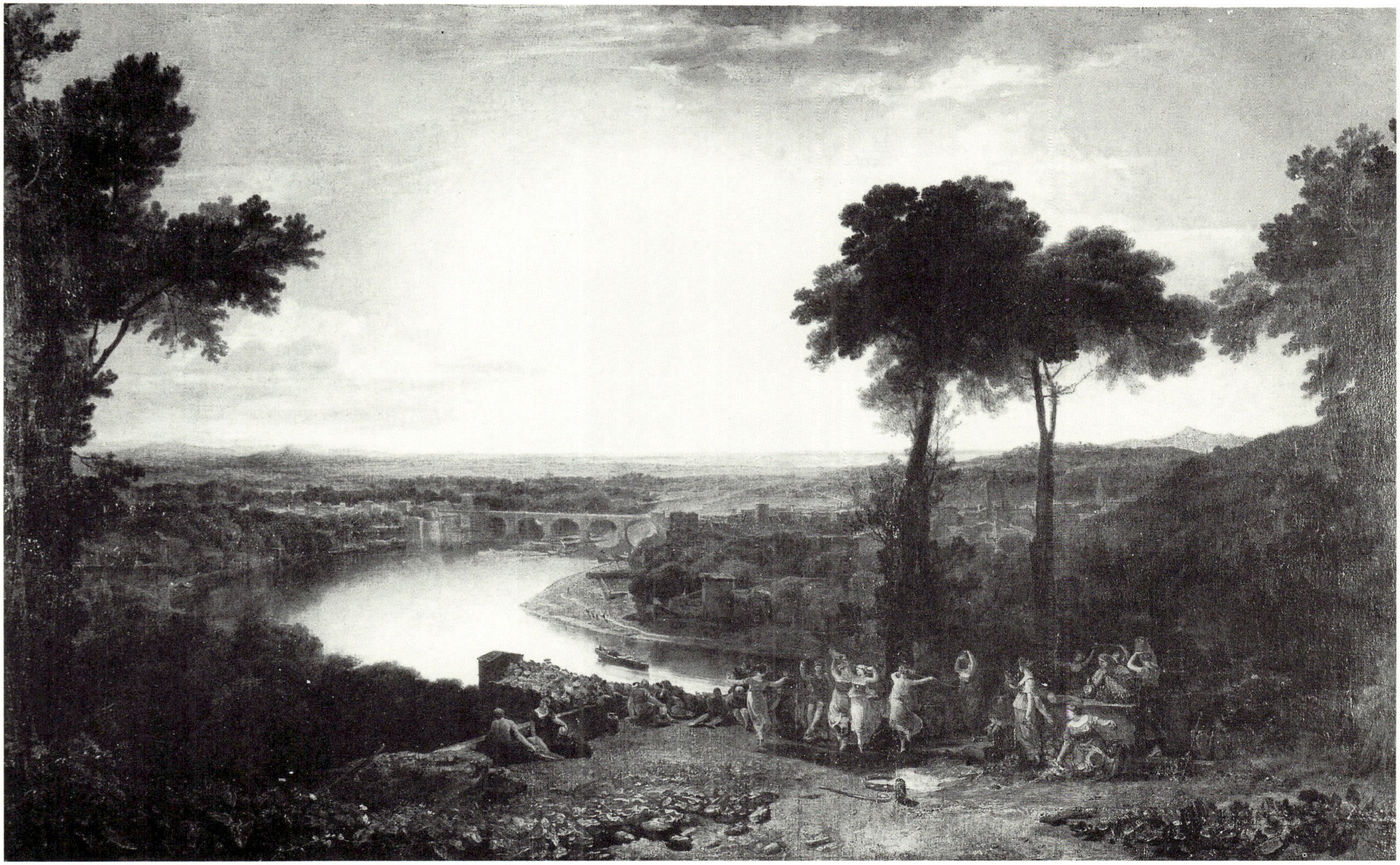

fig. 39 *The Festival upon the Opening of the Vintage of Macon* (BJ 47), R.A. 1803,
Oil on canvas 1460 × 2375 ($57\frac{1}{2} \times 93\frac{1}{2}$), Sheffield City Art Galleries

of Claude in his own 'Dido and Æneas' (BJ 129) at the Royal Academy a few months later the same year.

A further element in Turner's attack on the British Institution may have been the growing antagonism between the Royal Academy and the Institution. The Academy resented the Institution's encouragement of interest in the Old Masters, and were particularly resentful of the Institution for holding its annual exhibitions of Old Masters at the same time as the Academy's summer exhibition of contemporary artists, thus encouraging the relatively limited number of art patrons to purchase Old Masters rather than new.

For whatever reason, it is perhaps significant that Lord Egremont, who was to have been on the jury of the British Institution in 1814, failed to appear on the day. That there may have been some cooling off between artist and patron as a result of Turner's attack on the British Institution is suggested by the fact that there seems to have been no contact between the two men from 1814 until the mid 1820s, when Turner began to make regular visits to Petworth. Whatever ill feeling there may have been between the two men seems to have been finally put behind them by the time Turner made his second visit to Italy in 1828: on 11 August Turner wrote from Paris to Charles Eastlake in Rome asking Eastlake to have some canvases prepared for him as 'It would give me the greatest pleasure, independent of other feelings which modern art and of course artists, and I among the number, owe to Lord Egremont, that my first brush in Rome . . . should be to begin for him *con amore* a companion picture to his beautiful CLAUDE'. By this time in his career Turner had moved a long way from his earlier dependence upon Claude, but the scale of the likely candidate for the companion picture, 'Palestrina – Composition' (fig. 85; BJ 295), is the same, as is the general composition with its wide panorama. In fact, as we shall see, Lord Egremont never acquired this work, perhaps because, on this occasion, Turner's work departed too far from its model, or perhaps because Lord Egremont did not care to be reminded quite so sharply of the events of 1814.

Another probable early example of the influence of a work in Lord Egremont's collection on Turner is that of Thomas Gainsborough's 'Rocky Wooded Landscape with Rustic Lovers' (fig. 40) of the mid 1770s. Turner's 'Forest of Bere' (fig. 31; BJ 77), bought by Lord Egremont from Turner's gallery in 1808, reflects the influence of the Gainsborough in its general composition with figures by a pond, in its deep,

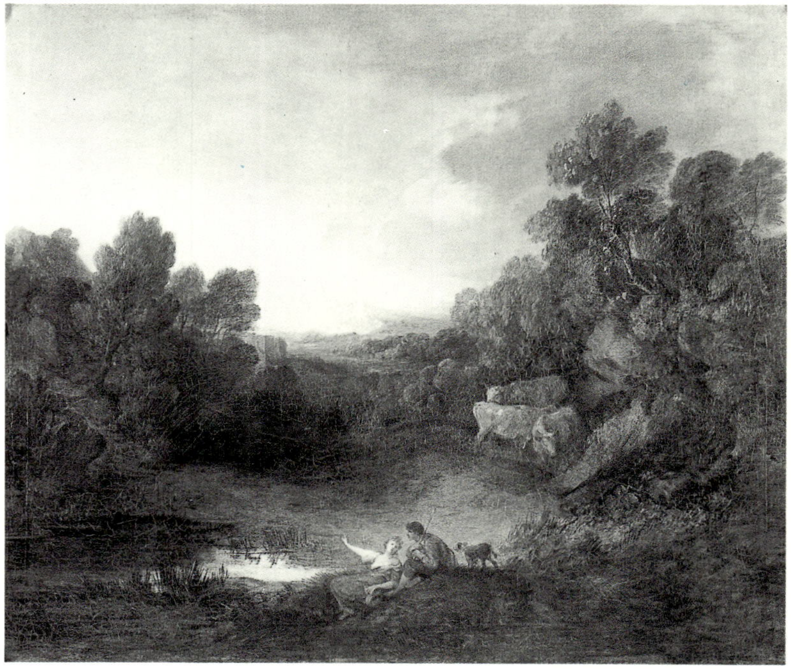

fig. 40 Thomas Gainsborough: *Rocky Wooded Landscape with Rustic Lovers*, *c.* 1775, Oil on canvas 1220 × 1450 (48 × 57), The National Trust, Petworth House

rich tonality, and in such details as the highlighting of the trees in yellow, some of these features being also found in 'The Thames near Windsor' (fig. 28; BJ 64), probably exhibited the year before. It may have been through Gainsborough rather than directly that Turner was also influenced at this time by the landscapes of Rubens.

Later, Turner was to be influenced by Gainsborough's great contemporary and rival, Sir Joshua Reynolds. Both the pose of Macbeth and the general composition of Reynolds's 'Macbeth and the Witches' (fig. 41) lie behind Turner's 'Vision of Medea', painted in Rome in 1828 (fig. 42; BJ 293); Turner showed the Reynolds painting hanging on the wall of the Square Dining Room in one of his Petworth gouaches (plate 2).

The importance of the influence of Watteau on Turner's work in the 1820s and early 1830s has been fully demonstrated, not least by Selby Whittingham.[8] The two paintings at Petworth, one a copy, were not

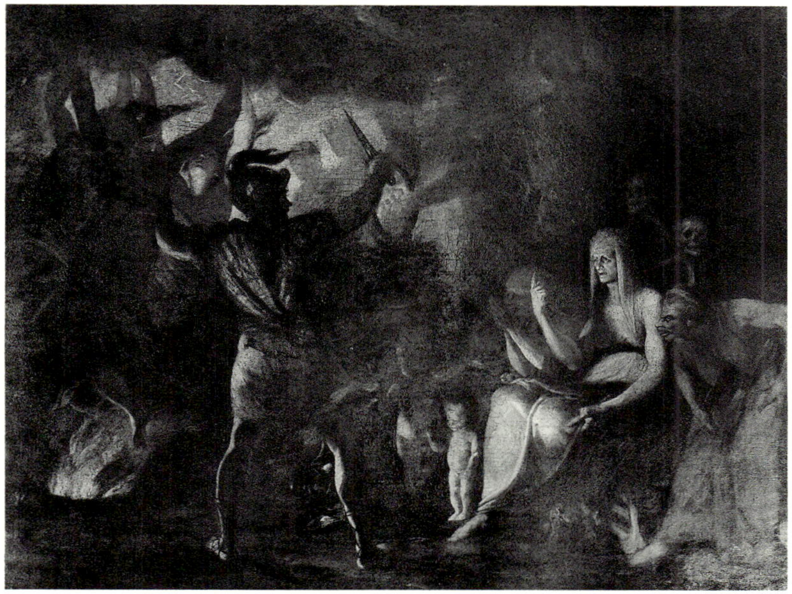

fig. 41 Sir Joshua Reynolds: *Macbeth and the Witches*, 1789, Oil on canvas 2680×3640 ($105\frac{1}{2} \times 143\frac{1}{4}$), The National Trust, Petworth House

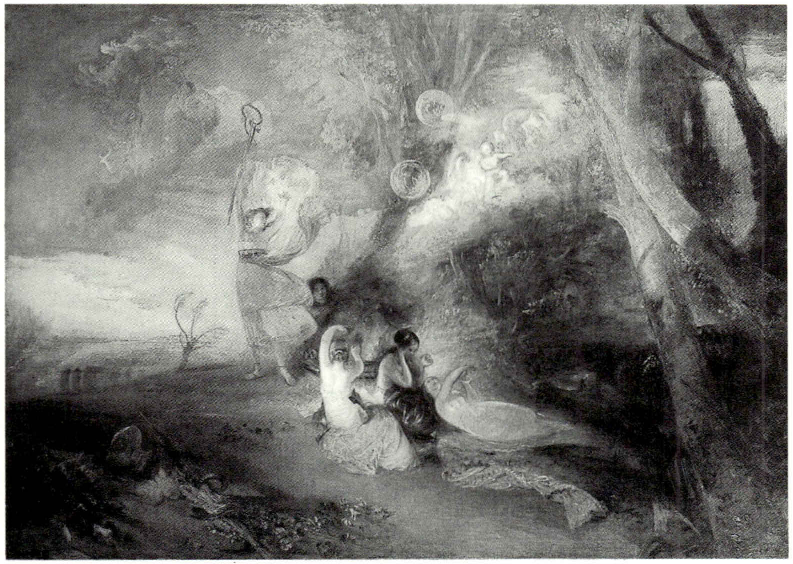

fig. 42 *Vision of Medea* (BJ 293), Rome 1828–9, R.A. 1831, Oil on canvas 1735×2410 ($68\frac{3}{8} \times 98$), Tate Gallery

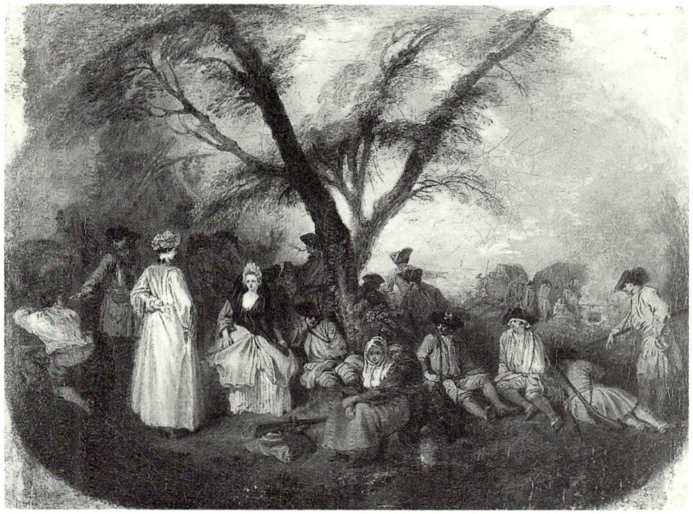

fig. 43 Watteau: *Alte*, *c.* 1710, Oil on canvas 320×425 ($12\frac{1}{2} \times 16\frac{3}{4}$), Thyssen-Bornemisza Collection

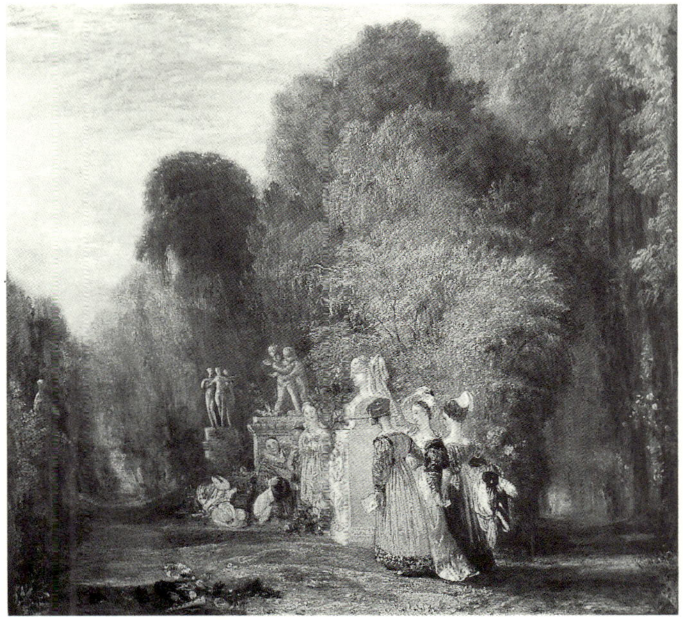

fig. 44 *What You Will!* (BJ 229), R.A. 1822, Oil on canvas 482×520 ($19 \times 20\frac{1}{2}$), Sir Michael Sobell

particularly representative but again an influence can be detected on Turner's 'What You Will' (fig. 44; BJ 229), almost certainly painted for Turner's friend Sir Francis Chantrey and exhibited at the Royal Academy in 1822. Although figures seen from behind are a regular feature of Watteau's work, that in the early painting 'Alte' (fig. 43), now in the Thyssen-Bornemisza collection but at Petworth until 1927, is particularly close to the corresponding figure in Turner's painting in such details as the squared-off cloth headgear. Other, more fundamental influences on this work from Watteau and also from Turner's friend Thomas Stothard have been demonstrated by Selby Whittingham.[9]

When it came to the Watteauesque painting by Turner most closely associated with Petworth, 'Watteau Study by Fresnoy's Rules' (fig. 93; BJ 340), exhibited at the Royal Academy in 1831, Turner found ample material in paintings by Watteau in other collections. In particular he included in the background copies of 'Les Plaisirs du Bal', which was already in the Dulwich College Picture Gallery (though Turner showed it greatly enlarged, and in reverse as in Gerard Scotin's engraving), and also in 'La Lorgneuse' which at that time belonged to Turner's friend Samuel Rogers.

In the companion painting at the 1831 Royal Academy exhibition, 'Lucy, Countess of Carlisle, and Dorothy Percy's visit to their father Lord Percy, when under Attainder upon the Supposition of his being concerned in the Gunpowder Plot' (fig. 94; BJ 338), it was the figures themselves that were copied from the appropriate portraits by Van Dyck at Petworth. The ninth Earl and Lucy Percy (on the left) are based on Van Dyck's three-quarter length portraits of the same sitters (figs. 54 and 55), while the woman standing behind the other two is based on another three-quarter length portrait, that of Ann Carr, Countess of Bedford (fig. 56). Only the third woman, that on the right, who is presumably Dorothy Percy, is not specifically related to the Van Dyck portrait of the sitter at Petworth. Another painting by Turner, the unfinished 'Lady in Van Dyck Costume' (fig. 91; BJ 444), is also based on the Van Dyck at Petworth of Ann Carr, Countess of Bedford.

Turner's habit of challenging both the artists of the past and his contemporaries is well known. In at least three cases works at Petworth seem to have acted as such challenges. Turner's 'The Fall of an Avalanche in the Grisons' (fig. 46; BJ 109), exhibited in his own gallery in 1810, was inspired by two works of the same subject by P. J. de Loutherbourg that belonged to Turner's two chief patrons of the time, Lord

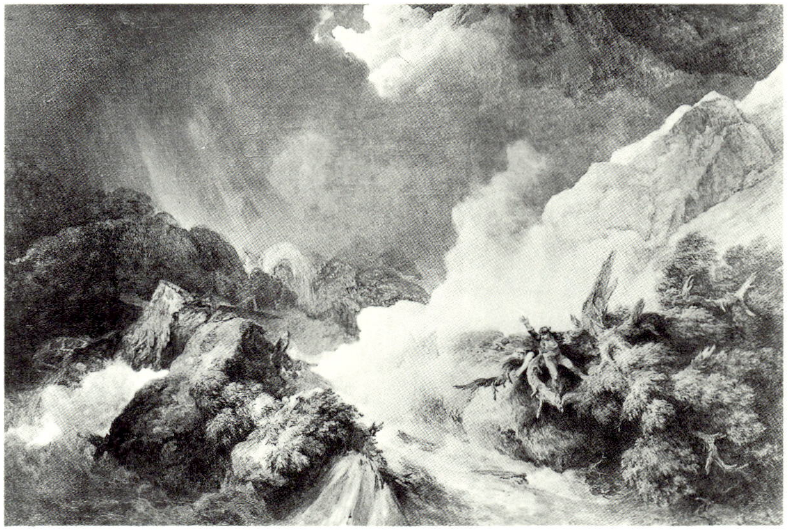

fig. 45 P. J. de Loutherbourg: *Avalanche*, *c.* 1800, Oil on canvas 1065 × 1575 (42 × 62), The National Trust, Petworth House

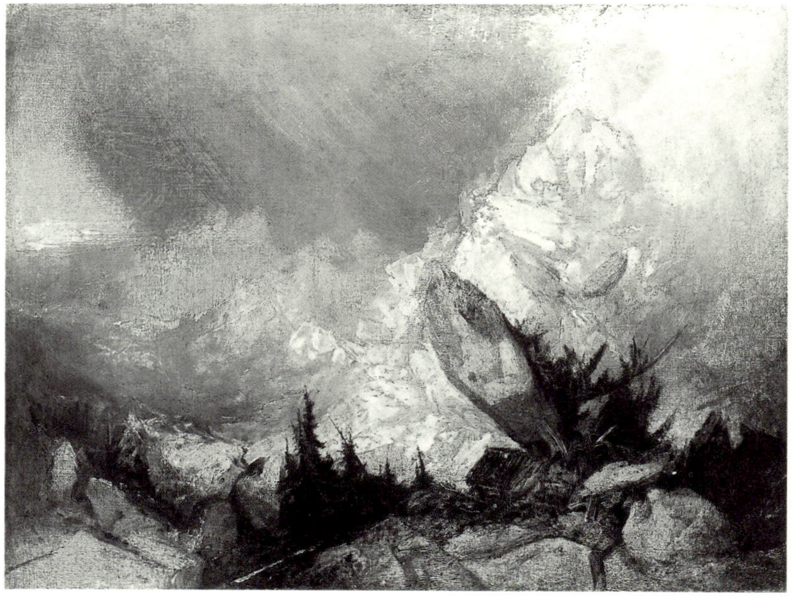

fig. 46 *The Fall of an Avalanche in the Grisons* (BJ 109), Turner's gallery 1810, Oil on canvas 900 × 1200 ($35\frac{1}{2} \times 47\frac{1}{4}$), Tate Gallery

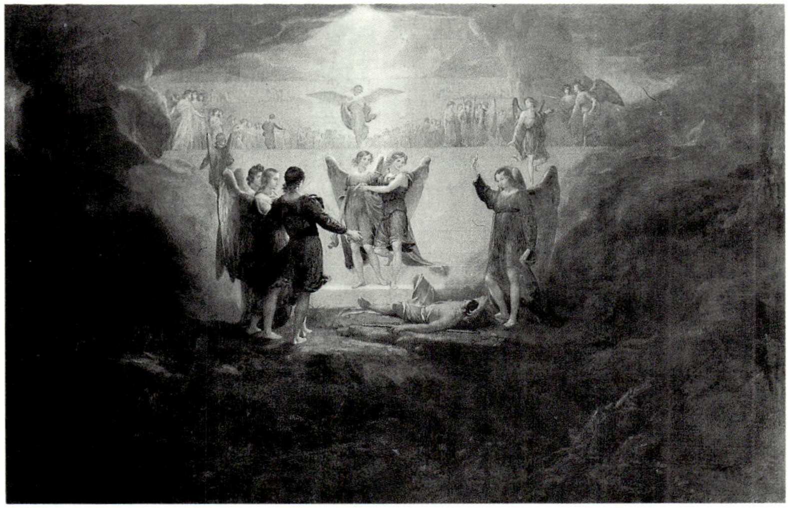

fig. 47 Washington Allston: *Jacob's Dream*, 1817, Oil on canvas 1575 × 2385 (62 × 94), The National Trust, Petworth House

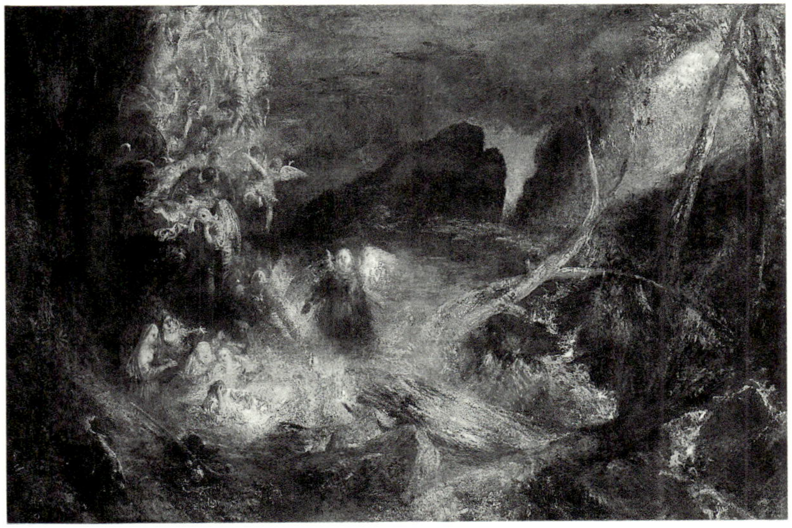

fig. 48 *The Vision of Jacob's Ladder* (BJ 435), *c.* 1800/*c.* 1830, Oil on canvas 1230 × 1880 (48½ × 74), Tate Gallery

Egremont and Sir John Leicester. De Loutherbourg's painting of an avalanche of *c.* 1800 still remains at Petworth (fig. 45); what seems to be a slightly later picture of the same subject, dated 1803, exhibited at the Royal Academy in 1804 and sold to Sir John Leicester in 1805, is now in the Tate Gallery.[10] Turner had visited the Alps in 1802 though it is unlikely that he visited the Grisons. His painting was probably in part at least a direct response to the avalanche that took place at Selva there in December 1808, but one also senses the spirit of competition with the older artist and neighbour, both in the choice of subject and, particularly in relation to the Tate Gallery painting, in actual detail and composition.

Another case of direct emulation seems to be 'The Vision of Jacob's Ladder' (fig. 48; BJ 435). This unfinished picture was never exhibited by Turner, and must at one time, standing with its face to the wall, have been used in an emergency as a palette, large lumps of paint having been found on the back of the canvas. It seems to have been begun in about 1800 but reworked considerably later, probably in about 1830. In this case it is the large painting, measuring 62 × 94 inches, of 'Jacob's Dream' (fig. 47) painted by the American artist Washington Allston for Lord Egremont in 1817 that seems to have spurred Turner on to add the specific subject matter to his own large canvas; Allston's painting was exhibited at the Royal Academy in 1819 and again at the British Institution in 1825. It occurs in the background of one of Turner's Petworth gouaches (plate 46) and the composition of Turner's main group of figures and the vision of light above may owe something to the American artist's work, though the influence of other artists, such as Salvador Rosa, is also clear.[11]

When the collection of Sir John Leicester, later Lord de Tabley, was sold in 1827 Lord Egremont acquired, besides Turner's own painting of 'Tabley, Cheshire, the seat of Sir J. F. Leicester, Bart.: Calm Morning', exhibited at the Royal Academy in 1809, John Hoppner's 'Sleeping Venus and Cupid' (fig. 49), commissioned by Sir John Leicester and exhibited at the Royal Academy in 1806. The year after this sale, Turner, while in Rome, besides painting 'Palestrina' for Lord Egremont, started on the large 'Reclining Venus' (fig. 50; BJ 296), which however remained unfinished. In part this is inspired by Titian's famous 'Venus of Urbino' which Turner would have seen in the Uffizi when he passed through Florence on the way to Rome in September 1828, but in certain significant points, such as the placing of the arms and the curve of the

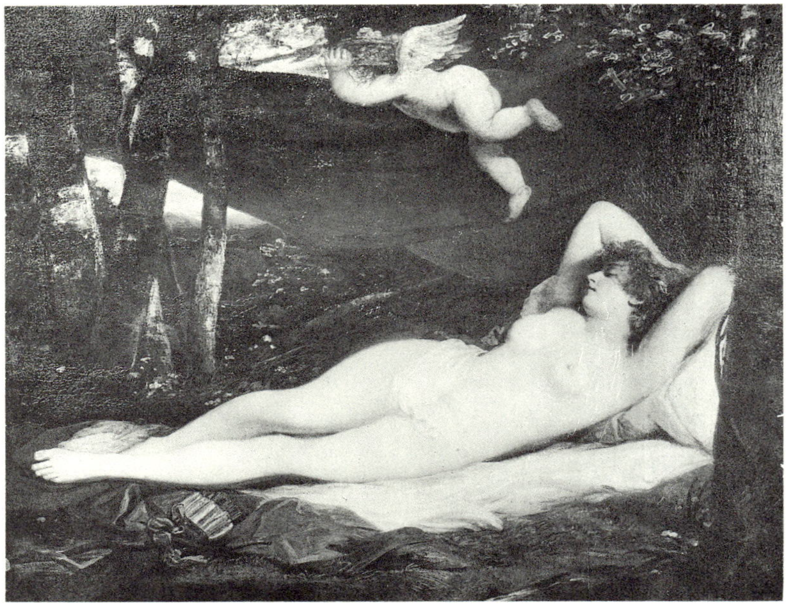

fig. 49 John Hoppner: *Sleeping Venus and Cupid*, R.A. 1806, Oil on canvas 1320 × 1675 (52 × 66), The National Trust, Petworth House

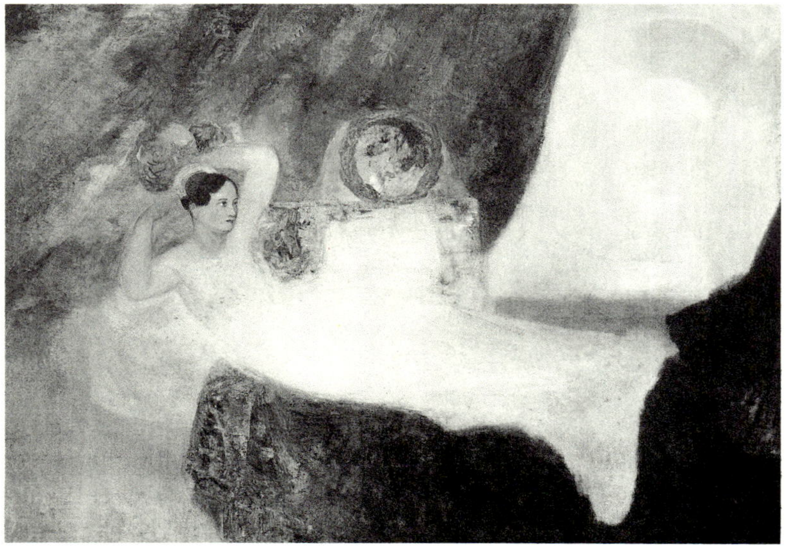

fig. 50 *Reclining Venus* (BJ 296), 1828, Oil on canvas 1750 × 2490 (69 × 98), Tate Gallery

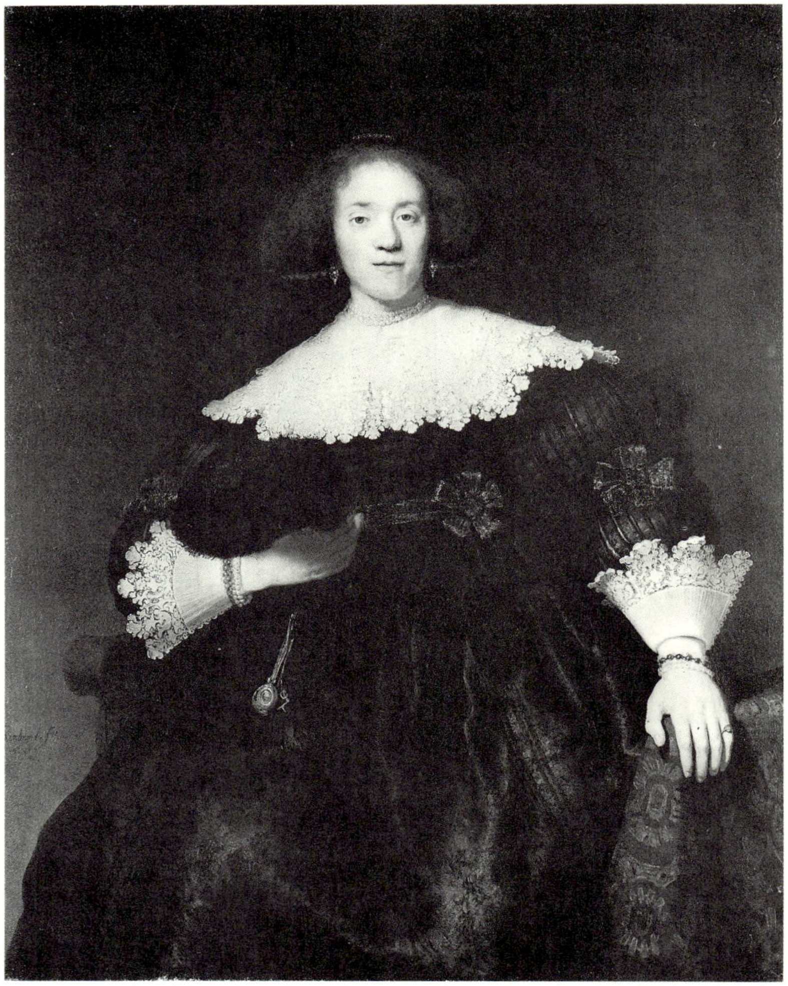

fig. 51 Rembrandt: *Lady with a Fan*, 1633, Oil on canvas 1255 × 1010 ($49\frac{1}{2} \times 39\frac{3}{4}$), Metropolitan Museum of Art, New York (Gift of Helen Swift Neilson 1943)

thigh, his nude is closer to that in the painting by Hoppner, though Hoppner's setting is an outdoors one rather than the interior shown in the works by Titian and Turner.

The painting that Lord Egremont seems to have purchased instead of 'Palestrina', that of 'Jessica' (fig. 92; BJ 333), exhibited at the Royal Academy in 1830, also pays tribute to a painting in the Petworth collection. A number of Rembrandts have been suggested as sources for the composition, including 'Young Woman at a Door', now in the Art Institute of Chicago, which was exhibited at the British Institution in 1818 and was sold at Christie's on 13 June 1829, and 'The Portrait of Agatha Bas' (also known as 'The Lady with a Fan') now in the Royal Collection, which was brought to England in 1814, sold at Christie's on 29 June of that year, and exhibited at the British Institution on three occasions in the 1820s. However, one of the Rembrandts sold from Petworth in 1927, also showing a 'Lady with a Fan' (fig. 51) would seem to be the model for at least the somewhat ungainly outstretched arm seen in foreshortening, and again would have been just the sort of painting to set Turner off in competition.[12]

Reynolds, in the closing paragraph of his Sixth Discourse, had exhorted his listeners, 'Study therefore the great works of the great Masters, forever. Study as nearly as you can, in the order, in the manner, and on the principles, on which they studied. Study nature attentively, but always with those Masters in your company; consider them as models which you are to imitate, and at the same time as rivals with whom you are to contend'. The Petworth collection gave Turner ample opportunity both to imitate and to contend.

Notes

1 All the works at Petworth during Turner's visits are recorded in C.H. Collins Baker, *Catalogue of the Petworth Collection of Pictures in the Possession of Lord Leconfield*, 1920. A copy on deposit in the Tate Gallery's library is annotated to show which works were sold in 1927.

2 See Martin Butlin, *The Paintings and Drawings of William Blake*, 1981, catalogue nos. 642, 662 and 811.

3 Beckett, vol. iii, 1965, p. 116.

4 Ibid, pp. 116–17.

5 Reprinted in Appendix to Youngblood, *Turner Studies*, p. 32.

6 Nicholson, 1980, pp. 679–84.

7 Repr. Nicholson 1980, fig. 32.

8 Selby Whittingham, 'What You Will: or some notes regarding the influence of Watteau on Turner and other British Artists', *Turner Studies*, vol v, no. 1, Summer 1985, pp. 2–24, and vol. v, no. 2, Winter 1985, pp. 28–48.

9 Whittingham in *Turner Studies*, vol. v, no. 1, Summer 1985, pp. 12–16.

10 For the Tate Gallery picture see *The Tate Gallery Report 1955–66*, 1966, pp. 19–20, repr. between pp. 12 and 13.

11 See Gage 1987, pp. 103–4, Salvator Rosa's 'Landscape with the Dream of Jacob' at Chatsworth repr. pl. 139.

12 For the relationship between Turner and Rembrandt see Michael Kitson, 'Turner and Rembrandt', *Turner Studies*, vol. viii, no. 1, Summer 1988, pp. 2–19. 'Jessica' is discussed on pp. 12–13.

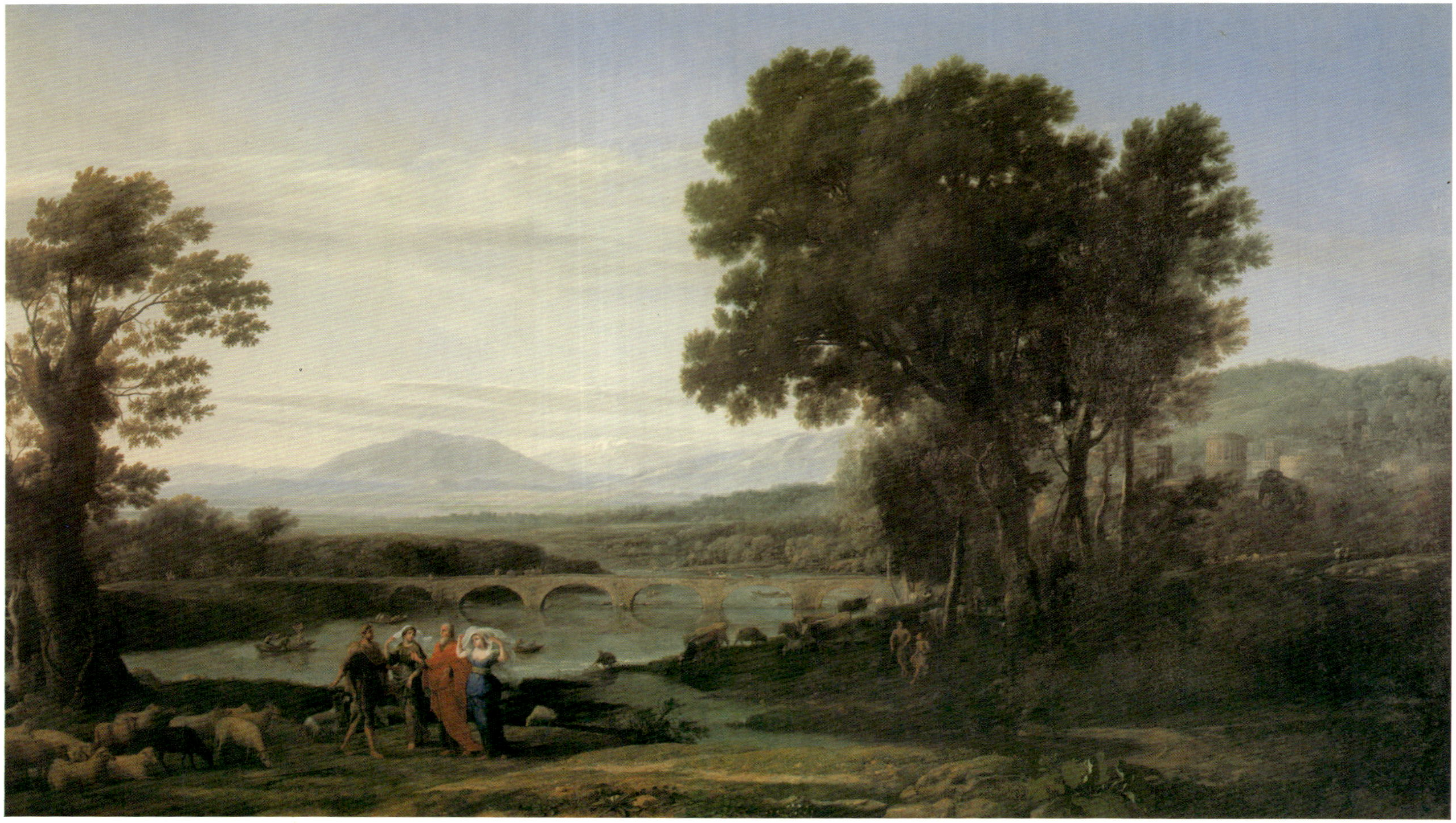

fig. 52 Claude: *Jacob with Laban and his Daughters*, *c.* 1655, Oil on canvas
1435 × 2515 (56½ × 99), The National Trust, Petworth House

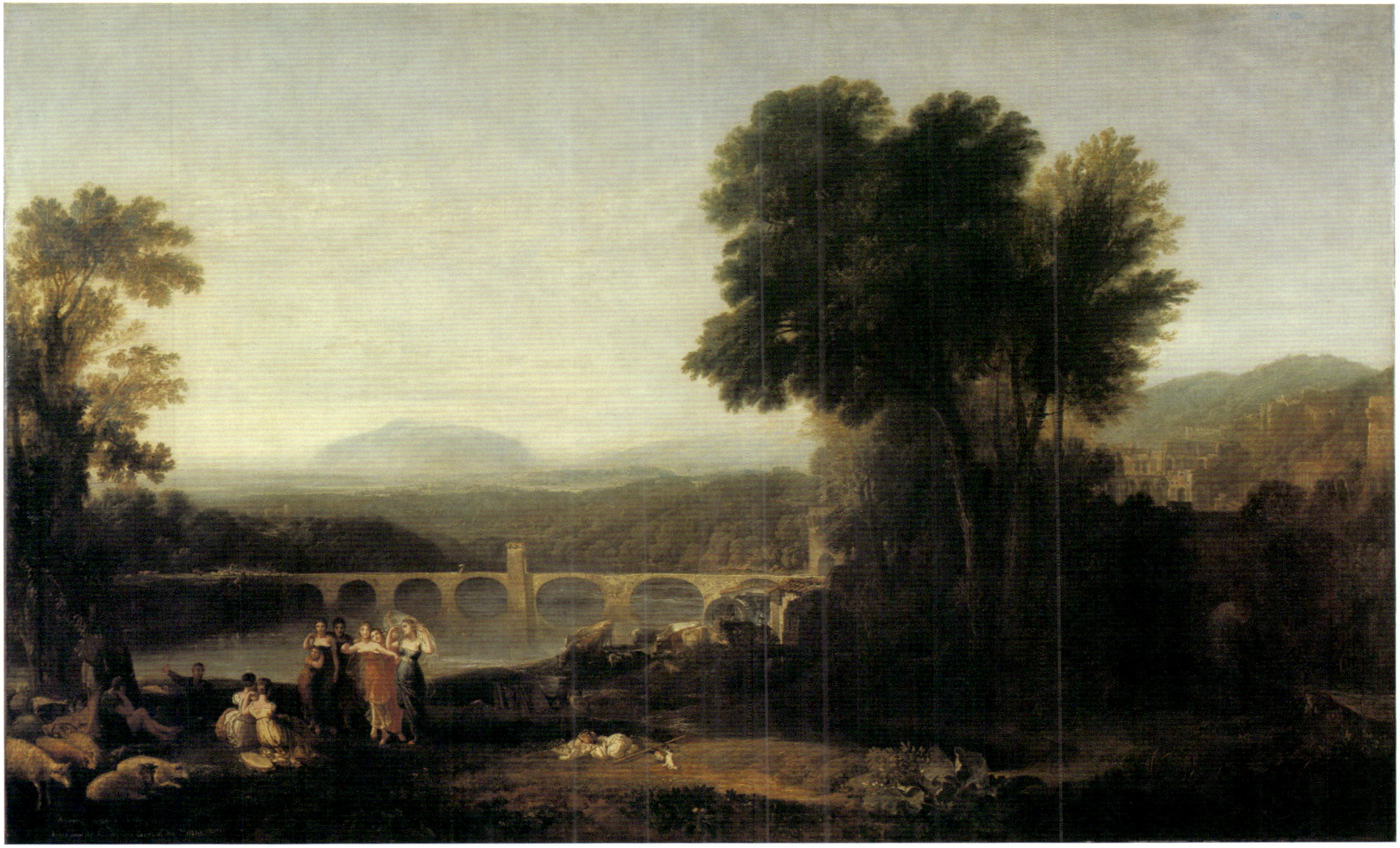

fig. 53 *Apullia in Search of Appullus vide Ovid* (BJ 128), British Institution 1814,
Oil on canvas 1460 × 2385 ($57\frac{1}{2} \times 93\frac{7}{8}$), Tate Gallery

fig. 54 Van Dyck: *The ninth Earl of Northumberland*, *c.* 1636–8,
Oil on canvas 1370 × 1195 (54 × 47),
The National Trust, Petworth House

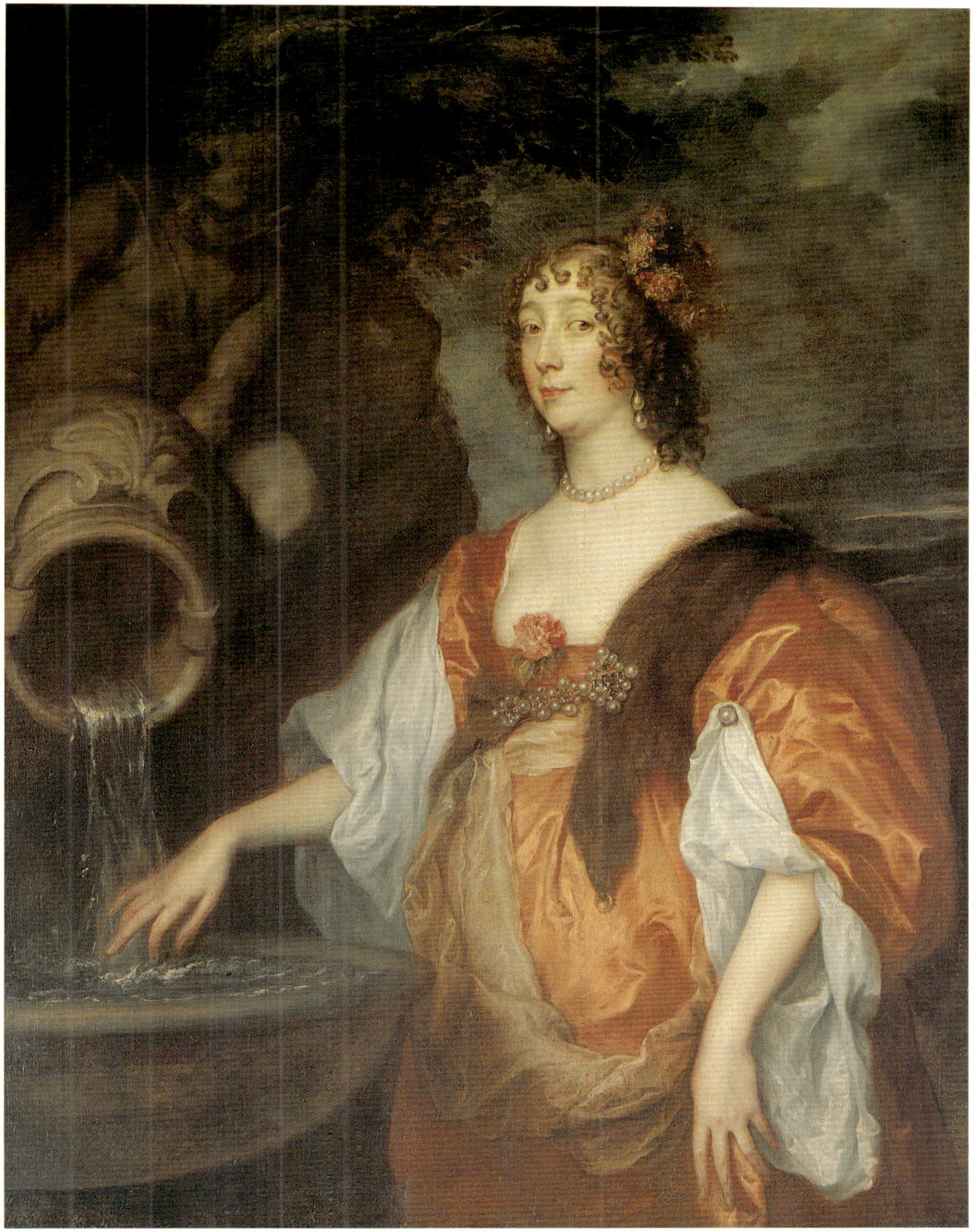

fig. 55 Van Dyck: *Lucy Percy, Countess of Carlisle*, *c.* 1637–40,
Oil on canvas 1360 × 1090 ($53\frac{1}{2} \times 43$),
Lord Egremont, Petworth House

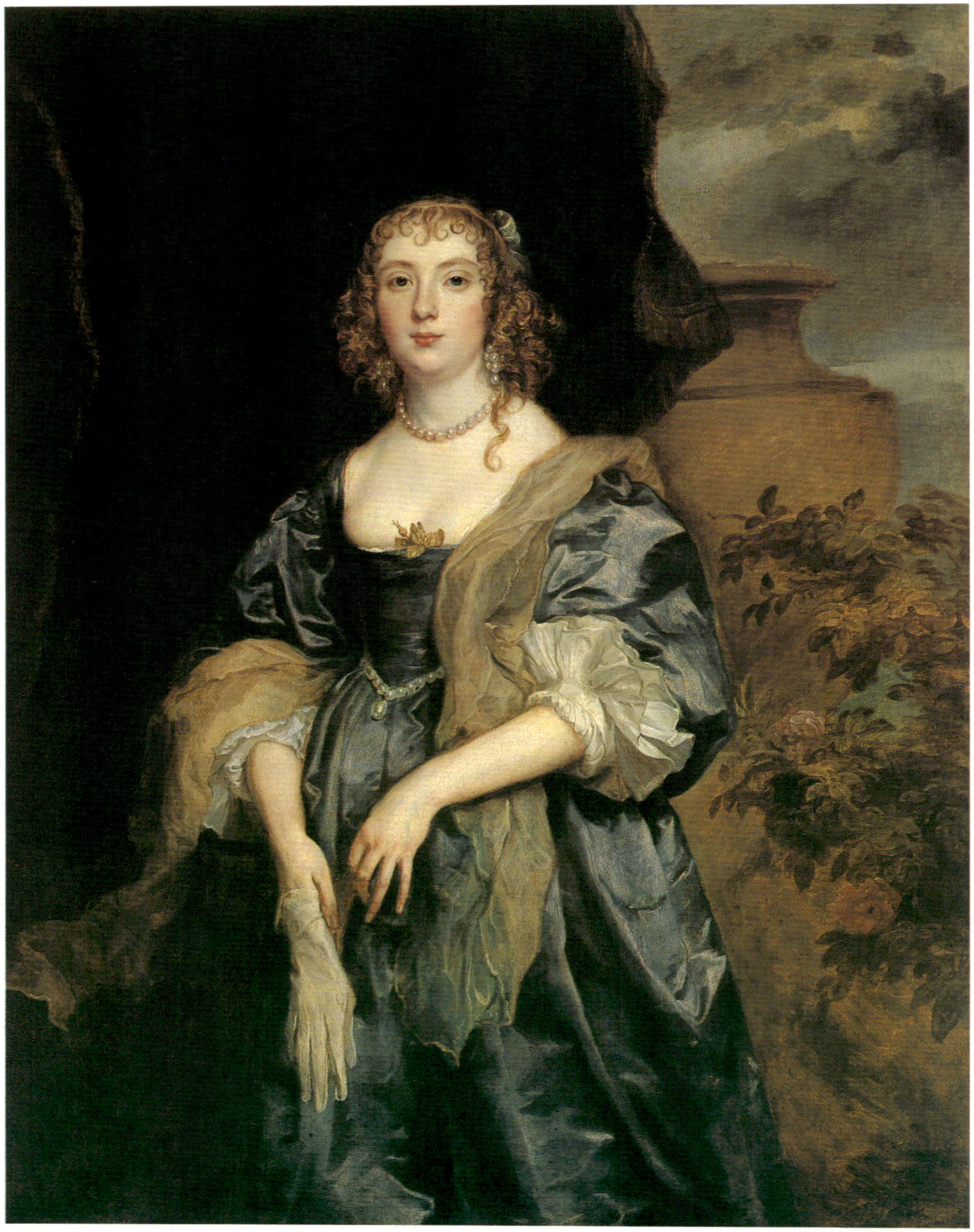

fig. 56 Van Dyck: *Ann Carr, Countess of Bedford*, *c.* 1635–40, Oil on canvas 1360 × 1080 ($53\frac{1}{2} \times 42\frac{1}{2}$), Lord Egremont, Petworth House

CHAPTER 4

The Petworth Gouache Drawings

'Rubbish', 'Inferior' and 'Worse' were Ruskin's verdicts on many of the large number of blue paper sheets which make up the group of Petworth gouache drawings.[1] Despite Ruskin's damning judgement, these small spontaneous sketches associated with Petworth have always proved very popular when shown in exhibitions drawing upon works from the Turner Bequest. Ruskin himself selected several subjects, mostly landscape views and the more finished interiors, for his grouping of Turner's work at the National Gallery towards the end of the nineteenth century, and other Petworth drawings were included in the various loan collections sent to the towns and cities of Britain: Dublin, Edinburgh, Leeds, Sheffield, Chester, and Bradford.[2] Since the beginning of this century works from the Petworth group have been seen around the world in destinations as far apart as Caracas and Osaka, and in 1970 the drawings actually returned to Petworth House itself in an exhibition arranged by the National Trust.[3]

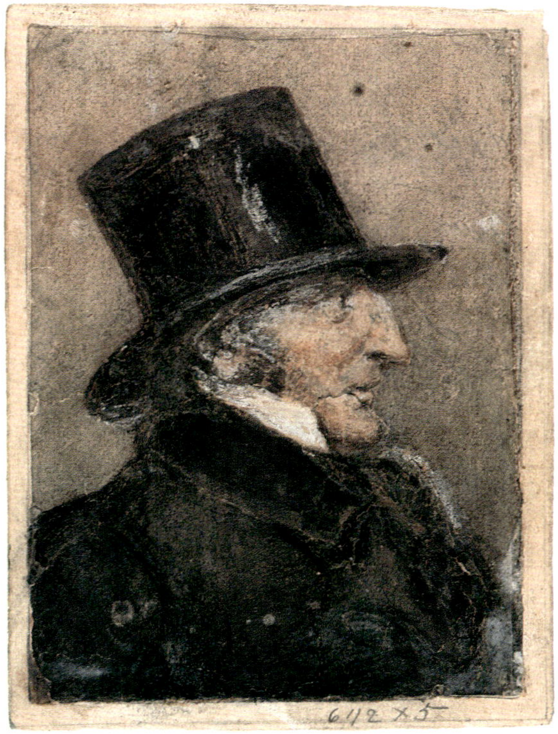

fig. 57 Charles Turner, *Portrait of J. M. W. Turner*, Gouache 89 × 63 (3½ × 2½), Tate Gallery

Despite their popularity, it is surprising that a large number of the group remain unpublished. Indeed, it is only in the last twenty years that the drawings have received any detailed discussion of their setting and subject matter. Here, for the first time, all one hundred and sixteen of the Turner Bequest group (TB CCXLIV) are reproduced, along with related drawings from other collections, and drawings from the Bequest which have proved to have a Petworth connection (plates 1–135). For anyone who has visited Petworth House and its great sweep of verdant parklands, Turner's drawings catch exactly the fleeting impressions not only of the physical details of the house, but of its ambience and atmosphere. Just as his famous watercolours of Venice colour our view of that city, Turner's vision of Petworth has become the lens through which we view the place – our experience merging with the images stored at the back of the retina. The opulent interiors of the house, decorated as much by the profusion of gold frames as by the pictures that fill them, are captured in moments of slanted and filtered sunlight. Outside the house, the parklands change colour by the second as the sun makes its slow decline towards the lake.

Taken together the drawings represent a cohesive record of a visit to the house. This cohesion suggests that Turner worked on the drawings very quickly, most probably all in the course of one visit. Although a couple of gouache drawings now linked with Petworth would seem to be of an earlier date than the main group (possibly as early as 1825), the majority of the drawings would appear to have been made in the late summer of 1827 before Turner went to stay at East Cowes Castle on the Isle of Wight, the home of the architect John Nash. The determining of what appears to be a precise dating for the main group of gouache subjects is largely due to discoveries connected with a series of alterations made to Petworth Church by Charles Barry beginning in 1827 (see p. 135). As well as the many scenes made inside Petworth House, the interior of the church is depicted from a number of viewpoints, most of which show a service in progress. As the church was closed from December 1827 until October 1829 it would have been impossible for Turner to have painted these scenes during this period. Moreover, the drawings capture the architecture of the church at the moment before Charles Barry began to re-shape the whole building therefore suggesting the summer of 1827 as the most likely date for the whole group. The slightly earlier pen-and-ink and gouache drawings, showing Fittleworth Mill on the River Rother (plate 122; TB CCLIX–41) and Petworth House from the lake (plate 67; TB CCLIX–5), relate to sketches in the 'Mortlake and Pullborough' sketchbook of 1825 (TB CCXIII), and are discussed more fully in the Appendices (p. 125).

Although the gouache drawings seem unprecedented in both their style and their subject matter, they in fact fit quite naturally into the pattern of Turner's work. He had made an extensive group of drawings for his friend and patron Walter Fawkes, showing the interior of the house and the countryside surrounding Fawkes's Yorkshire home, Farnley Hall.[4] These drawings are considerably larger and more precise than those made at Petworth, and record, with great accuracy, the contents of each room at Farnley Hall (fig. 58), whether this was the sculpture, the furniture, or the pictures, which included several of Turner's own paintings.

Four of the Petworth subjects resemble these more formal drawings in their meticulous treatment of the recorded interior (plates 35, 8, 42, and 2; TB CCXLIV–14, 16, 21 and 108). All four would seem to have been made at a time when natural daylight was allowed to fill the space, so that the drawing of the Square Dining-Room was presumably made in the bright morning light, while the other three drawings, depicting rooms on the west side of the house, were made in the course of a long sunny afternoon.

The Farnley drawings, also made in gouache on coloured paper, anticipate the Petworth formal room-studies by a decade, but it is in the freer, more spontaneous, sheets of Petworth that we appreciate both the informal intimacy of that environment and Turner's more relaxed style. In much of the material in the Turner Bequest of this period there is evidence of a broader handling of paint and a more confident use of economic effects, most notably in the 'French Rivers' (TB CCLIX) and in the vignette designs (TB CCLXXX), later used in their finished forms as the basis for engravings.

For the most part, the Petworth drawings are made on sheets of roughly torn blue paper, each of a size approximately 140 × 190mm ($5\frac{1}{2} \times 7\frac{1}{2}$ inches). One of the drawings, however, that traditionally called 'The Meet' (plate 69; TB CCXLIV–104), is on a sheet twice the size of all the other Petworth drawings (190 × 280mm; $7\frac{1}{2} \times 11$ inches), al-

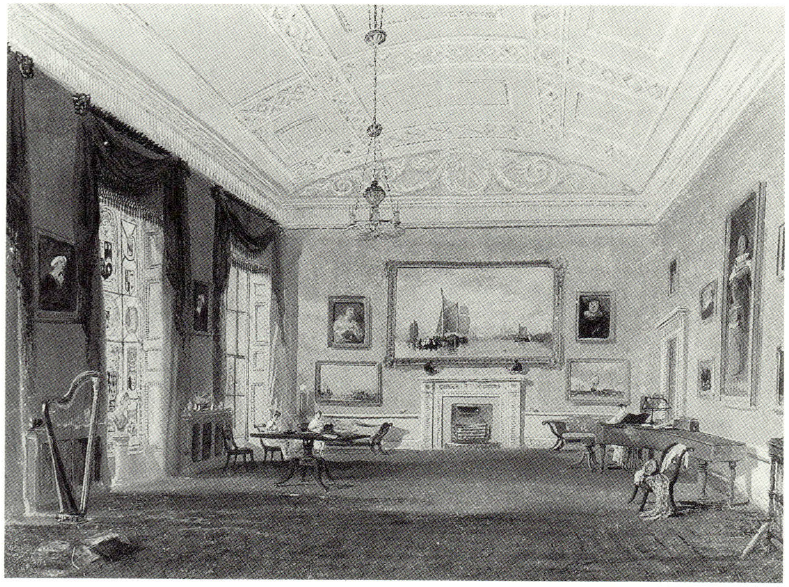

fig. 58 *The Drawing-Room, Farnley Hall*, 1818, Gouache on grey paper 315 × 412 ($12\frac{3}{8} \times 16\frac{1}{4}$), Private Collection (W.592)

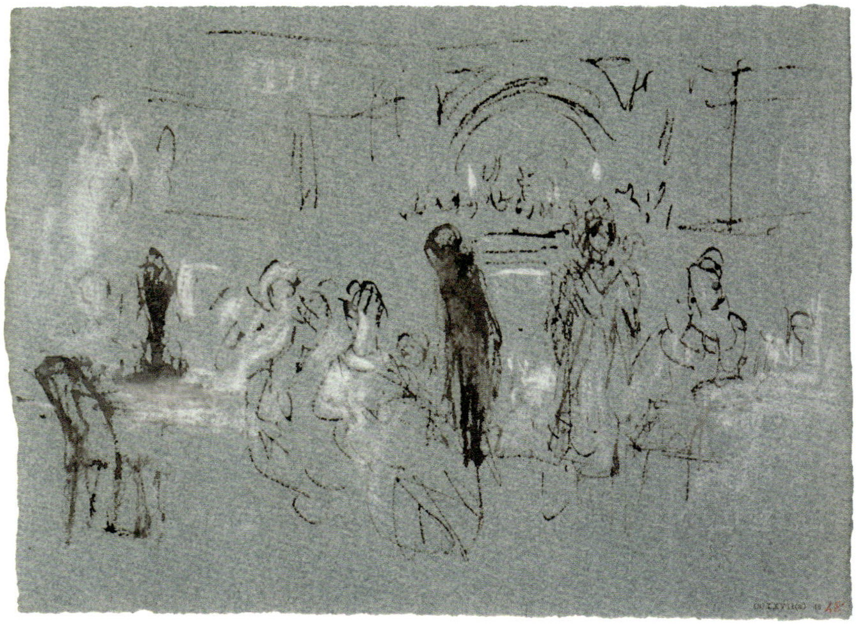

fig. 59 *Interior of the Library, East Cowes Castle*, 1827, Pen and ink, with some chalk, on blue paper 140 × 191 ($5\frac{1}{2} \times 7\frac{1}{2}$), Tate Gallery (TB CCXXVII(a)–48)

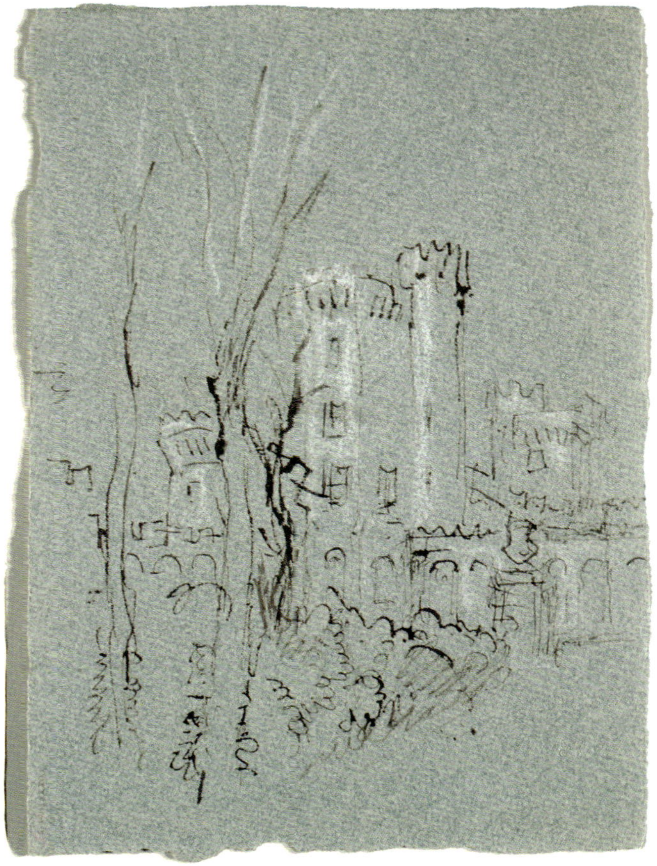

fig. 60 *East Cowes Castle from the West*, 1827, Pen and ink, with some chalk, on blue paper 193 × 140 ($7\frac{5}{8} \times 5\frac{1}{2}$), Tate Gallery (TB CCXXVII(a)–5)

though it is probable that this was also torn from a much larger piece of paper. Some of the sheets appear not to have been divided by Turner. This is indicated by Ruskin's description of a section of the main group as 'double sheets',[5] thereby implying that the sheets were folded in half and only subsequently separated for the purposes of exhibition (see plate 92: TB CCXCII–58/59).

Quite where the paper came from has not received much attention despite Turner's prolific use of this material throughout the late 1820s and the early 1830s. Large sheets of blue paper were used during Turner's lifetime as wrapping-paper, often for groceries and imported goods such as sugar, and were therefore both readily available and inexpensive. Turner's preference for this paper places him firmly within a long tradition of English artists for whom blue paper was a natural choice as drawing-paper. The blue colour was traditionally attained by dying the pulp paper with blue obtained from textiles such as sailors' clothes. Other means of achieving the same result in the process were reached through the addition of colourants such as ground blue glass or smalt, and various organic blues.[6]

The fresh blue of most of the Petworth sheets dramatically highlights the need for carefully arranged lighting conditions in which to show works of art on paper. Several of the drawings originally sent out for exhibition by Ruskin have suffered from being repeatedly exposed to the light for lengthy periods (see plates 3, 87, 125). On these sheets the original blue has become a washed-out yellow, with the true blue at the edge of the sheet (previously covered by a mount) testifying to the irreparable damage.

As implied earlier, Turner made extensive use of blue paper as the basis for his drawings in the years around 1830. The closest to Petworth in subject matter are those of East Cowes Castle, where, despite a handful of drawings showing the interior of the great architect's home (fig. 59; TB CCXXVII(a)–48), Turner concentrates on the relation of the castle to its setting, high above the River Medina (fig. 60; TB CCXXVII(a)–5). This was a theme he continued in the paintings he produced of the Regatta on the same visit (BJ nos. 242, 243, and nos. 260–268), for which he also made numerous pencil and chalk studies on blue paper of the yachts competing off the harbour at Cowes (TB CCXXVIII).

Other blue-paper drawings show scenes on European rivers, most notably the Seine, the Loire, the Meuse and the Moselle. For these works Turner used a variety of techniques and media, seeking constantly to challenge the achievements of his art. The earliest drawings associated with Petworth demonstrate a greater reliance on pen-and-ink work before the application of colour (plates 67, 122). One or two of the drawings dating from 1827 are made in pencil and white gouache (plate 118). However, in most of the Petworth drawings Turner reverts to gouache, the media he had used at Farnley. Gouache or bodycolour is the name given to watercolour when it has been made opaque by the addition of either lead or Chinese white. The conjunction of blue paper and gouache gives the colour in these drawings a vivid immediacy. Despite its resemblance to certain types of blotting-paper the blue paper is not particularly absorbent. This was presumably a quality Turner enjoyed in the paper as it created a greater distinction between paint and paper.

A certain amount of confusion over the identification of the subject matter of some drawings within the main group of Petworth subjects seems to have come about from the assumption that the media used could be related to a specific place. For example, the East Cowes Castle and Petworth drawings are largely distinct in that Turner tended to use ink and white gouache or chalk at East Cowes, whereas, at Petworth, he allowed himself freer expression, deploying rich colour. This view, while generally applicable, fails to take into account exceptions to its rule, and, as Patrick Youngblood has indicated,[7] some of those

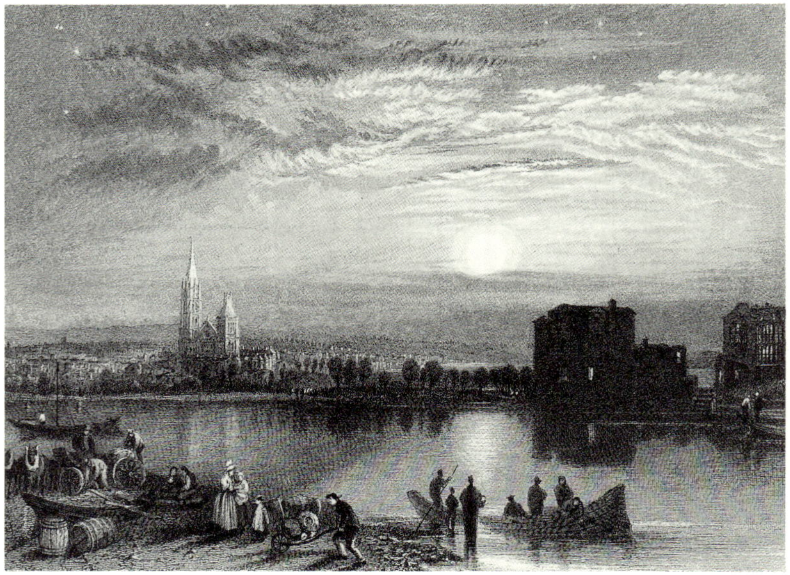

fig. 61 *St Denis*, 1835, Engraved by S. Fisher for *Turner's Annual Tour – The Seine* (R481) 100 × 138 ($3\frac{7}{8} \times 5\frac{7}{16}$) Image size, Tate Gallery

coloured sheets listed as Petworth subjects in fact show East Cowes Castle. This confusion is not altogether surprising. If the dating of the Petworth gouaches to the summer of 1827 suggested here is correct then the Petworth and East Cowes Castle subjects were made within weeks of each other, and it would be unlikely that Turner should make such a complete distinction in his choice of media.

Further confusion between the Petworth and the 'French Rivers' drawings results from a general stylistic similarity throughout the period. It is as well to point out a difference in motive behind these two important groups of drawings. The large number of subjects which concentrate on the scenery along the rivers of France, made from about 1825–27 onwards, were executed with an engraving project firmly in mind (figs. 62, 63).[8] The Petworth drawings, on the other hand, seem not to have been painted for any particular purpose other than for Turner's own pleasure and amusement. This may account in part for the sketchiness of a great many of the drawings. Neither were the majority of the drawings intended as a gift, nor were they part of a com-

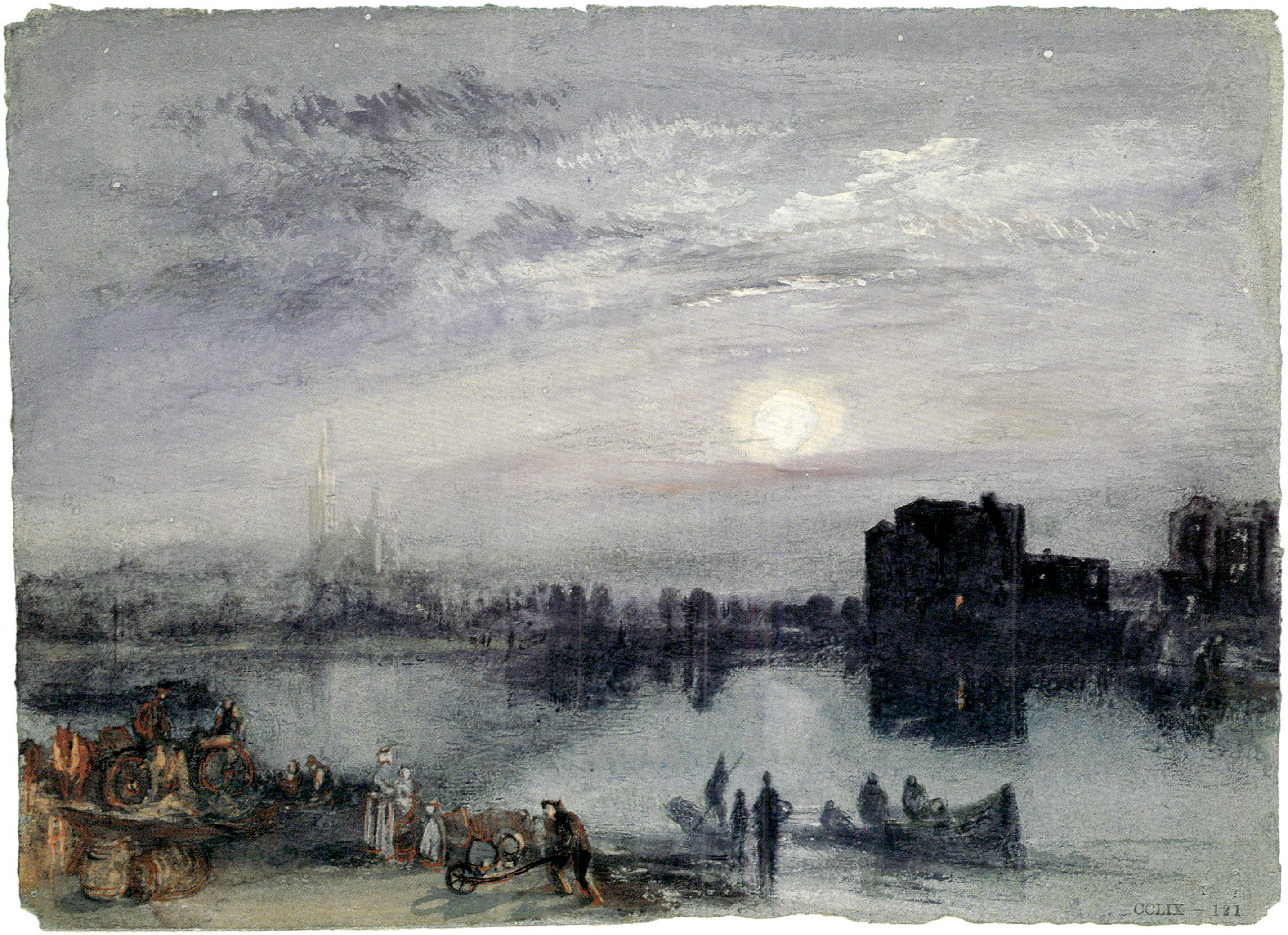

fig. 62 *St Denis*, *c.* 1832, Gouache and watercolour, with pen and ink
138 × 192 ($5\frac{7}{16} \times 7\frac{1}{2}$), Tate Gallery (TB CCLIX–121) (W. 979)

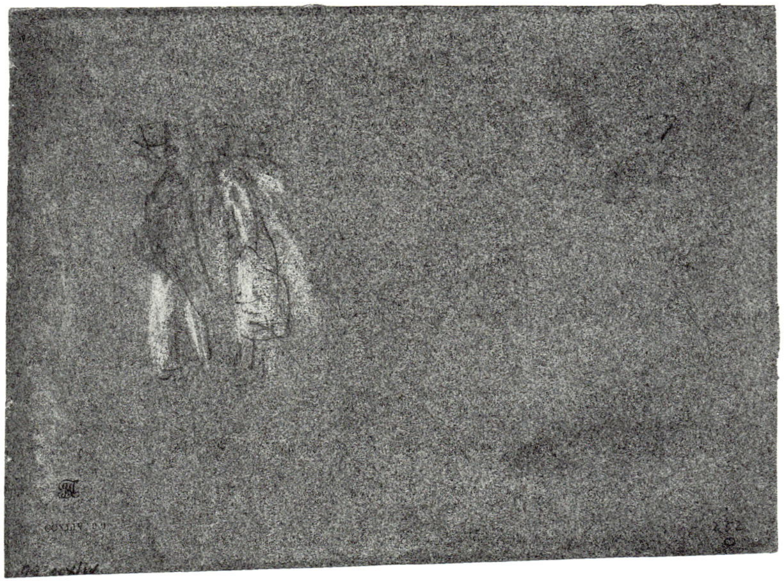

fig. 63 *Two Figures at East Cowes Castle*, 1827, Pencil and white gouache 144 × 190 ($5\frac{5}{8} \times 7\frac{1}{2}$), Tate Gallery (TB CCXLIV–99 verso)

mission undertaken for Lord Egremont along the lines of the subjects Turner had painted at Farnley for Walter Fawkes. Indeed, almost all the Petworth drawings remained in Turner's collection at his death.

There are seven Petworth drawings not in the Turner Bequest. These came to their present owners through collectors such as Henry Vaughan (plate 71) or J.E. Taylor (plate 72), or through more exceptional circumstances.[9] For example, the two drawings still at Petworth (plates 20, 121) recall an incident when Turner apparently spoilt the dress of the young Mrs Hasler (the niece of the third Earl, fig. 125) by spilling milk on it at breakfast. As a means of making amends he produced the two drawings after the meal. These few Petworth drawings outside the Bequest would seem to be of a similar date to the main group and are executed on the same paper.

It has been suggested that the group in the Turner Bequest may have been 'Studies for Pictures',[10] but this assertion seems largely unfounded in that only a handful of the sheets foreshadow in any real sense the finished pictures of Petworth Park, and the closeness of those sketches is mainly due to circumstances such as a coincidence of viewpoint. This is completely distinct from the purpose of those pencil studies made in the 'Petworth' sketchbook of 1827 (figs. 74, 71; TB CCXLIII–76v/77, 77v/78) and a couple of related loose sheets (figs. 72, 73; TB CCCXLI–225, 380), which set out the limits of the Petworth Park pictures in easily discernible stages.

The gouache drawings do, however, anticipate the crowded interiors of the late paintings associated with Petworth. This is another aspect of the Petworth work unique to its environment. At Farnley Turner seems to have been content to render the interiors of the manor house with a cool, almost disinterested, precision, so that one would hardly suspect his fondness for the place, or for its occupants. Indeed the occasional human element in the drawings is reduced to a subordinate level by the analytical study of a particular interior. This distancing of the Fawkes's household to the background is contrasted with the sheets of the Petworth drawings, which throng with characters realised with a succinct and masterly brushwork, as eloquent and perceptive as the subtly-crafted phrases of Jane Austen (plate 15; TB CCXLIV–101).

Although the sketchbooks in the Turner Bequest are filled with acutely-observed details of the people Turner noted on his travels, the Petworth gouache drawings are particularly striking in the economic means by which Turner has realised even the smallest nuance of social behaviour. His method of drawing these and the East Cowes figure subjects is most nearly anticipated in a group of studies in the 'Walmer Ferry' sketchbook (figs. 64, 65; TB CXLII–15, 16). These sketches show similar scenes of conversation and flirtation, drawn in pen and ink with a wash of gouache, but unlike the scenes of Petworth, they have less of the sense of a particular place.

The identity of some of the 'characters' shown can be guessed at in several instances. Lord Egremont seems to appear in at least two of the drawings, in one commanding the group of figures apparently waiting for dinner (plates 13, 16; TB CCXLIV–31, 87). The upright officer pacing the White Library in his red uniform could quite possibly be the Earl's son, Colonel Wyndham (plate 14; TB CCXLIV–22). Also seen in the White Library is the figure of an ungainly and towering cleric, who is likely to be the Rev. Thomas Sockett, Rector of Petworth (plate 17; TB CCXLIV–86), and presumably this is the same figure that we see in the series of drawings inside the church (plates 105, 109, and 107; TB CCXLIV–63, 64, 66).

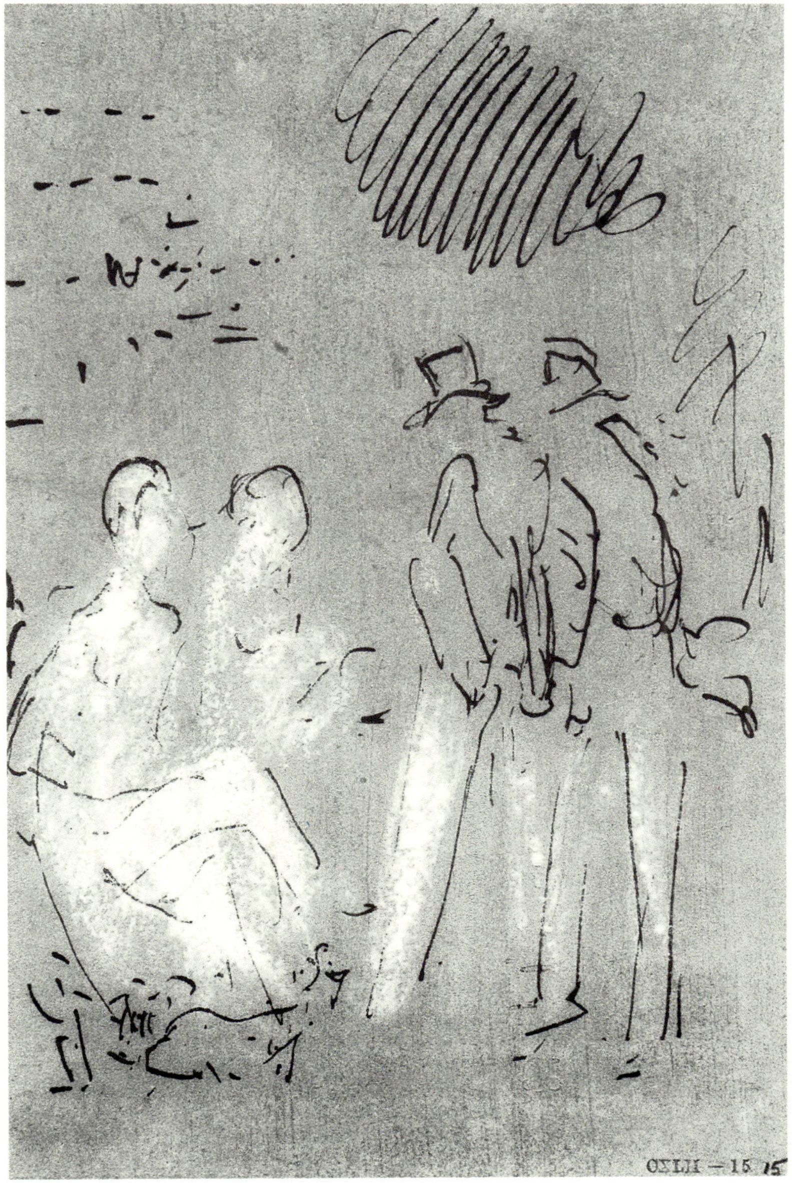

fig. 64 *A Conversation Group* ('Walmer Ferry' sketchbook, TB CXLII–15), *c.* 1817, Pen and ink and chalk on laid brown paper 160 × 114 ($6\frac{5}{16} \times 4\frac{1}{2}$), Tate Gallery

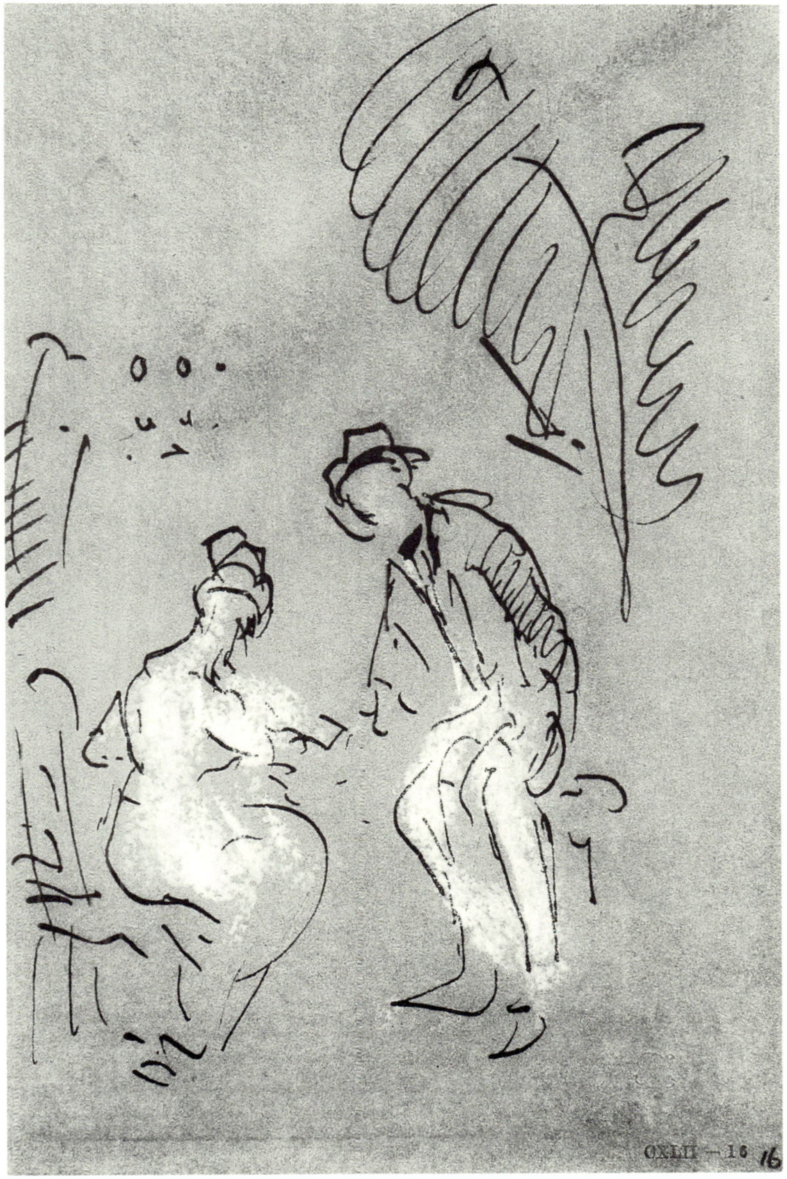

fig. 65 *A Flirtation* ('Walmer Ferry' sketchbook, TB CXLII–16), *c.* 1817, Pen and ink and chalk on laid brown paper 160 × 114 ($6\frac{5}{16} \times 4\frac{1}{2}$), Tate Gallery

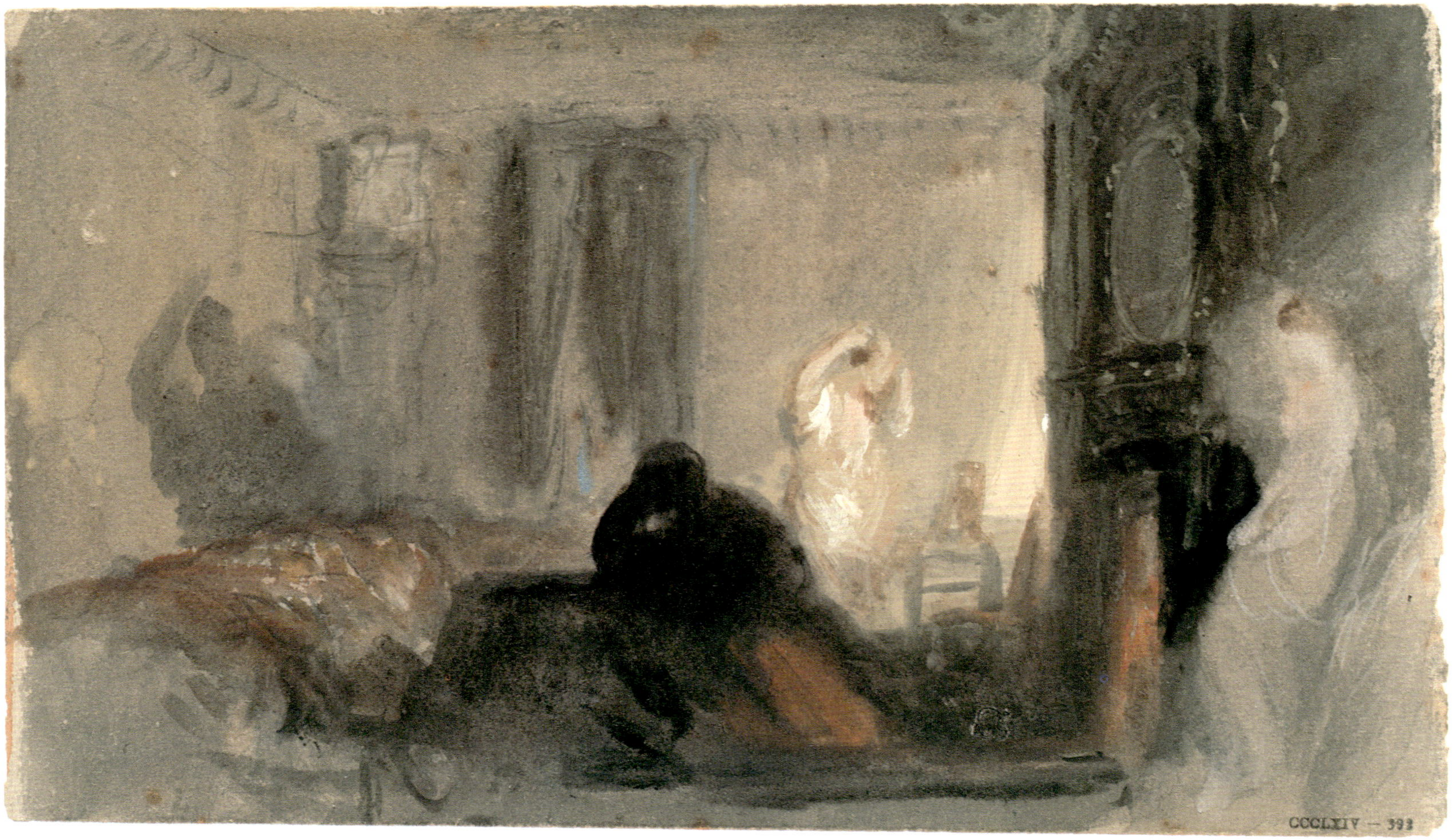

fig. 66 *Three Figures in a Darkened Room: Petworth (?)*, *c.* 1832, Gouache with traces of pencil and watercolour on grey paper 131 × 227 ($5\frac{1}{8} \times 8\frac{15}{16}$), Tate Gallery (TB CCCLXIV–392)

fig. 67 *Portrait of a Young Lady Playing the Fortepiano*, 1827, Gouache 192 × 140 ($7\frac{1}{2} \times 5\frac{1}{2}$), Tate Gallery (TB CCXLIV–39)

fig. 68 '*Brown Eyes*', ('Arundel and Shoreham' sketchbook, TB CCXLV, p. 54 verso), *c.* 1828–30, Pencil 67 × 110 ($2\frac{5}{8} \times 4\frac{1}{4}$), Tate Gallery

Another figure, that of the reclining man on the sofa, who appears in several of the drawings (plates 25, 60, 24, 17; TB CCXLIV–26, 77, 84, 86), has been thought to be the artist George Jones, who stayed at Petworth on many occasions.[11] This assumption relies on Jones's undated recollection that 'when on a visit to . . . Petworth with Turner, I hurt my leg, his anxiety to procure for me every attendance and convenience was like the attention of a parent to a child. His application to the housekeeper, butler and gardener for my comfort and gratification was unremitted'.[12] However, the dating for the gouache drawings suggested here would preclude this identification, for during this time Jones was travelling on the Continent, as his own travel notes and a letter in the Petworth House Archives bear witness.[13]

Over the other assorted figures and canine inhabitants there is a veil of mystery, vivid though these characters are: the rather large lady sitting among her court of attendant gossips; the many faceless beaux and belles; the lady whose face is created from one of Turner's thumbprints (plate 62; TB CCXLIV–79); the artists at their easels, as well as the musical young lady at the fortepiano. One drawing of this mysterious young lady at the piano seems almost a portrait, and it is curious to note that in a sketchbook of this date, used in the wider locality of Sussex, a similar face appears enigmatically inscribed, 'Brown Eyes' (figs. 67, 68).

As the drawings were not exhibited until after Turner's death no record of any contemporary reactions can be traced. However, Ruskin's statements, which shaped the attitude of a whole generation to Turner, are again interesting. His comments on the drawings that he did feel fit to show provide some indication of their reception, and highlight the significance of these blue paper drawings in Turner's relentless development. In talking of the erotic study of the folds of pink bedcurtains (plate 57; TB CCXLIV–15), Ruskin claims to have found the essence of Turner's middle period, while at the same time perceiving an affinity between Turner's drawing and the work of Tintoretto and Veronese. This drawing, which belongs with the more finished of the Petworth studies, coincides with Ruskin's view of the middle period as one of a stylistic 'Brilliancy, not without slight harshness'.[14] The drawings he rejects as untypical and below the standard he had set for Turner's art are to us more accessible thanks in part to subsequent developments in art, such as impressionism and abstraction, though to evaluate them by the standards of those movements is to misunderstand the motives behind their creation. As Ruskin saw, however, a transition is perceptible in the Petworth drawings towards the work of Turner's final years, made possible by reliance on colour that is at once 'pure', but 'always soft'.[15]

The drawings also mark a watershed in Turner's personal life. After the death of his friend Walter Fawkes in 1825, the return to Petworth heralds the end of a period of personal crisis and the beginning of what was to be a fruitful association with Petworth until Egremont's death in 1837. The burst of activity during the visit of 1827 is almost a song of joy at re-discovering a friendly environment to which he could escape after the loss of Farnley. Apart from their intrinsic merits and beauty as works of art, Turner's drawings provide the most privileged of insights into the remarkable and slightly eccentric behaviour of Petworth life. Here the peculiar mix of animals, artists, lords and ladies is captured in a sustained and unique vision that is both personal and popular in its appeal.

Notes

1 Finberg 1909, Vol. II, p. 744. Although the wrappers on which Ruskin recorded these comments have disappeared, it is still possible, in a number of cases, to establish which drawings Ruskin had in mind. On the versos of many drawings in the Turner Request Ruskin inscribed a group number. The relevant numbers for the Petworth drawings are '235', '238' and '239'. The list below includes all those drawings presently accessible:

'235: 46 double sheets = 8 rubbish'
TB CCXLIV–44, 45, 46, 47, 48, 49, 50, 51
'238: 62 Inferior'
TB CCXLIV–54, 55, 56, 63, 70, 71, 72, 89, 90, 92, 93, 97, 98, 102
'239: Worse'
TB CCXLIV–25, 26, 27, 28, 29, 31, 32, 34, 35, 36, 38, 39, 40, 41, 42, 43, 53, 58, 59, 60, 61, 62, 64, 68, 69, 73, 74, 77, 78, 79, 80, 82, 83, 84, 85, 86, 87, 94, 95, 100, 101, 103, 104.

2 All six loan collections travelled extensively and continuously from the late nineteenth century until the 1920s, which accounts for the tragic fading described below. The six towns listed are the first known port-of-call for the six collections respectively. I would like to thank Lucy Whitaker of the National Gallery for her help in tracing the many destinations the six loan collections visited.

3 See Clark 1949, 1970. Drawings from the Petworth group were also on display at the house in the autumn of 1979.

4 Wilton 1979, nos. 582–631.

5 Finberg 1909, Vol. II, p. 744.

6 I would like to thank Dr John Krill for discussing this aspect of the Petworth drawings with me. For the manufacture of paper in general see J. Krill, *English Artists' Paper; Renaissance to Regency*, 1987, p. 61.

7 Youngblood, *Burlington* 1983, p. 615–9.

8 See Wilton 1979, nos. 930–50 for *Turner's Annual Tour: The Loire*; and nos. 951–90 for *Turner's Annual Tour: The Seine.*

9 See Wilton 1979, nos. 906–12.

10 Wilkinson 1975, p. 51.

11 Youngblood, *Turner Studies* 1983, p. 33, n. 13.

12 George Jones, 'Recollections of J. M. W. Turner', transcribed in Gage 1980, p. 2.

13 West Sussex Record Office, PHA 5745, a letter from Jones to Egremont, dated 23 July 1827, proclaims 'I intend leaving London / for the Continent on Saturday'. The large group of cards in the Tate Gallery (A00219–A00701) on which Jones made costume studies on his travels includes one dated 2 October. This is inscribed Neustadt (card numbered 312), suggesting that Jones was abroad until quite late in the year.

14 Ruskin 1903–12, Vol. XIII, p. 287.

15 *Ibid.*

CHAPTER 5

The Petworth Landscapes of 1828 to 1829

The oil paintings of Petworth Park and Lake and other scenes nearby have always been held to be among Turner's masterpieces. They present however a number of unusual features which seem to arise out of the circumstances of their execution.

In the first place the landscapes fall into two main groups, similar in general composition and format but differing in degree of finish, one group apparently acting as sketches for the other. The four landscapes at Petworth are the more highly finished and show (as the pictures were never exhibited in Turner's life time, the titles are not the artist's own) 'The Lake, Petworth: Sunset, Fighting Bucks' (fig. 76; BJ 288), 'The Lake, Petworth: Sunset, A Stag Drinking' (fig. 78; BJ 289), 'Chichester Canal' (fig. 80; BJ 290) and 'Brighton from the Sea' (fig. 82; BJ 291). These were preceded by a series of less finished canvases which remained in Turner's possession and are now at the Tate Gallery. Four of them are earlier versions of the pictures at Petworth, and are known, respectively, as 'Petworth Park: Tillington Church in the Distance' (fig. 75; BJ 283), 'The Lake, Petworth, Sunset' (fig. 77; BJ 284), 'Chichester Canal' (fig. 79; BJ 285) and 'The Chain Pier, Brighton' (fig. 81; BJ 286). In addition there is a fifth composition, 'A Ship Aground' (fig. 83; BJ 287), presumably, in view of its place among other works that seem, as we shall see, to have resulted from a commission by Lord Egremont, a view on the south coast nearby. This composition, not used for the final series at Petworth, was developed in two paintings exhibited at the Royal Academy in 1831, 'Fort Vimieux' (BJ 341) and, to a lesser extent, 'Life-Boat and Manby Apparatus' (BJ 336).

As well as these nine canvases, the vertical dimensions of which range from $24\frac{1}{2}$ inches to 28 inches and the horizontal from 52 inches to $57\frac{1}{2}$ inches, there is a further canvas, $25\frac{5}{8} \times 52\frac{5}{8}$ inches (fig. 69; BJ 441), which Turner seems to have left unused until, some twenty years later, he used the prepared white ground as a basis for six sketches in grey paint, most if not all working out the composition of 'Dawn of Christianity (Flight into Egypt)' (BJ 394), exhibited at the Royal Academy in 1841. Turner clearly decided to have enough canvases ready in this unusual format and in the end found that he had one to spare.

In addition there is an earlier variant of the composition of the two versions of 'Chichester Canal', the work known as 'Evening Landscape, probably Chichester Canal' (fig. 84; BJ 282) in the Tate Gallery. This is exceptional as not having been one of the works handed over as part of the 'Turner Bequest' to the National Gallery in 1856. It was presented to the Tate Gallery in 1944 by Miss M.H. Turner, a collateral descendant of the artist, and was presumably one of the works that was given to Turner's next of kin at the time of his death as not being by his hand.[1] The attribution has indeed been doubted in the past, but the painting seems quite definitely to be by Turner. In style it seems to date from slightly earlier, in the mid 1820s. It is slightly narrower than the main group of Petworth paintings, measuring $25\frac{1}{2} \times 49\frac{1}{2}$ inches. In composition it is similar in a general way to the two later pictures, although the ship is placed further to the left, more is seen of the right-hand bank of the stretch of water, there is a peaked line of hills on the horizon very different in character to the rounded hills shown in the later paintings, and, most puzzling of all, there is no sign of Chichester Cathedral itself. Ian Warrell has pointed out the similarity to an earlier watercolour showing 'York Minster from the River Ouse' (fig. 70)[2] and it may indeed be that the 'Evening Landscape' was an intermediate stage in the composition with no specific reference to Chichester; after all, any view looking along a stretch of water between two banks is bound to be similar in its general points to any other. Turner would then have used this general idea for the more specific reference to Chichester in the landscapes that were designed for Petworth. However, this in itself would be an unusual way of working, from the

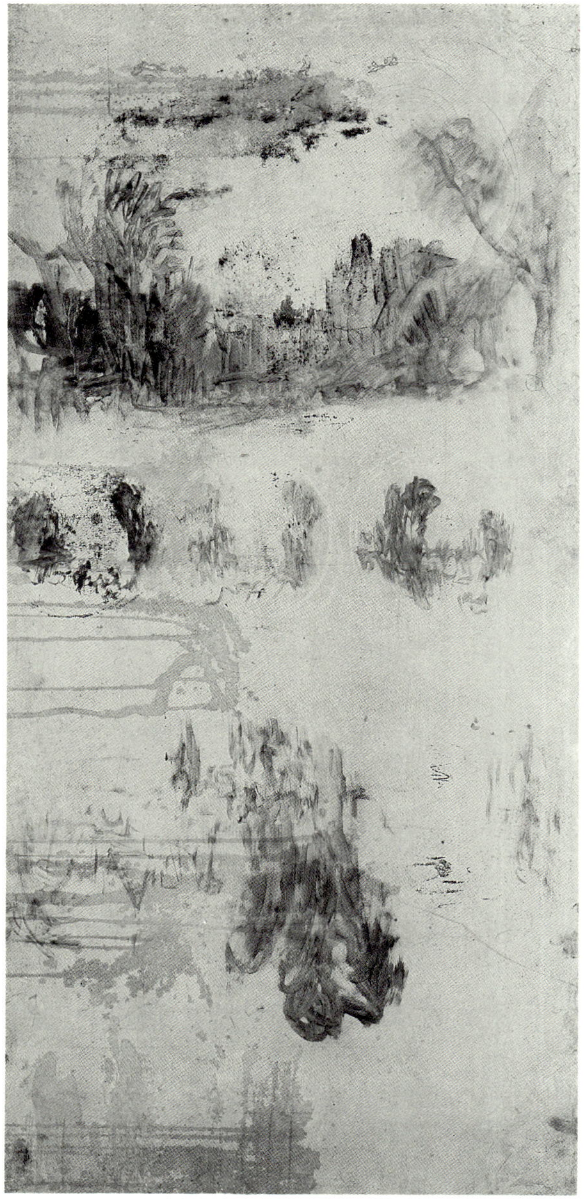

fig. 69 *Studies for 'Dawn of Christianity'* (BJ 441), *c.* 1841, Oil on canvas 1335 × 650 (52⅝ × 25⅝), Tate Gallery

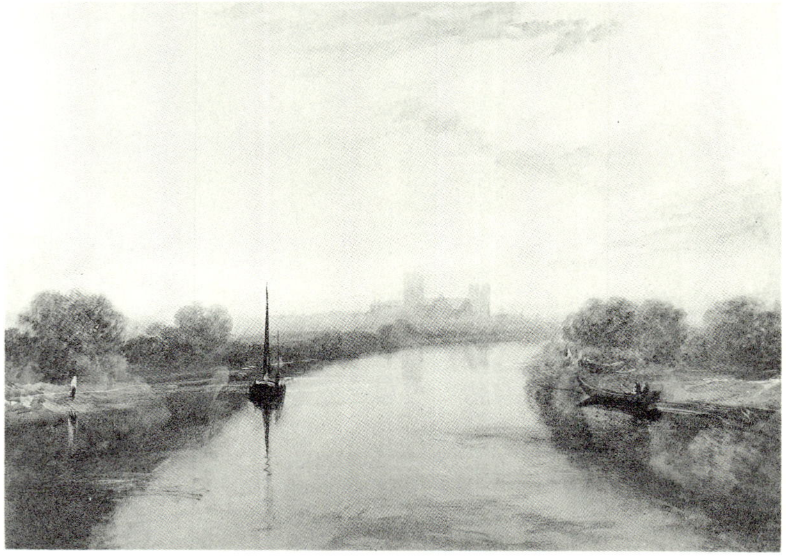

fig. 70 *York Minster from the River Ouse*, *c.* 1815, Watercolour with scratching-out, added white and gouache over traces of pencil 508 × 717 (20 × 28¼), Private Collection (W.275)

general to the particular, though there is a parallel case in one of the late unfinished oil paintings based on compositions in the *Liber Studiorum* which has been identified as a relatively exact depiction of 'The Ponte delle Torri, Spoleto' (BJ 518) but is based on the imaginary *Liber Studiorum* subject published much earlier, in 1812, as 'Bridge and Goats' (R 43) without any specific topographical reference.[3]

The landscapes still at Petworth are more highly finished than those now in the Tate Gallery, though for their period they are less detailed in finish than most of the works that Turner was exhibiting at the Royal Academy. In the case of 'The Lake, Petworth: Sunset, a Stag Drinking' at Petworth, Turner has added a considerable amount of detail in the form of a deer, swans and other birds, and also the boat-house and other garden furnishings shown on each side of the picture. The finished version of 'Brighton from the Sea' at Petworth again shows rather more detail: extra small boats on the right and various objects floating in the water. The Petworth version of 'Chichester Canal', probably the least finished of the later series, includes no extra features. The differences

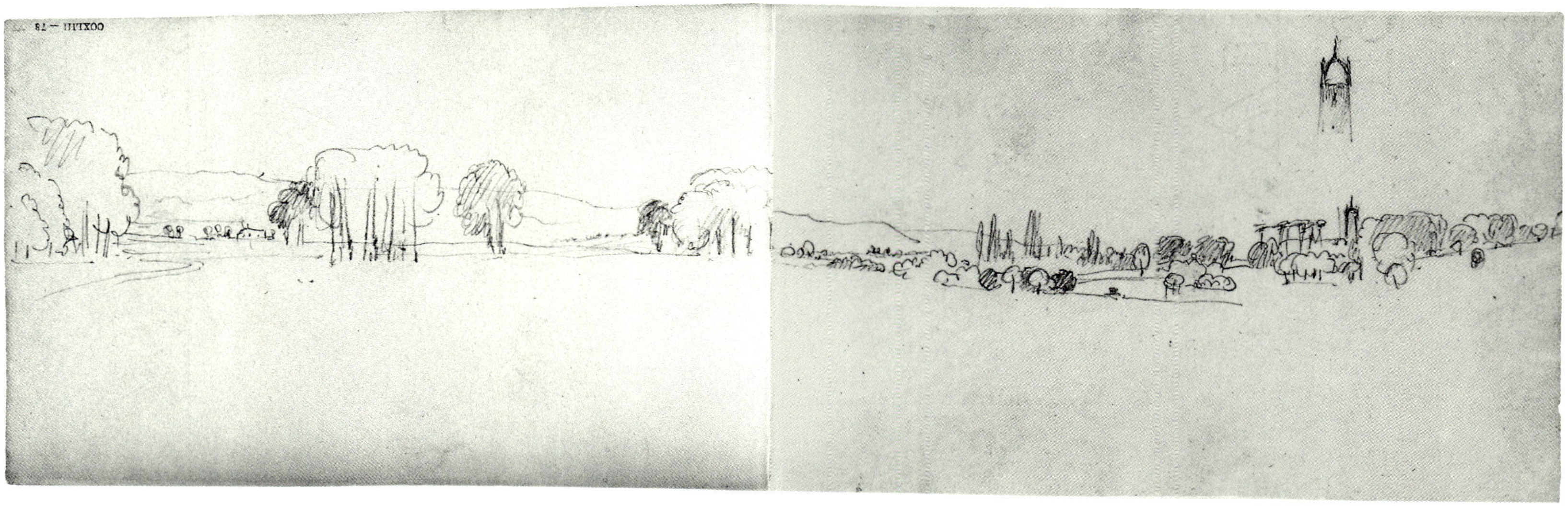

fig. 71 *Sketch for 'Petworth Park: Tillington Church in the Distance'* ('Petworth' sketchbook, TB CCXLIII, pp. 77 verso and 78), *c.* 1827, Pencil, page opening: 114 × 370 ($4\frac{1}{2} \times 14\frac{1}{2}$), Tate Gallery

between 'Petworth Park: Tillington Church in the Distance' and the more finished 'The Lake, Petworth: Sunset, Fighting Bucks' are more radical. Not only is the general viewpoint changed but so also are the main incidents depicted: the very personal touch in the earlier version of the returning Lord Egremont being greeted by his dogs rushing out from the terrace was replaced in the more finished version by a distant cricket match, and the later version also includes a greater number of deer and stags, including the incident of the two white fighting bucks that now gives the picture its title, and some of Lord Egremont's special black pigs (see p. 112).

Indeed, Turner seems to have used two different sketches of the general scene for the two pictures. For 'Petworth Park: Tillington Church in the Distance' he used a double page sketch in the 'Petworth' sketchbook (fig. 71; TB CCXLIII–77v/78), including a special detail of the top of the tower of Tillington Church. Indeed, as Ian Warrell points out on p. 126, there was a tradition that it was Turner himself who suggested that the tower, completed in 1807, should follow the unusual open lantern form with its flying arches. When Turner came to paint the more finished 'The Lake, Petworth: Sunset, Fighting Bucks', with its slightly different viewpoint, he seems to have used a different drawing (fig. 72; TB CCCXLI–225), done from somewhat to the right, with the result that the church tower appears more in the middle of the painting. This drawing seems to be from a dismembered sketchbook, another page of which (fig. 73; TB CCCXLI–380), as Ian Warrell has also pointed out, contains sketches used in three of the Petworth landscapes. That at the top shows the horizon at the right of 'The Lake, Petworth: Sunset, Fighting Bucks', with, rather more prominent than in the finished picture, the Upperton Monument. In the sketch in the middle the same tower appears but the configuration of the hills is closer to that in 'The Lake, Petworth: Sunset, a Stag Drinking', another of the finished pictures at Petworth. The sketch at the bottom, however, seems to be closest to one of the unfinished paintings, showing the path curving round between trees on the left of 'Petworth Park: Tillington Church in the Distance'. There is a further double-page sketch in the

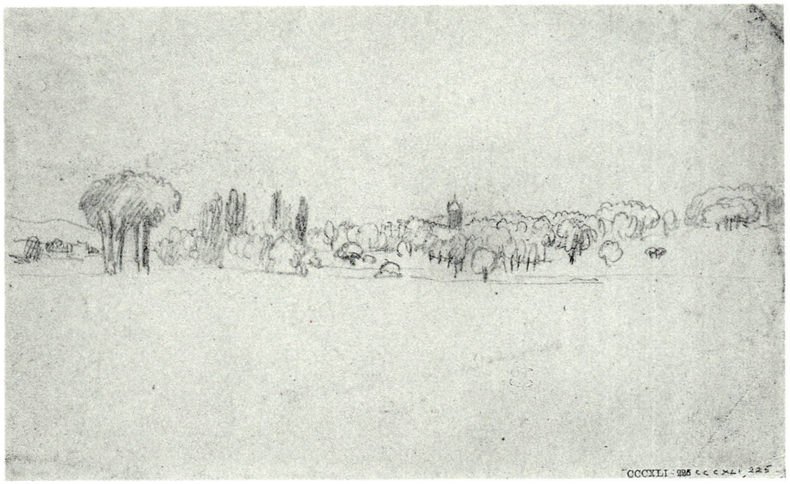

fig. 72 *Sketch for 'The Lake, Petworth: Sunset, Fighting Bucks'*, *c.* 1827, Pencil 113 × 184 ($4\frac{7}{16} \times 7\frac{1}{4}$), Tate Gallery (TB CCCXLI–225)

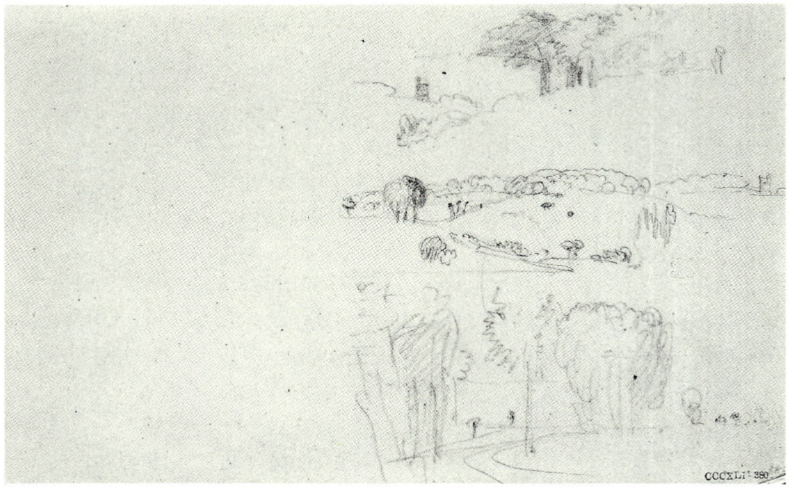

fig. 73 *Sketches for 'The Lake, Petworth: Sunset, Fighting Bucks'* (top), *'The Lake, Petworth: Sunset, a Stag Drinking'* (centre), and *'Petworth Park: Tillington Church in the Distance'* (bottom), *c.* 1827, Pencil 114 × 184 ($4\frac{1}{2} \times 7\frac{1}{4}$), Tate Gallery (TB CCCXLI–380)

'Petworth' sketchbook (fig. 74; TB CCXLIII–76v/77), adjacent to that for 'Petworth Park: Tillington Church in the Distance' already discussed, but in this case closer to 'The Lake, Petworth: Sunset, Fighting Bucks'. In this drawing however Turner does not seem to have been interested in the Upperton Monument which does not appear.

The final choice of subjects, as shown in the four pictures still at Petworth, presumably reflects the wishes of Lord Egremont. Indeed, Evelyn Joll has suggested that the extra subject at the Tate Gallery, 'A Ship Aground', may originally have been painted as a replacement of 'Chichester Canal', both versions of which record a venture from which Lord Egremont had withdrawn his money in 1826; in the event, 'Chichester Canal' was retained. 'The Chain Pier, Brighton' is also a depiction of an enterprise in which Lord Egremont was involved. His choice of the views in his own park suggest that he was well aware of Turner's activity in depicting the surroundings of his house in gouache (see plates 67–103).

The reason for the substitution of the pictures now at Petworth for those that remained in Turner's possession is not altogether clear; as will be seen, at least one of the less finished pictures was originally installed in the Carved Room. One suggestion is that the earlier sketches were rejected because they did not altogether fit in size, but this is unlikely in that some of the finished pictures match the dimensions of some of the ones now in the Tate Gallery. In any case, the panelling, already adapted from its original seventeenth-century setting by Jonathan Ritson at about the time that Turner's paintings were being installed, could presumably have been easily altered by an inch or so; many of the additions were removed again when the pictures were rehung in the adjacent Red Room in 1869. It seems more likely that Lord Egremont, whose taste by the later 1820s seems to have become even more conservative than earlier in his life, may have wanted a greater degree of finish. It was at this time that he purchased at the Lord de Tabley sale the much earlier landscape of 'Tabley', exhibited at the Royal Academy in 1809, and he was shortly to reject the landscape of 'Palestrina', specifically, it seems, painted for him in Rome in 1828, in favour of a figure subject, 'Jessica'. It seems odd, however, that Turner was not able to adapt his first versions; after all, he was to effect much greater transformations on the walls of the Royal Academy, or the British Institution working on paintings that were little more than lay-ins of the basic colours to produce finished works full of specific subject

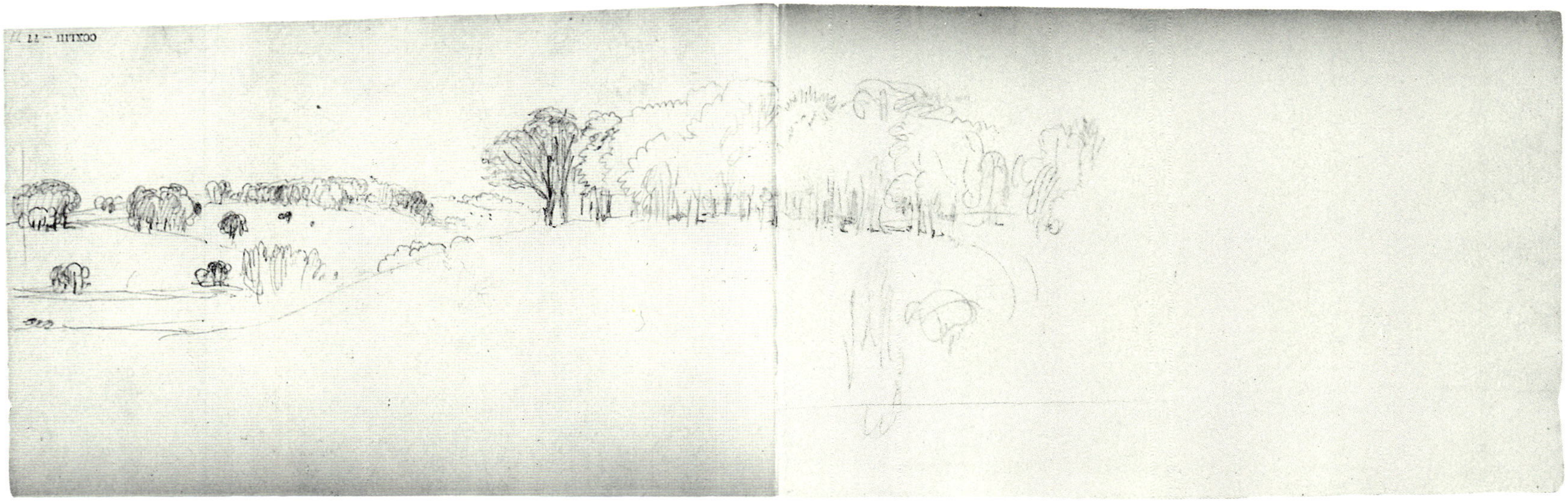

fig. 74 *Sketch for 'The Lake, Petworth: Sunset, Fighting Bucks'* ('Petworth' sketchbook, TB CCXLIII, pp. 76 verso and 77), *c.* 1827, Pencil, page opening: 114 × 370 ($4\frac{1}{2} \times 14\frac{1}{2}$), Tate Gallery

matter (see, for example, 'Regulus' and 'The Burning of the House of Lords and Commons', BJ 294 and 359).

It was rare, however, for Turner to paint pictures for so specific a setting as on this occasion. The only parallel case is that of the two views of 'Plompton Rocks' (BJ 26 and 27) painted for Harewood House in 1798. At Harewood House the paintings hung at a fairly normal height, but at Petworth they were placed rather like the predella panels on an Italian Renaissance altar-piece, below the full-length seventeenth-century portraits in the Carved Room (see fig. 115). The idea might have been suggested by the placing of landscape compositions below certain altarpieces in Bavarian churches, such as those in the late sixteenth-century Michaelskirche in Munich, though there is no record that Turner was in southern Germany until he passed through on his return from Venice in 1833.

A more practical reason for the unusual format of these landscapes may have been that that happened to be the space available. Thomas Creevey, in a letter to a Miss Ord of 18 August 1828, describing his visit to Petworth on the previous two days, gives a very matter-of-fact account of the circumstances. After describing the full-length portraits in the Carved Room Creevey goes on, 'Immense as these pictures are with all their garniture there are still panels to spare, and as he [Lord Egremont] always has artists ready in the house, in one of these compartments, you have Petworth Park by Turner, in another Lord Egremont taking a walk with nine dogs, that are his constant companions, by the same artist . . .'.

As well as describing the circumstances of Lord Egremont's commission, Creevey's letter also gives a date for when at least two of Turner's paintings were installed in the Carved Room. Surprisingly one of them at least must have been one of the less finished pictures that was to remain in Turner's possession and is now in the Tate Gallery: the second picture referred to can only be 'Petworth Park: Tillington Church in the Distance' which is alone in showing 'Lord Egremont taking a walk with nine dogs'. Various candidates have been suggested for the other painting mentioned by Creevey, including the equally unfinished

'Lake, Petworth, Sunset', now also in the Tate Gallery, or the more finished version of the same composition still at Petworth, 'The Lake, Petworth: Sunset, a Stag Drinking'.[4] Ian Warrell has suggested that the picture was 'The Lake, Petworth: Sunset, Fighting Bucks' which was, as he points out, engraved in 1859 as 'Petworth Park' and was always referred to by that title in the various inventories at Petworth. This would have meant that two versions of more or less the same composition, unfinished and finished, were set into the panelling in the Carved Room at the same time, perhaps to demonstrate the effect of the two degrees of finish or the two different depths of colour. Interestingly enough, it is 'Petworth Park: Tillington Church in the Distance' that is the most finished of the works that remained in Turner's possession. Moreover, this work shows definite signs of having been worked on in some kind of frame, presumably the Grinling Gibbons panelling in the Carved Room: a strip of the sky along the top of the picture, but excluding the vertical of the window frame on the left, and down the top part of the right-hand edge is much less finished than the rest. A similar effect can be seen along the top of the less finished, Tate Gallery version of 'Chichester Canal'. Perhaps this picture too was also partly painted *in situ* in the Carved Room. It seems probable that the rest of the work on these landscapes was done, at least in considerable part, in the Old Library at Petworth, giving occasion for the incident of Chantrey's imitation of Lord Egremont's peculiar step and knock described on p. 19.

At any event, the final installation of the landscapes now at Petworth cannot have taken place until after Turner returned from Italy in February 1829, he having been on his way to Rome when Creevey saw the unfinished 'Petworth Park: Tillington Church in the Distance' in the Carved Room. It may have been the difficulties caused by the placing of the landscapes so low in the panelled setting of the Carved Room, perhaps creating special lighting hazards, that led to Turner having to repeat his compositions; such a duplication is very rare in Turner's work.

The elongated format of these paintings seems to have inspired Turner to produce some of his most magical landscapes. The compositions echo, rather than attempt to counter, the long format, the emphasis being on the long line of the horizon and the wide vault of the sky. The framing trees at each side of some of the landscape compositions were strengthened in the more finished versions still at Petworth but still do little to contradict the openness of the view. In the case of 'Petworth Park: Tillington Church in the Distance' the strangeness of the format is if anything enhanced by Turner's extraordinary foreground: although the line of paving stones on the terrace in front of the house is explained rationally, forming a diagonal from the centre of the lower edge of the painting and running towards the left, this rectilinear stress is contradicted by the sweeping curve given to the whole of the foreground which is echoed by the vaulting clouds of the sunset sky. These curves serve to emphasize the diagonal emphasis of the dogs rushing into the picture to meet their master. The special features of this composition seem to have been developed from one of the gouaches (plate 70; TB CCXLIV–2) and also from the lowest of the three drawings on the page from a dismembered sketchbook already discussed (fig. 73). In none of the other paintings is there such an apparently imposed, arbitrary compositional device, though the central placing of the setting sun and the general symmetry of most of the pictures (an unconventional feature, countering text-book principles of design,[5] the effect of which was lessened in the finished versions) also seem to result from an attempt to control the unusually wide format. An interesting feature in the unfinished versions, again lessened in the more finished paintings still at Petworth, is the way in which Turner shows the optical effect of the setting sun apparently cutting into the solid form of the hills silhouetted against the horizon. The handling of the skies in these unfinished versions is also noticeable for its freedom.

These landscapes demonstrate the evocative power of Turner's work even in pure landscape with a minimum of figures. The setting suns, the silhouetting of a dark ship in 'Chichester Canal', the wan light of 'A Ship Aground' unite an unforced symbolism with a total control of form and colour to produce an overwhelming emotional effect. This exceptional degree of response to the forms of landscape may reflect Turner's return to his old patron, emotionally linked with the deaths of two of his other leading patrons, Walter Fawkes in 1825 and Sir John Leicester in 1827, and of his own father in 1829. These factors, and the general freedom of artistic activity at Petworth, seem to have produced something altogether exceptional in Turner's art.

Notes

[1] See 'The Turner Bequest' in Butlin and Joll 1984, p. xxii. Turner's will and its various codicils are reprinted in Walter Thornbury's *Life of J. M. W. Turner R.A.*, 1862, vol. ii, pp. 409–22, and 1877, pp. 620–33; there is also a much more legible contemporary printing of the documents on their own, of which copies can be found in the National Gallery library.

[2] Private Collection. See Wilton 1979, p. 330 no. 275, repr., where dated *c.* 1800, and David Hill, exhibition catalogue, *Turner in Yorkshire*, York City Art Gallery, 1980, p. 31 no. 37, where more convincingly dated *c.* 1815.

[3] Giovanni Carandente's identification of 'The Ponte delle Torri, Spoleto' (first published in the British Council's exhibition catalogue, *La Pittura Inglese da Hogarth a Turner (1730–1850)*, Palazzo Venezia, Rome, 1960, no. 59, and amplified in his article 'Un Viaggio di Turner in Umbria', *Spoletium*, vol. xi, no. 13, April 1968, pp. 20–21) has however been rejected by Cecilia Powell, *Turner in the South: Rome, Naples, Florence*, 1987, p. 34.

[4] Gage 1980, p. 250, and Butlin and Joll 1984, p. 165.

[5] See Lawrence Gowing, exhibition catalogue, *Turner: Imagination and Reality*, Museum of Modern Art, New York, 1966, p. 27, with illustrations of how not to compose a picture from Frank Howard's *The Sketchers Manual*, 1837.

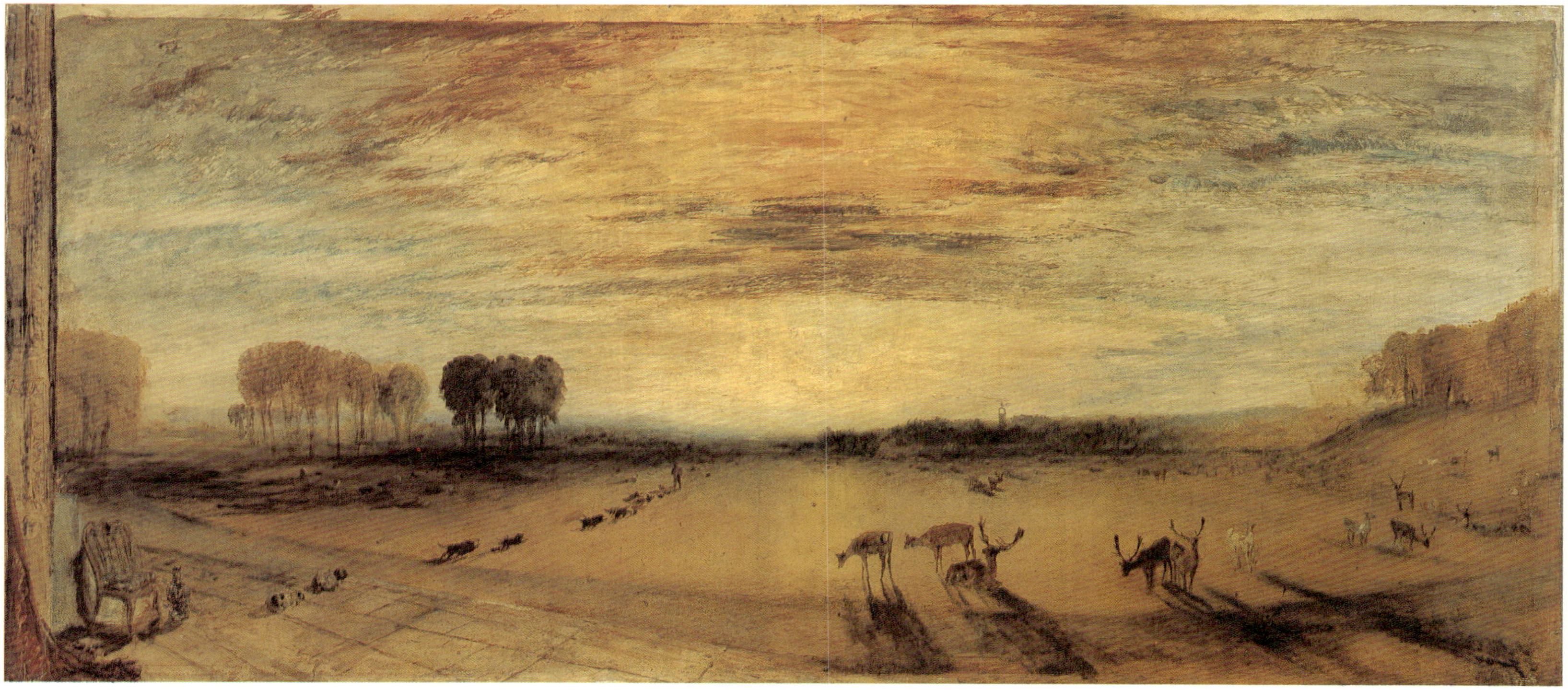

fig. 75 *Petworth Park: Tillington Church in the Distance* (BJ 283), 1827–28,
Oil on canvas 645 × 1455 ($25\frac{3}{8} \times 57\frac{3}{8}$), Tate Gallery

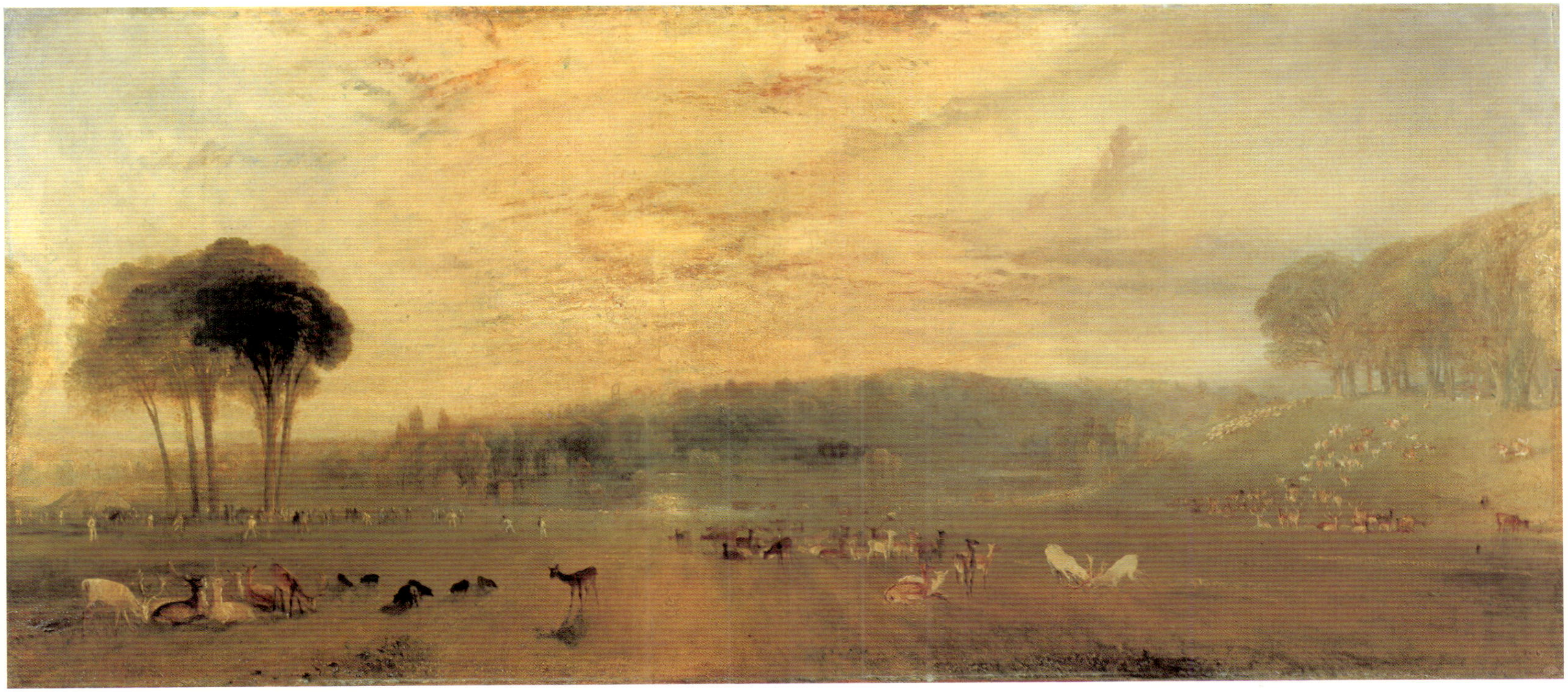

fig. 76 *The Lake, Petworth: Sunset, Fighting Bucks* (BJ 288), 1827–28,
Oil on canvas 620 × 1460 ($24\frac{1}{2} \times 57\frac{1}{2}$), Petworth House

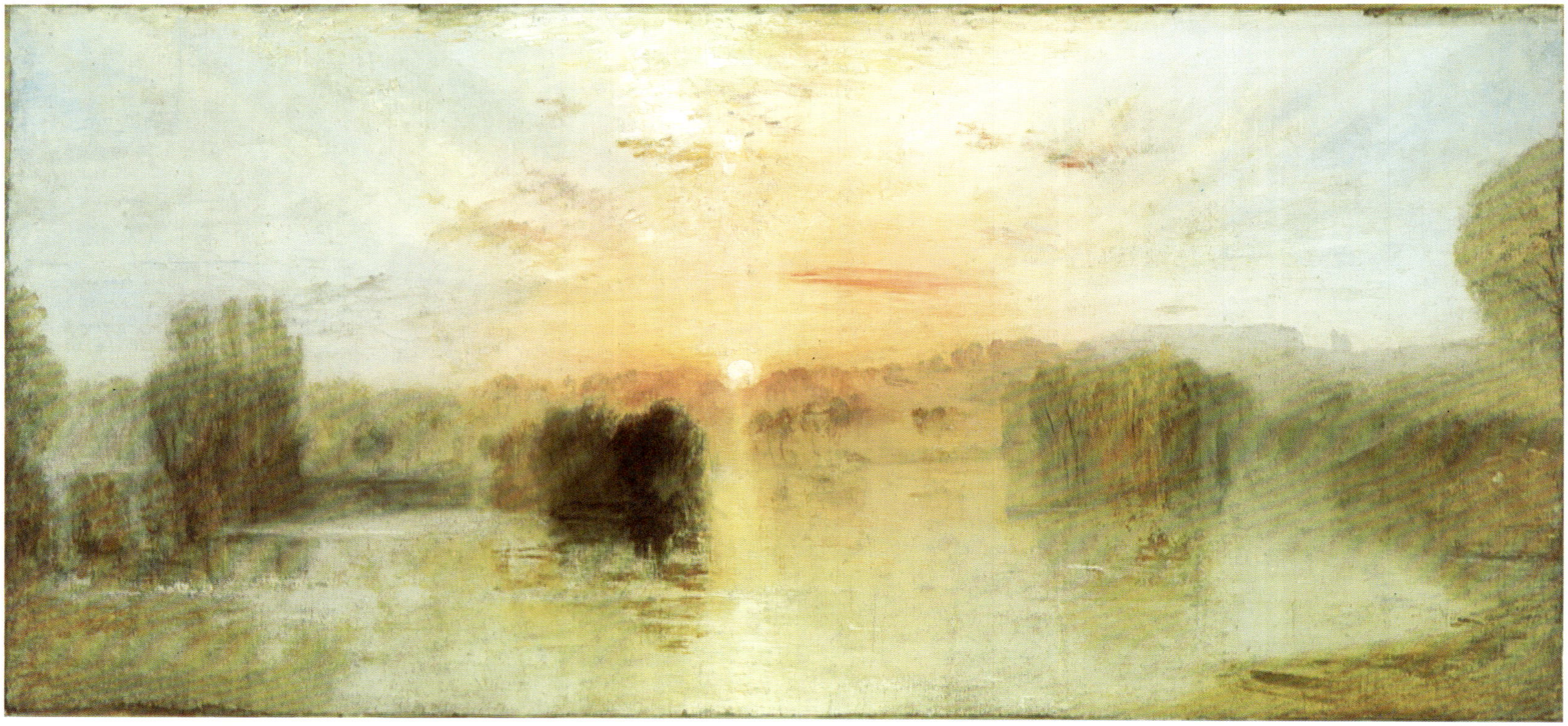

fig. 77 *The Lake, Petworth, Sunset* (BJ 284), *c.* 1828, Oil on canvas
650 × 1410 ($25\frac{1}{2} \times 55\frac{1}{2}$), Tate Gallery

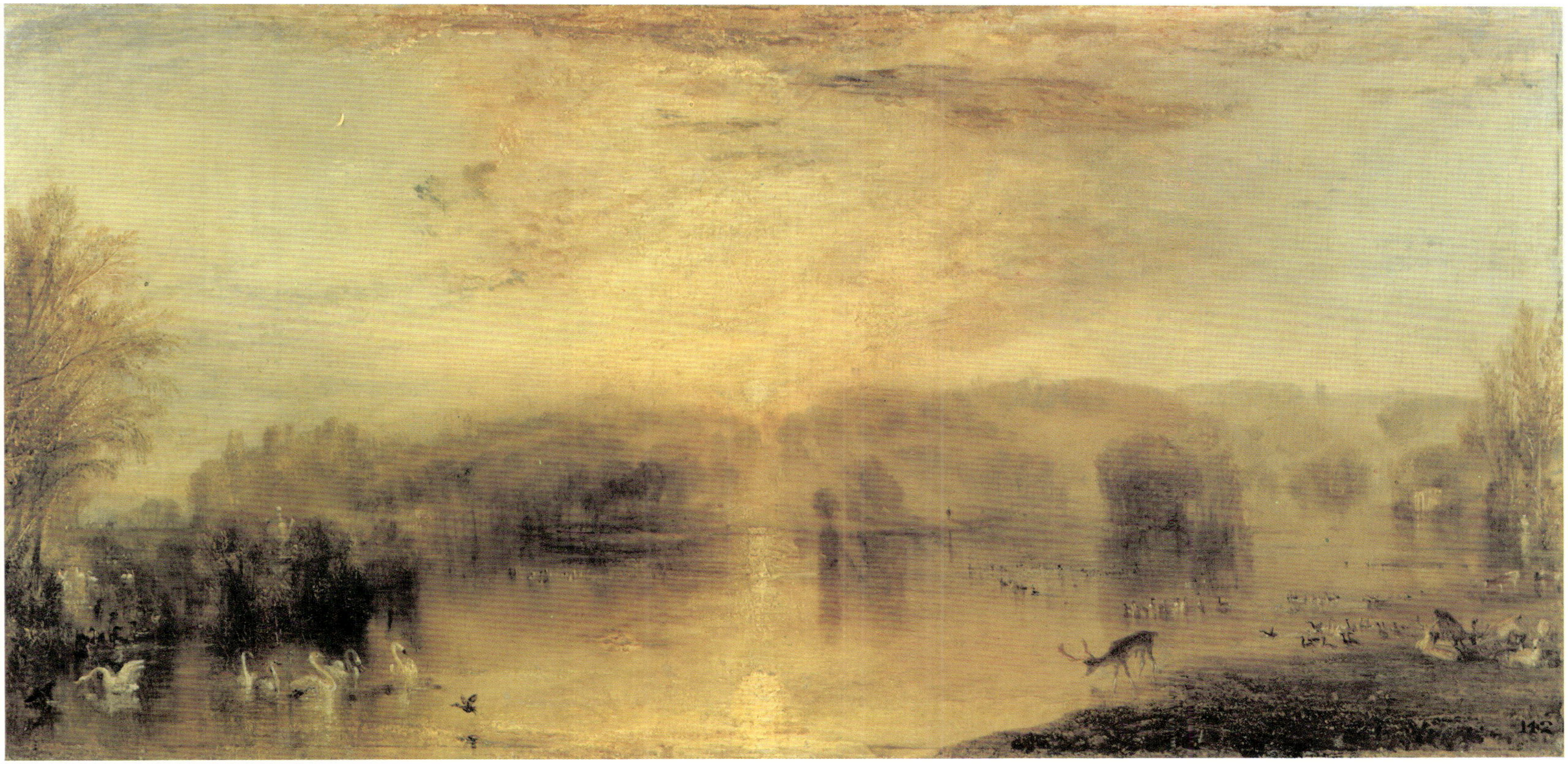

fig. 78 *The Lake, Petworth: Sunset, a Stag Drinking* (BJ 289), *c.* 1829,
Oil on canvas 635 × 1320 (25 × 52), Petworth House

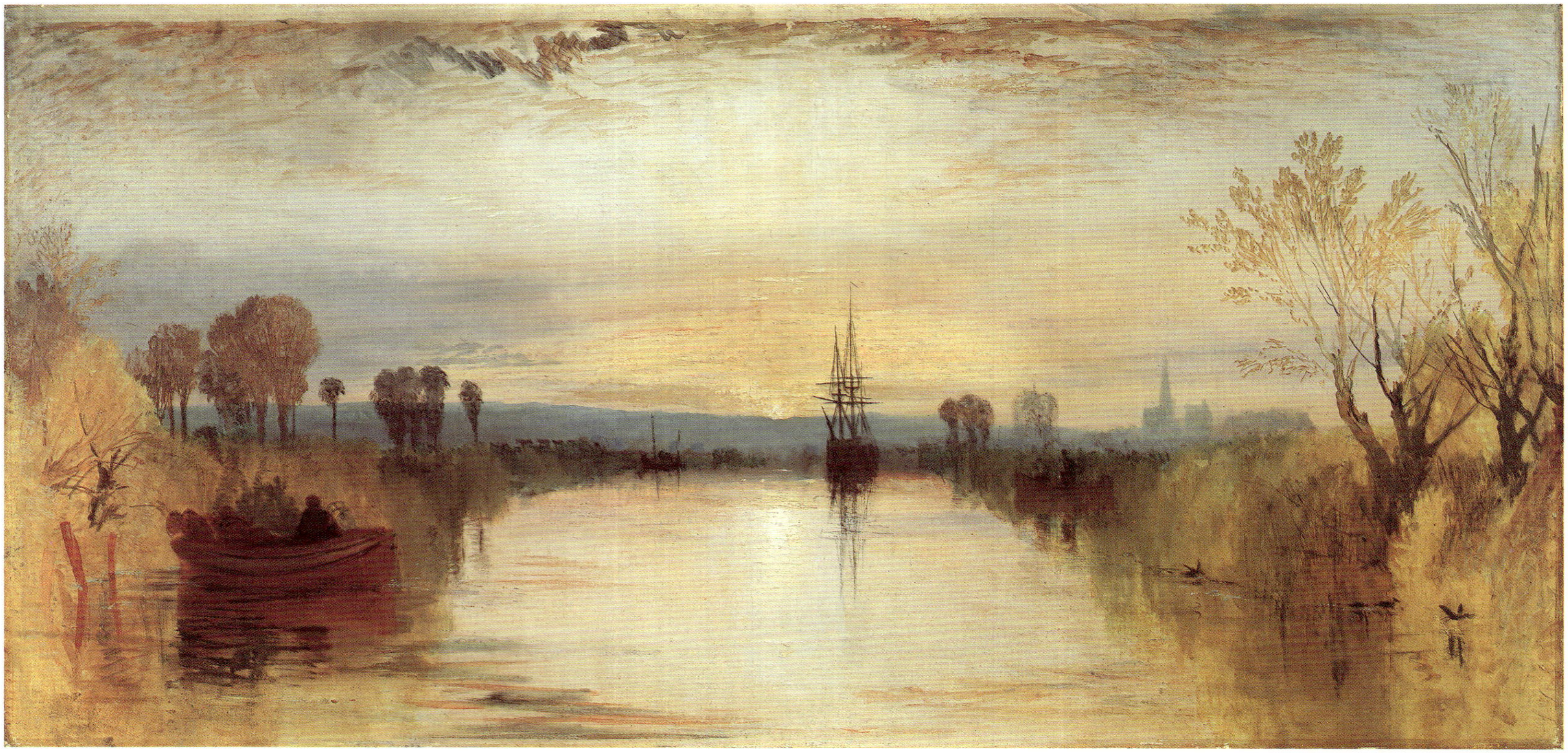

fig. 79 *Chichester Canal* (BJ 285), *c.* 1828, Oil on canvas 655 × 1345 ($25\frac{3}{4}$ × 53), Tate Gallery

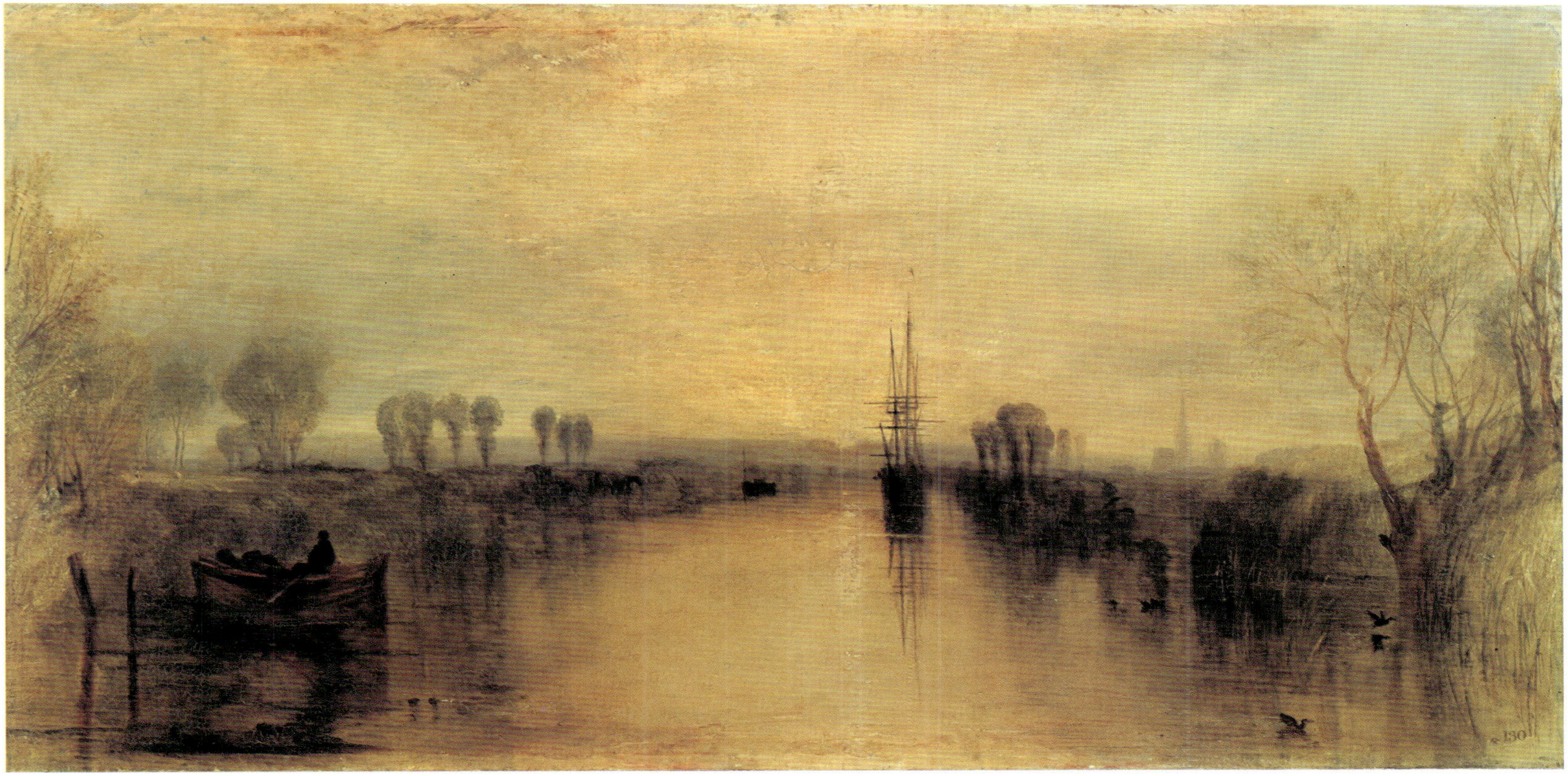

fig. 80 *Chichester Canal* (BJ 290), *c.* 1829, Oil on canvas 635 × 1320 (25 × 52), Petworth House

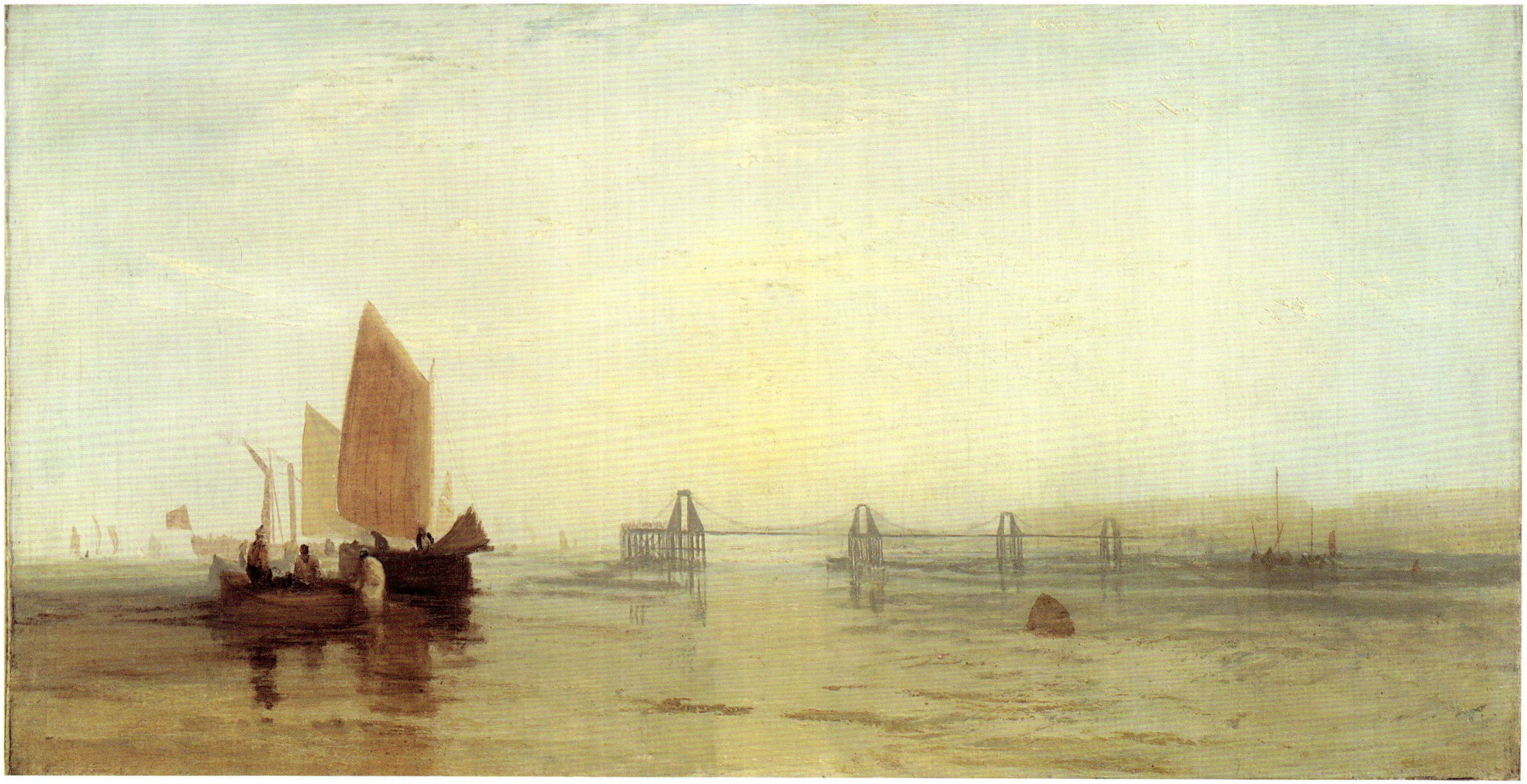

fig.81 *The Chain Pier, Brighton* (BJ 286), *c.* 1828, Oil on canvas 710 × 1365 (28 × 53¾), Tate Gallery

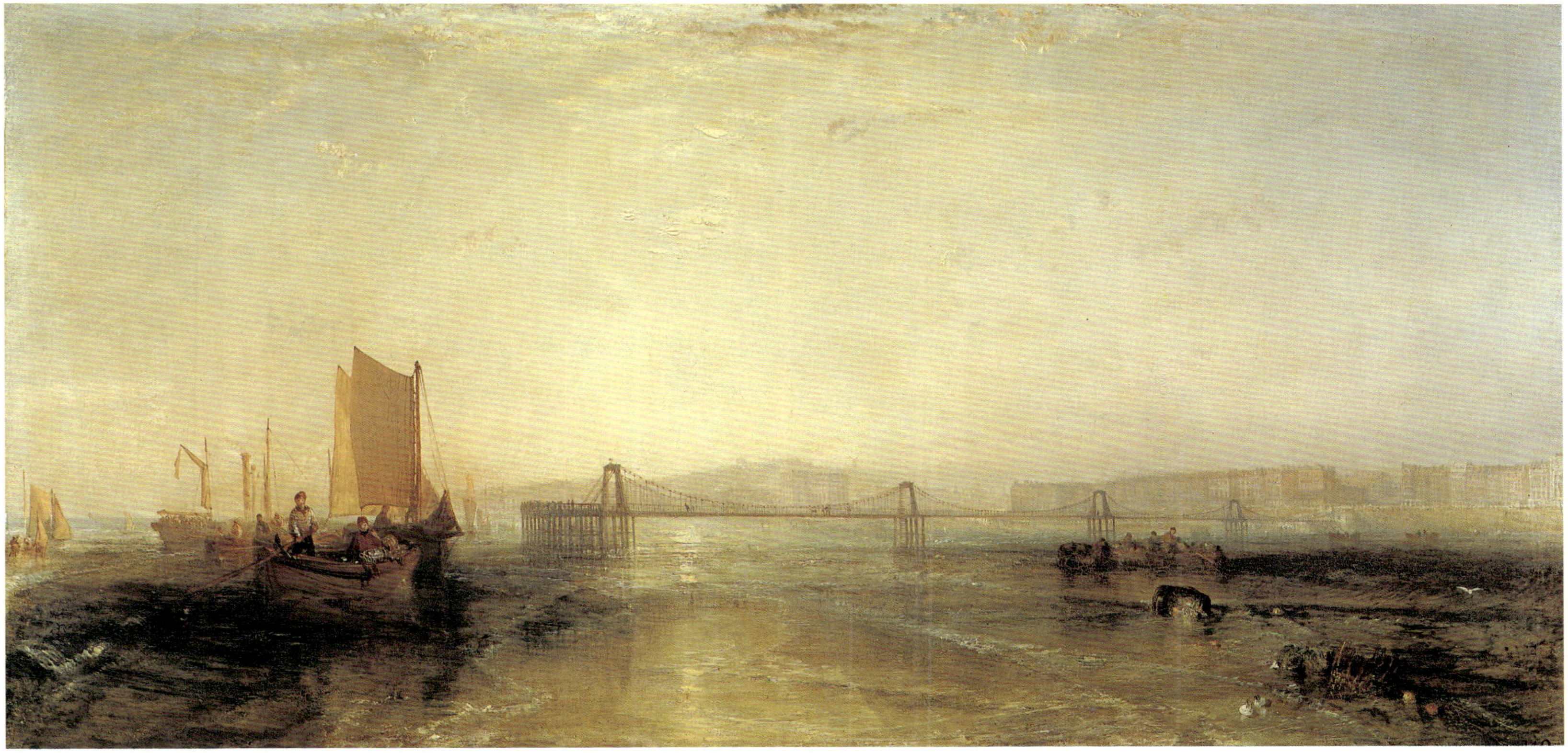

fig. 82 *Brighton from the Sea* (BJ 291), *c.* 1829. Oil on canvas 635 × 1320 (25 × 52), Petworth House

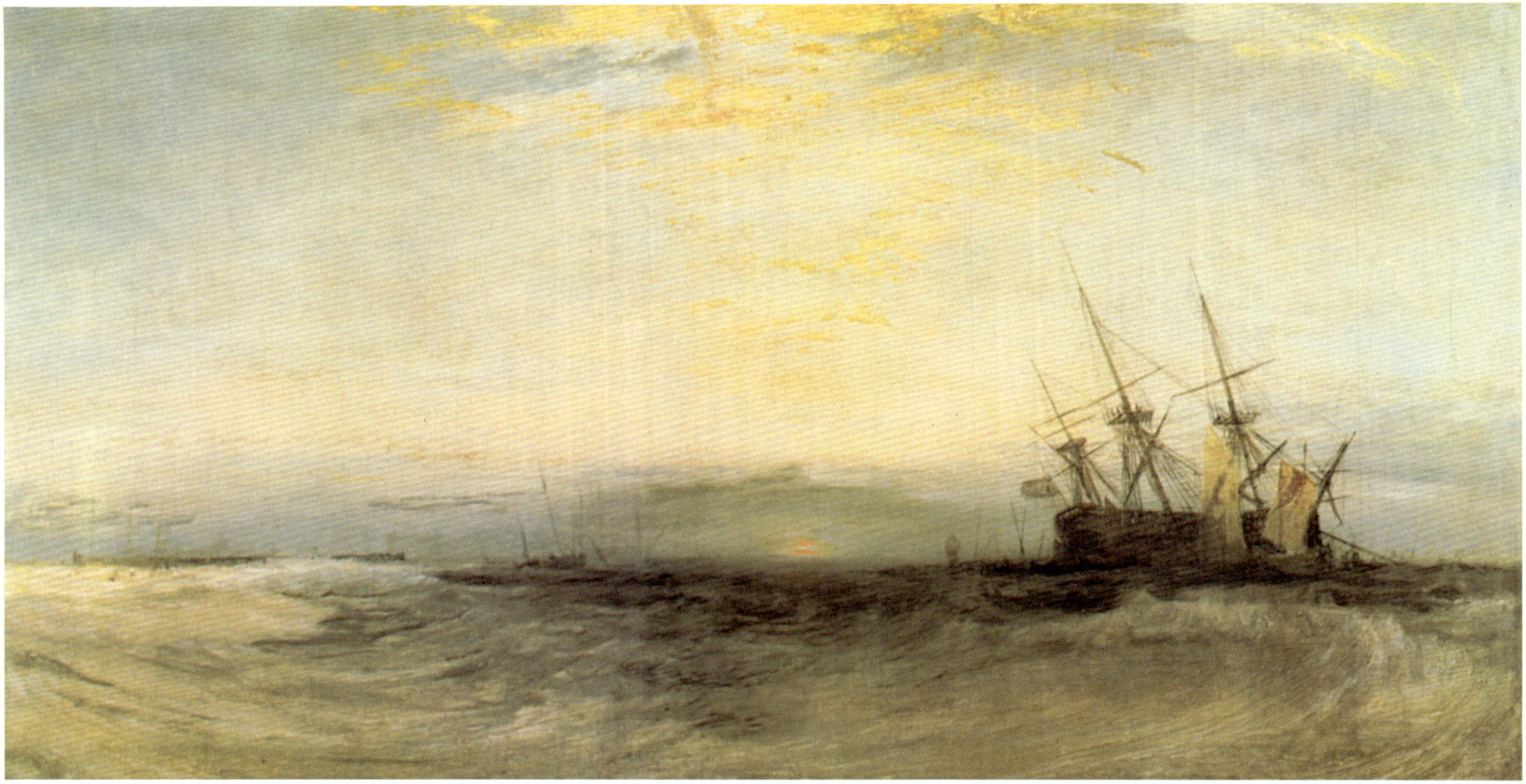

fig. 83 *A Ship Aground* (BJ 287), *c.* 1828, Oil on canvas 700 × 1360 ($27\frac{1}{2} \times 53\frac{1}{2}$),
Tate Gallery

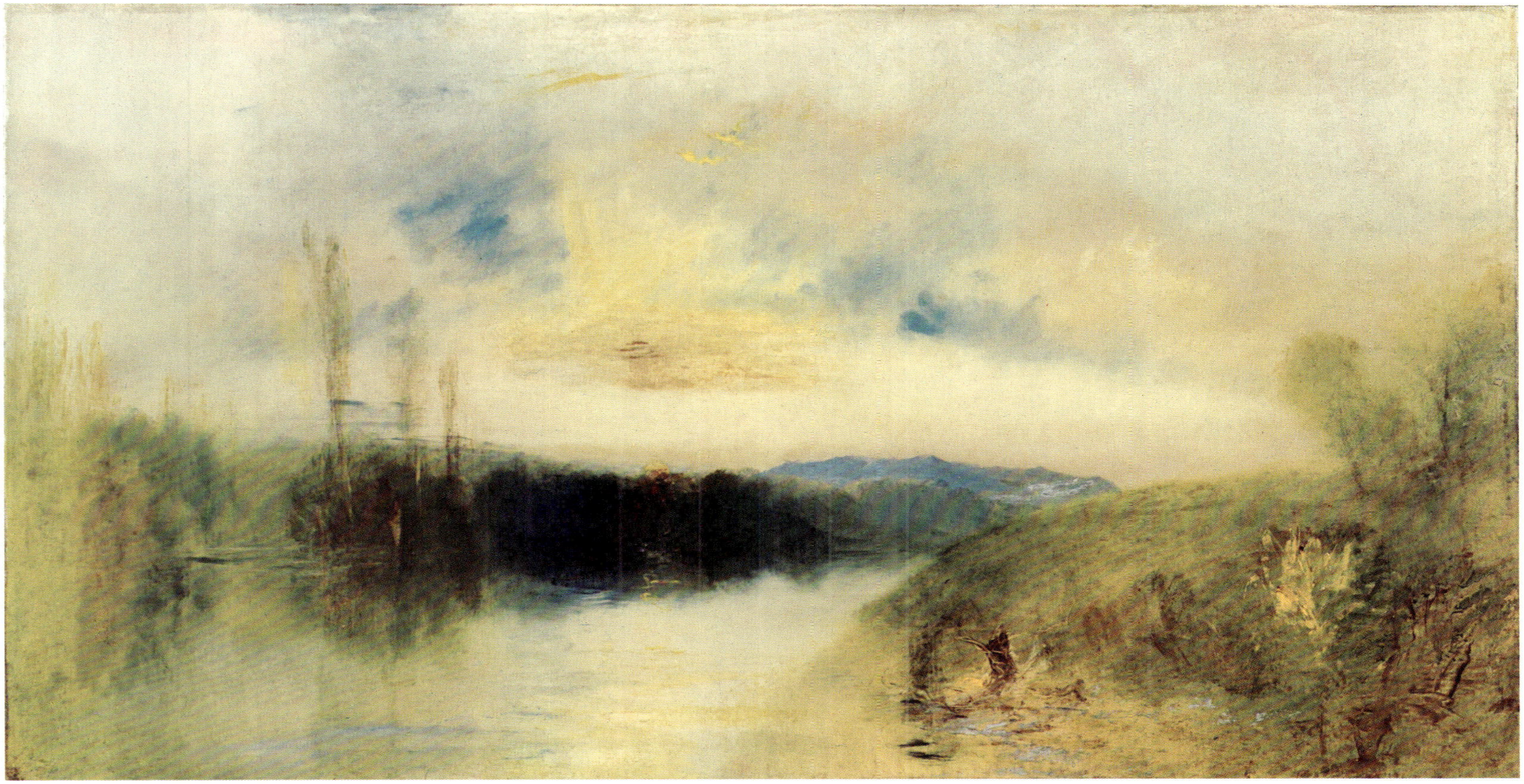

fig. 84 *Evening Landscape, probably Chichester Canal* (BJ 282), *c.* 1825–28, Oil on canvas 650 × 1260 ($25\frac{1}{2} \times 49\frac{1}{2}$), Tate Gallery

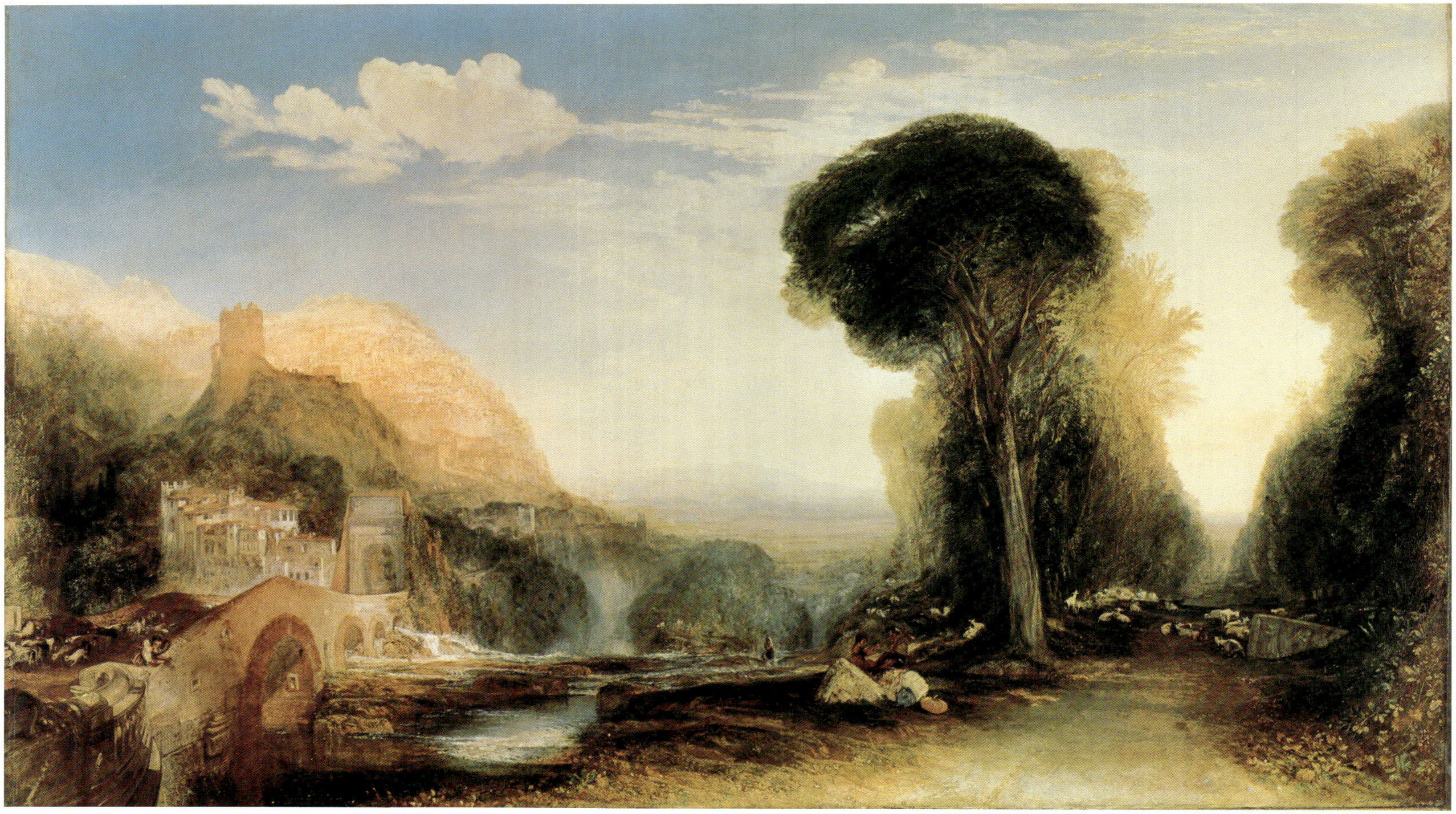

fig. 85 *Palestrina – Composition* (BJ 295), 1828, Oil on canvas
1405 × 2490 (55¼ × 98), Tate Gallery

CHAPTER 6

Interior and Figure Paintings at and associated with Petworth

The last phase of Turner's work for Lord Egremont began with a false start. While engaged on completing the landscapes for the Carved Room at Petworth Turner set off for his second visit to Rome. Leaving England in August 1828 he arrived in Rome in October, staying until early January 1829. Unlike his first visit, when he devoted himself to exploring the treasures of Rome through sketches and more finished watercolours, he spent much of his time on his second visit painting oils, renting a studio for this purpose at 12 Piazza Mignanelli, by the Spanish Steps. In December he exhibited three pictures at the Palazzo Trulli in Via del Quirinale near the Quattro Fontane: 'View of Orvieto, painted in Rome' (BJ 292), later exhibited again at the Royal Academy in 1830, 'Vision of Medea' (fig. 42; BJ 293), shown again at the Royal Academy in 1831, and 'Regulus' (BJ 294), exhibited again at the British Institution in 1837; in each case the picture seems to have been re-worked prior to being exhibited in London. According to Charles Eastlake Turner also began a further 'eight or ten pictures while he was in Rome' (see BJ 296–301).

En route, while in Paris, Turner had written to Charles Eastlake asking 'that the best of all possible grounds and canvass size 8 feet $2\frac{1}{2} \times$ 4 feet $11\frac{1}{4}$ inches to be if possible ready for me, two canvasses if possible', as 'It would give me the greatest pleasure, independent of other feelings which modern art and of course artists, and I among the number, owe to Lord Egremont, that my first brush in Rome . . . should be to begin for him *con amore* a companion picture to his beautiful CLAUDE'. As has already been discussed in chapter 3, this painting would have been yet another tribute to Claude's 'Jacob with Laban and his Daughters' (fig. 52), and it is generally accepted that the painting begun in Rome was 'Palestrina – Composition' (fig. 85; BJ 295), subsequently exhibited at the Royal Academy in 1830: it measures $55\frac{1}{4} \times$ 98 inches as compared to the $56\frac{1}{2} \times 99$ inches of the Claude. The only argument against this identification is the fact that 'Palestrina' is painted on a relatively fine canvas very different from the coarse Italian canvases of the other works known to have been painted in Rome. It may have been that Eastlake secured a fine canvas to await Turner's arrival but that the latter, having used this for 'Palestrina', switched to the locally more accessible coarse canvas for the other works he painted in Rome. Cecilia Powell[1] has suggested that Turner may in fact have experimented with four different compositions as possibilities for Lord Egremont, the other three being the three unfinished works on coarse canvas that remained in Turner's possession, 'Southern Landscape' (BJ 299), 'Southern Landscape with an Aqueduct and a Waterfall' (BJ 300), and 'Italian Landscape, probably Civita di Bagnoregio' (BJ 301); these are all roughly the same width as the Claude though the first is $69\frac{1}{2}$ inches in height and the other two approximately 59 inches, closer to the Claude. None of the compositions is particularly close to Claude's painting though 'Palestrina', with its relatively low horizon, is the closest.

In any event, none of the large Italian landscapes begun in Rome entered Lord Egremont's collection. Instead, his last acquisition of a work by Turner was 'Jessica' (fig. 92; BJ 333), exhibited at the Royal Academy in 1830 though not purchased by Lord Egremont until April 1831. The fact that Lord Egremont did not buy the picture until nearly a year after it was exhibited seems to contradict the otherwise attractive anecdote given by Lord Egremont's great-granddaughter, according to whom a fellow artist staying at Petworth with Turner chafed him on his predilection for yellow, saying 'A yellow background is all very well in landscapes, but would not be possible in our kind of pictures'; Turner is said to have replied that 'Subject pictures are not my style but I will undertake a picture of a woman's head with a yellow background if Lord Egremont will give it a place in his gallery'.

'Jessica' was exhibited at the Royal Academy with the following quotation purporting to come from Shakespeare: 'Shylock – "Jessica, shut the window I say" – *The Merchant of Venice*'. The quotation does not in fact occur in *The Merchant of Venice* but reflects Shylock's warning to Jessica: 'Lock up my doors . . . But stop my house's ears, I mean my casements.' It has also been suggested that the picture reflects the lines in Rogers's *Italy*:

> . . . Now Jessica
> Sung to her lute, her signal as she sate
> At her half-open window.

However, this duplication of sources seems unlikely, particularly as Jessica is neither singing nor holding a musical instrument. What the painting does reflect, visually, is the influence of Rembrandt, as we have seen in chapter 3. However, there may be a real-life source for the composition as well: Ian Warrell has pointed out the relevance of a small pencil drawing in the 'Birmingham and Coventry' sketchbook of *c.* 1829–30 (fig. 86; TB CCXL–7).

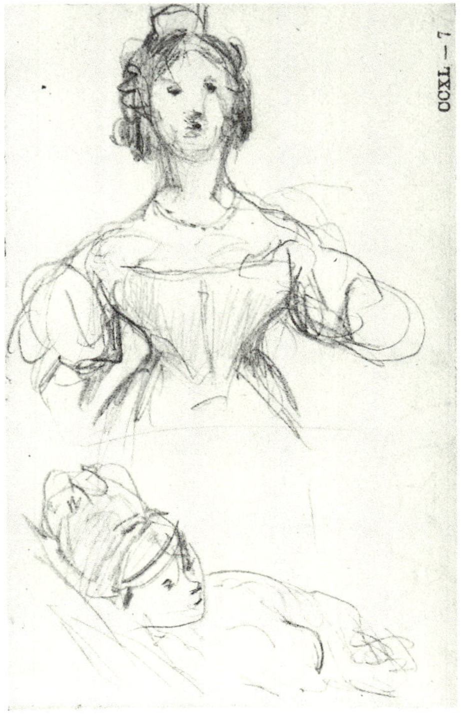

fig. 86 *Sketch for 'Jessica'* ('Birmingham and Coventry' sketchbook, TB CCXL, p. 7), *c.* 1829–30, Pencil 107 × 68 ($4\frac{1}{4} \times 2\frac{11}{16}$), Tate Gallery

Possibly designed as a pendant to this picture, but left unfinished, is 'A Lady in Van Dyck costume' (fig. 91; BJ 444); this remained in Turner's possession and is now in the Tate Gallery. Here the tribute to Rembrandt is replaced by one to Van Dyck, and again the model can be found among the pictures at Petworth, in Van Dyck's 'Ann Carr, Countess of Bedford' (fig. 56).

This portrait, and others by Van Dyck at Petworth, also lie behind Turner's 'Lucy, Countess of Carlisle, and Dorothy Percy's Visit to their Father Lord Percy, when under Attainder upon the Supposition of his being concerned in the Gunpowder Plot' (fig. 94; BJ 338), exhibited at the Royal Academy in 1831 together with its companion, 'Watteau Study by Fresnoy's Rules' (fig. 93; BJ 340). This supports a probable dating of 'A Lady in Van Dyck Costume' to the early 1830s.

'Lord Percy under Attainder', to give it a shorter title, though never purchased by Lord Egremont, is closely associated with him in subject as has been shown in Chapter 1. Henry Percy, ninth Earl of Northumberland, who was imprisoned in the Tower of London under suspicion of being involved in the Gunpowder Plot, was a direct ancestor of Lord Egremont. Lord Percy's eldest daughter Dorothy married Robert Sidney, second Earl of Leicester, while Lucy, after spending some time with her father in the Tower, married James Hay, later Earl of Carlisle. Turner has based the figures of Lord Percy and of Lucy, who stands on the left, on the three-quarter length portraits of the same sitters by Van Dyck at Petworth, while the woman standing slightly behind in the centre is based on the portrait of Ann Carr, Countess of Bedford; he had already copied the portrait of Lucy Percy, Countess of Carlisle, in one of his Petworth gouaches (plate 36; TB CCXLIV–100). The figure on the right is presumably Dorothy but is not specifically related to her portrait, seated, by Van Dyck, also at Petworth. Amongst the paintings on the right-hand wall are a view labelled 'TOWER OF LONDON' and a large picture of the Angel releasing St Peter from prison, of obvious relevance to the subject, and the interior in general relates, of course, to the series of Petworth interiors in gouache on blue paper.

Both 'Lord Percy under Attainder' and 'Watteau Study by Fresnoy's

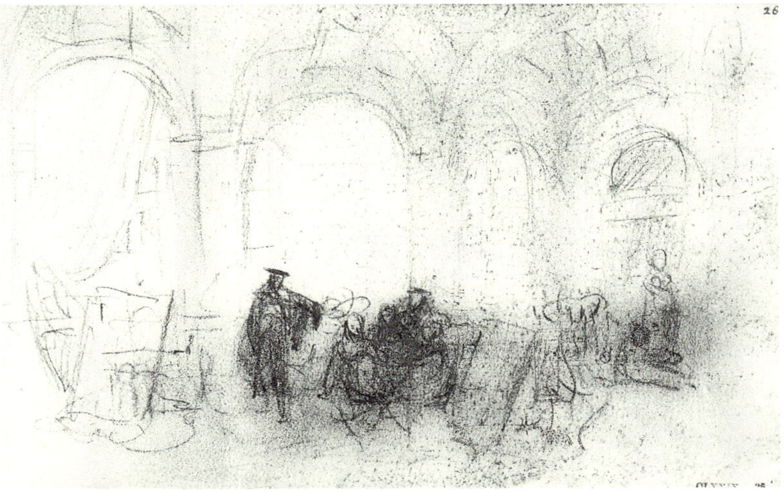

fig. 87 *Sketch for 'Rome from the Vatican'* ('Tivoli and Rome' sketchbook, TB CLXXIX, p. 26), 1819, Pencil 111 × 187 ($4\frac{3}{8} \times 7\frac{3}{8}$), Tate Gallery

Rules' are painted on what were originally cupboard doors; the inner frames of the paintings are in fact the frames around the door panels, and on the backs one can see where there used to be hinges. It would be a marvellous chance to discover a cupboard at Petworth lacking its doors, as clearly Turner turned to these supports in an emergency, lacking more orthodox materials.

The grouping of figures in an interior again relates 'Watteau Study' to the gouaches of interiors at Petworth, in particular those showing an artist at work in the Old Library, though there is no direct link between Petworth and the subject of the painting. This, as is made clear by a quotation in the Royal Academy catalogue, was a demonstration of colour theory of the kind that Turner later also displayed in his two oils illustrating Goethe's *Fahrbenlehre*, exhibited in 1843 (BJ 404 and 405). The quotation in the Royal Academy catalogue accompanying 'Watteau Study' reads:

> White, when it shines with unstained lustre clear,
> May bear an object back, or bring it near.
> Fresnoy's *Art of Painting*, 496

Just as 'Lord Percy under Attainder' was a tribute to Van Dyck, so this painting is a tribute to Watteau. Among the pictures shown in the background are Watteau's 'Les Plaisirs du Bal' and 'La Lorgneuse'. The figure of Watteau himself is developed from a drawing Turner had made over ten years earlier in the 'Tivoli and Rome' sketchbook (fig. 87; TB CLXXIX–26) for 'Rome, from the Vatican. Raffaelle, accompanied by La Fornarina, preparing his Pictures for the Decoration of the Loggia' (BJ 228), exhibited at the Royal Academy in 1820; this was, of course, another tribute to an artist admired by Turner, but it is perhaps surprising to see Raphael so nonchalantly transformed into Watteau.

Turner illustrates Charles du Fresnoy's *De Arte Graphica* by demonstrating the different spatial effects created by white according to where it is placed in the composition, but unfortunately the picture has darkened irredeemably: as the critic of the *Athenaeum* remarked, 'What a trifle in the tone would destroy the beauty!' The critic of the *Library of the Fine Arts* realised the intention of the painting, asking who but Turner could have painted this picture 'with its almost impossible effects produced on principles directly opposed to those generally adopted, his lights merging in depths, his depths thrown deeper by his lights, and this all in a mere sketch and apparently produced without effort?' The same critic picked out 'the flood of light pouring like water over the ledges of a cataract into Lord Percy's chamber, dispelling its sombre hue' in the companion picture, an effect that was to be carried much further in some of the interiors to be discussed below.

The other paintings that can be associated, more-or-less closely, with Petworth all remained unfinished in Turner's studio. This means, among other things, that he never gave them titles and that their identification with Petworth must, in each case, remain a matter of surmise. However, these paintings all seem to have arisen out of the flurry of activity that produced the Petworth interiors in gouache on blue paper together with, as has recently been made clear, those done in the house of another friend of Turner's at much the same time, the architect John Nash at East Cowes Castle.[2] The fact that the architecture in some of these pictures is derived from East Cowes Castle rather than Petworth is perhaps less significant than it might seem at first. Unlike the gouaches these oils were almost certainly painted back in London in Turner's studio and reflect his imagination as much as any specific interior that he might have seen.

This is particularly true of 'Music at East Cowes Castle' (fig. 95; BJ 447) as it must now be called,[3] and the other thickly painted upright

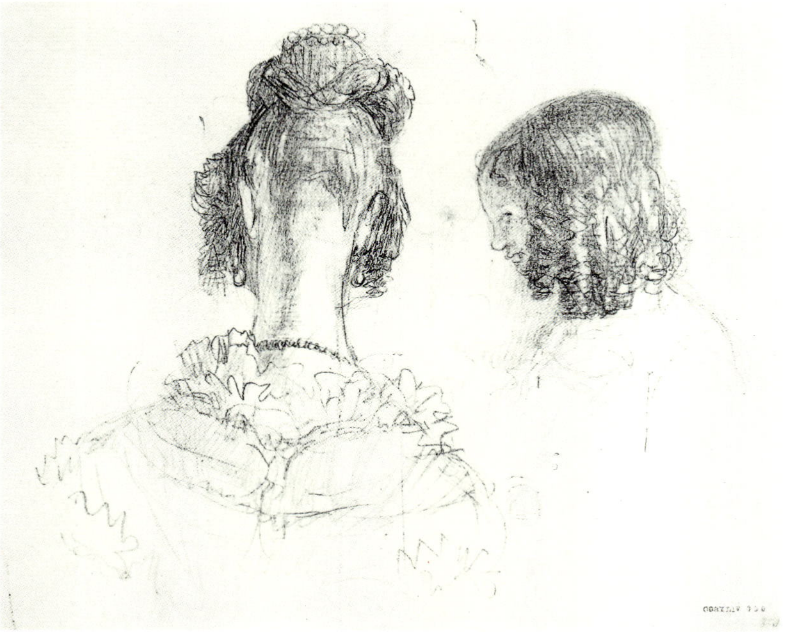

fig. 88 *Sketch for 'Two Women and a Letter'*, *c.* 1827–35, Pencil 159 × 201 ($6\frac{1}{4} \times 7\frac{7}{8}$), Tate Gallery (TB CCCXLIV–350)

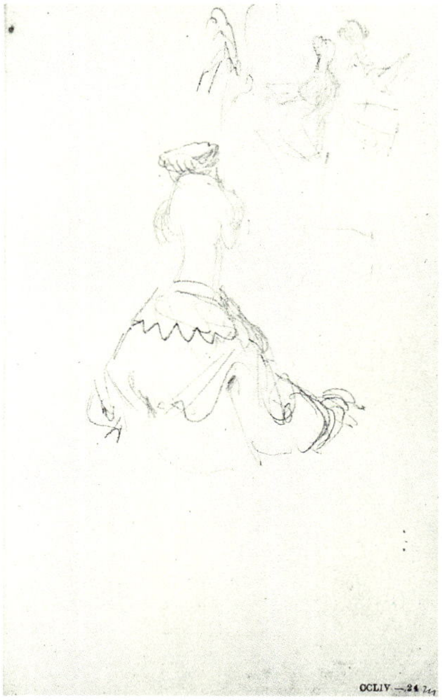

fig. 89 *Sketches for 'Music at East Cowes Castle' and 'Two Women and a Letter'* ('Seine and Paris' sketchbook, TB CCLIV, p. 24), ?1829, Pencil 110 × 175 ($4\frac{3}{8} \times 6\frac{7}{8}$), Tate Gallery

figure composition of the same type, 'Two Women and a Letter' (fig. 96; BJ 448). In their richness of colour and thickness of paint they seem to be somewhat later developments not only of the Petworth gouaches but of the oil paintings 'Jessica' and 'A Lady in Van Dyck Costume' and, before that, 'Rembrandt's Daughter' (BJ 238), exhibited at the Royal Academy in 1827 and purchased by Francis Hawksworth Fawkes, the son of Turner's great patron Walter Fawkes (now in the Fogg Art Museum, Harvard University). In 'Music at East Cowes Castle' a music party similar to that to be seen in some of the Petworth gouaches (plates 9, 19; TB CCXLIV–37, 90) is shown in an interior based on the Octagon Room at East Cowes Castle, demolished in 1949–50 but of which a photograph exists. To complicate things further, a study for the seated figure in black and gold, together with a small sketch of figures at music with an arch behind which could well be a first idea for this painting, appear on a page in the 'Seine and Paris' sketchbook (fig. 89; TB CCLIV–24) which Turner apparently used exclusively in France, probably in 1829. Turner is known to have visited East Cowes Castle in 1827 (a visit that gave rise to the two finished paintings, 'East Cowes Castle, the Seat of J. Nash Esq.; the Regatta beating to Windward' (BJ 242) and 'East Cowes Castle, the Seat of J. Nash Esq.; the Regatta starting for their Moorings' (BJ 243), exhibited at the Royal Academy in 1828 and now in the Indianapolis Museum of Art and the Victoria and Albert Museum respectively, together with the nine sketches of the Regatta and other subjects related to East Cowes and the Isle of Wight now in the Tate Gallery (BJ 260–68)) and again in 1832, but to see an exclusive dependence of this painting on Turner's experiences at East Cowes Castle alone would be to misjudge his practice.

The setting of 'Two Women and a Letter' has not been identified though the figure seen from behind seems to be based on the same drawing in the 'Seine and Paris' sketchbook (fig. 89) that was used for 'Music at East Cowes Castle', and also on a separate sheet containing two pencil drawings of heads (fig. 88; TB CCCXLIV–350). The concentration on the back of the neck below the upswept hair reminds one of the fetishism of Fuseli but has also been seen as a reflection of Watteau.[4] In any event, this painting, in which the woman seen from behind seems to be concealing a letter from her companion, the figures being pressed together in a spatially unexplained way against what appears to be a studded leather-backed chair with a wall and archway looming up behind, is one of the most powerful and unusual of Turner's images.

Recently identified as a view at Petworth is the picture formerly known as 'A Vaulted Hall' (fig. 90; BJ 450) but now held to show 'The Long Cellar, Petworth'.[5] This is a highly imaginative rendering with a flood of light that could never have reached the actual cellar from natural sources. The picture seems to show some form of gathering, particularly at the far end, but the cellar has apparently served a purely utilitarian function ever since it was first built under the same ninth Earl of Northumberland who appears in 'Lord Percy under Attainder', first for the storage of provisions, wine and beer, and later, in the present century, to house central-heating boilers. The painting, smaller in format than the rest of this group and on panel rather than on canvas, seems therefore to represent an imaginative peopling of a site known to Turner from actual experience.

More defined in their architectural forms, and with more clearly depicted richly dressed figures, are two paintings in Turner's standard three-foot by four-foot format, those known at present as 'Dinner in a Great Room' (fig. 97; BJ 445) and 'Figures in a Building' (fig. 98; BJ 446). Here the architectural forms, which seem to have been stripped down to a basic Piranesi-like monumentality, have not been identified but the general feeling is that of the Petworth interiors in gouache though with a weightier, more sombre mood. Again there are unexplained inroads of light that add to the air of mystery.

'Interior at Petworth' (fig. 99; BJ 449) seems to represent the culmination of this series of architectural interiors. Although the picture cannot be precisely dated, and although the room depicted is not in itself identifiable at Petworth, it has been convincingly suggested by David Thomas that this work is Turner's reaction to the death of his friend and patron Lord Egremont in 1837, an event that marked the end of an important period in his life: the suggestion of a catafalque with coat-of-arms hints at a lying in state, and the interior can be seen as a modification of the Marble Hall with the fireplace replaced by a large open arch. The frenzied dogs would seem to represent Lord Egremont's favourite pets, and sculptures from his collection appear flickeringly in odd corners of the room. Light floods in, not just emphasising the forms but dissolving them, and the whirlwind effect in the middle of the picture suggests dissolution. More recently it has been suggested that this picture should be paired, as 'The Apotheosis of Lord Egremont', with 'Dinner in a Great Room', reinterpreted as 'Mourners at Petworth', the setting again being likened, with less justification, to the Marble Hall.[6] But, given that all three paintings are of the same size and format, it is with 'Figures in a Building' that 'Dinner in a Great Room' should be paired: the scale of figures, the simplicity of the architectural setting and the sombre, relatively limited colouring are the same, and at strong variance to the flurry and explosive abundance of light and colour to be seen in 'Interior at Petworth'.

These great, evocative interiors had no successors in Turner's art. The last of Turner's exhibited paintings to give much importance to the figure was 'Shadrach, Meshech and Abednigo in the Burning Fiery Furnace' (BJ 346), exhibited in 1832, to which can be related the unfinished 'Christ Driving the Traders from the Temple' (BJ 436) of about the same date. Some Venetian interiors in gouache and watercolour showing St Mark's, theatres or hotel rooms[7] may date from as late as 1840 but lack the solemnity and weight of the last Petworth oil paintings; rather, they continue the tradition of the Petworth interiors in gouache. At the end of his life Turner, lacking the energy it would seem to complete new compositions for the Royal Academy, re-used a work from early in the century, overpainting much of it and exhibiting it in 1847 as 'The Hero of a Hundred Fights' (BJ 427) in celebration of the casting of Wyatt's equestrian statue of the Duke of Wellington. This too, like 'Interior at Petworth', shows material form being dissolved by the power of light and again, despite the fact that Turner was to exhibit one further, overpainted, painting in 1849 and four entirely new compositions in 1850, seems to mark the end of an era. As Turner is purported to have said on his deathbed, 'The sun is God', and it is in his depiction of light and colour, and the eventual impermanence of material things, that the ultimate significance of his art must be sought.

Notes

[1] Cecilia Powell, *Turner in the South: Rome, Naples, Florence*, 1987, p. 159.
[2] See Youngblood, *Burlington Magazine* 1983, pp. 615–19.
[3] Youngblood, *Burlington Magazine* 1983, pp. 615–16; see also Selby Whittingham, 'Turner's "Music Party" ', *Burlington Magazine*, vol. cxxvi, 1984, p. 92.
[4] Selby Whittingham, 'What You Will: or some notes regarding the influence of Watteau on Turner and other British Artists (1)', *Turner Studies*, vol. v, no. 1, Summer 1985, p. 19.
[5] Reid, 1987, pp. 393–94; the Long Cellar repr. fig. 58.
[6] Gage, 1987, p. 167.
[7] TB CCCXVIII–4, 7–9, 18, 20, 21. See Andrew Wilton, exhibition catalogue, *Turner in the British Museum*, British Museum, 1975, p. 146 nos. 248, repr., and 249, where dated 1840, and Lindsay Stainton, *Turner's Venice*, 1985, colour pls. 11, 14, 15, 19–21, 23, where tentatively dated '1833?'; in *Turner Watercolours*, 1987, p. 137 no. 61, Andrew Wilton also tentatively dates another of this group of Venetian gouaches on brown paper, 'Venice: the Salute from the Calle del Ridotto: night' (TB CCCXVIII–11) to '? 1833'.

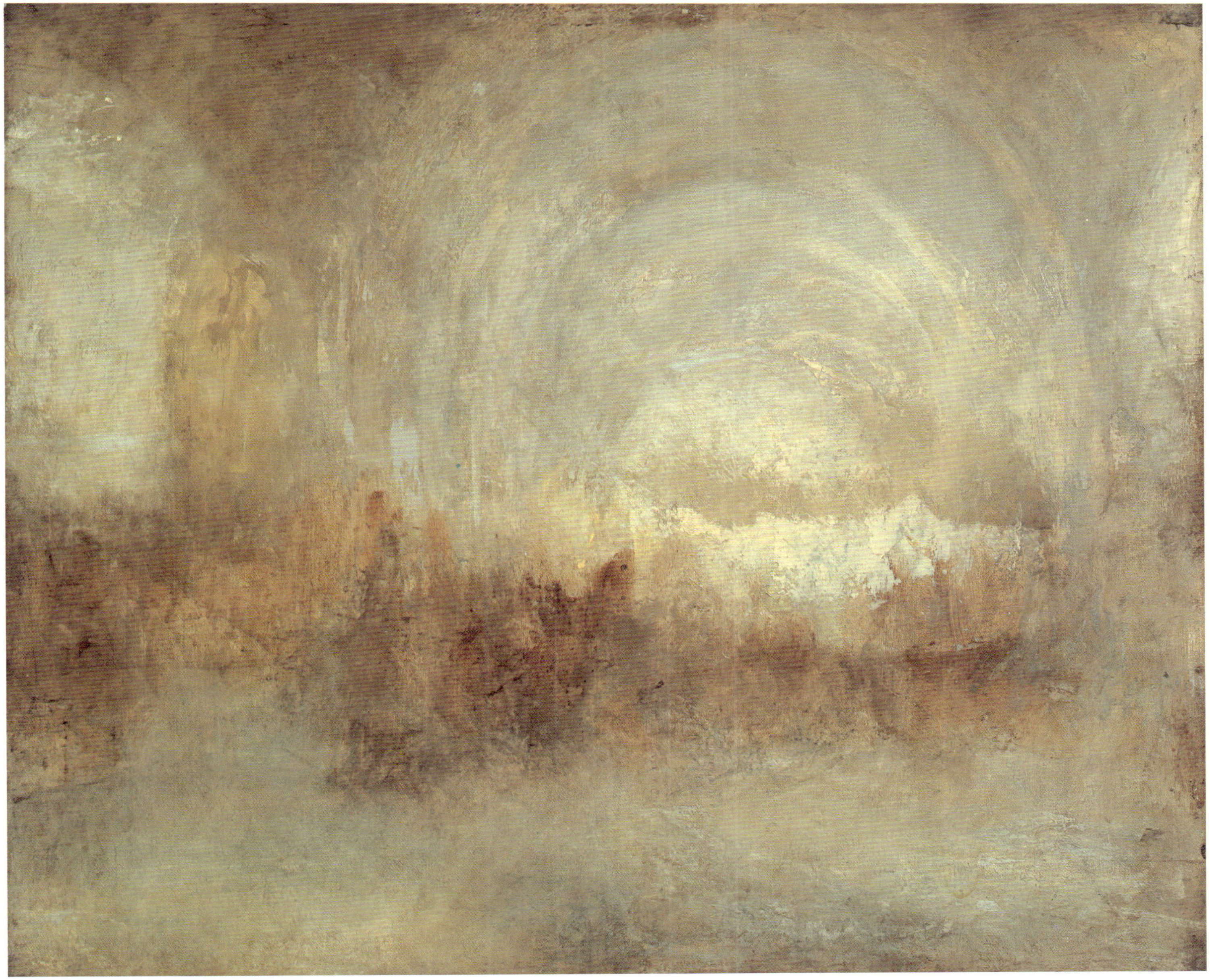

fig. 90 *The Long Cellar, Petworth* (*'A Vaulted Hall'*) (BJ 450), *c.* 1835, Oil on mahogany 750 × 915 (29½ × 36), Tate Gallery

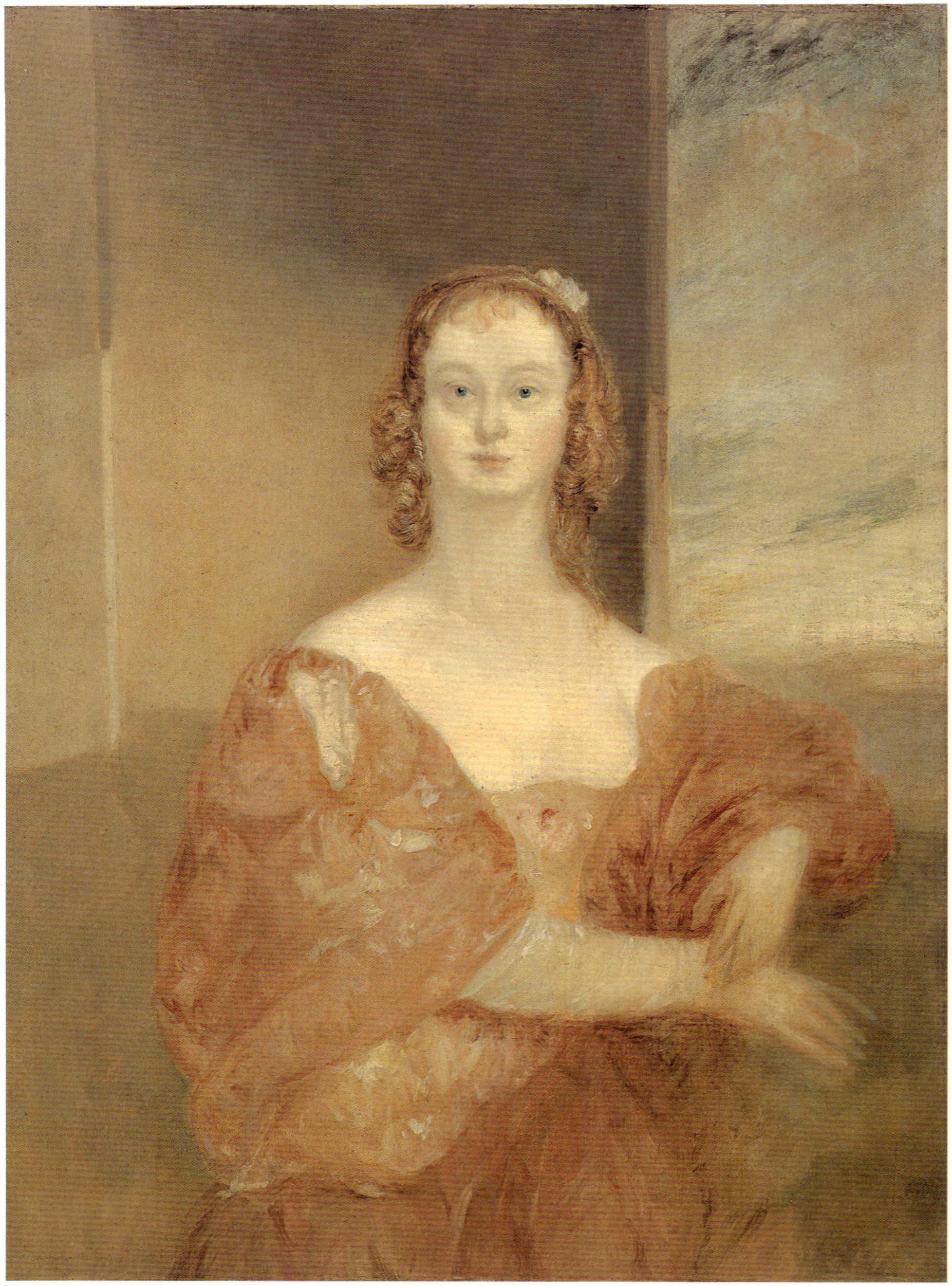

fig. 91 *A Lady in a Van Dyck Costume* (BJ 444), *c.* 1830,
Oil on canvas 1210 × 910 ($47\frac{3}{4} \times 35\frac{7}{8}$), Tate Gallery

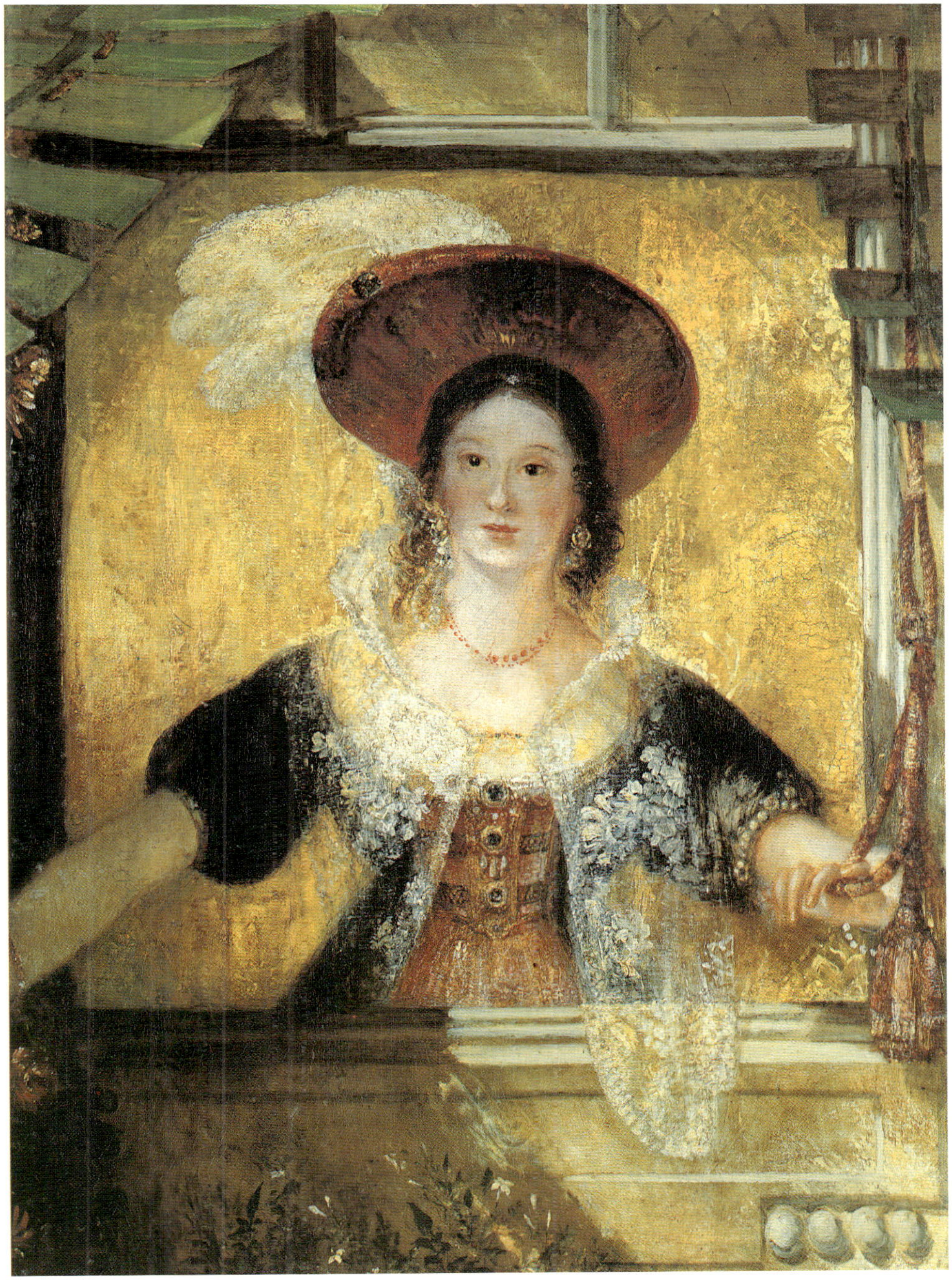

fig. 92 *Jessica* (BJ 333), R.A. 1830,
Oil on canvas 1220 × 915 (48 × 36), Petworth House

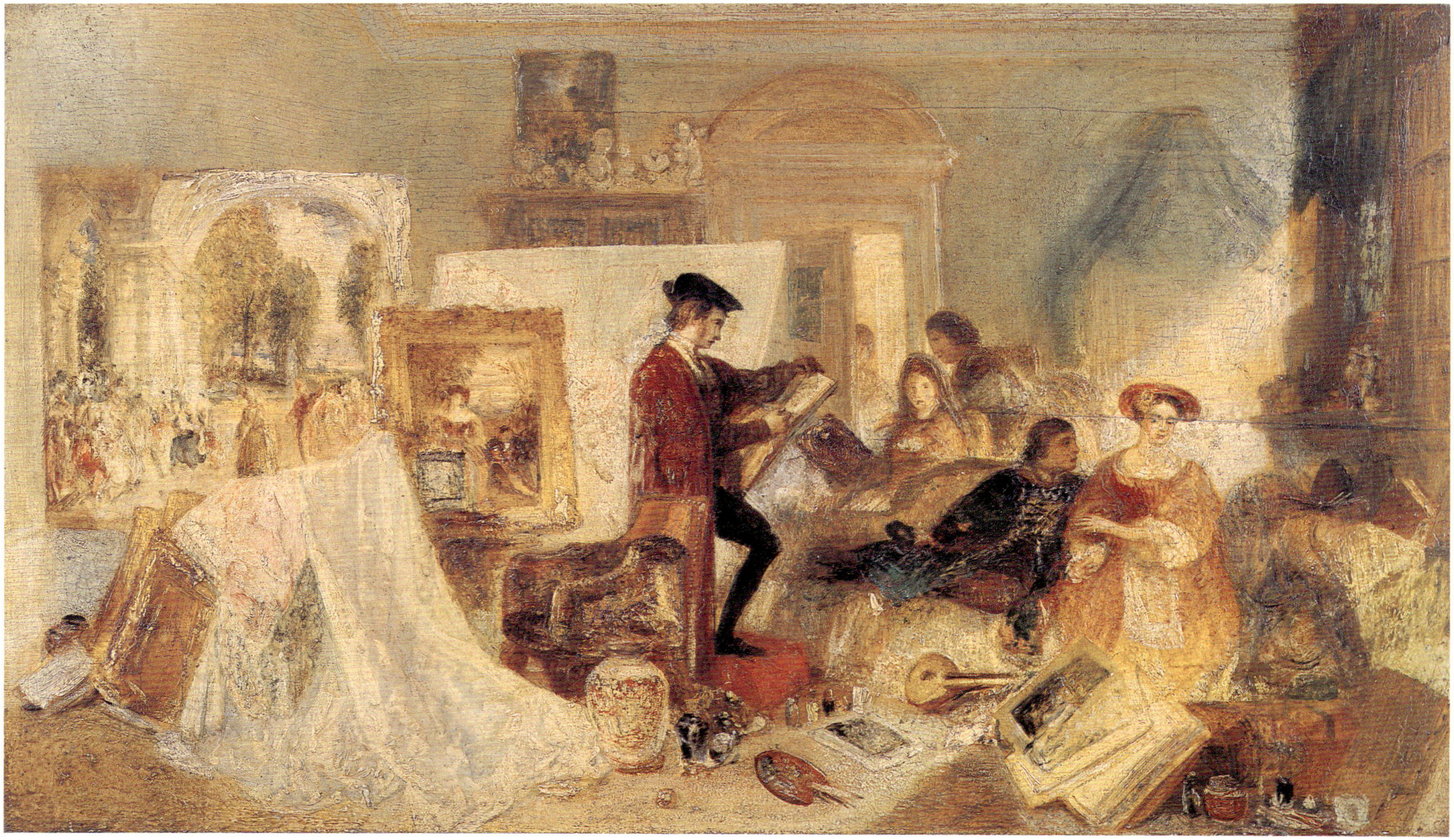

fig. 93 *Watteau Study by Fresnoy's Rules* (BJ 340), R.A. 1831, Oil on oak panel
approx: 400 × 695 ($15\frac{3}{4} \times 27\frac{1}{4}$), Tate Gallery

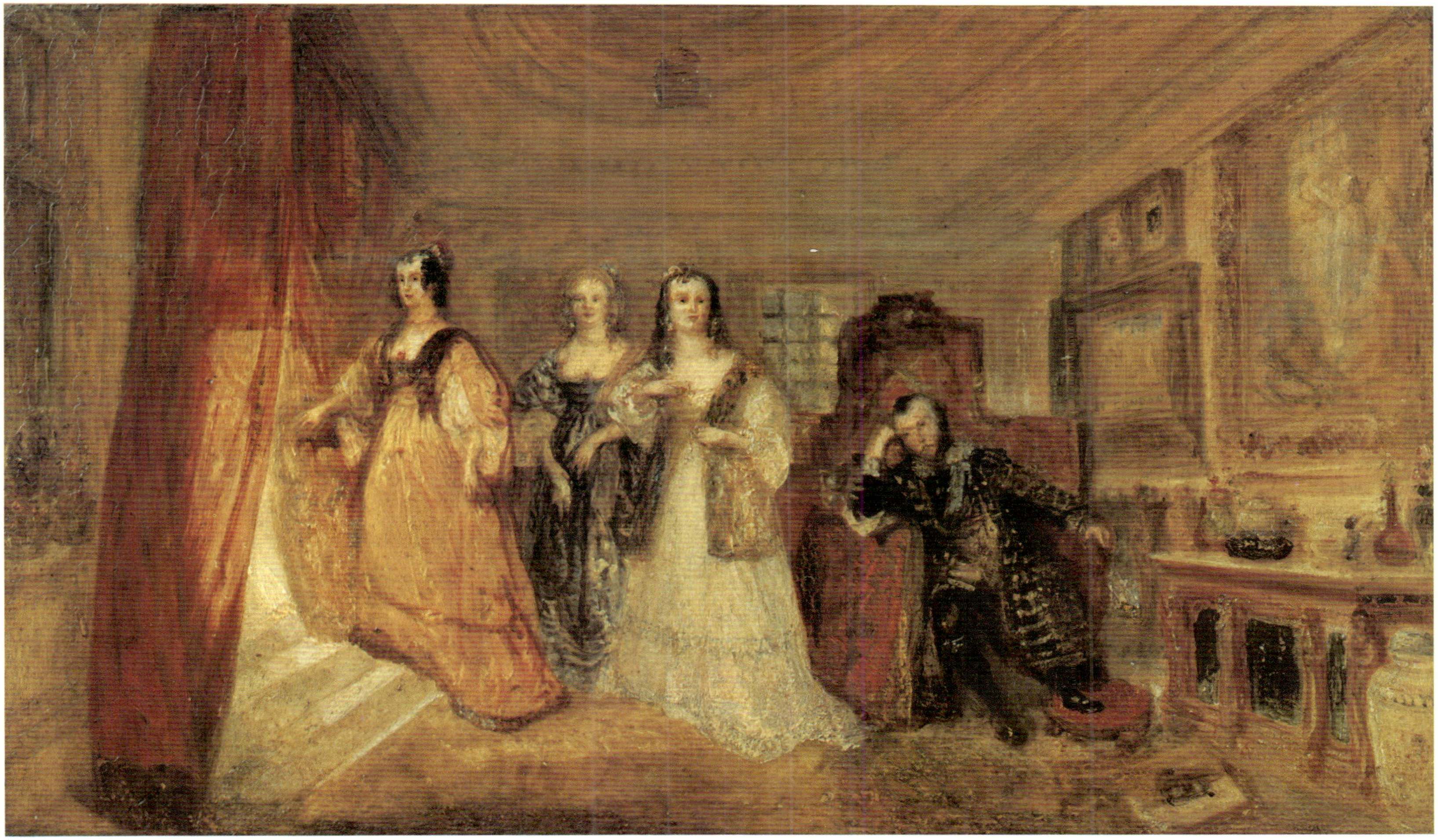

fig. 94 *Lucy, Countess of Carlisle, and Dorothy Percy's Visit to their Father Lord Percy, when under Attainder upon the Supposition of his being concerned in the Gunpowder Plot* (BJ 338), R.A. 1831, Oil on oak panel, approx: 400 × 695 ($15\frac{3}{4} \times 27\frac{1}{4}$), Tate Gallery

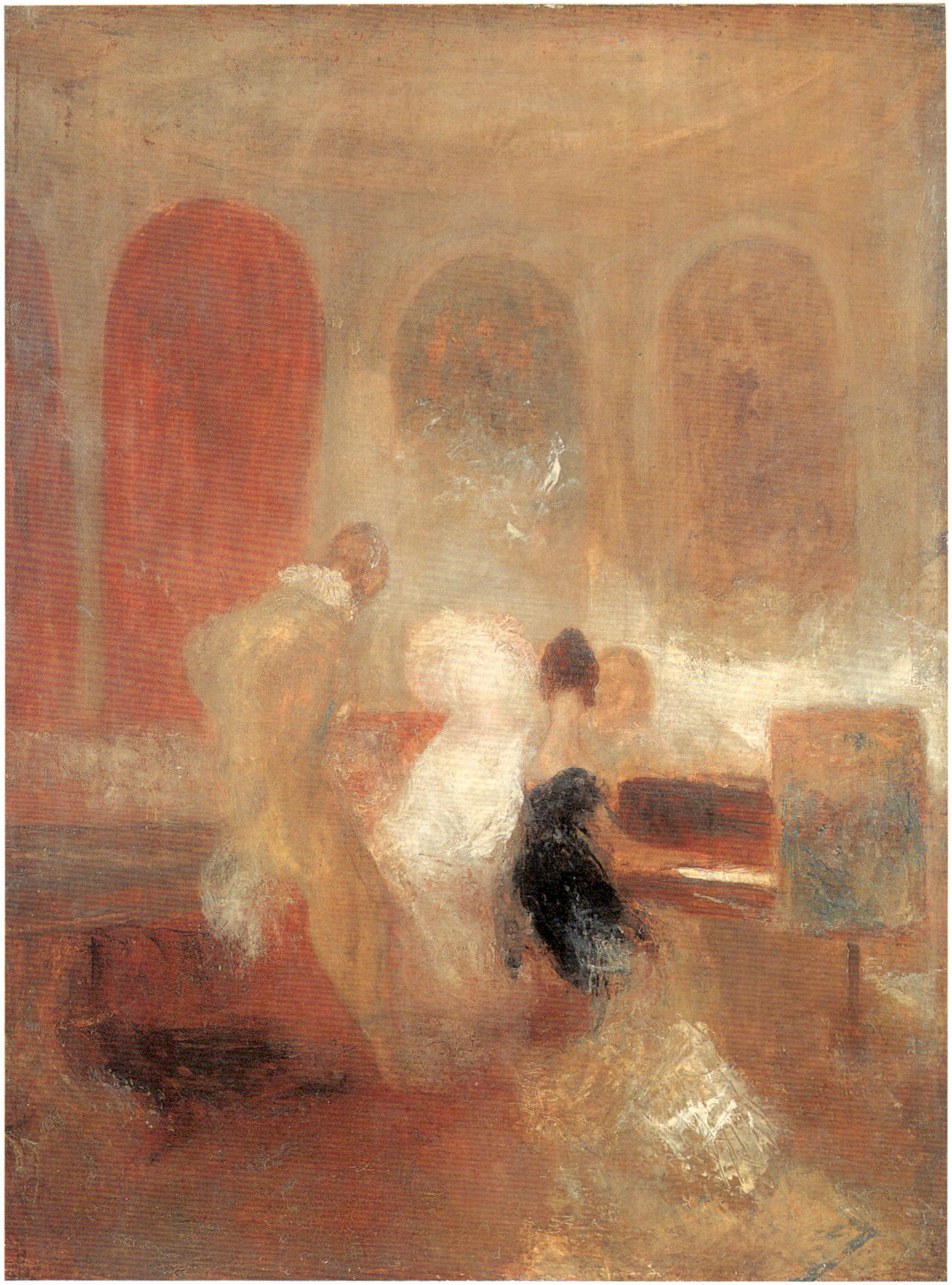

fig. 95 *Music at East Cowes Castle* (BJ 447), *c.* 1835, Oil on canvas 1210 × 905 ($47\frac{3}{4} \times 35\frac{5}{8}$), Tate Gallery

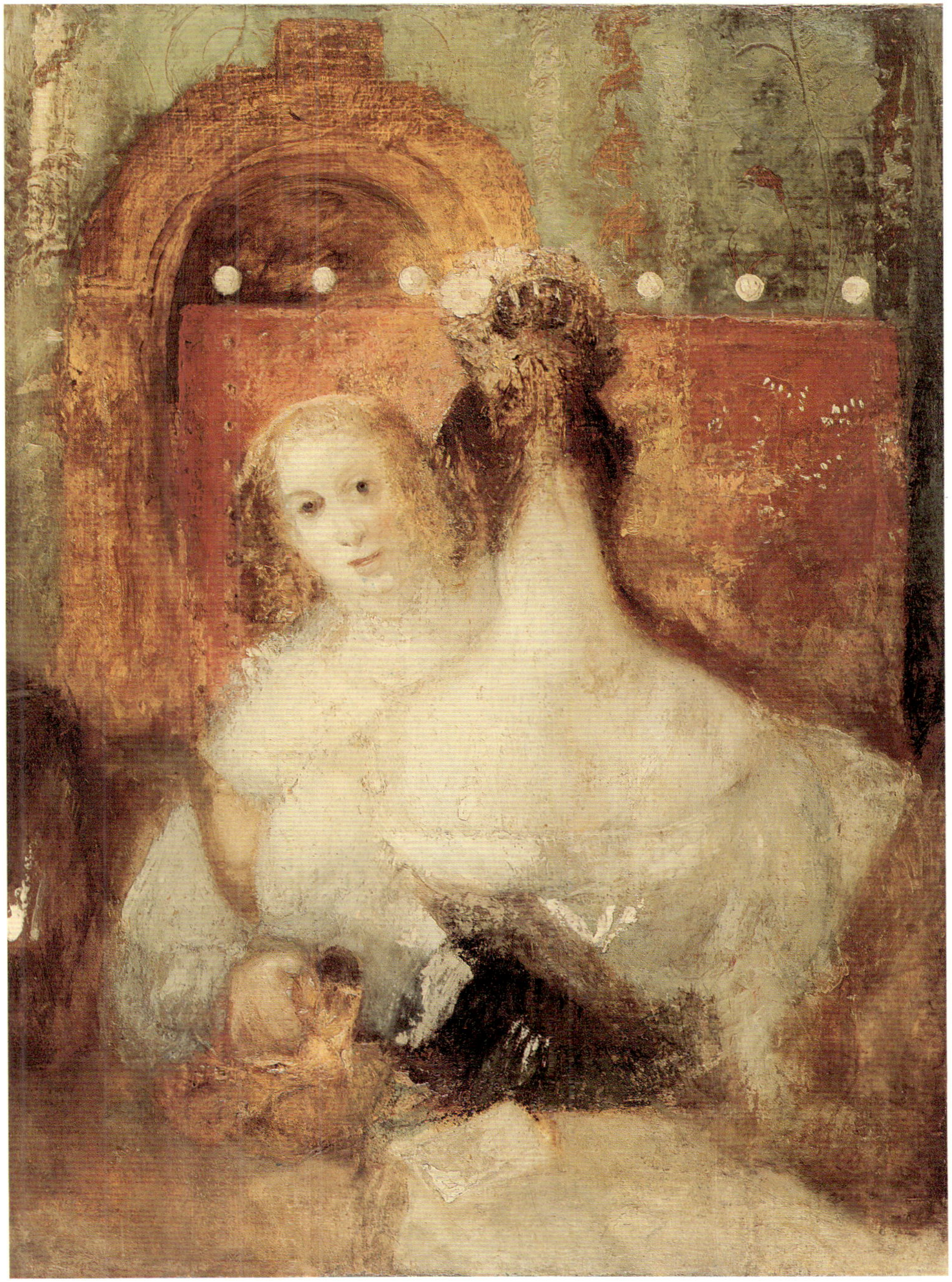

fig. 96 *Two Women and a Letter* (BJ 448), *c.* 1835, Oil on canvas **1220** × **915** (48 × 36), Tate Gallery

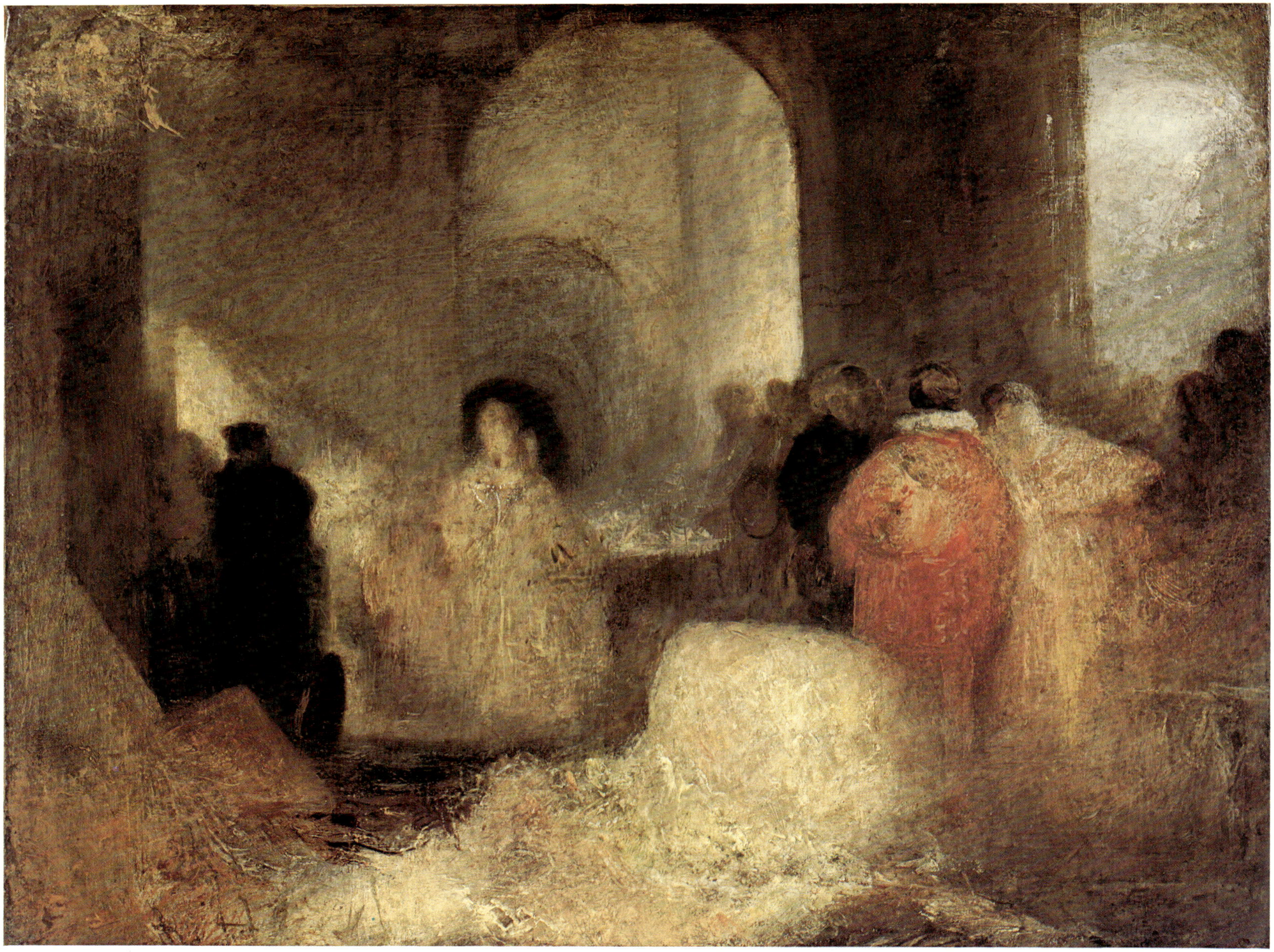

fig. 97 *Dinner in a Great Room with Figures in Costume* (BJ 445), *c.* 1830–35,
Oil on canvas 910 × 1220 ($35\frac{3}{4} \times 48$), Tate Gallery

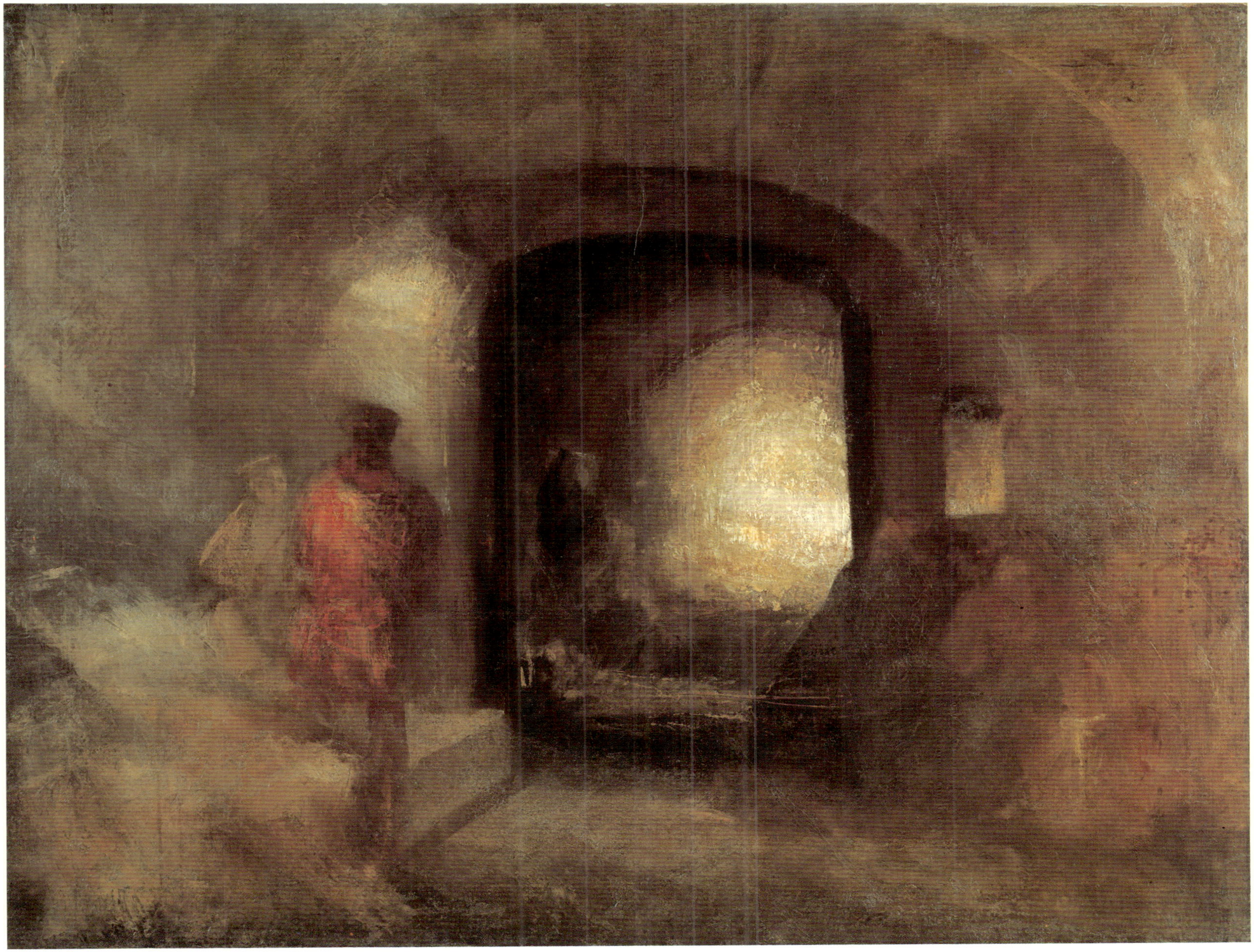

fig. 98 *Figures in a Building* (BJ 446), *c.* 1830–35, Oil on canvas
915 × 1220 (36 × 48), Tate Gallery

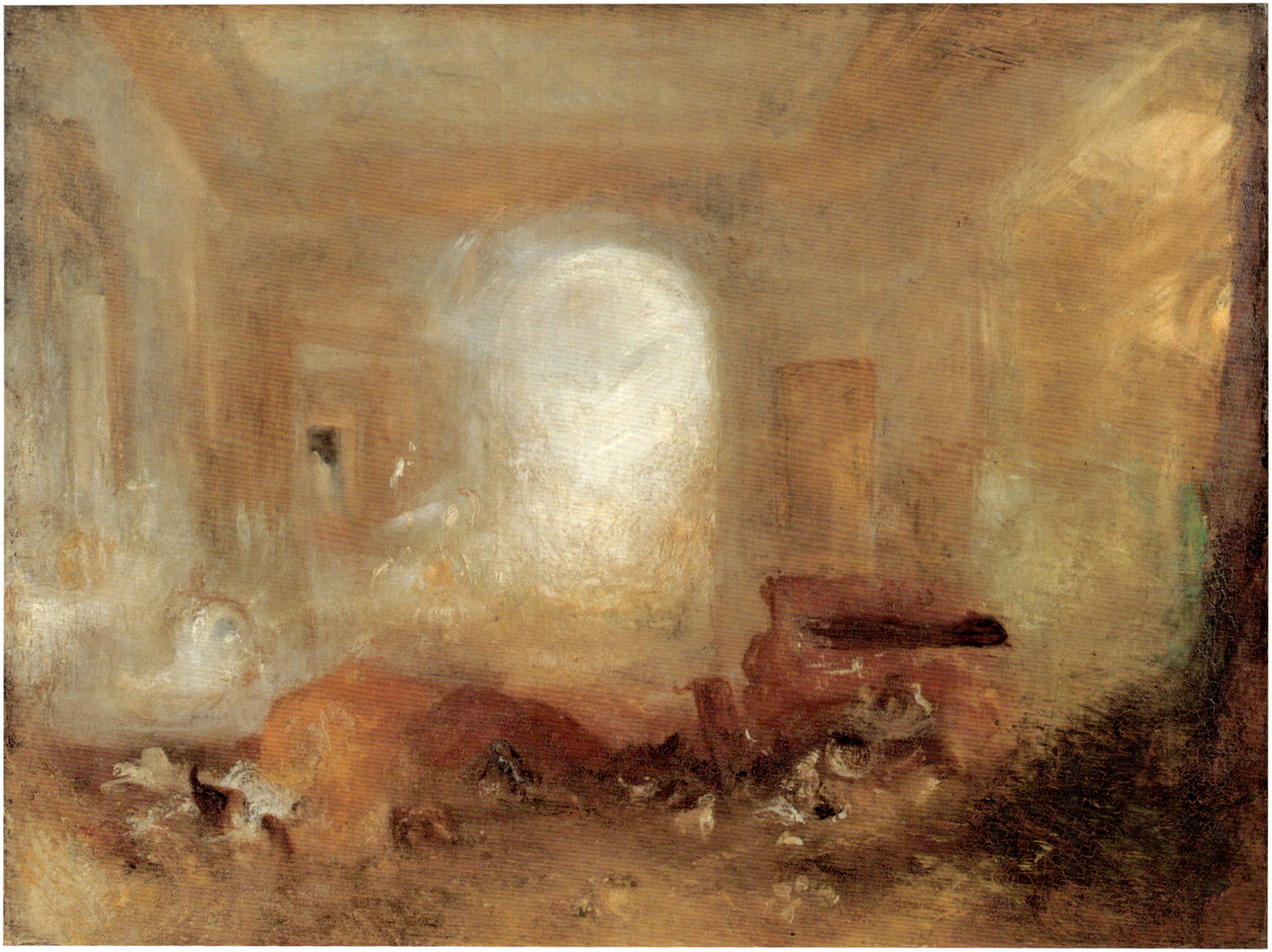

fig. 99 *Interior at Petworth* (BJ 449), *c.* 1837, Oil on canvas 910 × 1220 ($35\frac{3}{4} \times 48$), Tate Gallery

APPENDIX I

'Lord of the Soil': a re-appraisal of Turner's Petworth Patron

Heedless of pomp, to art and science dear,
Lord of the soil, see EGREMONT appear;
Firm in attachment to his native land,
No foreign feeling guides his fostering hand;
In judgement sound, in contemplation calm,
To gifted Britain still he gives the palm;
To pining genius still he points the way,
And merit ushers to the blaze of day.[1]

In examining the nature of Turner's connection with Petworth, most scholars have almost exclusively focused their attention on Lord Egremont's extensive patronage of Turner and other artists. Indeed, writing after his death local historians, awed by the extent of his artistic patronage, felt forced to draw a parallel with the patron of Horace and Virgil, referring to Egremont as a 'Sussex Mæcenas'.[2] However, it seems pertinent to re-examine the man – peer, farmer, entrepreneur, sportsman and philanthropist – and thereby provide a wider context for Turner's work at Petworth.

George O'Brien Wyndham (1751–1837), third Earl of Egremont, and Lord Lieutenant of Sussex between 1819 and 1835, was a man of wide interests with an income estimated at £100,000 per annum. Of this he spent some £20,000 per annum on charities of various kinds. This affluence also enabled him to investigate and enjoy the newest forms of art, literature, agriculture, science and sport. Such diverse interests meant that under his hand Petworth became not only a 'nursery of art', but also a thriving 'college of agriculture'.[3]

Turner's frequent sojourns at Petworth, recorded in the related group of oil-paintings, sketchbooks and gouache drawings, reflect the variety of life at the great house. Although, for the most part, the large group of drawings in the Turner Bequest contains intimate impressionistic scenes of the life of Petworth House,[4] about a third of the gouache drawings find Turner in the parklands of the great house, the town's church, or in the surrounding countryside. These drawings, and the paintings Turner made there, suggest that he was stimulated not only by the easy-going environment of this 'House of Art', as Constable termed it, but also by the ideas behind Egremont's ongoing improvements in Petworth and beyond. Most notably, the four paintings made for the Carved Room (figs. 76, 78, 80, 82) constitute a unique view of the Earl's lifelong innovatory endeavours.

Egremont was responsible for many innovations and improvements in the lives of the farming tenantry of Petworth and the other estates under his administration. This was clearly exceptional behaviour in an age when, as the *Dictionary of National Biography* states, 'The English landlords of [the] time were the least imaginative section of an unimaginative people'[5]; certainly a contentious statement, but one that indicates the outstanding scientific enterprise of men like Egremont. Indeed, in an appraisal of his reputation the Sussex historian, Mark Anthony Lower, hails Egremont as 'one of the fathers of modern English agriculture'.[6]

The famous agriculturalist, Arthur Young (1741–1820), was acquainted with Egremont and had visited Petworth in June 1793.[7] It is difficult in retrospect to establish the full extent of Young's influence on the developments at Petworth, for even before his first visit improvements were under way, although this may be attributable to his earlier writings on agricultural economy.[8] Nonetheless, a close friendship seems to have developed between Young and Egremont, so that by 1800 Young felt sufficiently confident of Egremont's opinion to write such direct advice as the following:

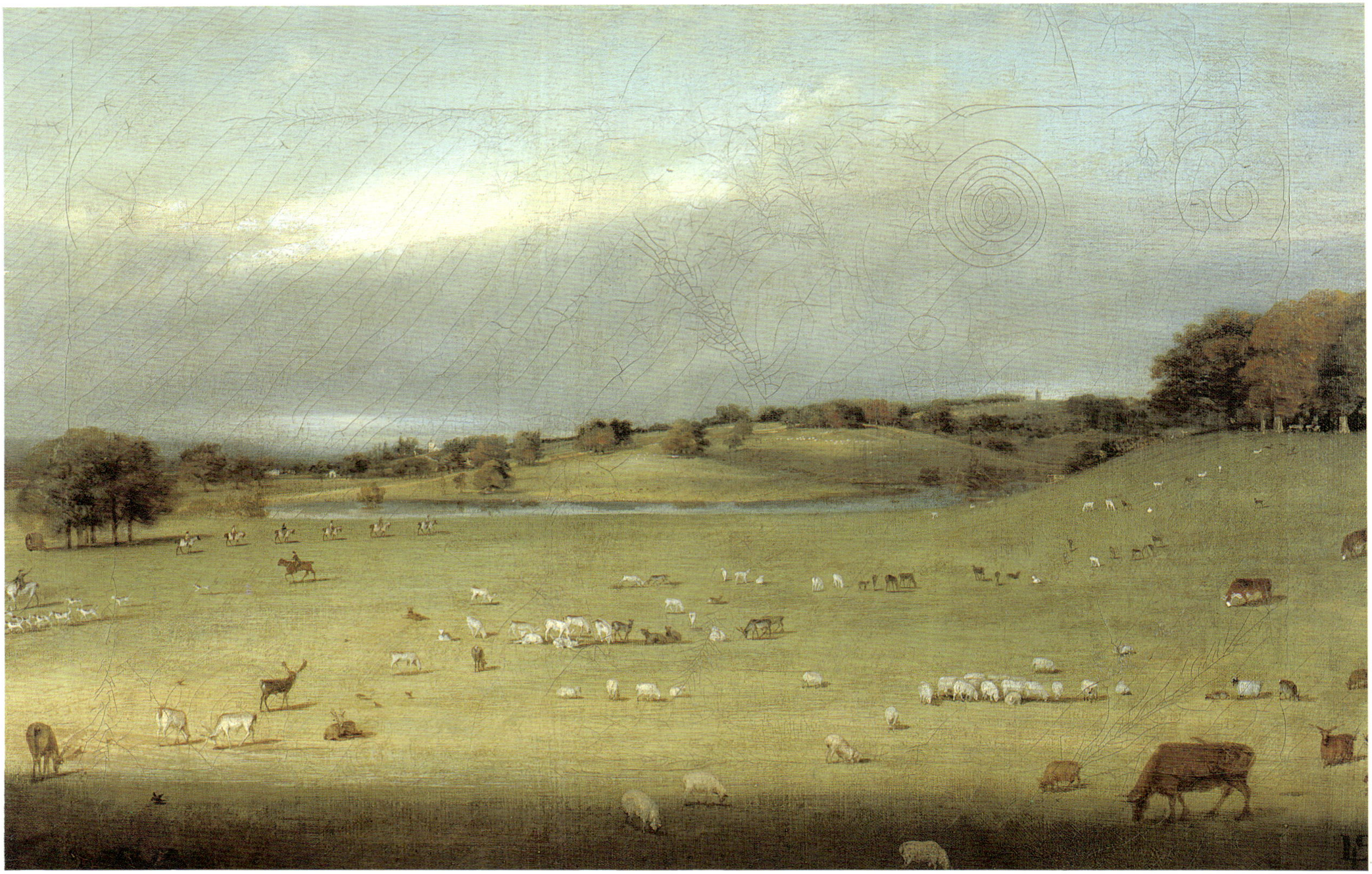

fig. 100 Thomas Phillips: *Petworth Park*, 1798, Oil on canvas 484 × 739 (19 × 29), Lord Egremont, Petworth House

I agree with you about the poor and prices & governt. They are infatuated: but such heads as yours should devise remedies; whether taken or not.[9]

Egremont had been a member of the Board of Agriculture since he was elected to its ranks in 1793, probably at Young's suggestion. He was also involved in another of Young's agricultural clubs at the Thatched House Club in Piccadilly, which became a meeting point for the Farmers' Club during the late 1790s. As Young's son, the Rev. Arthur Young noted, 'all the great improvements in our agriculture have been patronized and encouraged by gentlemen of large landed property and scientific exertions'.[10]

Widely admired for his innovative, if eclectic, methods at Petworth, Lord Egremont was suggested by Young and others as the obvious replacement for Sir John Sinclair after the latter was voted out of his post of President of the Board of Agriculture in 1798.[11] Pitt, then Prime Minister, had conceived the same idea and offered the post to Egremont, who rather typically declined it and the post eventually went to Lord Somerville.[12]

It was the *Sporting Magazine* which first proclaimed in 1795 that 'Everything is now conceded at Petworth to grazing and ploughing'.[13] At about the same time the Rev. Arthur Young, made a detailed and close inspection of all the 'Improvements' at Petworth, which he recorded in a eulogy to the disinterested patriotism of Lord Egremont in the 1808 volume of *A General View of the Agriculture of the County of Sussex*, presented to the Board of Agriculture. Despite an obvious bias in favour of Lord Egremont, this is the most extensive record of the development at Petworth.

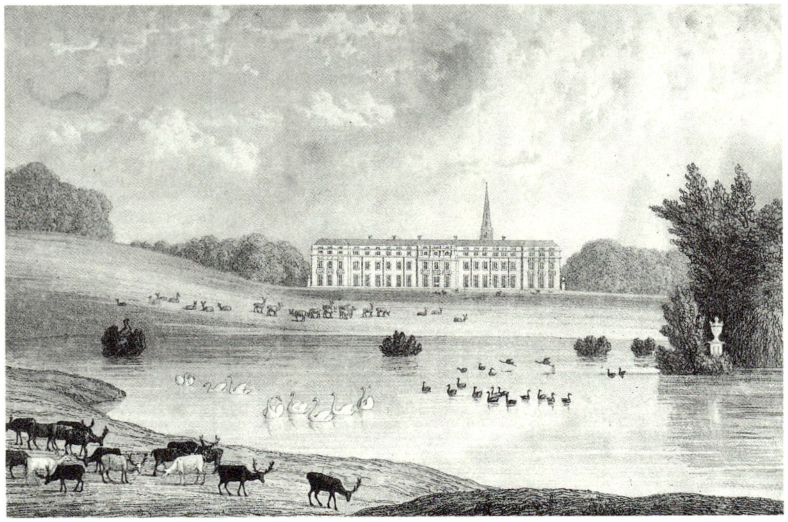

fig. 101 W. Westall A.R.A. after Thomas Henwood: *Petworth Park*, The Seat of the Right Honble the Earl of Egremont, by whom this plate is presented, engraving, *c.*1835, 204 × 262 (8 × 10¼), West Sussex Record Office, Chichester

Whilst radically improving the land he possessed, Egremont also pursued a policy of acquiring adjacent land through transfers, purchases and, more rarely in Sussex, enclosures.[14] It is estimated that altogether he owned 'upwards of 110,000 acres in the west of England, Cumberland, Yorkshire, Ireland, and West Sussex'.[15] A local expression mirrors the extent of Egremont's assets: 'not for all Lord Egremont's estate'.[16]

The potential of the acres of parkland surrounding his Petworth establishment was soon realised and by the early 1790s the immediate parklands and Stag Park were committed to agricultural uses. The Rev. Arthur Young notes the reclamation of the Stag Park as Egremont's principal achievement:

> Previously to its being improved, it was an entire forest scene, oversowed with bushes, furze, some timber, and rubbish; of no kind of use, if we except a few miserable and ragged stock which it annually reared; and would not have lett [sic] for more than 4s or at most 5s per acre. The undertaking of converting between 7 and 800 acres of land, was an exertion to be expected only from an animated and enlightened improver. It was begun about sixteen or seventeen years ago; the timber sold, the underwood grubbed, and burned into charcoal upon the spot; and every part of the park has been since drained in the most effectual manner: the whole of it enclosed and divided into proper fields.[17]

Alongside this extensive redevelopment of the Stag Park, the land closer to the house, and in particular the Pleasure Ground with its immense trees, was cultivated for recreation. Louis Simond commented upon the variety and size of this wooded area, seeing a resemblance to a heavy-timbered American forest'.[18] Tragically, many of these trees, some over three hundred years old, were uprooted by the hurricane of October 1987.

Elizabeth Frazer, the wife of the portrait painter, Thomas Phillips, made numerous watercolours of the park and the towering trees of the Pleasure Grounds on the many occasions the Phillips family stayed at Petworth (fig.102).[19] The Turner Bequest gouaches suggest Turner was also impressed by the trees in the park. In one group he seems to concentrate on the wilder growth (plates 99, 100, 101, 98; TB CCXLIV–53, 55, 56, 59), while in another group he lingers on the seductive beauty of the pastoral scene (plates 74, 82, 83; TB CCXLIV–11, 113, 114). Lit by slowly melting sunsets, the small artificial lakes (created by Lancelot 'Capability' Brown) become a motif for Turner to meditate on his favourite themes: light and colour.[20] Plate 95 (TB CCXLIV–12), showing the smaller lake in the Stag Park looking back towards the ridge, dwells on the magic of the reflected sunset, while in plate 90 (TB CCXLIV–3), Turner spreads the burning embers of the sun across the width of water and sky.[21]

In the spirit of his ancestor the ninth Earl of Northumberland, who originally set out the various gardens at Petworth, Egremont metamorphosed the parklands for the express design of 'experimental agriculture'.[22] The Rev. Young reports that far from resembling an agricultural laboratory, 'the whole of it is a garden'.[23] Despite the problems of draining the Stag Park, Egremont was able to plant all the cleared land. The planting rota was itself one of Egremont's innovations, for instead of following the old system of crop rotation on clay soil, Egremont proposed his own system, replacing the traditional fallow year with a turnip crop, which the Rev. Arthur Young insisted 'works well'.[24] Among a wide range of basic crops, Petworth also grew rhubarb and opium. In fact, according to Young, the 'largest quantity of this invaluable drug that was ever cured in this country, was raised in 1797 from the Earl of Egremont's garden at Petworth'. Both the rhubarb and the opium were, of course, for medicinal use.[25]

A flourishing part of the house during Egremont's lifetime was the Conservatory which led off the North Gallery. This was demolished sometime between 1838 and 1874 (fig.103). According to Louis Simond, the diversity of vigorous plant-life made the spacious growing area the 'finest conservatory immaginable'.[26] We see flowers, presumably from the Conservatory, in at least two of Turner's drawings (plates 50, 51; TB CCXLIV–20, 23). Plate 51 (TB CCXLIV–23), in particular, conveys the colour and splendour of the extensive range of species grown at Petworth.

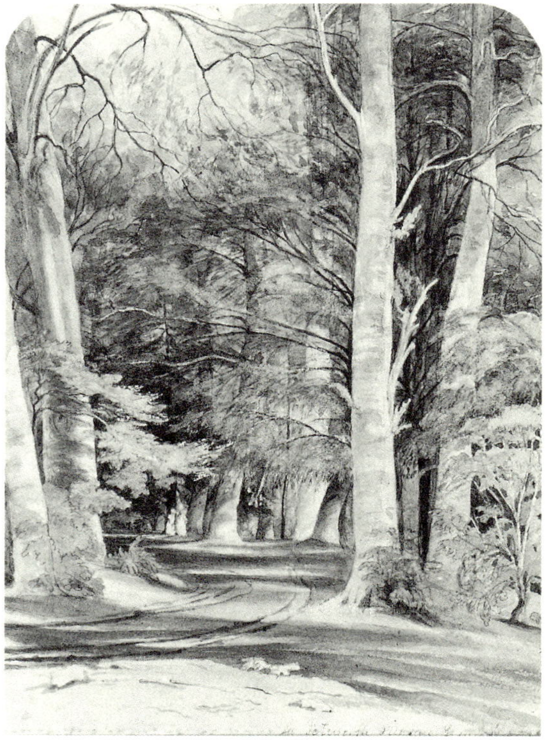

fig. 102 Mrs Elizabeth Phillips: *In Petworth Pleasure Grounds*, *c.* 1830, Pencil and watercolour on white wove paper 239 × 180 ($9\frac{3}{8} \times 7\frac{1}{8}$), Private Collection

Developments in the Stag Park were greatly aided by innovations Egremont made in the basic technology of Sussex farming. The Rev. Arthur Young had bemoaned that in 'the conduct of operations of so much consequence, and so depending upon the active knowledge and enlightened minds of individuals, it is indeed surprising that we find so little progress made in this branch of rural economy, and that we frequently see such a display of ignorance in agriculture tools'.[27] Egremont was not remiss on this point, for as well as introducing updated versions of planting tools such as the skim-coulter and the iron dibble,[28] he also built a threshing machine at Petworth, one of only three in the county.[29] The benefits of this were both economic and practical: straw made much better fodder after passing through the machine, whilst more of the wheat grain was delivered up.[30]

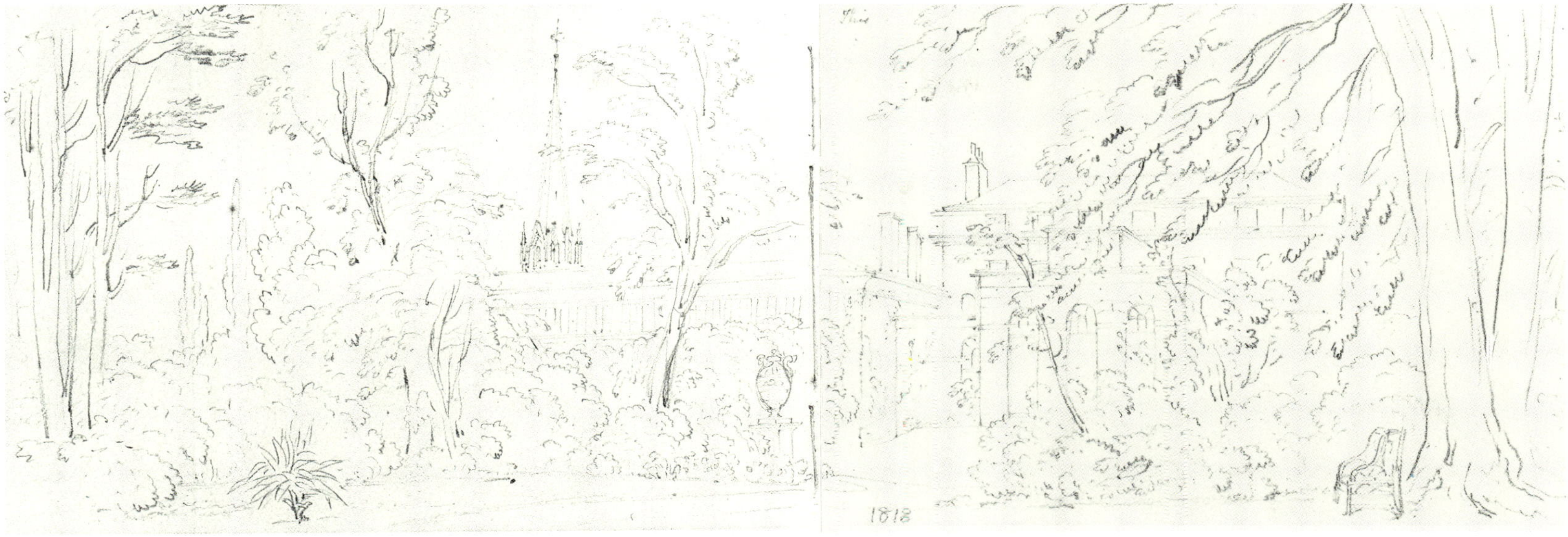

fig. 103 Unknown artist, *The Conservatory and North Gallery at Petworth from the North*, *c.* 1830, Pencil 167 × 254 (6½ × 10), West Sussex Record Office, Petworth House Archives (sketchbook once attribu:ed to Turner)

Egremont also imported the light Suffolk plough, perhaps on Arthur Young's recommendation. This proved to be greatly superior to the old Sussex wheel-turnrift plough, which William Marshall (1745–1818) had complained of in 1795 as an impediment to efficient farming.[31] The introduction of the Suffolk plough, along with a dynamically improved version by Young, and implements called the Mole and the Rotherham plough, do seem to have had an effect on Sussex agriculture beyond the confines of Lord Egremont's estate. The Rev. Arthur Young attests that these 'spread much in the neighbourhood'.[32] The many drawings of ploughing scenes in the Thames sketchbooks of the early years of the nineteenth century suggest that Turner was certainly aware both of traditional metho ls and of changes in this practice (fig 104).[33]

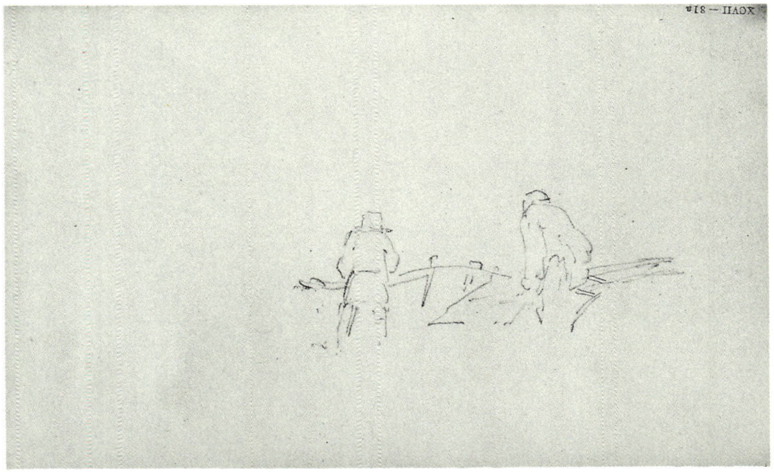

fig. 104 *Men ploughing* ('Windsor anc Eton' sketchbook, TB XCVII, p. 81a), *c.* 1807, Pencil 106 × 18c (4⅛ × 7), Tate Gallery

Another distinctive feature of Petworth agriculture was the use of teams of oxen to pull ploughs and farm waggons (fig. 105). William Marshall had protested that he had seen 'eight oxen, moving a snail's pace, in *stirring a light loamy fallow*, which any two of them, with a proper implement, might have done, faster, and better'.[34] Turner recorded a group of eight oxen harnessed to a cart in one of the gouache drawings in the Turner Bequest (plate 88; TB CCXLIV–98), whilst in a landscape watercolour of Petworth Park, he notes a similar team and waggon as a detail incidental to the brilliant sunset (plate 89).[35]

The rather curious sight of eight oxen pulling a cart does seem to have had its purpose, for it was the prescribed method of training young oxen. This was done 'between two pair of old steady oxen; one pair before, to prevent the steers from flying back, and one or two pair behind, to prevent them from pushing forward'.[36] In terms of practical economics, the amount of work an ox was made to do was proportional to his rate of growth (it being important not to stunt the growth of an ox during its first seven years) and his related saleable value. The Rev. Arthur Young notes the general pattern of use under these circumstances often involved as many as ten or twelve oxen in one action, although whenever more than eight were in use, the rest were being trained.[37] As a cheaper and more useful alternative for carting work, Young recommends jack-asses, advice Egremont may well have heeded as Turner also made drawings of donkeys in the Petworth series (plates 86, 87; TB CCXLIV–97, 107).

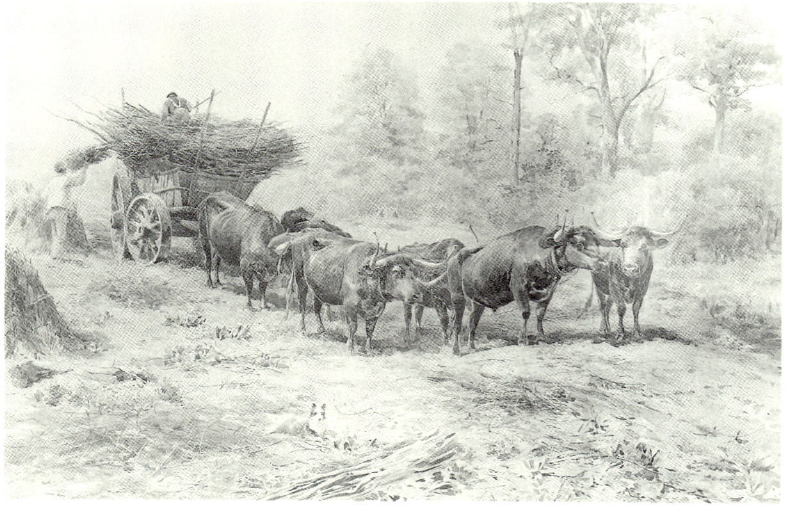

fig. 105 John Isaac Richardson: *Carting Faggots, Sussex*, Watercolour with gum arabic 662 × 1012 (26¼ × 40), Manchester City Art Gallery (1896.19)

As in other areas of his agricultural practice, Egremont pursued a series of experiments to convince himself of the efficacy of using oxen in farm work and, despite losing a ploughing race in which his eight oxen were pitted against a neighbour's three horses, Egremont held adamantly to his conviction of their merits.[38] His enthusiasm for propagating this method among the neighbouring tenantry was such that he offered a rebate of 'three per cent upon the annual rent' to all tenants who 'during the year, have done the whole work of their farms with oxen'.[39] The use of teams of oxen was therefore prolonged in the neighbourhood of Petworth by the Earl's financial encouragement, rather than because its practice proved effective. The drawings by Turner which included the eight oxen perhaps record something that was becoming an anachronism in the late 1820s, when Lord Egremont had apparently begun to encourage smaller teams.[40]

Despite this quirk of judgement, Lord Egremont had in fact contributed to an overall improvement in the quality of Sussex cattle. The Stag Park, which had formerly only produced 'ragged young stock', became the testing ground for cultivating stronger types of cattle, mostly descended from Devonshire and Hereford stock. By 1798 Marshall was already able to note the superiority of the Petworth cattle, to which, he felt, 'it is highly probable, the county, and the country at large, will, hereafter, look up for the point of excellence'.[41] Egremont's 'unequalled zeal' in improving the standard of Sussex cattle took a practical form in establishing a prize incentive at Petworth Fair for the finest bull and heifer. This 'zeal' was not confined to West Sussex only and, in 1797, he established a society at Lewes for the improvement of cattle.[42]

The collection at Petworth House includes a number of paintings related to the prize cattle.[43] Egremont's patronage of local artists in this kind of subject emphasises the compatibility of his agricultural and artistic passions. Most notably, Egremont was to cement his interest in Turner's art through the acquisition in 1808 of 'The Forest of Bere' (fig. 31). In this canvas Turner had depicted, with an element of professional shrewdness, workmen engaged in the practice of stripping bark from chestnut trees, thereby combining art and agriculture to the Earl's taste. In a similar vein to the pictures of the Petworth herd, an early representation of Petworth House and Park during the period of Egremont's improvements, made by Samuel Hieronymus Grimm (1734–1794), set an iconographic precedent by including Petworth's agriculture in the form of two cows at the centre of the view (fig. 106).

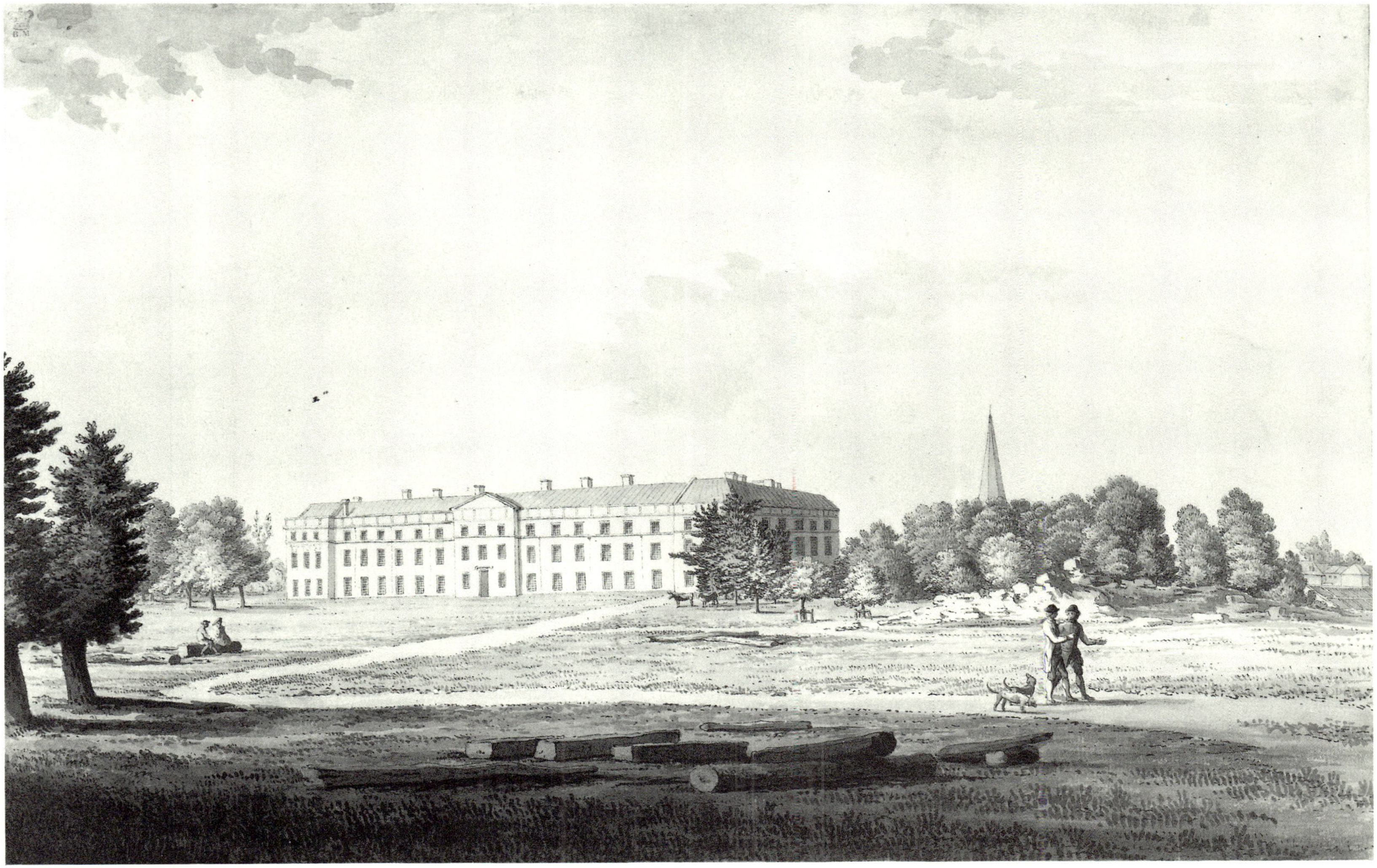

fig. 106 Samuel Hieronymus Grimm: *West and South Fronts of Petworth House, the Seat of Wyndham, Earl of Egremont*, 1780, Watercolour 307 × 484 (12 × 19), The Burrell Collection (Add Burrell, 5674, fol. 53), Department of Manuscripts, The British Library

Although this aspect of Petworth agriculture is evident in drawings in the Turner Bequest (plate 85; TB CCLIX–47), the cattle tend to be replaced, in later representations of the park made by Turner and other artists, by the more familiar deer (figs. 107, 108).

It is surprising that the Petworth deer, which form an inseparable part of Turner's landscapes of Petworth,[44] were not, as far as is known, the centre of an experimental investigation by Egremont. In the 1808 edition of *A General View of the Agriculture of Sussex*, the Rev. Arthur Young suggests an inquiry to discern 'in what degree this is an unprofitable stock'.[45] Shortly after the death of the third Earl, a census of the deer by the park-keeper, James Ward, showed there to be 512 deer, five of which were kept for fattening.[46] As well as the noble stag, Egremont's parklands were grazed by both sheep and pigs. The sheep were mostly South Downs, which in its hardiest form has a black fleece,[47] although there were also Wiltshire, Dorset and Somerset varieties. Egremont was keen to import other breeds and test their value against the home stock. Flocks of Leicester, Hereford, Nottinghamshire and Tiverton sheep were introduced, as well as more exotic Spanish breeds.

Thomas Phillips's view, 'Petworth Park, 1798' (fig. 100), gives an impressive idea of the diversity of livestock in the immediate parkland. It is interesting to note, in the lower right-hand corner of the picture, a goat which in all probability is one of the shawl goats of Tibet which Egremont introduced because of its highly prized fleece. These animals were not shorn. Instead, the wool was combed off and sold to hatters for a guinea a pound.[48]

One of the more unusual aspects of Egremont's husbandry was the erection of a piggery to the north of the house on the edge of the Pleasure Grounds (fig. 109).[49] Presumably this was developed in accordance with Arthur Young's printed views. In his 1771 *Six Week Tour of Sussex*, Young talks of the Suffolk method of grazing pigs;[50] while his *Essay on the Management of Hogs* (1774) also recommends grazing pigs on clover for the summer months, something which the parklands at Petworth offered in plenty and diversity.[51] On his 1795 visit Marshall noticed the Petworth practice of pasturing the pigs in the park as a peculiarity of West Sussex which he had not met with 'in any other part of the Island'.[52] In his view, 'The Lake, Petworth: Sunset, Fighting Bucks' (fig. 114), Turner includes a group of these grazing pigs, long thought to have been sheep, in the immediate foreground of the painting. The pigs were allowed to graze freely in the park all summer, right

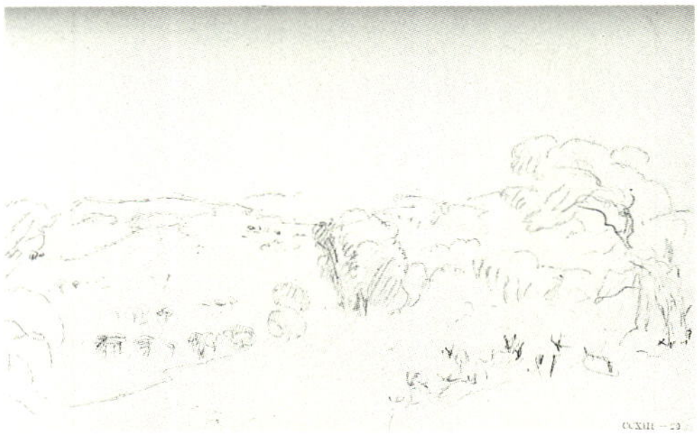

fig. 107 *Deer in Petworth Park* ('Mortlake and Pulborough' sketchbook, TB CCXIII, p. 20), 1825, Pencil 113 × 185 ($4\frac{7}{16} \times 7\frac{1}{4}$), Tate Gallery

fig. 108 *A pink deer*, 1827, Gouache 140 × 190 ($5\frac{1}{2} \times 7\frac{1}{2}$), Tate Gallery (TB CCXLIV–54 verso)

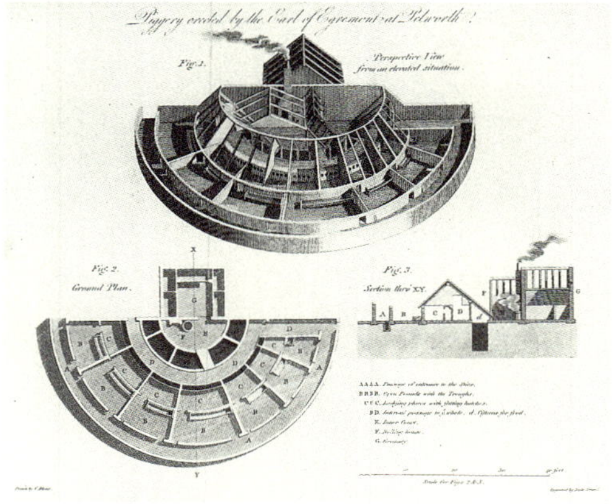

fig. 109 Neele Strand after C. Blunt: *Piggery erected by the Earl of Egremont at Petworth*, engraved for the Rev. Arthur Young's *A General View of the Agriculture in the County of Sussex*, c. 1808, The British Library

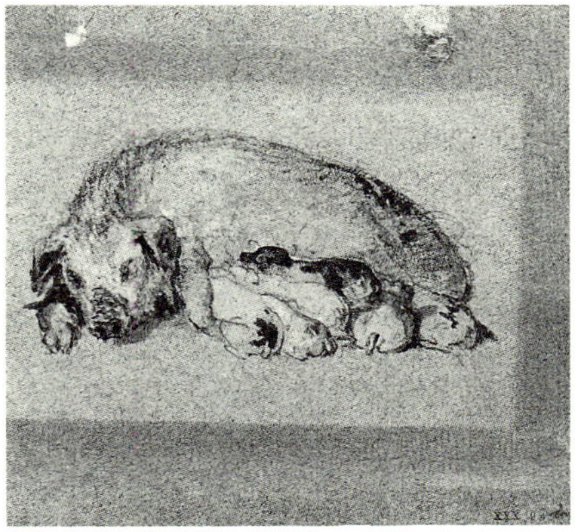

fig. 110 *A Group of Pigs* ('Studies near Brighton' sketchbook, TB XXX, p. 94), 1796, Gouache on a pink ground on blue paper, faded from exposure 125 × 118 ($4\frac{7}{8} \times 4\frac{1}{4}$), Tate Gallery

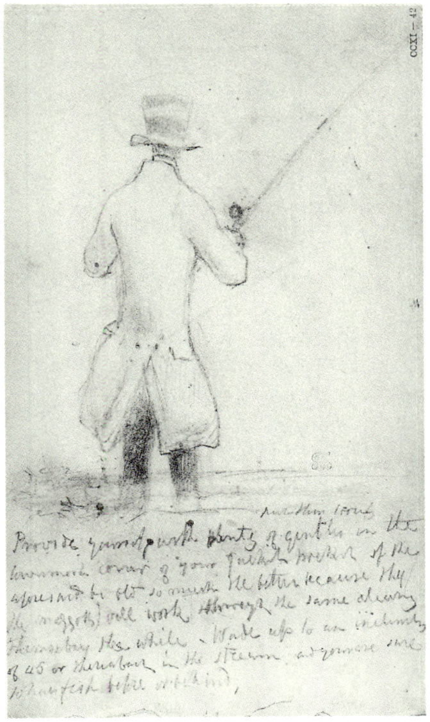

fig. 111 *A man fishing* ('Worcester and Shrewsbury' sketchbook, TB CCXXXIX, page inserted from the 'Paris, Seine and Dieppe' sketchbook, TB CCXI, p. 42), *c.* 1825–29, Pencil 113 × 190 ($4\frac{7}{16} \times 7\frac{3}{8}$), Tate Gallery

up to the house in fact, and were slaughtered in the autumn.

William Cobbett on his 1823 ride through the Sussex area noted that the pigs around Petworth were 'all *black, thin-haired*'.[53] The practice of grazing pigs in the park continued after Lord Egremont's time and was obviously successful, as is demonstrated by a plan in the Petworth House Archives proposing an extension to the existing piggery.[54] Perhaps in this, more than anything else, it is easy to appreciate Lord Egremont's obsession with agriculture, given the unconventional proximity of the piggery to the main house (fig. 110; TB XXX–94).

Constance Leconfield records an amusing story which bears some relation to this method. Whilst writing in the Library, Mrs George Wyndham (Lord Egremont's daughter-in-law, and later Mary, Lady Leconfield) happened to look down the enfilade of the house towards the North Gallery and was surprised to see a 'sow and her litter of pigs get in through a window and gallop down through the rooms'.[55] It was only after this incident that a protective iron fence was erected in front of the house along the road then leading to the Marble Hall entrance.

By all accounts, Egremont's agricultural endeavours seemed almost unable to fail, whether it was the poultry, whose eggs 'frequently astonished the company by their size',[56] or the variety of fish in the ponds. Several stories relate how Turner, a renowned fisherman, often spent time fishing on his Petworth visits (fig. 111; TB CCXI–42). On one occasion he is reputed to have caught a pike, whilst another guest and fishing rival, the sculptor, Sir Francis Chantrey, was unable by his scientific fishing methods to catch anything.[57]

In a mood of Petworth mania, the painter Benjamin Robert Haydon exalted that the 'very flies at Petworth seem to know there is room for their existence, that the windows are theirs', and that all the animals 'seemed happier than in any other spot on Earth – better fed, and their dumbness and helpless dependence on Man more humanely felt for . . .'[58] Indeed, Egremont's interest in animals was not limited to the domestic and agricultural, and there is a *Catalogue of the Quadrupeds and Birds contained in the British Zoological Museum*, in the Petworth Archives, which until recently was thought to have been written by him.[59]

Another cause for pride was Egremont's stable of fine racehorses, which his contemporaries saw as the pinnacle of his achievement (fig. 112). One friend wrote to him on an agricultural matter and professed a desire for Egremont to 'come at last to that degree of perfection in cattle, sheep and pigs, which your Lordship has so eminently reached in Horses'.[60] Horses from Egremont's stables competing in the Derby and Oaks won each event five times, more than any other owner could boast, and a record only shared in the Derby by the Aga Khan.[61] On one occasion at the Brighton Races Egremont owned three out of twenty runners. Like the Petworth deer, the racehorses form an integral part of images of Petworth Park in contemporary engravings as well as in the paintings of Phillips and Turner (figs. 100, 113). Indeed, until 1801, when Goodwood was established as a racing fixture, Egremont held an annual race-meeting in the park grounds. Like the prize cattle, several of Egremont's successful racehorses were recorded individually and these pictures remain in the collection at Petworth.[62] Such was the quality of Egremont's stable that by the 1860s Mark Anthony Lower could report that 'at the present day there hardly exists a racehorse of any celebrity that has not some of the Petworth blood in his veins'.[63]

Alongside the equine developments there was a keen sportsmanship manifest in the esteemed reputation of the Petworth Hunt amongst other sportsmen. Egremont had kept hounds at Petworth throughout his tenure and built up a well trained pack through astute purchases on his own part and by his huntsman, Luke Freeman. In retrospect Egremont was thought to have been 'one of the greatest sportsmen of his day'.[64]

By the mid 1820s, when Turner again began to visit Petworth, the Earl had allowed his son, Colonel George Wyndham (1787–1869), to assume the management of the hounds, so that the hunting study in the Turner Bequest (plate 69; TB CCXLIV–104) most probably shows the colonel and others before a hunt on the lawns of Petworth Park.[65] From a contemporary account of January 1824 the hunt seems to have been a large event with 'upwards of 200 horsemen being present'. The colonel obviously inherited his father's sporting passion, for it is reported that he 'rode very well to his hounds and his cheering hallo to them, in chase, would make an old man's heart feel glad'.[66]

The park was in many ways a village meeting ground, open to the people of the town. As Constance Leconfield recalled: 'there was a continual flow of people passing through on their way to and from the Park; one had to encounter this even to reach the kitchen garden', which was only a short distance to the south of the house.[67] Louis Simond, as a Frenchman, was apparently both amazed and shocked to

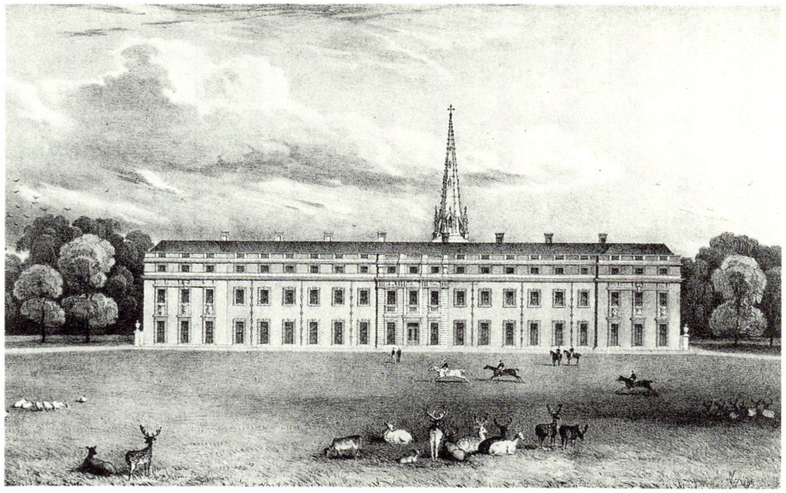

fig. 112 T.M. Baynes after Lady Burrell: *Petworth House, Sussex, The Seat of the Earl of Egremont*, lithograph 217 × 320 (8½ × 12½), West Sussex Record Office, Chichester

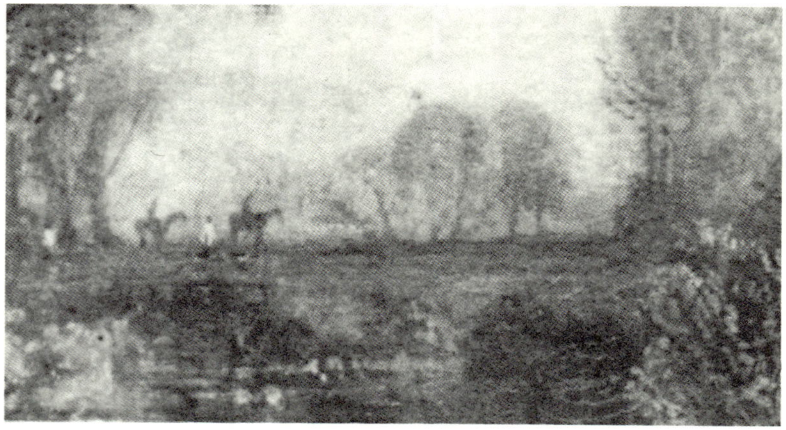

fig. 113 *The Lake, Petworth: Sunset, a Stag Drinking* (detail) (BJ 289), *c.* 1828, Oil on canvas 635 × 1321 (25 × 52), Petworth House

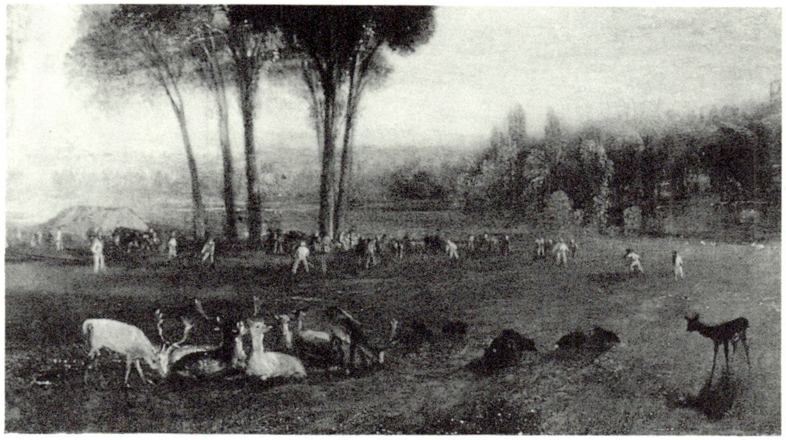

fig. 114 *The Lake, Petworth: Sunset, Fighting Bucks* (detail), (BJ 288), *c.* 1827–28, Oil on canvas 622 × 1460 (24½ × 57½), Petworth House

observe this practice: Egremont 'suffers the peasants of his village to play bowls and cricket on the lawn before the house; to scribble on the walls, and even on the glass of his windows'.[68] It is this sort of casual detail that Turner notes and uses for his picture of 'The Lake, Petworth: Sunset, Fighting Bucks' (fig. 76), replacing the racehorses Phillips had put into his view with a cricket-match (fig. 114), and thereby suggesting the public-spirited benevolence of the owner of the grounds. Other narratives linked with the park's history relate that during the 1790s when Napoleon's army was threatening to invade England, and again during the era of Waterloo, Egremont helped to establish the Petworth Yeomanry, by providing 'horses, uniforms, weapons and equipment', and allowing the troop to exercise in the grounds of Petworth Park.[69] William Frederick Witherington's picture, 'A Fête in Petworth Park' (fig. 15), memorably depicts one of the annual fêtes given for the people of the town on Egremont's birthday.

The 'Capability' Brown landscape seems to have remained largely unchanged in the thirty years between Thomas Phillips's view of 'Petworth Park' in 1798 and Turner's paintings of the late 1820s. The Phillips view is somewhat unconventional as a 'country-house portrait'. Up until this date, as Turner's work proves in the contemporaneous 'View of Fonthill House, Wiltshire' which he submitted to William Angus's 1800 volume of *Seats of the Nobility and Gentry in Great Britain and Wales*, the traditional way of representing such a subject was to show the patron's house set in its landscape. Typifying this tradition at Petworth was Grimm's drawing cited above, or Turner's own 'Petworth, Sussex, the Seat of the Earl of Egremont: Dewy Morning' of 1810 (fig. 35; BJ 113), and the many engravings and drawings of Petworth which take the house as their principal subject.

By depicting Petworth Park, instead of the more usual view of the house from the lake, Phillips creates a landscape portrait using each detail singly and collectively to represent the interests of his patron. When later painting the Petworth landscape in two of the four paintings for the Carved Room,[70] Turner may well have been aware of the Phillips picture hanging, with some of his own works, in the North Gallery, and this most probably compelled him to take up the challenge it presented.[71]

It is poignant at this point to recall comments Sir Horace Walpole made in conjunction with a visit to Petworth towards the end of the eighteenth century. Meditating on 'Capability' Brown's Petworth landscape in the 1784 edition of his *Essay on Modern Gardening*, Walpole pondered prophetically:

> Enough has been done to establish such a school of landscape, as cannot be found on the rest of the globe. If we have the seeds of a Claud [sic] or a Gasper amongst us, he must come forth. If wood, water, groves, vallies, glades, can inspire or poet or painter, this is the country, this is the age to produce them.

In retrospect it seems particularly apt that Turner, the closest England came to a painter of truly Claudean sensibilities, should have fulfilled this prophecy in actually rendering the Petworth landscape. Walpole's analysis continues by unconsciously noting the presence of the Petworth agriculture:

> The flocks, the herds, that now are admitted into, now graze on the borders of our cultivated plains, are ready before the painter's eyes, and group themselves to animate his picture. One misfortune in truth there is that throws a difficulty on the artist. A principal beauty in our gardens is the lawn and smoothness of turf: in a picture it becomes a dead and uniform spot, incapable of chiaro scuro, and to be broken insipidly by children, dogs, and other unmeaning figures.[72]

Turner was no doubt aware of this danger from Phillips's picture, which, though naturalistic, lacks the tension of a strong composition. The high vantage point means that the observer's eye is forced to rove over the cluttered foreground beyond the shadow of the house. Turner's first solution, 'Petworth Park with Tillington Church in the distance' (fig. 75; BJ 283), dramatically solves this problem by distorting the perspective into an encircling curve focusing on the figure of Lord Egremont. The line of dogs (perhaps hounds from the Petworth pack, or even the 'dozen black spaniels' mentioned by Haydon),[73] also serve to draw the observer into the landscape.

This painting was one of two pictures noted by Thomas Creevey on his visit in August 1828 as already installed in the Carved Room.[74] There has been much confusion among Turner scholars as to the identity of its companion. Neither Luke Herrmann nor John Gage agree with the solution proposed by Martin Butlin and Evelyn Joll, and each suggests a different coupling of pictures.[75] By re-examining the relevant passage of Creevey's correspondence it is possible to find only the briefest of clues. In comparison with the recognisable description of the Tate sketch noted above, Creevey refers simply to the other picture as 'Petworth Park by Turner'.[76] Of the various possibilities, it semes to have been overlooked that the most probable solution would, therefore, be the picture now called, 'The Lake, Petworth: Sunset, Fighting Bucks' (fig. 76; BJ 288), which was, in fact, engraved in 1859 as 'Petworth Park' and always referred to by this title in the various catalogues and wall plans of the picture collection at Petworth (fig. 115).[77] The present rather poetic titles for the two Petworth landscapes still at the house (figs. 76, 78) fail to differentiate significantly between the view of the park and that of the lake. These titles were, in fact, only introduced in 1920 by C.H. Collins Baker in his catalogue of the Petworth Collection.

The coupling of pictures suggested here leads one to conclude that Turner's 'study' of the park, with Egremont and his dogs (fig. 75), and his 'finished' painting, still at Petworth (fig. 76), briefly hung side-by-side and were probably executed at much the same time. That the sketch hung beside the finished version is peculiarly unprecedented in Turner's practice. A reason for this arrangement might have been that

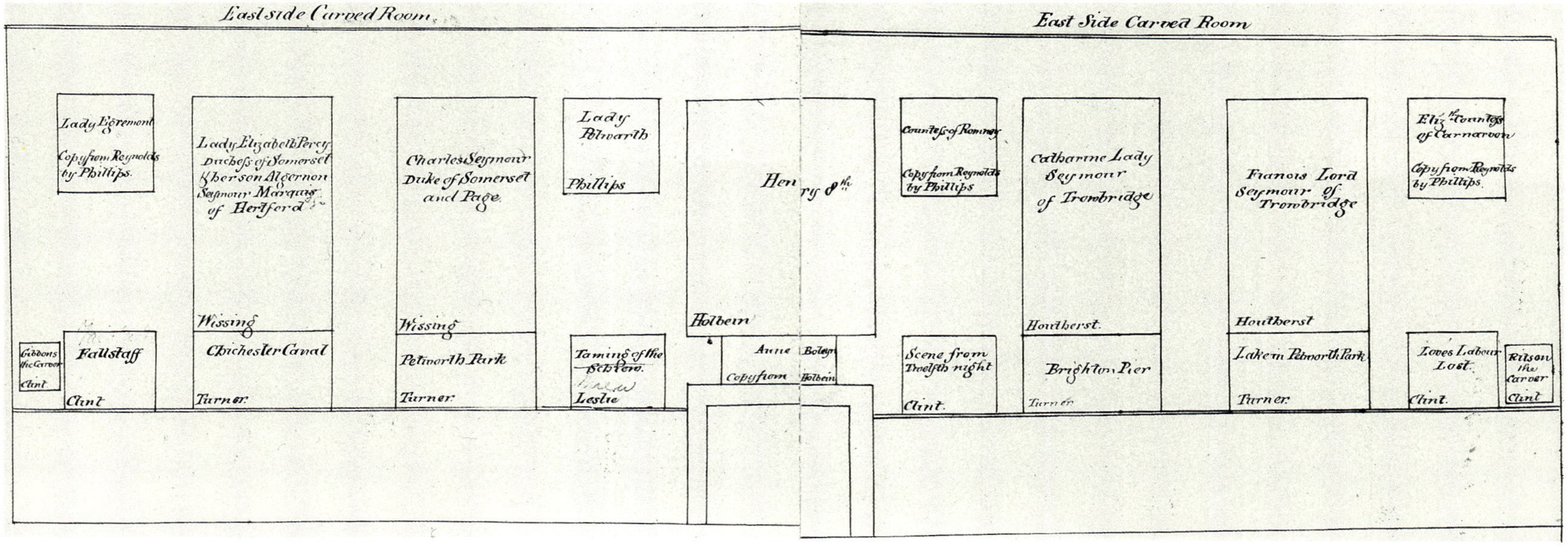

fig. 115 *Wall Plan of the East Side of the Carved Room, c.* 1835, Petworth House Archives (7518–19)

this provided an early indication, for both painter and patron, of how the projected scheme of four paintings would look within Grinling Gibbons's carved-frame surroundings.

Both the study (BJ 283) and the finished picture (BJ 288) are portraits of Lord Egremont, literally and metaphorically respectively, placing him in the landscape he has shaped. In the finished version, Turner creates an idyllic Claudean pastoral, conveying something of the ideals of Virgil's *Georgics*. Both the mood and the setting celebrate Egremont as the architect of this Petworth arcadia. The picture would also serve as an illustration of the words of that English Virgil, Alexander Pope:

> Whose cheerful tenants bless their yearly toil,
> Yet to their Lord owe more than to the soil;
> Whose ample lawns are not ashamed to feed
> The milky heifer and deserving steed;
> Whose rising forests, not for pride or show,
> But future buildings, future navies grow.

Pope's 'Epistle to Richard Boyle, Earl of Burlington' was a poem Turner undoubtedly knew, for in his 'Backgrounds' lecture at the Royal Academy as Professor of Perspective he alluded to Pope's judgement of the painter Verrio which appears some forty lines above the passage quoted.[78]

Martin Butlin has suggested in the catalogue of the 1974–75 *Turner* bicentenary exhibition[79] that Egremont instigated the inclusion in the picture of livestock and cricket match to create a more conventional image. It is quite likely that the figure of the Earl with his dogs in the 'sketch' version was felt to be too personal for display in so prominent a position. 'Petworth Park with Tillington Church' also raises the possibility that Egremont, a man of intense pride, might not have relished being reminded in so public an image of his own decline and of the nearness of death, conjured by the associations of the setting sun. C.C.F. Greville acutely noticed the dilemma Egremont faced over the continuance of his title, given the illegitimacy of most of his heirs: 'The Earl's course, however, is nearly run, and he has the mortification of feeling that, though surrounded with children and grandchildren, he is almost the last of his race, and that his family is about to be extinct'.[80]

This view of Egremont may well have been apparent to those who met him at this period, as is attested by the numerous comments remarking with awe on his aged sprightliness. Egremont's resistance to his declining health is perhaps the key to his continued energy and enthusiasm for introducing and consolidating his earlier policies of change. Indeed the pursuit of anything which might 'confer a national good', as the *Sussex Agricultural Express* observed, seemed to be Egremont's obsession.[81] He expressed the view that 'almost every great improvement in society is counterbalanced by some evil arising from it, which is not thought of till it happens', but felt that it was essential to have the 'good sense and good temper to make the best of it and enjoy it, even if it should subside without any fatal effect'.[82]

Beyond the immediate world of Petworth, Egremont was keen to stimulate improvements in the basic communications systems of Sussex, thereby augmenting the local agricultural development he had instigated by providing easily reached markets for produce. This strategy largely meant exploiting the untapped potential of the county's rivers in a series of canal schemes. In total Egremont was to spend £100,000 on canal projects.[83] By the 1820s he was already seen as 'the original projector and indefatigable promoter of many undertakings of this nature for the general benefit'.[84]

In 1787 the Arun canal had been opened as far as Newbridge. This was the dawn of the canal age, for during the 1780s canals were constructed that linked the Thames with the Severn, and the Trent with the Mersey. In 1791 Egremont had submitted a proposal in Parliament to 'make and maintain the river Rother navigable, from the town of Midhurst to a certain meadow called the railed pieces, or Stopham meadow; and a navigable cut from the said river, to the river Arun, at or near Stopham Bridge . . .'.[85] This would link the area surrounding the Rother (including Petworth which in 1793 was provided with a cut off the Rother coming within half a mile of the town) with the River Arun, and hence with the sea.

This proposal could be effected with benefits for all. It provided employment for an army of up to two hundred local workmen, thereby involving less expense to the employer and consequently greater wages for the workman (14 or 15 shillings instead of only 8 or 9).[86] The immediate advantages were a swifter movement of crops such as corn, and an increased value in heavier products such as timber, iron (for the docks), chalk, lime, marl, limestone (for agriculture) and Petworth marble, mined at Kindford from quarries owned by Egremont.[87] This would also help the export of bricks, made in kilns near Petworth, which were sent to the West Indies.[88] Most important for Egremont, as an agriculturalist, was the distribution of chalk and lime which could be used in manuring. The Rev. Arthur Young notes in 1808 that at least '40,000 tons are dispersed in the neighbourhood of the Rother and Arun',[89] and that 'by this most useful and public spirited undertaking, many thousand acres of land are necessarily rendered more valuable to the proprietors'.[90]

The improvement of navigation on the Rother had been a relatively easy operation: the project had generally followed the natural course of the river by falling fifty-four feet to the level of the River Arun via eight locks. Altogether, there were less than two miles of artificial waterway introduced.[91] The whole venture including the link to Petworth cost Egremont £18,300, and it is a mark of his benevolence that he introduced tolls and wharfage at a rate well below the payments on the Arun or other navigations.[92]

Egremont's commitment to canal-building increased with a proposal in 1807 to amend the navigation of the River Adur,[93] and his involvement in the 1811 prospectus, printed in *The Times*,[94] for a Wey–Arun junction canal which would effectively link London with the sea. The prospectus estimated that the 1,200,000 tons which annually travelled via land and sea from London to Portsmouth could be carried much more cheaply via canal. On top of this freight they also calculated a local traffic of up to 30,000 tons.[95] Once again Egremont was the principal subscriber contributing £20,000 to the scheme. In just a month one hundred and thirty-two subscribers had been found. The enthusiasm for this venture is mirrored in the rapidity with which it was concluded. The actual building took only three years, and the canal opened on 29 September 1816. One immediate effect meant a reduction in the price of Guildford coal from three guineas to fifty shillings a chaldron.[96]

Visiting the Petworth area in the early 1830s, Constable made several watercolours of the country surrounding the Rivers Rother and Arun.[97] Like Constable, Turner was certainly familiar with the expansion of waterways across the country.[98] On the visit to West Sussex dating from 1809, he seems to have made several drawings on the River Arun,[99] while in the early 1820s he made a watercolour of the London barge traffic on the river south of Arundel (fig. 116; TB CCVIII–F). A gouache and pen-and-ink drawing, listed as 'A water mill' under the 'French Rivers' series of the Turner Bequest, in fact depicts Fittleworth Mill on the River Rother (plate 122; TB CCLIX–41), although the building has since been much altered making identification difficult.[100] Closely related to drawings in the 'Mortlake and Pulborough' sketchbook of 1825,[101] this is possibly one of the earliest drawings made on blue paper which can be directly linked with Petworth.

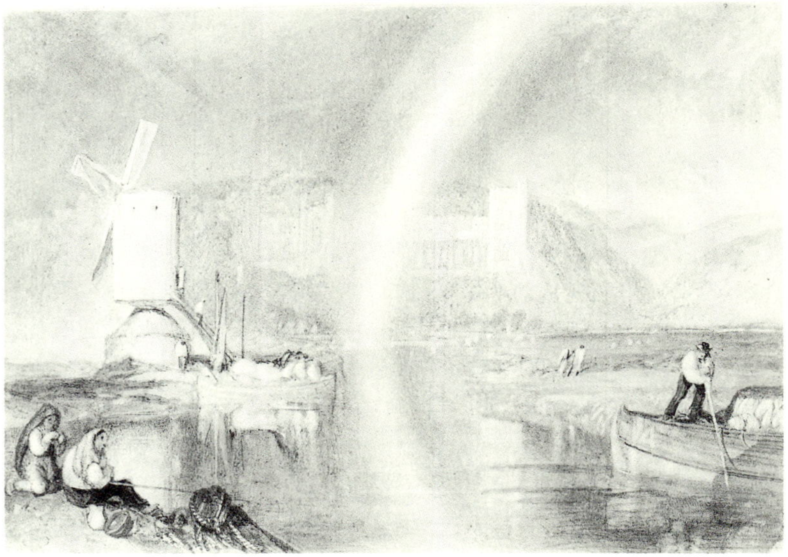

fig. 116 *Arundel Castle, on the River Arun, with rainbow*, *c.* 1823, Watercolour 160 × 230 ($6\frac{1}{4}$ × 9), Tate Gallery (TB CCVIII–F) (W.748)

Some of the views formerly identified as depictions of Petworth Lake could more plausibly be views on the Rother or Arun. Indeed plate 124 (TB CCXLIV–4) seems not to be a scene at Petworth at all, for there is nothing which resembles the tower-like form at the edge of the water in the drawing, and this strange outcrop is surely too large to compare with the statue by Carew of one of Lord Egremont's favourite dogs, which still sits rather forlornly on its island in the lake. Other drawings, such as plate 76 (TB CCXLIV–18) and plate 125 (TB CCXLIV–106), also have the feeling of a river rather than the strip of water at Petworth, although it is possible that plate 76 (TB CCXLIV–18) could be related to the 'Chichester Canal' paintings (figs. 79, 80, 84,).

Basking in the success of the Wey and Arun Canal project, Egremont embarked on the projected Portsmouth and Arundel Canal under the Act of 1817, and subscribed three hundred and twenty shares (at £1 per share). The canal temporarily linked Portsmouth with the River Arun just below Arundel at Ford. A small subsidiary canal from the main navigation was built to Chichester. The first Act was supplemented by the Act of 1818 which allowed the subscribers to build the Chichester and Portsea sections of the canal as ship-canals, of a depth of eight foot to carry up to one hundred and fifty ton burdens, which would avoid trans-shipment. The estimated cost rose to about £137,268, towards which Lord Egremont offered a personal guarantee of £40,000 against the failure of the project. Although the Portsmouth and Arundel Canal was completed in 1823, at a time when the Wey and Arun Canal was paying dividends, the project was to lose Egremont at least £55,000. No doubt Egremont and the other investors were blinded by the apparent success of the Wey and Arun scheme. The opening ceremony of the Portsmouth and Arundel Canal itself cast an ill-omen on his prospects in the venture: 'The procession from Milton consisting of three barges, two sailing vessels, and eleven rowing boats towed by the tug *Egremont* ran aground on a mud bank in Emsworth Channel and never arrived'.[102]

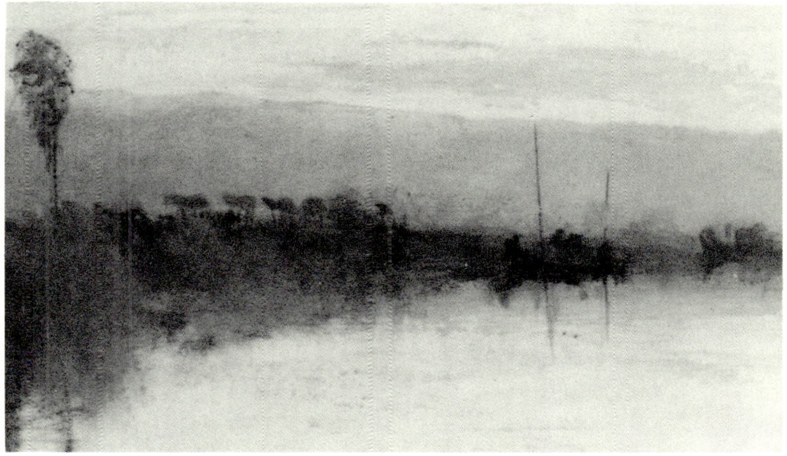

fig. 117 *Chichester Canal* (detail), (BJ 285), *c.* 1828, Oil on canvas 656 × 1345 ($25\frac{3}{4}$ × 53), Tate Gallery

As a speculative link with London the Portsmouth and Arundel Canal foundered, and from 1840 traffic between London and Portsmouth had essentially ceased. As P.A.L. Vine has suggested in his book, *London's Lost Route to the Sea*,[103] Egremont's judgement was perhaps blurred by his view that the canal would improve the agriculture of the surrounding countryside through a wider availability of manure, as well as providing various incentives for local crafts and industry to develop. Egremont did redeem some self-esteem by withdrawing, in 1826, from the increasingly troubled company, although at a considerable cost to himself. After relinquishing his three hundred and fifteen shares and paying off the company's £40,000 mortgage,[104] it seems somewhat surprising that Egremont should choose to be reminded of this misadventure in Turner's 'Chichester Canal' (fig. 80), presumably a subject he sanctioned. Apparently begun some time after 1828, at a time when Egremont was no longer involved with the navigation, the reasons for the picture remain enigmatic.

It has been noted that the square-rigged ship, possibly a collier-brig, would have been unable to enter the shallow waters of the canal.[105] The width of the channel in the picture is also clearly exaggerated, implying a low angle from which it would be almost impossible to see the cathedral. Another curious effect recalls the criticism by one of Turner's contemporaries that he never saw sunsets of the sort Turner managed to capture and may here have some justification, for in all three Chichester Canal views (including fig. 84: BJ 282), the sun appears to be setting to the north, over the ridge of the South Downs. Turner may have caught, with visionary intensity, the sun's last rays, but he has arranged the golden disk and the other elements in the picture very much to suit his purpose and the demands of poetic licence.

It may be mere coincidence that a watercolour of 'York Minster seen from the River Ouse' (fig. 70) bears a general resemblance to the composition of the Chichester pictures. This watercolour was painted around 1815 when the River Ouse faced the renewed prospect of canal navigation. At the same time, Egremont was privately criticising the Ouse Navigation Committee for the self-interest which, he felt, lay behind their plans.[106] Such criticism was to become more widespread in 1823 when the Committee built themselves a Banqueting House at Naburn Lock.[107] In the Chichester picture it is possible that Turner recalled his watercolour while making a mental contrast between Egremont and the committee members of the Ouse project. Certainly the painting seems to refer to the wider agricultural implications of Egremont's initiation of river improvement in the silhouettes of cattle on the left bank in the Tate sketch (fig. 79).

The other picture, completing the quartet of landscapes for the Carved Room, that of the Chain Pier at Brighton (fig. 82), also suggests the theme of entrepreneurial expansion. The pier, only the second to be constructed in this country, was proposed in Parliament in 1822 and built by Captain Samuel Brown at an estimated cost of £30,000. It opened in November 1823 and was viewed as 'gratifying evidence of the resources and the intellect of our country'.[108] Egremont had three shares at £100 each[109] and, though not extensively involved in the project, it is perhaps significant that he was among those toasted by the crowd at the opening ceremony.[110]

As Butlin and Joll note, Constable had exhibited his picture of the Chain Pier at the Royal Academy in 1827 (fig. 118),[111] and amongst the Petworth gouache drawings it is interesting to note two drawings of the pier taken from very much the same angle (plates 126, 127; TB CCXLIV–110, 111). Constable's picture was something that must have been fresh in Turner's mind as it had hung in the Academy with five of his own paintings. He had already noted the particulars of the pier in the early 1820s in the 'Brighton and Arundel' sketchbook,[112] but until 1827, when he made these gouache drawings, he had not drawn it in the way in which these studies echo Constable's painting. In his finished picture of the pier, however, Turner deliberately changed the viewpoint from Constable's landlocked shoreline to a low view from the sea with the pier extending across our line of vision.

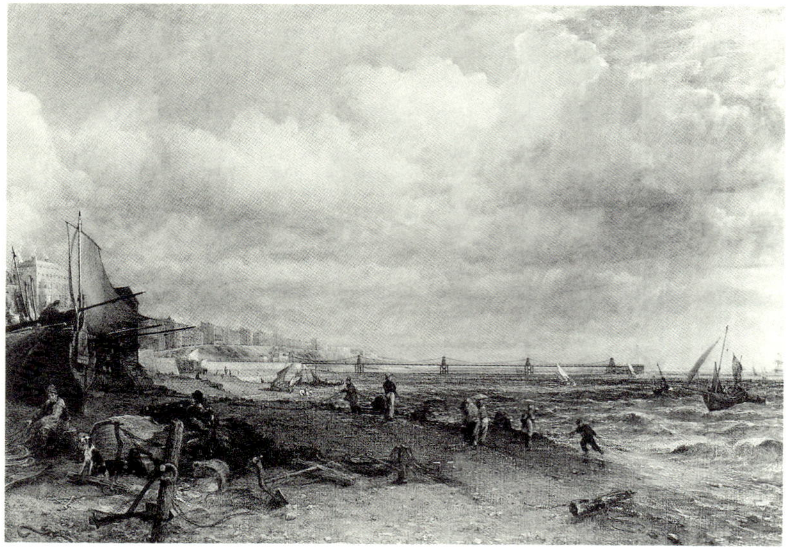

fig. 118 John Constable: *Chain Pier, Brighton*, 1826–27, R.A. 1827, Oil on canvas 1270 × 1829 (50 × 72), Tate Gallery

As well as TB CCXLIV–110 and 111, the Turner Bequest contains, among the 'French Rivers' series, two sketches very similar in style showing the Chain Pier at Brighton (plates 128, 129; TB CCLIX–250, 271). Once more they illustrate a confusion of the subjects amid the gouache and ink drawings made on blue paper during the late 1820s.[113] As well as the two beach scenes showing the distinctive structure of the Chain Pier from the east side, the 'French Rivers' group contains a series of drawings of figures on the beach which seem related to the Brighton scenes, perhaps suggesting that Turner actually worked on the beach there, something the sketchiness of the drawings would bear out.[114] Whether these were made in England or France is difficult to prove conclusively, although Constable's studies of the fisher-folk on Brighton beach show figures dressed in similar costumes. It would have been easy for Turner to visit Brighton from Petworth, especially since Egremont kept a residence there, and it is also possible that Turner may have used Brighton as a departure point for the Continent. The voyage to Dieppe took eight hours and was available daily.[115]

Closer to his real home at Petworth, Egremont was the architect and instigator of much local philanthropy. He introduced a forcing-engine on the River Rother which, worked by water-wheel at Coultershawl Mill, raised enough water over the one hundred and seventy-eight feet to the town to supply, through iron pipes, 'every street, without cost to the inhabitants'.[116] Because of a steady rise in the local population, Egremont made the provision for four houses a year to be built in the vicinity.[117] The Market-house and Court Room were also built under Egremont's jurisdiction in 1793, while over forty years later the Earl, still concerned for local improvement, was involved in the erection of the town's gas works. He contributed financially to the building of the County Hospital in Brighton, as well as an Infirmary at Chichester.[118] In Petworth he appointed a surgeon-apothecary to minister to the poor,[119] as well as providing funds for the training of a midwife and an innoculation nurse.[120] During the last decade of the eighteenth century, when repeated bad harvests pushed the price of corn beyond the means of the poor, Egremont attempted to effect a short-term solution, by experimenting with potatoes and rice, to try and provide a nourishing alternative to real bread.

Yet despite this concern for his fellow man, visitors to Petworth House today can immediately perceive, among the splendours of the collection of paintings and sculpture, how Egremont's scientific endeavours and projects of national improvement have been eclipsed by the monumental scale of his artistic patronage. As the Reverend Thomas Sockett, rector of Petworth, wrote in his journal, above all else, Egremont was a patron.[121] Contemporary accounts balanced this munificence with 'his immense benevolence' in Petworth and glorified his acts directed at the nation's improvement,[122] and if amid the glory of Petworth, Turner's paintings and drawings help us to contemplate the diversity of industries – the agricultural, scientific, botanical and social concerns pursued by Lord Egremont with such animated energy – then Turner's work is a fitting tribute to his patron and friend.

Notes

1 Quoted in Horsfield 1835, Vol. II, p. 179. I wish to thank Mr Alun Howkins for drawing my attention to this poem.

2 Arnold 1864, p. 40.

3 Lower 1865, p. 90.

4 Patrick Youngblood's article in *Turner Studies* is the fullest account of the artistic life in Petworth House.

5 See *Dictionary of National Biography*, under Arthur Young, p. 1277.

6 Lower 1865, p. 90. Among the other 'fathers' listed were Francis Russell, fifth Duke of Bedford and a Mr J. C. Curwen, MP. The Duke of Bedford was the creator of a model farm at Woburn Abbey, where, like Egremont, he conducted agricultural experiments on the various breeds of sheep to determine their respective merits. He also had sheep-shearing exhibitions and ploughing competitions. *Dictionary of National Biography*, pp. 435–36.

7 West Sussex Record Office, Chichester, PHA 91; Letter 15 June 1793; 'Pray allow me to express my sincere thanks for the kind reception & valuable information I met at Petworth. I think of it with pleasure, and should not feel pleasantly if I did not hope for a renewal of it sometime or other'.

8 See Arthur Young, *Rural Oeconomy; or Essays on the practical parts of husbandry*, 1770: a copy of this book is in the Library at Petworth.

9 West Sussex Record Office, Chichester, PHA 91; letter postmarked 6 October 1800.

10 Young 1808, p. 17. Another of Turner's patrons, Walter Fawkes (1769–1825), could just as easily fit this description, for among many unusual species of livestock there are reported to have been zebras at his Caley Park estate (Lindsay 1966, p. 112).

11 West Sussex Record Office, Chichester, PHA 91: 'Pray my Lord think of this; and remember yt it is a duty you owe to yr country. You can serve it essentially the consequence is you ought to do it – You are not at liberty to refuse it. I must write warmly when I write from conviction.' Dated 26 January 1798.

12 Arthur Young, *The Autobiography of Arthur Young, with Selections from his Correspondence*, edited by M. Betham-Edwards, 1898, pp. 323–24. Egremont disliked 'ribbons and higher titles' and repeatedly refused the honour of the Garter (Wyndham 1950, p. 223).

13 Quoted in Wyndham 1950, p. 246.

14 In West Sussex his acquisitions consisted of 14,000 acres by purchase, 1,200 by exchange, and only 150 acres by enclosure (Wyndham 1950, p. 300); see also Dallaway 1819, vol. 2, part 1, pp. xi, 195, 210, 213, 246, 295; Horsfield 1835, p. 179; A. Young, *Autobiography*, 1898, p. 179.

15 Wyndham 1950, p. 245.

16 Jerrome 1976, p. 54 and p. 60.

17 Young 1808, p. 188–89.

18 Simond 1815, ii, 250–51.

19 Sotheby's 10 April 1980, lots 17 and 18 contained a number of Petworth subjects by Mrs Phillips.

20 Plates 77, 78, 79; TB CCXLIV–105, 57 and 54 seem to be stages in a sunset series.

21 Plate 94; TB CCXX–X also resembles other drawings of the lake and has therefore been included here.

22 Dallaway 1819, p. 295.

23 Young 1808, p. 189.

24 *Ibid.*, p. 78.

25 *Ibid.*, p. 141–42.

26 Simond 1815, ii, p. 249.

27 Young 1808, p. 55.

28 West Sussex Record Office, Chichester, PHA 91: letter dated 22 March 1797 points out that the efficacy of the improved iron dibble had given Egremont cause to write a paper on its merits.

29 This had been recommended to him by John Austin, see undated letter with plan, PHA 90; and letter from Arthur Young, PHA 91 dated 7 October 1797; the other two threshing machines were owned by Sir Richard Hotham at Bognor and Mr Pennington at Ashburnham, see G. E. Fussell, 'Four Centuries of Farming Systems in Sussex', *Sussex Archaeological Collections*, vol. XC, Oxford University Press, 1982.

30 Young 1808, p. 90–91; In the 'rick-burning' scenes of the 1830s there was a sad irony that mechanisation such as the threshing machine, which had been thought of as an improvement, was destroyed by the rioters as one of the contributory evils of unemployment (Wyndham 1950, p. 351).

31 Marshall 1795, p. 171; and Young 1808, p. 55.

32 Young 1808, p. 60.

33 See the 'Windsor and Eton' sketchbook (TB XCVII–29, 30, 31, 66a, 68a, 81a, 82a); the 'Spithead' sketchbook (TB C–35a, 38, 40); and the 'Boats, Ice' sketchbook (TB CI–89, 90). John Gage's most recent book (Gage 1987, pp. 213–14 and p. 234) comments on the proliferation of ploughing images in Turner's work.

34 Marshall 1795, p. 171.

35 See Wilton 1979, catalogue no. 912 'Petworth Park, Sunset, with a cart'. A watercolour in the 'Fonthill' sketchbook (TB XLVII–46) shows an arrangement of six oxen pulling a cart, whilst 'The Vale of Ashburnham' in the British Museum's Salting

Bequest has a group of possibly eight (1910–2–12–272; W.425).

36 Young 1808, p.275.

37 *Ibid.*, p.277.

38 Determined to be proved right he had repeated the ploughing competition using two strong eleven-year-old oxen, who managed to plough an acre of clover in under six hours (Wyndham 1950, p.248).

39 Young 1808, p.283; Wyndham 1950, p.258, reveals that this was resented by his tenants in Ireland who felt they were equally entitled to agricultural encouragement of this kind.

40 Wyndham 1950, p.249.

41 Marshall 1795, p.195.

42 Goodsall 1963, p.100. The society (at Egremont's suggestion) also provided incentives to encourage industry amongst the poor.

43 Collins Baker 1920. This catalogue lists a number of works by J. Bolteby (or Boultbee) of various breeds of cattle. Several of these pictures include the distinctive features of the Petworth landscape in their backgrounds: no. 546, 'Sussex Bull and cow, South Down Ram and ewes' (1797), for example, actually includes Petworth House, whilst no. 544, 'Hereford Bull and Cow and Ryland Ewe' (1797), seems to show the lake. There are also works listed by an artist called Eltham.

44 Deer appear in several of Turner's paintings: 'Petworth Park: Tillington Church in the distance' (fig.75; BJ 283); 'The Lake, Petworth Park; Sunset, Fighting Bucks' (fig.76; BJ 288); 'The Lake, Petworth: Sunset, a Stag Drinking' (fig. 78; BJ 289); and in the drawings: fig. 24 (TB CIX–5), plate 73 (TB CCXLIV–7), fig. 108 (TB CCXLIV–54 verso), plate 83 (TB CCXLIV–114), and possibly also in plates 70, 100, 77 (TB CCXLIV–2, 55, 105). Two of the drawings outside the Bequest also depict deer: plates 72 and 75. The 'Mortlake and Pulborough' sketchbook includes deer in a number of the views taken from the Upperton Monument (TB CCXIII–18, 20, 20V).

45 Young 1808, p.403.

46 West Sussex Record Office, Chichester, PHA 1304.

47 Dallaway 1815, vol.I, p.cxliii.

48 Young 1808, p.375.

49 There is an early design for the piggery in the West Sussex Record Office, Chichester, PHA 7941.

50 Young 1771, p.218.

51 Arthur Young, *Essay on the management of Hogs including Experiments on rearing and fattening them* (first edition 1779, p.77; revised second edition 1780, p.xiii).

52 Marshall 1795, p.203.

53 Cobbett 1830, p.116.

54 West Sussex Record Office, Chichester, PHA: Uncatalogued plan of extension to the existing piggery, dating from *c.*1845. I am grateful to Alison McCann and Heather Warne for bringing this to my attention. On an earlier visit to this area, Turner made a group of beautiful studies of livestock including two watercolours of various pigs; see 'Studies near Brighton' sketchbook, TB XXX ff. 93 & 94 (fig. 110). The 'Spithead' sketchbook (TB C–57a) includes a diagram of a pig sty, as well as various drawings of pigs and cattle.

55 Leconfield 1938, p.48–49.

56 Young 1808, p.392.

57 Ruskin 1903, vol.XXXV, 571–72; here Ruskin quotes a letter from C.R. Leslie's son. For the most extensive account of the Leslie family's connection with Petworth see Hamlyn 1984.

58 Haydon 1963, vol.III, p.167 & vol.IV, p.449. Haydon's account of Petworth life, though widely quoted, has obvious limitations in that most of his information is repeated on almost all occasions: the idea of Egremont as the magnanimous Sun King is repeated p.167 & p.168; the story of Lady Londonderry and her page appears both on p.163 and again on p.171. Ironically, Haydon unconsciously records a series of *faux pas* he commits, and needless to say, the visit in 1826 appears to be the only one Haydon made to Petworth. Petworth House contains only one painting as a result of Egremont's benevolence towards Haydon (that commissioned in 1826, 'Alexander the Great taming Bucephalus', Collins Baker 1920, no.660).

59 West Sussex Record Office, Chichester, PHA 5315. In fact this was written by the Rev. Robert Ferryman, whom Egremont had employed to establish a private museum at Petworth.

60 West Sussex Record Office, Chichester, PHA 90; letter dated 26 July 1800 from a Mr Parsons.

61 Derby winners were: Assassin (1782); Hannibal (1804); Cardinal Beaufort (1805); Election (1807); Lapdog (1826). The Oaks were won by: Nightshade (1788); Tag (1789); Platina (1795); Ephemera (1800); and Caroline (1820). I would like to thank Sue Anderson of the Jockey club for providing this and other information.

62 Collins Baker 1920: J. Bolteby: 625 'Gohanna, the Racehorse, and his Groom, T. Bird, 1797' – Gohanna, the chief stud, is depicted in the park with the lodge gates in the distance; Richard Barrett Davis: 580 ' "Camel" a Racehorse' (1826); 626 ' "Whalebone" a Racehorse'; 674 ' "Skim" a greyhorse'; Benjamin Marshall: 688 'Racehorse and Groom'. A statue of the racehorse 'Whalebone' appears in Thomas Phillips's portrait of Lord Egremont (fig.13); there is also a portrait by Thomas Phillips of the racing owner and banker, Robert Ladbroke (Collins Baker 1920, no.260).

63 Lower 1865, p.90.

64 *Victoria History* 1907, Vol.2, p.444.

65 Plate 14 (TB CCXLIV–22) perhaps shows the colonel in his red uniform.

66 *Victoria History* 1907, p.445.

67 Leconfield 1939, p.45. The park had been enclosed during Henry VIII's reign. See Peter Jerrome, *Cloakbag and Common Purse. Enclosure and Copyhold in Sixteenth Century Petworth*, 1979.

68 Simond 1815, p.ii, 250. In her notes in the British Museum, Prints and Drawings copy of the *Inventory of the Turner Bequest*, Lady Leconfield has annotated drawing plate 83 (TB CCXLIV–114) as 'the old cricket ground'. However, this drawing seems to be a view from the north-west of the house, looking back across the lake, whereas the cricket-ground today and in Turner's painting is to the south-west.

69 See Vine 1965, pp.36–37; and Arnold 1864, p.92.

70 'The Lake, Petworth: Sunset, Fighting Bucks' (fig. 76; BJ 288); 'The Lake, Petworth: Sunset, a Stag Drinking' (fig.78; BJ 289).

71 Phillips's picture is no.44 in Henry Phillips's 1835 catalogue. By 1856 it had been moved to the Buff Room as no.43 (Sockett 1856) and, in a later catalogue, to the Hertford Room (PHA 5272–3: *c.*1836–1901, no.43).

72 Walpole 1784, p.85.

73 Haydon 1963, vol.III, p.167. See Collins Baker 1920: Clint, no.599; Phillips nos. 57 and 695, for portraits of Egremont with his dogs.

74 Creevey 1948, p.293.

75 Butlin & Joll 1984, pp.164–65; no.284; the two pictures suggested here are BJ 283 and BJ 284 (or even 289). Gage suggests that the two pictures hanging on Creevey's visit were BJ 288 and BJ 289 (Gage 1980, p.250). Herrmann concludes that the two studies were hanging at this time to be replaced later by their smaller finished versions (BJ 283 and BJ 284; Herrmann 1986, p.34).

76 Creevey 1948, p.293.

77 The Turner paintings are consistently referred to by the following titles in the catalogues of the pictures at Petworth: 'Chichester Canal' (fig.80; BJ 290); 'Petworth Park' (fig.76; BJ 288); 'Brighton from the Sea' (fig.82; BJ 291); and 'Petworth Lake', or 'The Lake in Petworth Park' (fig.78; BJ 289). See Phillips 1835, nos. 129, 131, 139, 141; Sockett 1856, nos. 130, 132, 140, 142; and the MS Catalogue of Pictures, *c.*1836–1901, PHA 5272–3, nos. 130, 132, 140, 142.

78 J. Ziff, ' "Backgrounds, Introduction of Architecture and Landscape": A Lecture by J.M.W. Turner', *Journal of the Warburg and Courtauld Institute*, vol.XXVI, 1963, p.142.

79 RA 1974–75, p.70, no.149.

80 Greville 1888, vol. II, p. 345. There was a nephew who inherited the title, but he left no descendants to continue the line.
81 *Sussex Agricultural Express*, 18 November 1837.
82 Leslie 1978, pp. 122–23.
83 Vine 1965, p. 127; Vine's book offers the most useful and thorough guide to the development of waterways in Sussex.
84 *Excursions* 1822, p. 5.
85 Quoted in Dallaway 1815, p. clxi.
86 Young 1808, pp. 423–24.
87 Dallaway 1819, p. 330.
88 Young 1808, p. 436.
89 *Ibid.*, p. 202.
90 *Ibid.*, p. 422.
91 Vine 1965, p. 2.
92 *Ibid.*, p. 38.
93 Dallaway 1815, p. clxi; Egremont was pressured into joining the Arun Canal Committee in order to protect the interests of the Rother which seemed threatened by proposed changes to the course of the Arun navigation at Stopham, where Rother and Arun meet; Vine 1965, pp. 38–41.
94 *The Times*, 17 October 1811.
95 Vine 1965, p. 50.
96 Wyndham 1950, p. 252; Vine 1965, p. 67.
97 See Reynolds 1984, especially nos. 34.31; 34.41; 34.45; 34.46; 34.53; 35.13; 35.16 for the River Rother; 35.18 and 35.19 depict views on the Arun.
98 See the painting, 'Grand Junction Canal at Southall Mill' ('Windmill and Lock'; BJ 101) and watercolours such as the 'Canal Tunnel near Leeds', W. 325.
99 TB CIX–1, 2, 3.
100 Cf. Constable's drawings: Reynolds 1984, nos. 34.46; 34.45; 35.13; 35.16.
101 TB CCXIII–23, 23a, 24. The book contains drawings of Petworth House from the park with pinnacles visible on the church. This would suggest that the book was in use before 1827 when this feature of the church was removed. The sketches for the Mortlake pictures (BJ 235 and BJ 239) which were exhibited in 1826 and 1827 imply that the drawings were probably made some time in 1825.
102 Vine 1965, pp. 81–82.
103 *Ibid.*, p. 127.
104 *Ibid.*, p. 89.
105 Heneghan 1958, p. 16.
106 Wyndham 1950, p. 333; Vine 1965, pp. 37–38; PHA 671 also contains several copies of the *Report of the Knaresborough Railway Committee*, *c.* 1818, a venture which succeeded the canal developments.
107 I owe this information to Mrs R. J. Freedman of York City Archives, who also informs me that Walter Fawkes, possibly Turner's patron, was appointed to the committee in April 1787, so that it is possible to assume Turner was aware of these developments at first hand.
108 Simes 1830, p. 10.
109 *Brighthelmston Suspension Pier Company Register of Shareholders*, Brighton Reference Library, share nos. 4, 5, 6.
110 Bishop 1896.
111 Butlin and Joll 1984, p. 168 (231). Constable's picture, 'Chain Pier, Brighton', RA 1827, no. 186, is now in the Tate Gallery (N 05957. Reynolds 1984, no. 27.1). Although the pier had been completed in 1823, Constable's painting seems to be the first image of it to have been exhibited at the Royal Academy.
112 See the 'Brighton and Arundel' sketchbook, TB CCX–15v, 20, 21, 22, 22v, 27, 28, 31, 31v/32, 33, 34v, 35v; and again later the 'Arundel and Shoreham' sketchbook, TB CCXLV–18, 22v/23, 67v/68.
113 The division between the Petworth, French Rivers and East Cowes groups seems to have been made on the assumption that they are each technically distinct; however, as the drawings already noted above suggest, this is not an adequate criteria for judging locations. Plate 130 (TB CCXLIV–10), traditionally thought to depict the lake in Petworth Park, seems not to relate to Petworth and perhaps shows a greater affinity with the Meuse-Moselle subjects, which it resembles stylistically (cf. TB CCXCII–35, 68, 76). Unusually for the Petworth drawings, it is inscribed illegibly in chalk on the verso. None of the other sheets which depict Petworth scenes have this kind of marking, although several of the French Rivers subjects have similar inscriptions or even mathematical calculations on their versi (TB CCLIX–177, 86, 100, 38; TB CCXXII–K).
114 Cf. TB CCLIX–26, 27, 54, 55, 57, 58, 59, 61, 62, 63, 64, 65, 66, 67, 68, 225, 226, 229, 232, 245.
115 *Sussex Weekly Advertiser*, 31 July 1826.
116 Dallaway 1819, p. 298.
117 Wyndham 1950, p. 308.
118 *Sussex Weekly Advertiser*, 31 January 1825. Egremont was the chief subscriber contributing £20,000.
119 Young 1808, p. 447.
120 Wyndham 1950, p. 308, recounts the first, rather unsuccessful attempt at introducing a vaccine against small-pox which resulted in two villagers contracting the disease, one of whom died. Petworth House was used during this crisis as an isolation ward.
121 West Sussex Record Office, Chichester: PHA 1679.
122 *Brighton Patriot*, no. 14, 1837.

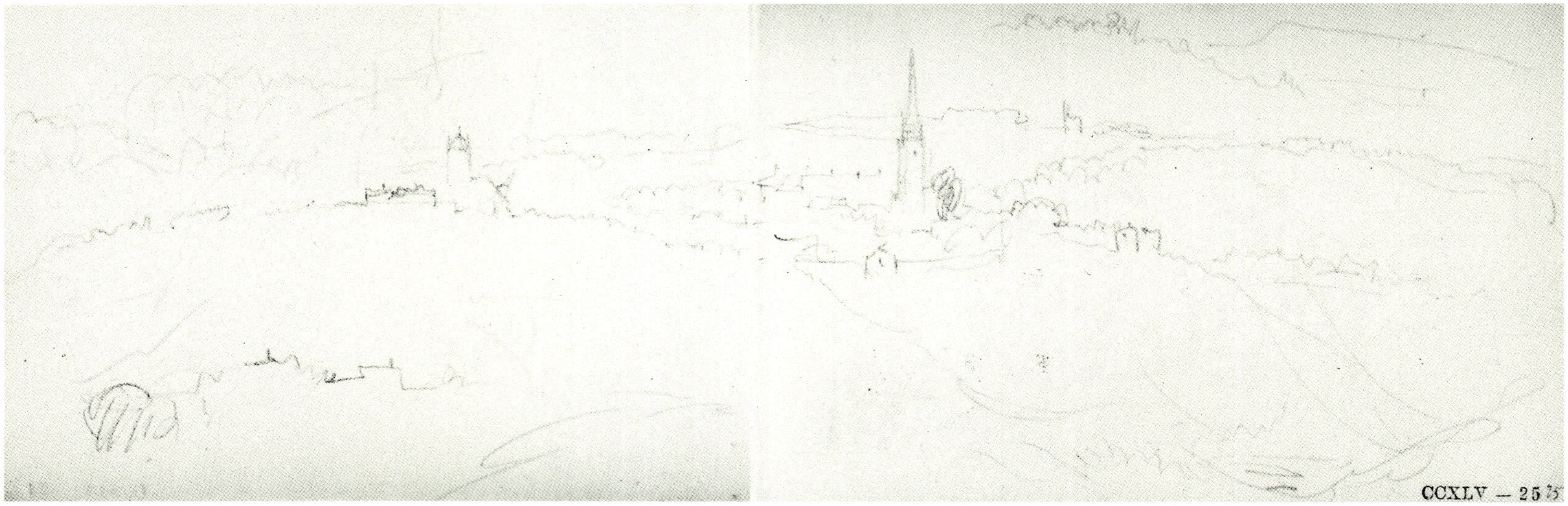

fig. 119 *Petworth from the East* ('Arundel and Shoreham' sketchbook, TB CCXLV, pp. 24v/25) *c.* 1828–30, Pencil, Page opening: 67 × 220 ($2\frac{5}{8} \times 8\frac{1}{2}$), Tate Gallery

APPENDIX II

Petworth's Architectural Landscape

The large group of gouache drawings on blue paper in the Turner Bequest (reproduced at the end of the book) are justly renowned for the insight they provide into the life of Petworth House during the years of the third Earl of Egremont. Clearly this was an environment to which Turner responded with warmth and sympathy, recording both the human incident and the architectural splendour. For the most part, the drawings made at Petworth House concentrate on its interior, with the exception of a small group which depict a service taking place in Petworth Church. This is in marked contrast with the drawings of East Cowes Castle, made at roughly the same date, which place a greater emphasis on the exterior features. The Turner scholar Patrick Youngblood has suggested that the 'exceptionally monotonous'[1] façade of Petworth House was a deterrent to any sort of satisfactory artistic representation of its external architecture. Indeed, the crisp pencil studies (figs. 3, 24; TB CIX–4 and 5), made in 1809 as preparatory notes for the painting 'Petworth, Sussex, the Seat of the Earl of Egremont: Dewy Morning' (fig. 35; BJ 113), are the most detailed record of the house Turner was tempted to make, but it would be a mistake to blame him for failing to delineate more exhaustively the exterior of the house. As a landscape painter the enfolding expanse of Petworth Park with its ethereal sunsets proved a much more conducive subject. This is not to suggest that he ceased to be interested in architecture beyond the walls of the house. Indeed, a number of previously unidentified works in the Turner Bequest testify to his wider interest in the architectural forms visible in the park and from the surrounding countryside. Most importantly, these features help to provide more precise dates for Turner's visits to Petworth.

It is interesting to look briefly at Turner's response to the façade of the house he was to visit so often. The seventeenth-century design was not such a monotonous expanse of masonry in Turner's day, although changes were afoot which contributed to its present appearance. Samuel Hieronymus Grimm's watercolour of the house made in 1780 shows a handsome pediment over the central bay breaking the otherwise unrelieved order (fig. 106). This is a detail Turner also recorded, both in his pencil sketch of 1809 (fig. 3) and in his painting 'Dewy Morning' of the following year (fig. 35). However, around 1814 Egremont consulted the architect Sir John Soane with regard to the possible introduction of a portico above the Marble Hall entrance. Soane submitted three proposals[2] and, although none of these was built, it seems probable that the central pediment was removed at this time.[3] Certainly the pediment was gone by the 1820s when contemporary engravings began to show the regular lines of the dull but imposing façade evident today (figs. 101, 134).

Turner's reaction to the loss of this pediment can perhaps be estimated from a pen-and-ink and gouache sketch (plate 67; TB CCLIX–5) related to a pencil outline in the 'Mortlake and Pulborough' sketchbook of 1825.[4] This sketch shows the house as seen from the lake, and is probably the earliest Petworth subject Turner made on blue paper. The distinctive view of the house, the lake and one of several urns which Egremont introduced into the parklands, has been metamorphosed into a 'French château, with dark trees and river'. A.J. Finberg's title for this drawing in his *Inventory of the Turner Bequest* reveals how effective the artist was at disguising the bland architecture of the great house.

Apart from the house, Turner notes other architectural features prominent in Petworth's landscape, dwelling on them in his pictures with the charged significance of *leitmotifs*. He sets out the five principal features of this landscape on the pages of the 'Arundel and Shoreham' sketchbook from a spot to the north-east of the town (fig. 119; TB CCXLV–24v/25). This view shows: the tower of Tillington church, Petworth windmill, Petworth House, the Church of St Mary the Virgin, and the prospect tower to Petworth Park, also known as the Upperton Monument.

Turner's paintings of Petworth Park usually include Tillington church and the Upperton Monument as silhouettes on the horizon of the park. Both buildings also feature in an earlier work by the portrait painter Thomas Phillips, 'Petworth Park, 1798' (fig. 100). In this picture Tillington Church appears not to have been crossed by its distinctive flying-arched tower. Nairn and Pevsner record an 'unfounded tradition' which holds that this detail was designed by Turner at Lord Egremont's behest.[5] Lady Leconfield's notes on the Petworth drawings in the British Museum's copy of Finberg's *Inventory* declare that it was always supposed that Egremont built the tower at Turner's suggestion.

Whatever the authorship, the tower was completed and paid for by 1807 in the style of those at Newcastle upon Tyne and St Dunstan-in-the-East, London.[6] Until the discovery of two watercolours showing Petworth Church made in 1792–93 (discussed below) it had seemed that Turner made his first visit to Petworth in 1809,[7] thereby making any involvement in the Tillington scheme unlikely. Given Turner's active interest in architecture from the first decade of the nineteenth century, when he began planning the construction of his villa in Twickenham, it is not altogether impossible that he may have offered his advice concerning the decoration of Tillington Church tower. In the course of his 1801 tour in the North of England, Turner had seen and recorded the tower of Newcastle Cathedral in the 'Helmsley' sketchbook,[8] which could have served as an influence on the design of Tillington.

However, if Turner did have a connection with the Tillington church scheme, it is surprising not to find a fully developed architectural drawing of the sort he made of the East Lodge Gates at Farnley Hall, which he designed for Walter Fawkes,[9] or a picturesque watercolour of the church, such as that by John Constable (fig. 120). Those drawings he has made of this subject show the church tower as a distant, yet prominent feature. The 'Petworth' sketchbook of 1827, for example, contains two double spreads with pencil drawings (fig. 74, 71; TB CCXLIII–76v/77; 77v/78) which relate to the picture 'The Lake, Petworth: Sunset; Fighting Bucks' (fig. 76; BJ 288), painted for the Carved Room.[10] In one of these the tower of Tillington Church is depicted above the main sketch as a detail he appears particularly keen to capture

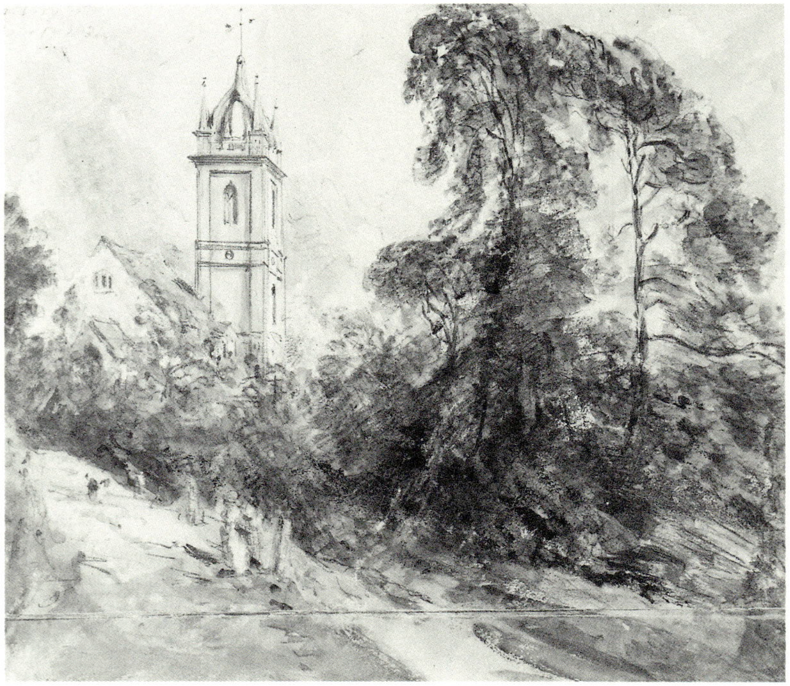

fig. 120 John Constable: *Tillington Church*, 17 September 1834, Pencil and watercolour 232 × 264 ($9\frac{1}{8} \times 10\frac{3}{8}$), Department of Prints and Drawings (1888–2–15–49), The British Museum

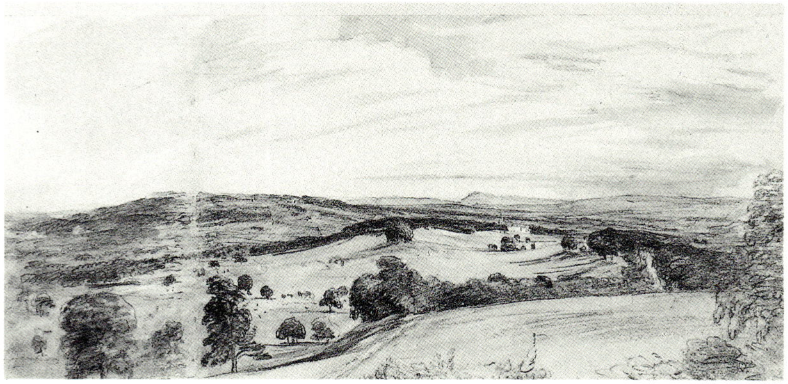

fig. 121 John Constable: *Petworth Park*, 1834, Pencil and watercolour 129 × 279 ($5\frac{1}{8} \times 11$), Department of Prints and Drawings (1887–10–10–3), The British Museum

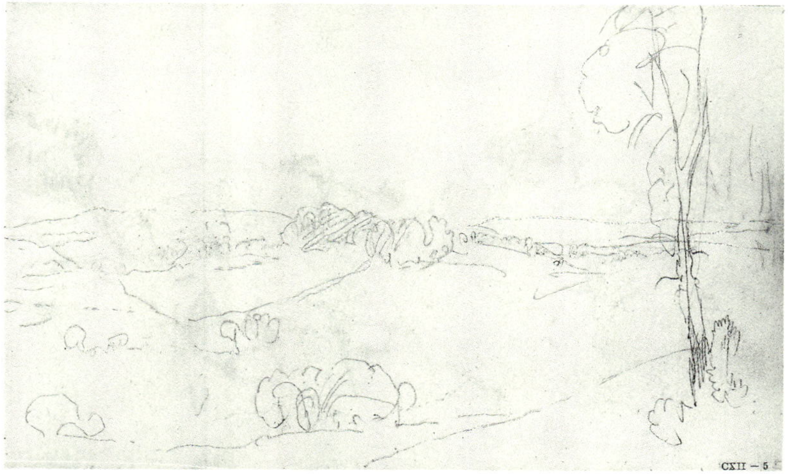

fig. 122 *Petworth Park from the Upperton Monument* ('Frittlewell' sketchbook, TB CXII, p. 5), 1809, Pencil 106 × 182 ($4\frac{1}{8} \times 7\frac{1}{8}$), Tate Gallery

fig. 123 *The Upperton Monument* ('Mortlake and Pulborough' Sketchbook, TB CCXIII, p. 19), 1825, Pencil 113 × 185 ($4\frac{7}{16} \times 7\frac{1}{4}$), Tate Gallery

(fig. 71). The tower is visible yet again in the 'Mortlake and Pulborough' sketchbook (fig. 131; TB CCXIII–18). Slight though this is as evidence of Turner's authorship of the tower, it is curious that most of the vistas of the town and park should include the tower in such a way as to suggest that it held some special significance for him. Indeed, its prominence in these paintings and drawings is strikingly disproportionate to the tower's modest size.

As well as Tillington church, Thomas Phillips's 1798 landscape shows a building which seems to approximate to the prospect tower, known as the Upperton Monument, still visible from the park today.[11] If this prospect tower was erected for Egremont in about 1815 to a design by Sir John Soane, as suggested by Gervase Jackson-Stops,[12] the tower depicted by Phillips cannot be the same building. This would seem to imply that there must have already been a similar folly on this spot at the earlier date, a conclusion which is to some extent confirmed by a picture in the Petworth Collection. The picture by the artist J. Bolteby shows an agricultural grouping of 'Two Hereford Oxen and a Ewe' dating from 1797 and includes a structure very like that in Phillips's picture on a hill beyond the cattle.[13]

One of the watercolour drawings by Constable in the British Museum associated with Petworth is a view simply entitled, 'Petworth Park' (fig. 121). This watercolour appears to have been taken from the high point in the park on which the Upperton Monument is built, perhaps actually from the top of the tower. Petworth House and church can be seen beyond the lake, which is reduced to a slight stretch of water. Turner also used this vantage point to make a series of drawings firstly in 1809 in the 'Frittlewell' sketchbook (fig. 122; TB CXII–5)[14] and again on several pages of the 'Mortlake and Pulborough' sketchbook, one of which actually includes the tower itself (fig. 123; TB CCXIII–19). This second group of unidentified drawings most probably date from 1825, thereby suggesting an earlier dating for Turner's return to Petworth after his alleged estrangement from Lord Egremont.[15]

As noted above, the Upperton Monument is present in most of Turner's paintings of the park. Two coloured drawings in the Turner Bequest also seem to depict its distinctive outline. In the first (plate 93; TB CCLIX–234) it appears high above the viewer, silhouetted against the sky. Another drawing (plate 92; TB CCXCII–58/9) shows the building from a position higher up the wooded downland on which the tower is built, but the composition is almost the same as the sketch in the 'Mort-

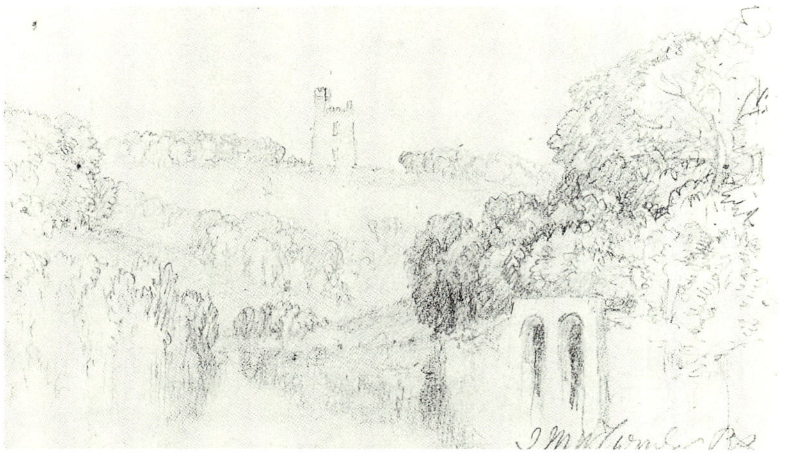

fig. 124 *The Upperton Monument seen from the Lake, Petworth Park*, 1827–28, Pencil 100 × 165 (4 × 6½), Private Collection (photograph Sotheby's)

lake and Pulborough' sketchbook (fig. 123). The style and grey paper of this subject suggests that it was made sometime later, most probably in the early 1830s.

The Upperton Monument is also depicted in one of the few Petworth gouache drawings outside the Turner Bequest (plate 91). This drawing reverses the position of the turret, so that it appears on the right-hand side instead of the left of the tower. The viewpoint in this drawing corresponds with a sheet in the Turner Bequest in which the boathouse (erected by Egremont) is seen at the right, while the monument, though surely visible to the viewer, is omitted (plate 90; TB CCXLIV–3).

An interesting drawing, remarkably similar to the latter two views, has only recently come to light on the London art market (fig. 124). This was made at the request of Mrs William Wyndham, who asked Turner and another of Egremont's visiting artists, Sir William Beechey, to make drawings for her sketching album. Taken from the lake, with the boathouse in the right-hand foreground, the drawing is exquisitely finished and complemented, rather uncharacteristically, by Turner's florid signature.[16] According to the letter accompanying the pencil drawing, both artists were then at work on pictures for Mrs Wyndham's brother-in-law, Lord Egremont. The pencil drawing for Mrs Wyndham would, therefore, seem to have been made at the time of Turner's return visit to Petworth in the autumn of 1827. This dating is partly confirmed by one of the Petworth drawings in the Turner Bequest (plate 50; TB CCXLIV–20), which shows an artist seated in front of the unfinished painting, 'Mrs Hasler as Flora' (fig. 125). This was the picture that Beechey was engaged upon during this year and the last work he was to complete for Egremont. If the dating suggested here is correct it is most likely that Turner began the pictures of Petworth Park towards the end of 1827, and the fruits of his labours were the two canvases observed by Thomas Creevey adorning the Carved Room in August 1828.[17]

The subject of Beechey's picture has another connection with Turner's work. A gouache drawing still in the Petworth Collection, known as 'Spilt Milk' (plate 20), shows Mrs Hasler, Egremont's niece.[18] Turner painted this little sheet as reparation for an accident he had caused to the young lady's dress.[19] Both this story and the apparently unpaid-for drawing made for Mrs Wyndham provide a marked contrast with an incident at Tabley House, the home of Sir John Leicester, where the artist charged Sir John for an impromptu painting lesson.[20] This once again serves to emphasise the unique attitude Turner had for all things associated with Petworth.

Almost incidental in Turner's views of the town is its windmill. This is seen in the vista of the town in the 'Arundel and Shoreham' sketchbook (fig. 119) and is also found in drawings in the slightly earlier 'Petworth' sketchbook (fig. 136; TB CCXLIII–1).[21] The windmill is more clearly discernible, however, in another watercolour by Constable (fig. 126). Two gouache studies included in the Petworth group depict windmills: one silhouetted against the sunset (plate 117; TB CCXLIV–1); the other with the moon rising behind it (plate 116; TB CCXLIV–61). However, neither seems to approximate to that recorded in the sketchbooks, suggesting that their association with Petworth is perhaps fanciful.

Of the architectural features at Petworth by far the most prominent in the pencil and gouache views is the Church of St Mary the Virgin. The church has a complex history of additions and alterations, and dates originally from Saxon times. As implied earlier, two hitherto unidentified watercolours in the Turner Bequest can be established as drawings of the church made in 1792–93. This fact was no doubt obscured by the many changes which have taken place to the church spire since 1800. Samuel Hieronymus Grimm's topographical drawing of Petworth Church in 1789 shows the original tall leaded spire from the north-east (fig. 128). The tower beneath the steeple is partly obscured by the east

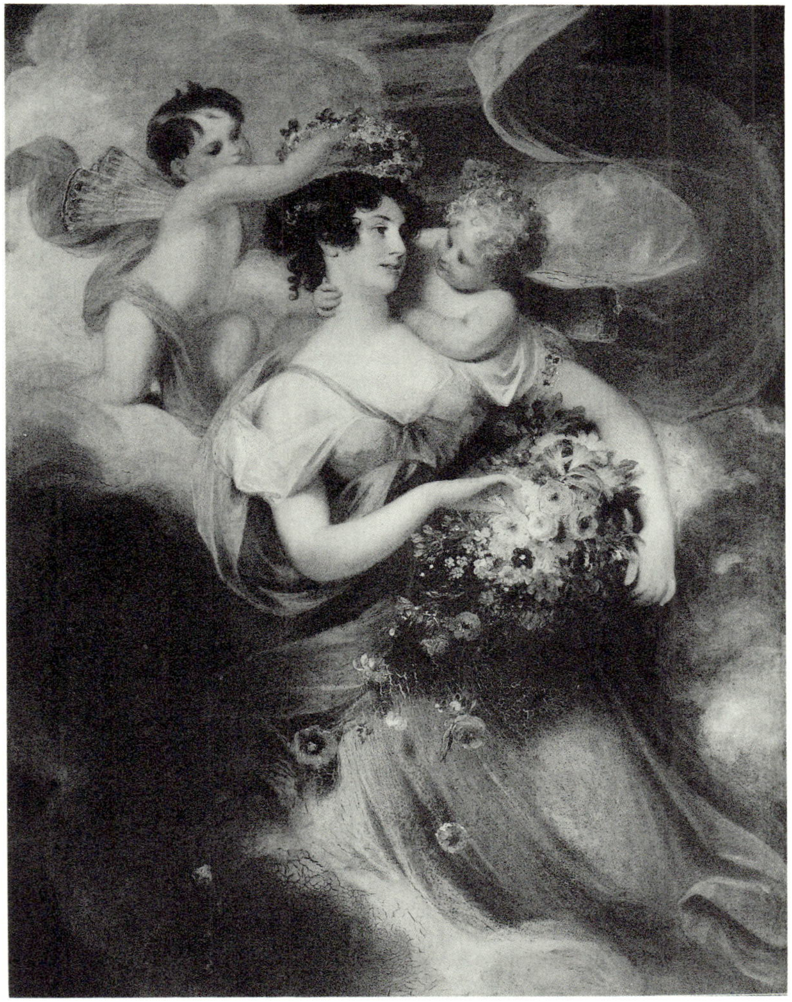

fig. 125 Sir William Beechey: *Mrs Hasler as Flora*, 1827–28, Oil on canvas 1530 × 1225 (60 × 48), Lord Egremont, Petworth House

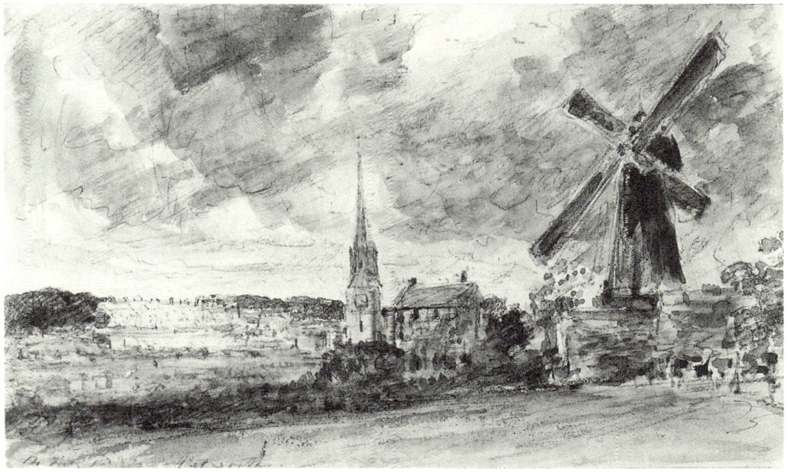

fig. 126 John Constable: *Petworth Church and Windmill*, 14 July 1834, Watercolour and pencil 137 × 231 ($5\frac{3}{8} \times 9\frac{1}{8}$), Department of Prints and Drawings (1888–2–15–60), The British Museum

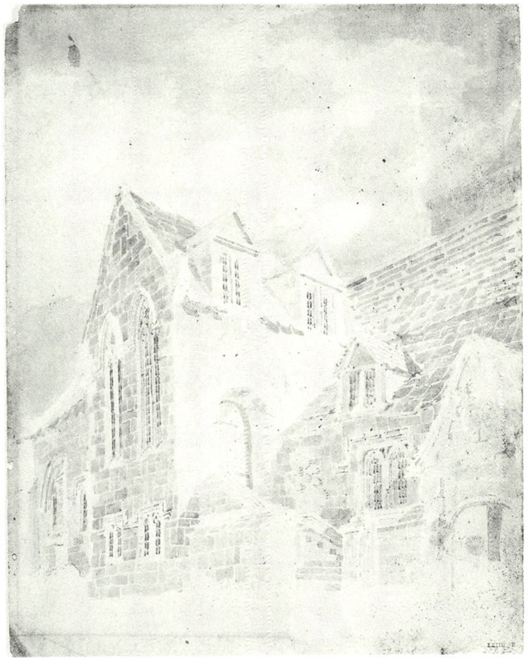

fig. 127 *Petworth Church*, 1792–94, Watercolour 270 × 212 ($10\frac{5}{8} \times 5\frac{5}{16}$), Tate Gallery (TB XXIII–E)

window of the St Thomas's Chapel in the church. The first of the two Turner Bequest drawings does not appear to have been made by Turner himself (fig. 129; TB XXVIII–I). This shows the church from very much the same angle as the Grimm drawing. In both the Grimm and the Bequest drawing the tower staircase-turret is present, a feature retained after the first spire was taken down. Both this and the distinctive baroque monument, which dominates the area in front of the chapel of St Thomas, are still evident today. The Turner Bequest drawing is crude in execution with none of the subtlety of the young Turner's topographical manner. The complex planes of the intersecting parts of the building have not been realised with any firm sense of perspective, and the drawing is quite possibly the work of one of Turner's pupils.

The other early watercolour, this time by Turner, listed by Finberg as 'Buildings in a Cathedral Close' (fig. 127; TB XXIII–E), shows the church from the north-west at a low angle close to the building, so that the building commands the full attention of the viewer. Turner has fastidiously rendered each brick of the building, as well as the effect of light passing over its surface, in a technique reminiscent of other drawings made in his late adolescence, perhaps influenced by the work of topographers such as Thomas Malton and Michael Angelo Rooker. The steps in the drawing rise to a door in the private gallery of the Egremont family, one of the oldest parts of the building. A tower and spire, the original leaded one seen in Grimm's watercolour, are only just perceptible in the top right-hand corner. Despite some alterations it is still possible to see the gabled roof above the doorway on this part of the building. A contemporary watercolour, made by Henry Petrie in 1804 (fig. 130), shows the whole church from this angle with the same details evident, although the spire by this date had been replaced by four pinnacles.[22]

The various changes made to the spire are of considerable importance to the dating of Turner's various visits to Petworth, and reveal earlier dates than have hitherto been accepted for both his first visit to the town, and for the time of his return to Petworth in the 1820s. The church had been in need of improvement for some time before Egremont's decision to remove the old spire in 1800. This spire had once been of legendary status in local rhyme:

Proud Petworth; poor people,
High Church; crooked steeple.[23]

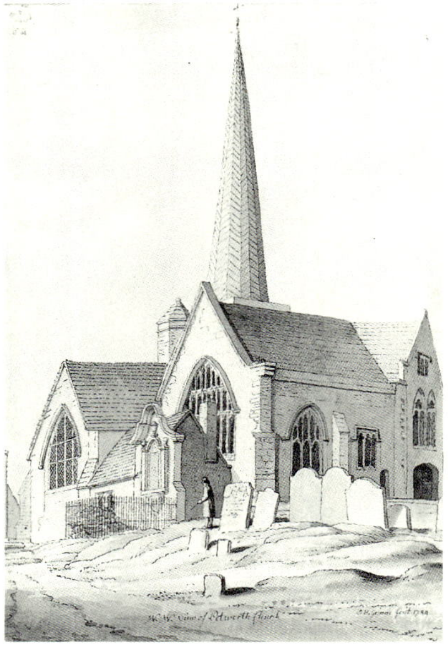

fig. 128 Samuel Hieronymus Grimm: *A North-East View of Petworth Church*, 1789, Watercolour 267 × 191 ($10\frac{1}{2} \times 7\frac{1}{2}$), The Burrell Collection (Add Burrell, 5674, fol. 54), Department of Manuscripts, The British Library

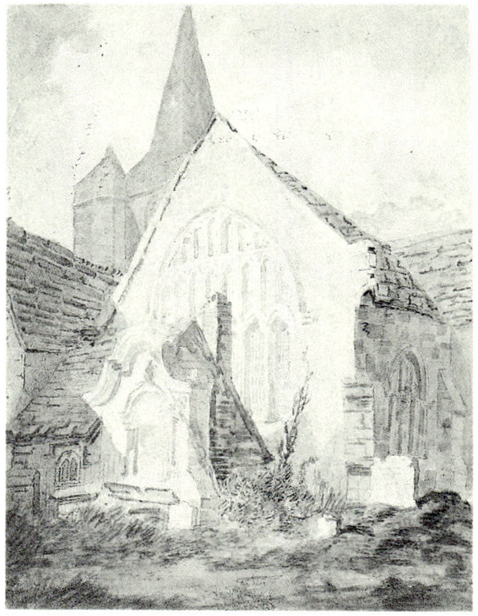

fig. 129 Unknown artist: *Petworth Church from the North-East*, *c.* 1792–94, Pencil and watercolour 272 × 212 ($10\frac{3}{4} \times 8\frac{5}{16}$), Tate Gallery (TB XXVIII–I)

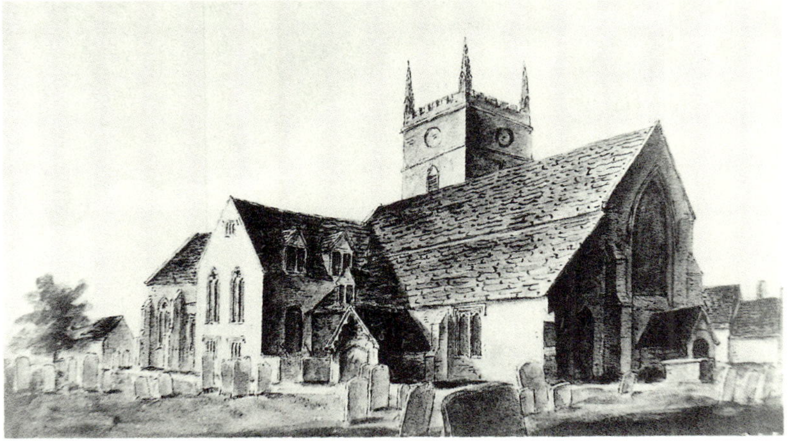

fig. 130 Henry Petrie: *Petworth Church from the North-West*, *c.* 1804, Formerly in the Sharpe Collection of Drawings, now untraced. Photograph in Brighton Reference Library

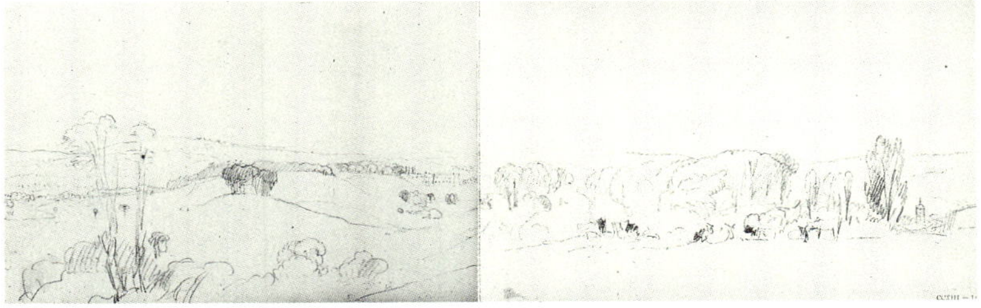

fig. 131 *Petworth Park from the Upperton Monument* ('Mortlake and Pulborough' sketchbook, TB CCXIII, pp. 17v/18), 1825, Pencil, Page opening: 113 × 370 ($4\frac{7}{16} \times 14\frac{1}{2}$), Tate Gallery

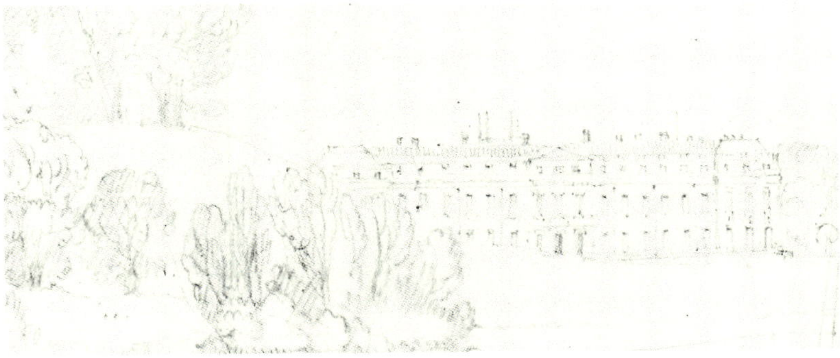

fig. 132 *Sketch for 'Dewy Morning'* (detail) ('Petworth' sketchbook, TB CIX, p. 4), 1809, Pencil 225 × 370 ($8\frac{7}{8} \times 14\frac{1}{2}$), Tate Gallery

The spire gone, the tower was 'finished off with pinnacles'[24] and remained so until March 1827 when the construction of a new spire began.

As well as preparatory drawings for the two 'Mortlake' paintings (BJ 235, exh. 1826, and BJ 239, exh. 1827), the 'Mortlake and Pulborough' sketchbook contains a group of pencil views made at the Upperton Monument,[25] presumably in 1825, the year before Turner exhibited the first of the 'Mortlake' subjects. In a panoramic view looking down to Petworth House from the Upperton Monument, Turner defines the pinnacles of the church tower with particular care (fig. 131; TB CCXIII–17v/18). It is not really surprising to find him recording this kind of detail, albeit very much as secondary information to his main concern; one of Turner's earliest biographers, Walter Thornbury, wrote that he was insistent on recording every visible feature of a landscape down to the last church spire.[26]

Turner had also recorded the four pinnacles on the church tower in 1809 when drafting a preparatory sketch (fig. 132) of the view of Petworth House from the lake for 'Dewy Morning' (fig. 133). It is therefore rather curious that while the pencil drawing of 1809 has pinnacles, the painting exhibited at the Royal Academy in the following year clearly shows a spire which resembles that erected in 1827 by Sir Charles Barry (fig. 138). The discrepancy between drawing and painting seems to be undocumented in any records at Petworth House.[27] It is perhaps most likely, therefore, that Turner simply painted in this feature on a later

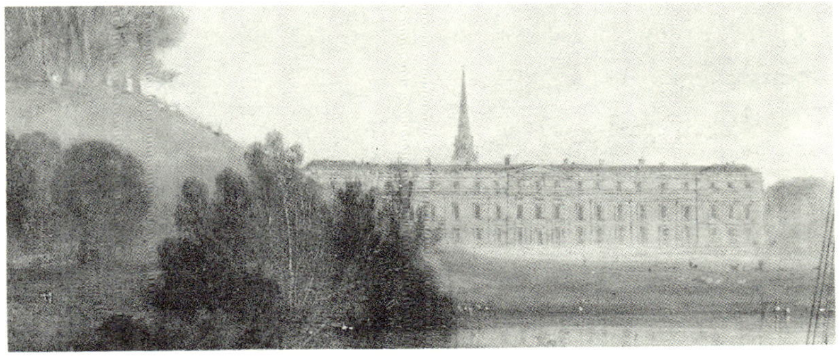

fig. 133 *Dewy Morning* (detail) (BJ 113), 1810, Oil on canvas 914 × 1206 ($36 \times 47\frac{1}{2}$), Petworth House

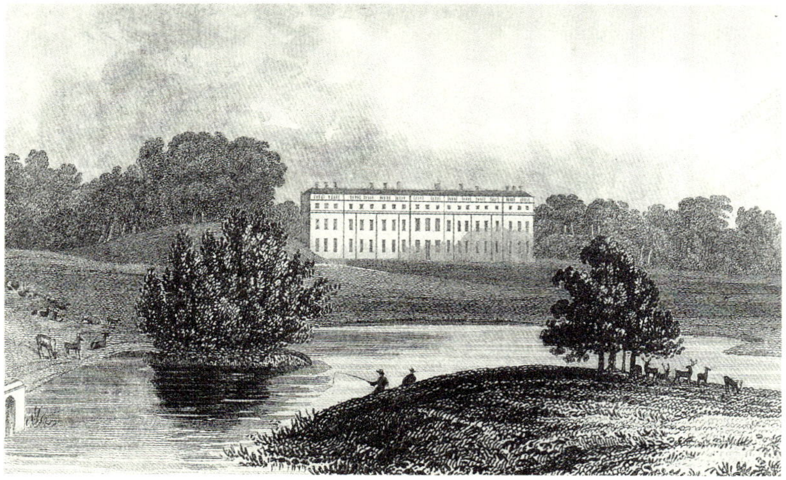

fig. 134 *Petworth House, Sussex. The Seat of the Earl of Egremont*, 65 × 110 ($2\frac{1}{2} \times 4\frac{1}{4}$), West Sussex Record Office, Chichester

visit once Barry's spire had been completed, thus making the picture a more precise record of Egremont's improvements to his estate, while also offering a vertical interest to the composition. Moreover, on close inspection, there is in fact evidence of some repainting to the canvas. It is interesting to note at this point that contemporary engravings show the view from the lake, in compositions reminiscent of Turner's painting, with neither spire nor pinnacles (fig. 134). Recent commentators on the architecture of Petworth, most notably Nairn and Pevsner, have found the idea of a spire appearing behind the house strangely 'puzzling',[28] but Turner's contemporaries felt that the church spire was an essential feature, breaking the rigid horizontal lines of the house. Indeed, according to Murray's *Handbook for Travellers in Kent and Sussex*, the façade was no better than 'a strip from an indifferent London terrace'.[29] The need for the upward relief that the church spire provided was surely an opinion with which Turner agreed, for in one of his vignettes, executed to illustrate the poems of Thomas Campbell, he included a incidental study of the house with Charles Barry's new spire behind it (fig. 135).[30]

Despite the evidence for Turner's return to Petworth in 1825, it is only from 1827 that he seems to have renewed with any frequency his

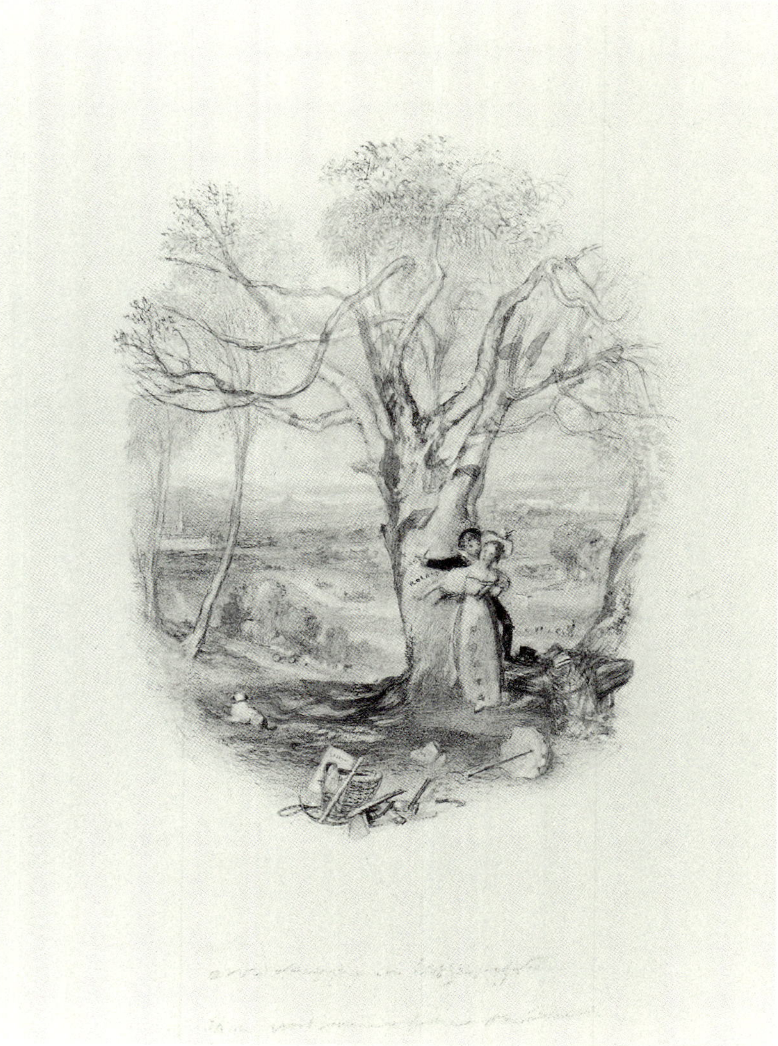

fig. 135 *The Beech Tree's Petition*, *c.* 1835, Watercolour 130 × 110 vignette ($5\frac{1}{8} \times 4\frac{5}{16}$), National Galleries of Scotland, Edinburgh (w.1286)

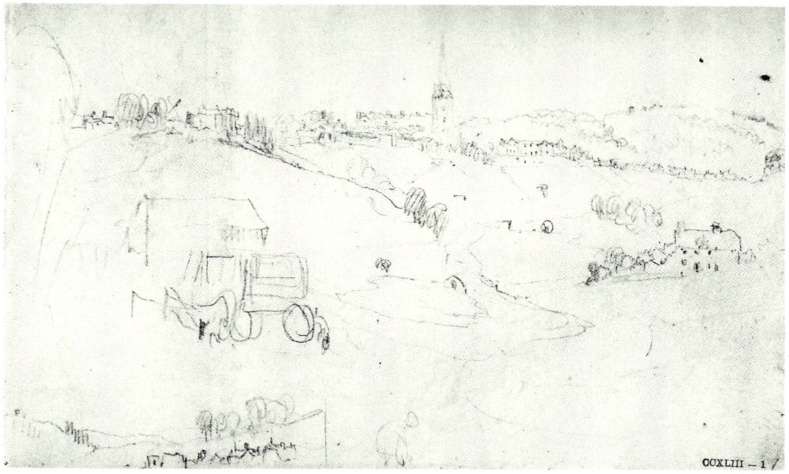

fig. 136 *Petworth from the East* ('Petworth' sketchbook, TB CCXLIII, p. 1), 1827, Pencil 113×188 ($4\frac{1}{2} \times 7\frac{3}{8}$), Tate Gallery

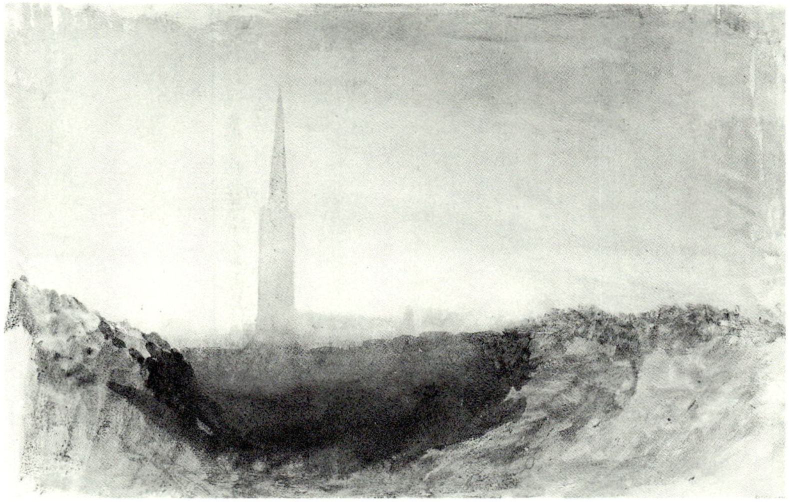

fig. 137 *?Petworth Church*, *c.* 1828–30, Watercolour 308×487 ($12\frac{1}{8} \times 19\frac{1}{8}$), Tate Gallery (TB CCLXIII–304)

old association with Egremont and Petworth. This was the year that Turner apparently visited the house both in late July, before he went to East Cowes Castle, and in October on his return.[31] The renewal of Turner's connection with Egremont prior to these visits was no doubt strengthened when the two men met at the Tabley House picture sale on 7 July, at which Lord Egremont bought 'Tabley, Cheshire: the Seat of Sir J. F. Leicester, Bart: Calm Morning' (fig. 34; BJ 99). It is quite possible that an invitation to Petworth House was extended at this time and Turner interrupted his journey to the Isle of Wight by spending a few days with a sympathetic host.

The renewed association is reflected both in the large group of gouache subjects and in pencil drawings in the Turner Bequest sketchbooks which show him inspecting the town from the surrounding countryside. In a group of pencil sketches in the 1827 'Petworth' sketchbook[32] the outline of the newly erected steeple of Petworth Church appears in its towering glory as a beacon proclaiming Egremont's country seat (fig. 136; TB CCXLIII–1). The spire was an impressive one hundred and eighty feet high and easily replaced the old crooked spire as a local landmark. The gouache drawings of the park and countryside often include it as an outcrop appearing above the trees and hills of the rustic arcadia (plates 84, 119, 120, 121, 123). Among the large number of drawings known as 'Colour Beginnings' in the Turner Bequest, there is a watercolour which seems to be closely related to at least two of these Petworth gouaches (fig. 137; TB CCLXIII–304). In particular, it appears very close in composition to TB CCXLIV–5 (plate 120), where the outline of Petworth House is defined with a cluster of peaks at the right resembling its chimneys, a motif repeated in the 'Colour Beginning'. It is perhaps possible that Turner may have considered using a finished design, based on this watercolour, as an engraved plate for his *Picturesque Views in England and Wales.*

The spire of Petworth Church was designed by Charles Barry at an early stage in the architect's career (fig. 138). Upon winning a public competition Barry had received a commission for the design of Brighton's new church, St Peter's, and work on this project had begun in 1824 when plans were sent to the Royal Academy.[33] The original conception of St Peter's included a proposal for a steeple, the design for which was exhibited at the Royal Academy in 1826, although this was never built.[34] It seems to have been this design which brought the young Barry to Egremont's attention and resulted in a commission and the exhibited steeple design for St Mary's, Petworth,[35] as well as proposals for alterations to Petworth House itself.[36]

As noted above, work on the spire began in March 1827 and continued throughout that summer. The Turner Bequest includes a gouache drawing of the church spire during the period of its construction (plate 104; TB CCXLIV–52), as well as a pencil outline on the verso of TB CCXLIV–16 (fig. 139). The view in the gouache drawing is taken from the Fountain Court, a space created by the walls of the house, the Conservatory, the Service block and a covered corridor, but which is no longer evident. In the centre of the sketch we see figures around the Triton Fountain, based on a statue by Giambologna, which gave the little court its name.[37] The fountain stood outside the windows of the Square Dining-Room, as seen in the watercolour by Thomas Phillips's wife, Elizabeth Frazer (fig. 140),[38] although it was later removed in 1869 to the green on the south side of the house, where it remains today.[39] Beyond the fountain in Turner's drawing looms the unfinished steeple of the church, apparently still incomplete at this stage.

The progress of work on the spire also has a significant bearing on the dates of Turner's visits that year. In the Petworth House Archives' list of *Works done at the Church of Petworth at the cost of George Obrien Earl of Egremont*, the entry for 15 October 1827 reads, 'Vane was fixed on the spire' suggesting the apparent completion of the project.[40] Although the vane and peak of the steeple are not visible in drawing TB CCXLIV–52, the unfinished condition of the structure seems to indicate that the drawing must have been made at some time previous to this date. As most scholars are agreed that the main series of Petworth gouaches were executed all on one visit,[41] this would mean dating the group to the brief period of time before Turner went to East Cowes Castle. By providing a date sufficiently close to the time at which the gouache and pen-and-ink drawings of East Cowes Castle were made, an explanation is found which helps to account for the confusion over the identification of some of the blue paper sheets made at Petworth and on the Isle of Wight.[42]

Work done on the spire soon after its completion does not contradict the apparent solution to the problems of dating the drawing of the unfinished spire. Murray's *Handbook* notes that once the spire was finished Barry 'took down the tower beneath it and reconstructed it, leaving the spire meanwhile under-pinned by scaffolding'.[43] Turner's drawing, however, shows the spire under construction, the tower beneath it ap-

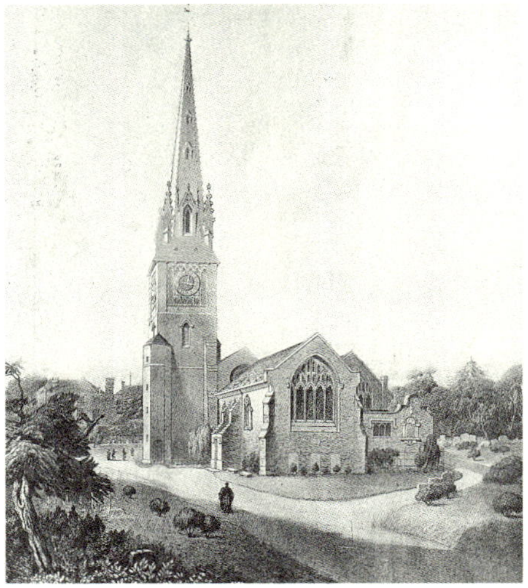

fig. 138 After Thomas Henwood: *Petworth Church with the New Spire Designed by Charles Barry, Esq.*, c. 1830, 446 × 352 (17½ × 13¾), West Sussex Record Office, Chichester

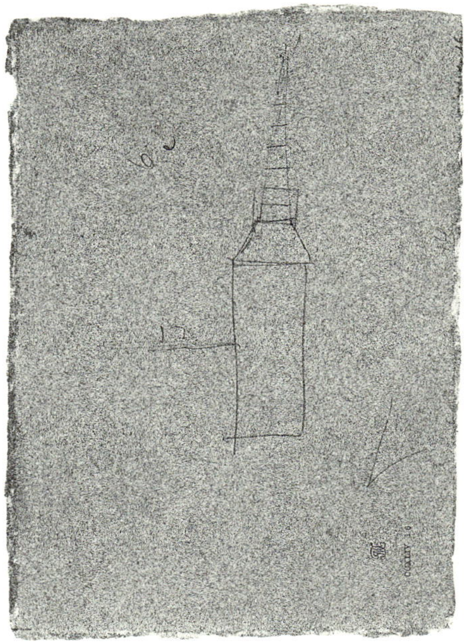

fig. 139 *The Outline of Petworth Church Tower and Spire*, 1827, Pencil on blue paper 190 × 140 (7½ × 5½), Tate Gallery (TB CCXLIV–16 verso)

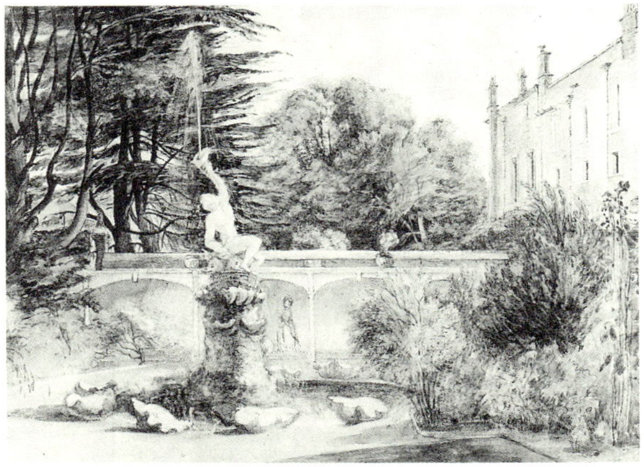

fig. 140 Mrs Elizabeth Phillips: *The Fountain Court, Petworth*, 1829, Pencil and watercolour with white highlight 210 × 306 (8¼ × 12), Private Collection

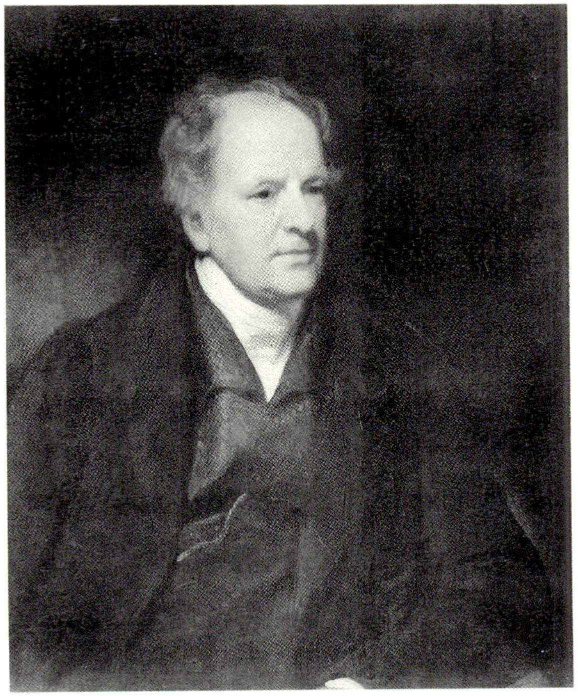

fig. 141 Thomas Phillips: *Rev. Thomas Sockett*, 1841, Oil on canvas 765 × 510 (30 × 25), Lord Egremont, Petworth House

pearing to be sound. The Petworth House Archives' list of *Works done at the Church* again verifies this conclusion. At first it was thought that the walls of the old tower were of a thickness to support the extra weight of the new spire. However, the entry immediately after the erection of the weathervane records that:

> the tower having cracked above the arch in the church, and on examination been reported unsafe Lord Egremont gave orders to have it effectually strengthened – for which purpose it was deemed necessary to close the Church, and a licence was obtained from the Bishop to have divine service in the Town Hall – Sunday Dec 31st / [18]27 was the last time the Church was used, and it remained closed until Oct 4 1829.[44]

The closure of the Church between 1827 and 1829 also has an important bearing on the dating of the gouache drawings of the interior, which clearly show a service in progress seeming to confirm the dating to 1827. The identification of the subject of these drawings has understandably eluded scholars until comparatively recently,[45] due largely to the two sets of alterations which have since taken place: the 1827–29 alterations by Lord Egremont and Sir Charles Barry, and those of 1903–4 by Lord Leconfield and Thomas Kempe.

The man responsible for Petworth Church at this time was the Reverend Thomas Sockett (1777–1859) (fig. 141). Sockett had come to the Petworth household through his association with experimental science, rather than for any spiritual values Egremont might have divined in him. Sockett's father possessed an electrical machine which was said to cure illness.[46] On hearing of this Egremont was naturally intrigued and brought the young Sockett, a man whose 'acquaintance with experimental science was accurate and extensive',[47] to Petworth where he was engaged to help supervise the education of Egremont's own children before being sent to Oxford in 1806 at the Earl's expense. He was ordained in 1809 while still an undergraduate,[48] and after brief tenures in livings at Tadcaster and in Lincolnshire he returned to Sussex in 1811 as curate of Northchapel, an appointment which was augmented four years later by the offer of the Rectory at Duncton.[49] This was followed on the death of the Rev. Charles Dunster in 1816 by his appointment as Rector of Petworth. The living was then one of the richest in Sussex with an estimated annual income of upwards of £1700.[50]

As well as completing a catalogue of the picture collection of Petworth House, Sockett administered a project which helped the poor of Petworth and its neighbouring towns to emigrate to Canada. Egremont met the costs for this project from his own purse, with passage rates at £15 per adult and £8.10 per child (including new outfits for each individual). A total of seven hundred and thirty individuals travelled to Canada under these conditions in 1832 and 1833.[51] As Sockett wrote in the pamphlet propagating the idea of emigration, this method proved highly popular with the emigrees who found that,

> by enduring a few weeks of inconvenience and fatigue, they are elevated to a class in society, far above that they before occupied. *Here* they are regarded by many as an incumbrance, and their rapid encrease [*sic*] as a national evil: in *Upper Canada* they are looked upon as the main strength of the country, and a national benefit.[52]

Despite the apparent harmony of interests, local tradition asserts that there was friction between the house and the rectory.[53] Certainly Sockett was banned from the house at the time of Egremont's death apparently because Egremont felt that Sockett's conduct in the 1837 election was unacceptable.[54] The Turner Bequest drawing TB CCXLIV–86 (plate 17), referred to as the 'Vicar on the Hearthrug' since the *Inventory of the Turner Bequest* of 1909, most probably shows Sockett with some guests in the White Library, although other visitors to Petworth recalled the presence of various clerical visitors as a usual feature of the house.[55]

The presence of clergy, however, does not seem to have ensured the practice of religious ceremony in Petworth House. Indeed a comment made by Arthur Young in 1797 reveals the lack of religious observance in its chapel, which had anyway become a studio for the sculptor, Edward Carew, by the 1820s:

> Yet Egremont does all that could be wished as far as humanity, charity, and doing moral benefit can – but no religion. In the chapel, no worship, no hats off but my own – dreadful example to a great family and to his children and to the 2,500 people in the town.[56]

Former identifications of those gouache drawings showing a service in progress as of Petworth Chapel are therefore historically improbable, and, as the rest of this chapter will demonstrate, equally as impossible from an architectural viewpoint.

Admittedly, once inside the church, to try to locate the particular position from which Turner made his drawings can be, as Nairn and Pevsner said of the church as a whole, an 'exasperating puzzle'.[57] The Wyndham Family Gallery, in the north transept adjoining the Chapel of St Thomas, is the oldest part of the fabric, and provides the easiest point from which to get the bearings of the church as it is depicted in Turner's sketches. In TB CCXLIV–63 (plate 105), Turner gives a view from Egremont's balcony-pew with richly-dressed figures kneeling, while the figure of a parson arrayed in black, presumably that of the Rev. Thomas Sockett, gesticulates with apocalyptic fervour. His high pulpit is positioned on the south side of the nave in a central position where it remained until the present one was placed on the north side of the church at the beginning of the twentieth century.

Another drawing (plate 107; TB CCXLIV–66) shows Sockett in the upper pulpit with the chancel behind framed by a low arch. This arch was rebuilt and heightened in the 1827 alterations. To the right of the pulpit in TB CCXLIV–63 is the arch of the south transept, on which the church tower is built. This also appears in TB CCXLIV–65 (plate 106). In both these views the first of three south windows in the chancel is apparent. Both transept-arch and chancel-window are now blocked by the addition of the present organ. The corresponding chancel-window as well as small windows above the chancel-arch can be seen in a watercolour of *c.*1804 by Henry Petrie (fig.142) of the exterior of the church. In TB CCXLIV–65 these small windows are also apparent, although during the 1827 alterations they were replaced by a rose-window of German glass.

The pulpit is seen again in TB CCXLIV–62 and 64 (plates 108, 109). The first of these is a view from the north-east, below the Egremont family gallery, showing the cramped galleries in the south aisle of the nave. The second drawing, TB CCXLIV–64, presents more of a problem in that the organ depicted is no longer present in the church to provide any clues. There was, however, at this time a two-tiered balcony across the west end of the nave complete with organ loft.[58] The drawing must have been made from behind the pulpit in the chancel looking down the length of the nave, although Turner has neglected to draw the nave arches that must have been visible.

A view looking across the nave to the south shows the old high-

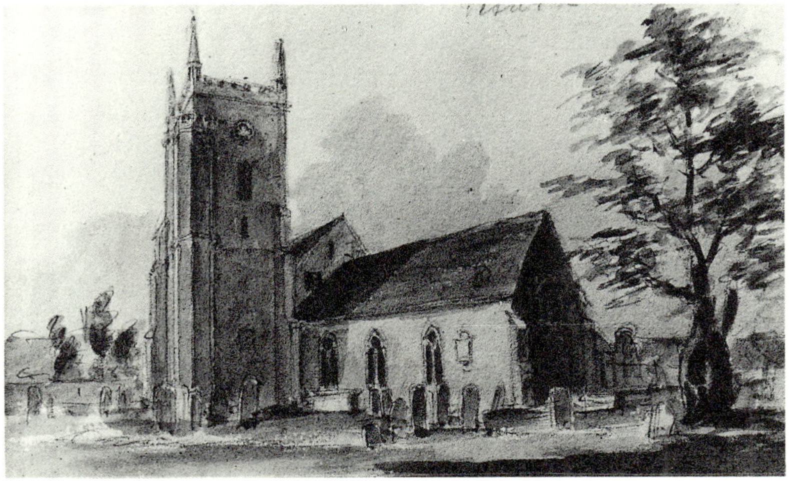

fig. 142 Henry Petrie: *Petworth Church from the South-East*, *c.* 1804, Watercolour 110 × 180 ($4\frac{5}{16} \times 7\frac{1}{8}$), The Sharpe Collection (no. 256), Michelham Priory

backed pews with their carved *fleur-de-lys* heads (plate 110; TB CCXLIV–68). In this and TB CCXLIV–67 (plate 111) the gallery can be seen running round the church. Despite Egremont's expensive additions in 1827, only the west end of the church is galleried now. The drawing on sheet TB CCXLIV–35 (plate 112) appears to show a view from the south balcony. In this scene the reddish-brown box at the centre-left of the drawing resembles the pulpit in TB CCXLIV–65. Some idea of how the church must have looked before the alterations were made which destroyed the symmetry of the aisles can be gained from TB CCXLIV–67, in which the fourteenth-century arches appear still intact throughout the building.

Other subjects linked with the church (plates 115, 114; TB CCXLIV–88, 91)[59] are in fact probably impossible to place with certainty. However TB CCXLIV–71 (plate 113), which has been variously identified as the Hall or the Chapel of Petworth House, in fact seems to show the chancel and altar of the church. The white form in the centre of the drawing suggests the bulk of a piece of sculpture, in outline reminiscent of the copy of Michelangelo's 'Pietà', which is now placed in the chapel corridor of Petworth House.[60] The author of the 1821 guidebook, *Excursions in the County of Sussex*, refers to a work in the church which had 'a claim to the character of the curious, rather than the excellent'. This statue depicted 'a female, supporting the nude figure of a man with a beard, on her knees and her left arm'.[61] Furthermore, the author of the guidebook notes that the statue 'has been mischievously mutilated since its erection here', and the sculpture now in Petworth House has, sadly, lost several fingers and toes. As there is no sculpture in the church which fits these descriptions, the identification of the sculpture as the 'Pietà' seems most probable. The window above the wooden reredos in TB CCXLIV–71 also relates to the small altar-window evident in the Henry Petrie watercolour of the church (fig. 142), predating any of the major structural alterations. The Petworth Church Logbook notes that in 1827 'a new gothic stone window with stained glass was erected at the East end of the Chancel, instead of the wooden framed one formerly there'.[62]

Somewhat inevitably Egremont's improvements to the church of 1827–29 changed the original structure, but these were not the first alterations he had instigated. As well as removing the dangerous old spire in 1800, Egremont had paid for stained-glass windows in the south bays, and then in 1812 he had introduced an organ between the arches of the St Thomas Chapel at a cost of between £500–600.[63] Changes due to lack of pew space occurred in 1816,[64] and during the 1827 alterations Egremont seems to have availed himself of the opportunity to expand the seating further. This was obviously a pressing point among the local parishioners, as a letter in the Petworth House Archives, petitioning Lord Egremont for improved seating, testifies.[65] The extent of these repairs involved replacing the south and west walls, putting in a new west window and door, and revising the gallery arrangements, as well as providing a new roof, new pews, windows and heating.[66]

This enlarged seating, by the addition of two hundred and seventy-four making a total of something like one thousand seats, transformed the appearance of the building most dramatically. Many felt that it suffered what amounted to a virtual rebuilding in the Victorian 'Gothic' style. Murray's *Handbook* bemoaned the 'numerous and heavy' galleries which gave the church a 'most theatrical appearance'.[67]

Despite criticisms of this kind, Egremont's achievement in rebuilding a church that was becoming increasingly decayed must be borne in mind. The total cost for the 1827 spire and the various improvements came to more than £16,000, which, contemporary sources insist, gave the church a 'style of convenience and accommodation, which no other church in the county, and few in any other can equal',[68] and a photograph taken before the most recent alterations of 1903 shows that the church did have a certain unity that it no longer possesses (fig. 143).[69]

Unlike the Earl's artistic patronage, the fruits of his architectural improvement have, unfortunately, been somewhat lost to time. With the different demands of a new century, the church Egremont shaped has been greatly transformed, almost beyond recognition. Many of the rooms of Petworth House, however, testify to the good taste which lay behind the internal modifications he made. The park also bears the stamp of the Earl's hand, both in the buildings he chose to erect there and in equally significant features such as the classical urns placed about the parklands with picturesque ease. The success of Petworth's landscape – the consumately created natural prospect augmented by buildings of memorable simplicity – is at its most pervasive in Turner's depictions. In the many paintings and drawings of Petworth Turner reflects its architectural landscape in his own distinctive vision creating a unique and near perfect synthesis of art and nature.

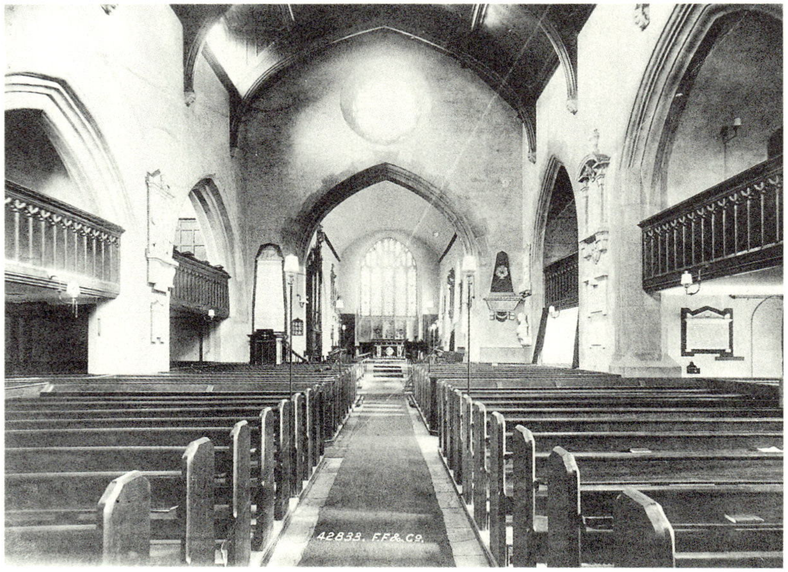

fig. 143 Francis Frith: *Petworth Church before the alterations by Thomas Kempe*, *c.* 1899, Photograph. Worthing Reference Library (P1194)

Notes

1 Youngblood *Turner Studies* 1983, p. 16.
2 Jackson-Stops 1977 (1), p. 332.
3 Sockett 1856. Sockett confirms that it was Egremont who removed the 'quadrangular roof in the form of a truncated pyramid', p. xxii.
4 This appears to be related to a sketch in the 'Mortlake and Pulborough' sketchbook, TB CCXIII–22a. The 'Mortlake' paintings (BJ 235 and BJ 239) based on sketches in this sketchbook suggest a date at least as early as 1825. Andrew Wilton appears to have been the first to identify correctly the pen-and-ink and gouache sketch as a view of Petworth House (BM 1977–78, p. 43, no. 24).
5 Nairn and Pevsner 1970, p. 351.
6 Dallaway 1819, vol. II, part 1, p. 266. Horsfield 1835, vol. II, p. 181.
7 Butlin and Joll 1984, pp. 79–80.
8 TB LIII–94a/95.
9 Wilton 1979, p. 638, no. 589, 'Gate and Lodges, Farnley'. This was based on a sketch in the Turner Bequest, TB CLIII–13/14.
10 There are also two loose sheets in the Turner Bequest of around this date (figs. 72, 73; TB CCCXLI–225, 380) which relate to the Petworth Park pictures. These drawings could perhaps have been aids to Turner whilst composing the paintings of the wide expanse of Petworth Park. The first condenses the central part of the view from the four pages used in the sketchbook to one sheet, while the second drawing breaks the picture-space down into three sections: two of which concentrate on the areas which eventually become peripheral in the finished painting: the trees and road leading off at the right of the image, and the distant monument beyond the gentle slopes of the hill at the left. Although both sheets are roughly the same size as the pages of the sketchbook, they do not seem to have been part of the book at any stage: the paper is of a much coarser quality and without the watermark in the sketchbook ('A Lee 1819').
11 B. Jones, *Follies and Grottoes*, 1974, p. 402. 'Tillington. Upperton Monument. Tower, late eighteenth century (SU 9722). A three-storey plain stone castellated tower, rectangular in plan, with round-headed windows and a taller octagonal staircase turret; probably a prospect tower to Petworth'.
12 Jackson-Stops 1977 (1), pp. 324–33.
13 Collins Baker 1920, p. 8, no. 547. I would like to thank Mrs Leyland of Petworth House for helping locate this and several other pictures and Lord Egremont for kindly allowing me to see them.
14 Finberg calls this the 'Frittlewell' sketchbook through an erroneous reading of the inscription on f. 6. The drawing on this page shows Fittleworth Church, recognisable despite substantial alterations in the nineteenth century.
15 For the possible causes behind the estrangement of artist and patron see Nicholson 1980, pp. 679–84.
16 Sotheby's, 14 July 1988, lot 14; the drawing came complete with a letter giving its history, dated 22 March 1872, written by Emily Lewes, the niece of the third Earl of Egremont.
17 For a discussion of the possible identity of the two pictures seen by Creevey see pp. 116–17.
18 Julia Hasler appears to be Egremont's niece, not his grand-daughter as stated erroneously on the verso of

the drawing and in Wilton 1979, p. 404, no. 906. I am grateful to Alison McCann for confirming this, and providing help over the identity of Emily Lewes (see n. 16).

19 This information is given on the verso of the drawing.

20 W. Jerdan, *An Autobiography*, 1852, vol. II, p. 260, quoted in Gage 1987, p. 163.

21 See also TB CCXLIII–1V and 2.

22 This work is at present untraced. The image shown in fig. 130 is reproduced from a photograph stored at Brighton Reference Library among a survey of Sussex Churches. Like fig. 142, it may have belonged to the Sharpe Collection, now at Michelham Priory. Part of this collection was sold off in the late 1930s. Carolyn Jacob at Brighton Reference Library provided much help in locating this and other material.

23 Arnold 1864, p. 62.

24 *Ibid.*

25 Drawings on ff. 17a–22a of the 'Mortlake and Pulborough' sketchbook (TB CCXIII).

26 Thornbury 1862, vol. 2, p. 153.

27 Wilkinson 1974, p. 98. Wilkinson is surprisingly the only writer on Turner at Petworth who has commented on this peculiarity, but he assumes that the pinnacles are something to do with the house itself.

28 Nairn and Pevsner 1970, p. 302.

29 Murray 1877, p. 115.

30 The reason for the inclusion of the Petworth architecture in this vignette may be attributable to a fond nostalgia for the place where Turner had completed a similar series of vignettes for the poet Samuel Rogers. See Gage 1980, pp. 278–79.

31 Butlin and Joll, 1984, p. 165 cite Gage for August 1827. See also Wilton 1987, p. 166, which says Turner visited Petworth in August and October. As the Cowes Regatta began in the first week of August, Turner's stay can only have been brief at this time and most probably took place in the last week of July.

32 TB CCXLIII–1, 1V, 2.

33 Royal Academy, 1824 (955), 'View of the Church now building at Brighton, as it will appear from the Steyne'.

34 Royal Academy, 1826 (914), 'Elevation of the New Church at Brighton, with the proposed spire'. There is a drawing of the spire in the RIBA collection, listed under J. Murray, *Tracings from Charles Barry: 'Gothic and Italian'*.

35 Royal Academy, 1827 (496), 'View of the new steeple now being added to the parish church of Petworth, at the expense of the Right Honourable the Earl of Egremont'. Local tradition maintains, probably because of the similarity in their design, that the unused Brighton design was built onto the Petworth tower.

36 *On the Architectural Career of the late Sir Charles Barry by M. Digby-Wyatt, V.P.*, a lecture delivered at RIBA 21 May 1860, p. 4. As well as designing the present bannisters on the Grand Stairs of Petworth House, Barry was also involved in the building of the Sussex County Hospital in Brighton which would have brought him into contact again with Egremont, who was financially involved with its construction.

37 Several plans of the house with this feature can be found. The most accessible are: Phillips 1835 and Leconfield 1938.

38 The watercolour was also drawn on stone for the lithographic process by J. D. Harding and printed by C. Hallmandel.

39 Leconfield 1938, p. 43. Strood 1977, p. 339, reproduces the statue.

40 West Sussex Record Office, Chichester, PHA 2979.

41 See RA 1974–5, p. 111; BM 1975, pp. 116–18 (116); Gage 1980, p. 250.

42 See Youngblood *Burlington* 1983, pp. 615–19; see also p. 64 and p. 120.

43 Murray 1877, p. 114.

44 West Sussex Record Office, Chichester, PHA 2979.

45 Finberg's *Inventory* 1909, vol. II, p. 745, refers to the drawings as 'church interiors', but his *Life of J. M. W. Turner* (1969, p. 325) suggests he thought them to be of the 'interior of the Chapel'. The RA 1974–75 catalogue, p. 112 also follows this idea, as does BM 1975, p. 86 (125). The catalogue for the exhibition which toured America in 1977–78 identified the drawings correctly (BM 1977–78). See also Youngblood *Turner Studies* 1983, p. 29.

46 Leslie 1978, pp. 249–50.

47 Arnold 1864, p. 71.

48 Povey 1928, p. 40.

49 Horsfield 1835, p. 179. I would also like to thank Alison McCann for much of this information.

50 *Excursions* 1822, p. 118.

51 Sockett 1833, p. 5.

52 *Ibid.*, p. 16.

53 Jerrome 1976, p. 44; Goodsall 1963, p. 102.

54 Gundry 1981, p. 31.

55 Leslie 1978, p. 249–50; Creevey notes the presence of a chaplain at dinner (Creevey 1948, p. 291) and Haydon is careful to record a 'Mr Crow' who was 'the butt of the family, though a nice fellow' (Haydon 1963, vol. III, p. 169). Alison McCann has suggested that this may be the Rev. William Crow / Crole, Vicar of Kirdford, who was one of Egremont's illegitimate sons.

56 A. Young, *Autobiography and Correspondence*, p. 299, 26 November 1797.

57 Nairn and Pevsner 1970, p. 294.

58 Logbook in the Vestry at Petworth Church for alterations made, including pew appropriation plans. Also a photograph showing the church from the chancel, taken some time before 1903, shows the organ gallery as it was after Egremont's alterations. My thanks to the Rev. J. Green and Dr Hume for making this material readily available to me.

59 Youngblood *Turner Studies* 1983, p. 29.

60 The 'Pietà' was bought by the Proud Duke of Somerset from the Arundel Collection: see Blunt 1980, p. 130.

61 *Excursions* 1822, p. 118.

62 Logbook Petworth Church, p. 42.

63 Arnold 1864, p. 63 quotes the sum of £600, whilst the *Excursions* 1822, p. 118, suggests £500. Leconfield 1938, recalls the position of the new organ on p. 30 and p. 79.

64 Dallaway 1819, p. 301.

65 West Sussex Record Office, Chichester, PHA 6492.

66 West Sussex Record Office, Chichester, PHA 5199. This contains a full description of works done by Charles Barry in 1827–29 at Petworth Church.

67 Murray 1877, p. 114.

68 Dallaway 1832, p. 336.

69 My thanks to Martin Hayes of Worthing Reference Library for helping locate this and other early photographs of Petworth.

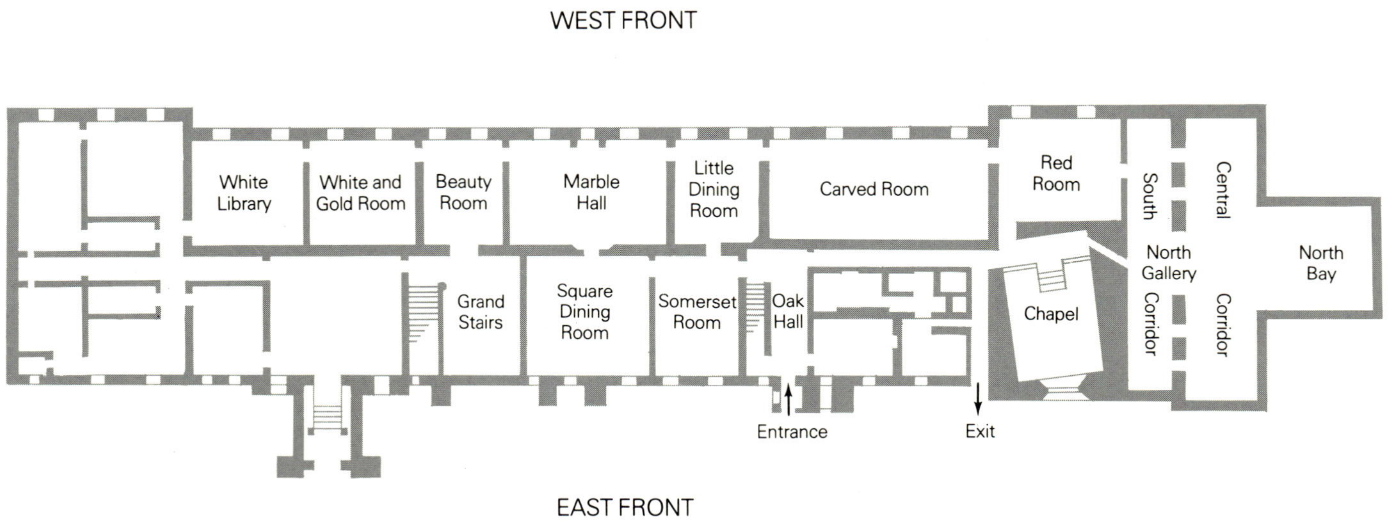

Plan of Petworth House

The Petworth Gouache Drawings

Notes on the Plates

The Somerset Room

The Somerset Room originally formed a part of the Duke of Somerset's Dining-Room and, along with the Square Dining-Room, was created by the third Earl's division of the much larger room in 1794–5.

Turner appears to have made only one drawing of the Somerset Room, and even this shows little of the room except the furnishings on either side of the door leading into the Square Dining-Room. In this drawing the painting at the left above the fireplace is Romney's picture, 'The Egremont Family', of 1795 (fig. 7). This shows the Countess of Egremont (the third Earl's wife and sometime mistress, Elizabeth Iliffe) and her four children, one of whom, George (later first Lord Leconfield, 1787–1869) is clearly seen with his bow and arrow in Turner's drawing.

[Plate 1]

The Square Dining-Room

The decoration of the Square Dining-Room was the responsibility of the third Earl. Turner's drawing of this room is one of four very precise interiors he made at Petworth lit by bright day-light. The large painting on the far south wall is a late work by Sir Joshua Reynolds, 'Macbeth and the Witches' (fig. 41). Above it is an oval picture, most probably a portrait, hung in eighteenth-century fashion from the cornice. Much of the furniture seen in the drawing can still be found in the house. This is arranged in the style of the eighteenth century with a central space created by placing the furniture at the sides of the room. According to the inventories of furniture and paintings in Petworth House, the long white console-table and chairs date from the original dining-room before its alteration. Above the smaller console-table, the picture hanging on the elongated right wall appears to be Van Dyck's 'Algernon Percy, tenth Earl of Northumberland, Lady Ann Cecil, his first wife, and their Daughter'. The room seems to have been used as a dining-room on occasions when the larger and more formal setting of the Carved Room was not needed. Writing of the social procedures of the house at the end of the eighteenth century the local poet, William Hayley, records that the artist guests dined with both their host and his wife when a large company was gathered, but that on occasions when the company was not so great the artists dined with 'Mrs Wyndham only' (this was the title by which Elizabeth Iliffe was known until her marriage to the third Earl in 1801)

[Plate 2]

Marble Hall

Despite the third Earl's consultation with Sir John Soane in *c.* 1815–17 over possible alterations to make the Marble Hall more functional as the main entrance to the house, the room remains largely as it was created by the Duke of Somerset in the seventeenth century. The decoration is chiefly of a French or Dutch baroque style with the conspicuous crest of the Duke of Somerset supported by bull and unicorn, a feature which can be seen above the fireplace in Turner's drawings.

One of these drawings shows the north side of this room (plate 3). Although the room was used as an entrance hall in the first two decades of the nineteenth century, as seen in Thomas Phillips's painting of the 'The Allied Sovereigns at Petworth, June 24, 1814', by the time of Turner's visit in 1827 a billiard-table seems to have been introduced, and the purpose of the room had changed sufficiently for H. W. Phillips (Thomas Phillips's son, also a painter) to describe it as the 'Billiard Room' in his 1835 picture-inventory.

Another drawing of the room (plate 4) shows a group of men gathered around the fireplace on the south wall, perhaps late in the evening after dinner. The light from the fire silhouettes the figures, casting long shadows over the stone floor. The painting hanging above the fireplace on the south wall was thought, at the time of its acquisition, to be 'The Duke of Urbino' by Raphael, a picture Lord Egremont valued highly enough to pay an annuity of £100 a year for life to Ozias Humphry, who sold it to him. The south and east walls in this drawing merge into each other as Turner traces the bright light falling across the room.

[Plates 3–5]

Grand Staircase

The richly painted walls of the Grand Staircase are the work of Louis Laguerre and date from after a fire in 1714 which destroyed much of this part of the house, including the old staircase.

Turner made two drawings specifically of the Grand Staircase, but it can also be seen in the drawing of the Square Dining-Room from the Somerset Room, where the right-hand door on the south wall of the Square Dining-Room is open onto the staircase hall (plate 1). Until the middle of the nineteenth century there was also a door under the stairs on the east wall which functioned as the usual entrance to the house for visitors. Both this and the door into the Square Dining-Room were sealed in 1869 and painted over, as was a small oval window under the staircase, which can also be seen in Turner's drawing (plate 6).

As in many of the scenes depicting the house and church, Turner has distorted the space in his picture so that the ceiling, the painted side-walls, and the floor can all be seen in one glance. It is impossible even to begin to try to find the place from where he made this view, but the drawing highlights Turner's technical skill in making the space in his image seem real and three-dimensional. Although Turner manages to suggest part of Laguerre's mural with the Duchess of Somerset's triumphal chariot-procession on the right wall, it is curious that the other drawing, made from the top of the Grand Staircase looking down the first-floor bedroom corridor towards the south (plate 7), does not show the mural in a more fully realised way, given the more convenient position.

[Plates 6–7]

White Library

The room was originally known as the King of Spain's Bedchamber, after a visit by the future Emperor Charles VI in 1703. During the years of the third Earl it served as the main sitting-room, and it is not surprising that its relaxed atmosphere provided the setting for many of the Petworth subjects. The White Library seen in Turner's drawings is a larger room than it is today. The third Earl had made alterations to the room, converting the former bedroom into a library, and at the same time incorporating a dressing-room further to the south, which resulted in the arched alcove on the south side of the room. However, the alcove was dispensed with at the end of the nineteenth century. Another room, the Red Library, a little further along the south end of the house, was during this period the bedroom of the third Earl, so that the adjacent White Library became a natural meeting point for those living around the ageing peer.

One of the more detailed Petworth drawings shows the view from the alcove in the Library looking through the open door down the grand *enfilade* of the house towards the North Gallery (plate 8). In the foreground is a fortepiano which is seen in several of the other drawings being played by a young woman whose long neck is reminiscent of the work of Henry Fuseli (plates 9, 19). The small portraits, mostly by Thomas Phillips, shown hanging above the bookshelves, and the busts of philosophers are still in place today, as is the circular wind-dial which is seen above the picture hanging over the chimneypiece.

Other drawings show the many inhabitants pre-occupied by their pastimes in an incredibly diverse range of lighting effects, from the even wash of bright daylight to more atmospheric moods of fire and lamplight. In many the red walls and the placings of the pictures are only loosely suggested. In these drawings Turner is concentrating on an atmosphere of convivial *bonhomie* beyond mere notations of human and canine activity. The overwhelming number of drawings of this room emphasise its importance in the life of Petworth once the sun had set and the park gates had closed. This is the heart of the third Earl's Petworth, and Turner seems to have shown him in at least two of these drawings as very much the centre of his world (plates, 13, 16).

[Plates 8–34]

White and Gold Room

Probably the most splendid of Petworth's interiors, the White and Gold Room, with its French design, was decorated during the years of the second Earl of Egremont. The room was originally intended as a drawing-room for the main state bedchamber before fashion turned against ground-floor bedrooms.

Turner's drawing (plate 35) dazzles the viewer as much as does the real room – with the brilliancy of daylight reflecting from the ivory and gilt decoration. This effect was no doubt heightened by the application of a wash of white gouache to the blue paper before work on the details of the room was begun. Again, like the drawing of the Square Dining-Room, this sheet shows the eighteenth-century fashion for uncluttered decoration with the furniture arranged around the sides of the room. The portraits seen hanging here are by Van Dyck: that on the east wall is most probably of 'Dorothy Percy, Countess of Leicester', while on the north wall the portrait seems to be that of 'Ann Carr, Countess of Bedford' (fig. 56). Amongst the other gouache drawings Turner also made a detailed copy of Van Dyck's portrait of 'Lucy Percy, Countess of Carlisle' (plate 36; see fig. 55), which, like 'Ann Carr', served as the stimulus for a figure in Turner's picture 'Lord Percy under Attainder' (fig. 94). Below the Van Dyck portraits two landscape-sized paintings hang, in much the same arrangement that Turner's four landscapes were originally hung in the Carved Room.

Another drawing of this room (plate 37) shows a man in front of the giltwood console-table and rococo pier-glass between the windows. Behind him an open door allows us to look through into the White Library, where the arch of the alcove can be seen.

[Plates 35–37]

Little Dining-Room

Originally called the Van Dyck Room, this room was used for smaller dinner-parties, and it is quite likely that the painter Benjamin Robert Haydon was entertained here when he stayed at Petworth. He boasts in his *Diary* entry for 15 November 1826 that he dined with the 'finest Van Dyck's in the world'. The Petworth picture collection seems to have been constantly on the move, for while Haydon claims one of the Van Dyck portraits to have been of 'Ann Carr, Countess of Bedford' (fig. 56), Turner seems to show this in the White and Gold Room in his drawing of a year later (plate 35).

The Turner sketch which shows this interior (plate 38) includes an impressive group of paintings, presumably the Van Dyck canvases which gave the room its name. There are also an assortment of figures whose poses suggest they are musicians. Through the open door there is a view of the Carved Room, in which a banquet is taking place, and for which the musicians are providing entertainment.

[Plate 38]

The Carved Room

The Carved Room was created as a result of the third Earl's alterations to the house interior at the end of the eighteenth century. For this he knocked two smaller chambers into one great state-room. This was not to be the end of his modifications to the room, for he commissioned Jonathan Ritson to re-position the existing carved limewood panels by Grinling Gibbons and John Seldon in the greatly enlarged environment. For this purpose some carvings were also brought from other rooms in the house; other gaps were filled by Ritson himself.

A painting by Charles Robert Leslie, now in the Tate Gallery (fig. 11), shows the north-west end of the room as it was before the wooden panels were stripped of the white and gilt paintwork. Work on this process seems to have begun *c.* 1827, at the time of Turner's sketching visit, and his drawings show the room decorated in much the same fashion as in Leslie's picture.

Besides the view of the Carved Room, seen through the open door in the drawing of the Little Dining-Room (plate 38), Turner made three other drawings of this room. The most extensive view seems to be a continuation of that done in the Little Dining-Room, almost as if Turner has stepped through the door and drawn the banquet he had already shown to be in progress (plate 39). The intricate carvings are suggested merely by a gridwork of gouache lines, which also establish the long perspective of the room. Another drawing shows what appears to be a number of figures sitting at the long table (plate 40). Constable's visit in 1834 led him to write to Leslie of the long dining-table weighed down with 'magnificent gold and silver plate'. As well as being used for banquets the Carved Room seems to have served as the focus of less formal gatherings. A local tradition records how Lord Egremont invited a troupe of travelling actors to give a performance in the Carved Room of *She Stoops to Conquer*, to which nearly 'all the townspeople of respectability' were invited.

The furnishings of the room come in for closer scrutiny in a drawing of a giltwood sidetable and two large blue and white china jars of the K'ang-hsi period (plate 41). Above the Louis XIV-style table, the Gibbons carvings can be seen on either side of a picture, probably one of the family portraits which later hung above Turner's landscapes, while a bust to the right rests on a bracket above the table.

It is entirely consistent with Egremont's enthusiasm for detail that, in his lengthy improvements to the room, he should have engaged Turner to make four panoramic landscapes to complete the decoration (figs. 76, 78, 80, 82). How far work had progressed with the stripping of the walls at the time Turner was painting the four landscapes cannot be established. However, it seems possible that Turner took into account the rich dark colour of the bare limewood carvings when painting for this room, a factor which helps to explain the differences in colour between those versions at Petworth and those at the Tate Gallery. Indeed, visiting Petworth House in the mid-1800s, the correspondent G. Storey (quoted in Thornbury's *Life of Turner*) observed that a black line needed to be painted around the canvases in order to make them more distinct from their surroundings. Another painter, George Price Boyce, commented on his visit in 1857 that the pictures were of a 'crude yellow', and it may be that their exposure on the east wall resulted in the general darkening of colour and cracking in the paintings.

Some idea of how the finished pictures would have looked hanging as pendants to the family portraits can be gained from a watercolour of the Carved Room by Mrs Percy Wyndham, executed before Turner's work was brought together in the old Red Room.

[Plates 39–41]

The Red Room (Turner Room)

Largely the product of the Proud Duke of Somerset's decoration, the room has been known as the Red, the Oak and (most recently) the Turner Room. Turner's drawing (plate 42) shows it with the warm red walls fashionable in the early part of the nineteenth century in a view looking across the room from the windows at the southern end. Tastes inevitably change and the 'horrible crimson' (as Anthony Blunt called it) was replaced in the early twentieth century by the present ochre colour as part of a programme of re-decoration by Constance, Lady Leconfield.

The portraits on either side of the door leading into the North Gallery are by Van Dyck. The sitters for these works, Sir Robert and Lady Shirley, are seen in oriental costume – Sir Robert having been an agent of the Shah of Persia.

Another portrait, this time by Reynolds, hangs above the door. This is of Georges Brydes, Admiral Lord Rodney. Other objects included in the drawing, such as the blue china and the marble busts in front of the pier-glass and at the far right, can still be found in the house.

[Plate 42]

The North Gallery

Turner's return to Petworth during the 1820s coincided with the recent completion of the North Gallery. This had been built in three stages. The corridor furthest south had been converted from the Old Chapel Cloisters by the second Earl some time after 1754 as a means of storing some of the extensive collection of antique sculpture acquired on his Grand Tour in Europe. At the end of the eighteenth century the third Earl greatly expanded this space by adding a second wider corridor, and to this he added the North Bay in 1824. Lord Egremont's rapidly increasing collection of contemporary British art was the main reason for this expansion into the area to the north of the house. Not only does the gallery house antique sculpture from the second Earl's vast collection, such as the 'Seated Statue of a Philosopher', visible in one of Turner's drawings (plate 43), but it also contains important large-scale works by contemporary sculptors. Most notably John Flaxman's 'St Michael Overcoming Satan' (fig. 14) dominates the gallery in both of Turner's drawings. This was a work of obvious interest in that it had only been completed in 1826, the year before Turner's visit.

Turner had designed and opened his own picture gallery at 47 Queen Anne Street West in 1822, and was probably interested in the improvements that had taken place to Lord Egremont's gallery since his last visit. The drawings of the gallery, made with a rare use of pencil and ink outlines, tend to dramatise the method devised for lighting pictures, a problem to which Turner had given considerable thought in his own designs for the Queen Anne Street gallery. In these Petworth drawings he pays close attention to the skylight and the lunette windows at the top of the walls in the North Bay. These semi-circular windows are no longer apparent and seem to have had a short-life, for by 1835 they had been blocked, perhaps because with both skylight and lunettes there was more than enough light, but more probably because the wall space was needed for hanging new pictures.

[Plates 43–44]

The Old Library Staircase

This staircase is in an area of the house not open to the public, leading from the first floor up to apartments at the north end of the building. Turner's drawing conveys the darkness of this part of the house, lit only by light from beyond the limits of the picture-space at the top right and from the open doorway halfway up the stairs. This is the door to the Old Library, the room which became Turner's studio on his visits to Petworth. George Jones recalled how possessive Turner was of the room during the period when the latter frequently worked at Petworth:

> When Turner painted a series of landscapes at Petworth, for the dining-room, he worked with his door locked against everybody but the master of the house. Chantrey was there at the time, and determined to see what Turner was doing; he imitated Lord Egremont's peculiar step, and the two distinct raps on the door by which his lordship was accustomed to announce himself; and the key being immediately turned, he slipped into the room before the artist could shut him out, which joke was mutually enjoyed by the two attached friends.

Another Petworth gouache drawing (plate 51) depicts the inside of the Old Library door, which has a hinged-panel that can be opened to scrutinize the visitor. This is traditionally associated with Turner's visits to Petworth and can perhaps be related to the episode above.

[Plate 45]

The Old Library

Despite the story of Turner's exclusive use of the Old Library as a personal studio, his drawings show various other artists at work on canvases or sitting in front of pictures, something which confirms the likelihood that this group of drawings records the first of many visits made from 1827 onwards before he had asserted his rights to the room.

The Old Library is built above the Chapel, the oldest part of the house, which is not on quite the same east–west bearings as the rest of the house, a factor which means that the huge fan-light in the Old Library is at enough of an angle to catch a north-east light, ideal for painting (see fig. 5). This distinctive window appears in two of the drawings but with interesting discrepancies between the forms of the window. In one (plate 48) a studious figure pores over a book, while behind him a large picture hangs above the bookshelves. The lower half of the window here is partly blocked in an attempt to restrict the amount of light coming into the room. More importantly the horizontal grid of the window resembles that still in place today. In the other drawing (plate 49), showing an artist at his canvas watched by three demure ladies, the fanlight has a grid of concentric lines and is altogether more attractive, but it is not consistent with that in the first drawing. Why Turner should change the information he had already recorded – except for reasons of aesthetic perfection – is difficult to explain satisfactorily. The drawing has often been thought to show Turner himself at the easel. If the drawing is a fantasy, perhaps made slightly after the main group of drawings, it would not be surprising for Turner to change some of the 'facts' to suit his image.

All the drawings show the room cluttered with the apparatus of painting: frames and pictures, as well as dusty volumes from the library shelves. As Patrick Youngblood has explained, Turner and other artists staying at Petworth were permitted to bring paintings up to this room or to their bedrooms. In the background of one of the drawings, which shows the north wall of the Library (plate 46), hangs the painting 'Jacob's Dream', by the American painter Washington Allston (fig. 47). It seems possible that this was brought up to the Old Library by Turner, for he also made a gouache variation on its subject which has not previously been connected with the Petworth drawings (plate 47).

Other recognisable objects from the Petworth Collection appear in these drawings, including the statue by Nollekens, 'Seated Venus' (plate 46). This was acquired by Egremont in 1823 at Christie's. It also appears behind the still-life study of a vase of flowers, probably grown in the now demolished conservatory, which led off the North Gallery (plate 51). This study is almost without a precedent in Turner's oeuvre, and seems to record an episode in the work of another Petworth artist, Sir William Beechey. A drawing (plate 50), showing the south side of the Library, depicts an artist, almost certainly Beechey himself, seated before a picture on an easel; the bowl of flowers sits on the table to the left of the painting. The canvas the artist is working on is the portrait of 'Mrs. Hasler as Flora' by Beechey still at Petworth (fig. 125), which the artist executed during 1827 in preparation for its exhibition at the Royal Academy in the following year. The flowers on the table beside the canvas are presumably there to aid Beechey in his study as he paints Mrs Hasler's floral basket into his unfinished canvas. Turner's sketch indicates that he also found their colour and variety irresistible.

[Plates 46–52]

The Bedrooms

'He has placed me in one of the most magnificent bedrooms I ever saw!', Benjamin Robert Haydon confided to his *Diary* on 15 November 1826. Other artists met with similar hospitality during their visits to the house. As well as being able to move works from the Petworth collection up to the Old Library, Egremont permitted the artists to take pictures to their bedrooms. All Turner's drawings of bedroom interiors show these temporary arrangements of the huge collection of pictures and *objets d'art*. Haydon's description of his bedroom serves to evoke the opulence of the setting: 'On the left of the bed hangs a portrait of William, Ld. Marquis of Hertford . . . over the chimney is a nobleman kneeling – a lady of high rank to the right. Opposite Queen Mary. Over the door a head. On the right of the cabinet, Sir Somebody, & over the door of entrance another head. The bed curtains are difft. coloured velvets, let in on white satin. The walls green damask, sofas, easy chairs, carpet, & a beautiful view of the Park out of the high window'.

Although Turner seems to have had the run of the house, which presumably included the State Bedroom with its grand rococo four-poster bed (plate 53), most of the drawings concentrate on one bedroom. Next to the bed in this room appears a Japanese lacquer cabinet on top of a carved gilt-stand. In at least two drawings this piece of furniture, surmounted by a blue vase, can be seen in the same place, although the colour of the bedcurtains changes from yellow to green between the two (plates 54, 55). Other drawings show the bed with red, pink, or even blue curtains, as if Turner is creating a suitable aesthetic environment, perhaps as the setting for erotic fantasies.

Whether the drawings show real or imagined scenes, it is impossible to say with any surety. However, this group of drawings would seem to form an unfolding drama, ending with a drawing showing an empty bed on which the sheets have been thoroughly disturbed (plate 65). Another drawing shows a pile of clothes on a nearby chair, perhaps suggesting a careless *deshabillé*, while an apparently naked form peers from the bed (plate 64). This kind of intimacy was a theme subsequently renewed in Turner's work on later visits to the house, notably in two small sketchbooks of colour notes used in about 1834 (TB CCXCI(b), CCXCI(c)), which show similar scenes as well as featuring the furniture and fireplaces of the Petworth bedrooms.

[Plates 53–66]

Petworth Park

The park as we see it today has changed little since Turner's time, although the once balanced clumps of beech, oak and chestnut trees, which surmount the sloping hills, have recently been uprooted by the destructive hurricane of October 1987. The fan-like sweep of the park, with its artificially created 'stunning natural prospect', was the vision of the great eighteenth-century landscape gardener Lancelot 'Capability' Brown (1715–1783). The second Earl of Egremont first sought Brown's design for the park in 1751 and had established a working contract for the project by 1753. The centre-piece of the design, and its triumph, is the lake created through damming a stream which had formerly fed a series of small ponds. The calculated wildness is enhanced by the herd of fallow deer living in the park and often venturing right up to the windows of the house.

Turner captured the view from the house towards the lake, and the lake itself, in two of his most lyrical paintings (figs. 75, 77). His drawings, however, explore the more distant reaches of the park, with the old spire of Petworth church often appearing above the heavily wooded hills as a familiar landmark (plate 84). Nor does Turner restrict himself to the serpentine lake in front of the house: several of the drawings find him taking his viewpoint from the smaller pond to the north of the house in the stag park (plate 95).

As noted elsewhere in this book (p. 114), the park was very much a village meeting ground. Activities permitted by the third Earl included cricket matches, fêtes, firework displays, and the whole space was even turned over to the local defence corps as a training ground. The Petworth Hunt also met here, as seen in Turner's drawing (plate 69). A peculiarity of Egremont's benevolence towards his staff was that he apparently allowed them to ride in the hunt along with the local gentry.

As in the oil paintings of the park, Turner is interested in its livestock and he makes drawings of oxen, donkeys, horses and dogs, as well as the deer, which often appear silhouetted against the sunsets in the park. Turner is especially captivated by the sunset-light that defines these landscape views, and we can follow his fascination in a particular sunset as he traces the waning embers of its light through a series of drawings (plates 77, 78, 79).

[Plates 67–103]

The Church of St Mary the Virgin, Petworth

The one-hundred-and-eighty foot spire of Petworth Church, designed by Sir Charles Barry (fig. 138), appears in many of the drawings of the park and countryside. It was taken down shortly after the last war and replaced by the present tower. Turner, himself an architect *manqué*, would no doubt have been interested in the construction work taking place during his visit to Petworth in 1827 (see also p. 133). One drawing (plate 104) shows the spire, still incomplete, in a view from the Fountain Court, while another hastily sketched outline (fig. 139) conjectures the final form of the spire. The drawings of a service in progress are taken from various points inside the church, and one is forced to wonder whether Turner took his sheets of blue paper and his painting equipment into church to relieve the longeurs of a dull sermon, or whether he made them later from memory. The latter private procedure is the more likely. As in the drawings of the house interior, those of the church are most effective when they depict the intruding rays of sunlight.

[Plates 104–115]

The Countryside around Petworth

Both in his sketchbook pencil notes (figs. 119, 136) and in the group of gouache drawings, Turner depicts the town from the surrounding countryside. The newly-built spire of Petworth Church acts as a beacon for the town and clearly could be seen for miles in the neighbouring country. On an earlier visit Turner seems to have looked for familiar landmarks as he approached the town, and a drawing on page 22 verso of the 'Mortlake and Pulborough' sketchbook shows him pinpointing Petworth with obvious affection in a distant landscape. Other drawings made in the area quite possibly find Turner on the Rivers Arun and Rother, or even on the Chichester Canal (plates 76, 124, 125).

Several of the blue-paper drawings depict beach scenes at Brighton with the Chain Pier (built in 1823) in the background (plates 126, 127, 128, 129). These may be designs for a projected series of engravings called 'THE ENGLISH CHANNEL or LA MANCHE', which was advertised in 1827, but which failed to materialise. As there was a daily crossing from Brighton to Dieppe from the end of the pier it is quite possible that Brighton was the embarkation point for some of Turner's visits to the Continent.

[Plates 116–129]

East Cowes and Other Locations

The reidentification of various Petworth drawings and the painting, 'Music at East Cowes Castle' (fig. 95), by Patrick Youngblood in 1983 has meant that greater attention has been focused on the identity of a number of previously problematic Petworth drawings. Given Turner's interest in architecture, and particularly in the interiors of his hosts' houses (one thinks of Farnley, Petworth and Abbotsford), it would have been surprising had Turner not made more sketches of the interior of East Cowes Castle than those listed by A. J. Finberg (TB CCXXVII(a)).

Turner stayed at John Nash's house on the Isle of Wight in the late summer of 1827 in between visits to Petworth. The castle was largely complete by 1798, although Nash rebuilt and added various turrets and features such as the conservatory at later dates. Despite its rather grand exterior, the castle was in fact quite a small house. Unfortunately it was demolished in 1949–50. However, the group of drawings by Turner, made on identical blue paper to that used for the Petworth drawings, provide the most extensive contemporary record of the castle as it was during Nash's occupancy. As these drawings demonstrate, the chief attraction of the castle was its setting high above the estuary of the River Medina.

Patrick Youngblood identifies two of the Petworth drawings as studies of rooms at East Cowes Castle (plates 132, 133). Other so-called Petworth drawings should also more probably be identified with East Cowes. One appears to show the Library with a gathering assembled to hear a harp recital (plate 134), possibly one stimulus for the 'Music at East Cowes Castle' picture.

Of the drawings associated with Petworth Park, several seem incongruous in that grouping. One appears to show a river subject, perhaps associated with the Meuse-Moselle drawings Turner made in the early-1830s (plate 130). Another, though traditionally thought to show a game being played in Petworth Park, appears to relate to East Cowes (plate 131). Despite stories of the many recreational uses of the park, it seems unlikely that the blue stretch beyond the trees represents the lake and it is more probable that this is the sea seen from East Cowes Castle. The mood of the drawing is also similar to the *fête champêtre* of Turner's picture, 'Boccaccio relating the tale of the Birdcage' (BJ 244), which depicts East Cowes Castle, and to the atmosphere of some of the East Cowes drawings.

As well as a huge number of shipping subjects, other East Cowes subjects on blue paper have been found among drawings more usually connected with France (TB CCLX–5, 9, 11, 12, 25–30, 32).

[Plates 130–135]

The Plates

Unless otherwise stated, the drawings have been painted using a combination of gouache and watercolour on sheets of roughly-torn blue paper, each measuring approximately 140 × 190 ($5\frac{1}{2} \times 7\frac{1}{2}$).

All the drawings would seem to date from Turner's visit to Petworth in 1827 with the exception of plates 67 and 123 which were most probably made a year or two earlier.

With the exception of plates 20, 71, 72, 75, 89, 91 and 121, all the drawings reproduced form part of the Turner Bequest and were first catalogued by A. J. Finberg in his *Complete Inventory of the Drawings in the Turner Bequest*, 1909. Where appropriate the original titles given to the drawings by Finberg have been retained, although in many cases they have been revised in the light of recent research.

A concordance can be found at the end of the book to enable rapid cross-reference between the plate order and the sequence listed in Finberg's *Inventory*.

The drawings depicting Petworth House are organised by room in the order a visitor to the House today might pass through the sequence of state rooms (see plan of Petworth House, fig. 144), with the drawings of the parklands and church following on at the end of this grouping.

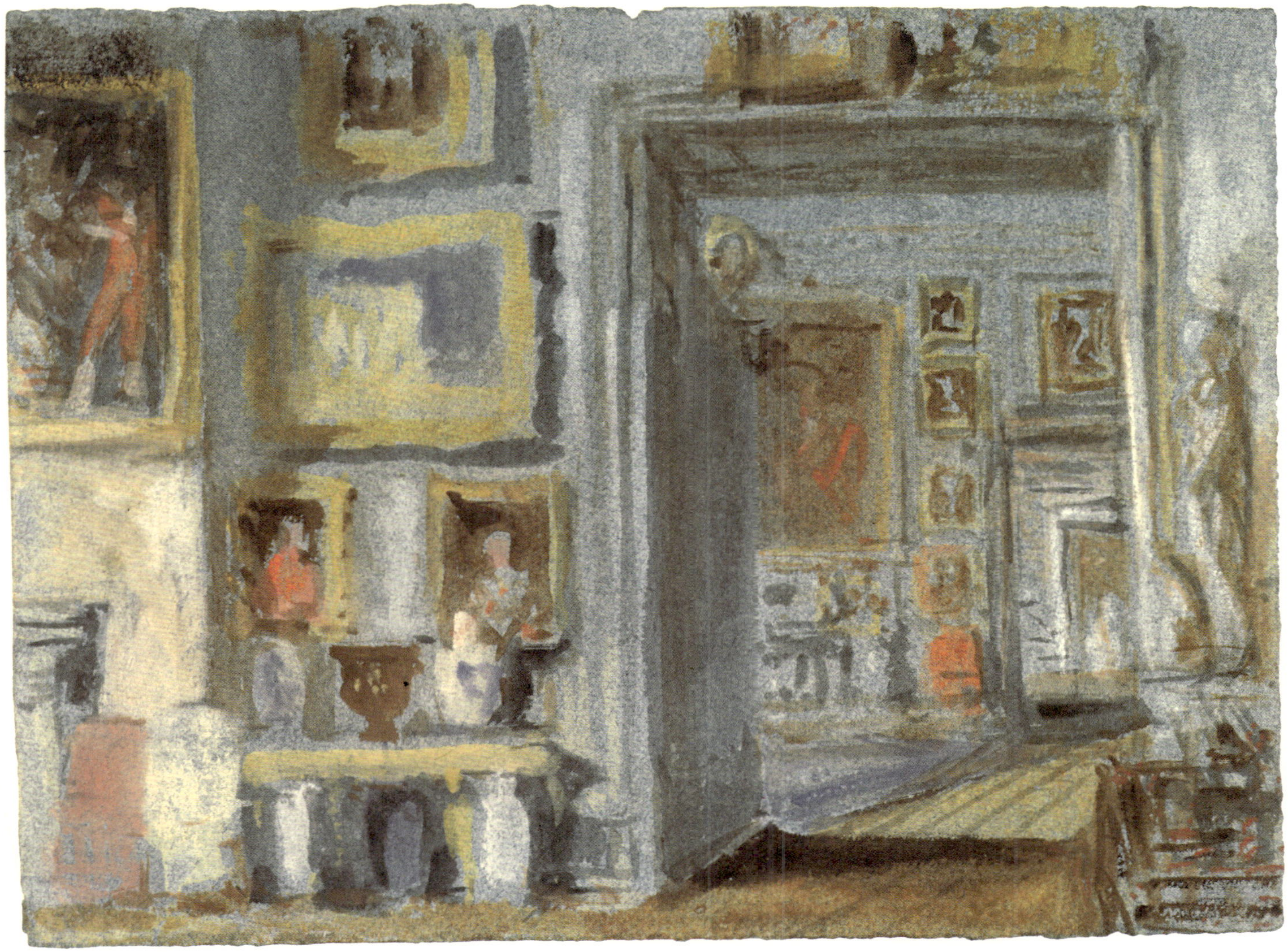

PLATE 1

The Somerset Room: looking into the Square Dining-Room and beyond onto the Grand Staircase

TB CCXLIV–73

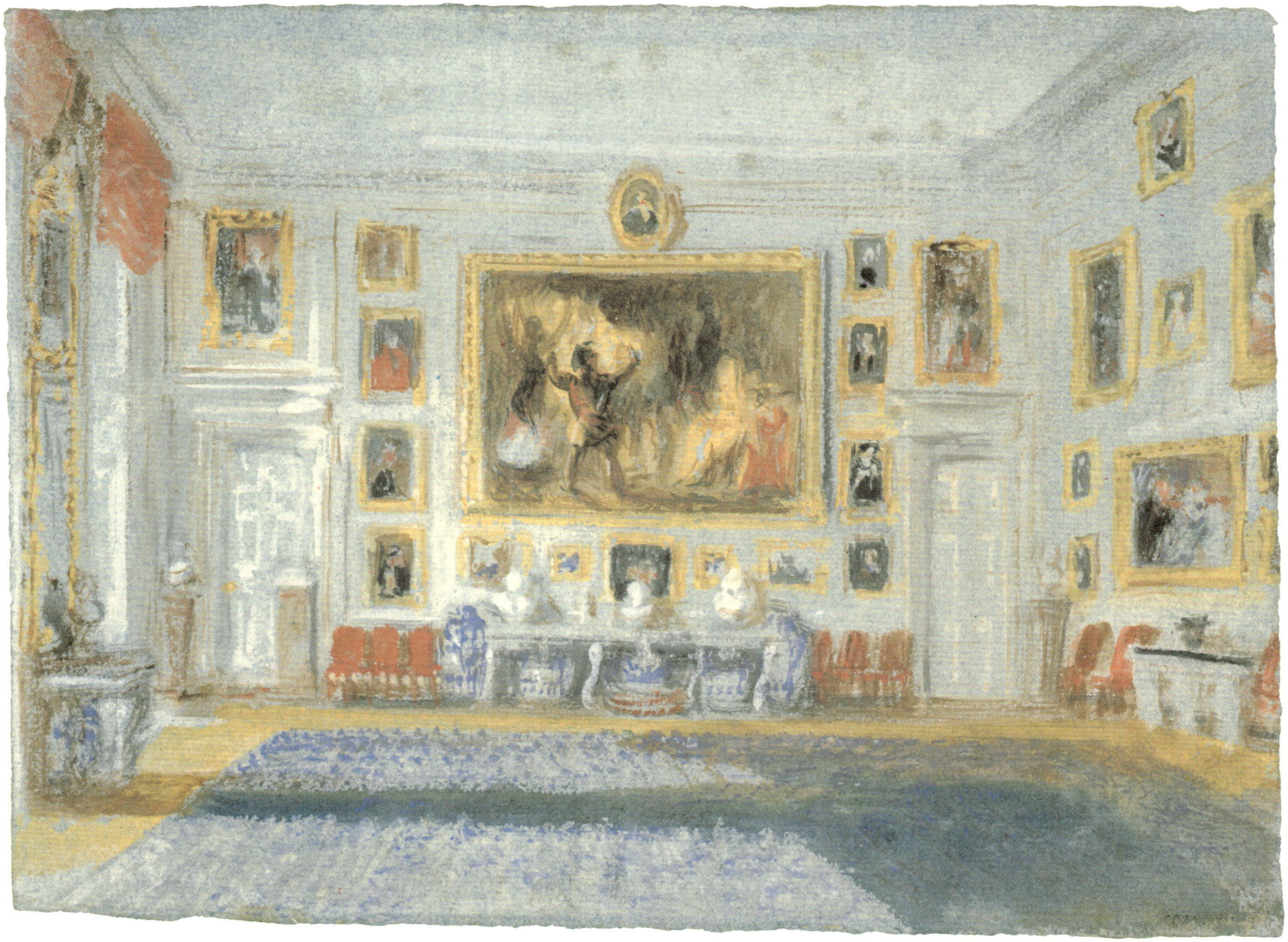

PLATE 2

The South Wall of the Square Dining-Room

TB CCXLIV–108

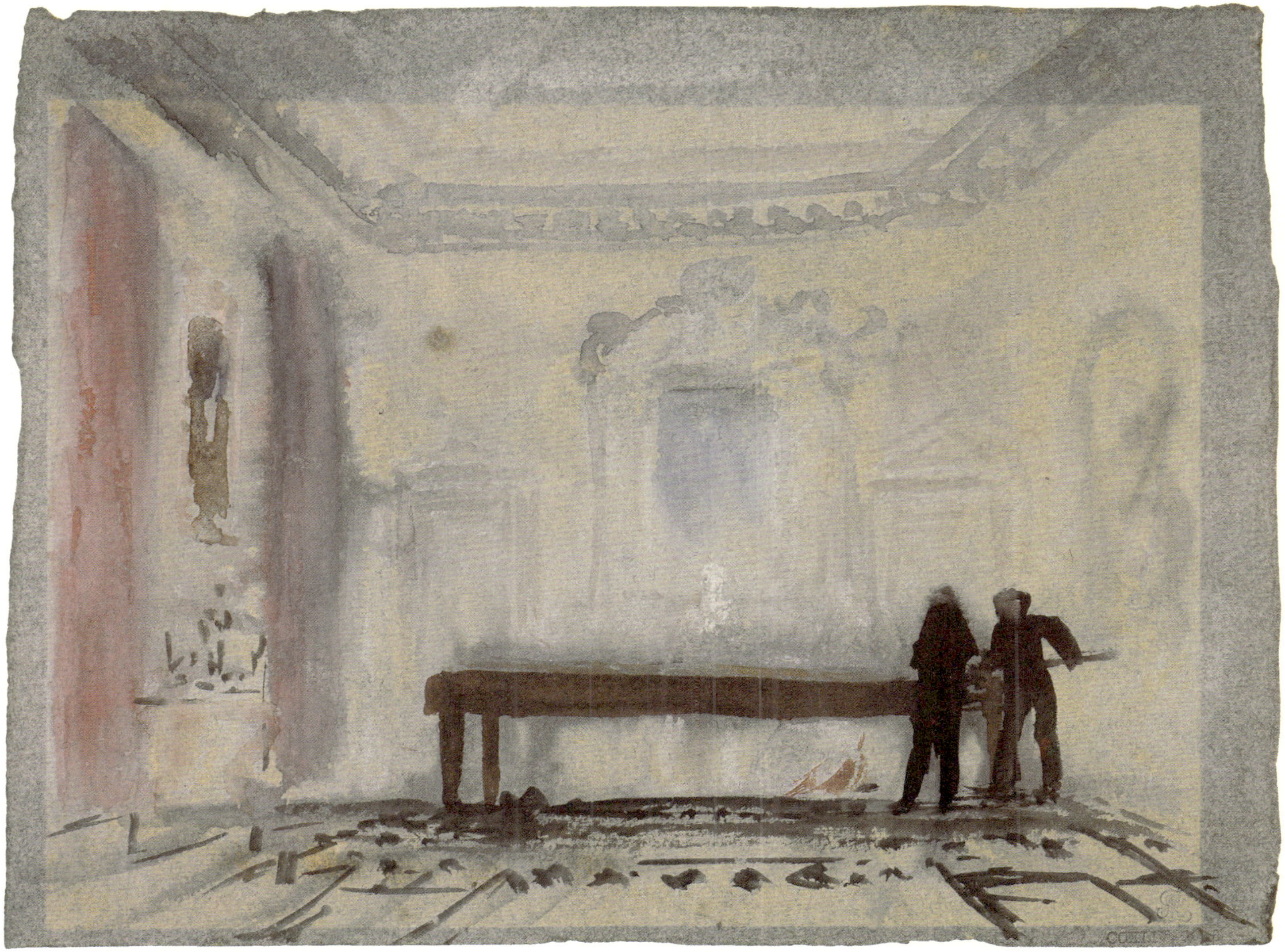

PLATE 3
The Billiard Players
TB CCXLIV–116

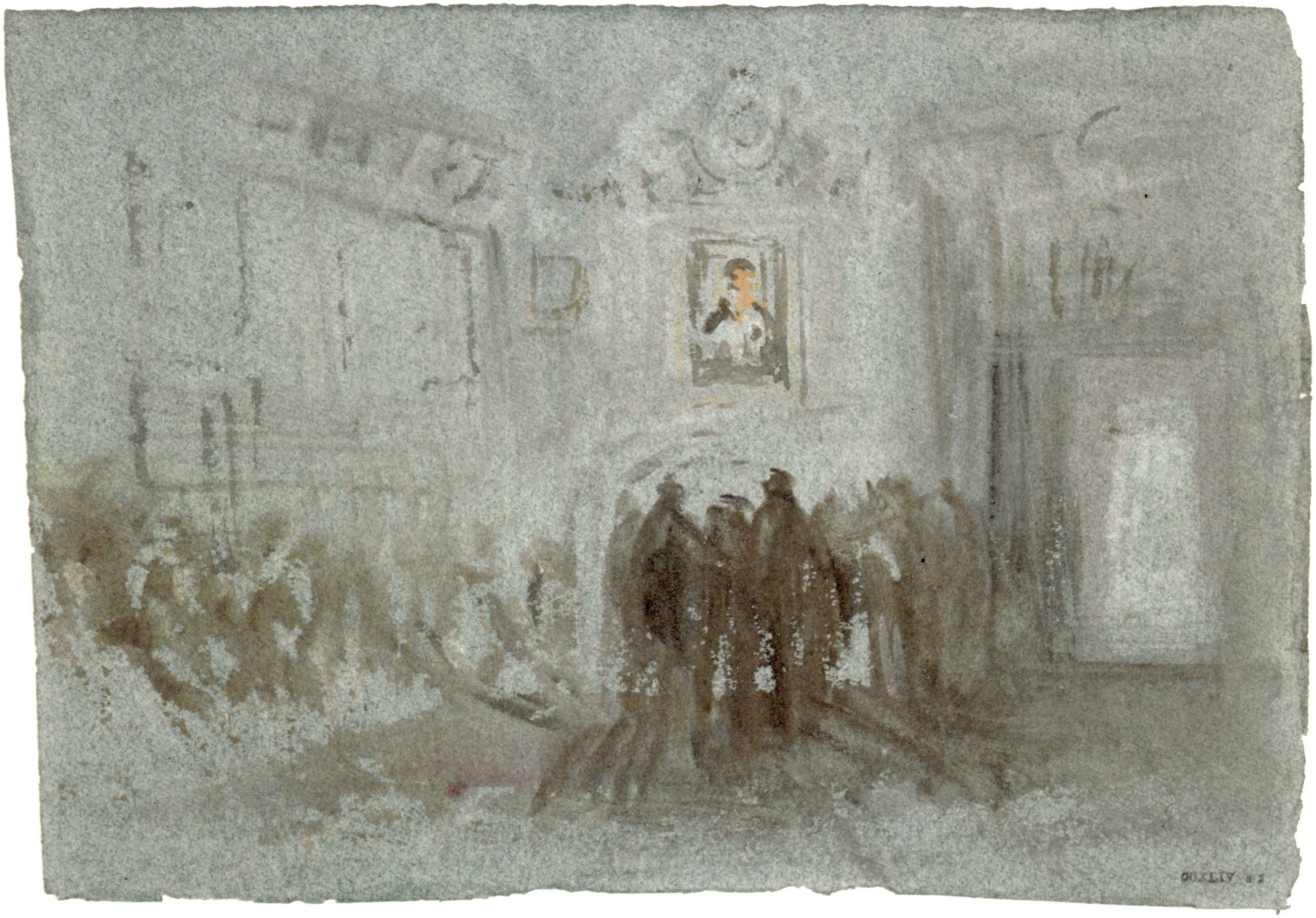

PLATE 4

Men Chatting around a Fireplace

TB CCXLIV–82

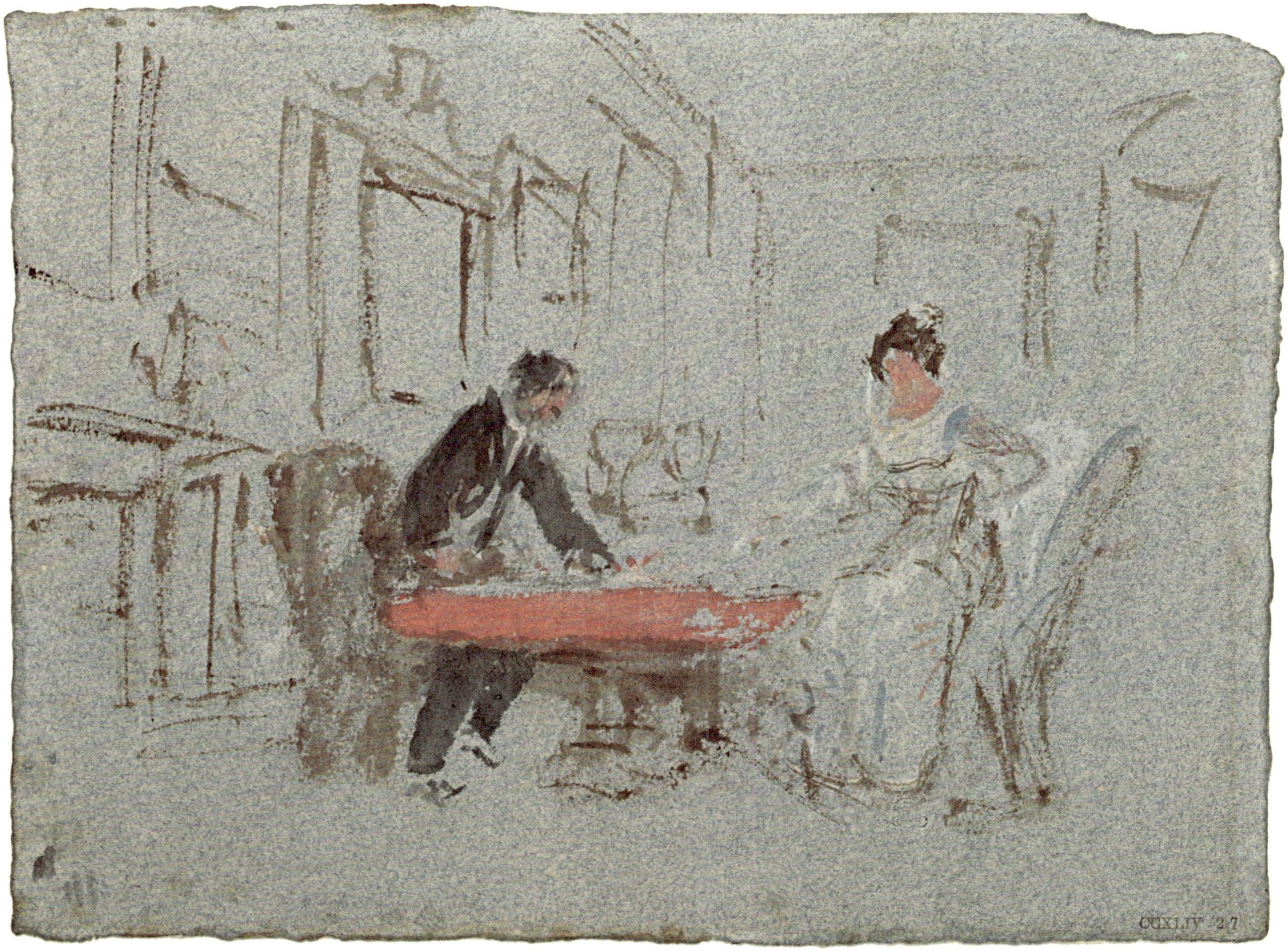

PLATE 5
The Backgammon Players
TB CCXLIV–27

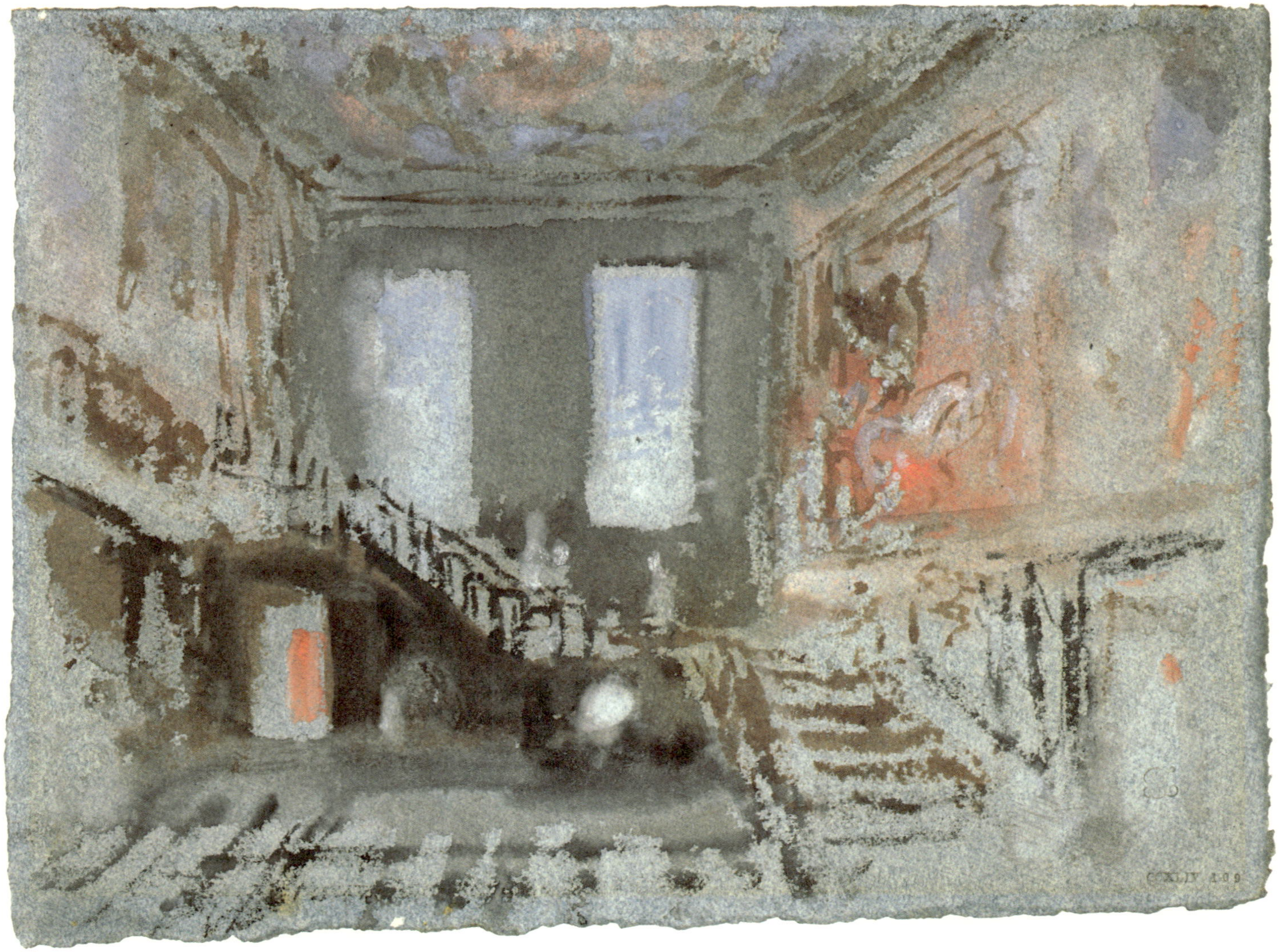

PLATE 6

The Grand Staircase: from the West

TB CCXLIV–109

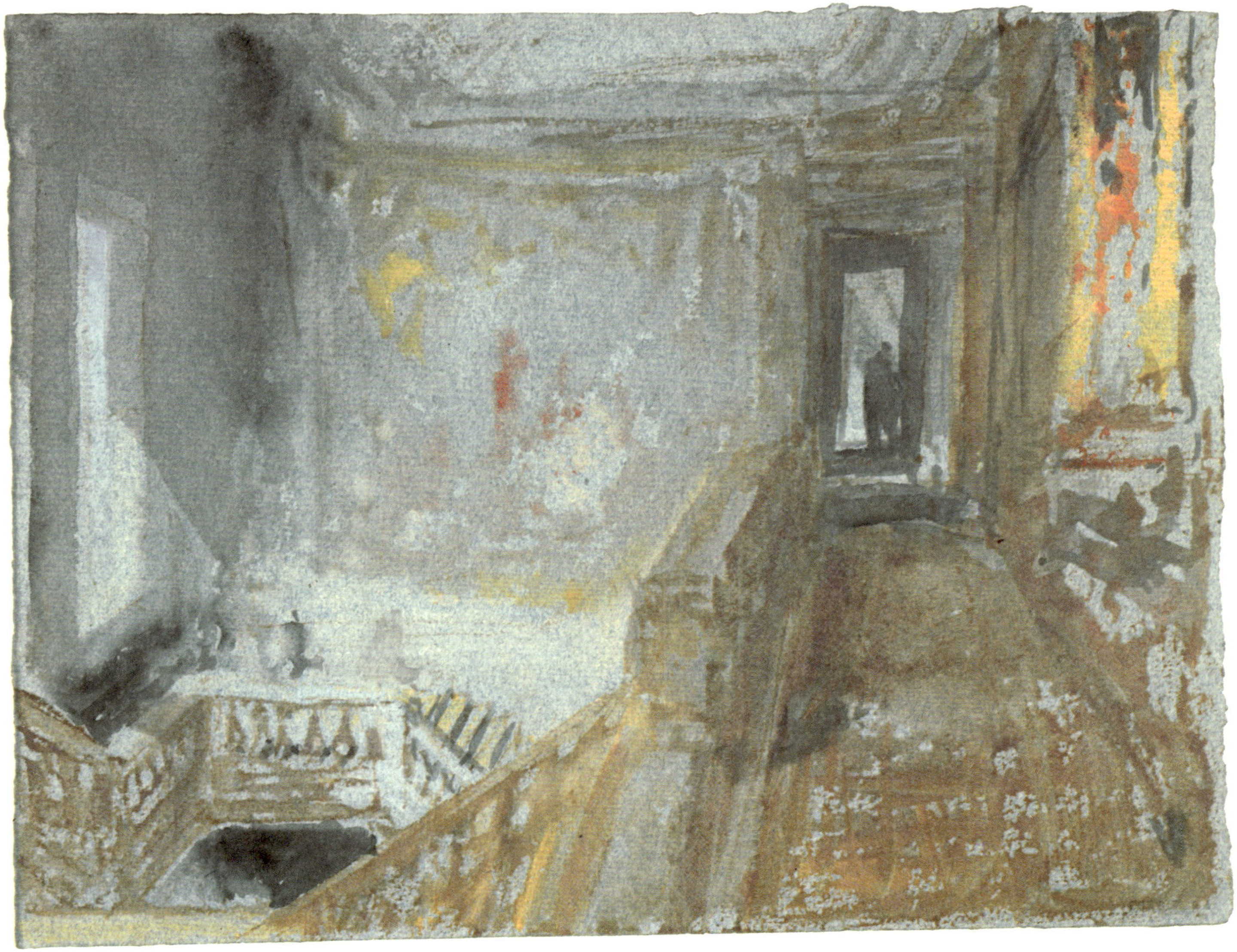

PLATE 7
The Grand Staircase: from the bedroom landing
TB CCXLIV–94

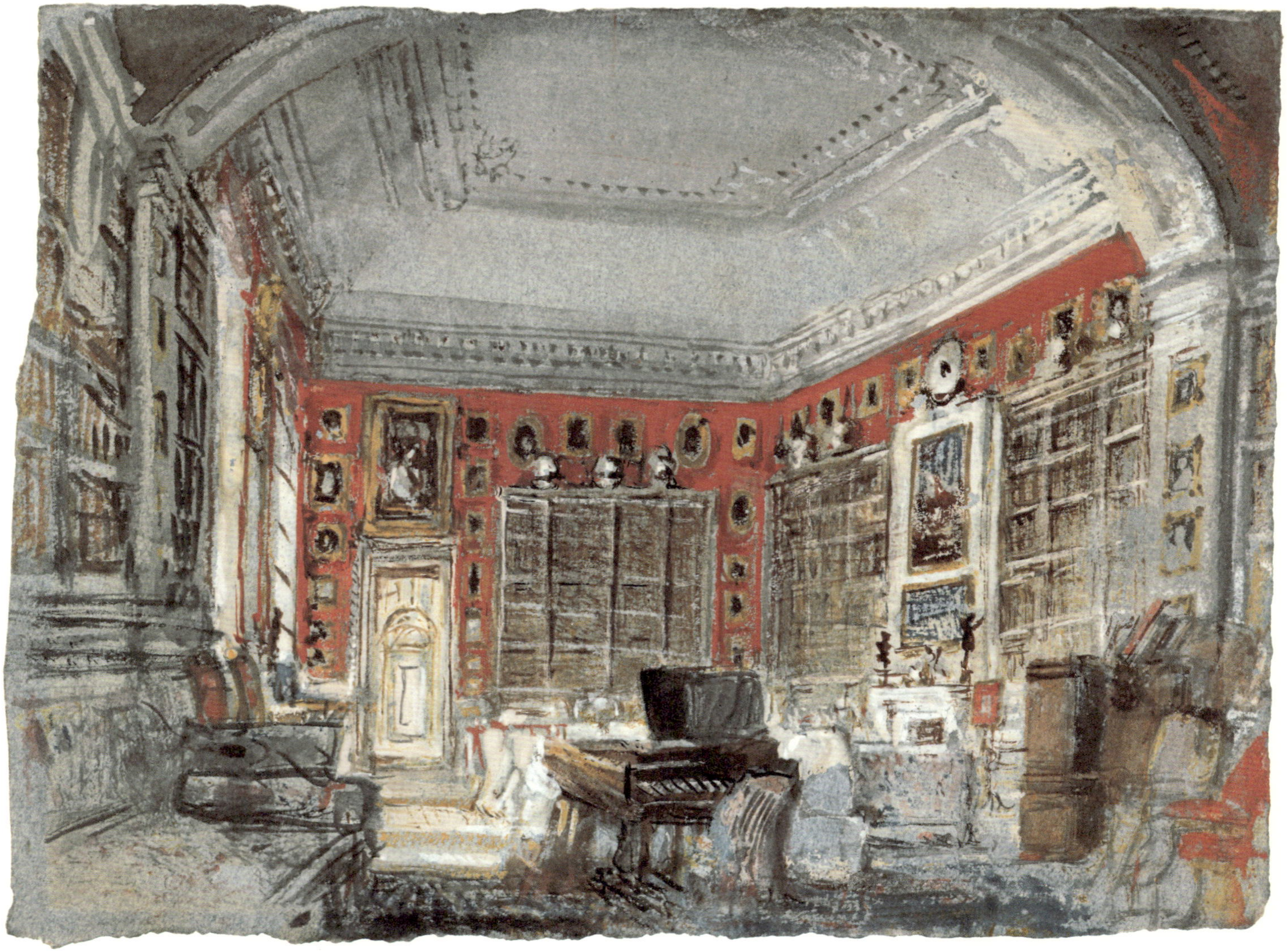

PLATE 8

The White Library: looking down the enfilade from the alcove

TB CCXLIV–16

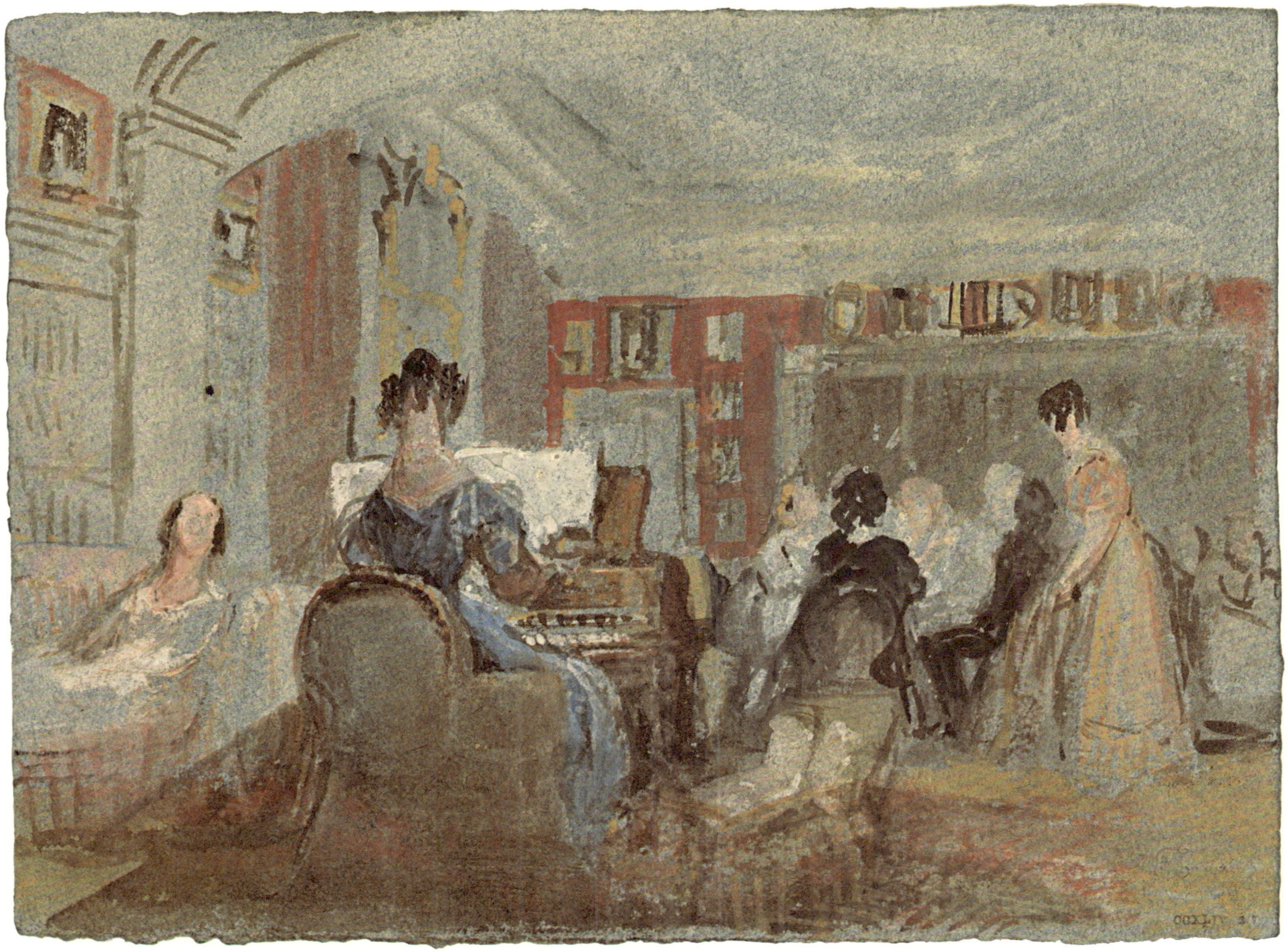

PLATE 9

Music in the White Library

TB CCXLIV–37

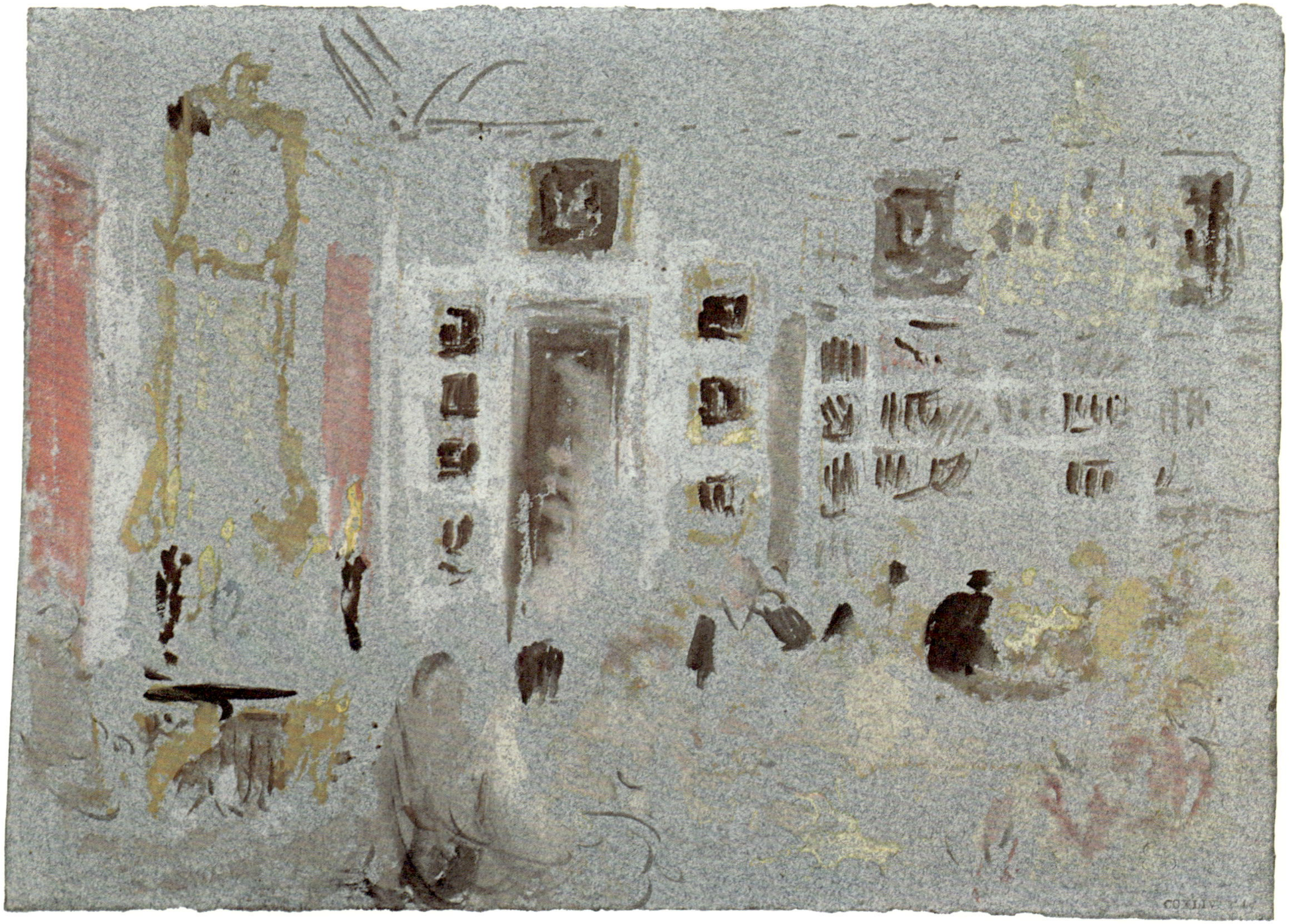

PLATE 10

Bookshelves and a Rococo Pier-glass, with several Figures

TB CCXLIV–24

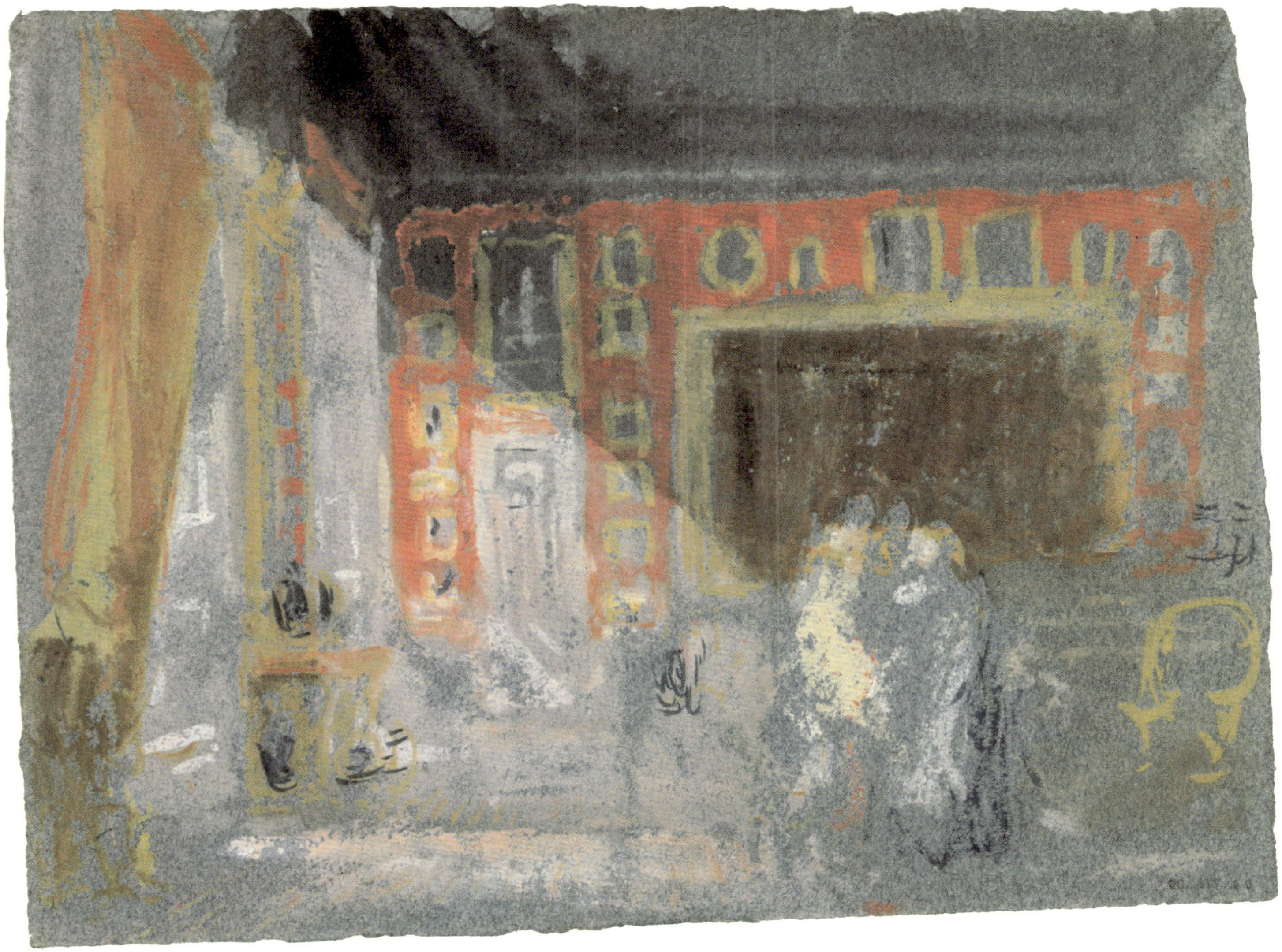

PLATE 11
Sunlight and Figures in the White Library
TB CCXLIV–96

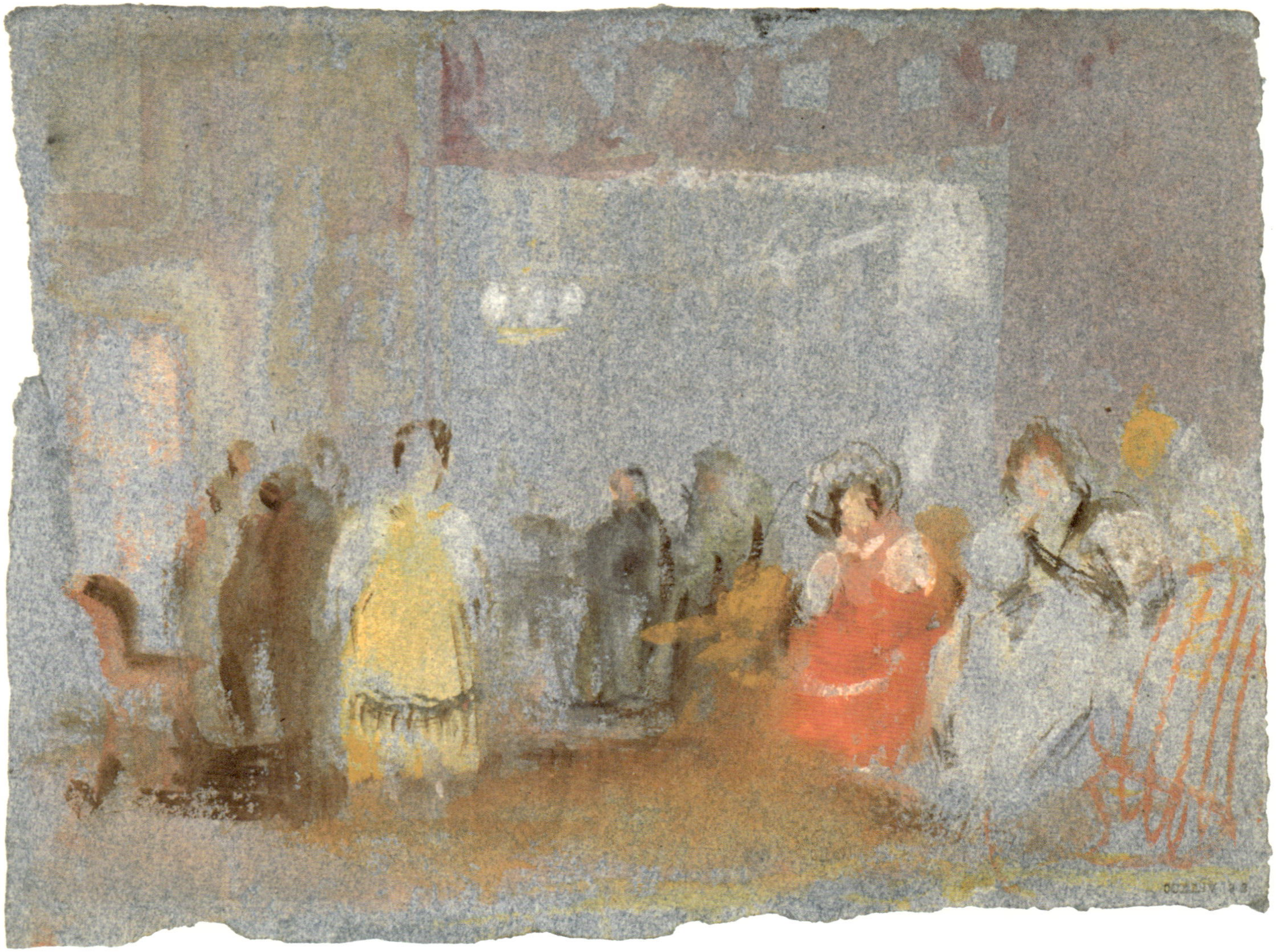

PLATE 12
An Assembly of Ladies
TB CCXLIV–92

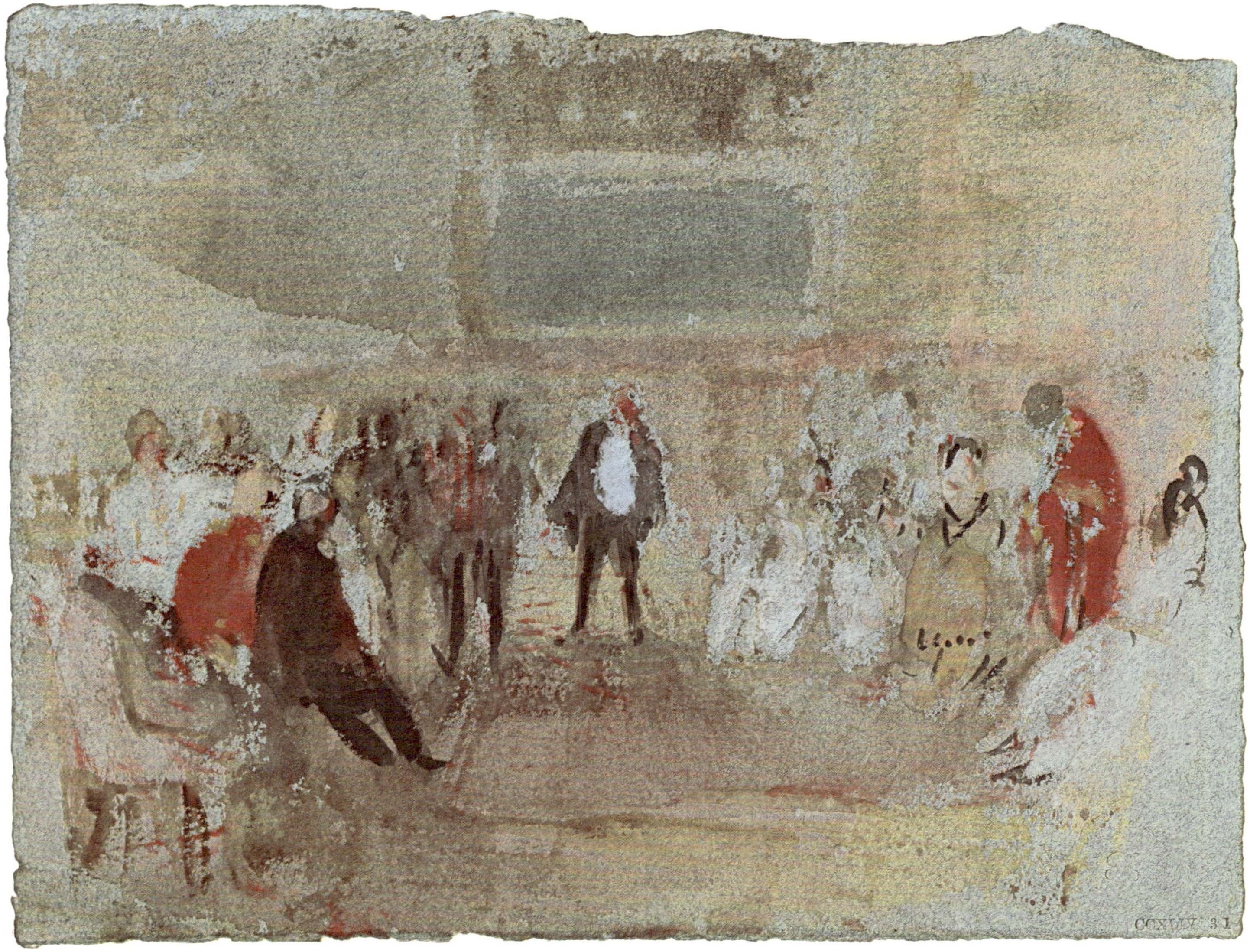

PLATE 13
Waiting for Dinner
TB CCXLIV–31

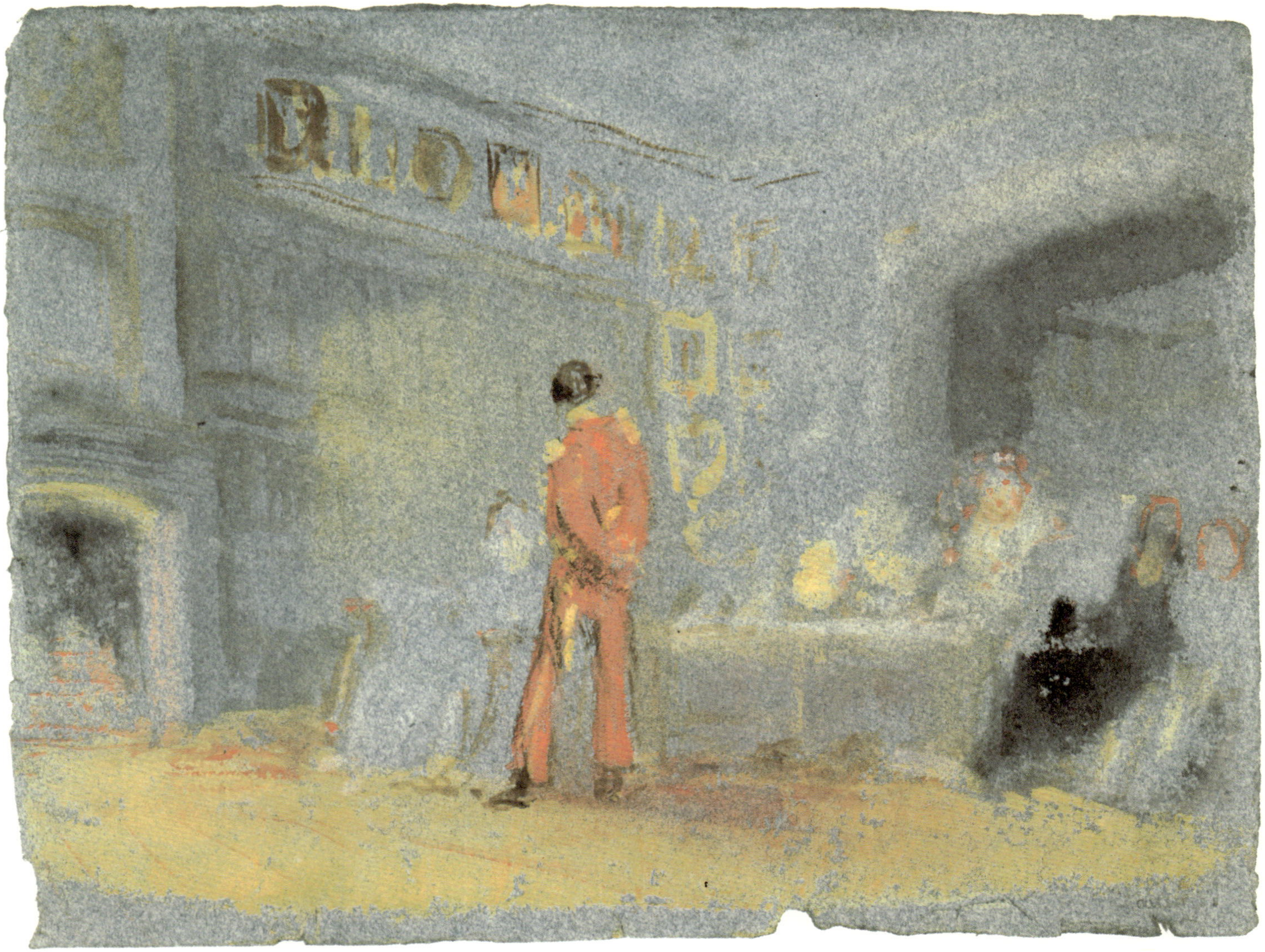

PLATE 14
The Red Uniform
TB CCXLIV–22

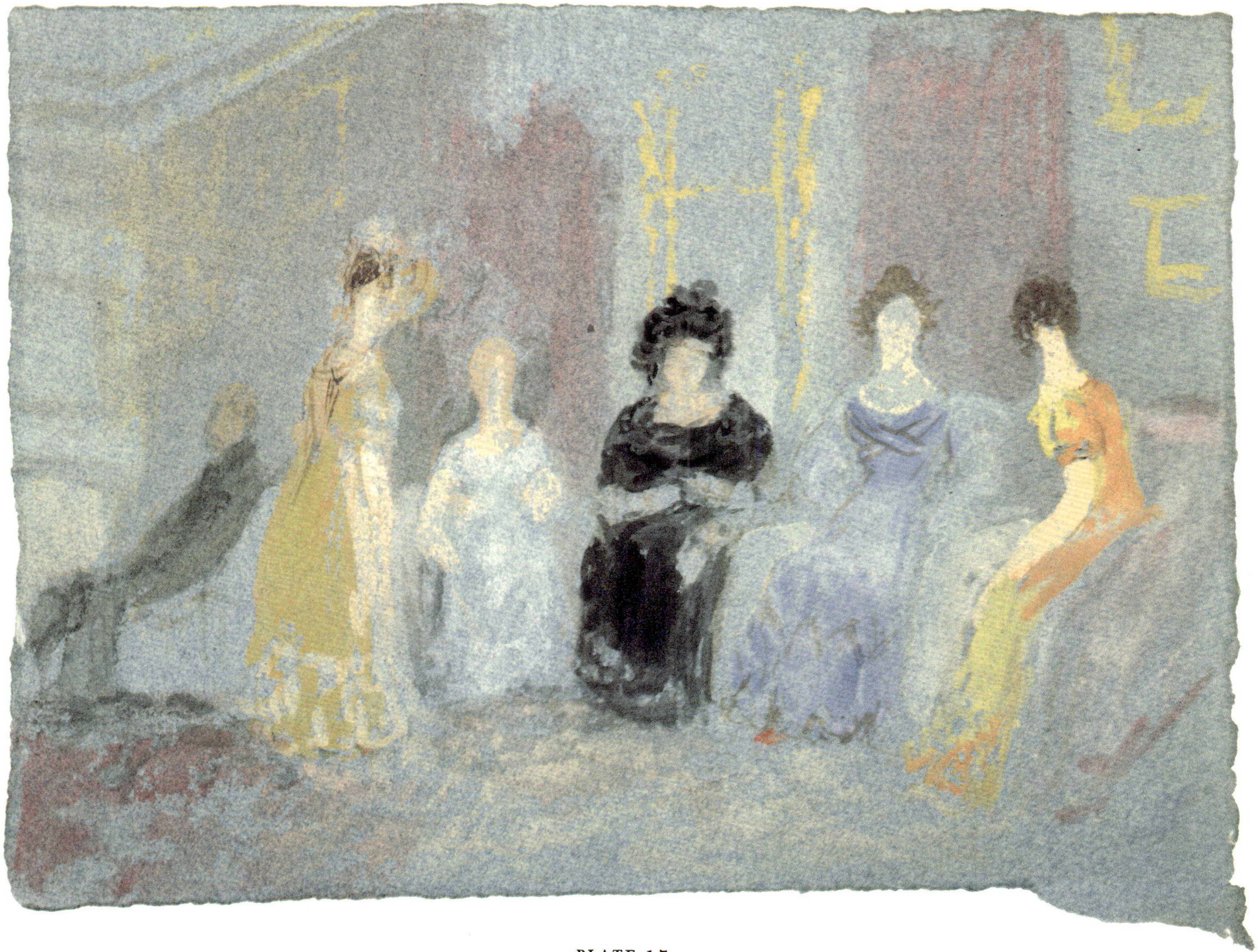

PLATE 15
A Bevy of Beautiful Women
TB CCXLIV–101

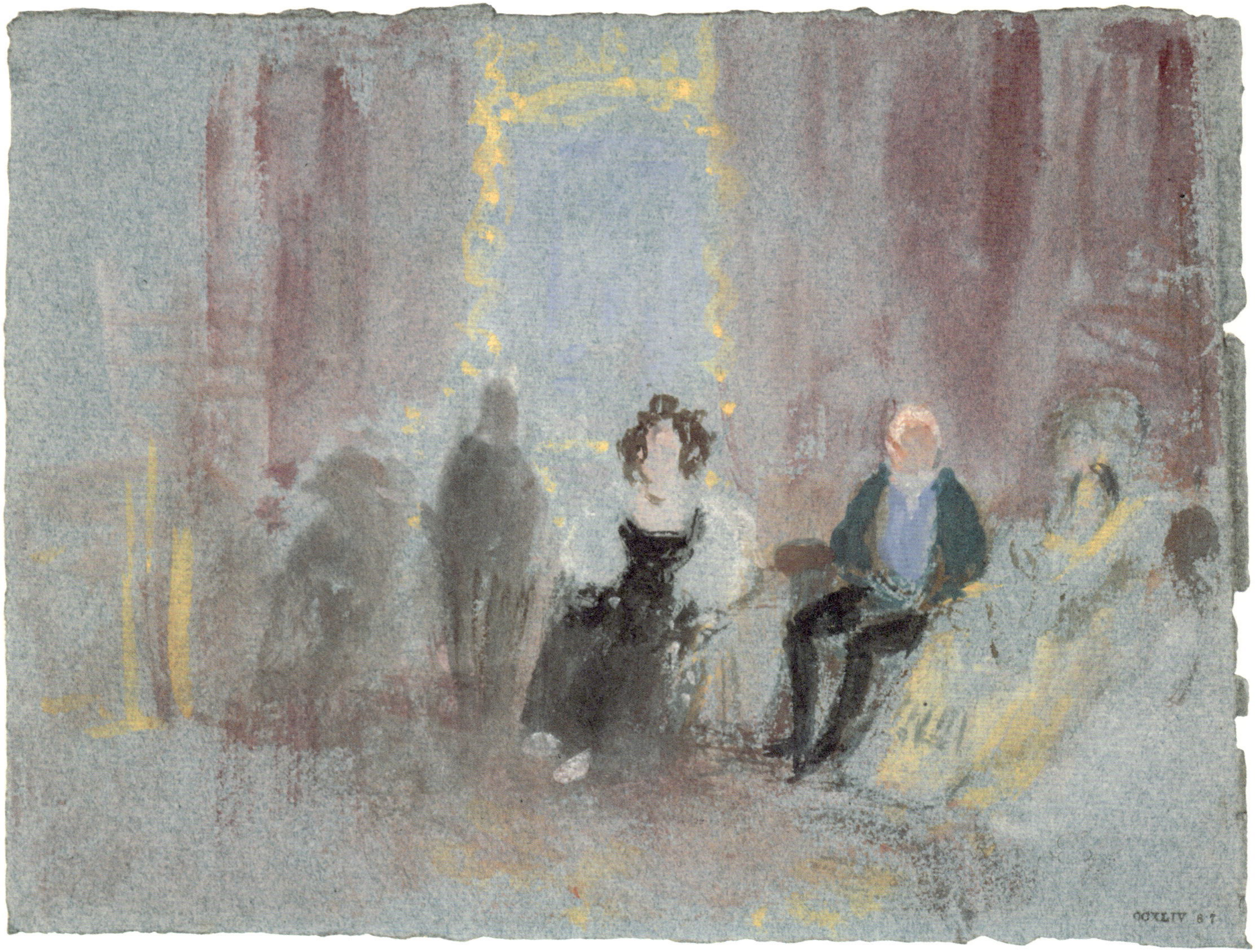

PLATE 16

The White Library: Lord Egremont (?) among his guests

TB CCXLIV–87

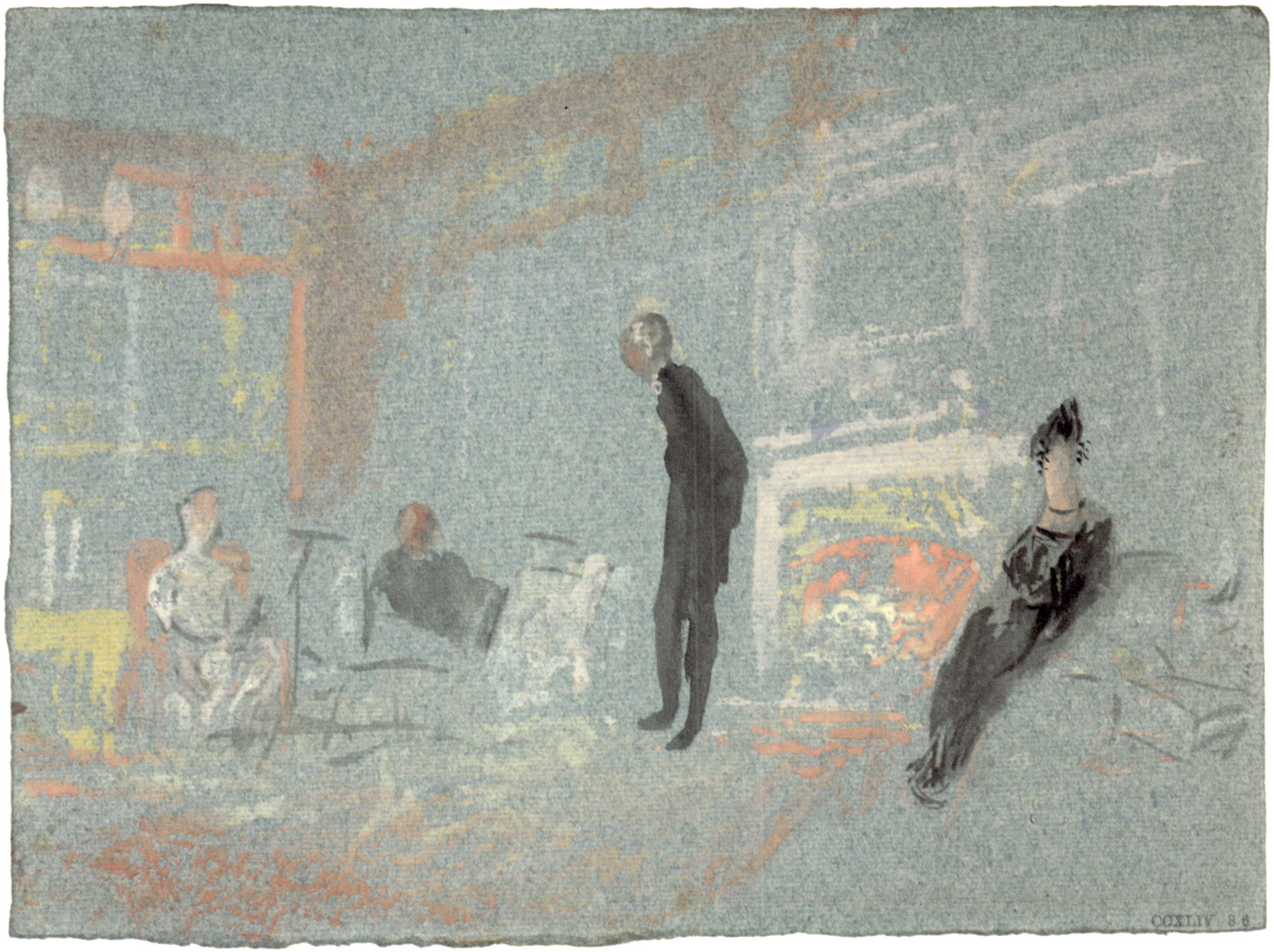

PLATE 17
The Vicar on the Hearthrug
TB CCXLIV–86

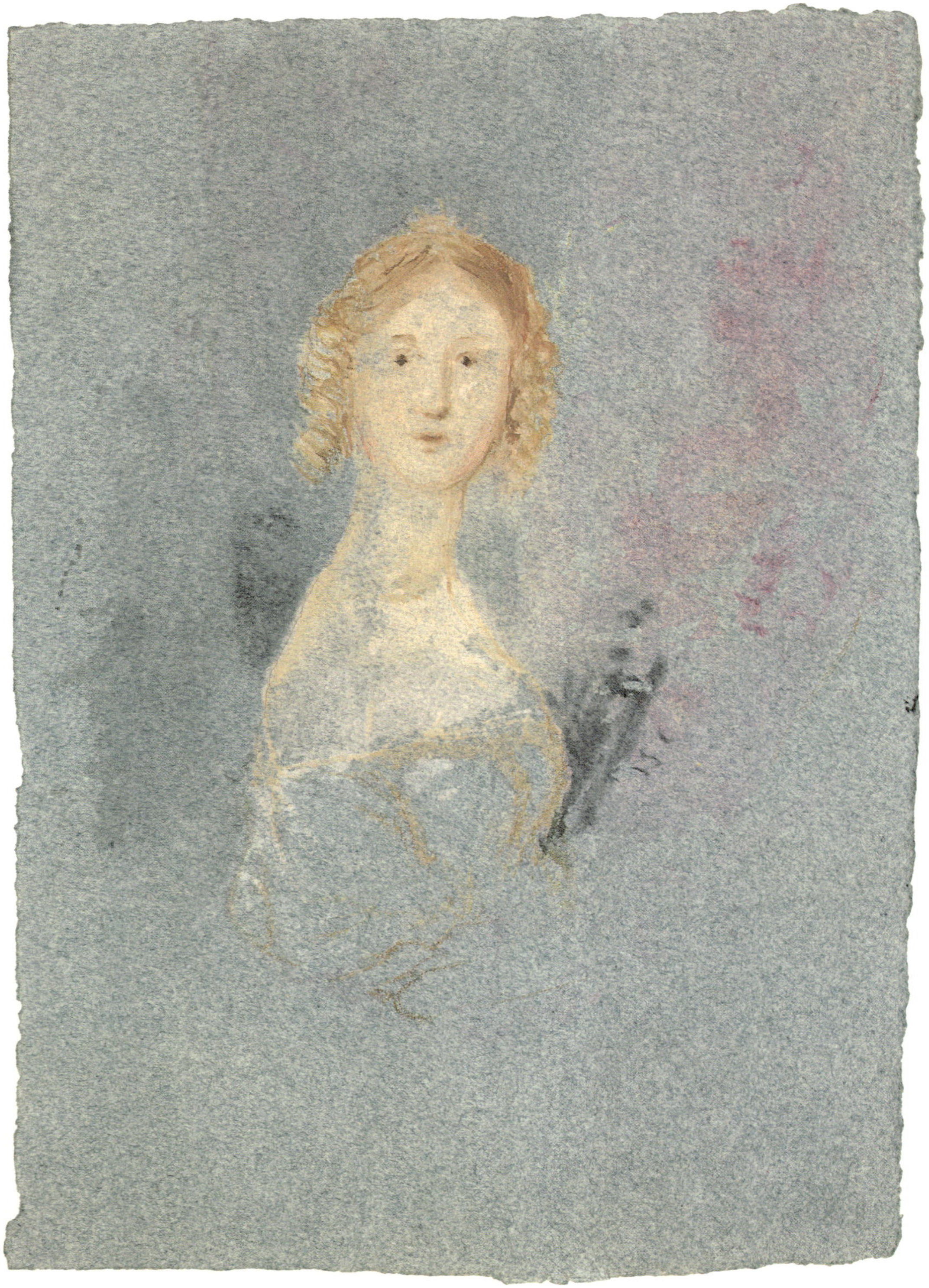

PLATE 18
Portrait of a Young Lady Playing the Fortepiano
TB CCXLIV–39

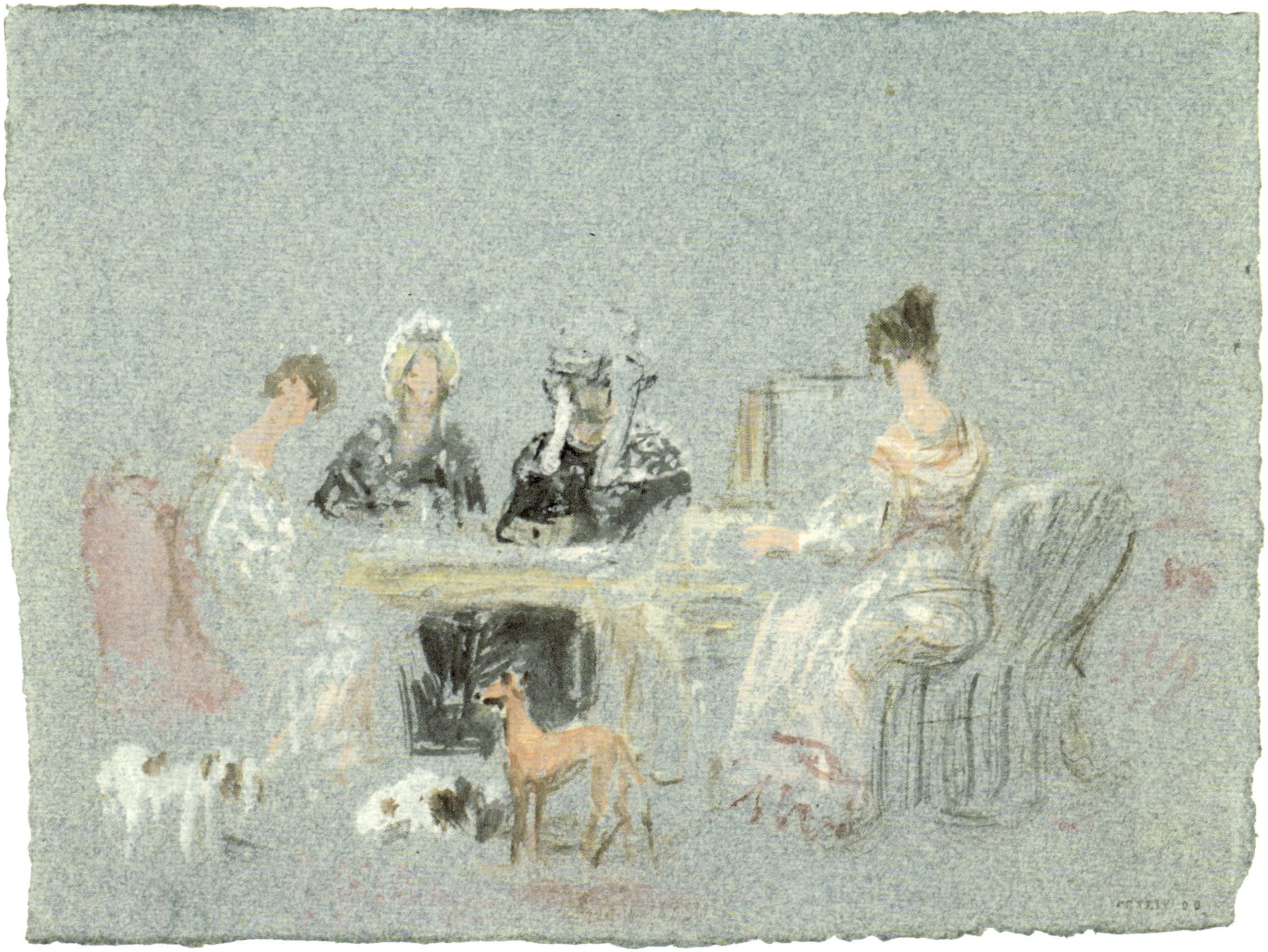

PLATE 19
A Dames' Party
TB CCXLIV–90

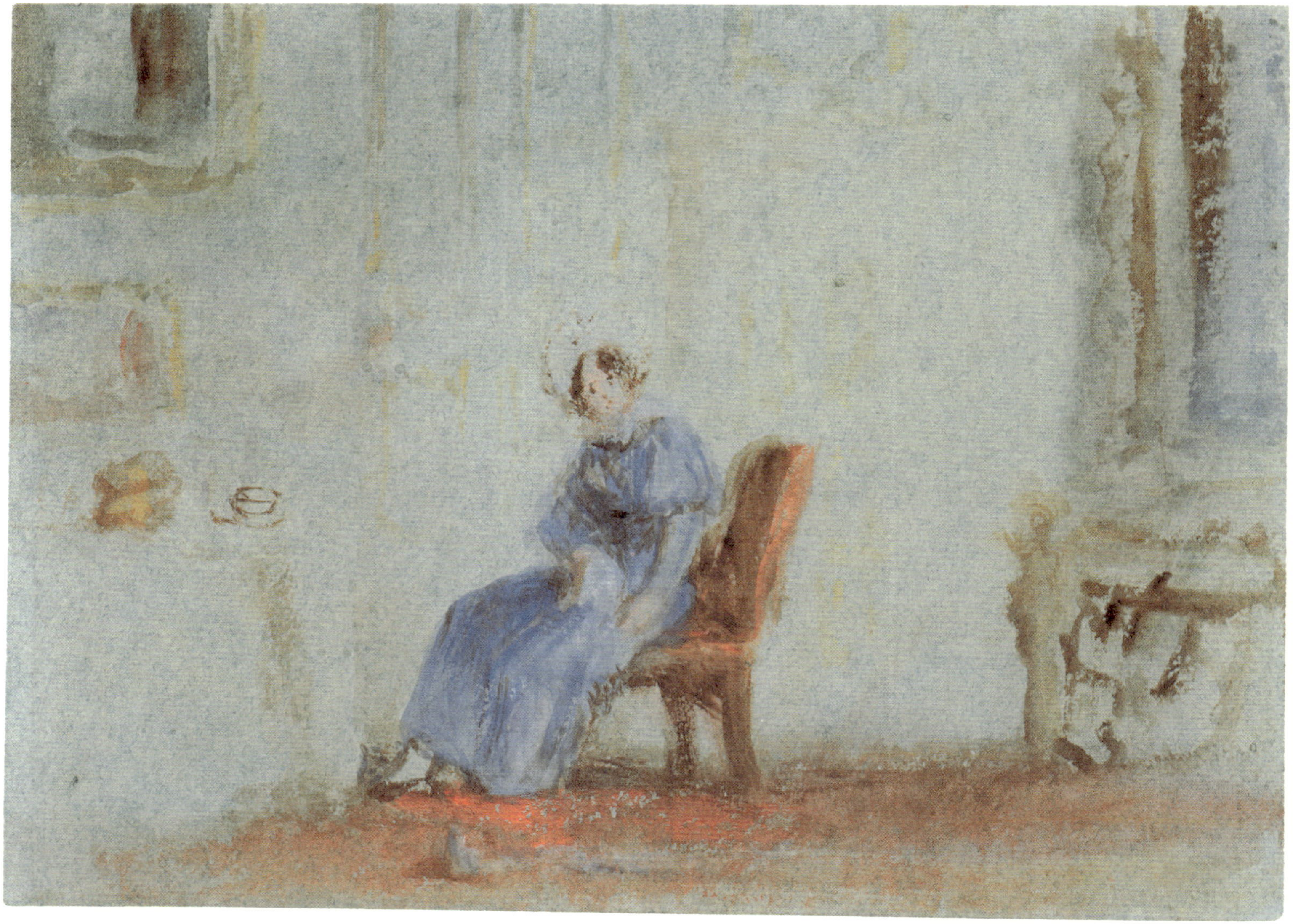

PLATE 20
Spilt Milk 534×588
Lord Egremont, Petworth House (W.906)

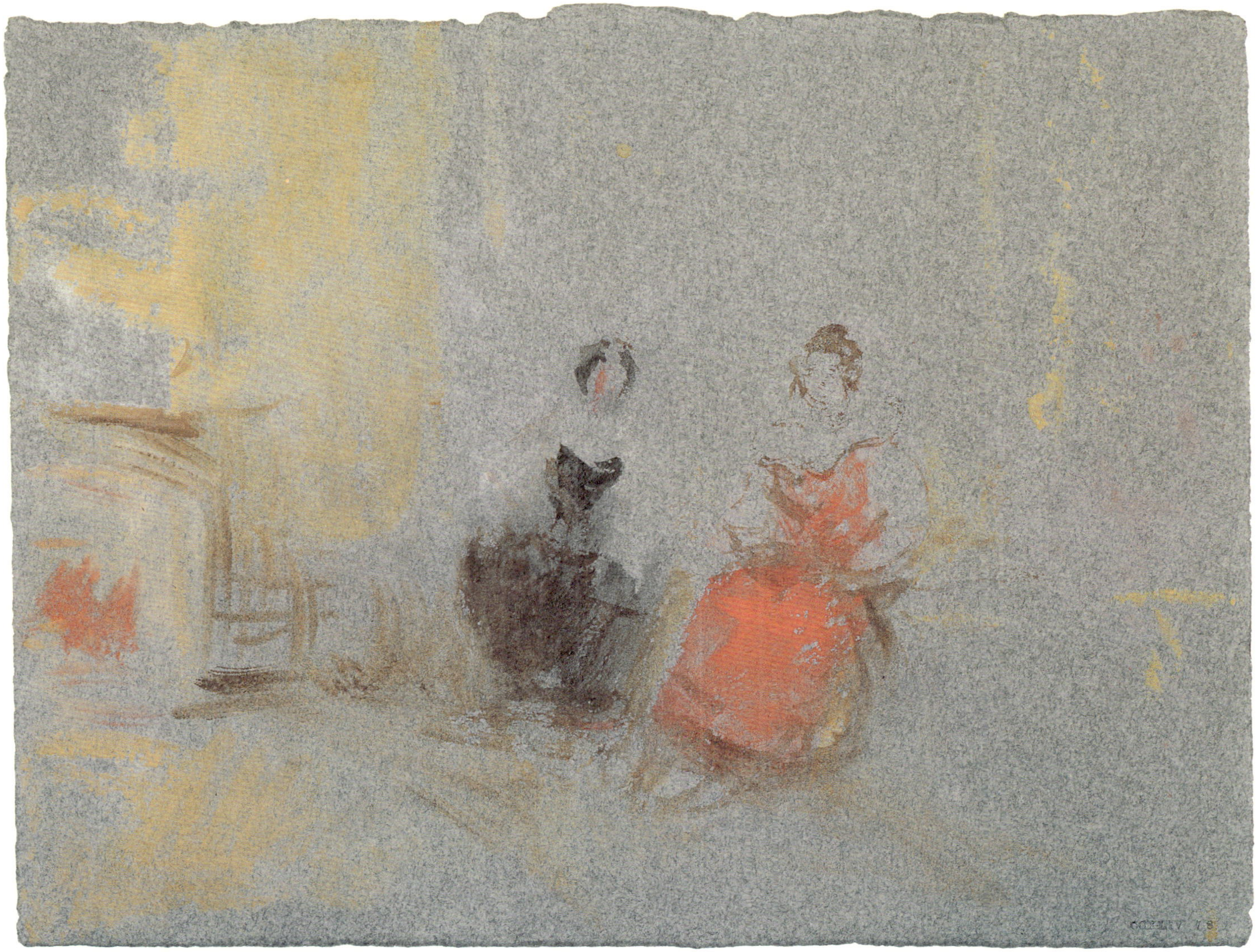

PLATE 21
Two Ladies Sitting by the Fire
TB CCXLIV–78

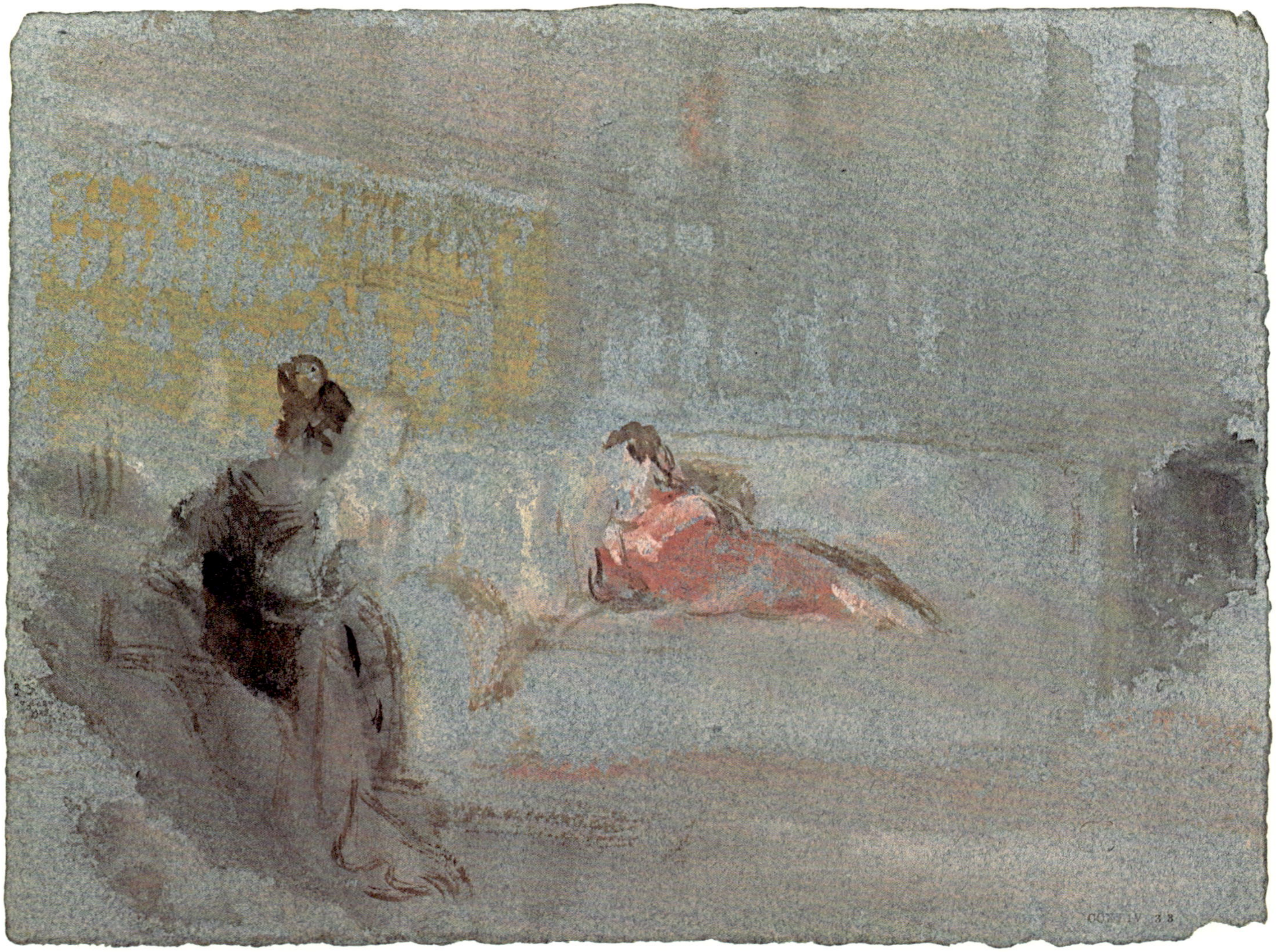

PLATE 22
The Red Lady on a Couch
TB CCXLIV–33

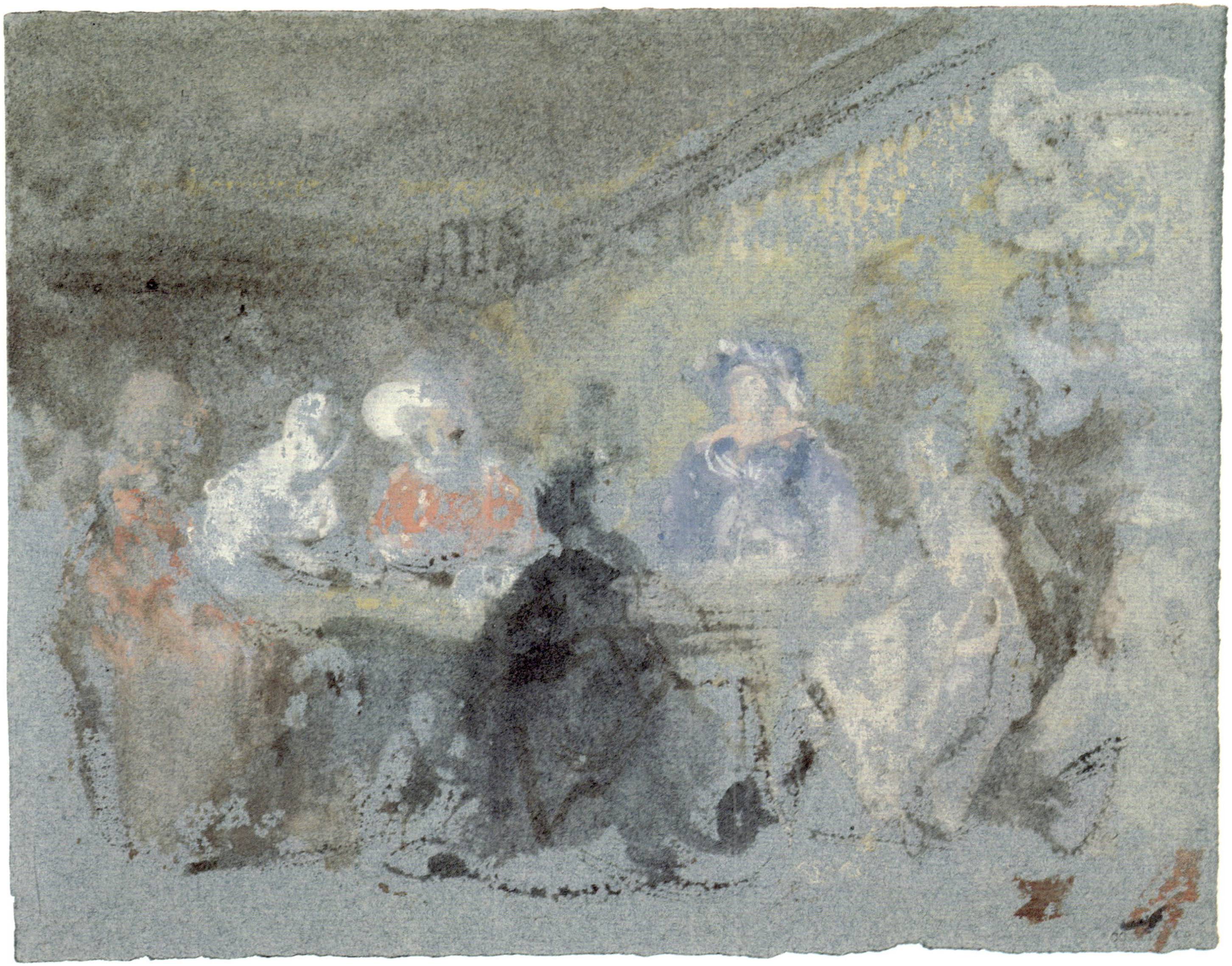

PLATE 23

Ladies Seated round a Table

TB CCXLIV–40

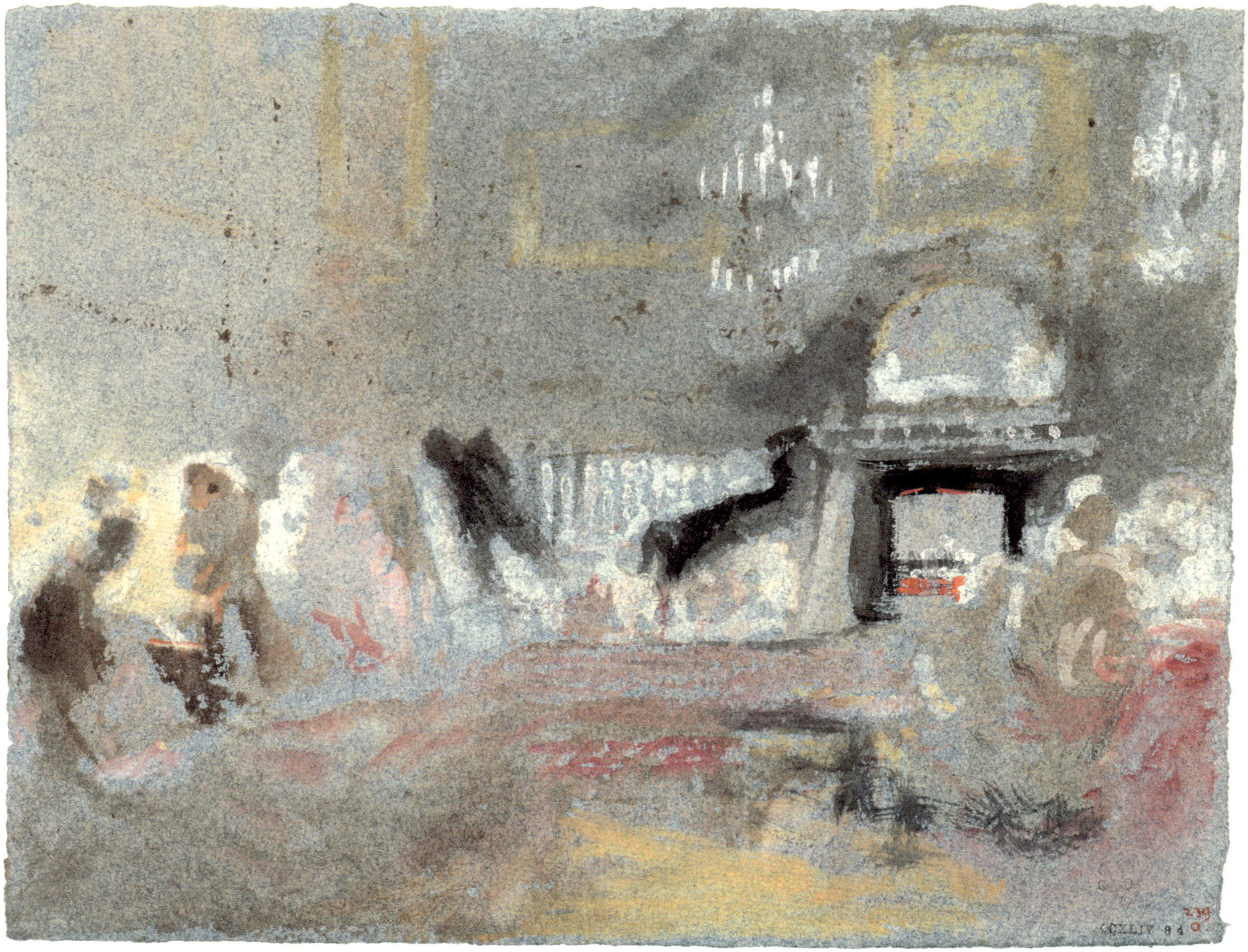

PLATE 24
After Dinner
TB CCXLIV–84

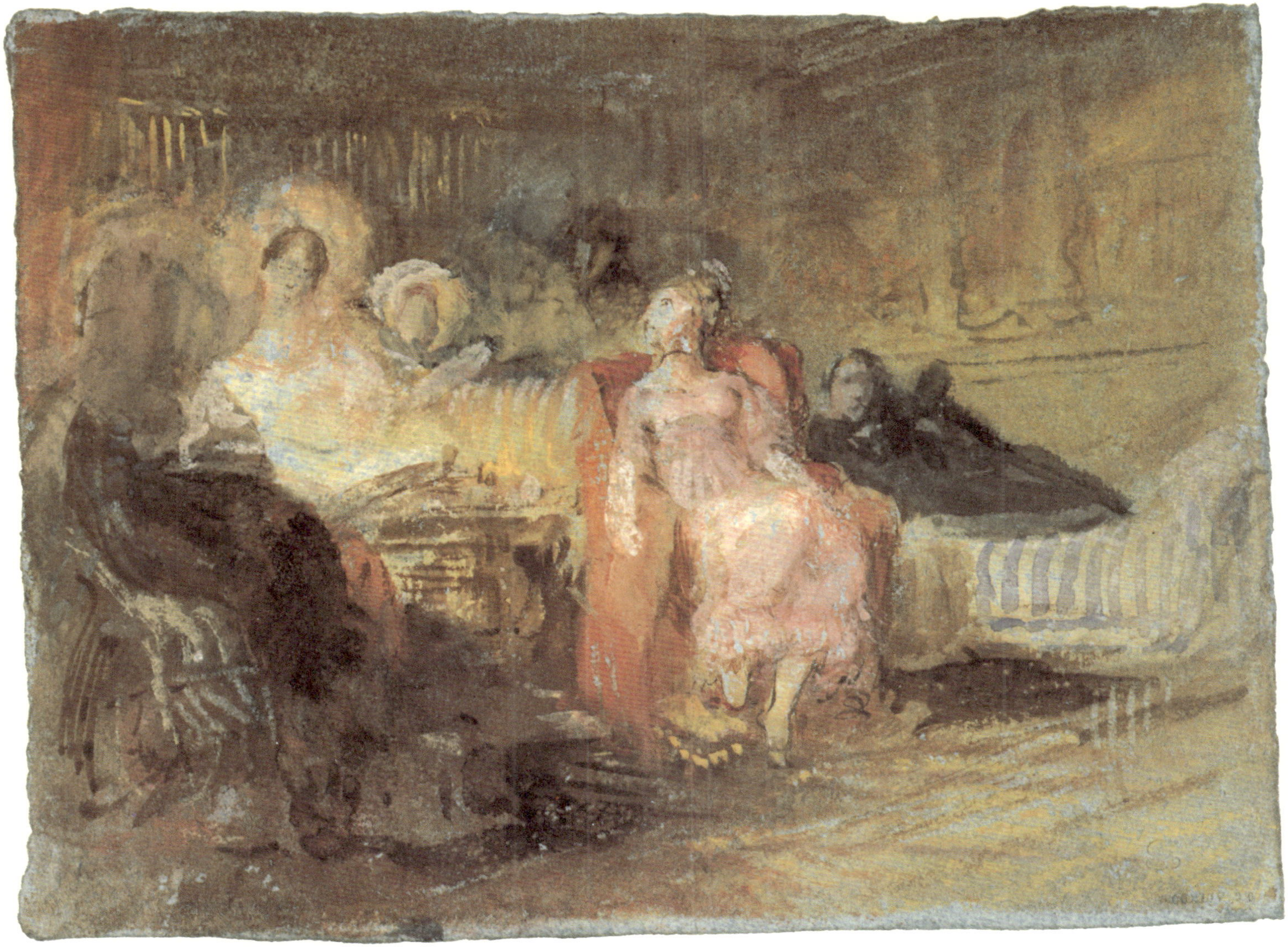

PLATE 25

The Lady in Pink: conversation in the White Library

TB CCXLIV–26 Pen and brown ink with gouache and watercolour

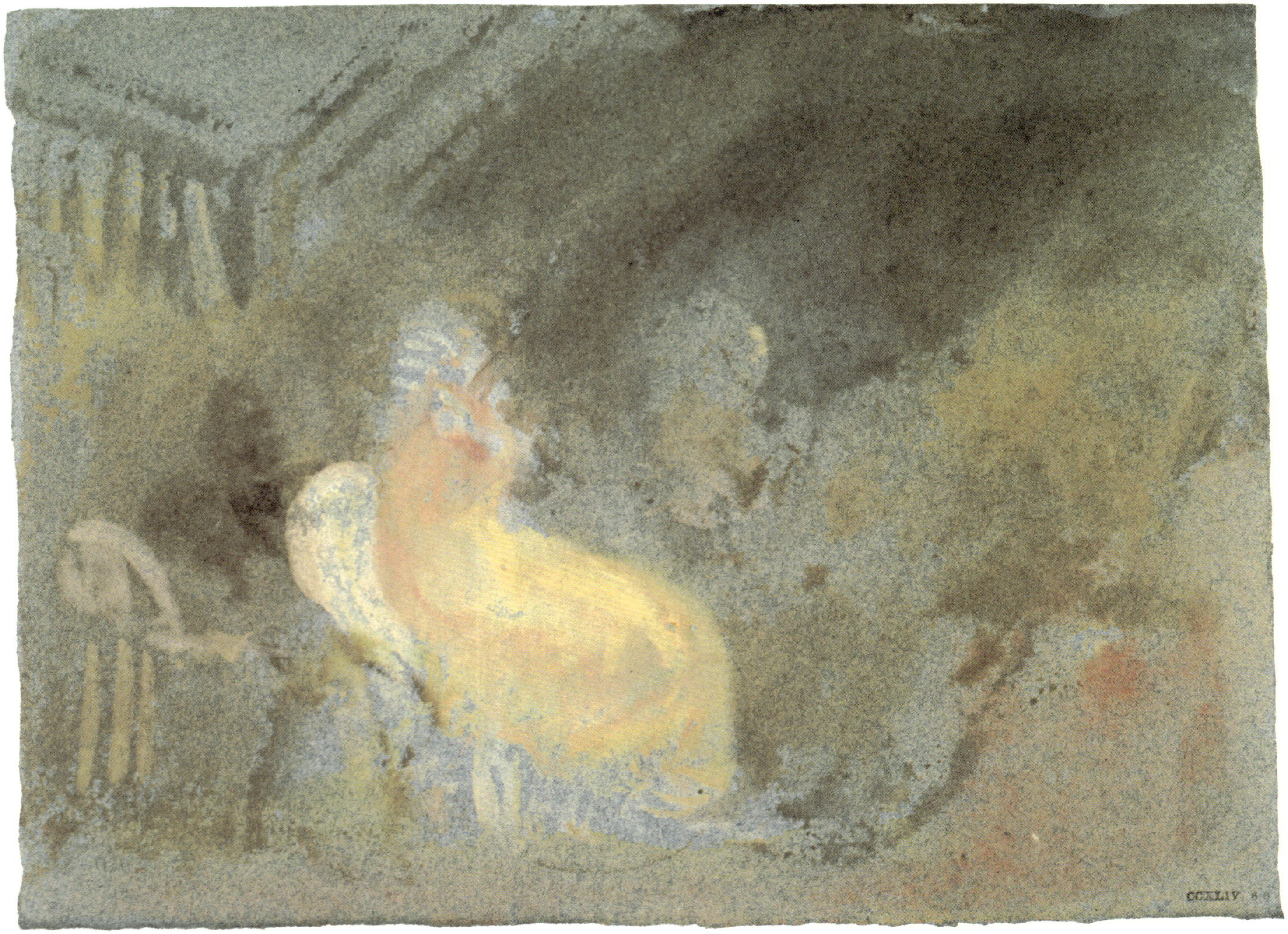

PLATE 26
A Seated Figure in a Yellow Dress
TB CCXLIV–80

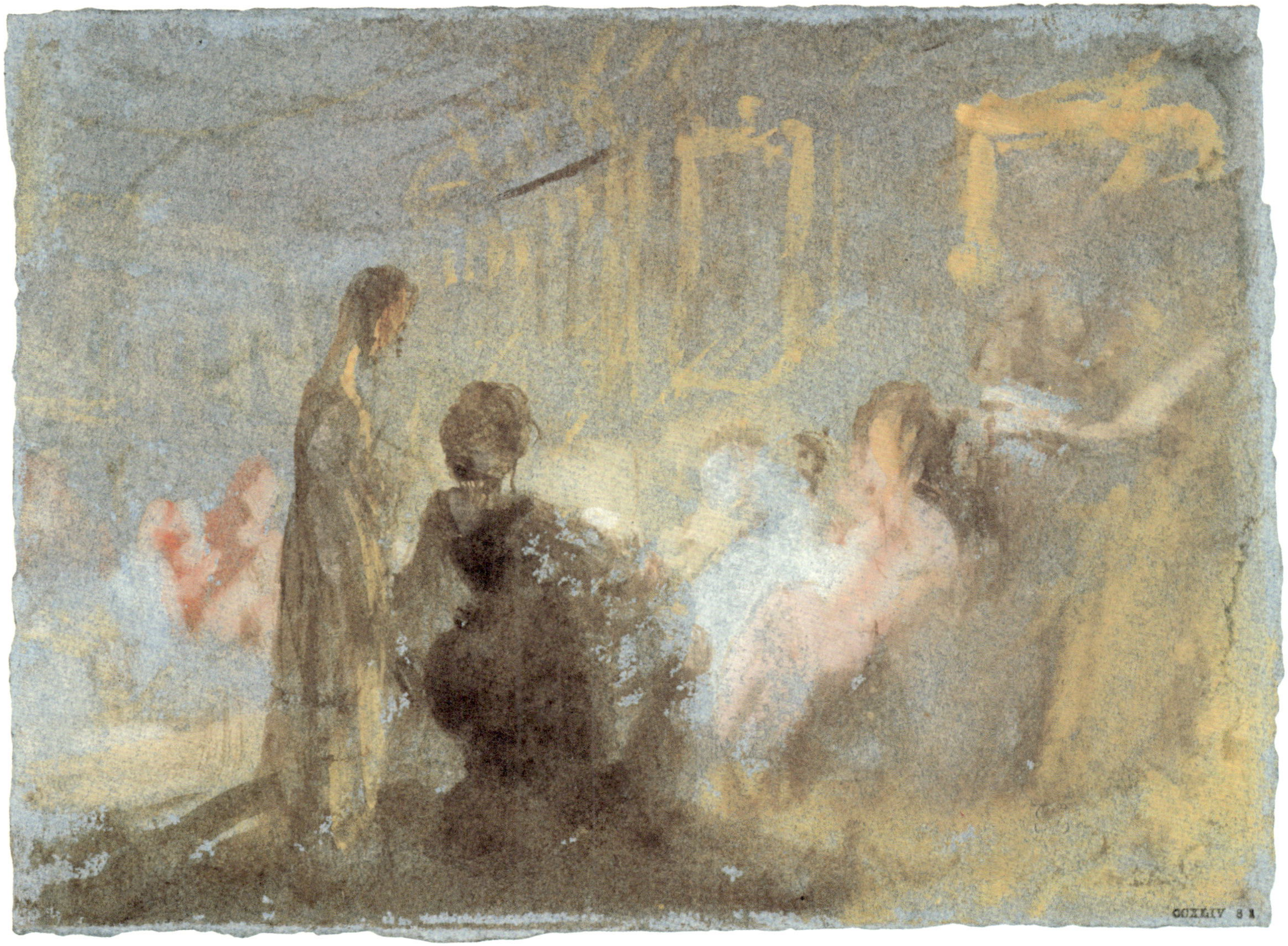

PLATE 27
A Conversation Group
TB CCXLIV–81

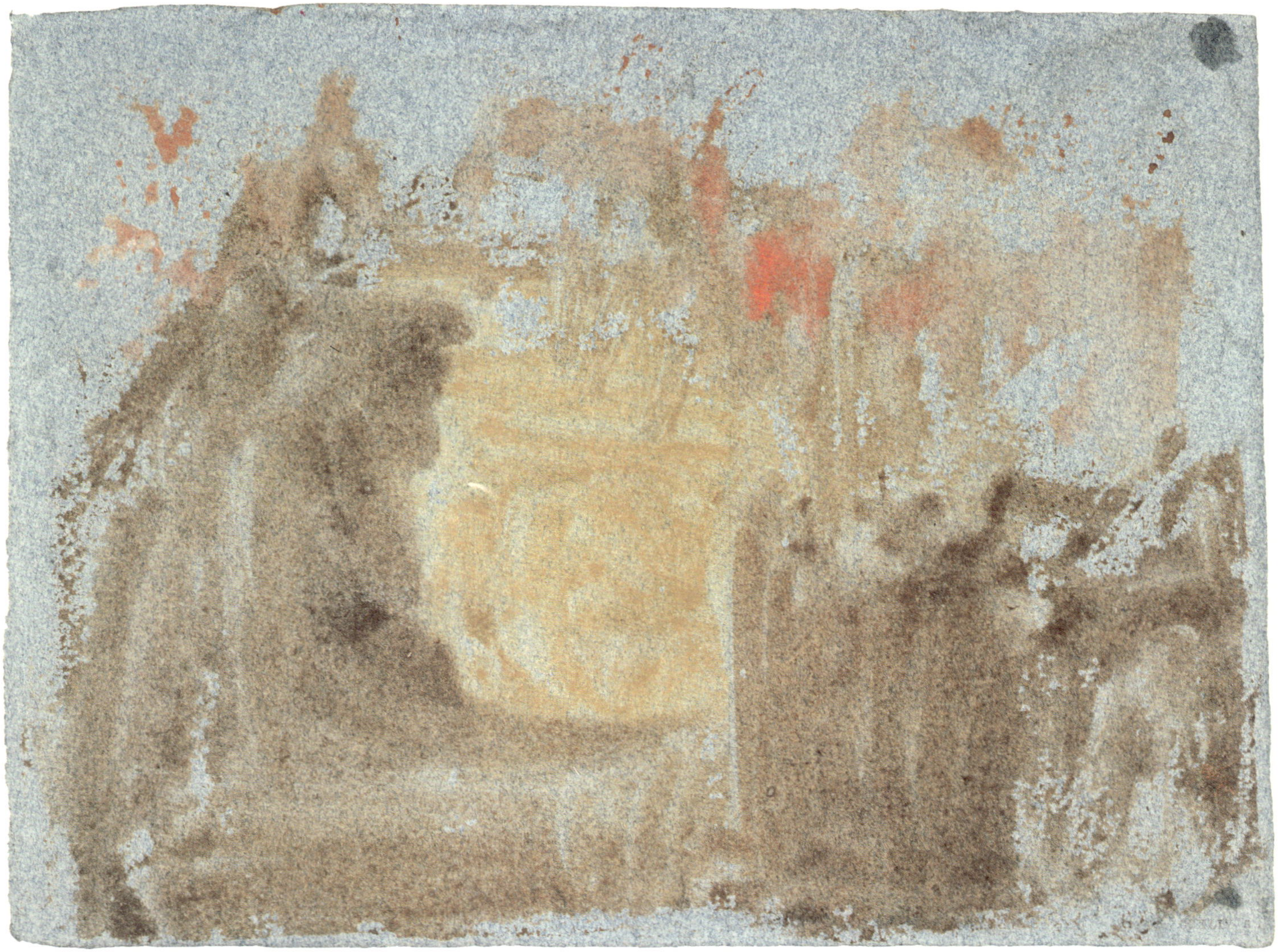

PLATE 28
Colour Trial or Colour Beginning: an interior
TB CCXLIV–51

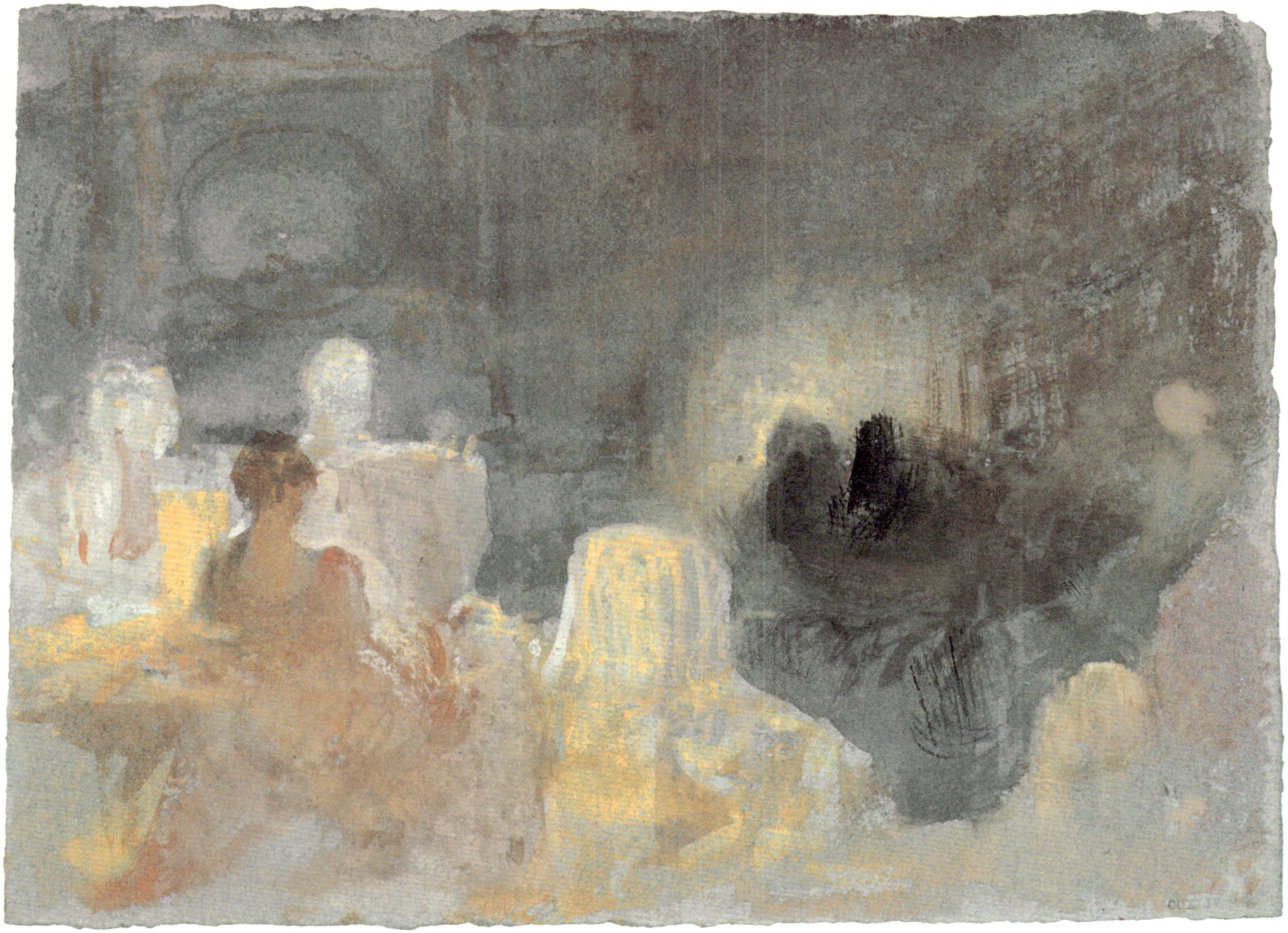

PLATE 29
Fire-light and Lamp-light
TB CCXLIV–41

PLATE 30
Figures
TB CCXLIV–93

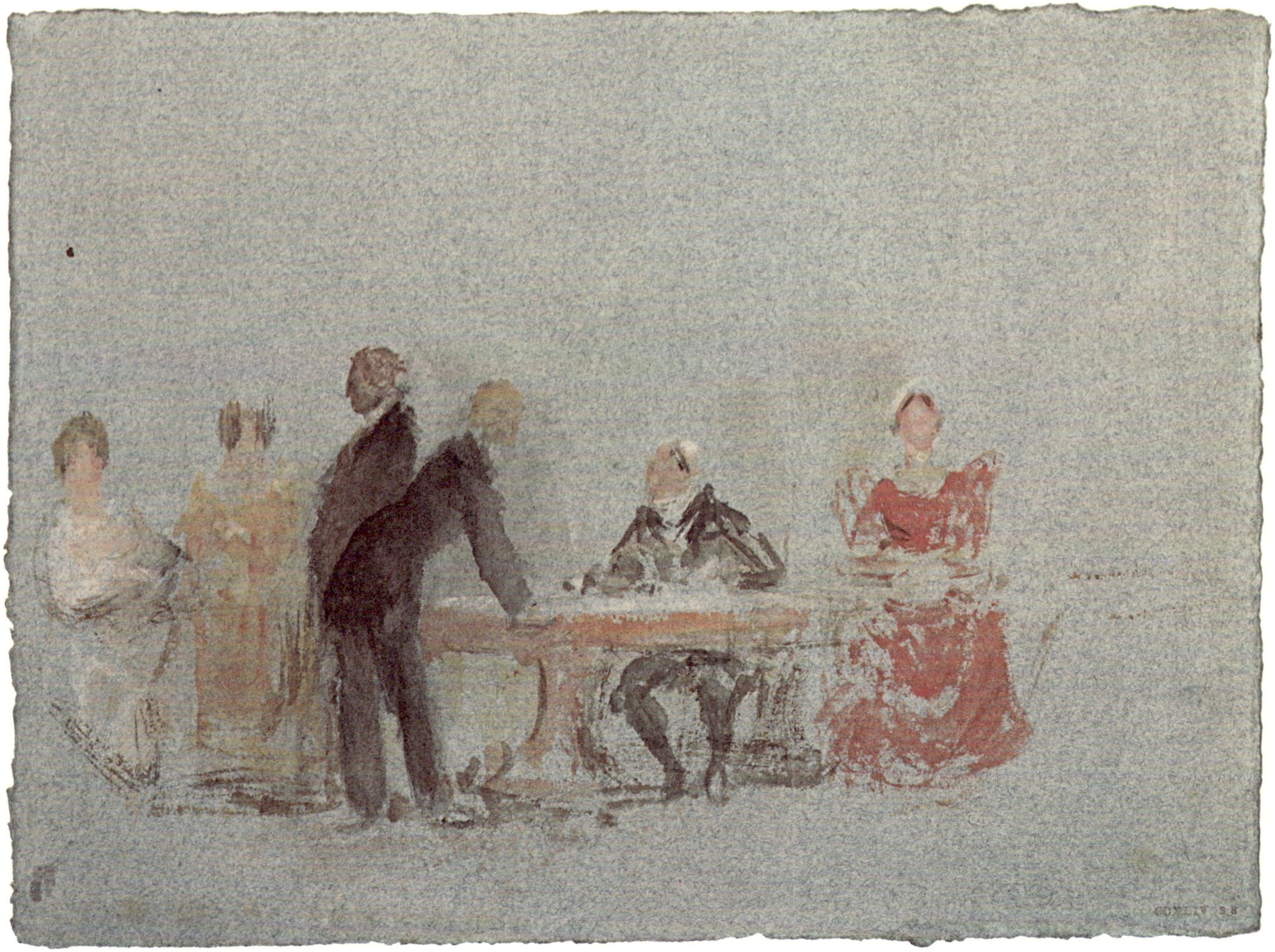

PLATE 31
Seated and Standing Figures
TB CCXLIV–38

PLATE 32
Seated Figures
TB CCXLIV–89

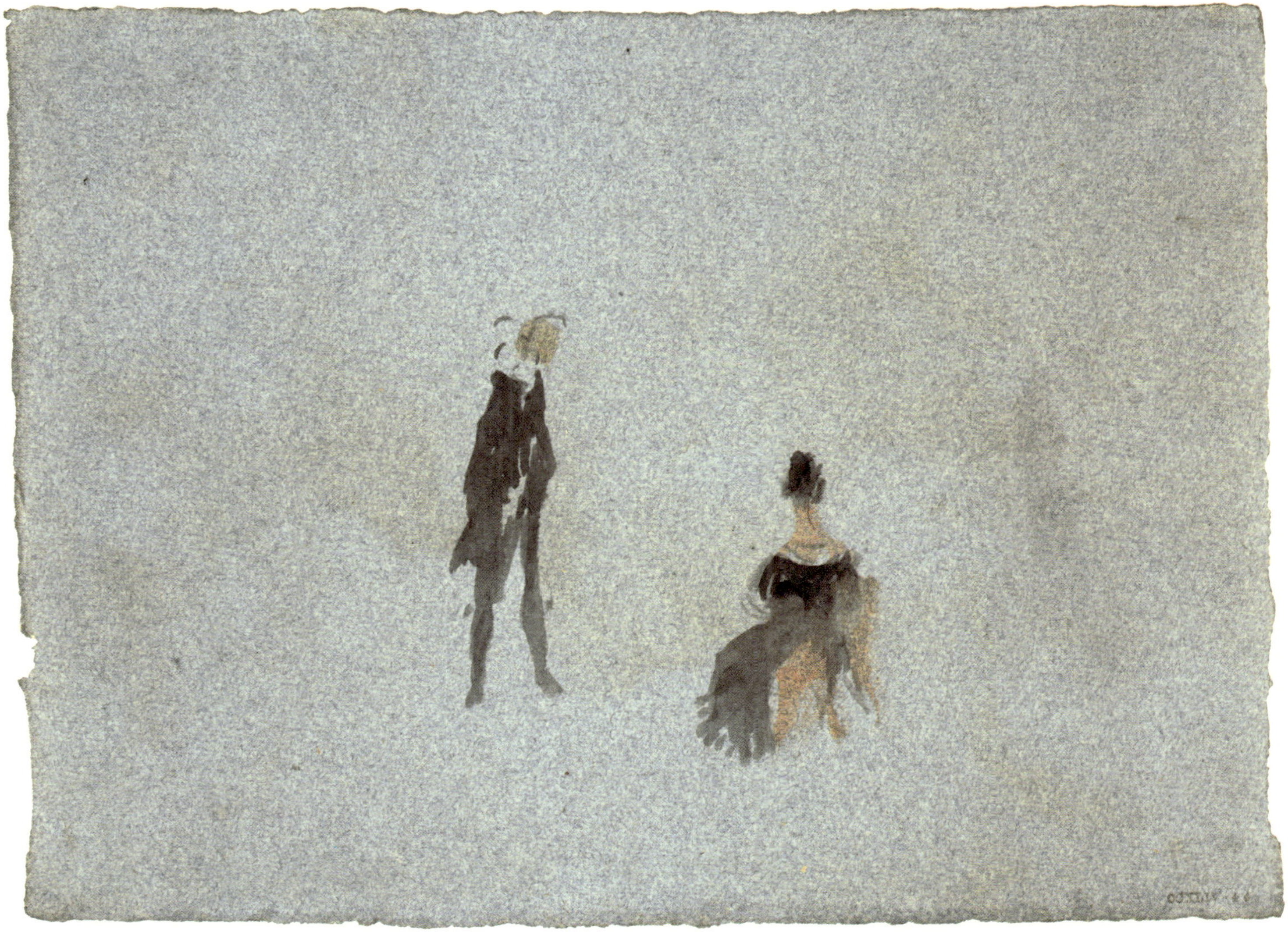

PLATE 33
Two Figures
TB CCXLIV–44

PLATE 34
A Single Figure
TB CCXLIV–47

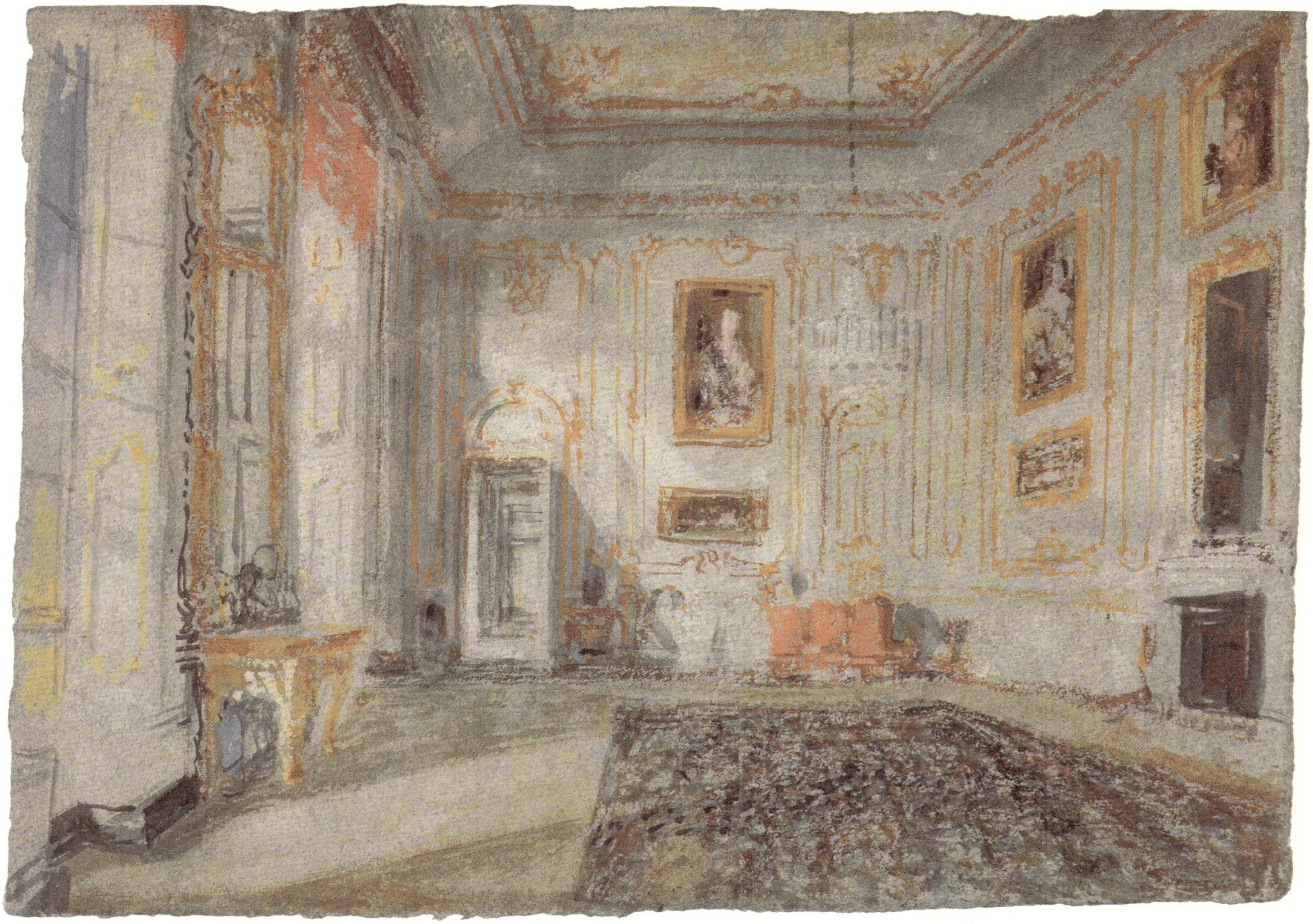

PLATE 35
The White and Gold Room (with Van Dyck portraits)
TB CCXLIV–14

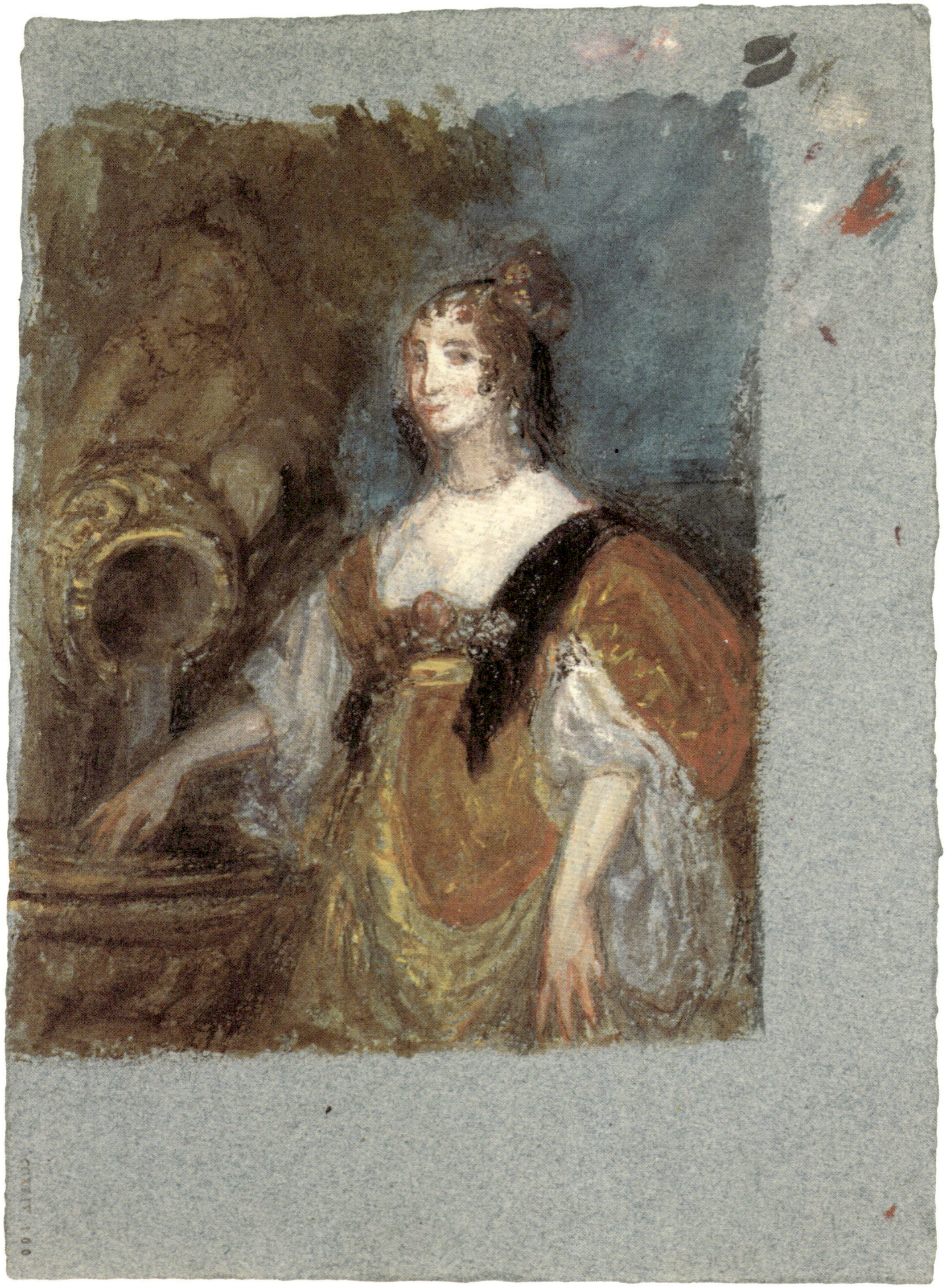

PLATE 36
A Copy of Van Dyck's Portrait of Lucy Percy, Countess of Carlisle (see fig. 55)
TB CCXLIV–100

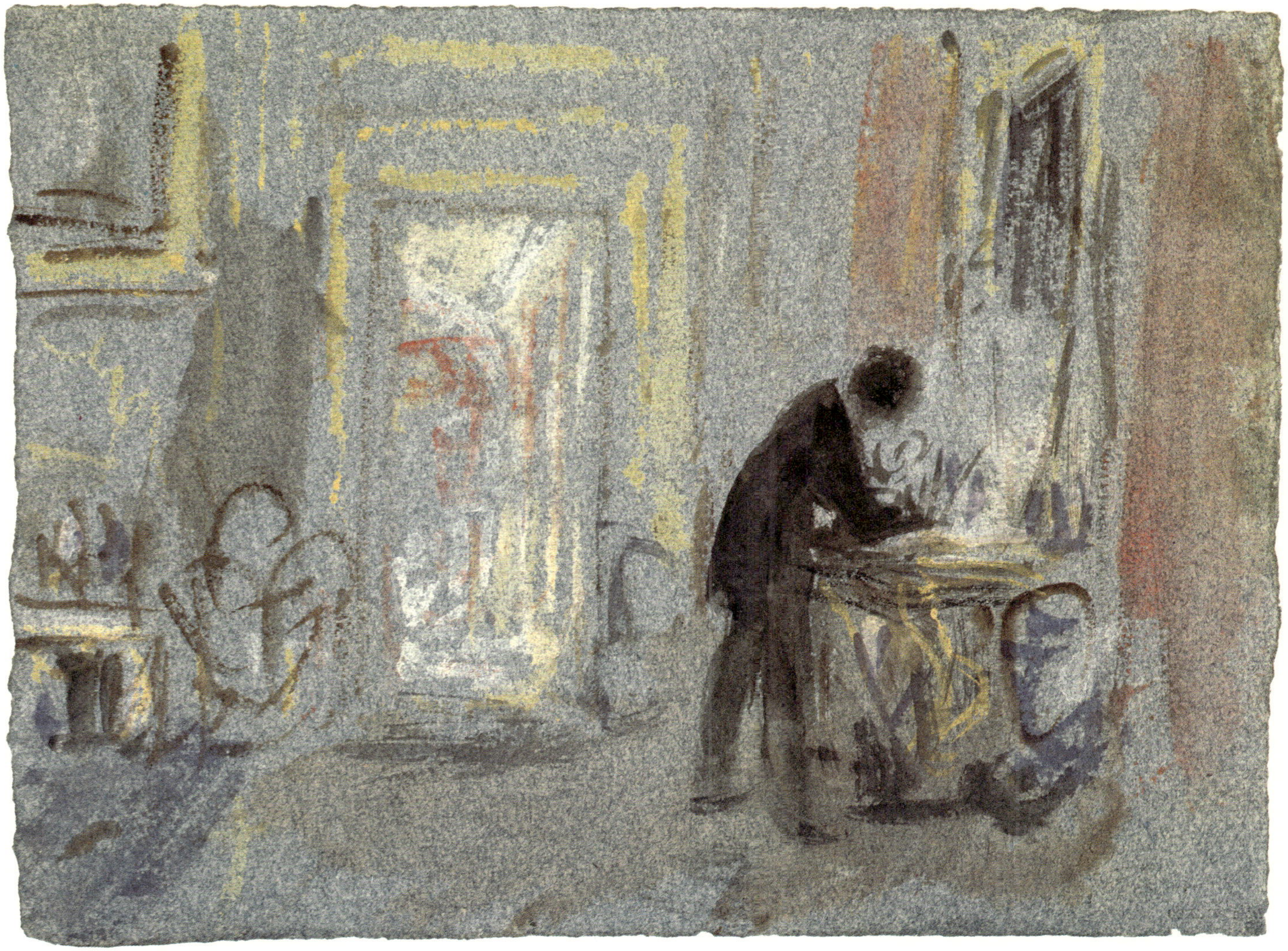

PLATE 37
A Man Standing at a Console Table in the White and Gold Room: the White Library seen through the open door. Formerly known as 'The Toilet'
TB CCXLIV–30

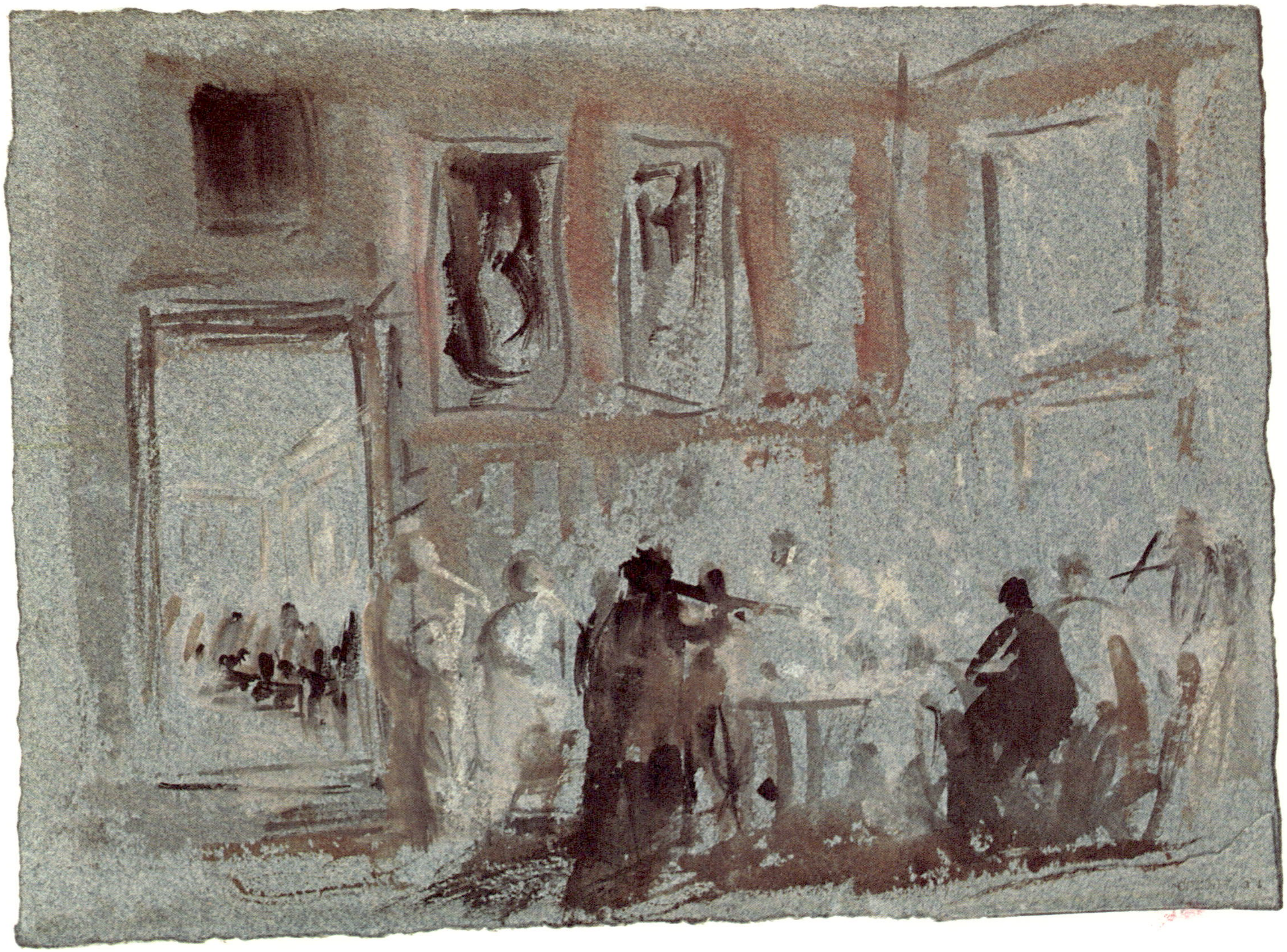

PLATE 38
Musicians
TB CCXLIV–34

PLATE 39
At Dinner
TB CCXLIV–36

PLATE 40
Figures at Table
TB CCXLIV–36

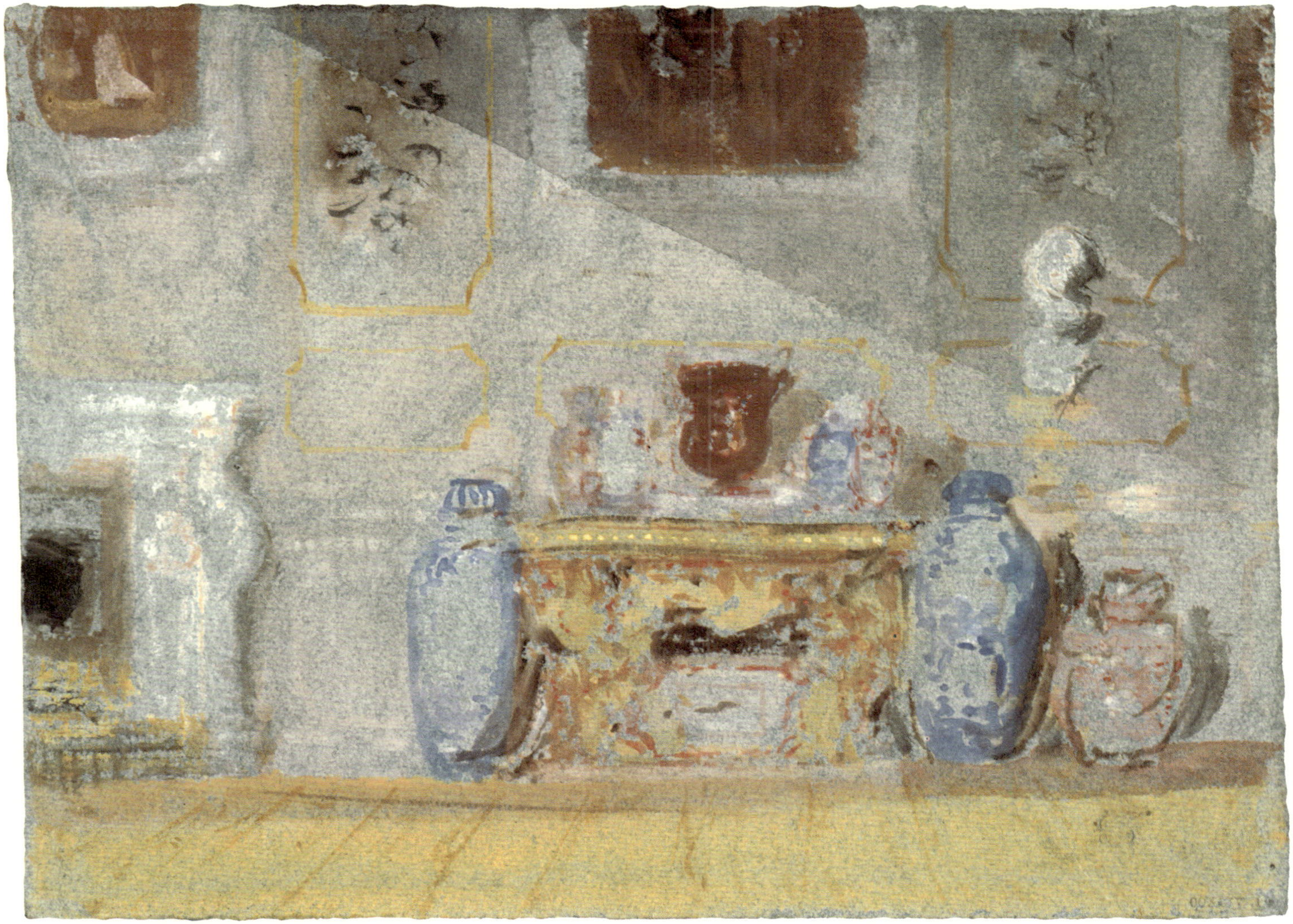

PLATE 41
Blue and White China Jars Flanking a Gilt Console Table: carvings by Grinling Gibbons
TB CCXLIV–19

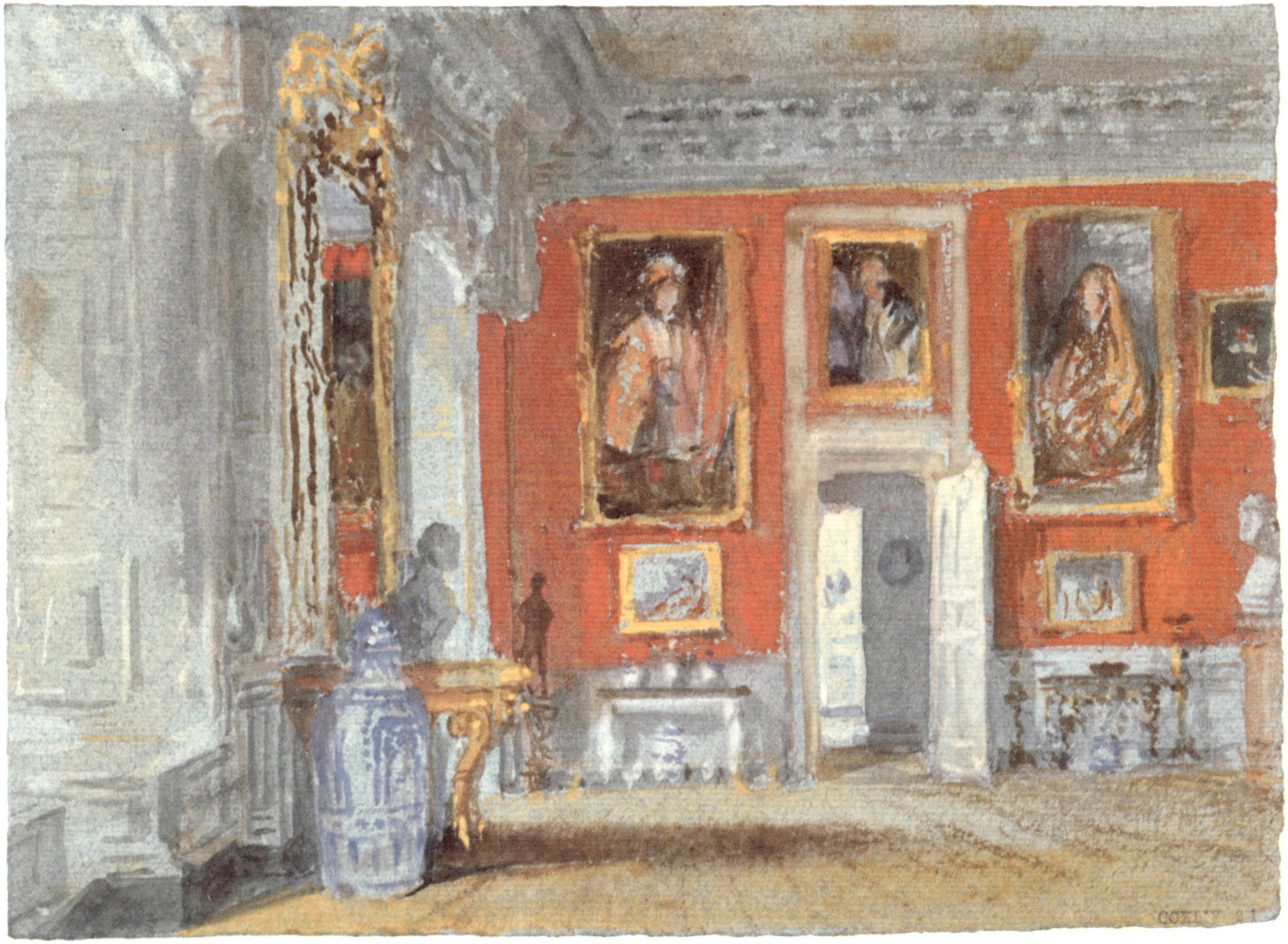

PLATE 42
The Red Room
TB CCXLIV–21

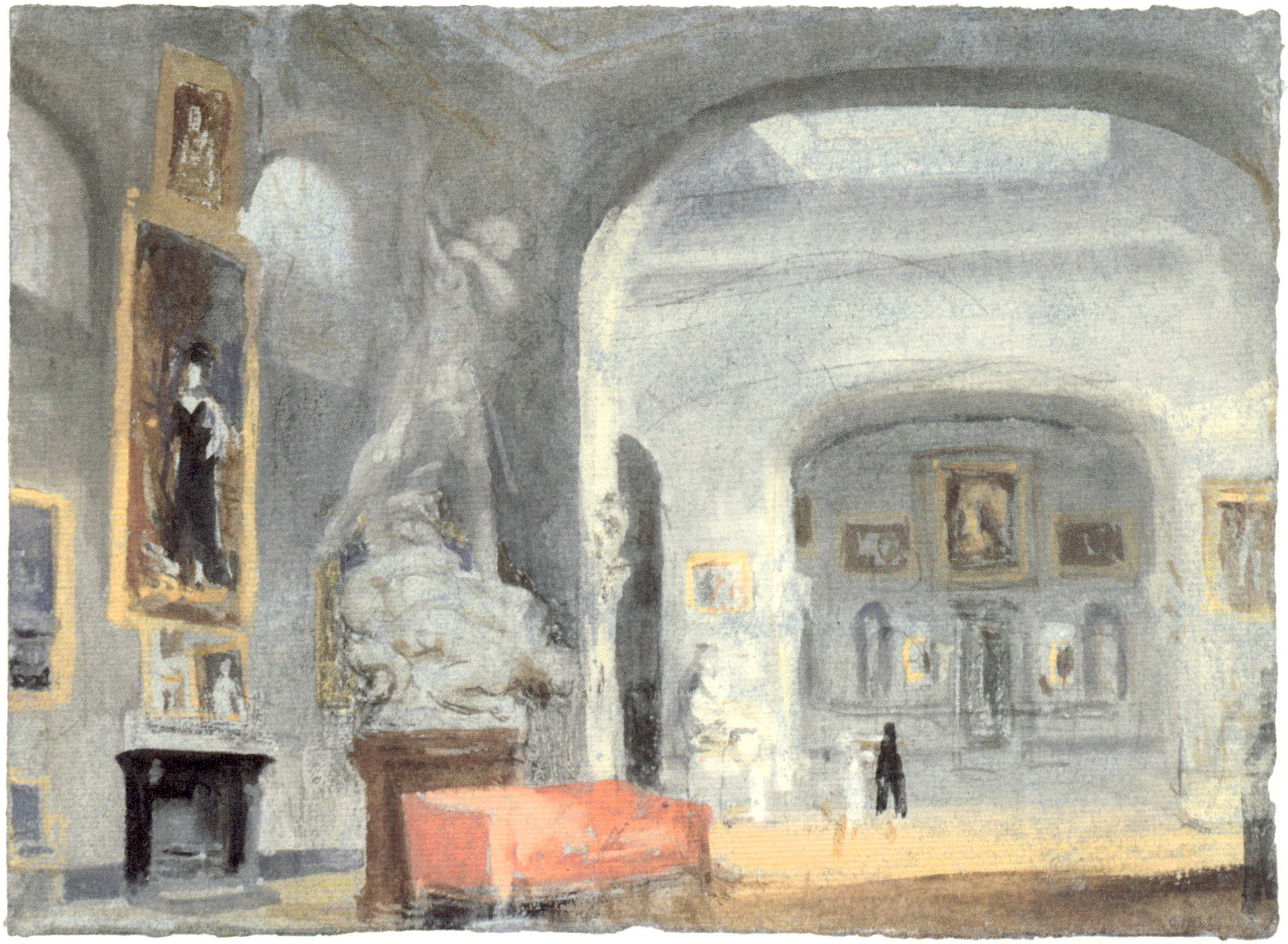

PLATE 43
The North Gallery from the North Bay
Owen's portrait of Mrs Robinson hangs to the left of
Flaxman's 'St Michael Overcoming Satan' (fig. 14)
TB CCXLIV–13 Watercolour and gouache over pencil outlines

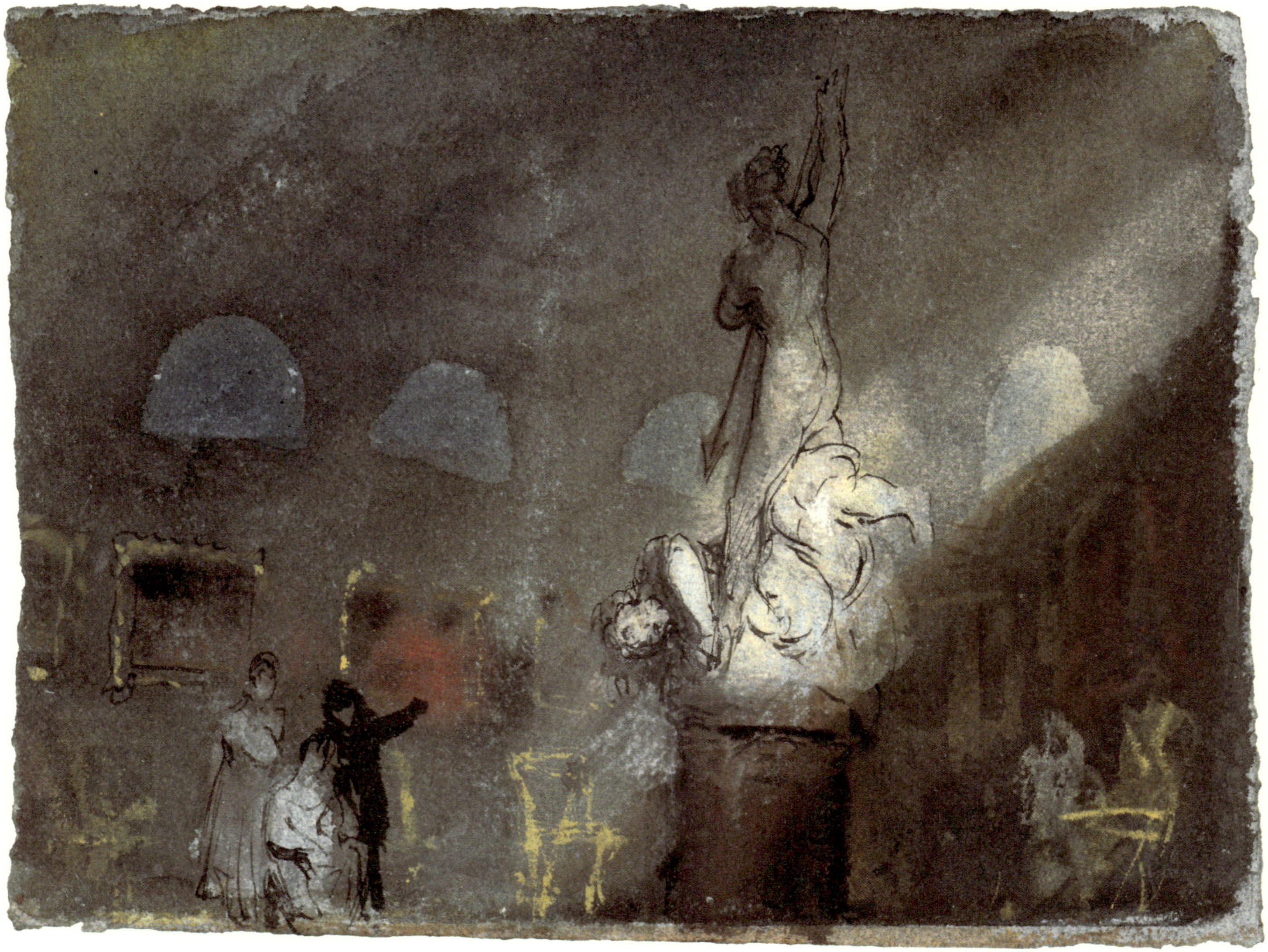

PLATE 44

The North Gallery at Night Figures contemplating Flaxman's newly completed statue, 'St Michael Overcoming Satan' (fig. 14)
TB CCXLIV–25 Pen and black ink with watercolour and gouache and some scraping-out

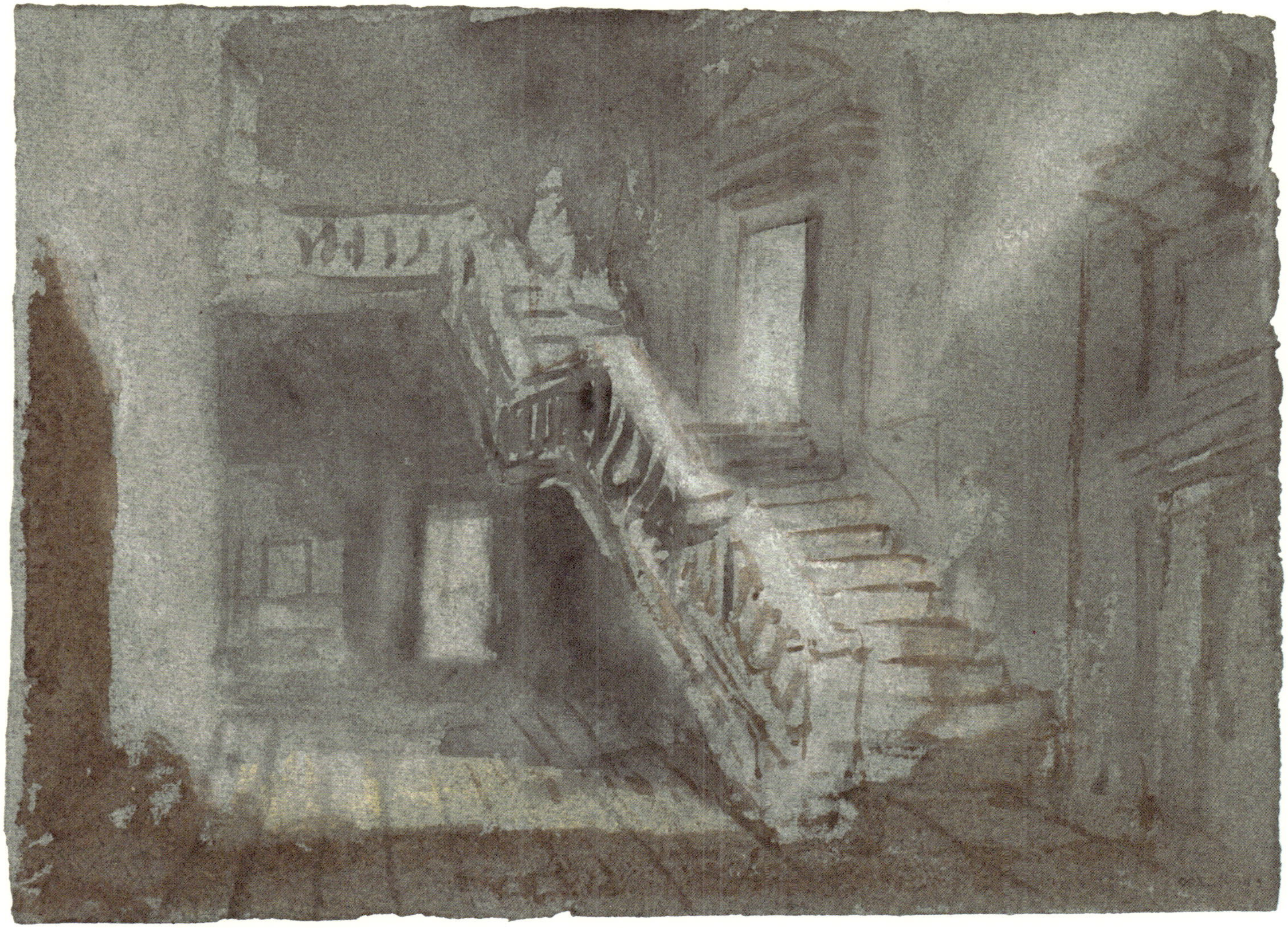

PLATE 45
The Old Library Staircase
TB CCXLIV–95

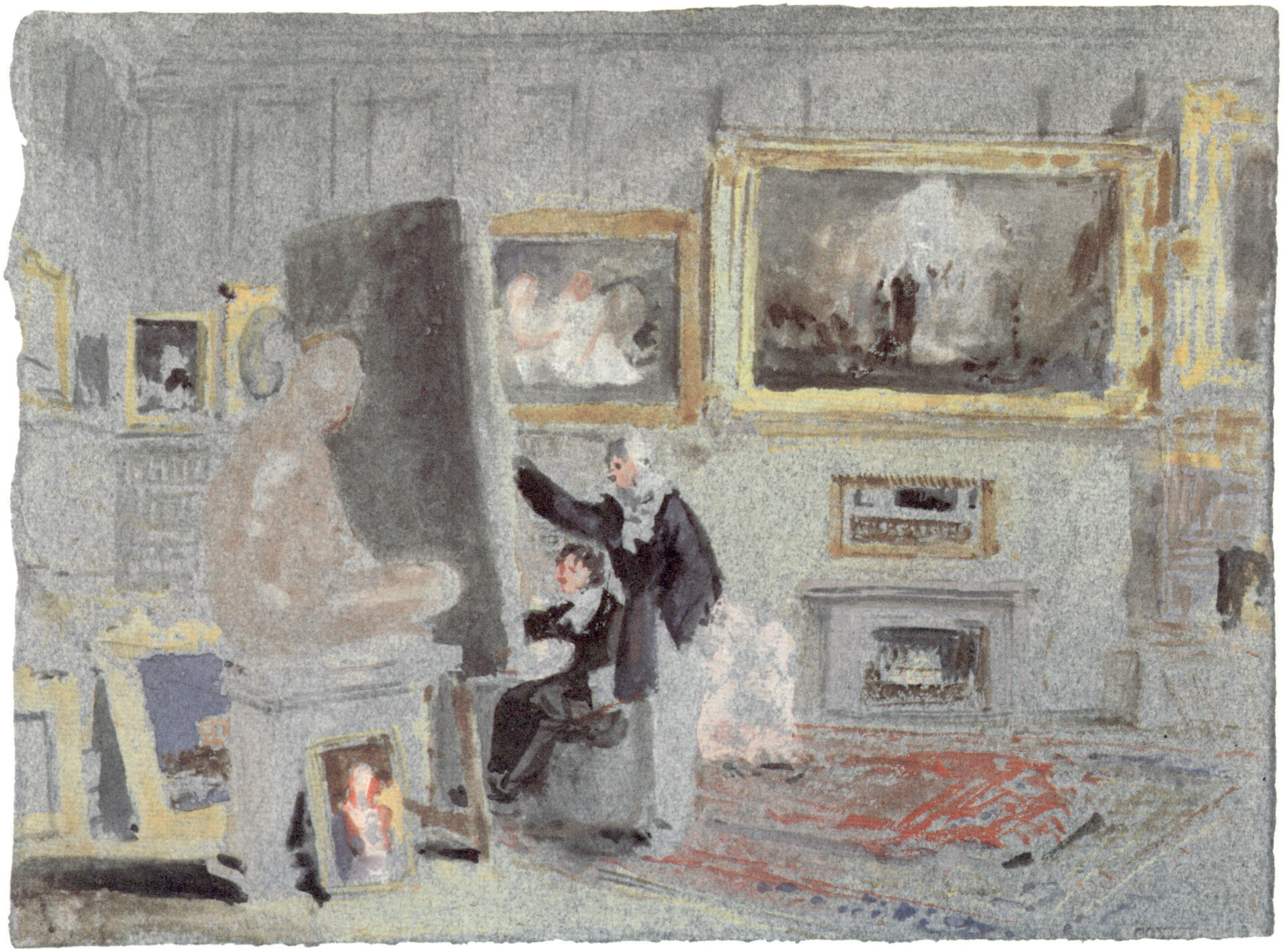

PLATE 46

Two Artists in the Old Library Formerly known as 'The Artist and the Amateur'. Washington Allston's picture, 'Jacob's Dream' (fig. 47), hangs over the fireplace

TB CCXLIV–103

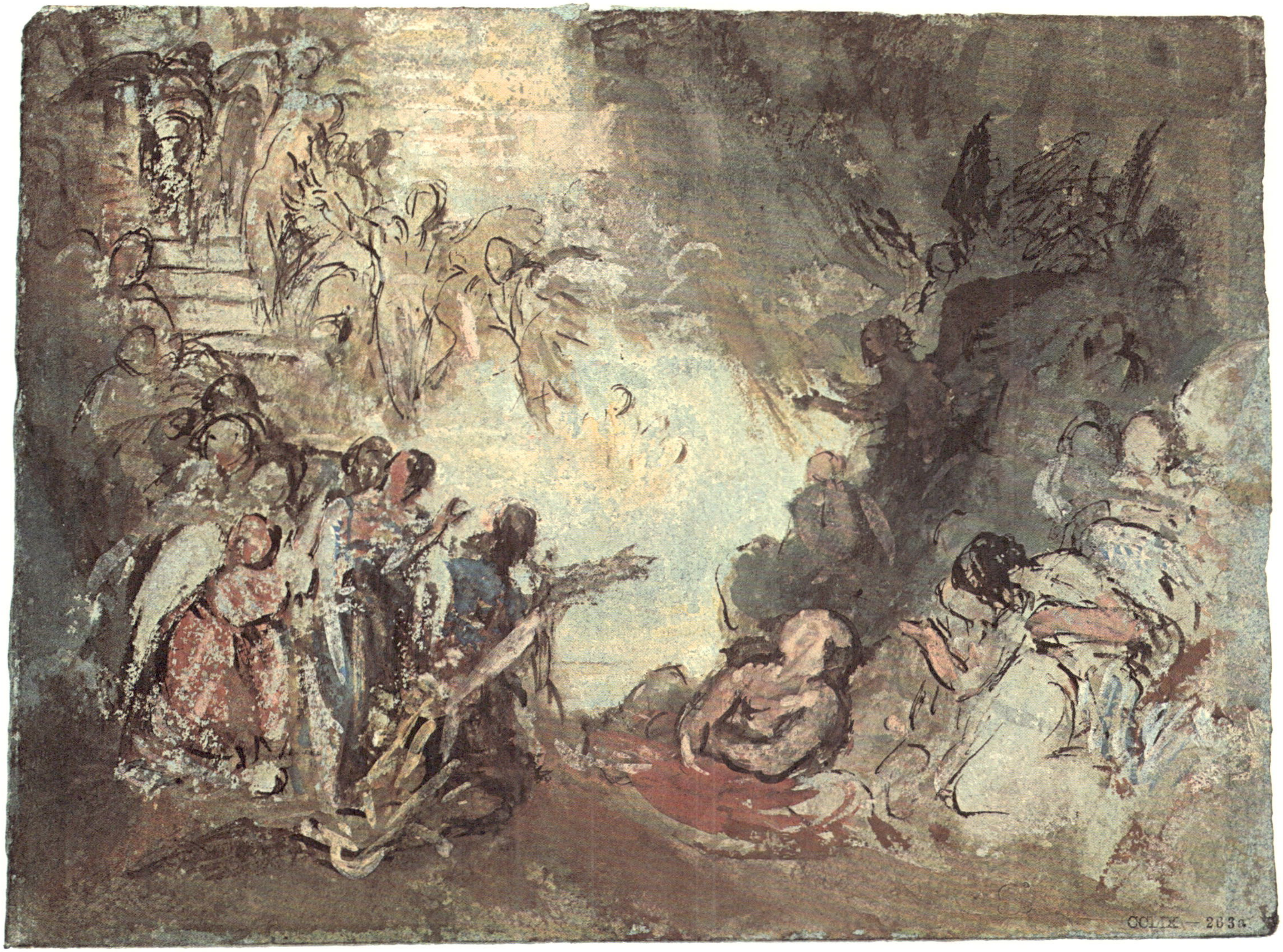

PLATE 47

A Variation on Washington Allston's 'Jacob's Dream'

TB CCLIX–263a Pen and brown ink with watercolour and gouache

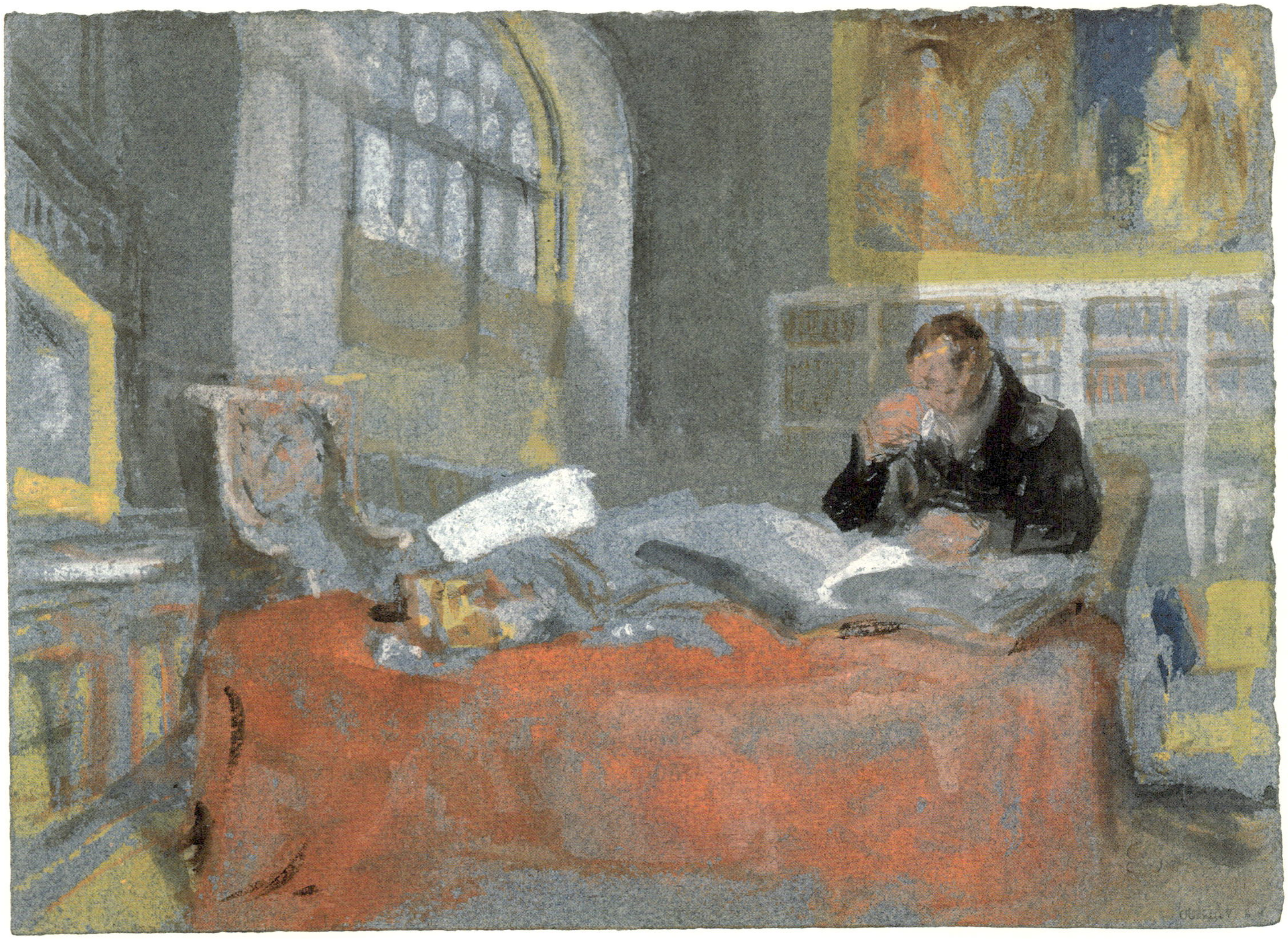

PLATE 48
A Man Seated at a Table in the Old Library
Formerly known as 'The Student'
TB CCXLIV–29

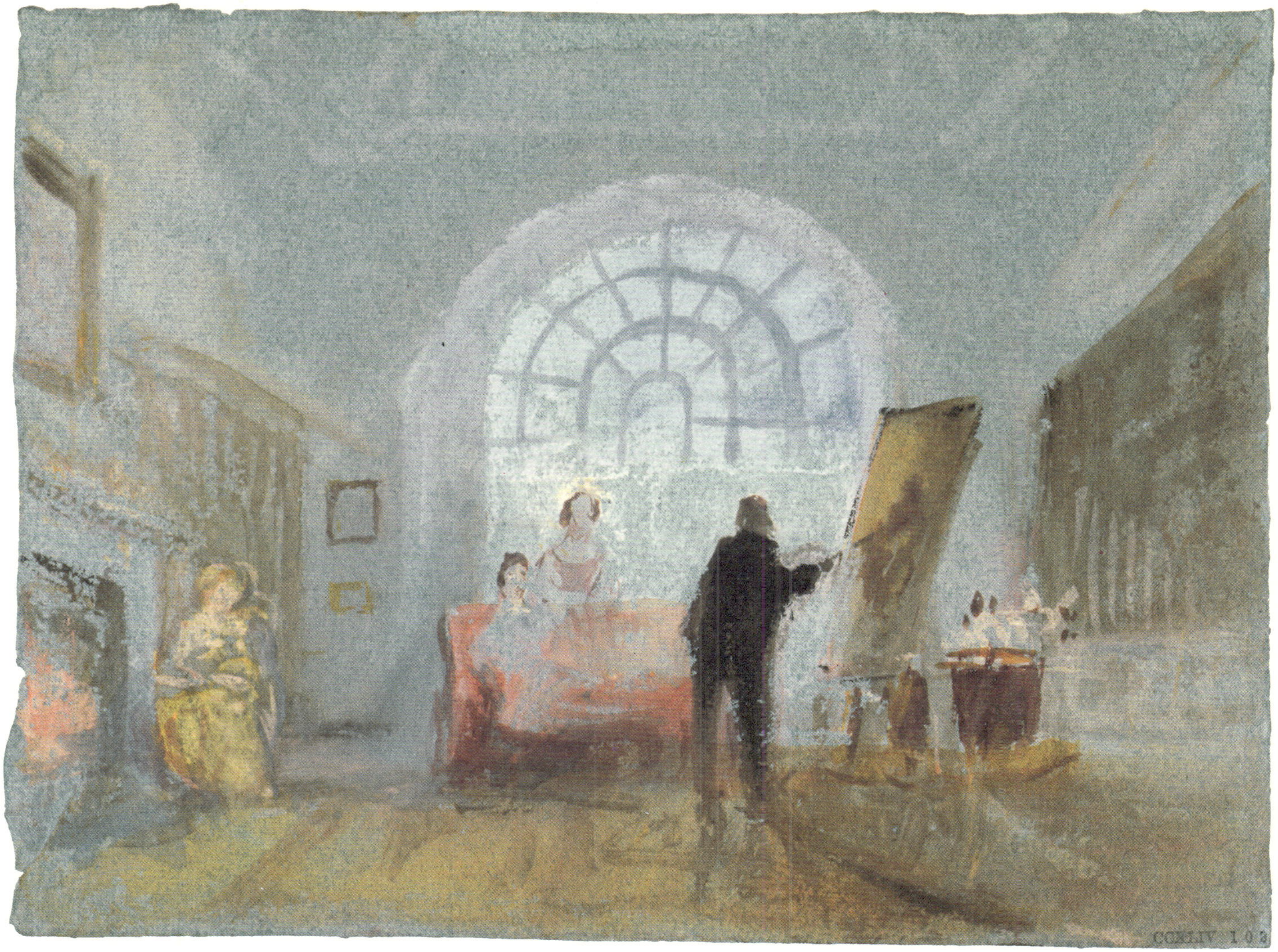

PLATE 49
The Artist and his Admirers
TB CCXLIV–102

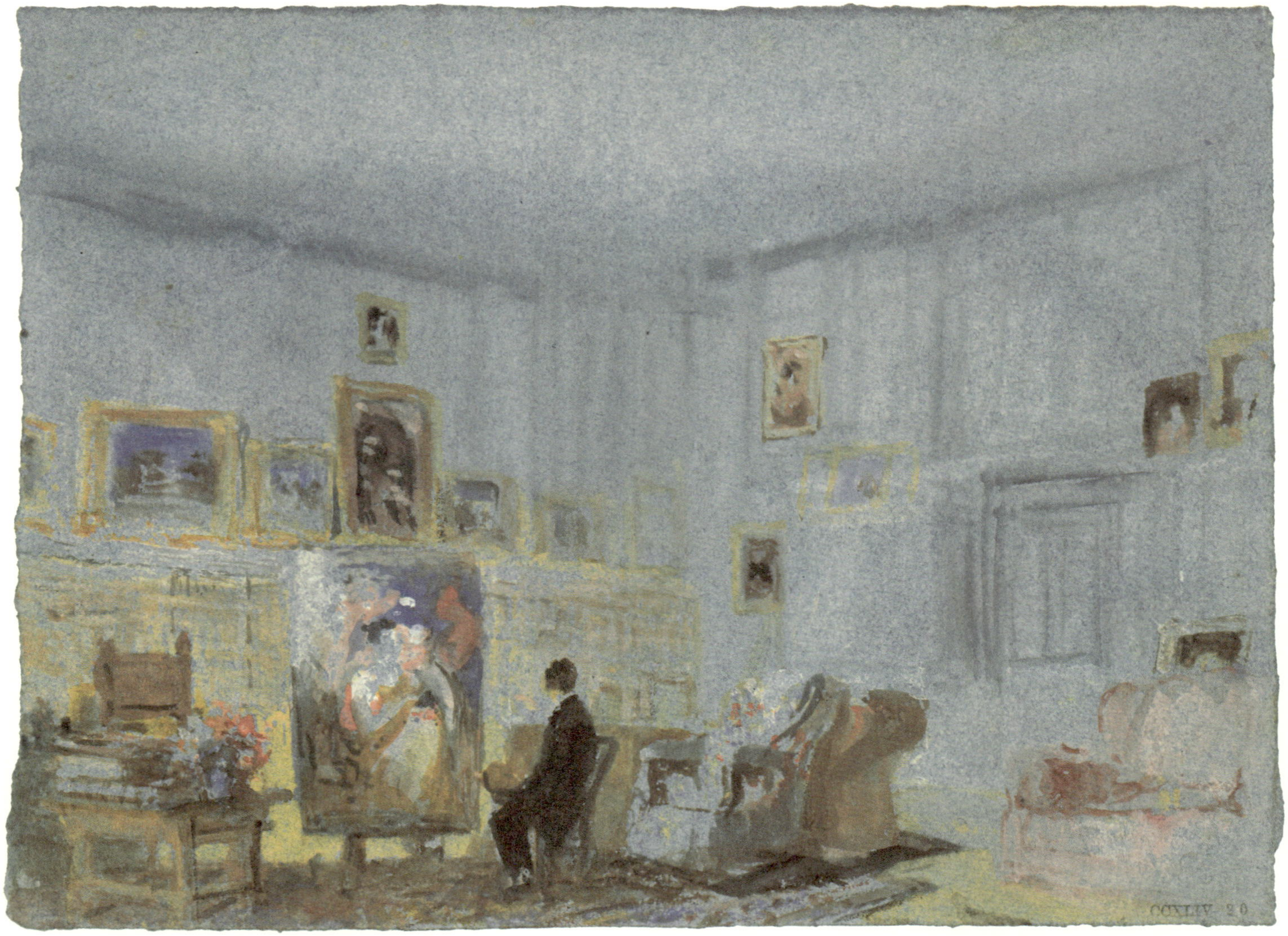

PLATE 50

An Artist Seated before Sir William Beechey's Portrait
'Mrs Hasler as Flora'

TB CCXLIV–20

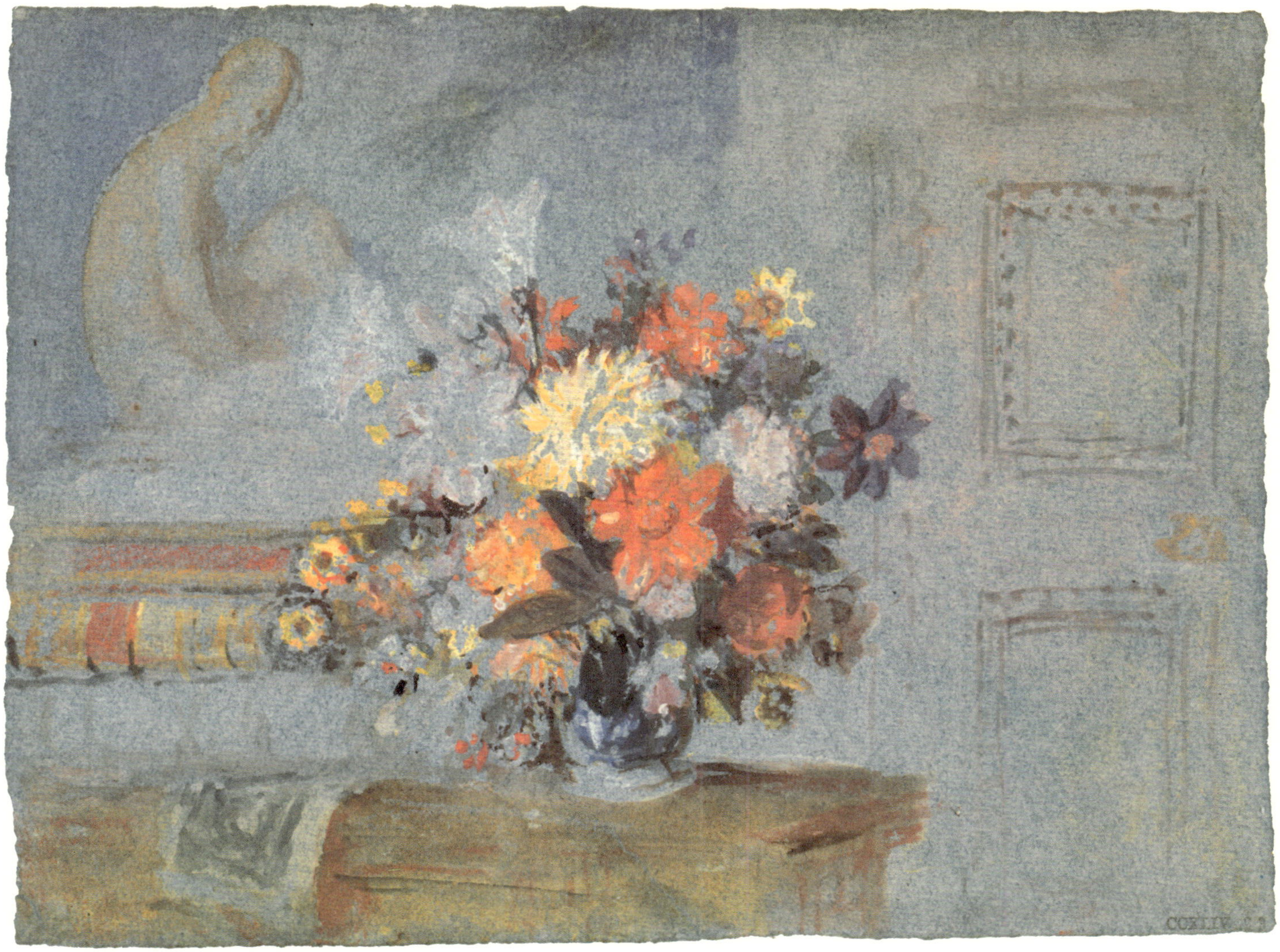

PLATE 51

A Vase of Lilies, Dahlias and Other Flowers A statue of Venus by Nollekens appears in the background

TB CCXLIV–23

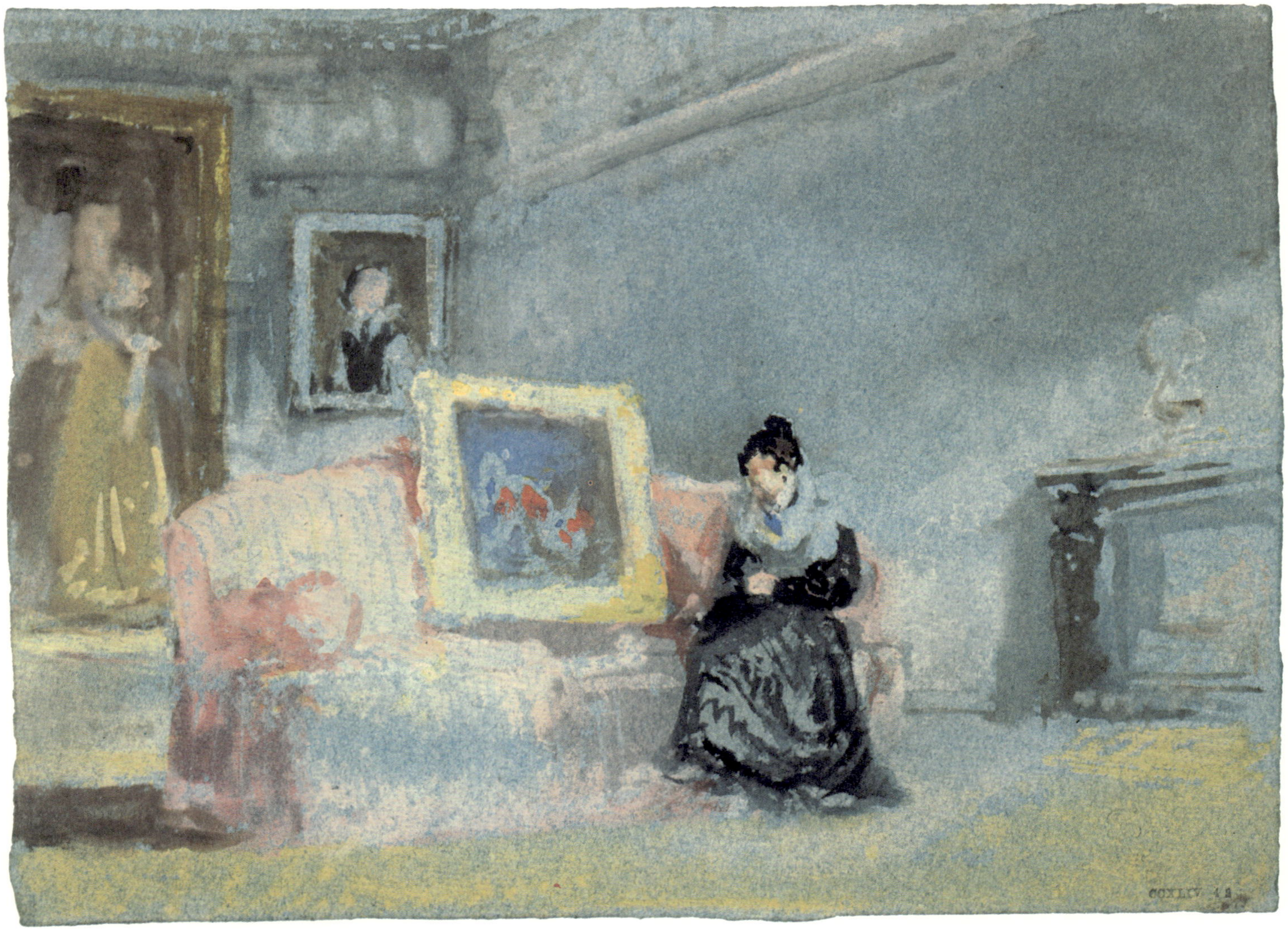

PLATE 52
A Lady in a Black Silk Dress Seated on a Pink Sofa
TB CCXLIV–42

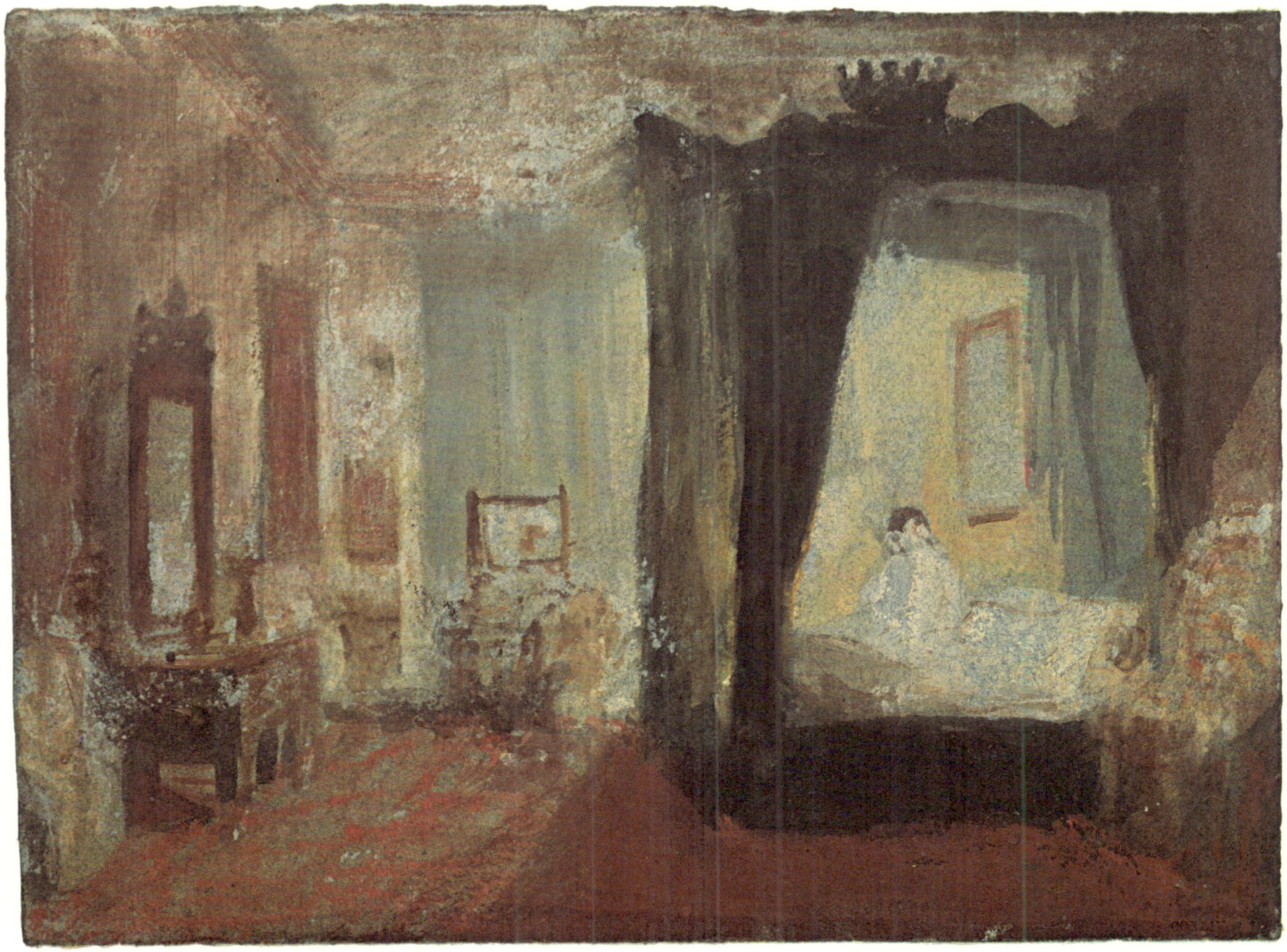

PLATE 53

A Bedroom with a Large Four-Poster Bed: ?The Petworth State Bed

TB CCXLIV–17

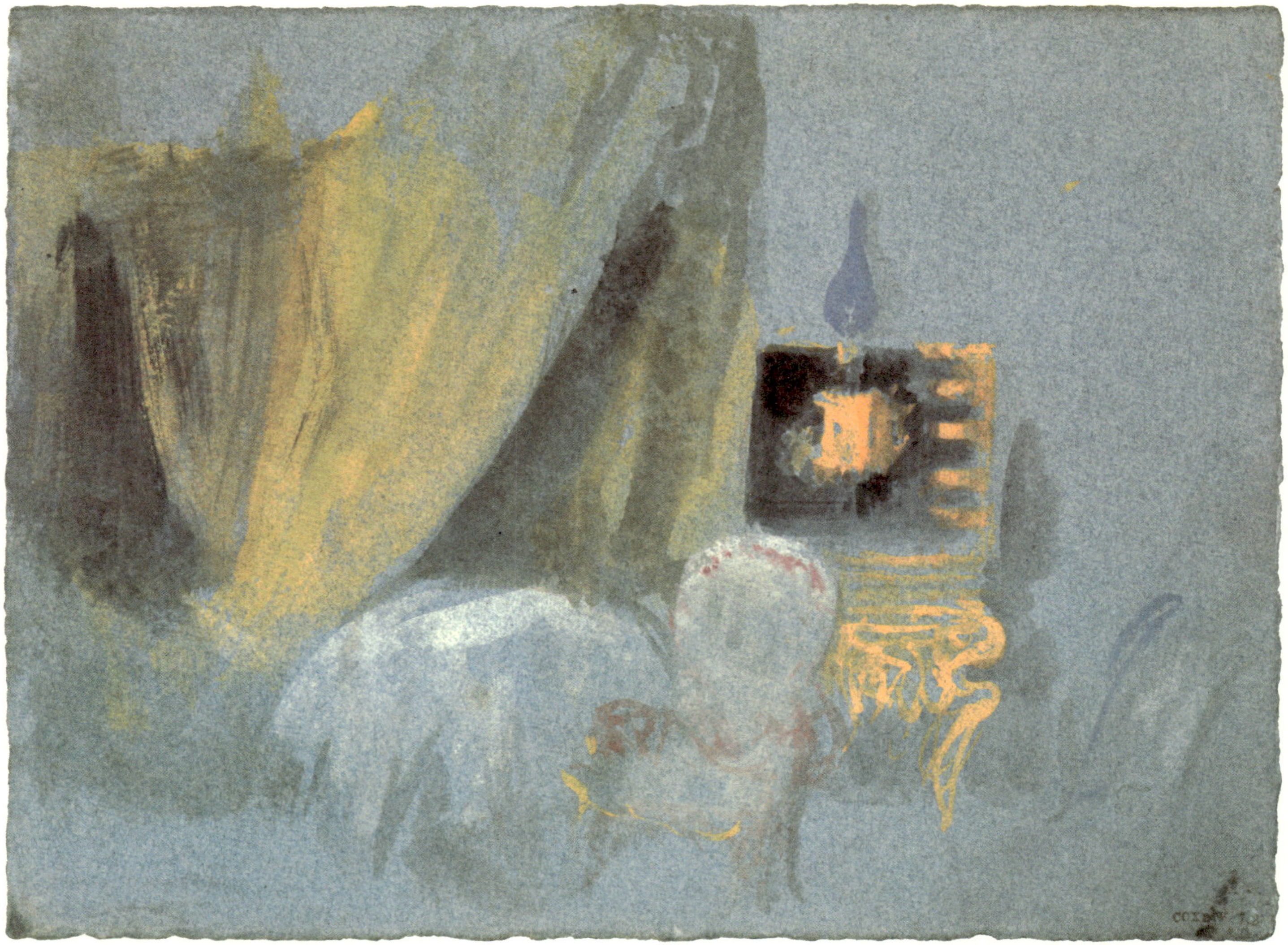

PLATE 54
A Japanese Lacquer Cabinet: a bed with yellow curtains
TB CCXLIV–72

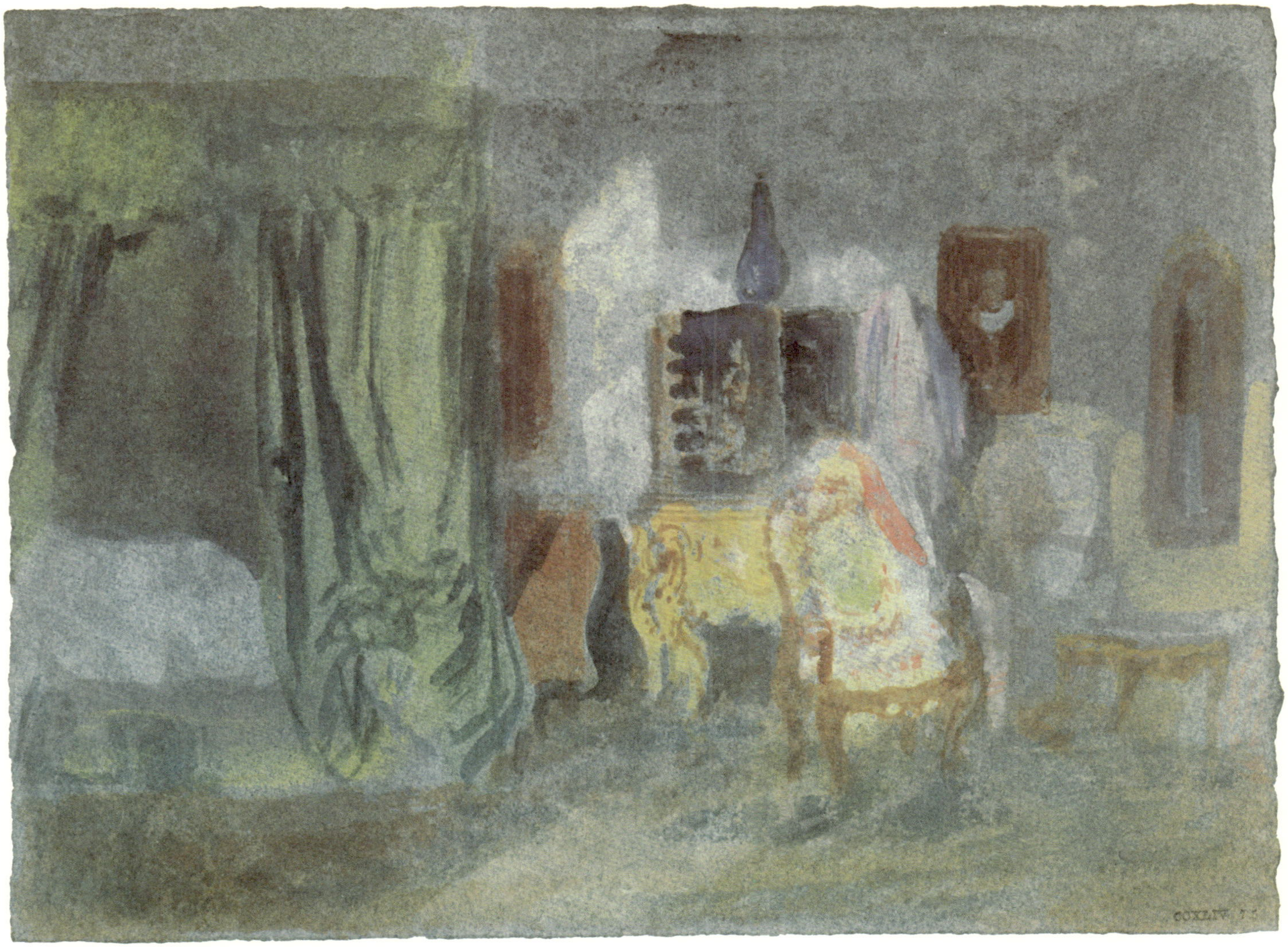

PLATE 55

A Japanese Lacquer Cabinet: a bed with green curtains

TB CCXLIV–75

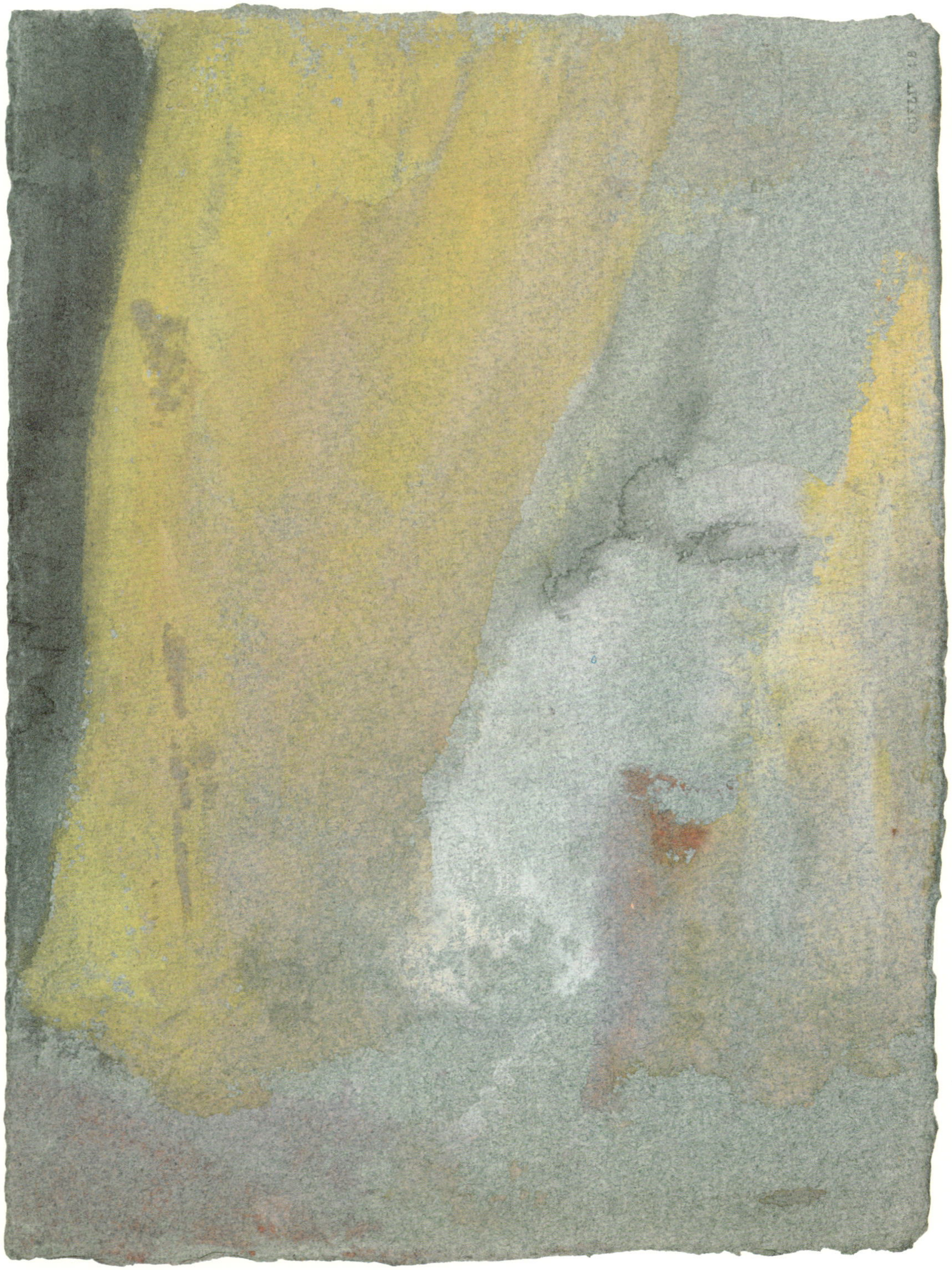

PLATE 56
Yellow Curtains
TB CCXLIV–48

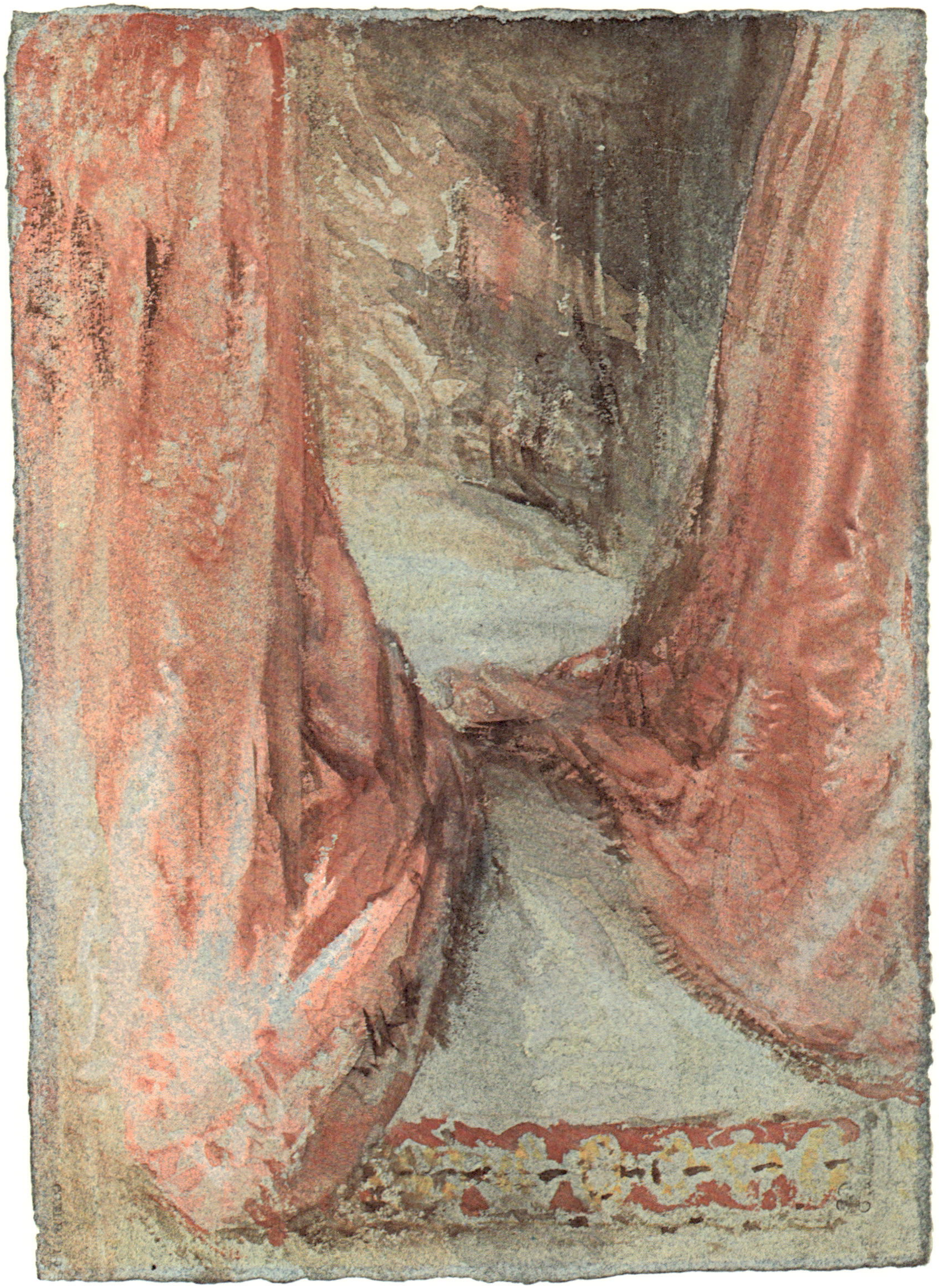

PLATE 57
Study of Pink Bed-Curtains
TB CCXLIV–15

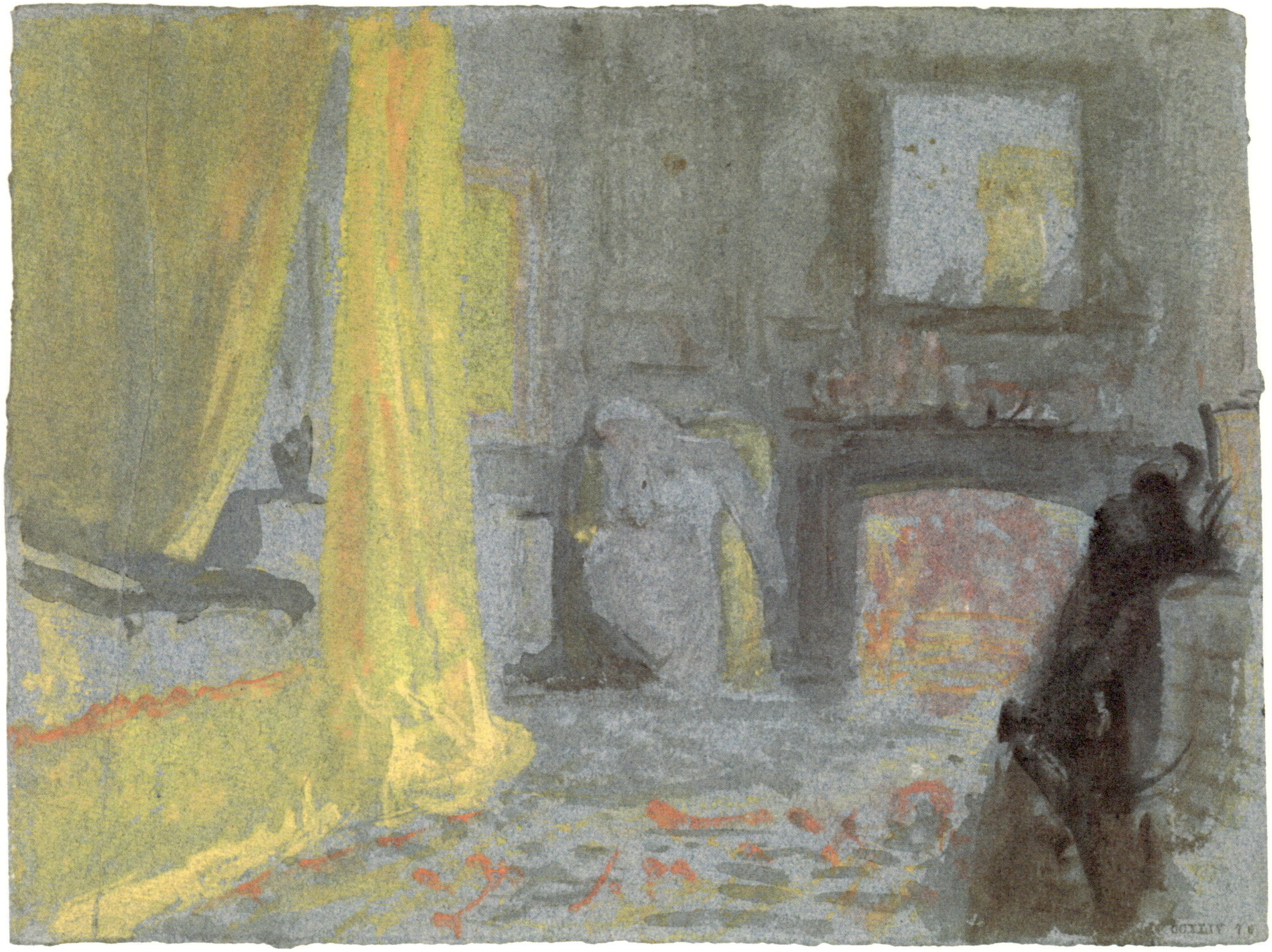

PLATE 58
A Bedroom: with a fire burning, and a bed with yellow curtains
TB CCXLIV–76

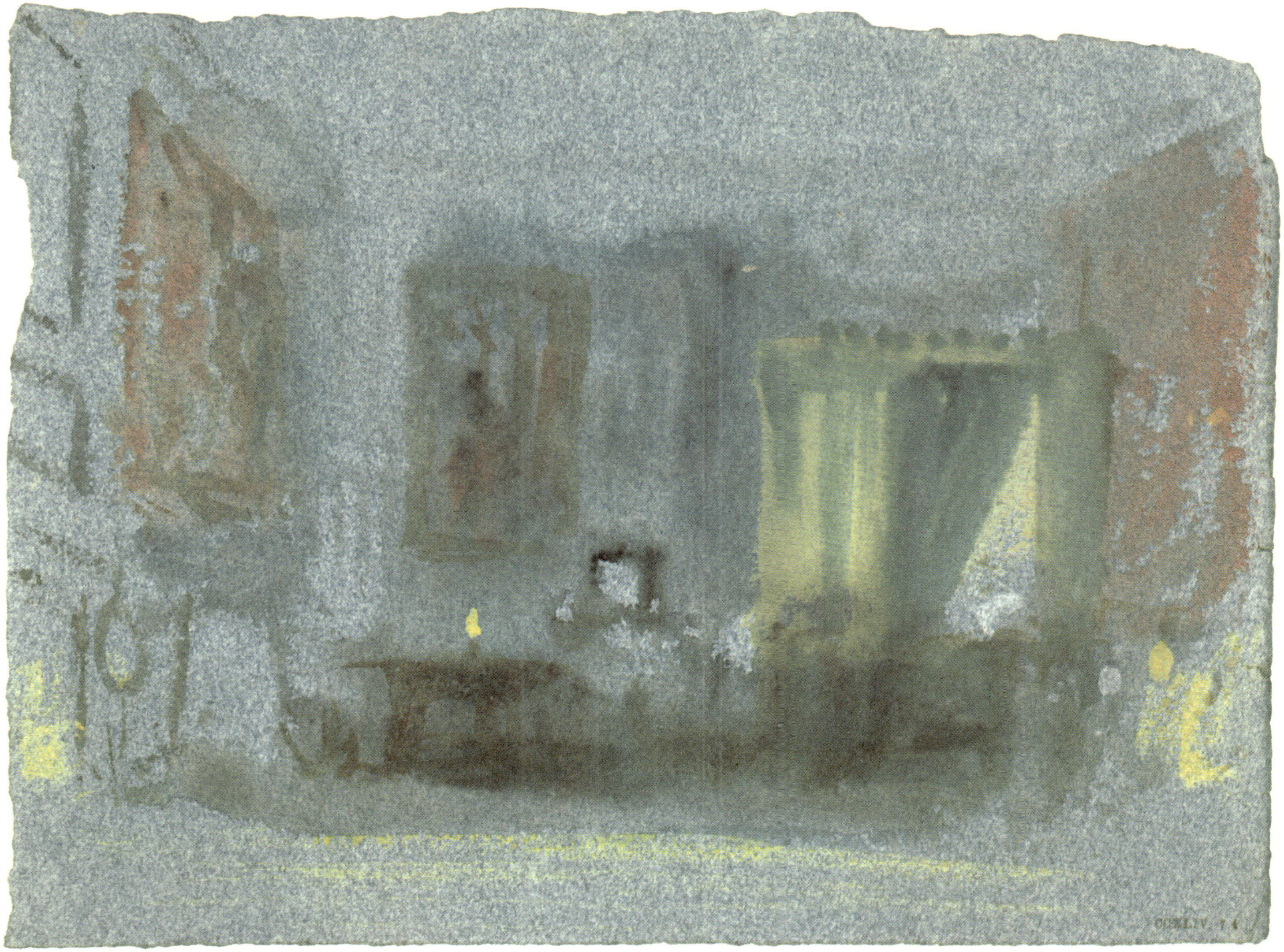

PLATE 59

A Bedroom: a lamp burning on a table

TB CCXLIV–74

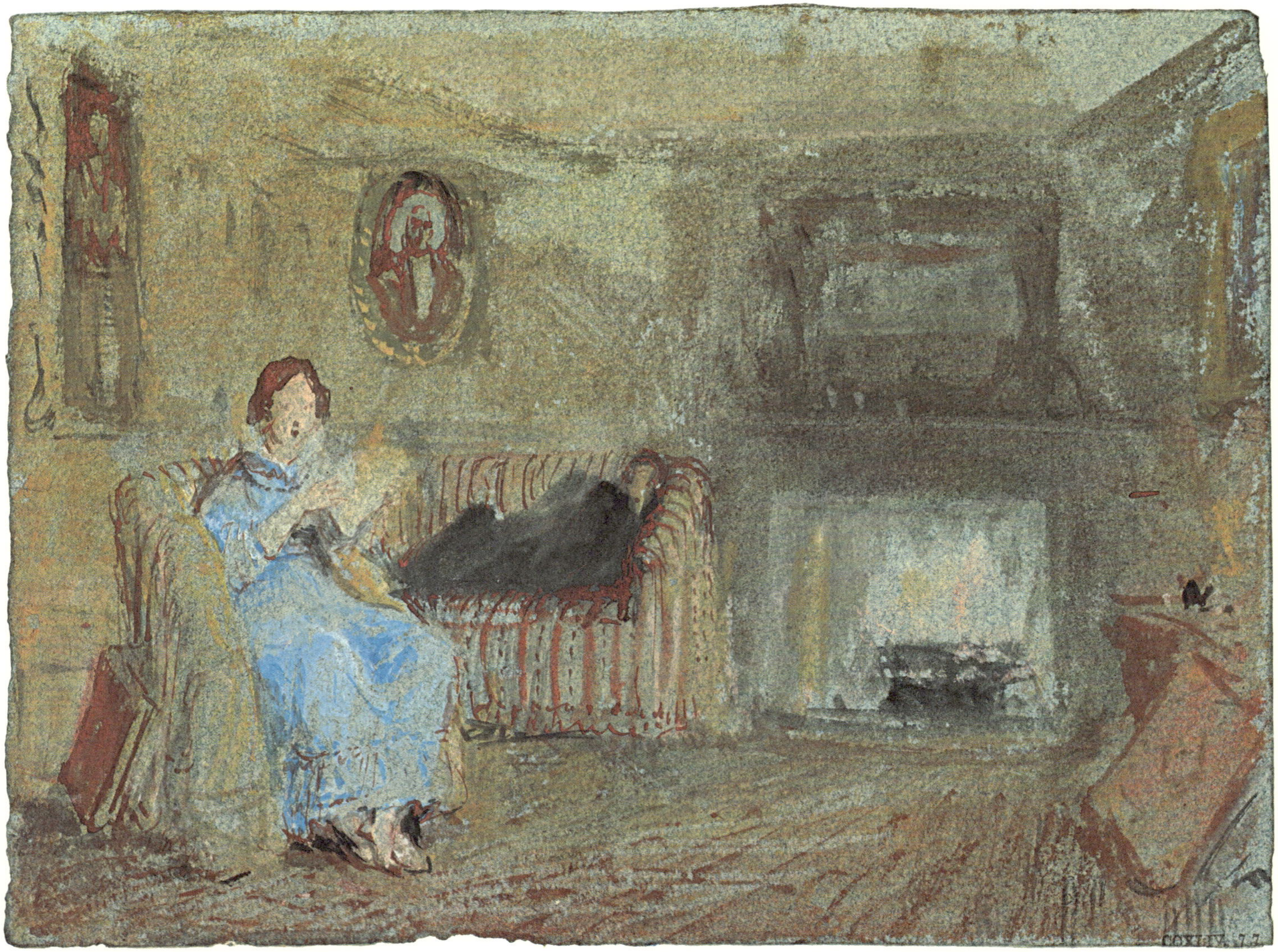

PLATE 60
A Bedroom: with a fire burning and a woman reading to a man lying on a sofa
TB CCXLIV–77

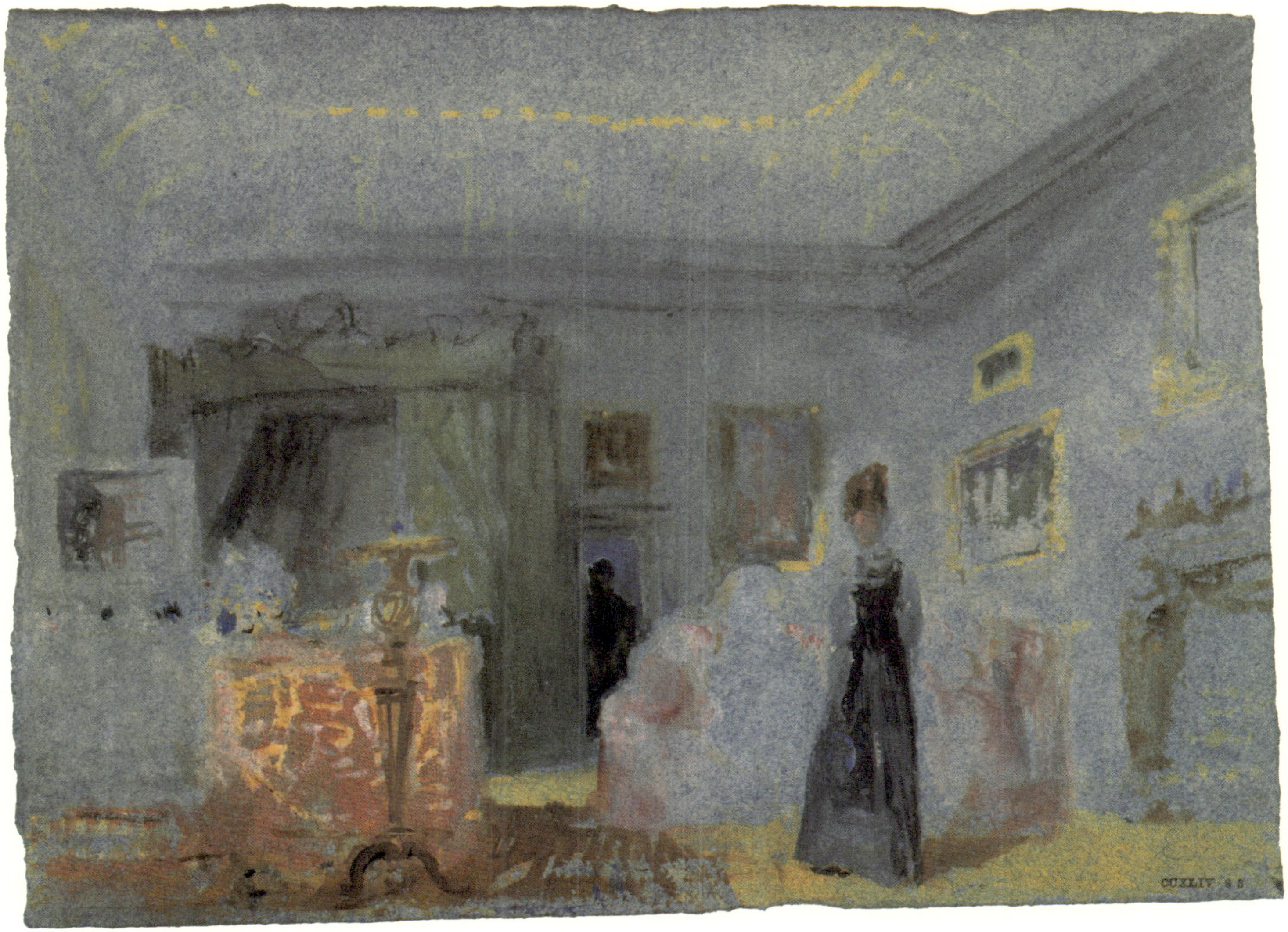

PLATE 61

A Bedroom: a lady dressed in black standing in a room with a green-curtained bed – a figure in the doorway

TB CCXLIV–83

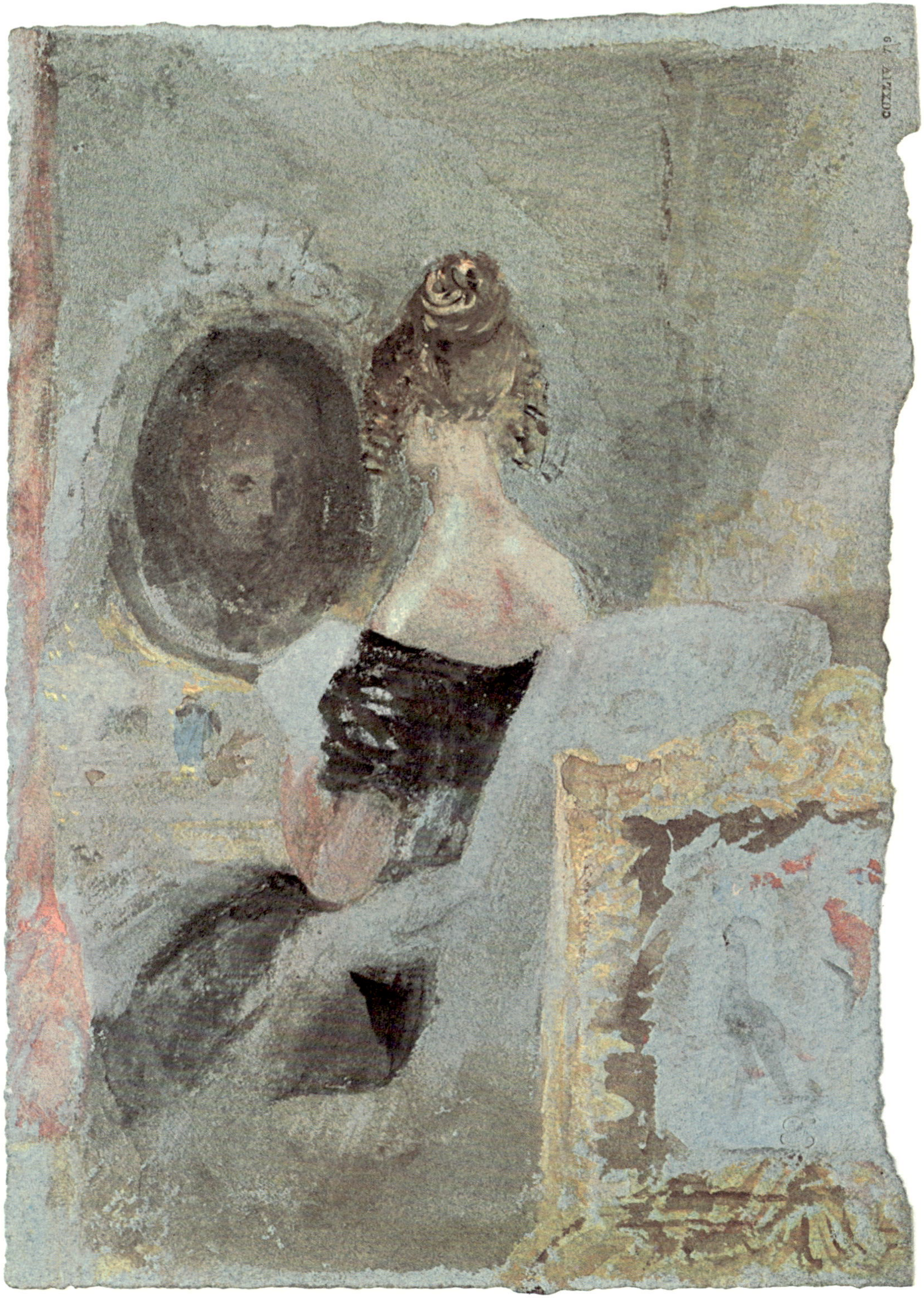

PLATE 62
A Lady in a Black Dress at her Toilet
TB CCXLIV–79

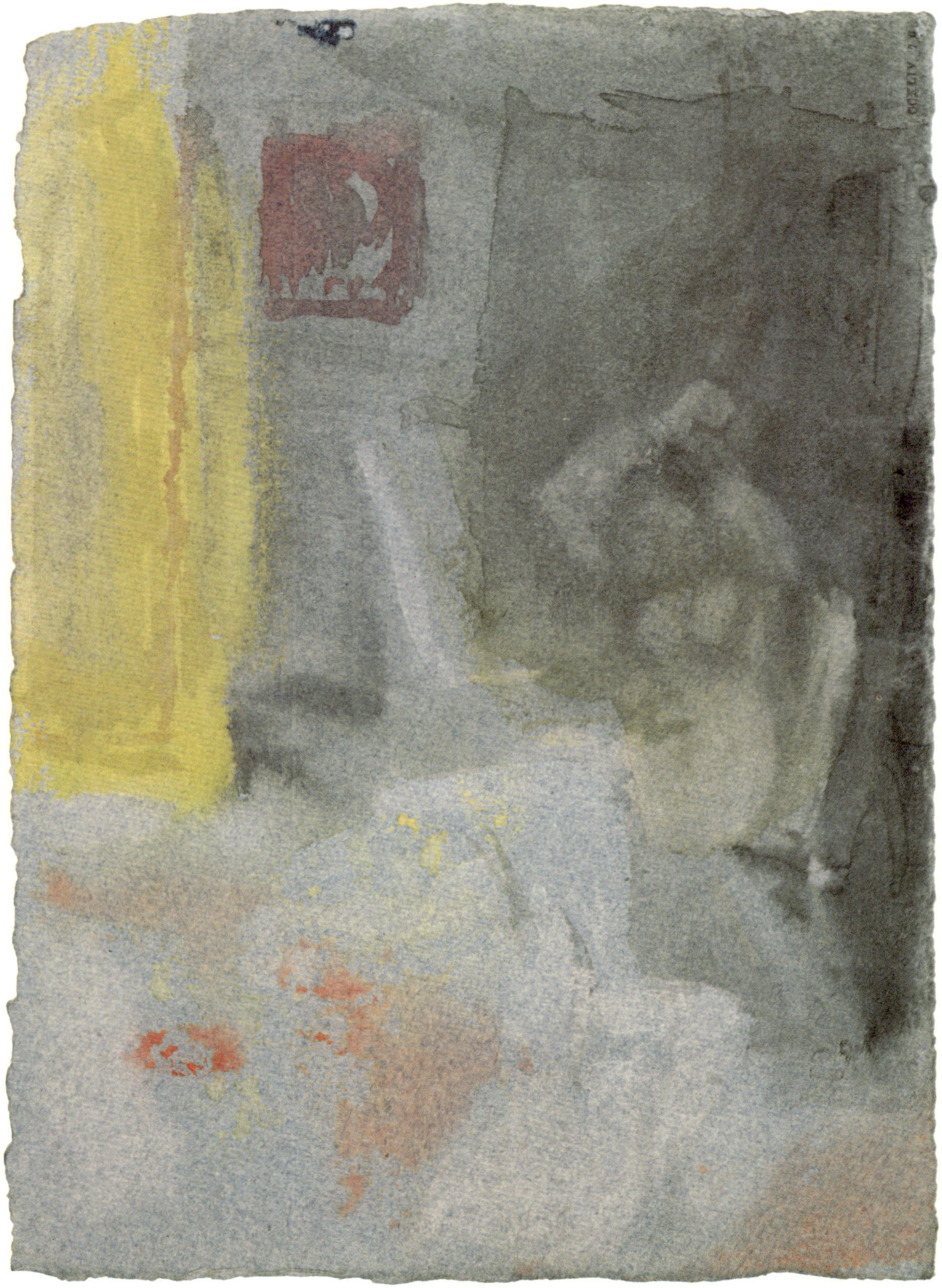

PLATE 63
A Bedroom with a Female Nude
TB CCXLIV–70

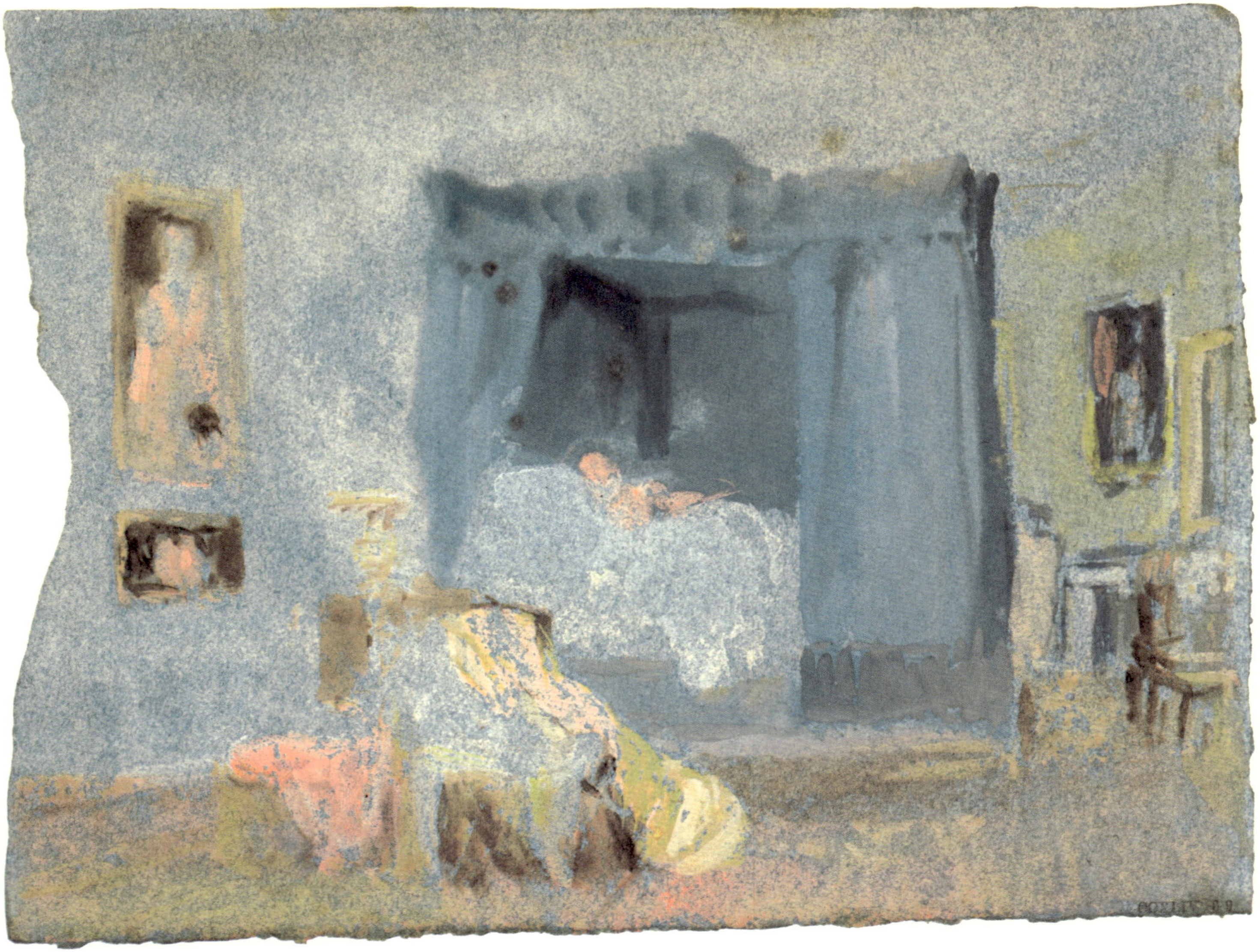

PLATE 64
A Bedroom: a figure in bed
TB CCXLIV–69

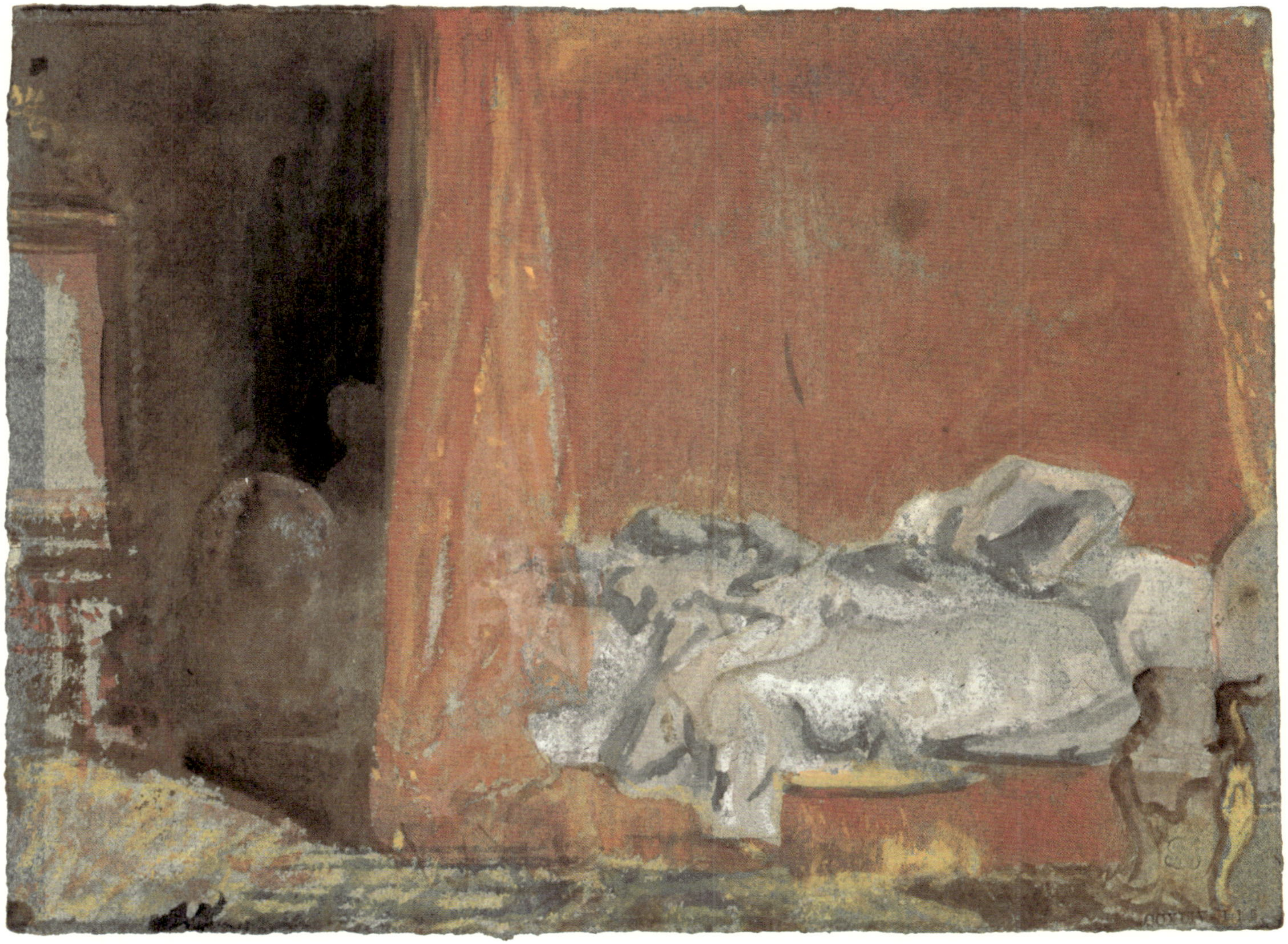

PLATE 65
A Bedroom: the empty bed
TB CCXLIV–115

PLATE 66
At Petworth: morning light through the windows
TB CCXLIV–112

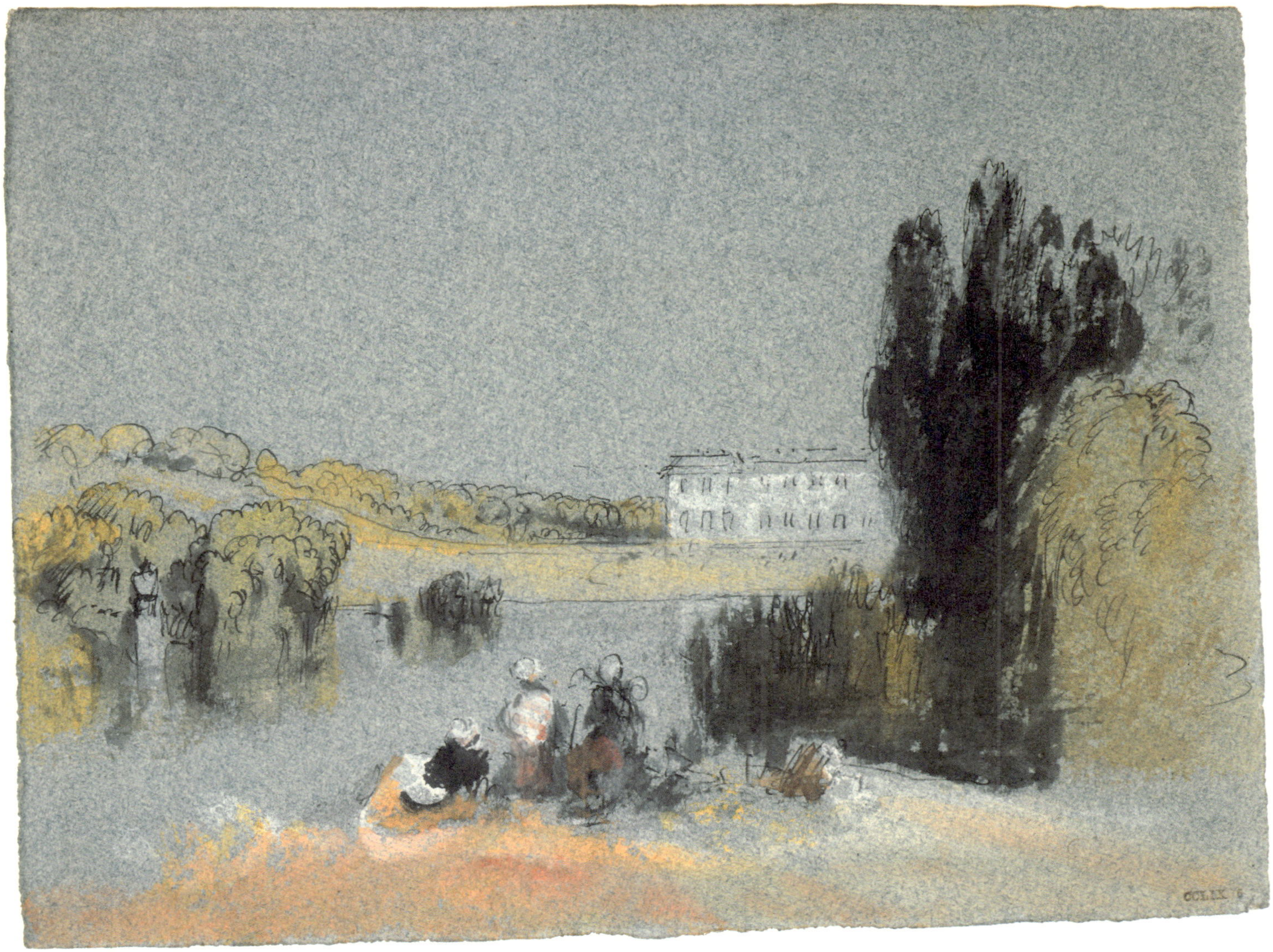

PLATE 67

Petworth House from the Lake, with Figures

TB CCLIX–5 Pen and black ink with watercolour and gouache

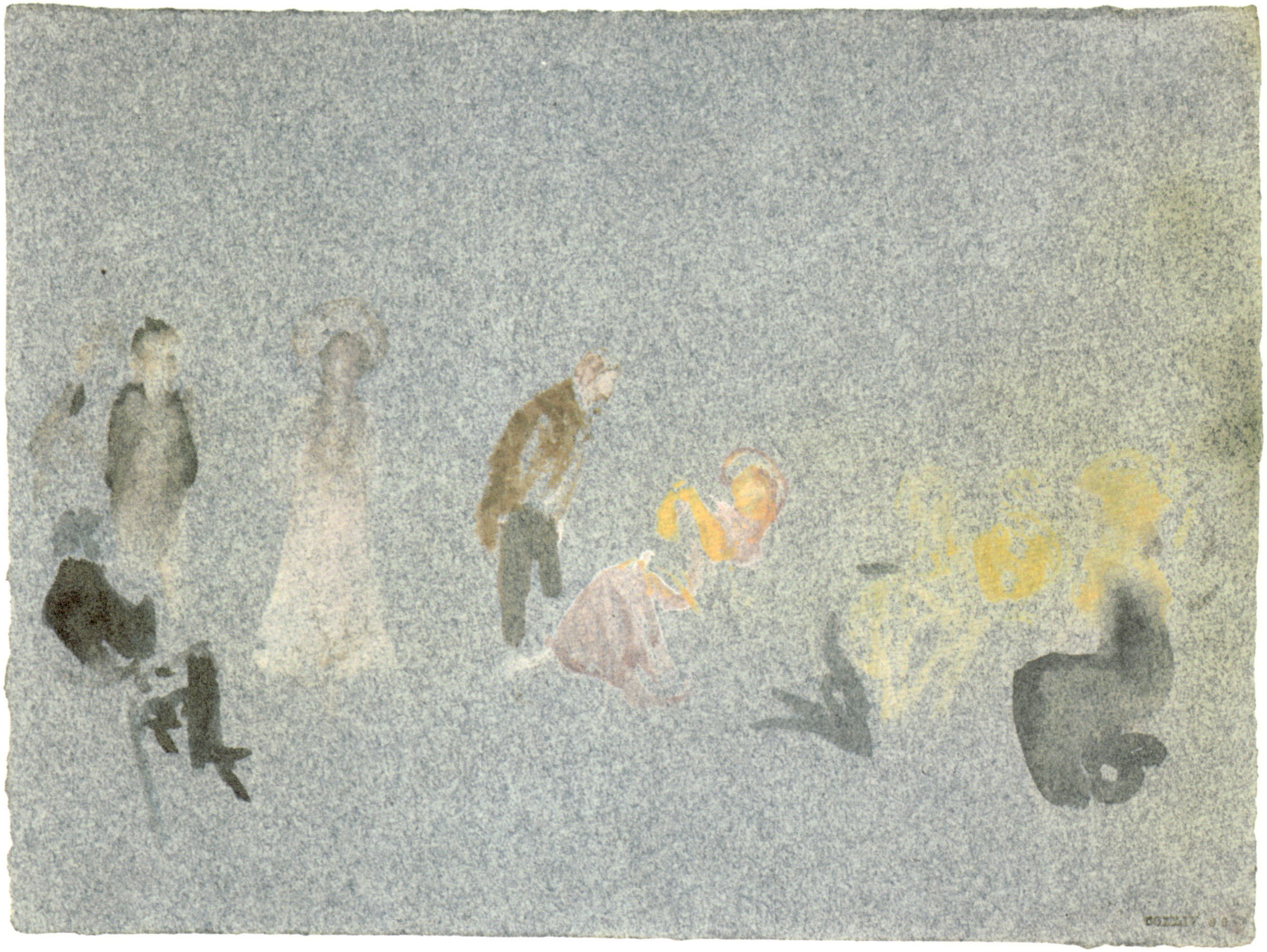

PLATE 68
Chatting with the Ladies
TB CCXLIV–85

PLATE 69
The Meet
TB CCXLIV–104, 190×280

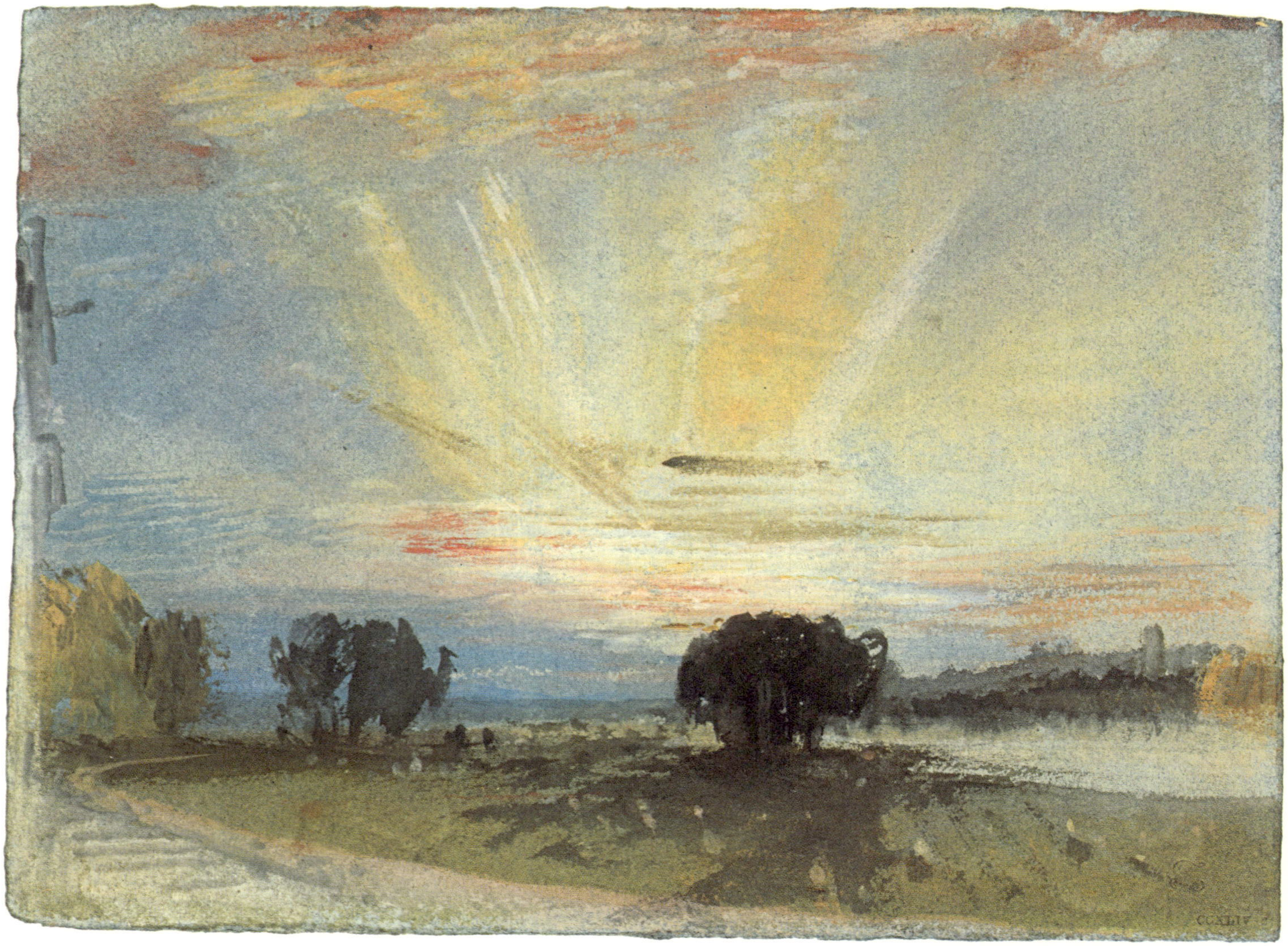

PLATE 70
Sunset across the Park from the Terrace of Petworth House
TB CCXLIV–2

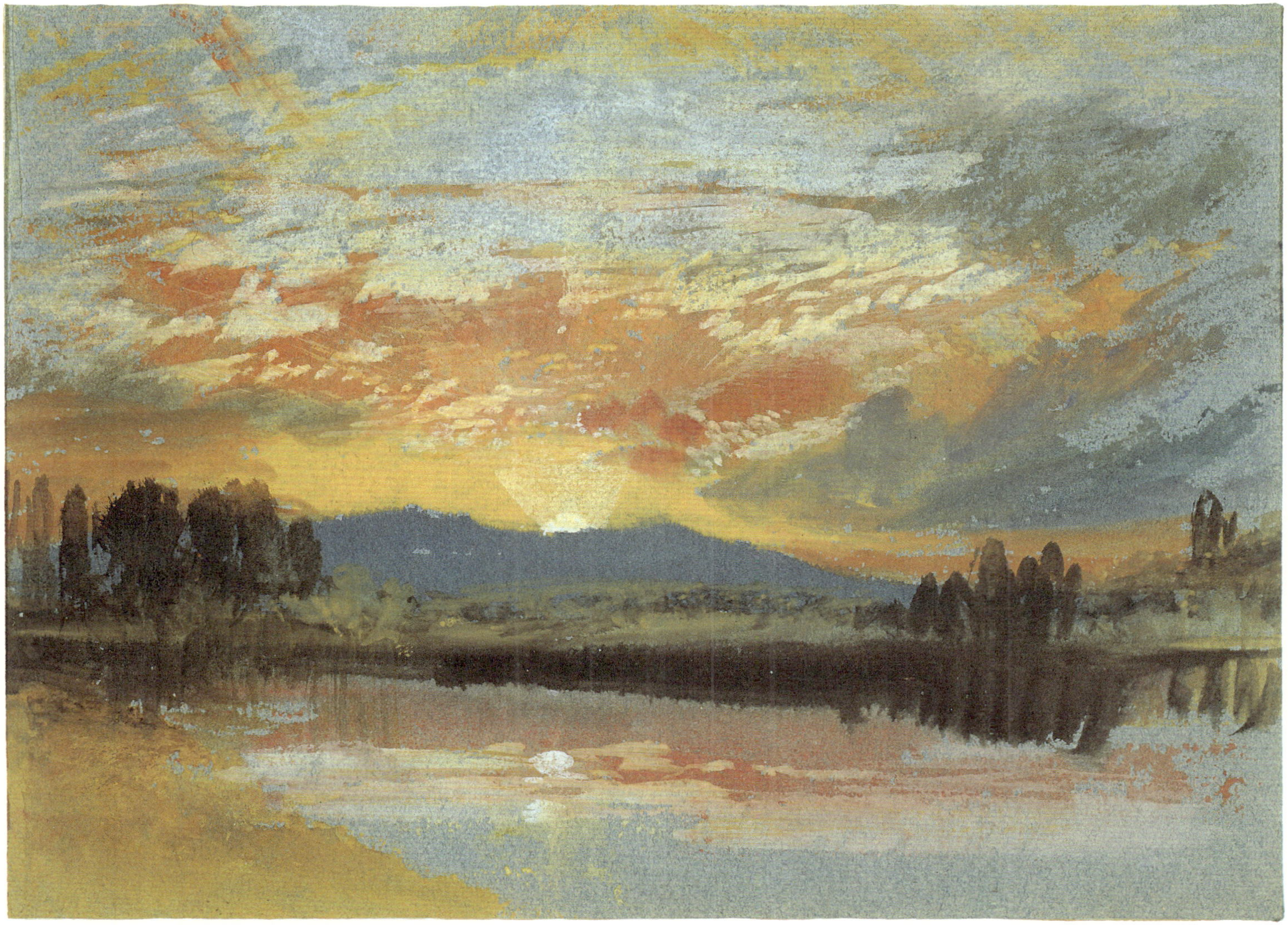

PLATE 71
Petworth Park, Sussex
National Gallery of Ireland, Dublin; 2430 (W.908)

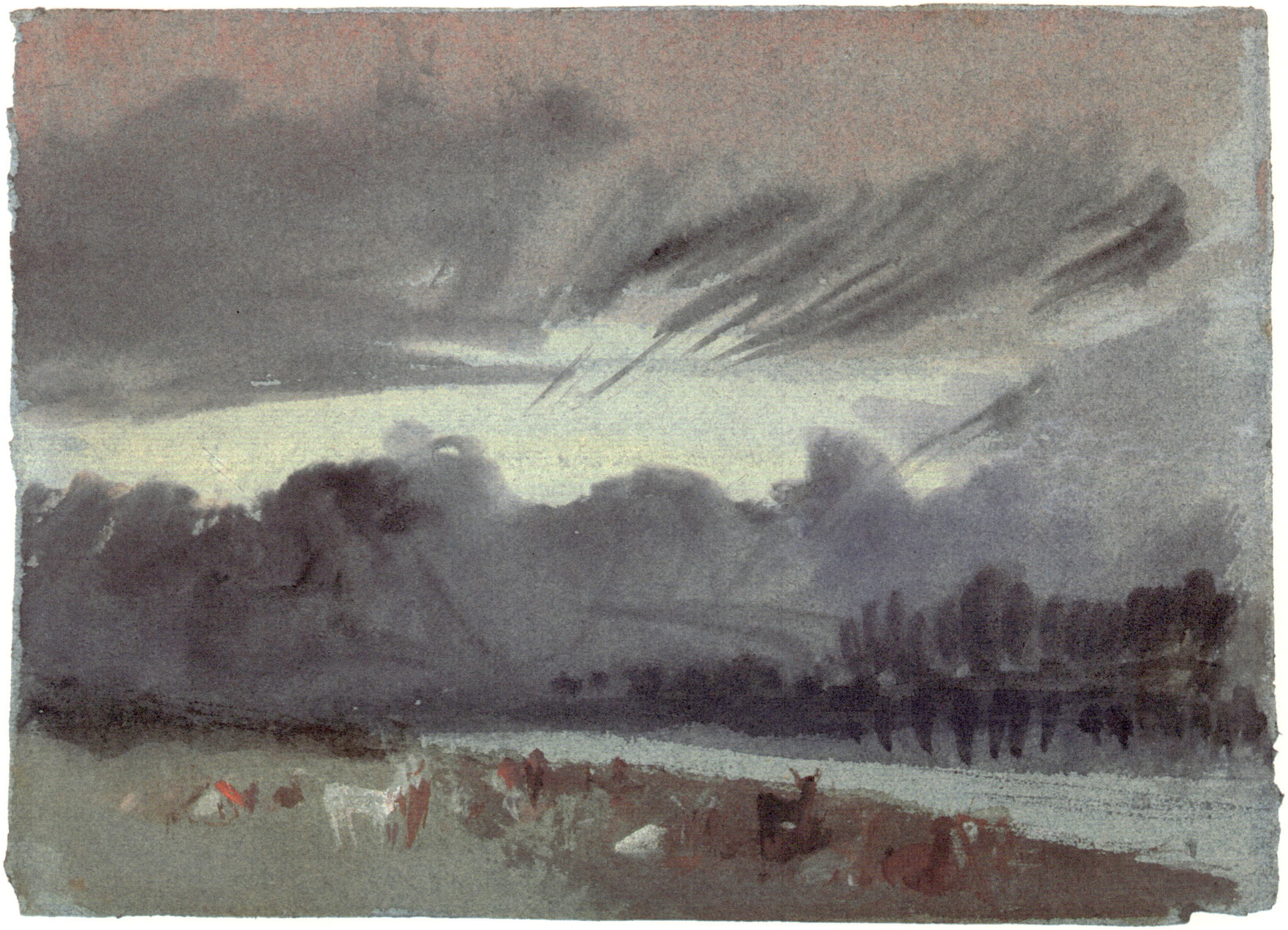

PLATE 72
Petworth Park, Sussex
Whitworth Art Gallery, University of Manchester: D.91.1892 (W.909)

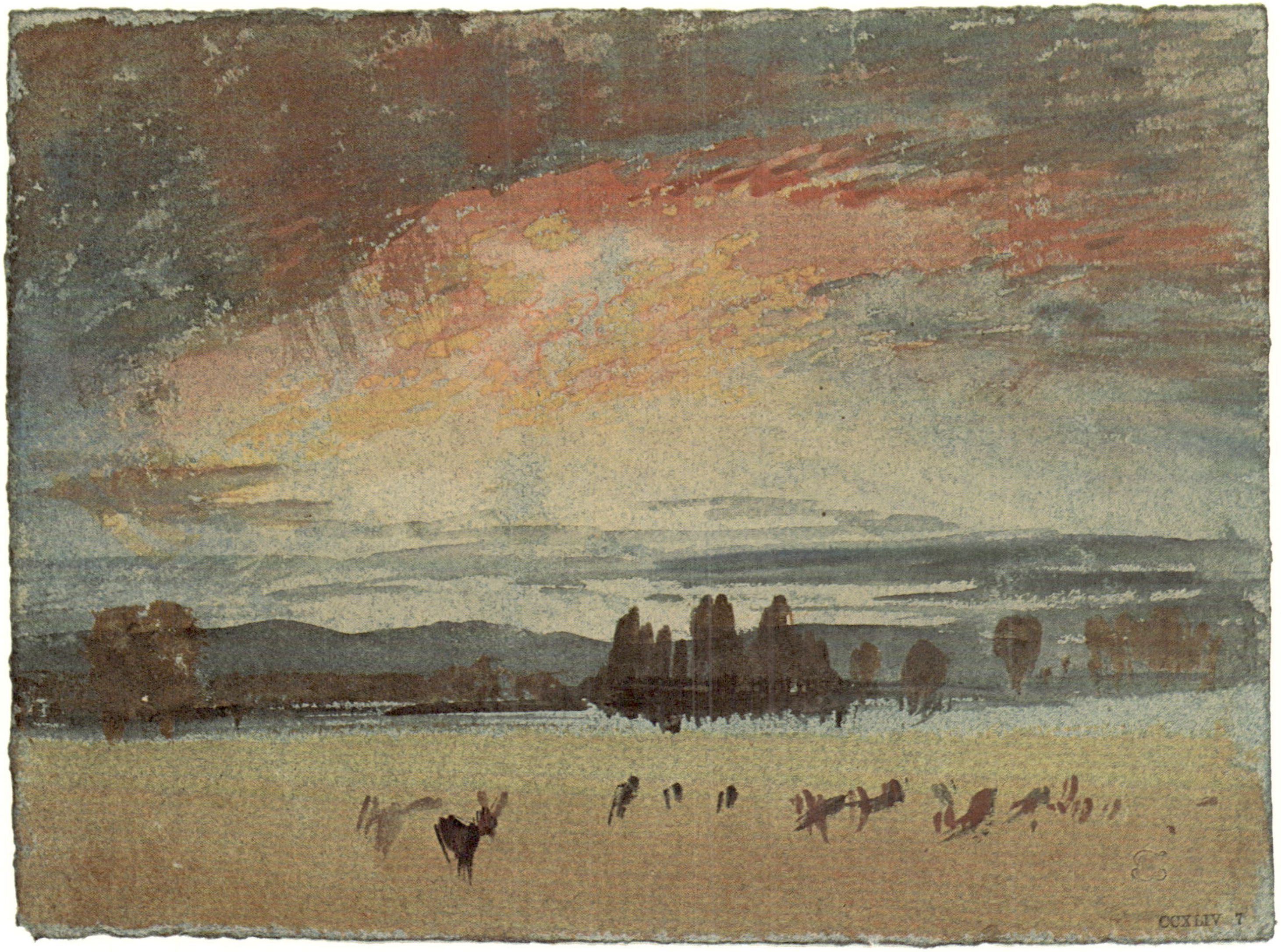

PLATE 73
The Deer in Petworth Park
TB CCXLIV–7

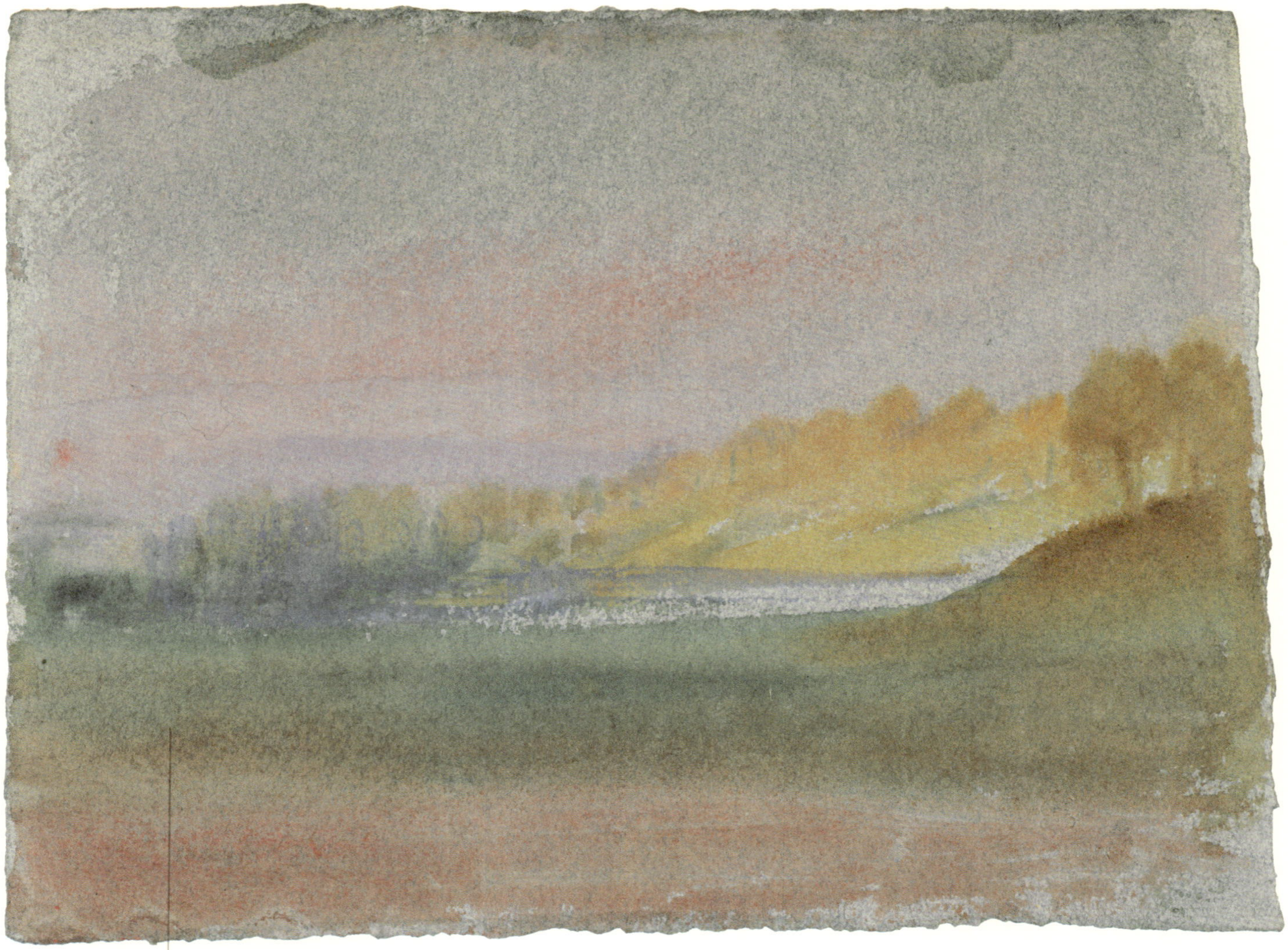

PLATE 74
The View from Petworth House, with Lawn Hill and Petworth Lake
TB CCXLIV–11

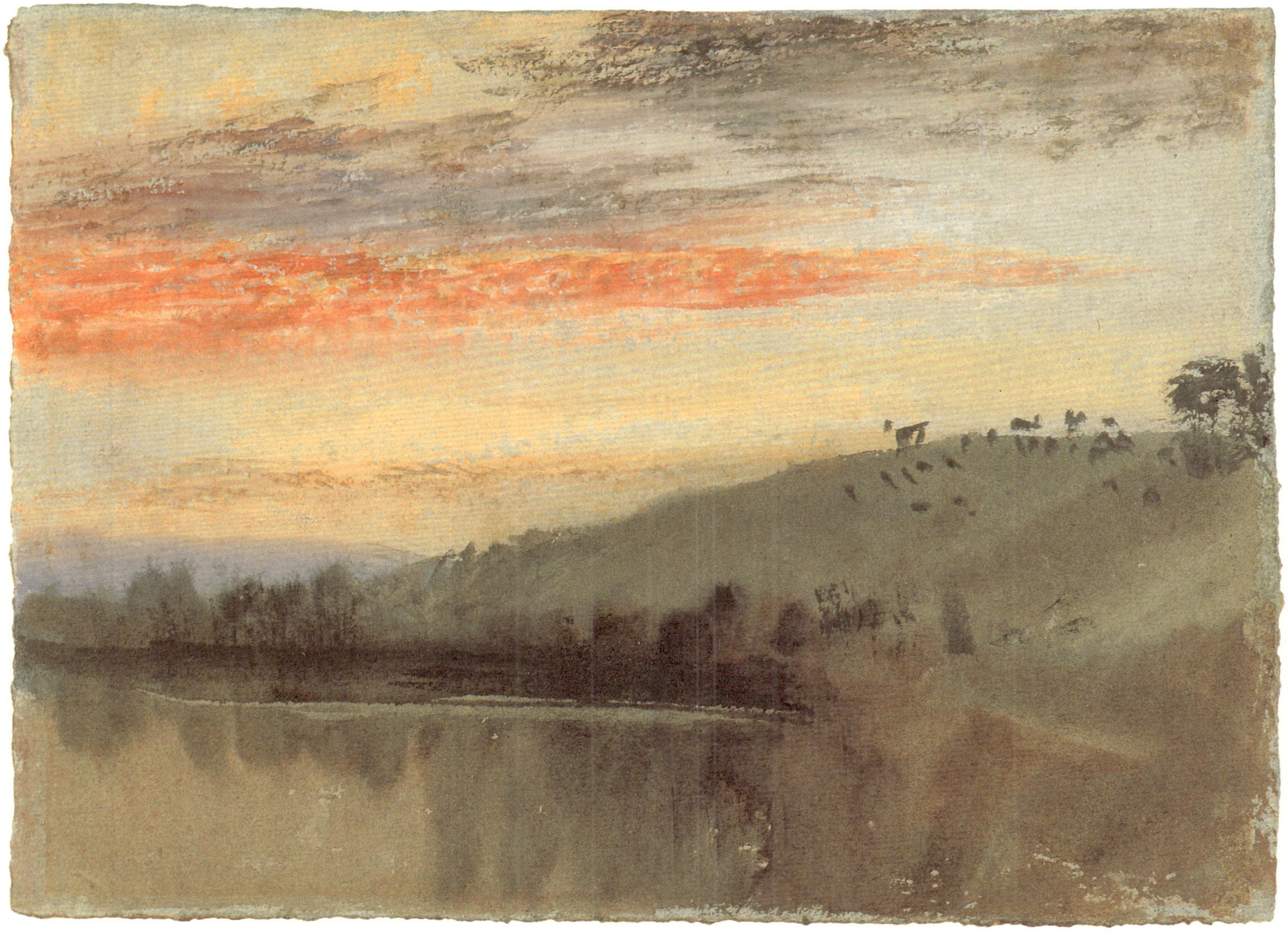

PLATE 75
Sunset in Petworth Park: deer grazing on a ridge near the lake
Private Collection (W.910)

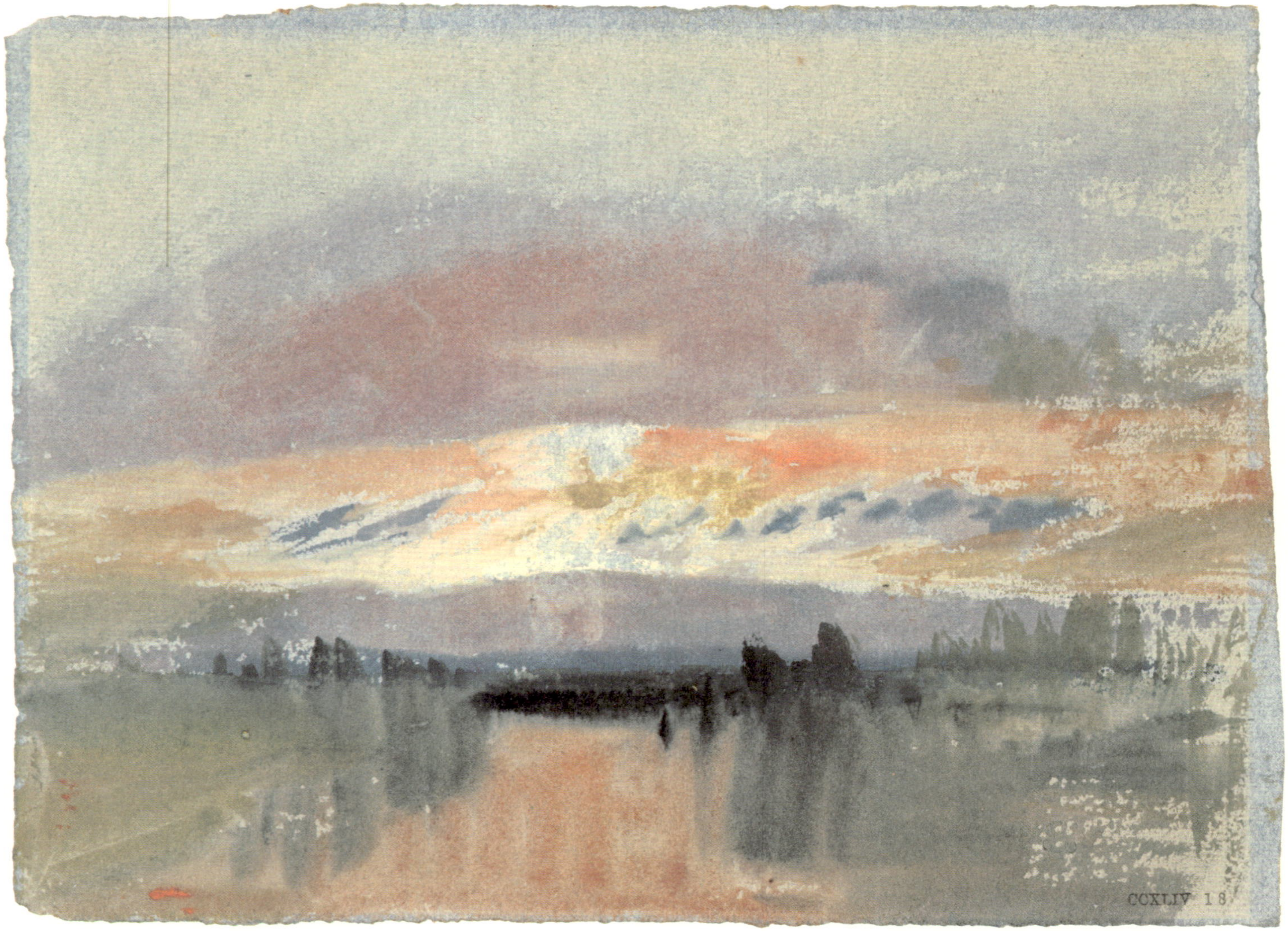

PLATE 76
Twilight: a lake or river scene (possibly Chichester Canal)
TB CCXLIV–18

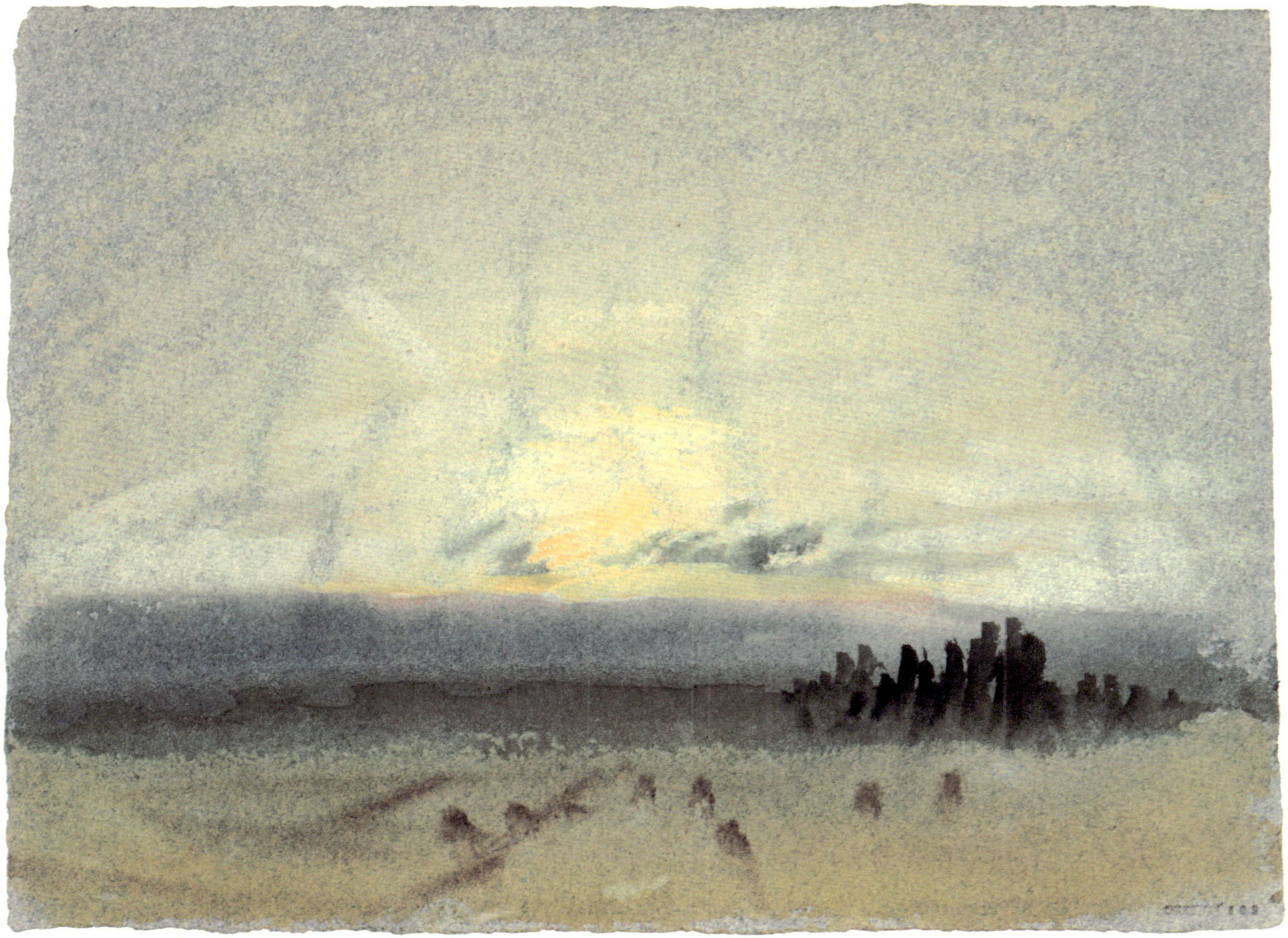

PLATE 77
Glade and Greensward
TB CCXLIV–105

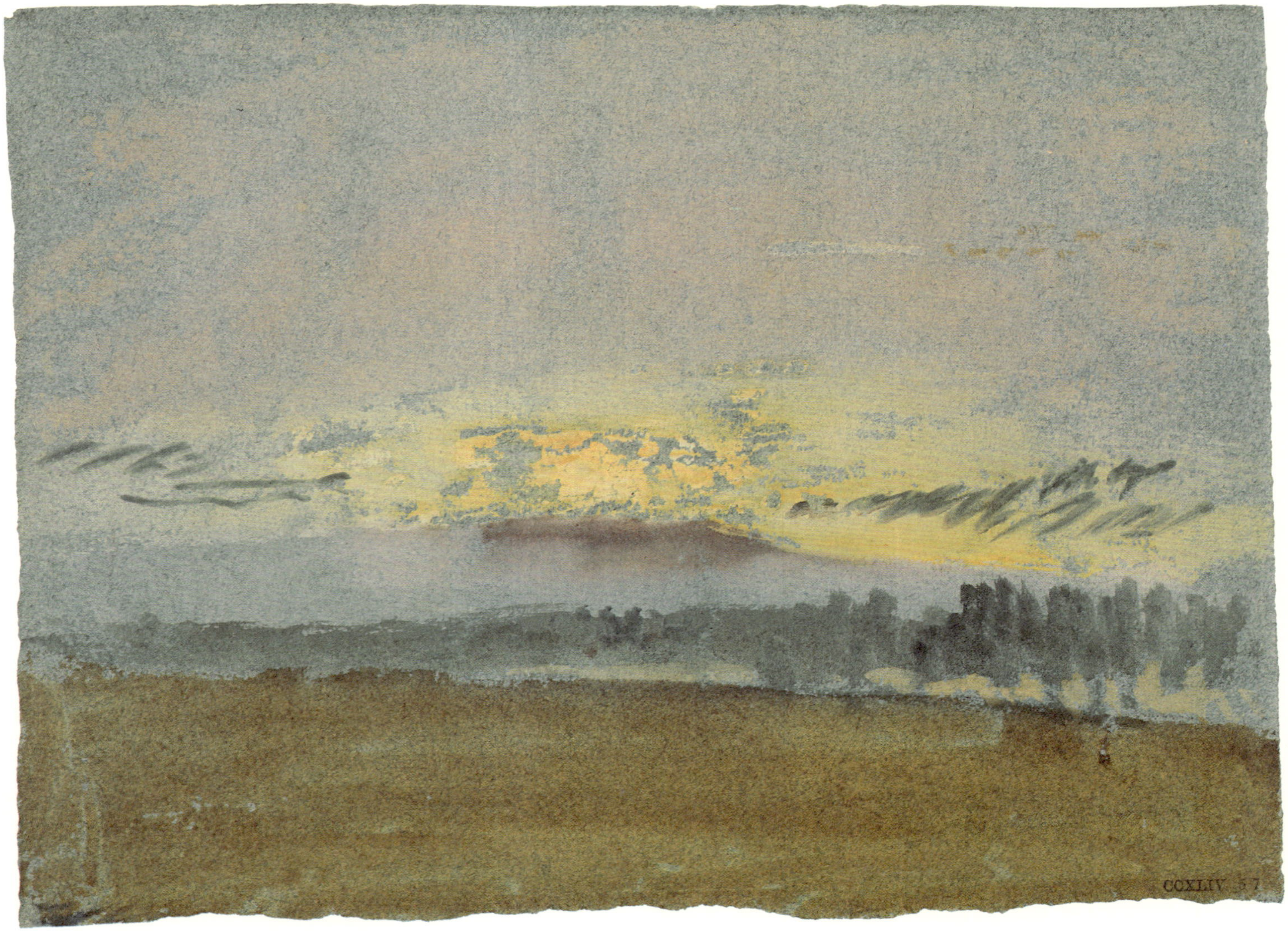

PLATE 78
The Setting Sun over Petworth Park
TB CCXLIV–57

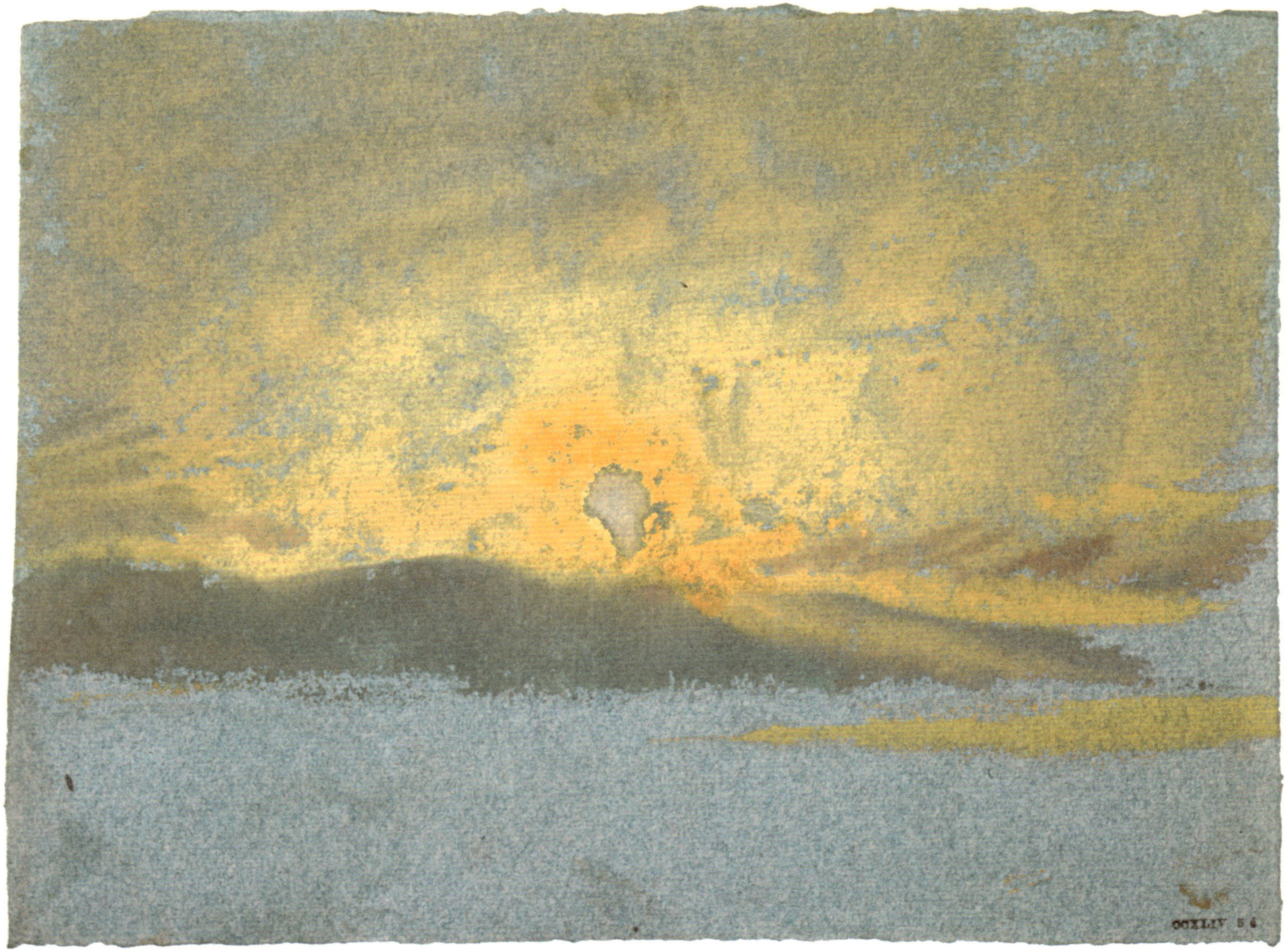

PLATE 79
Setting Sun
TB CCXLIV–54

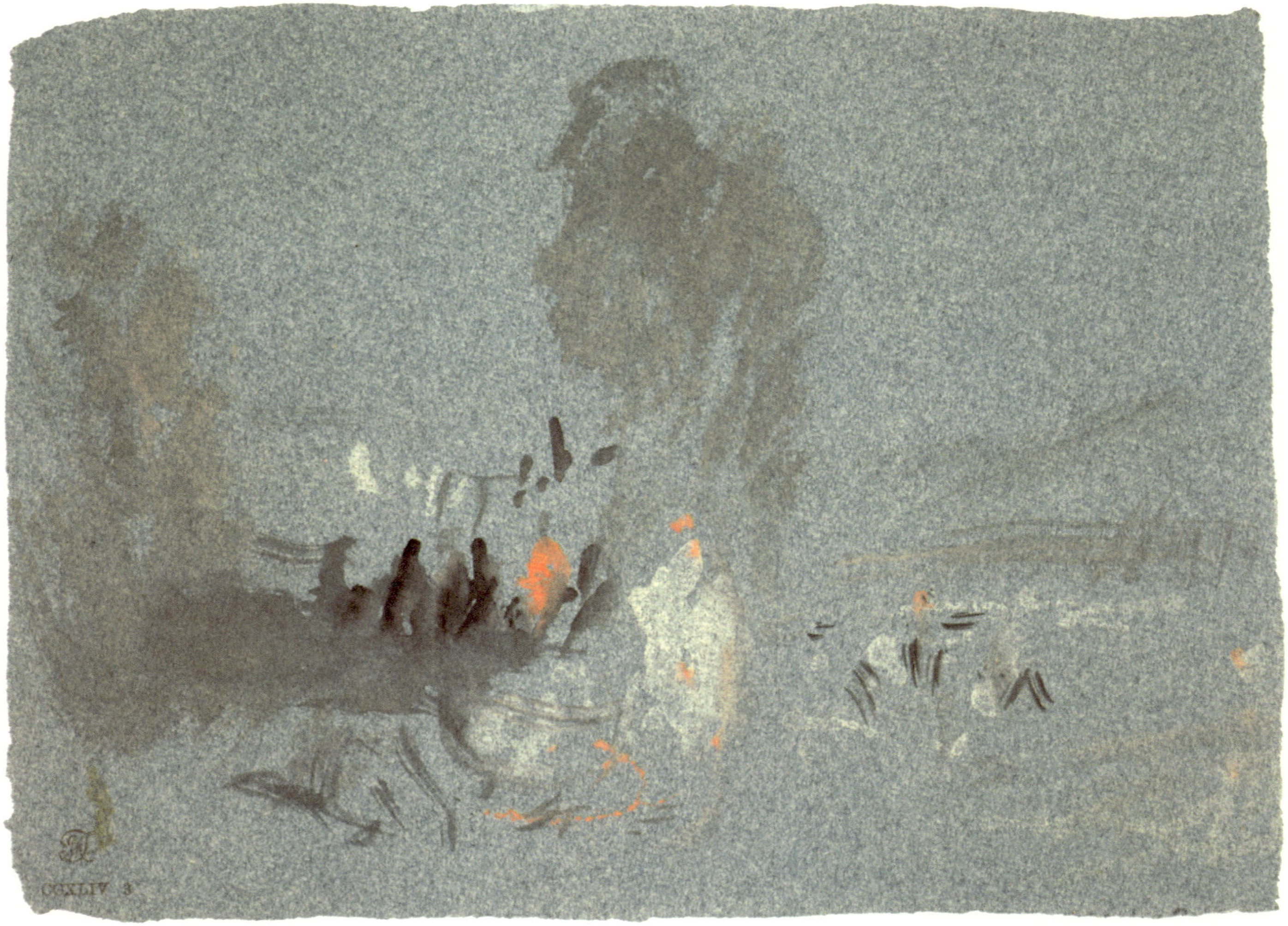

PLATE 80

?Figures in the Park

TB CCXLIV–3 verso

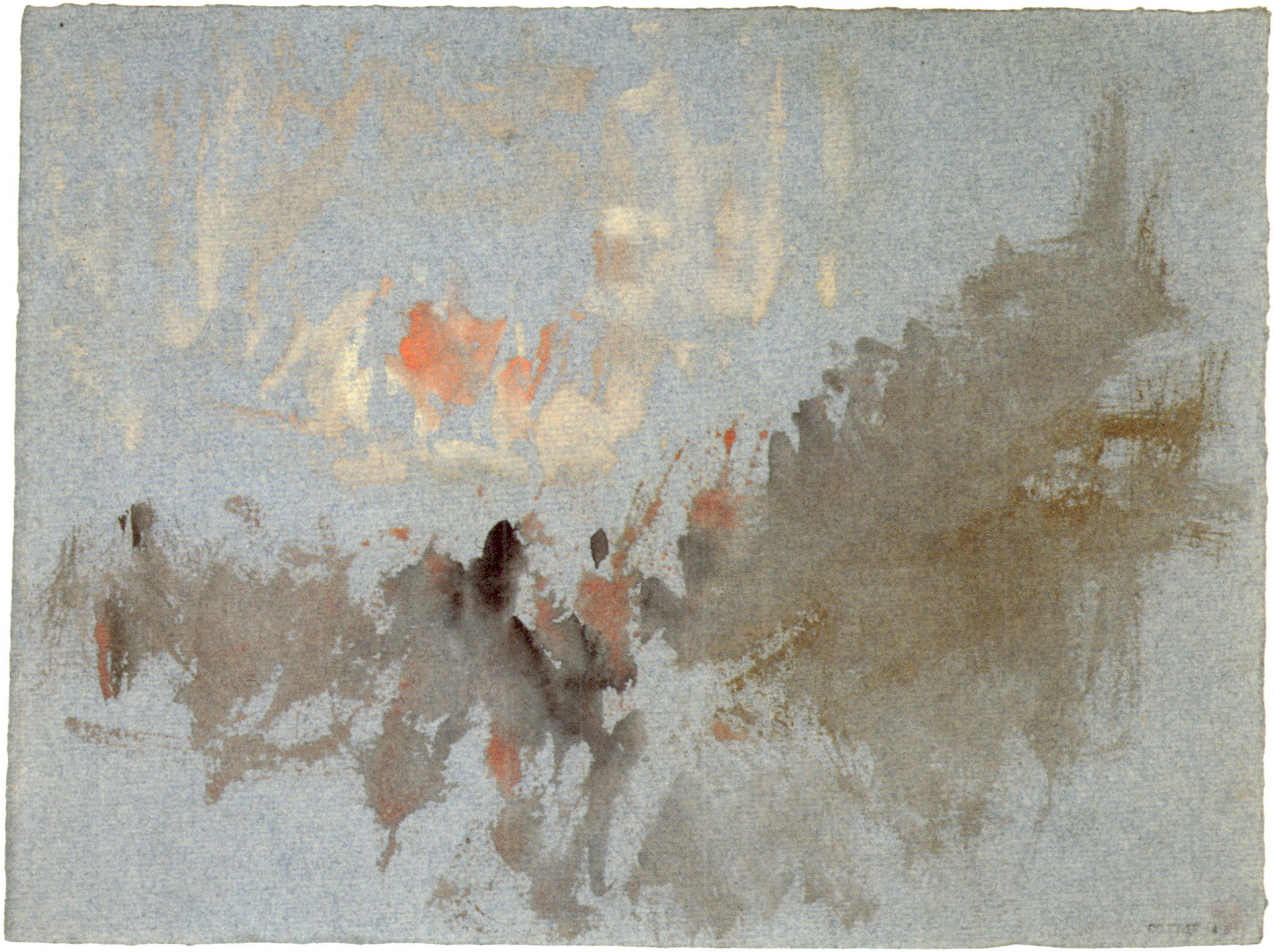

PLATE 81
Amateur Theatricals
TB CCXLIV–45

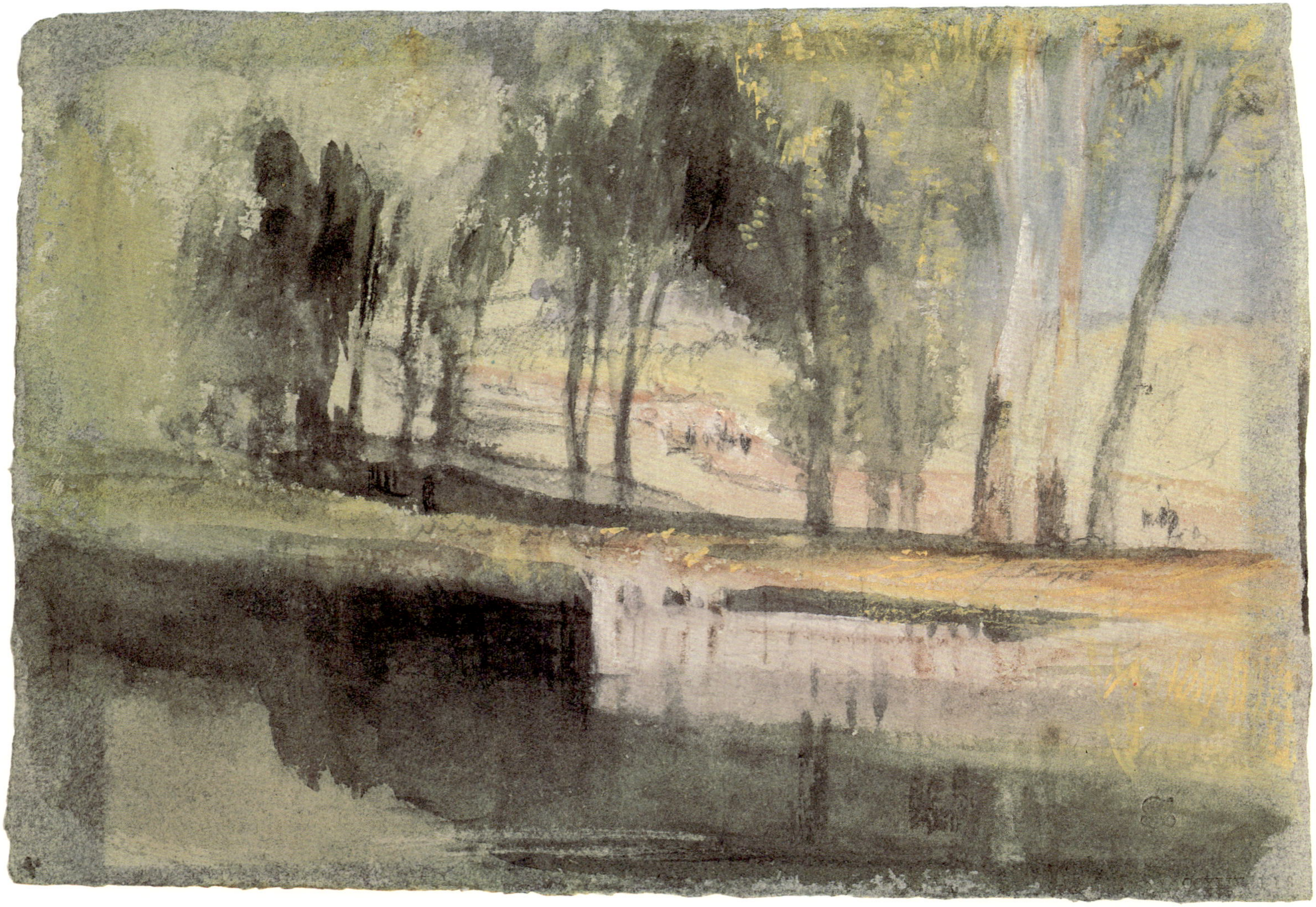

PLATE 82
Reflections in Petworth Lake: a rider glimpsed through trees
TB CCXLIV–113 Gouache and watercolour over traces of pencil

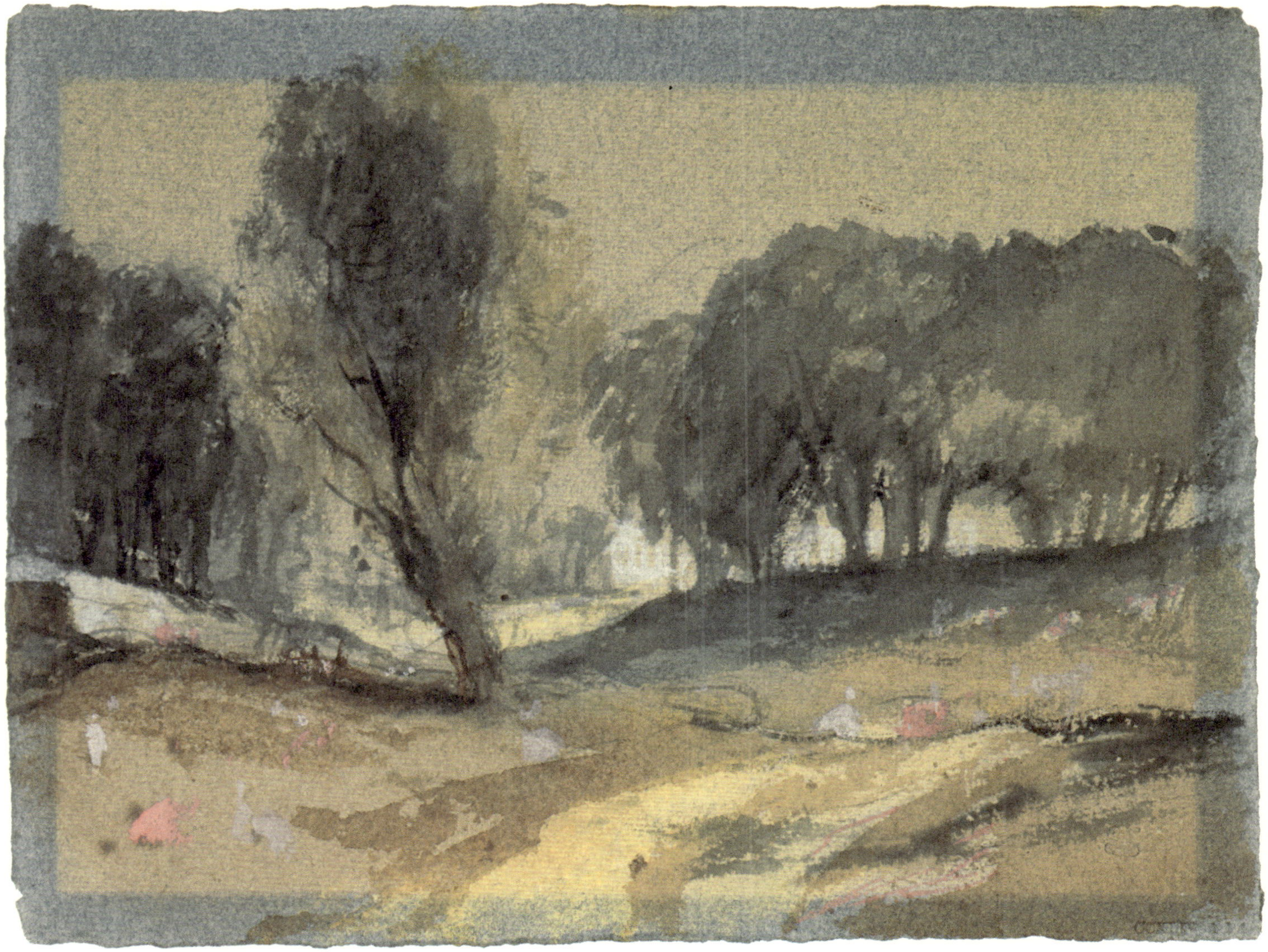

PLATE 83
Deer in Petworth Park: Petworth House seen beyond the trees
TB CCXLIV–114

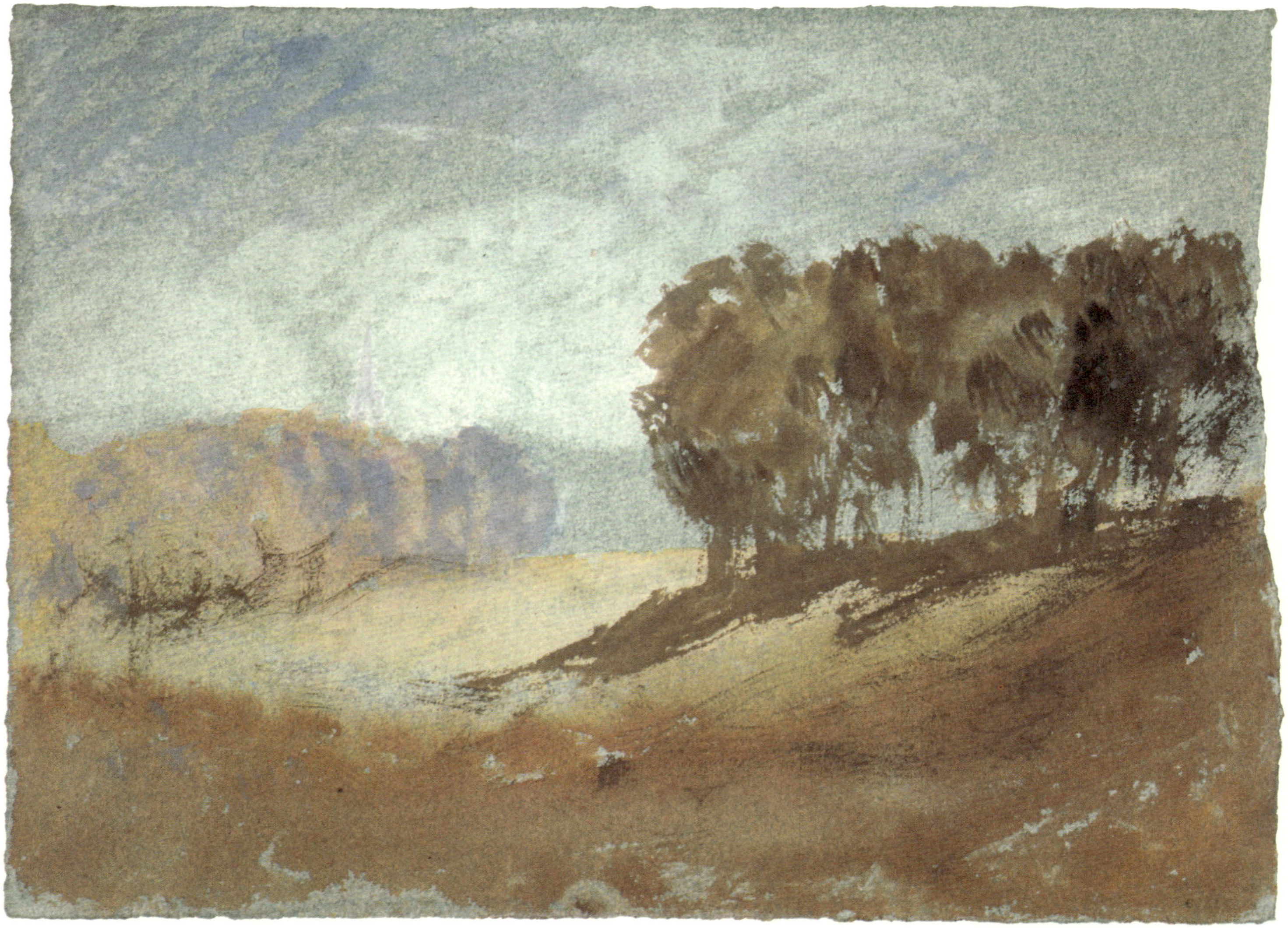

PLATE 84
Petworth Church seen from the Park
TB CCXLIV–9

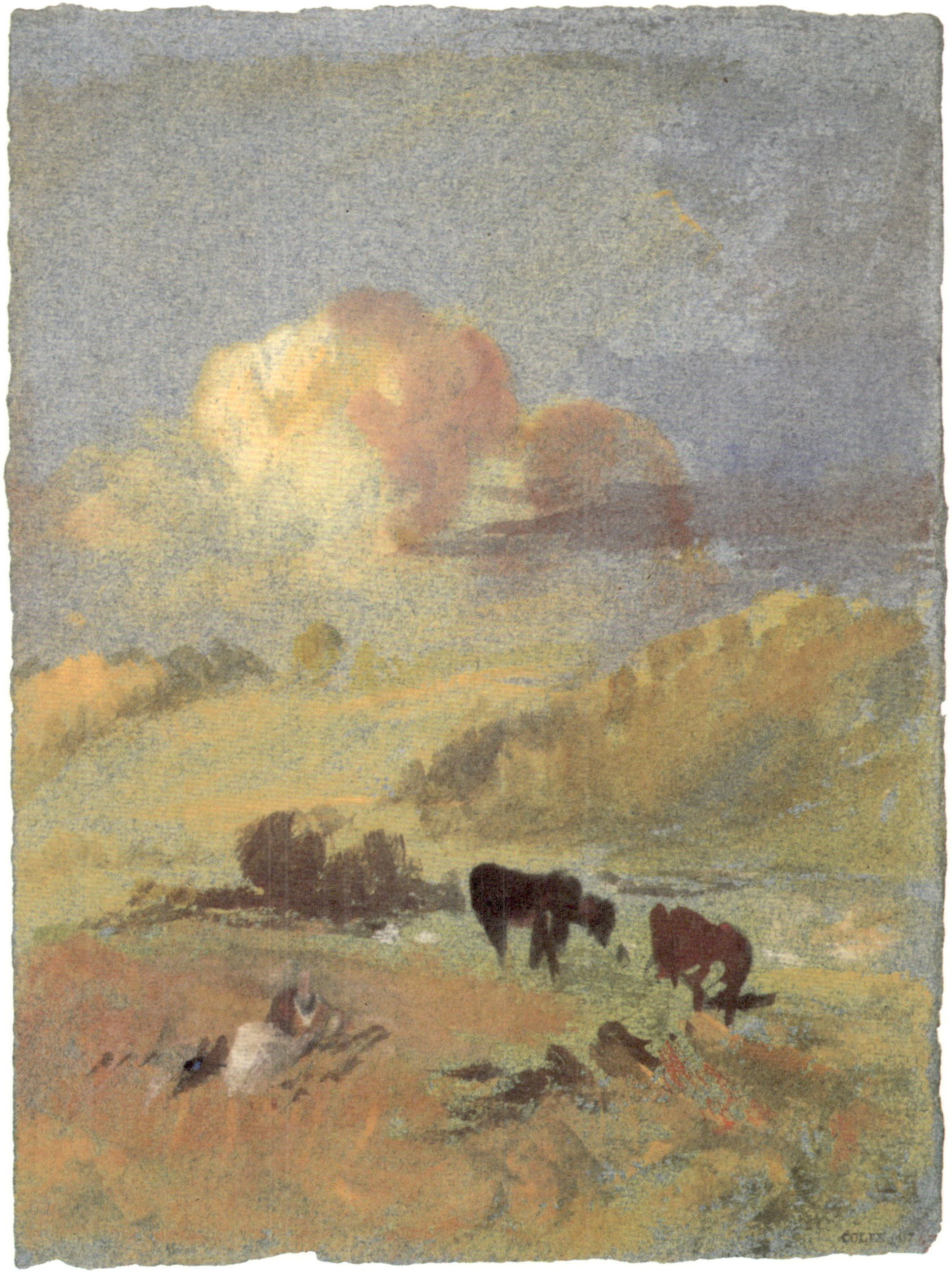

PLATE 85
Figures and Cattle in Petworth Park
TB CCLIX–47

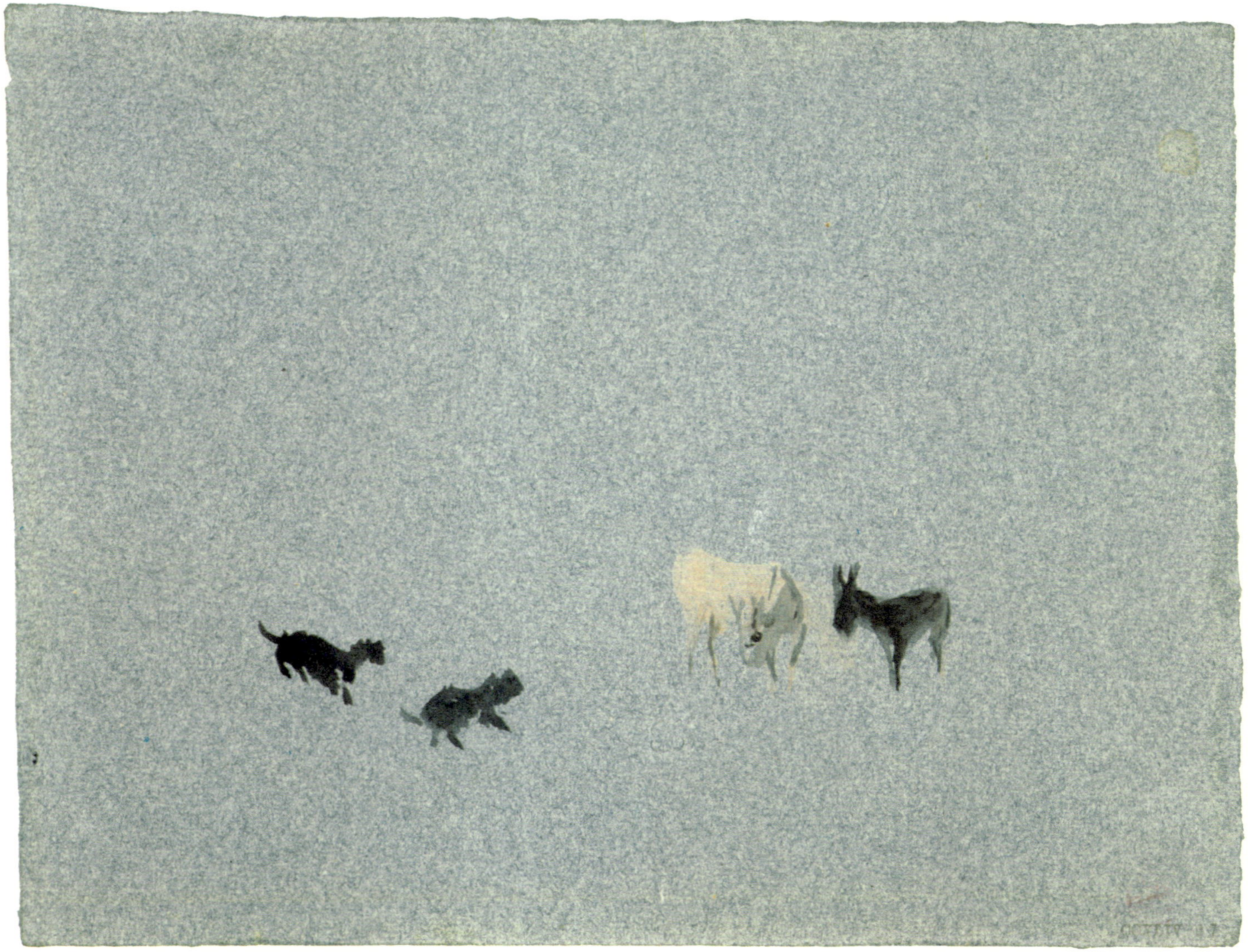

PLATE 86
Teasing the Donkey
TB CCXLIV–97

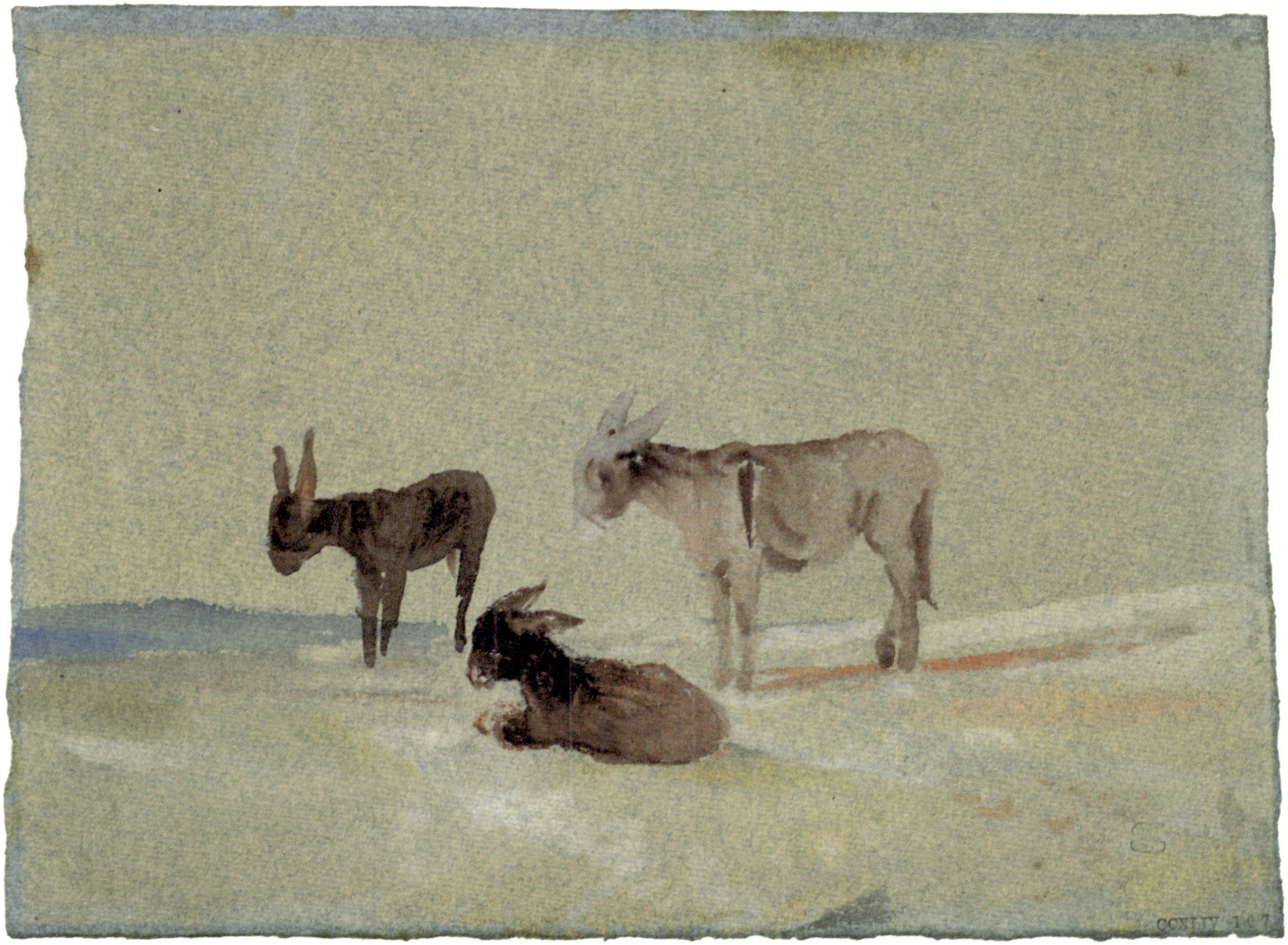

PLATE 87

Three Donkeys

TB CCXLIV–107

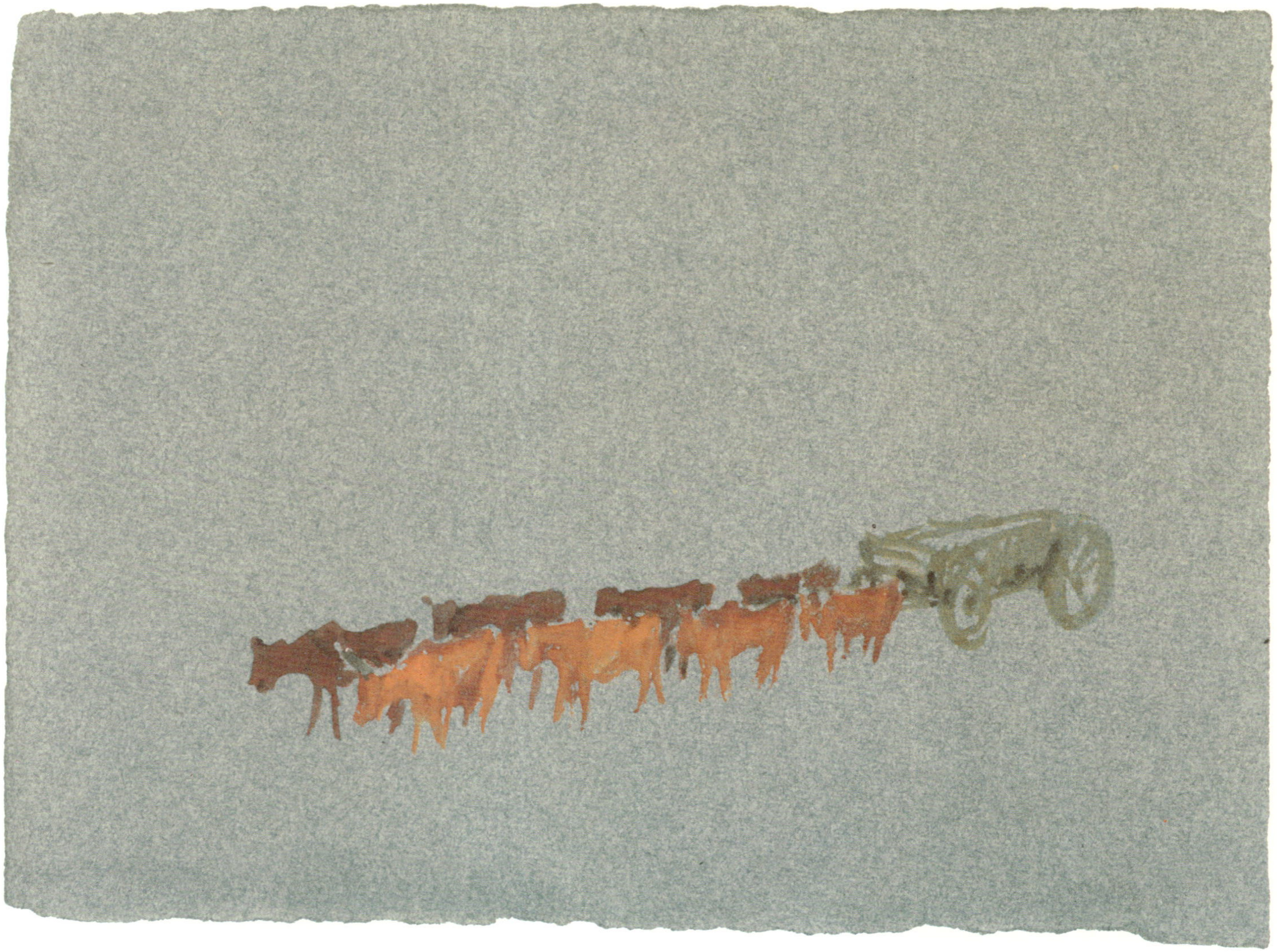

PLATE 88
A Team of Eight Cattle Pulling a Wagon Also known as
'The Bullock Wagon'
TB CCXLIV–98

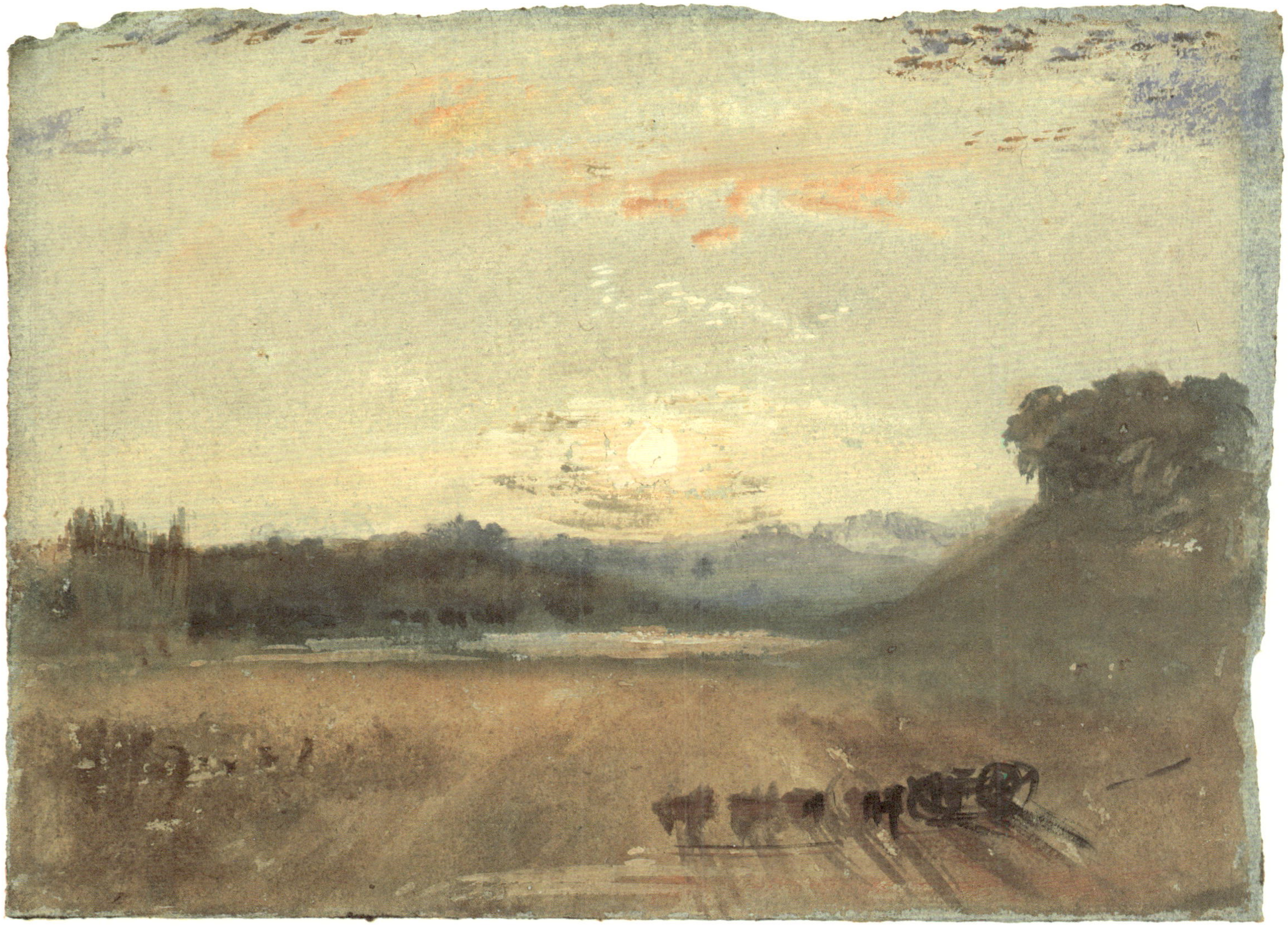

PLATE 89
Petworth Park, Sunset: with a cart
The Harry and Mary Dalton Collection, Mint Museum,
Charlotte, North Carolina (W.912)

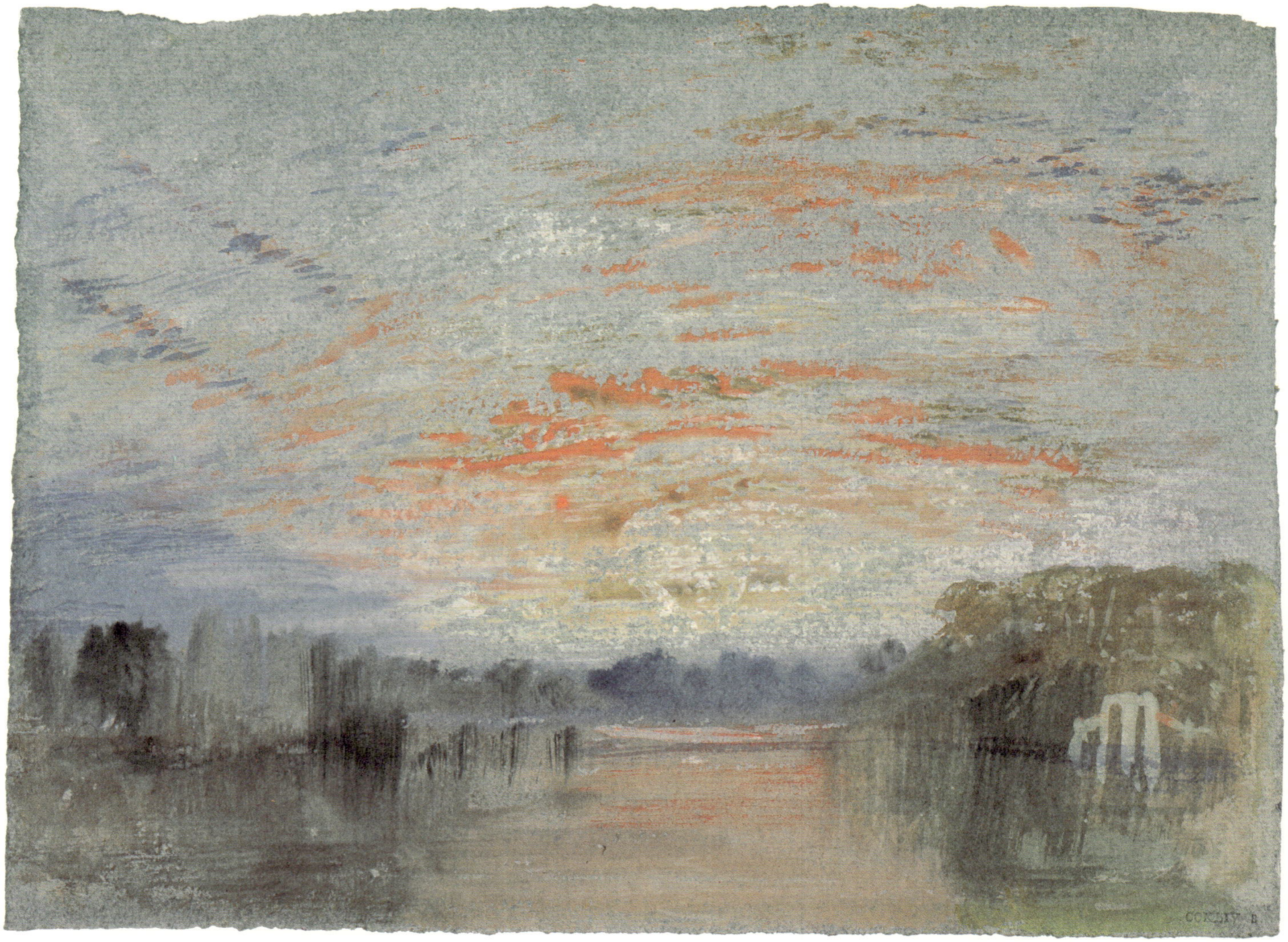

PLATE 90

Sunset Sky over the Lake: the boathouse on the right

TB CCXLIV–3

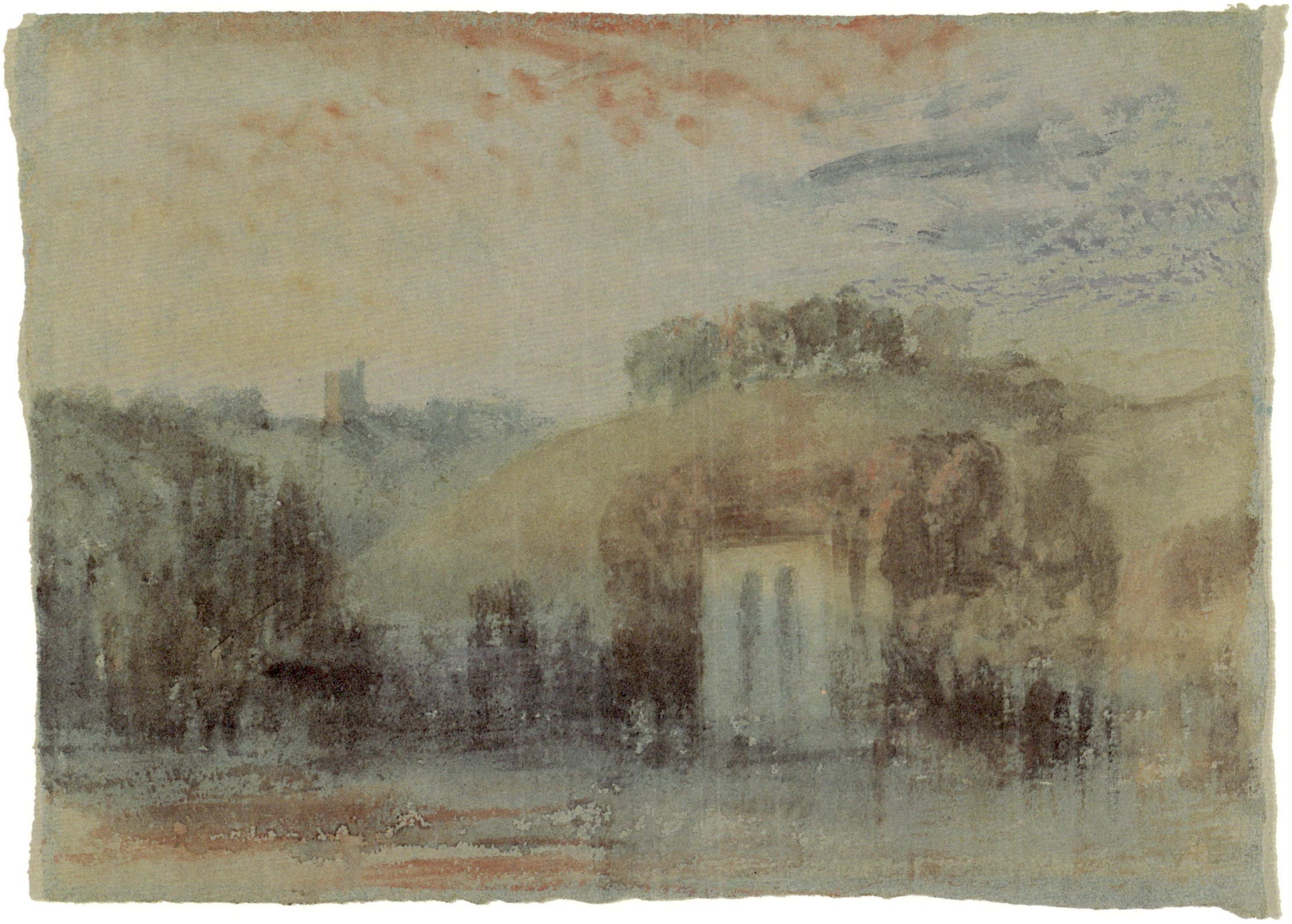

PLATE 91

The Lake, Petworth Park

Anonymous Gift, Museum of Art, Rhode Island School of Design, Providence, R.I. (70.118.55) (W.911)

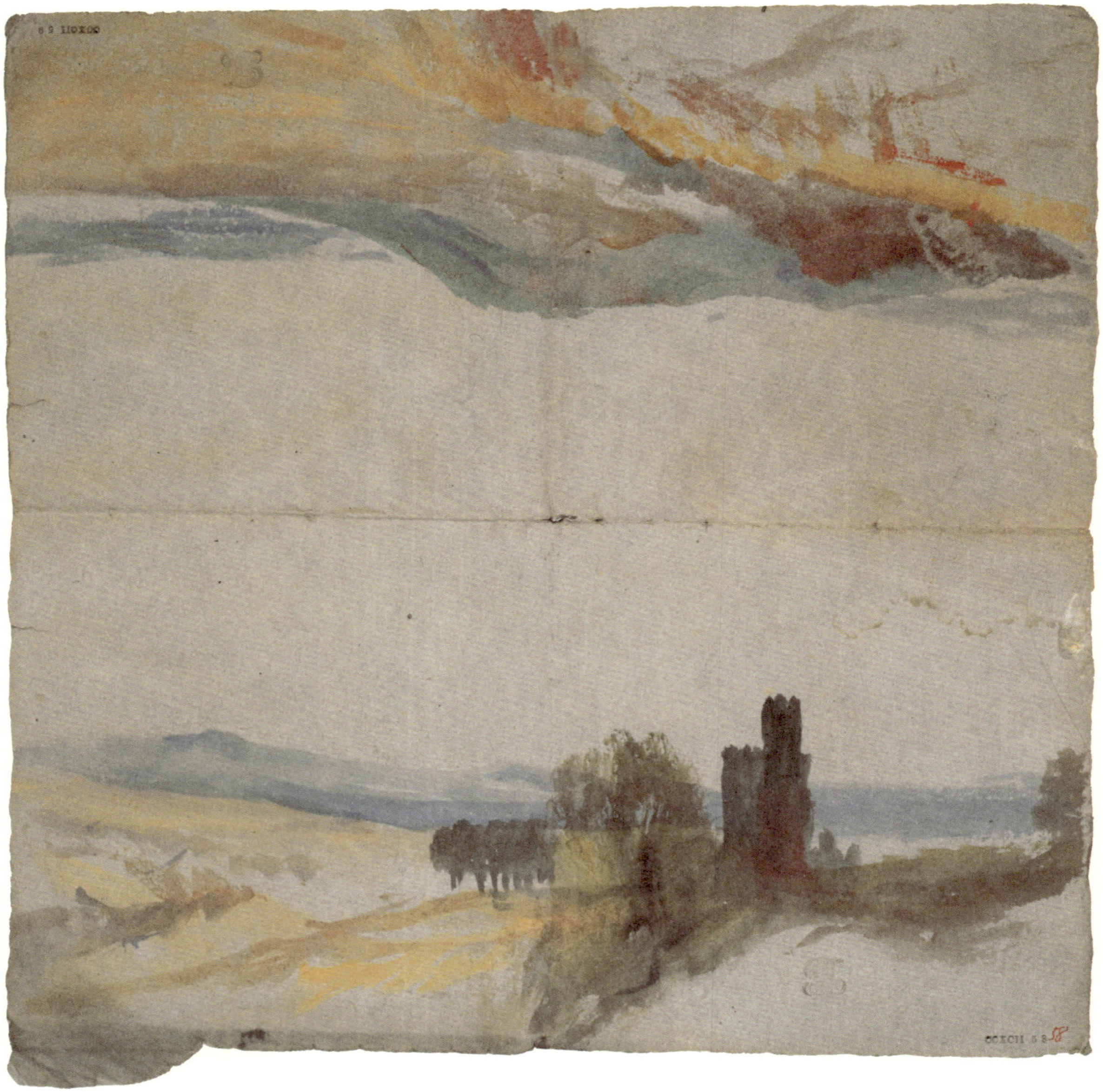

PLATE 92

The Upperton Monument, looking down towards Petworth Park; and (upside down) *a view along the Sussex Downs c.* 1832

TB CCXCII–58/9, 200 × 202, Gouache and watercolour on grey paper

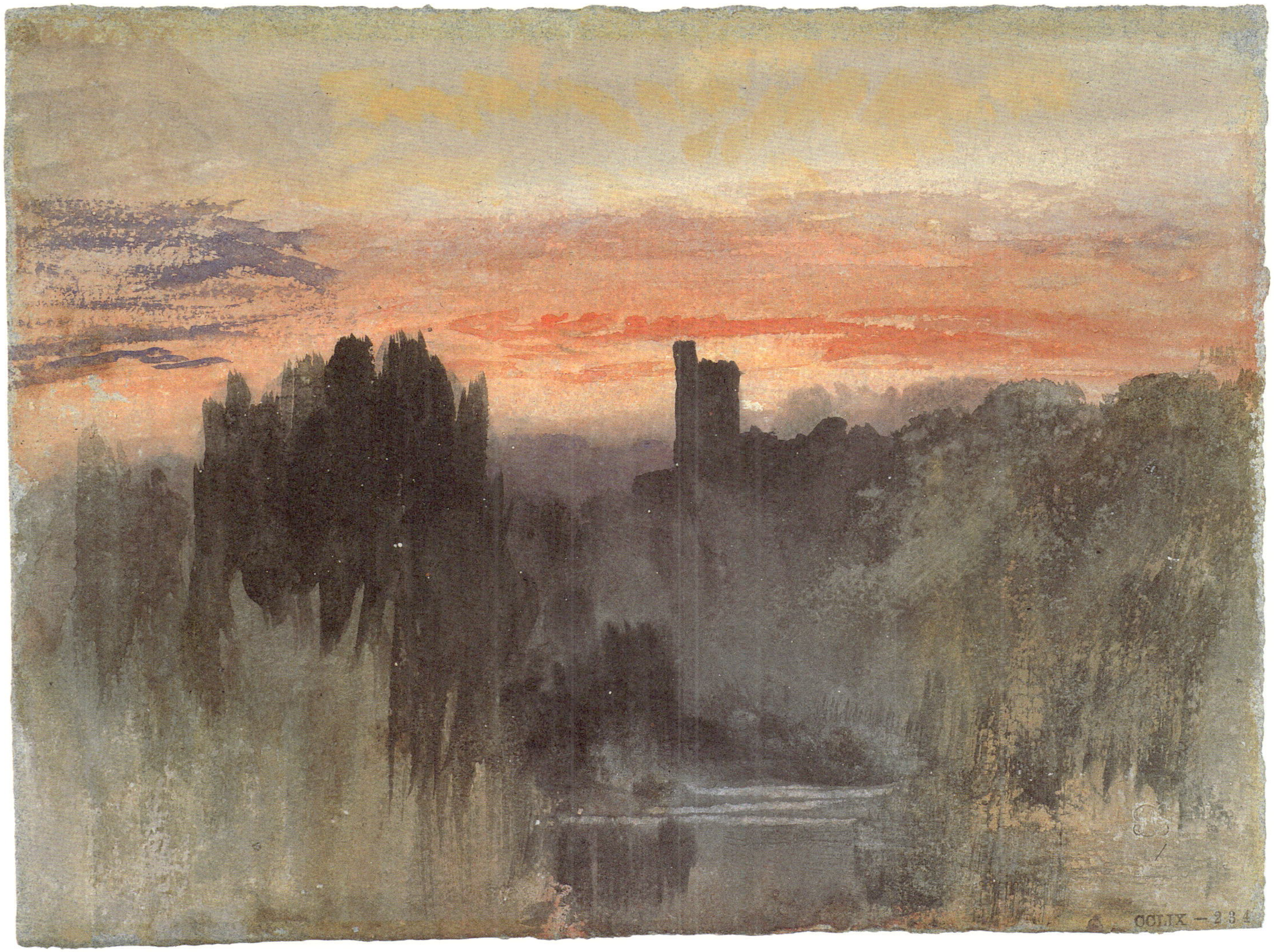

PLATE 93
The Upperton Monument (?) seen from Petworth Park
TB CCLIX–234

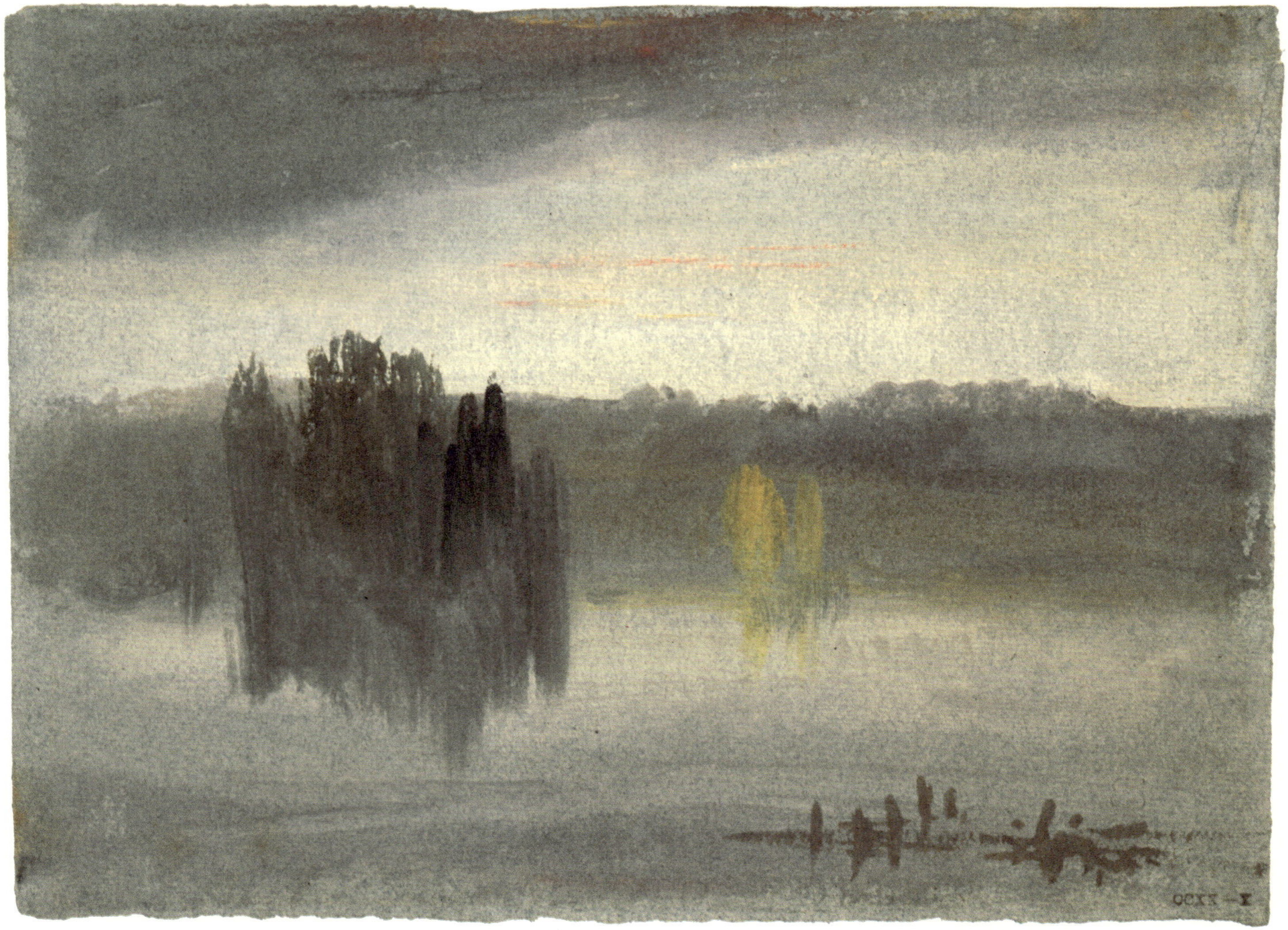

PLATE 94
A River Scene, possibly Petworth Lake
TB CCXX–X

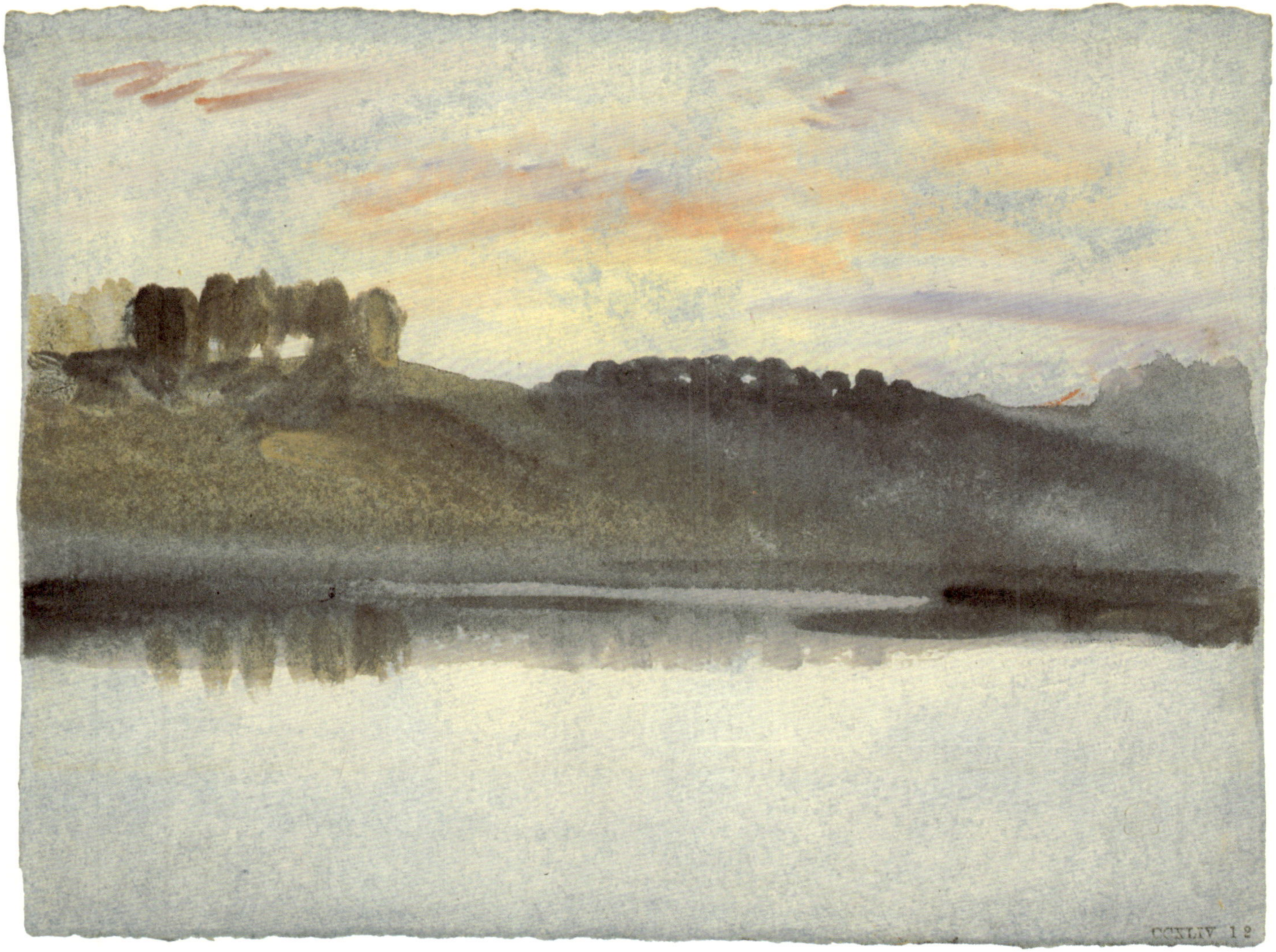

PLATE 95

Sunset over the ridge: seen from the north pond in Petworth Park

TB CCXLIV–12

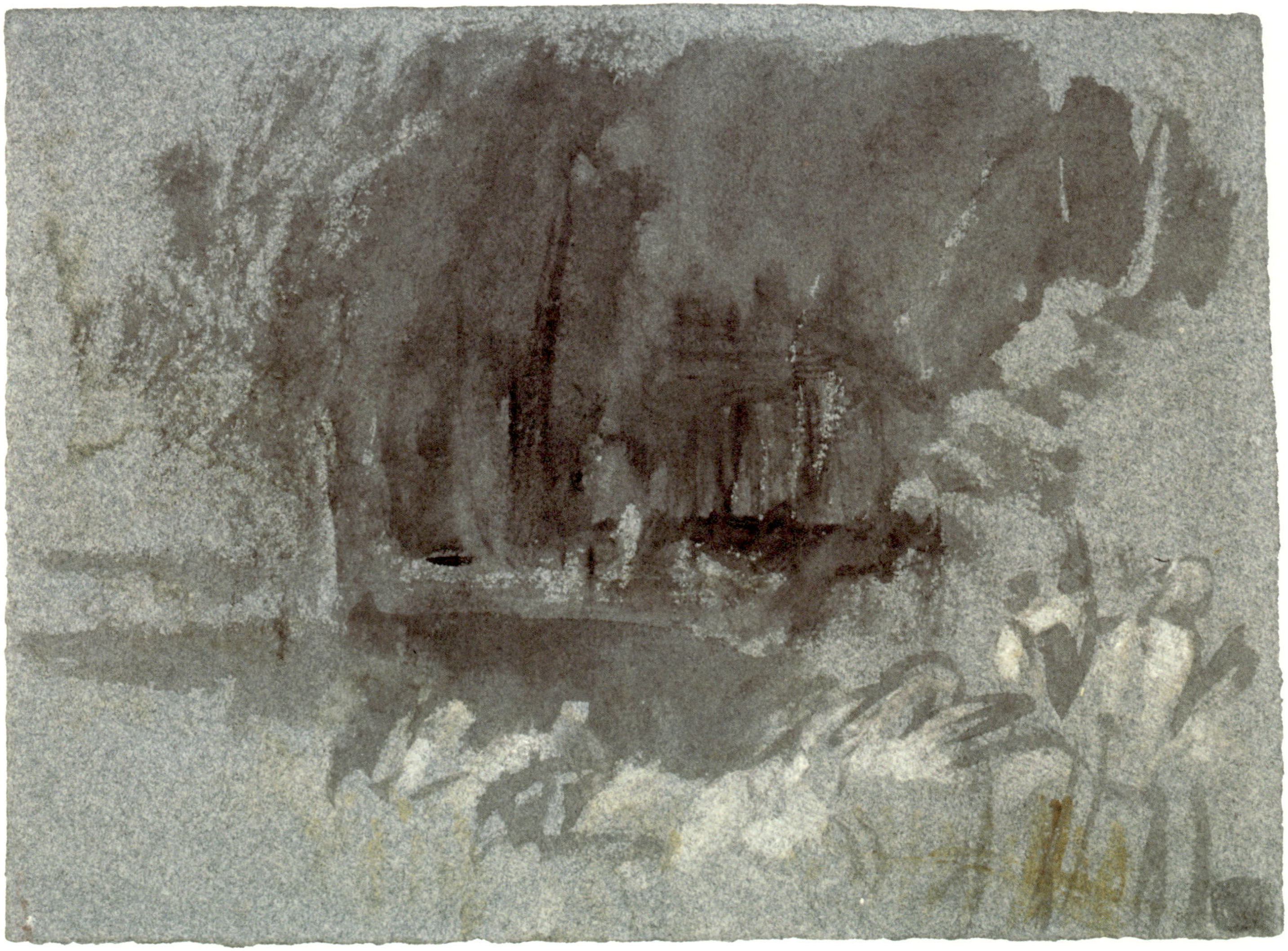

PLATE 96
A Wooded Glade: colour beginning
TB CCXLIV–49

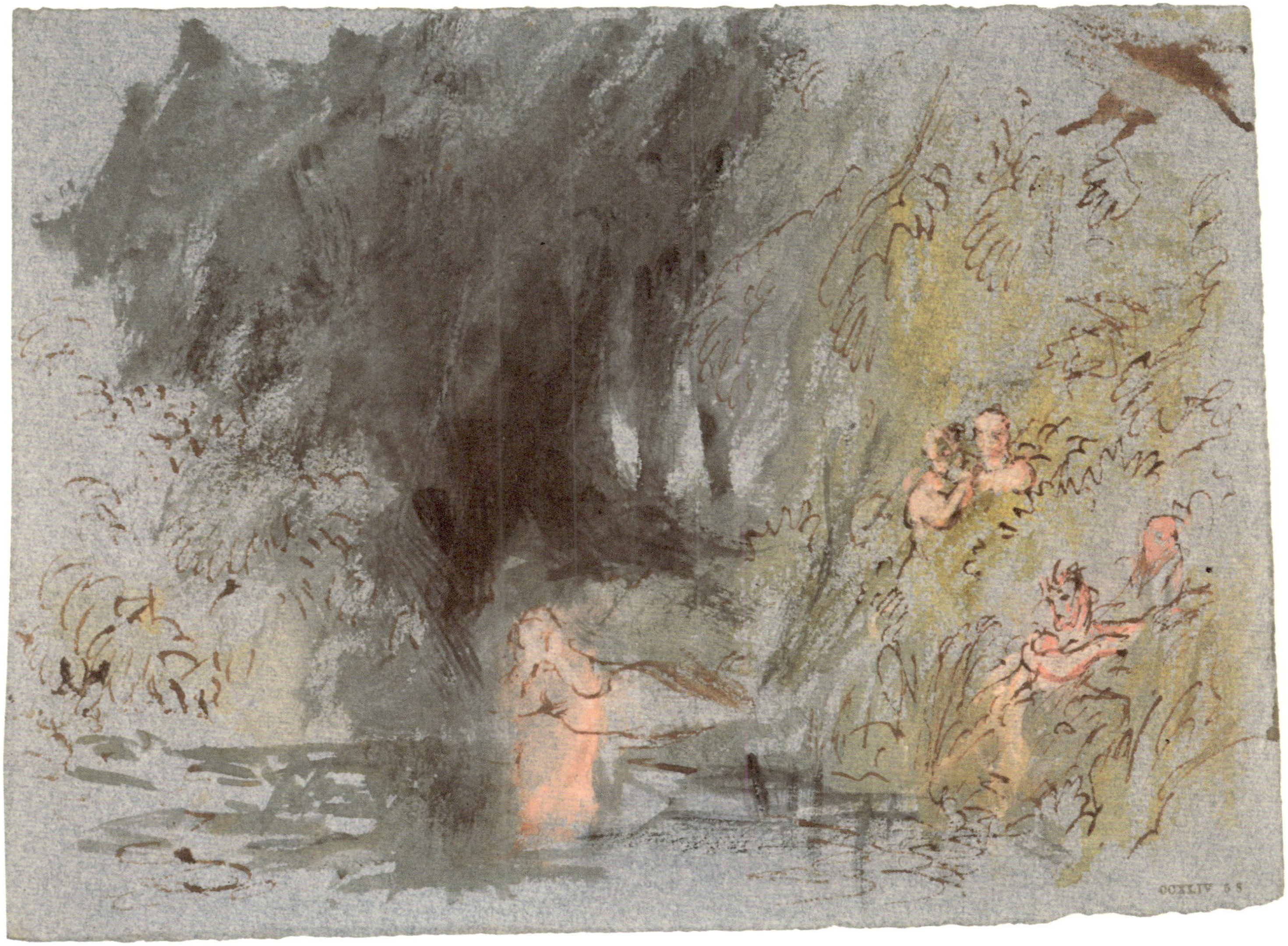

PLATE 97

Lake with Classical Figures [cf plate 96]

TB CCXLIV–58 Pen and brown ink with watercolour and gouache

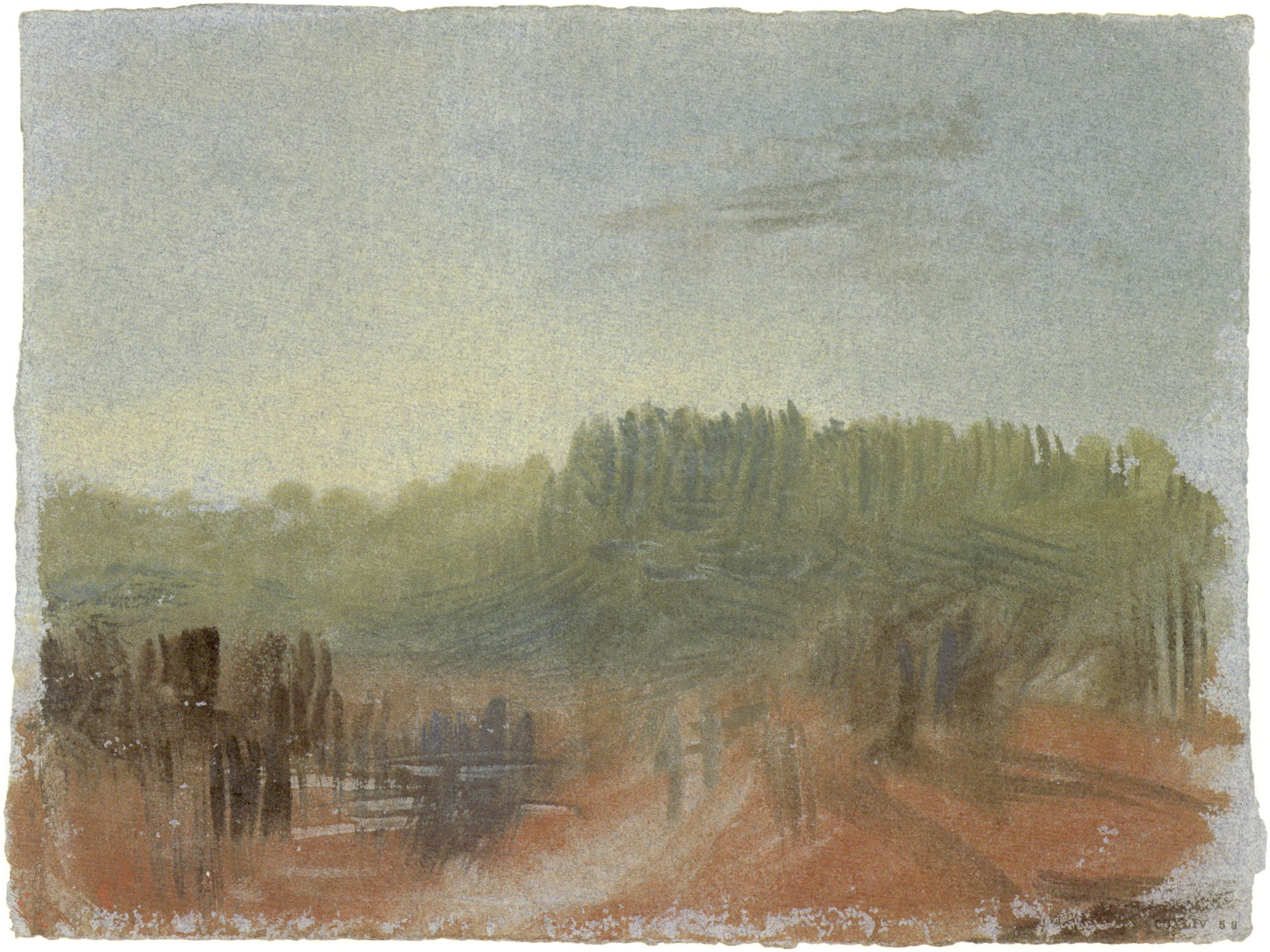

PLATE 98
Landscape at Petworth: ?the Stag Park
TB CCXLIV–59

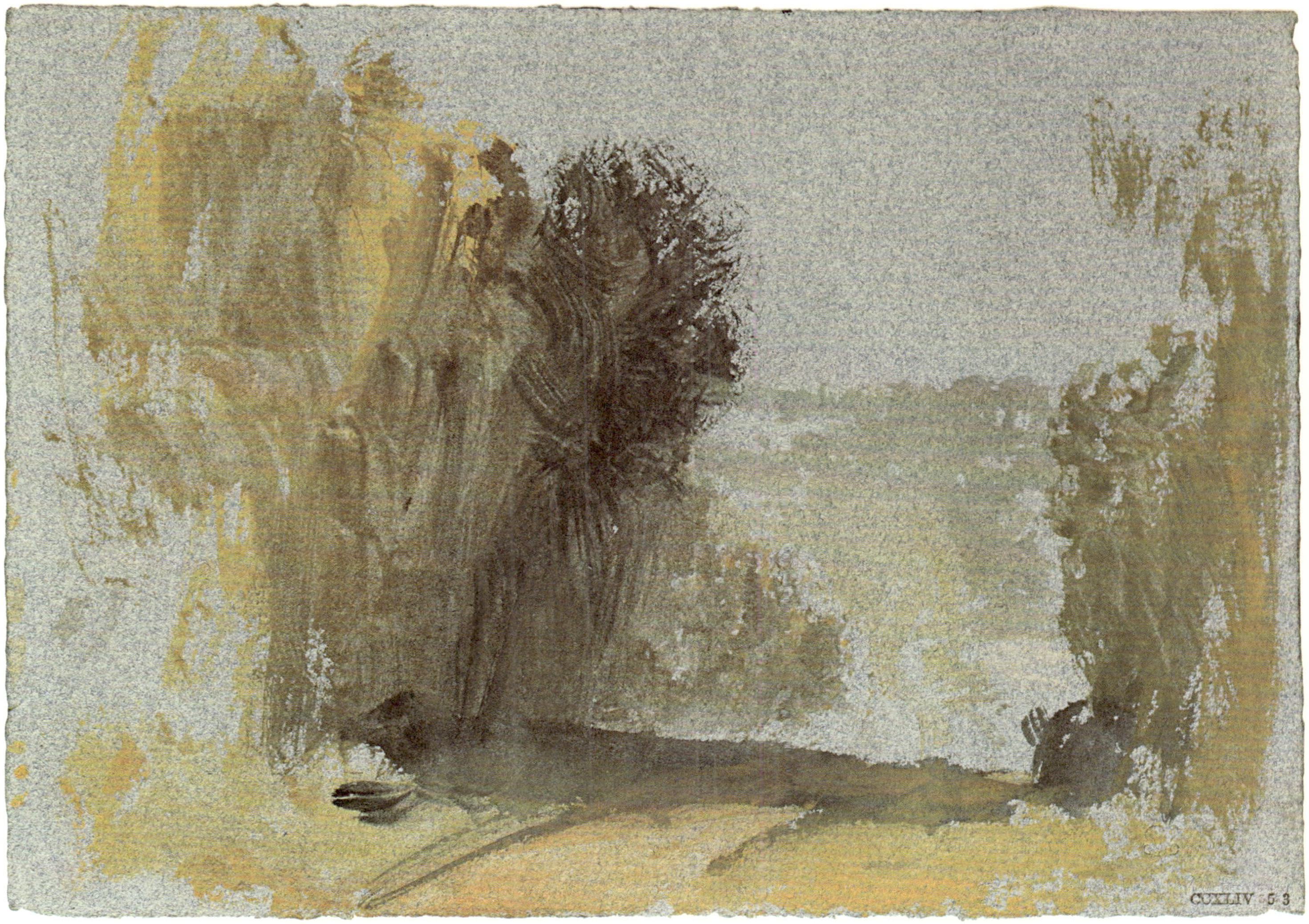

PLATE 99
Roadway Bordered by Trees
TB CCXLIV–53

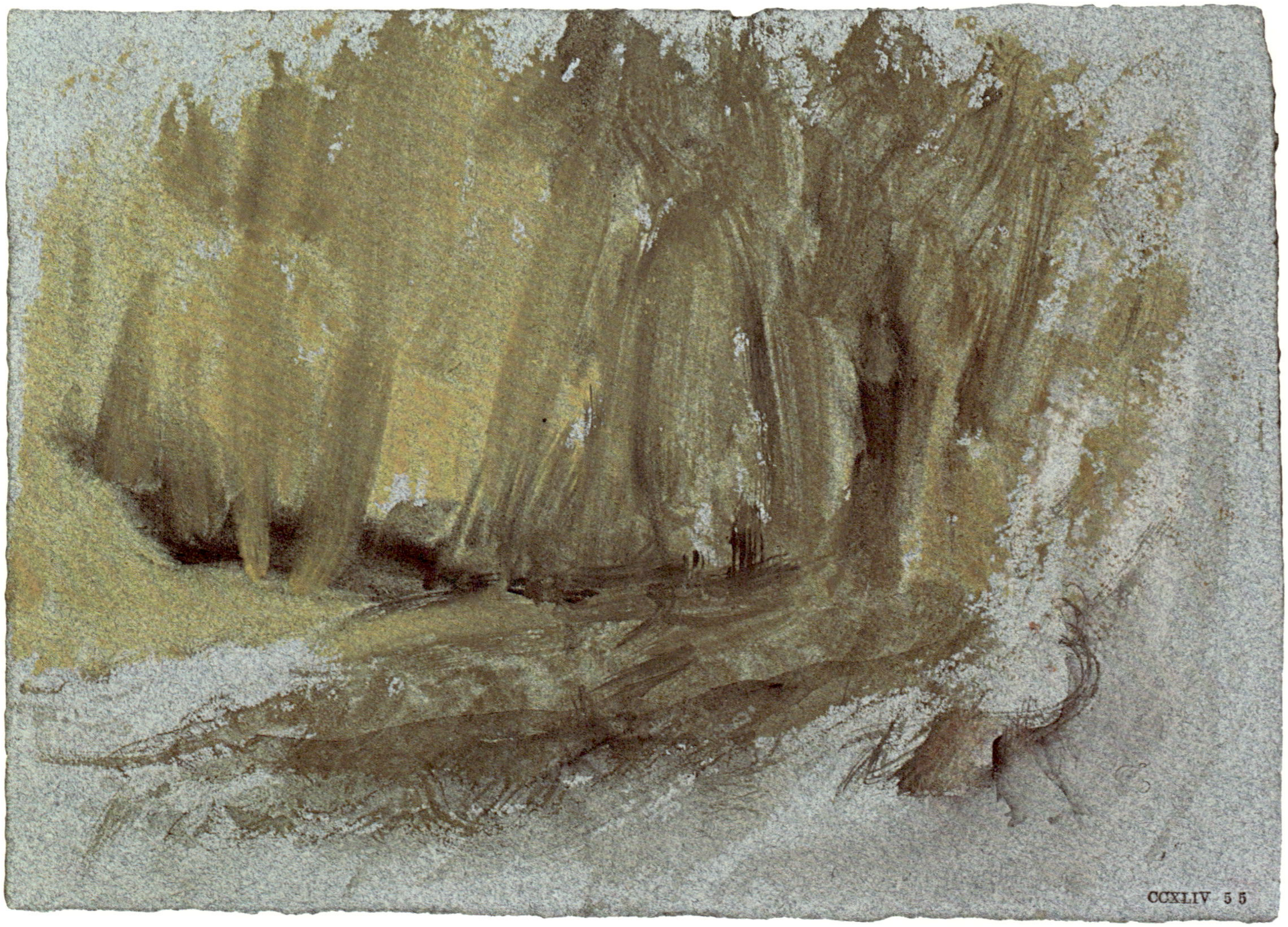

PLATE 100
A Group of Trees
TB CCXLIV–55

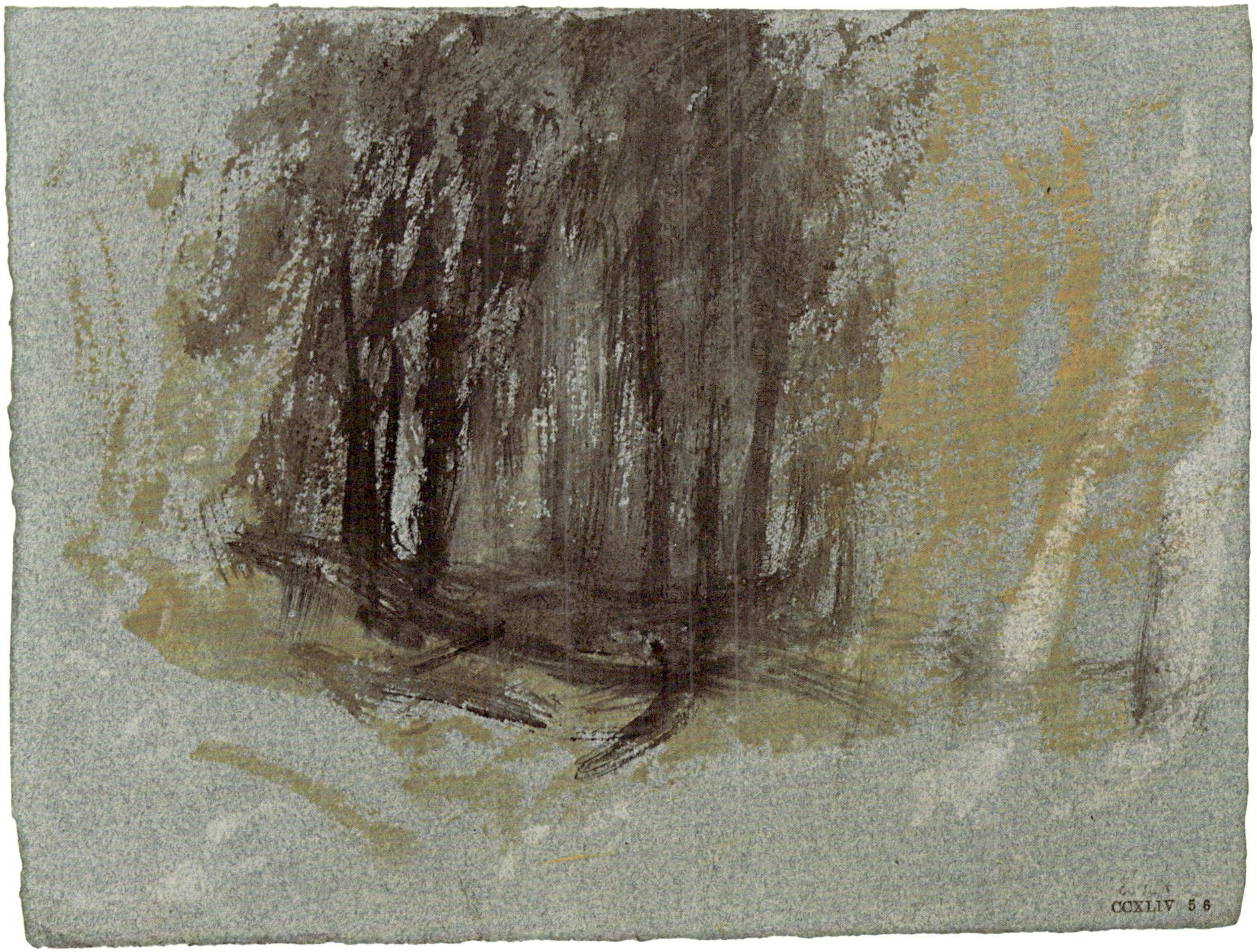

PLATE 101
Landscape with Trees
TB CCXLIV–56

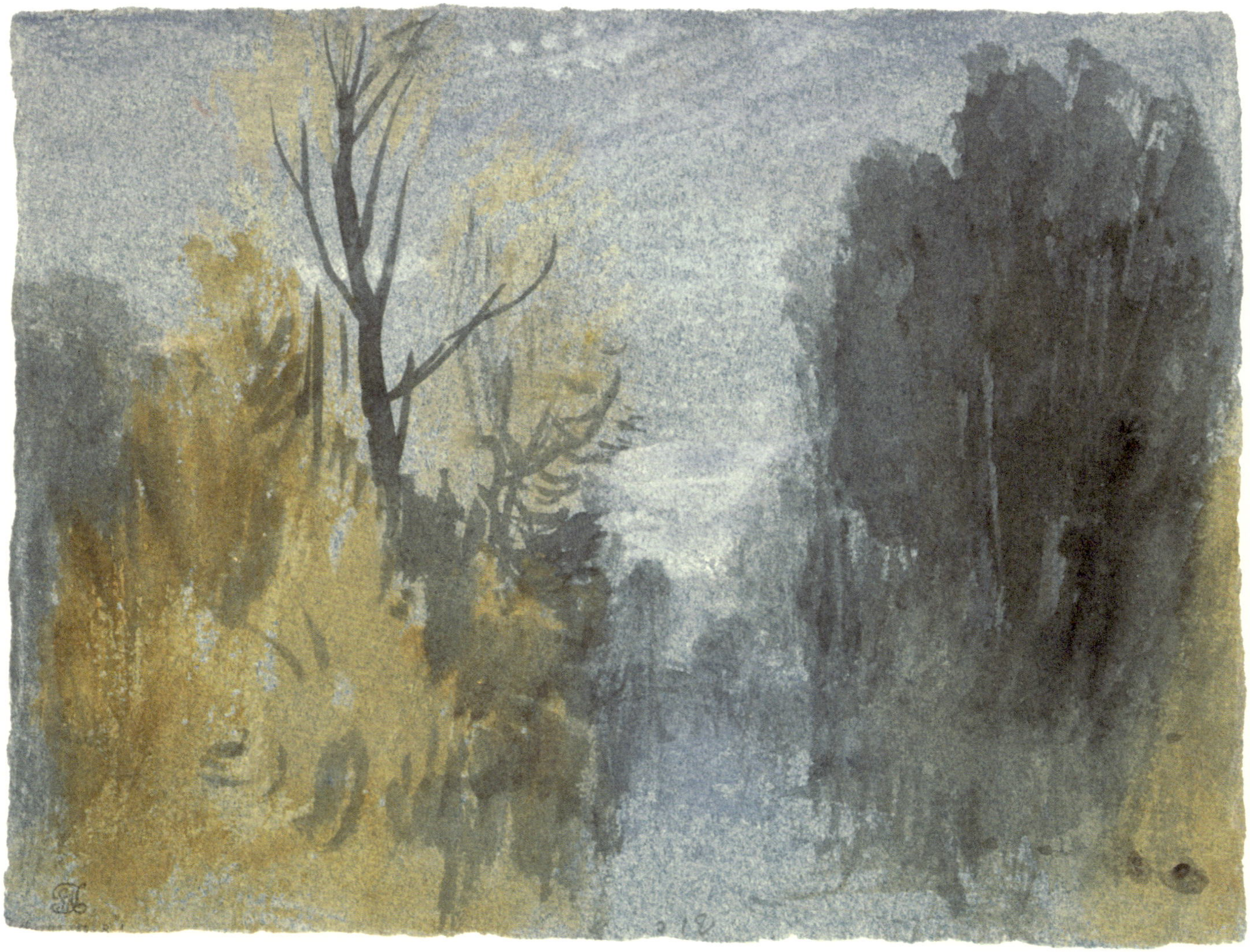

PLATE 102
Landscape with Lake and Trees
TB CCXLIV–84 verso

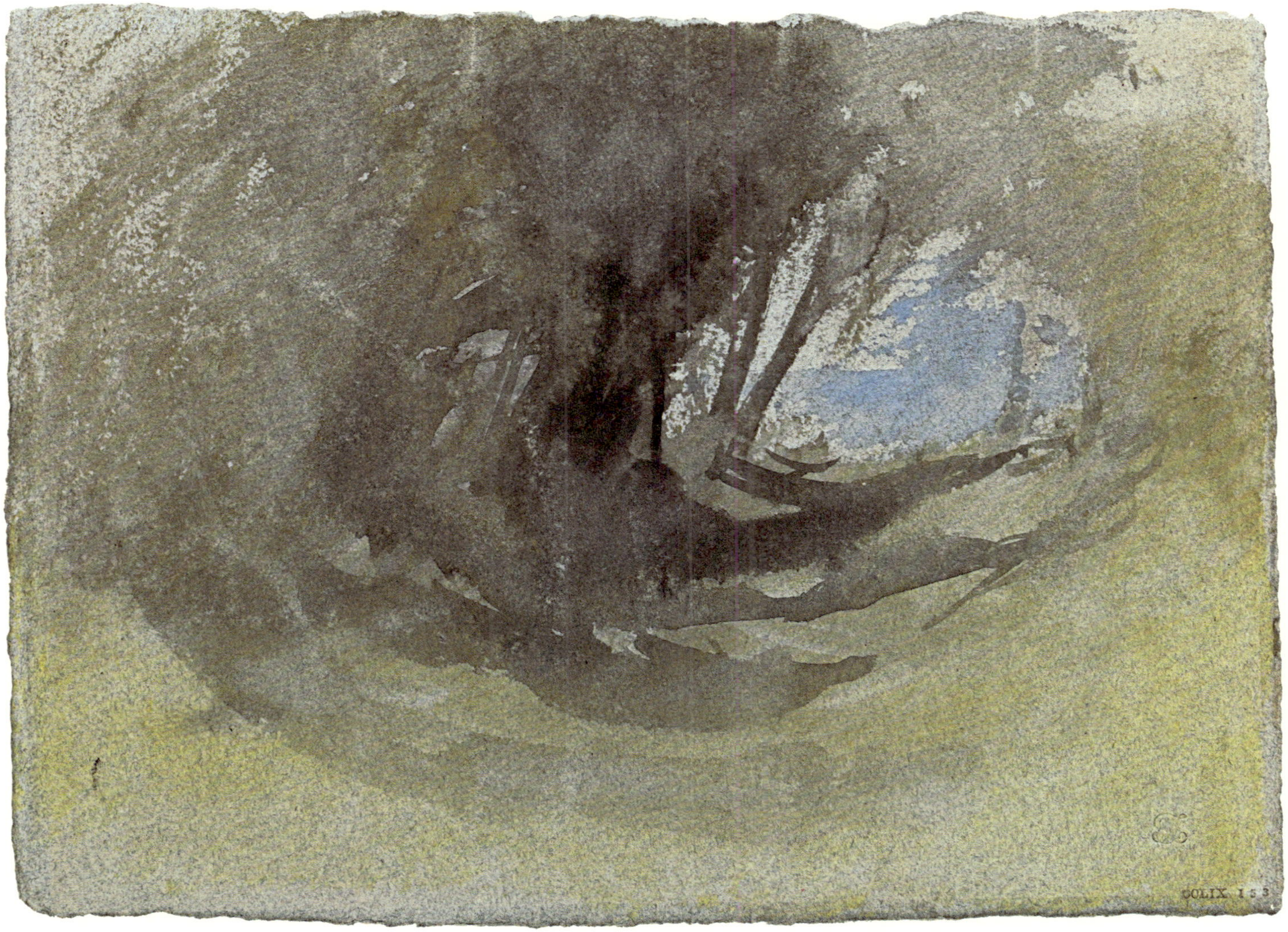

PLATE 103
A Wooded Glade
TB CCLIX–153

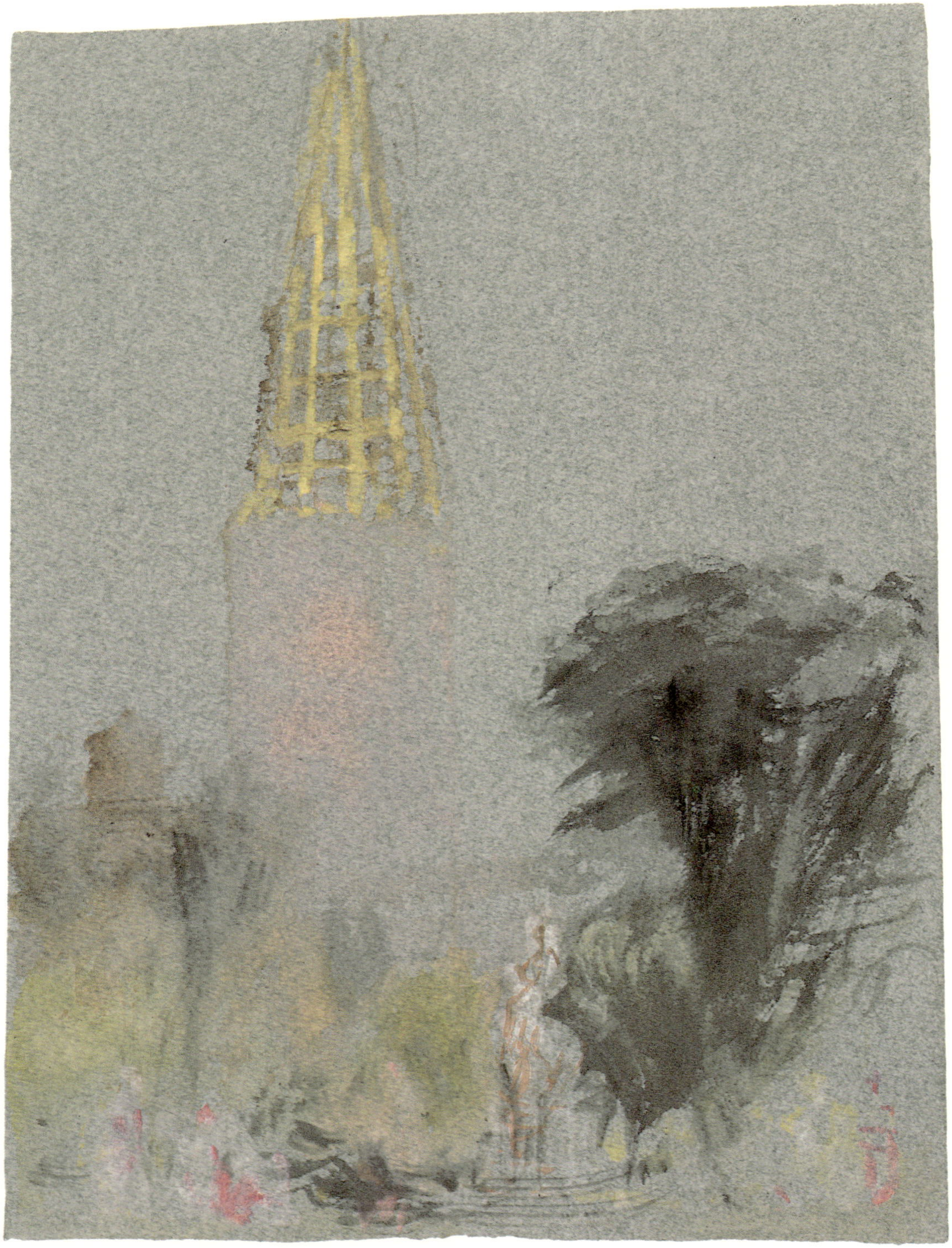

PLATE 104
The Spire of St Mary's, Petworth under Construction: seen from the Fountain Court of Petworth House
TB CCXLIV–52

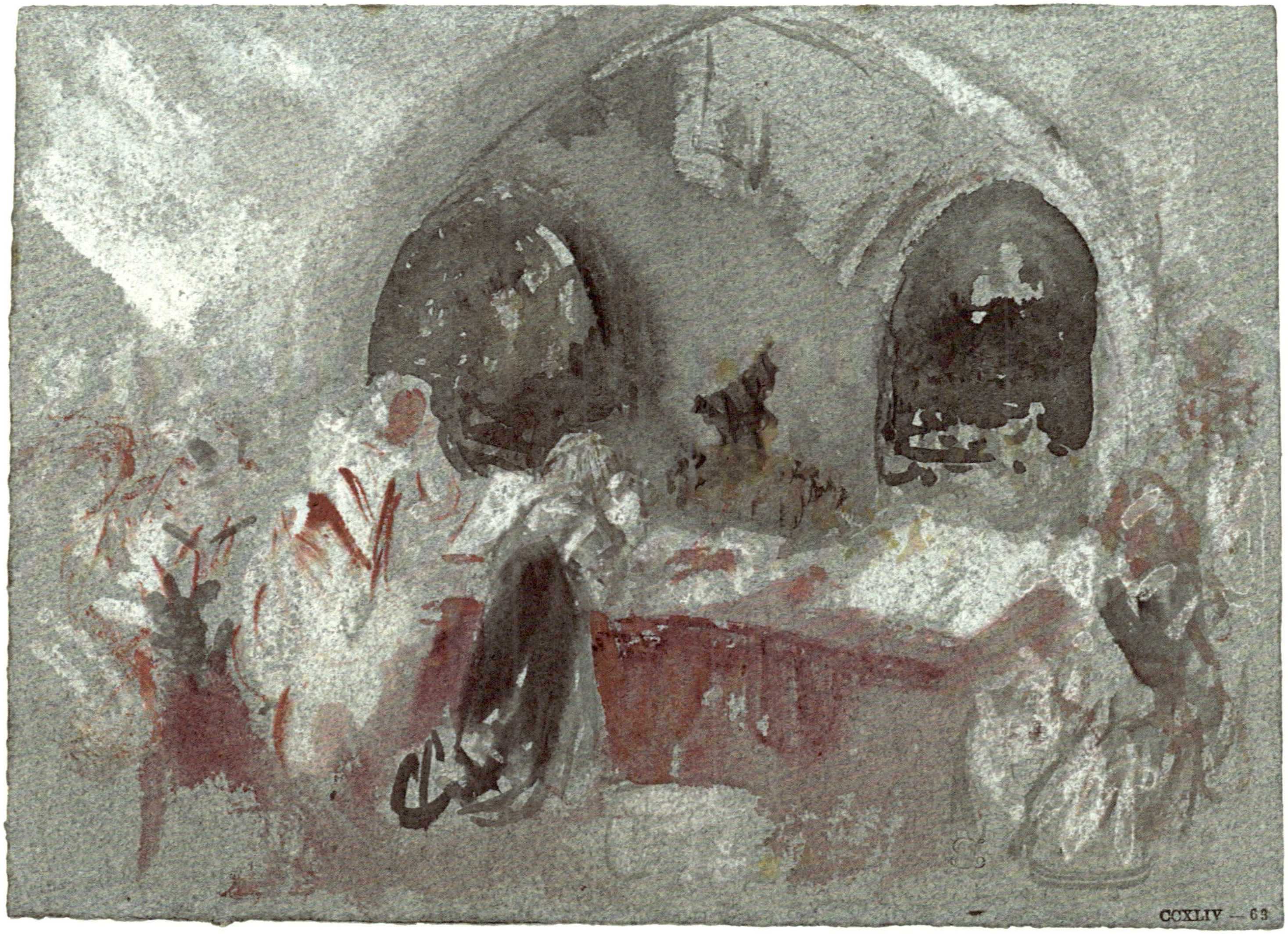

PLATE 105

The Interior of Petworth Church seen from the Egremont Family Gallery

TB CCXLIV–63

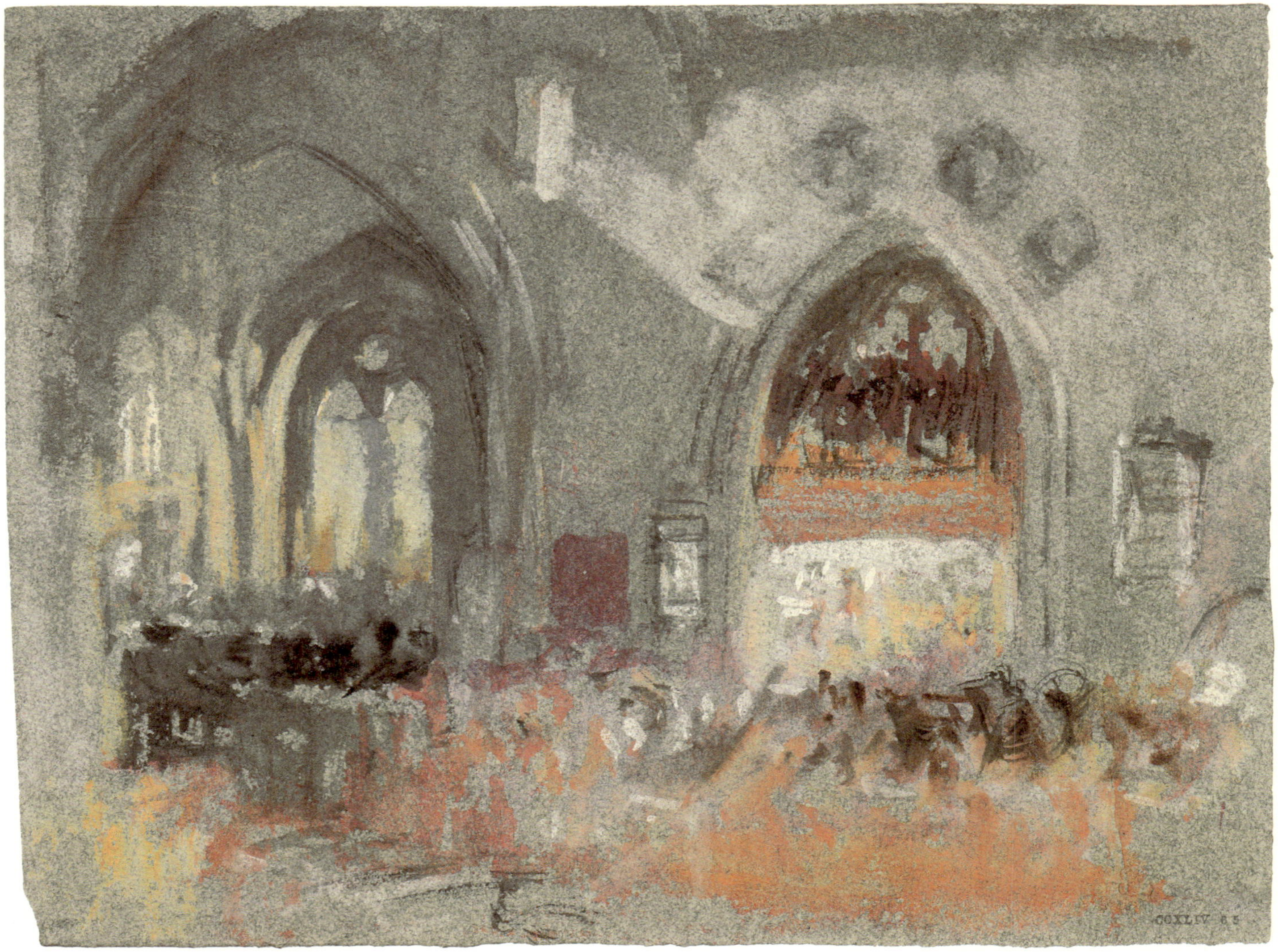

PLATE 106

Looking across the Nave into the Chancel and South Transept

TB CCXLIV–65

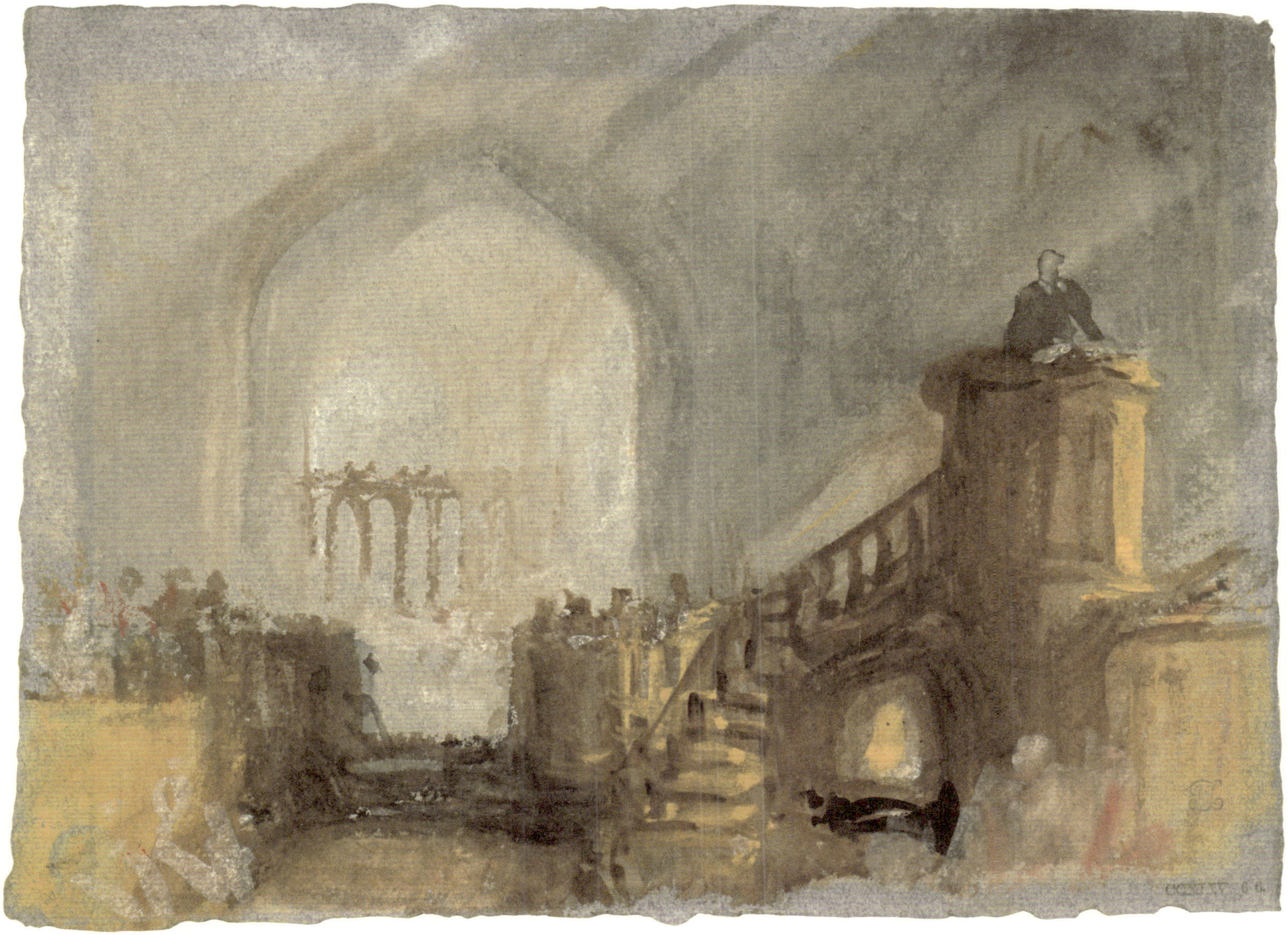

PLATE 107

A Sermon from the High Pulpit: the Chancel behind

TB CCXLIV–66

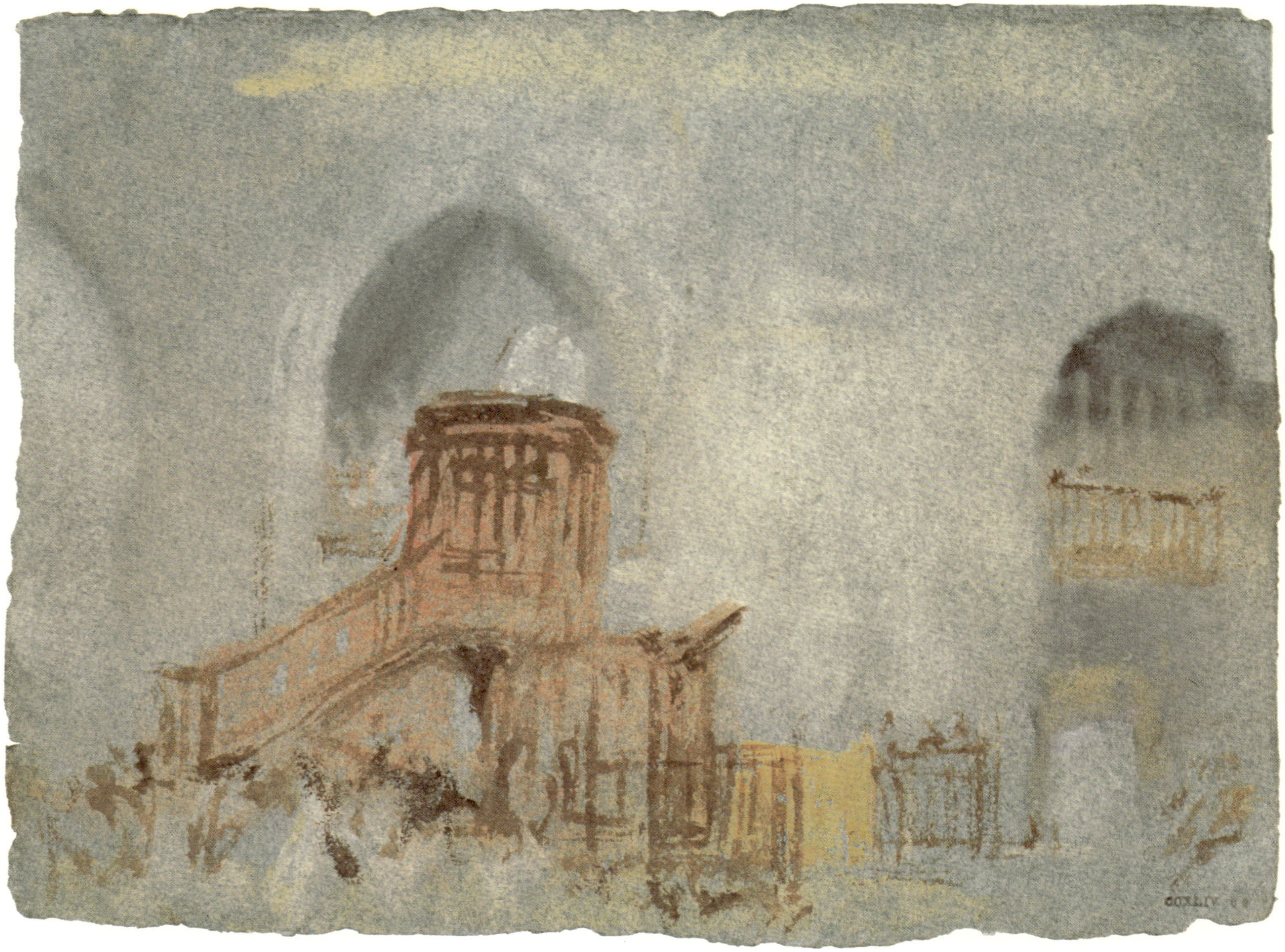

PLATE 108

The Pulpit and South Side of Petworth Church

TB CCXLIV–62

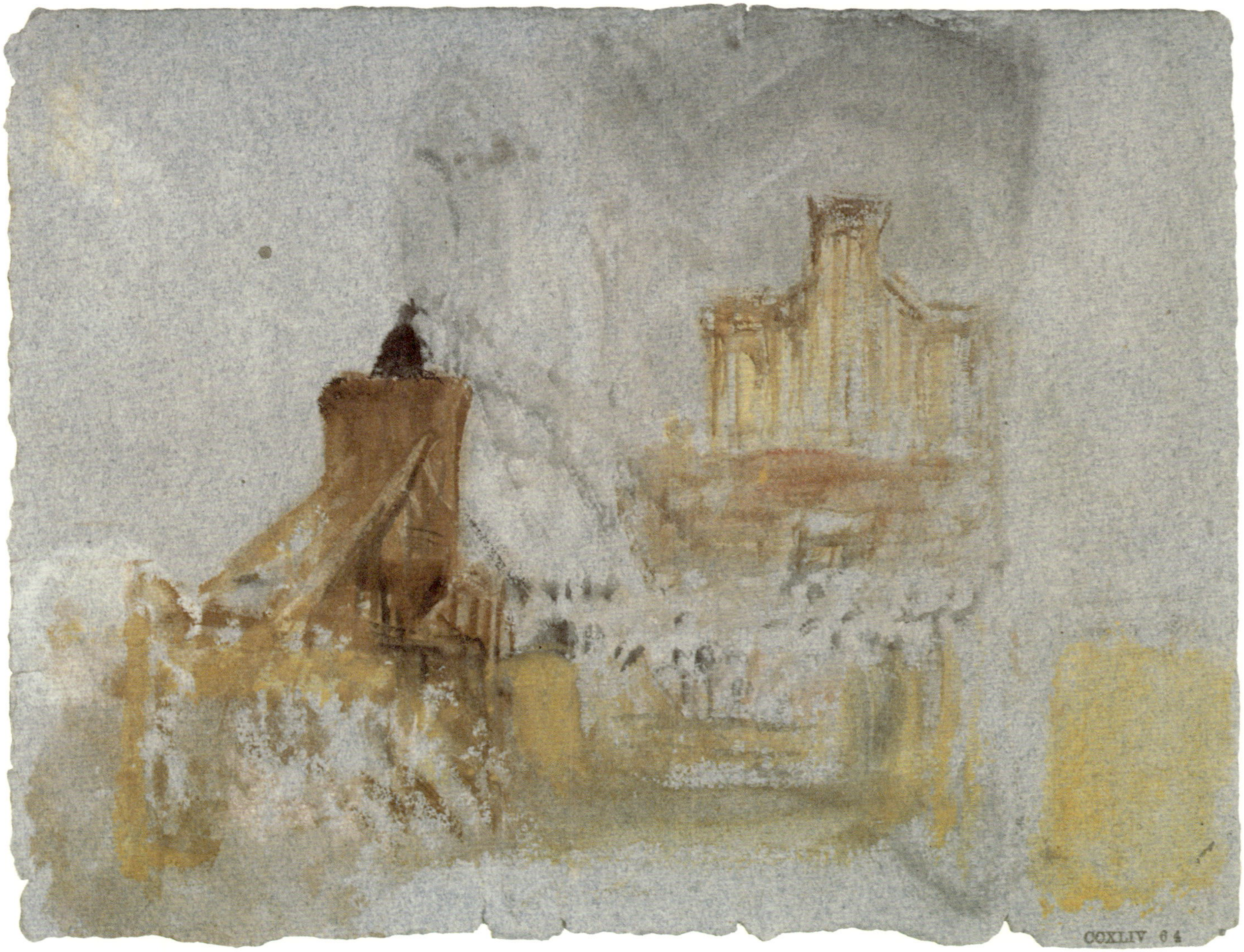

PLATE 109

Looking towards the West End of Petworth Church: the Organ Gallery

TB CCXLIV–64

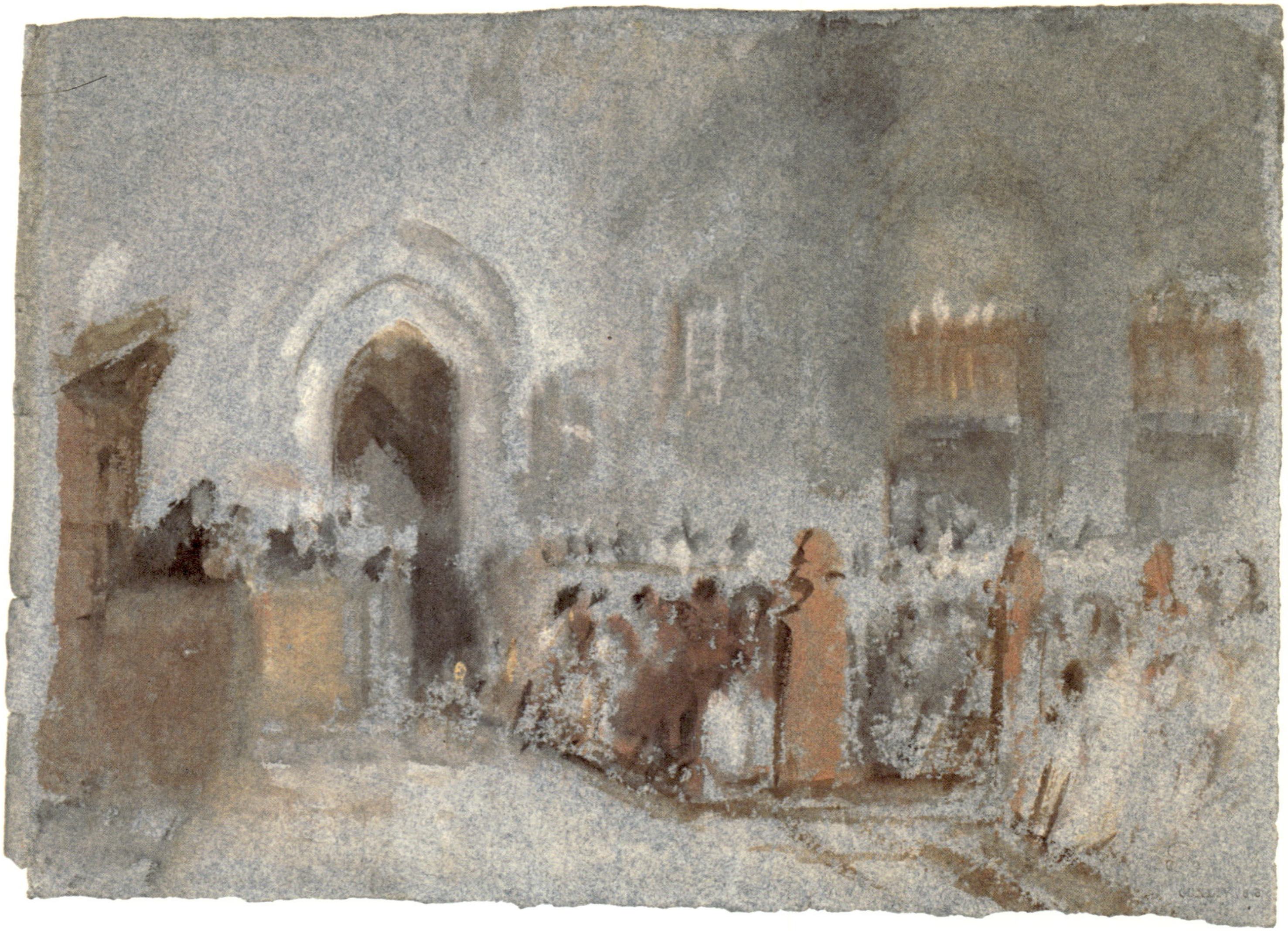

PLATE 110
The Congregation during the Sermon
TB CCXLIV–68

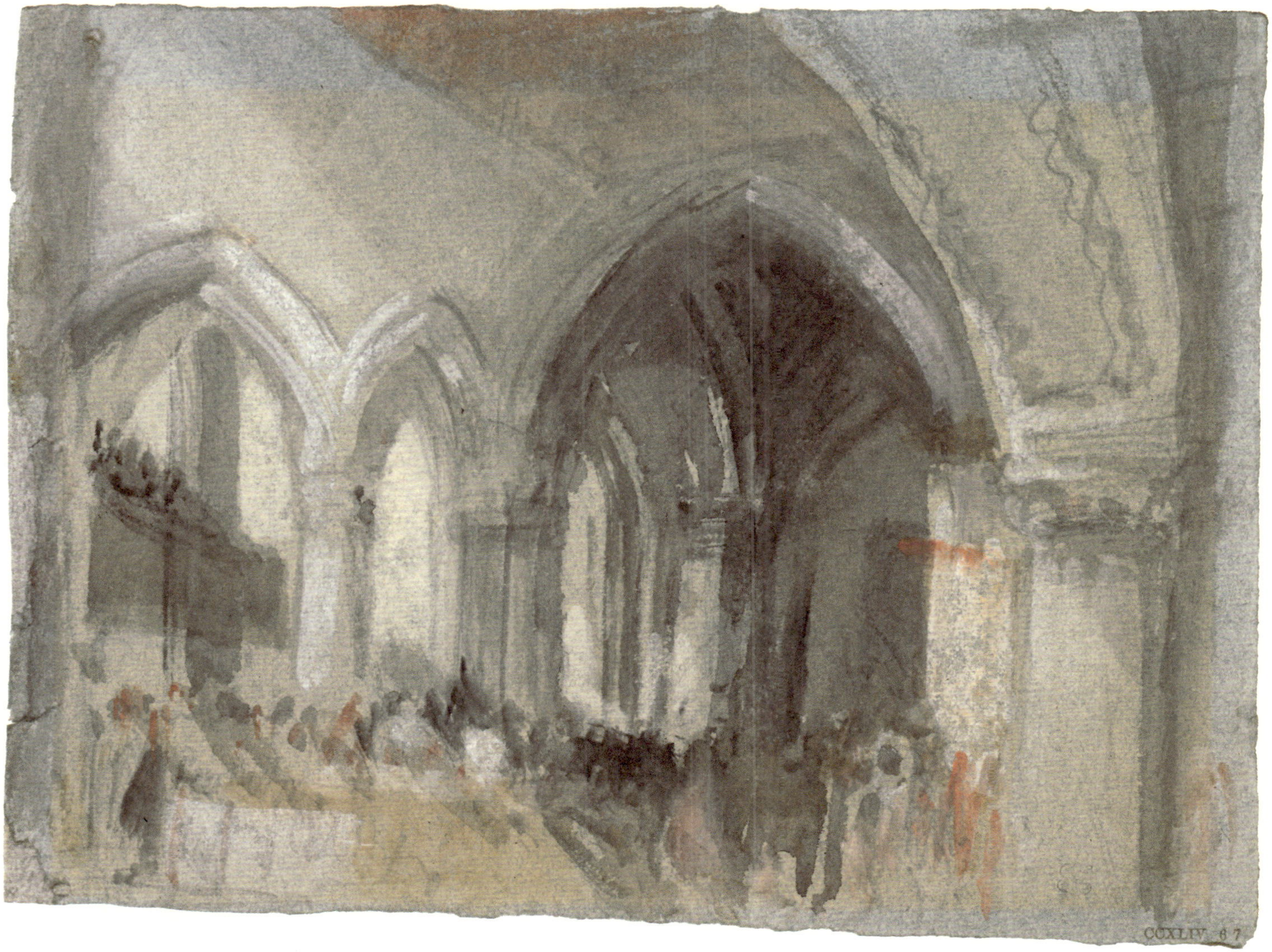

PLATE 111

The Original Arches of Petworth Church

TB CCXLIV–67 Gouache and watercolour over traces of pencil

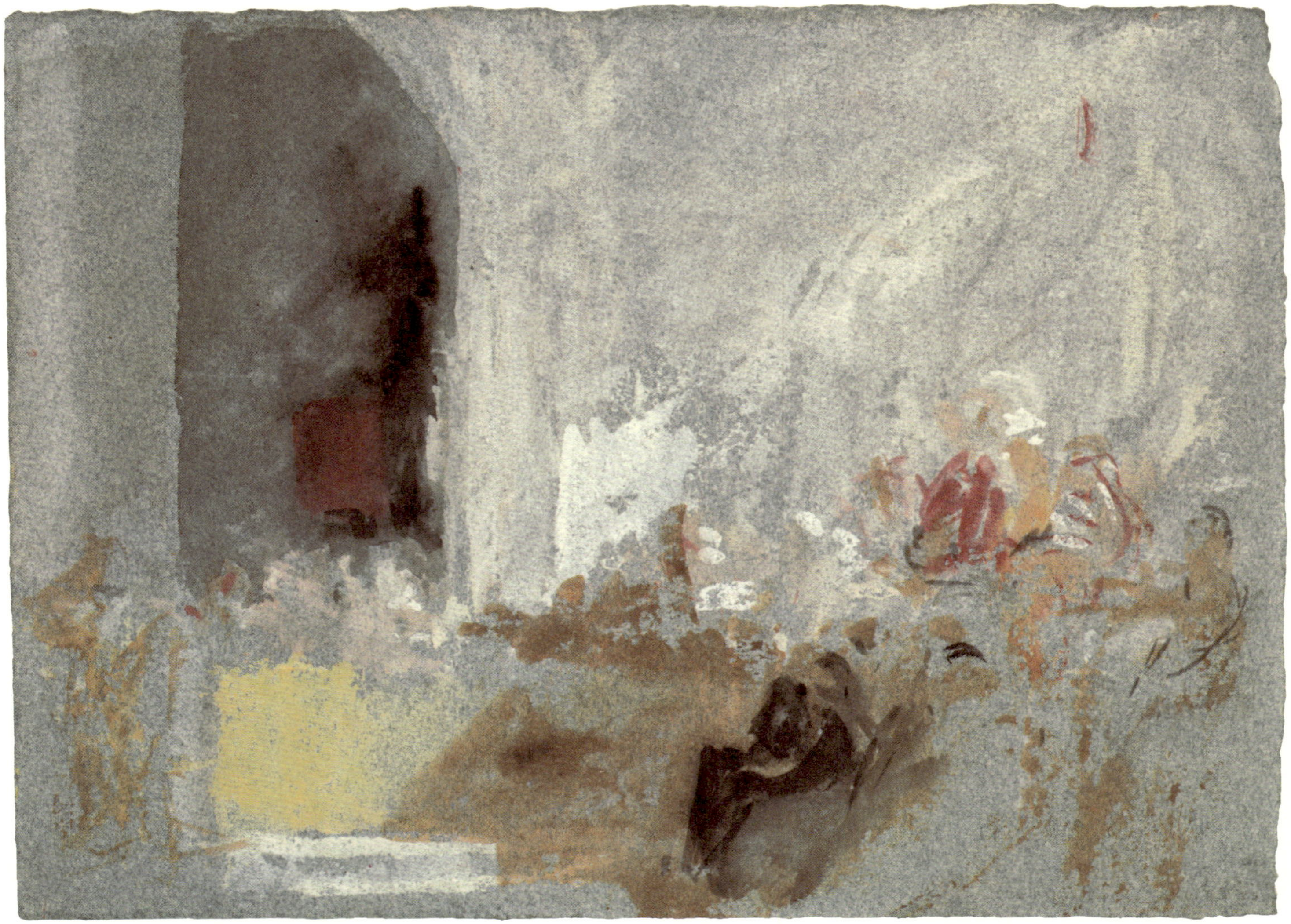

PLATE 112
The South Gallery of Petworth Church: the pulpit on the left
TB CCXLIV–35

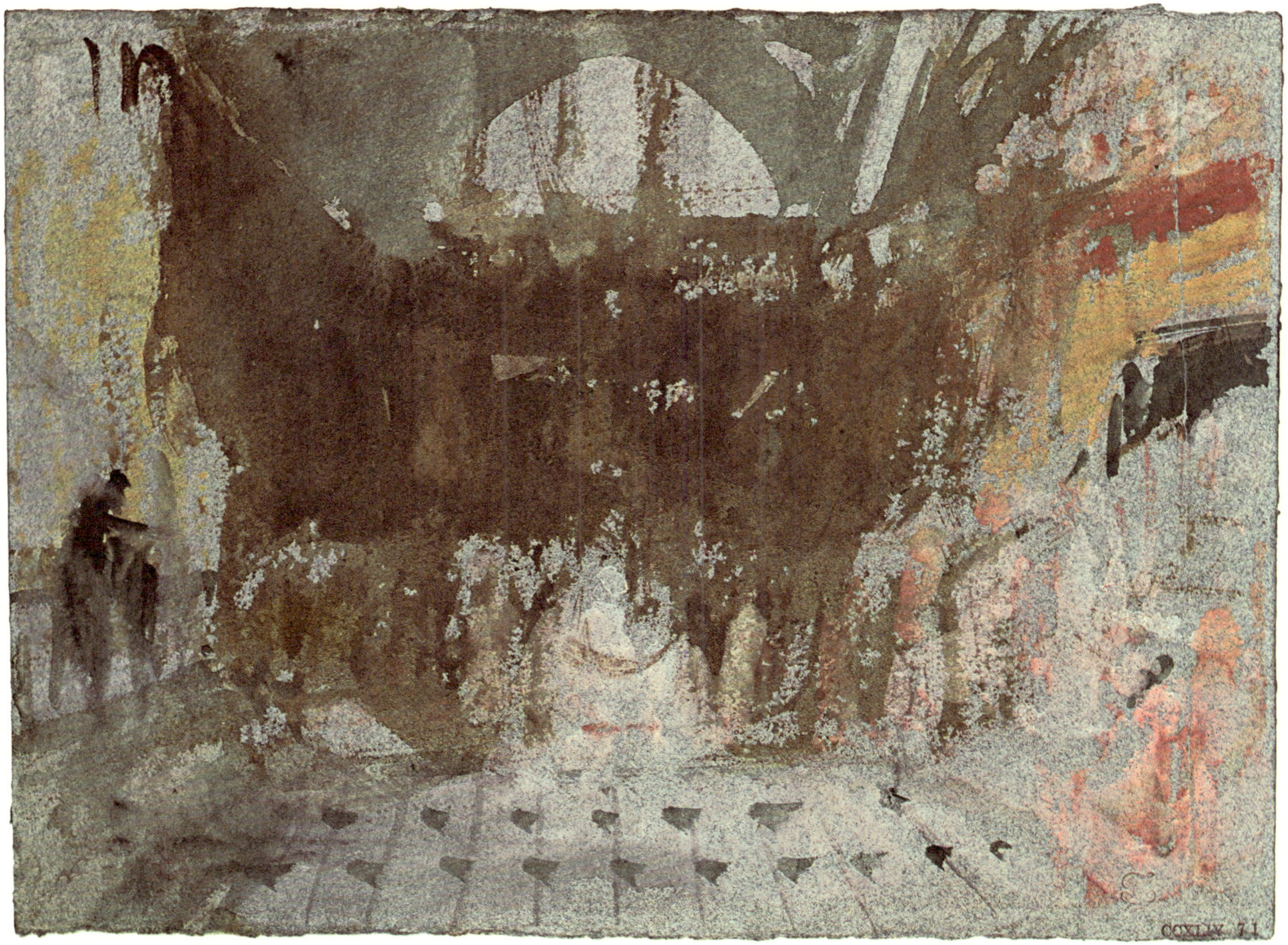

PLATE 113
The Chancel of Petworth Church: a copy of Michaelangelo's 'Pietà'
TB CCXLIV–71

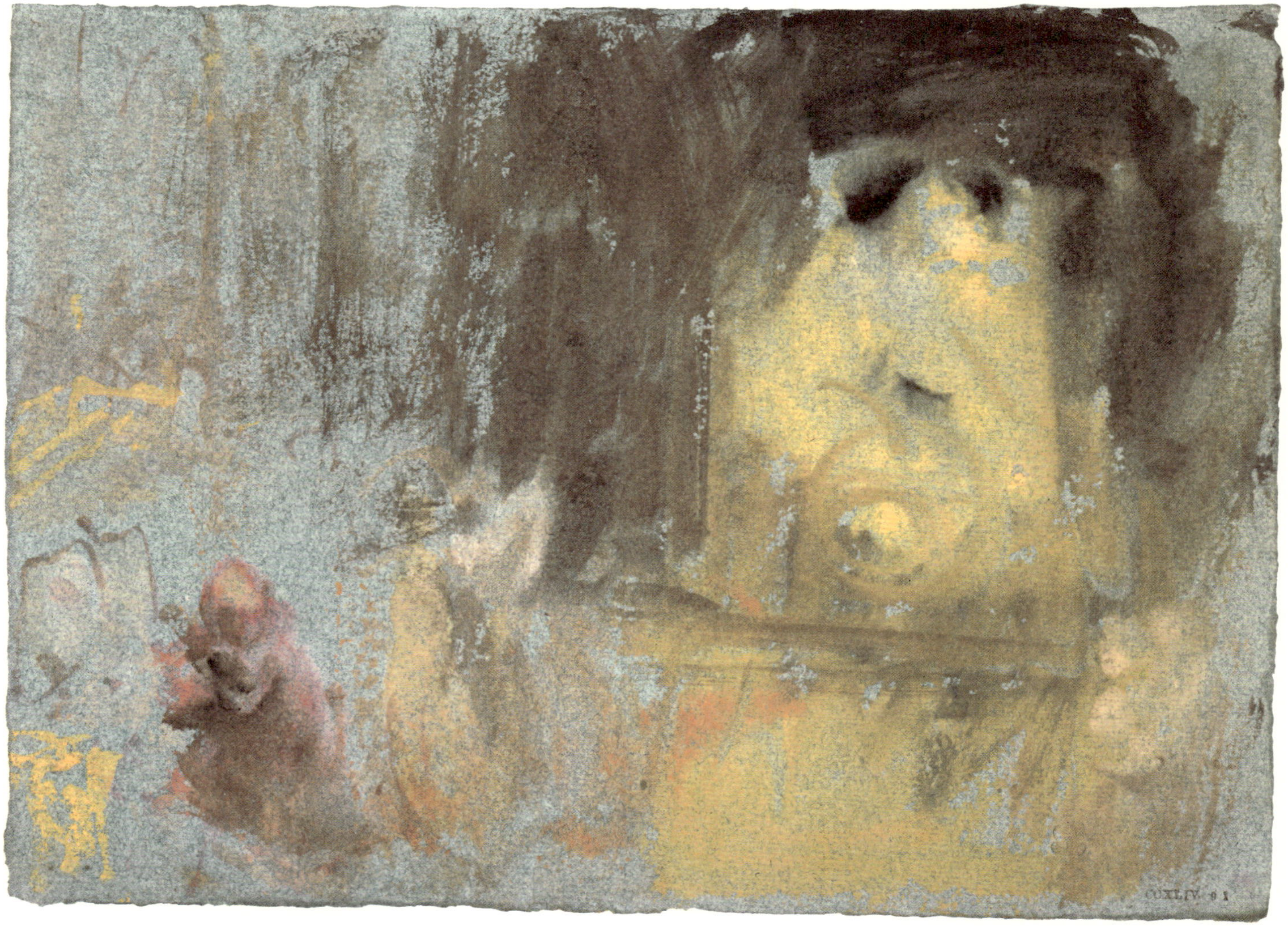

PLATE 114

An Imaginative Subject: Petworth Church (?)

TB CCXLIV–91

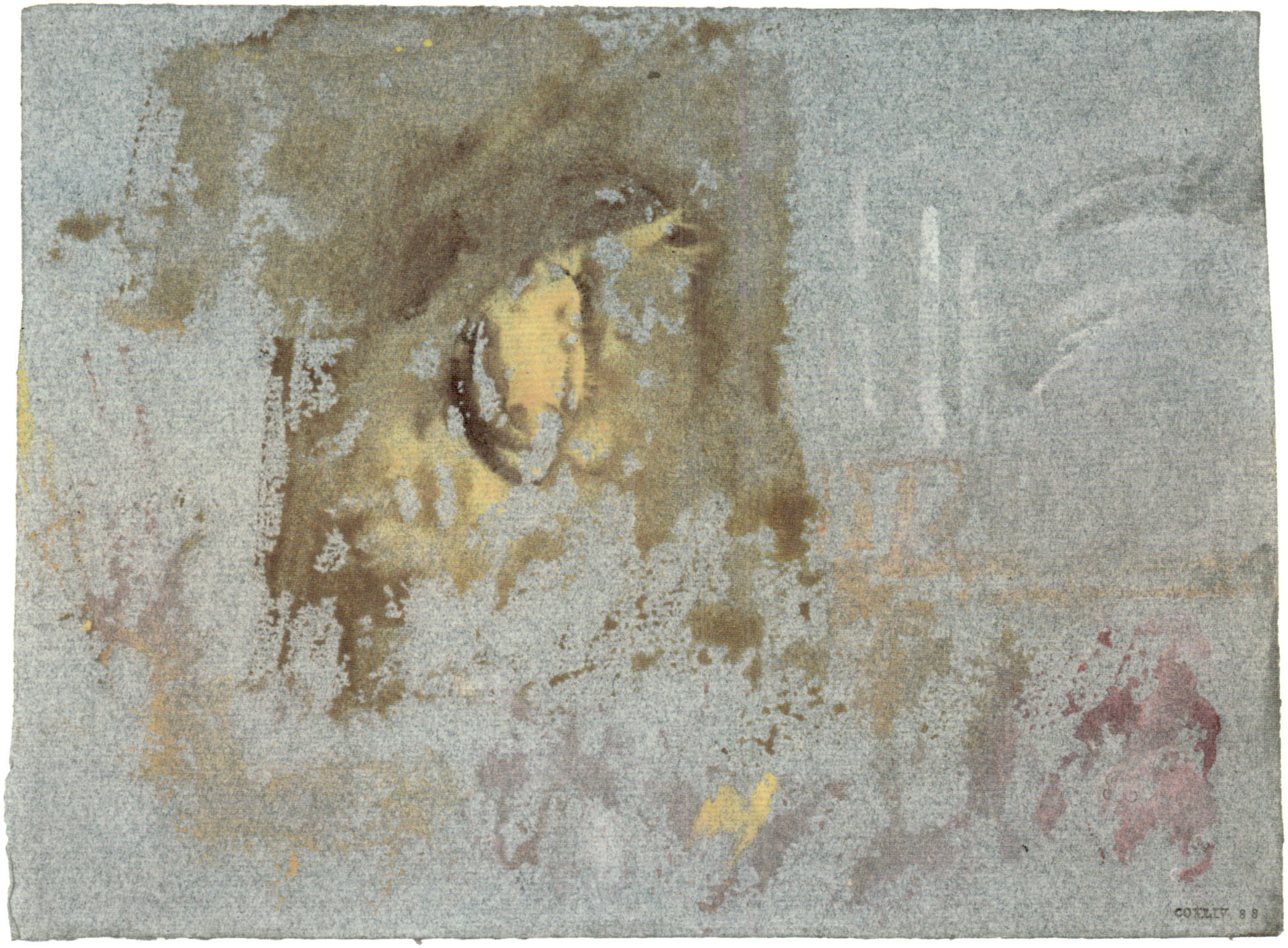

PLATE 115

An Interior: Petworth Church (?)

TB CCXLIV–88

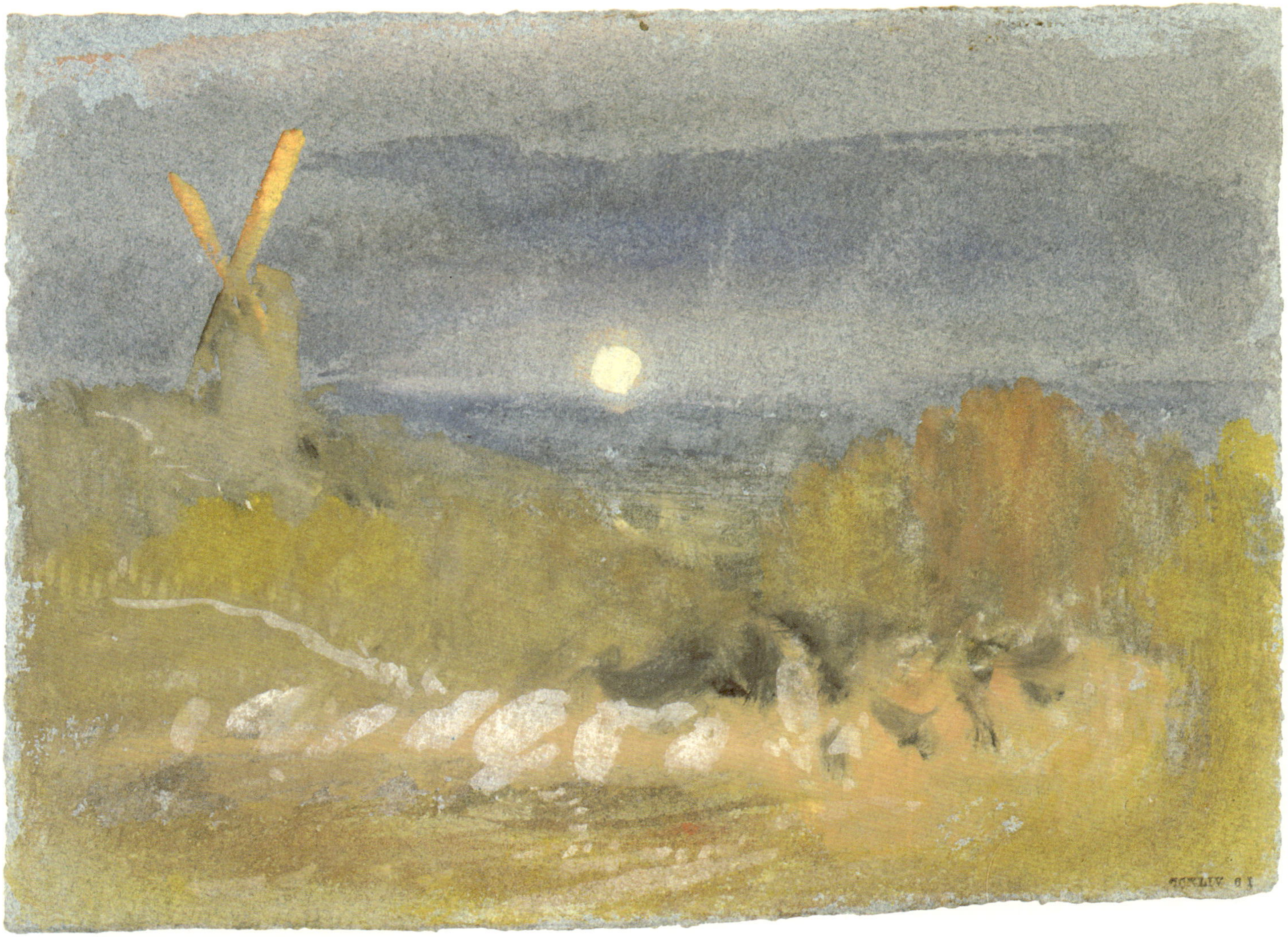

PLATE 116
Landscape with Windmill: twilight
TB CCXLIV–61

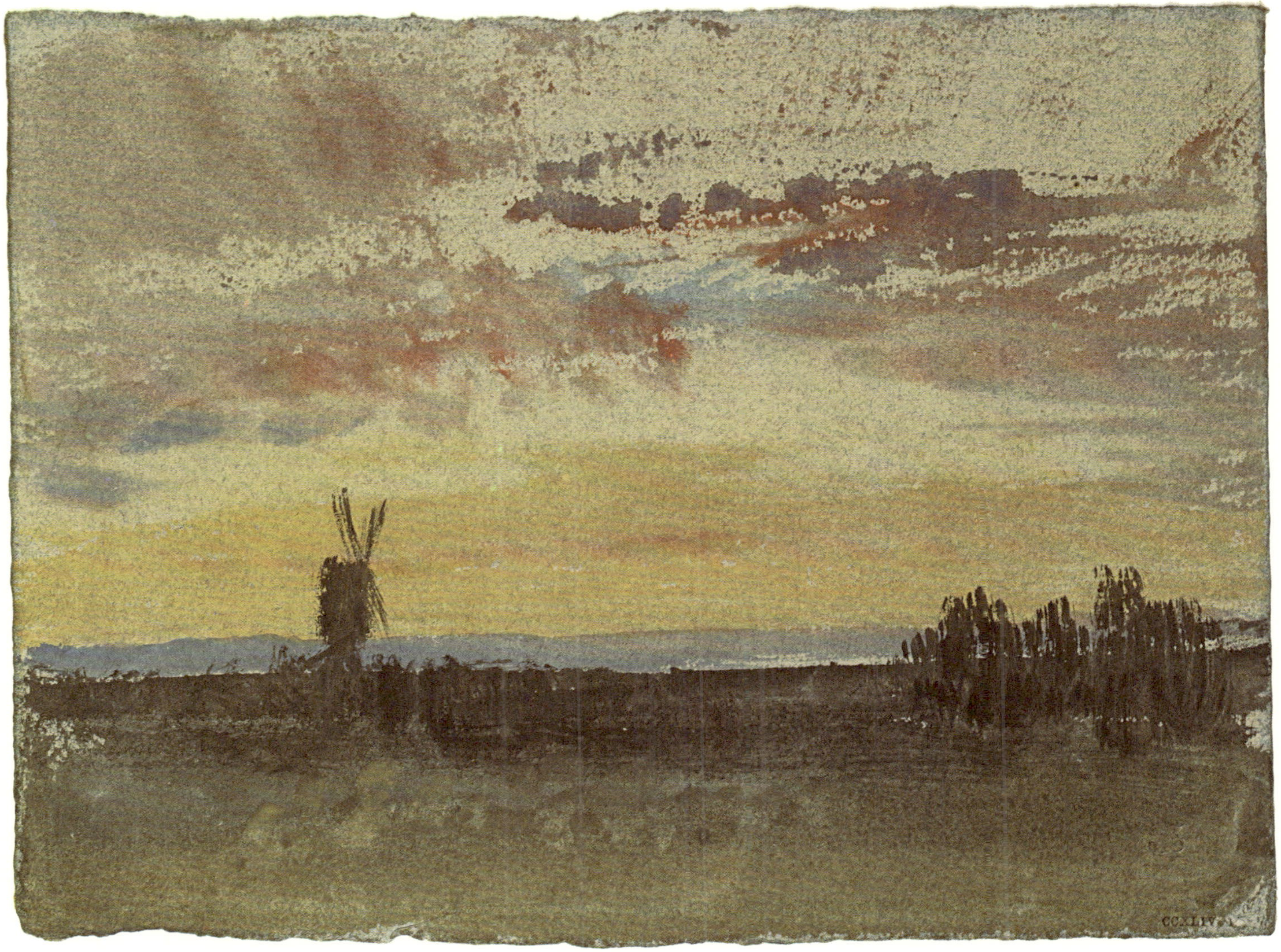

PLATE 117
Evening: a windmill at sunset
TB CCXLIV–1

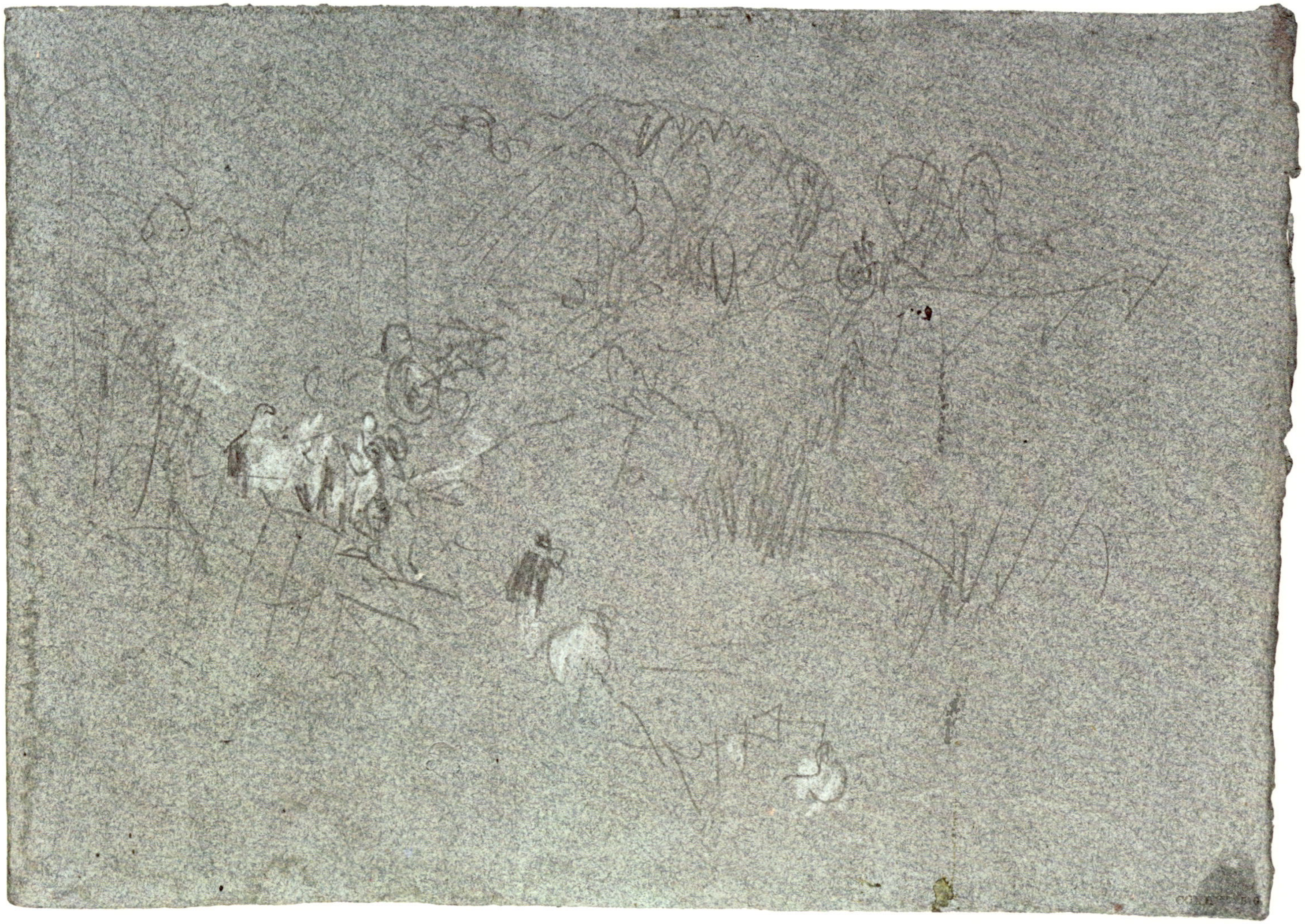

PLATE 118
The Pond: figures watching a swan
TB CCXLIV–50 Pencil and gouache

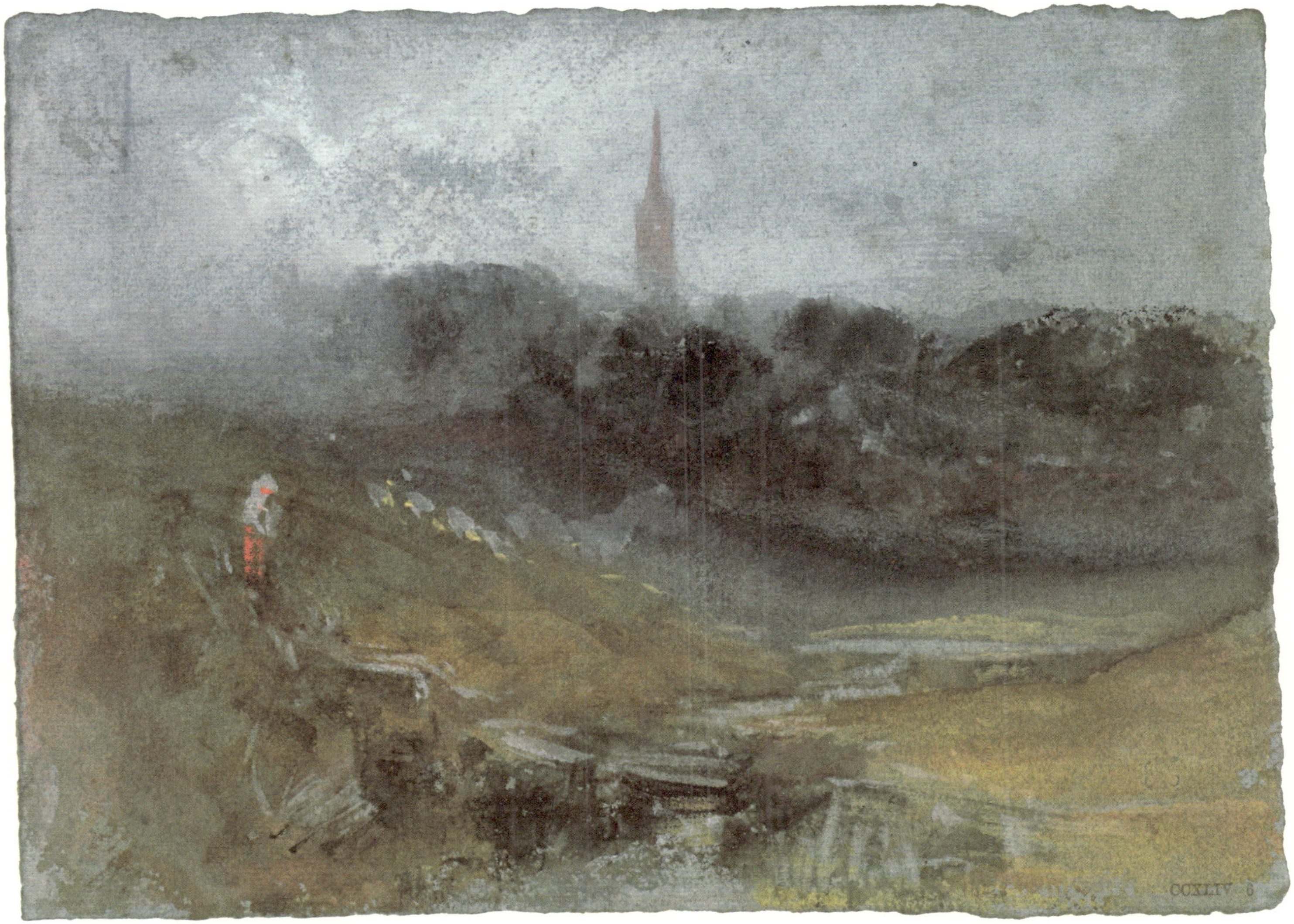

PLATE 119
Petworth Church seen from Rectory Meadows
TB CCXLIV–6

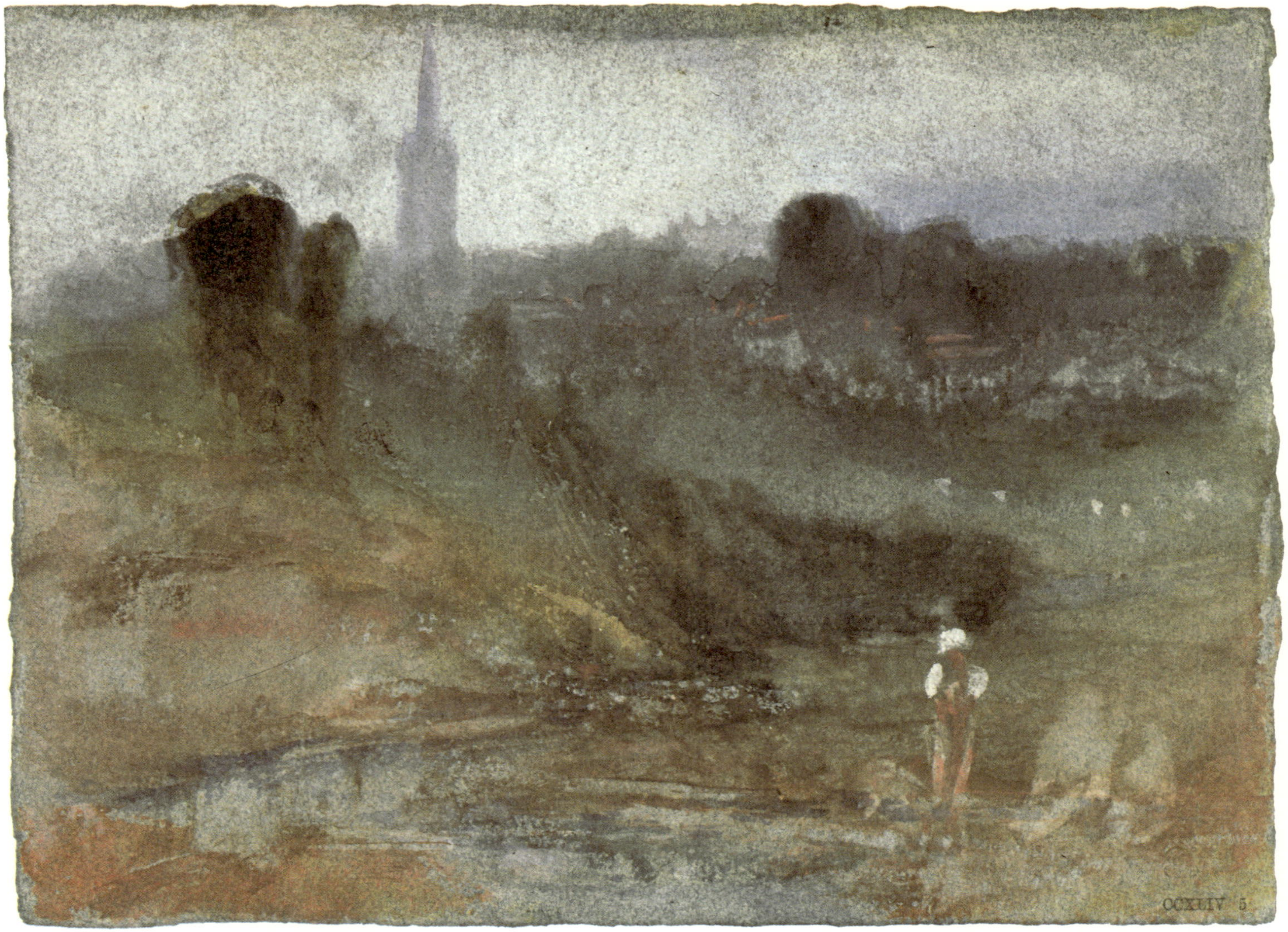

PLATE 120
A Closer View of Petworth Church
The chimneys of Petworth House visible to the right of the spire
TB CCXLIV–5

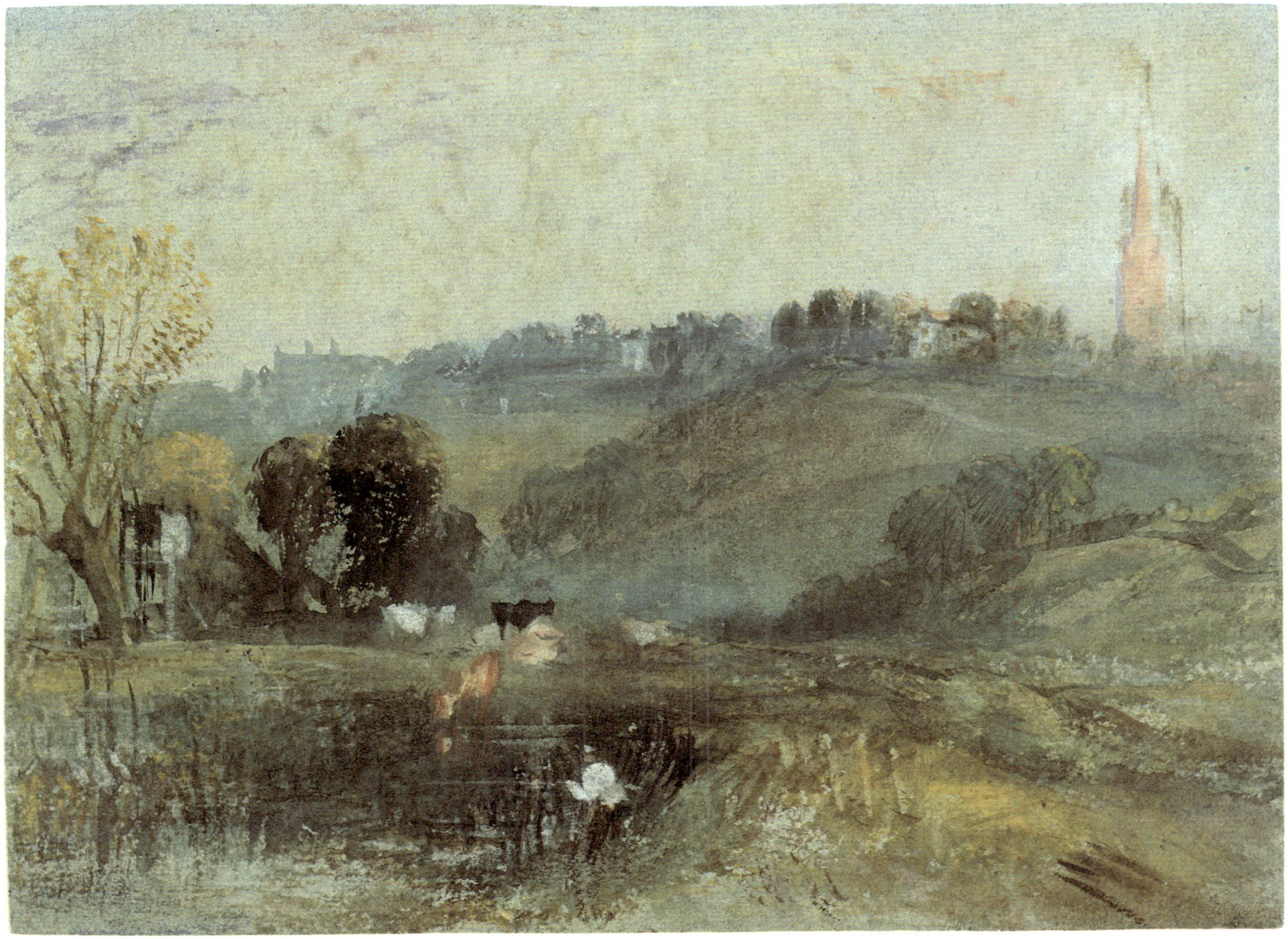

PLATE 121
Landscape near Petworth
Lord Egremont, Petworth House (w.907)

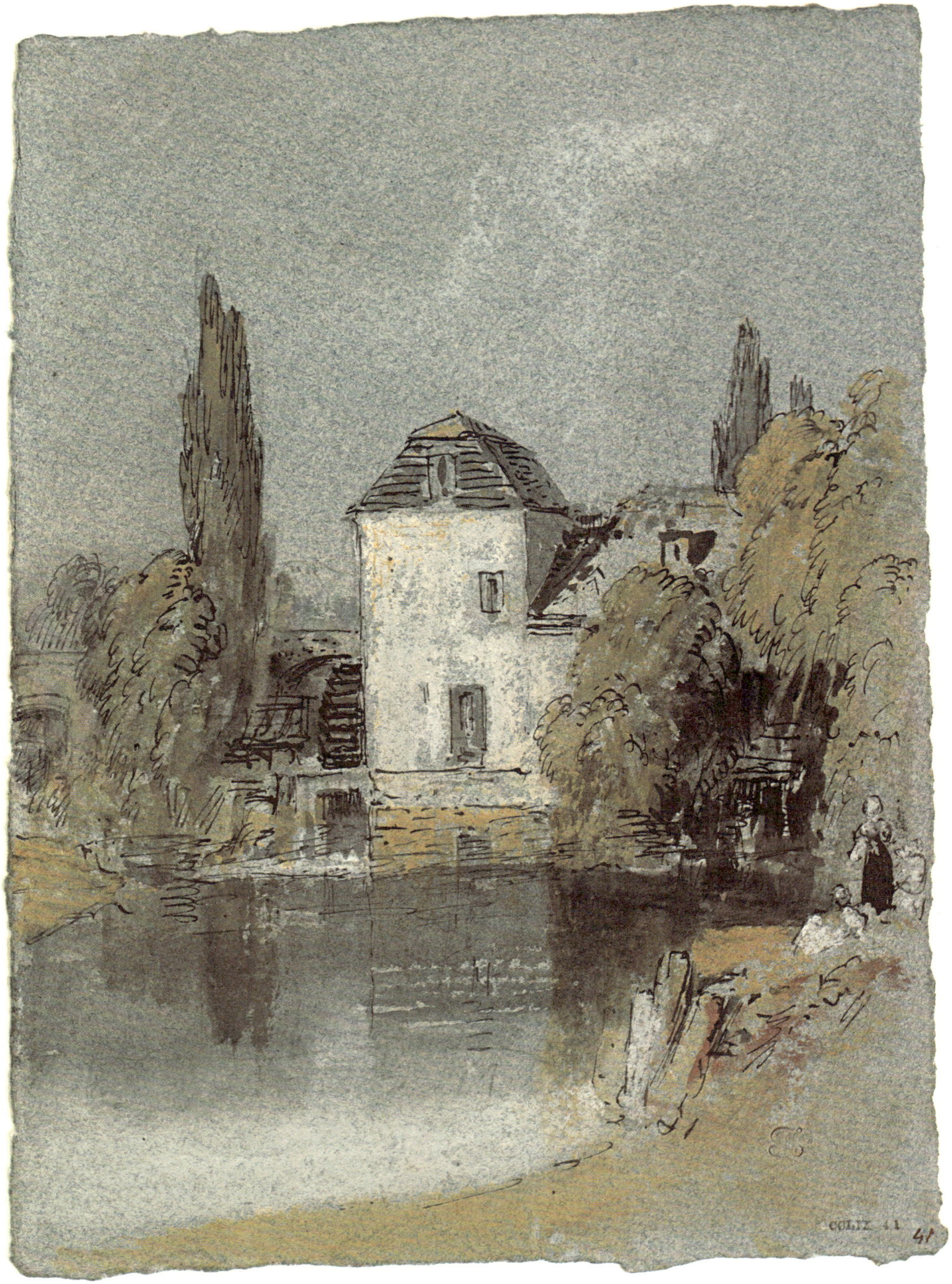

PLATE 122
Fittleworth Mill on the River Rother
TB CCLIX–41 Pen and ink
with watercolour and gouache

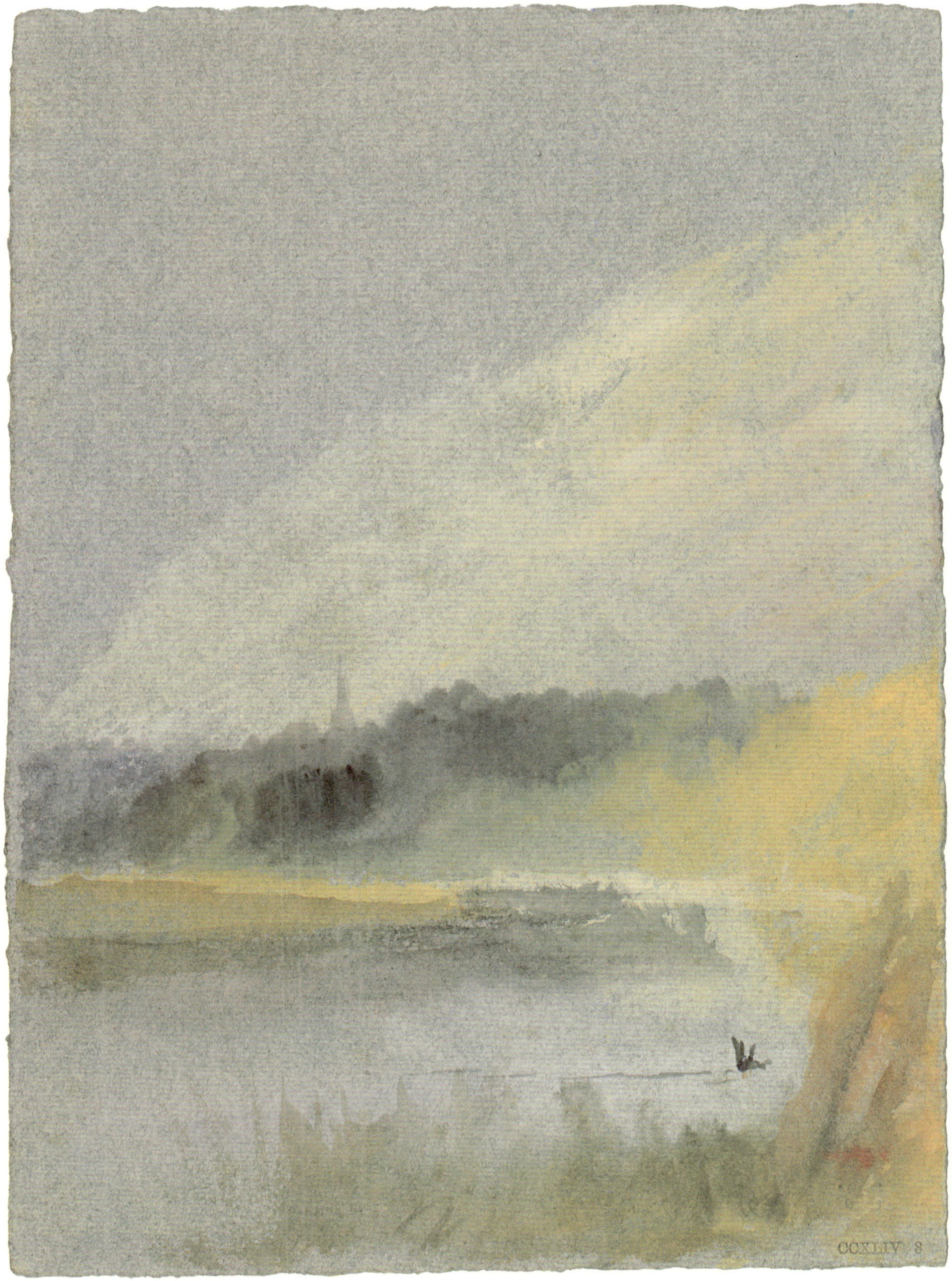

PLATE 123

Petworth Church from the River Rother (?)

TB CCXLIV–8

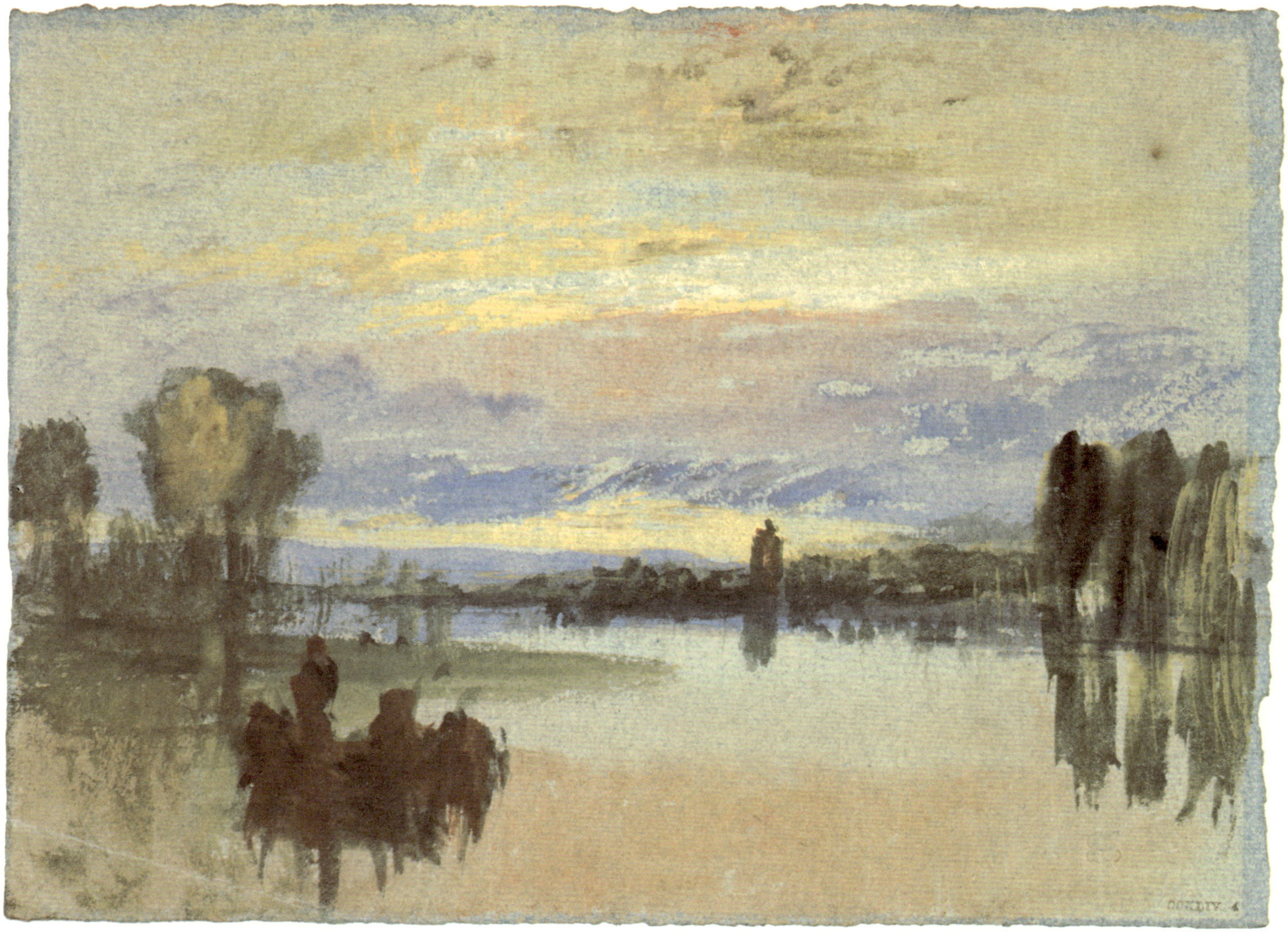

PLATE 124

Evening: a boat on a river with a distant tower

TB CCXLIV–4

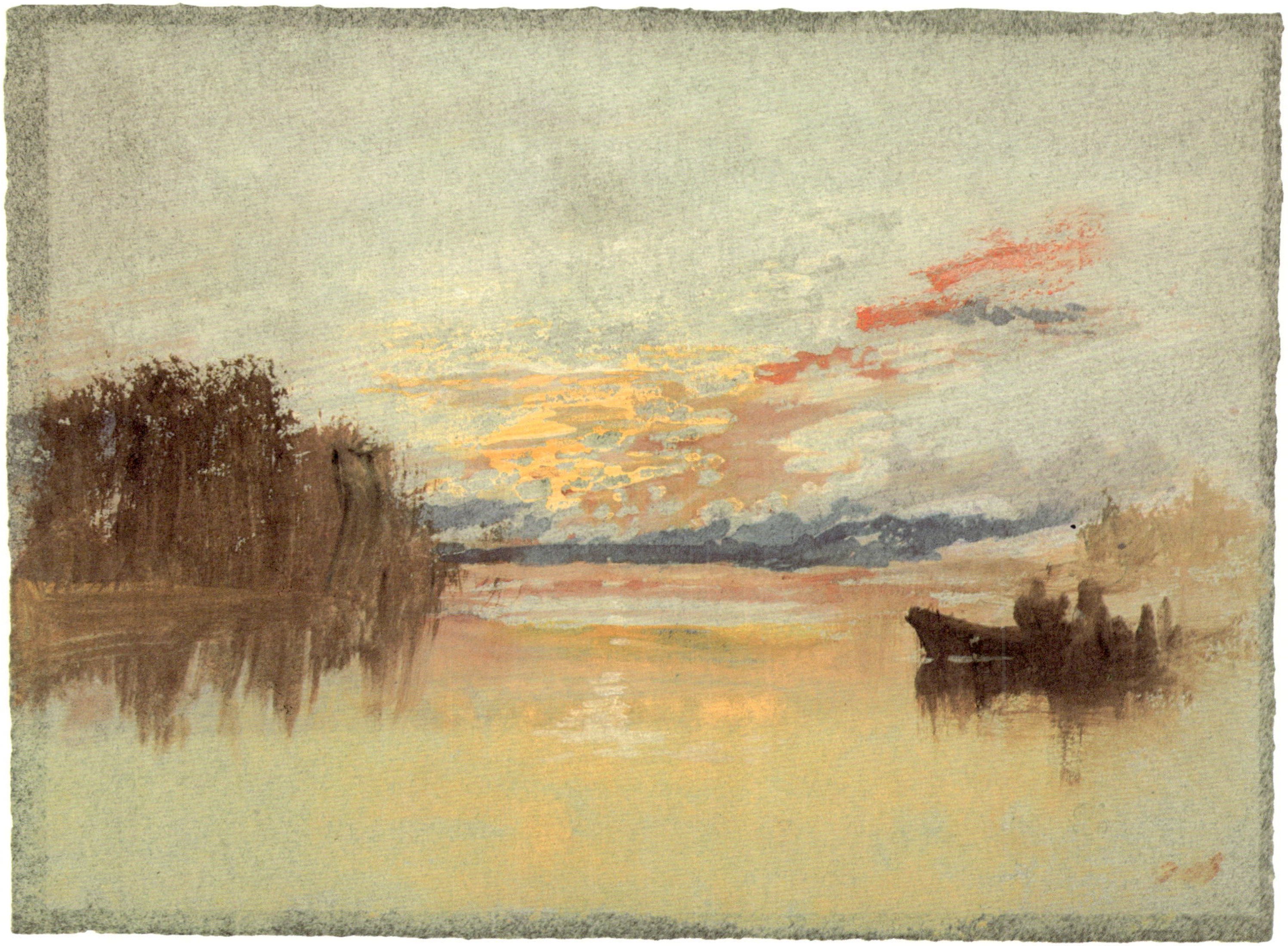

PLATE 125
Sunset: a boat on a river
TB CCXLIV–106

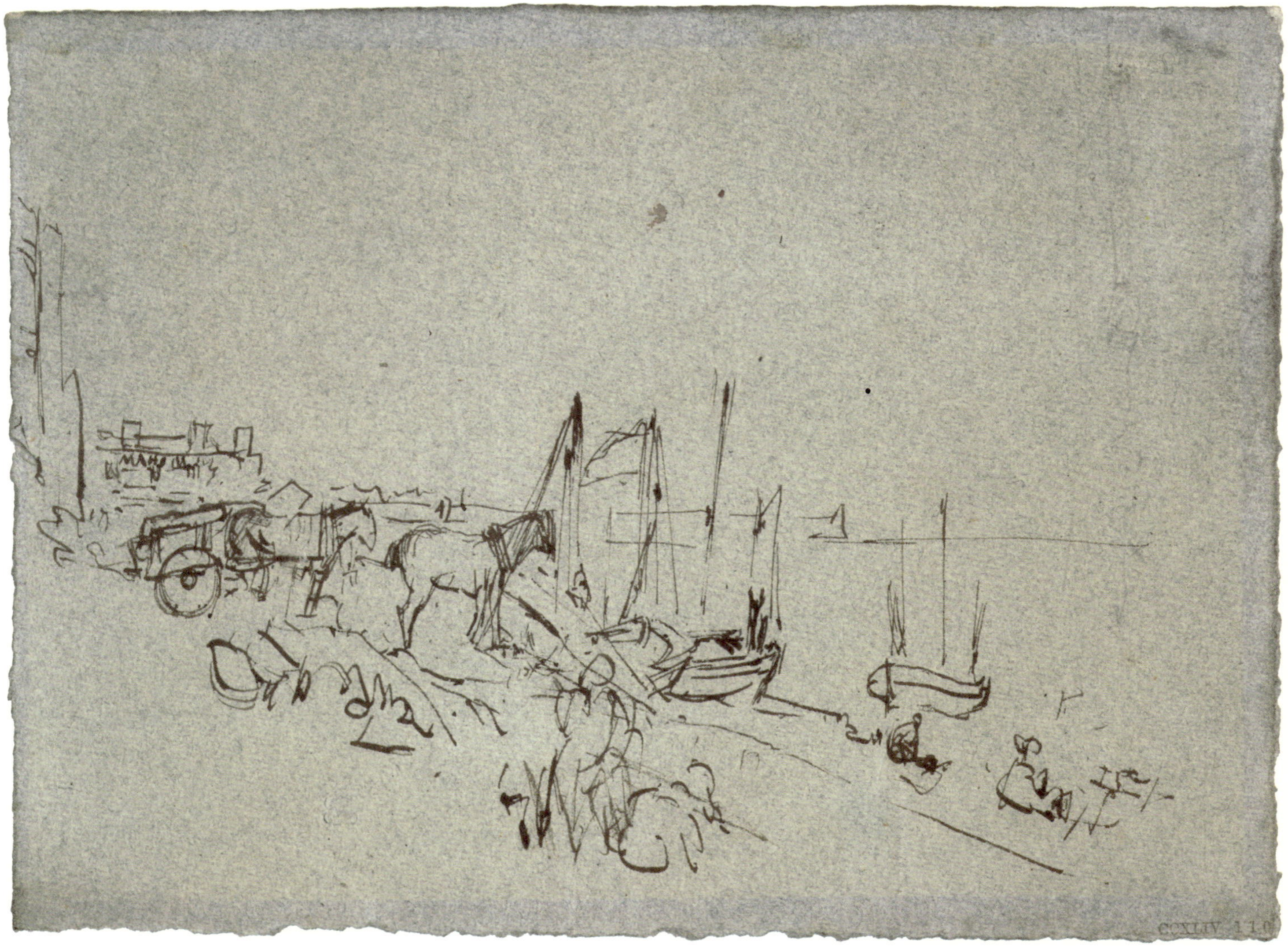

PLATE 126
On the Coast at Brighton
TB CCXLIV–110 Pen and black ink

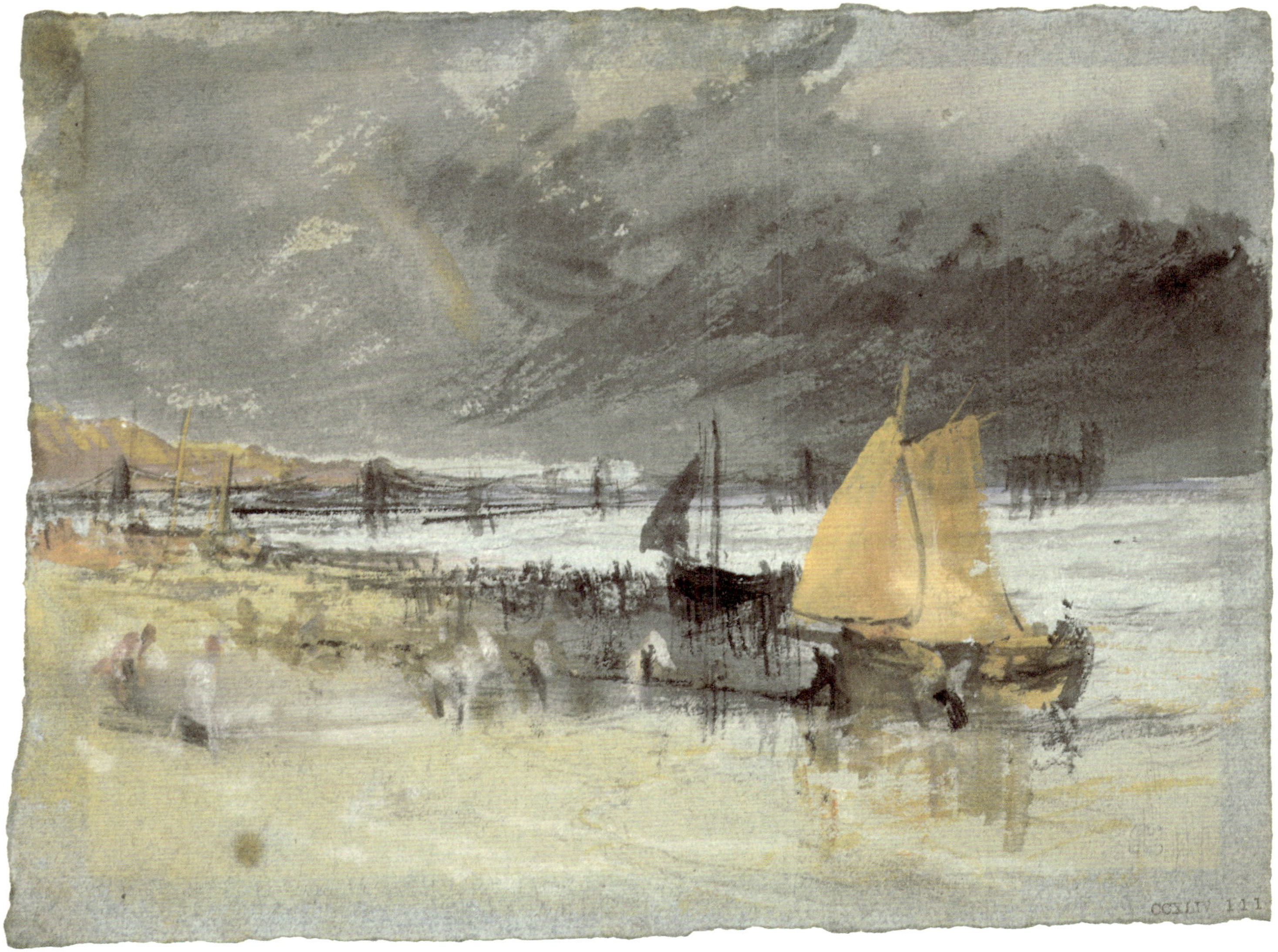

PLATE 127
The Old Chain Pier, Brighton
TB CCXLIV–111

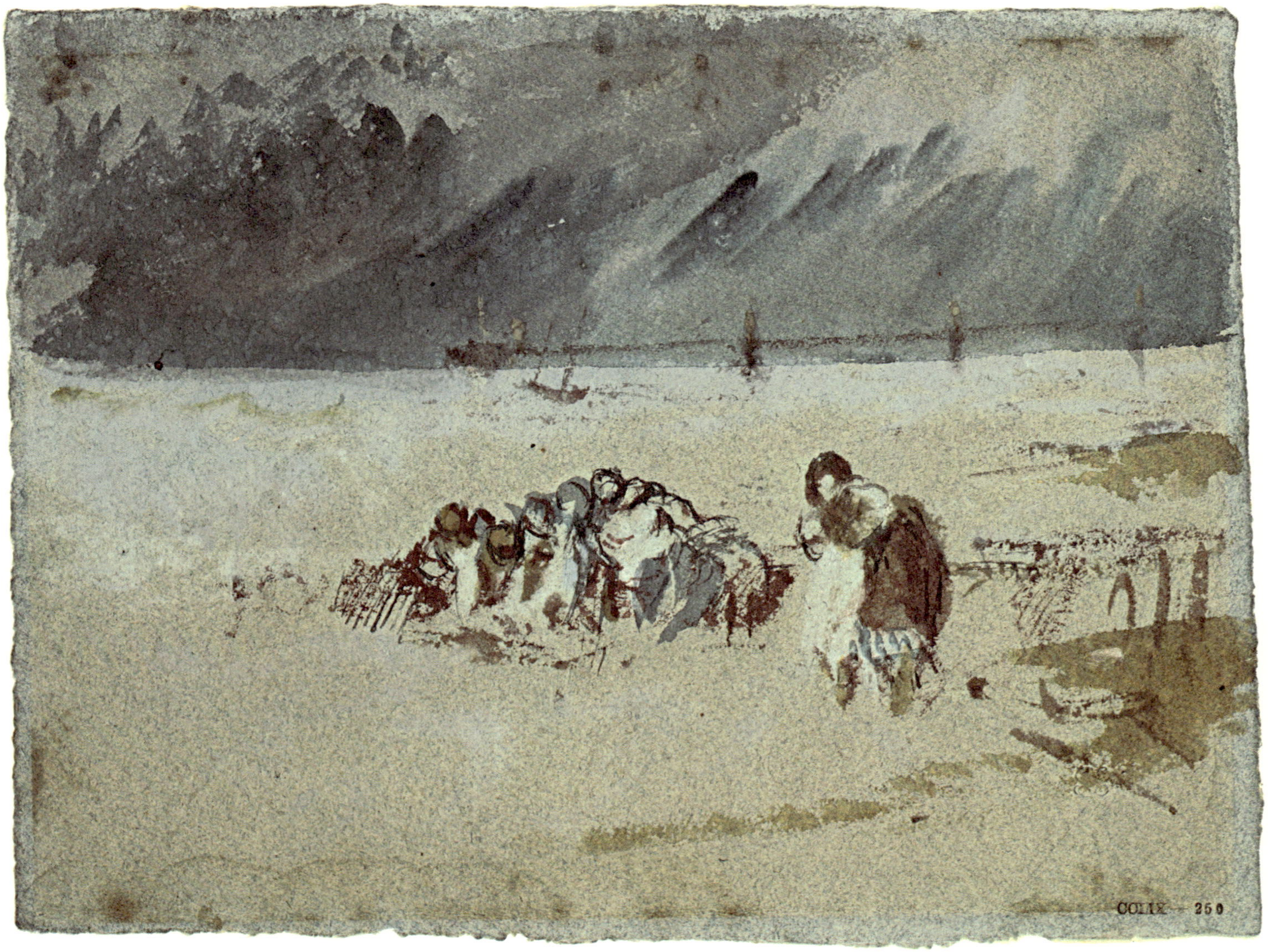

PLATE 128
Fishermen on the Shore at Brighton
TB CCLIX–250

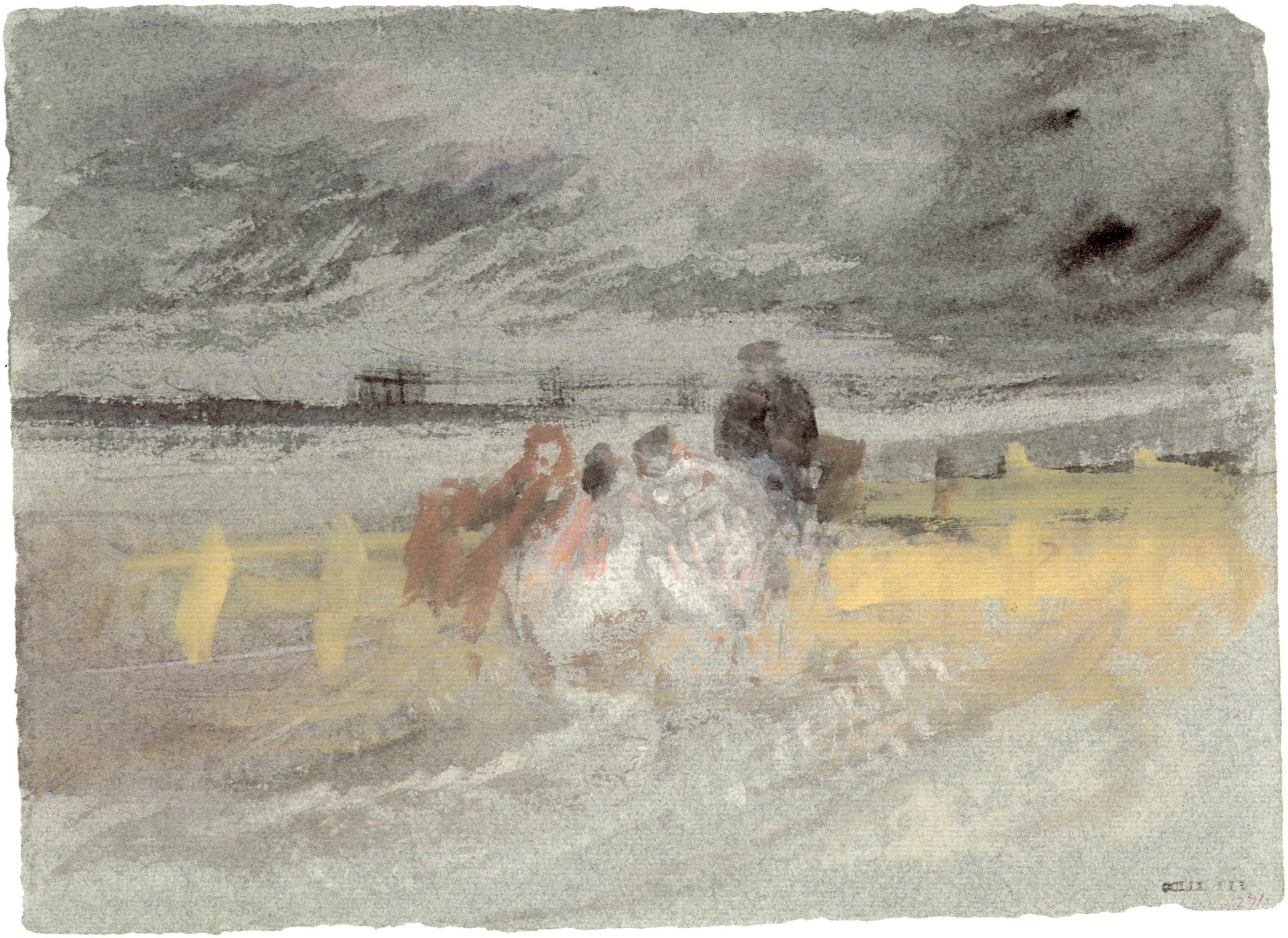

PLATE 129
Fishermen at Brighton
TB CCLIX–271

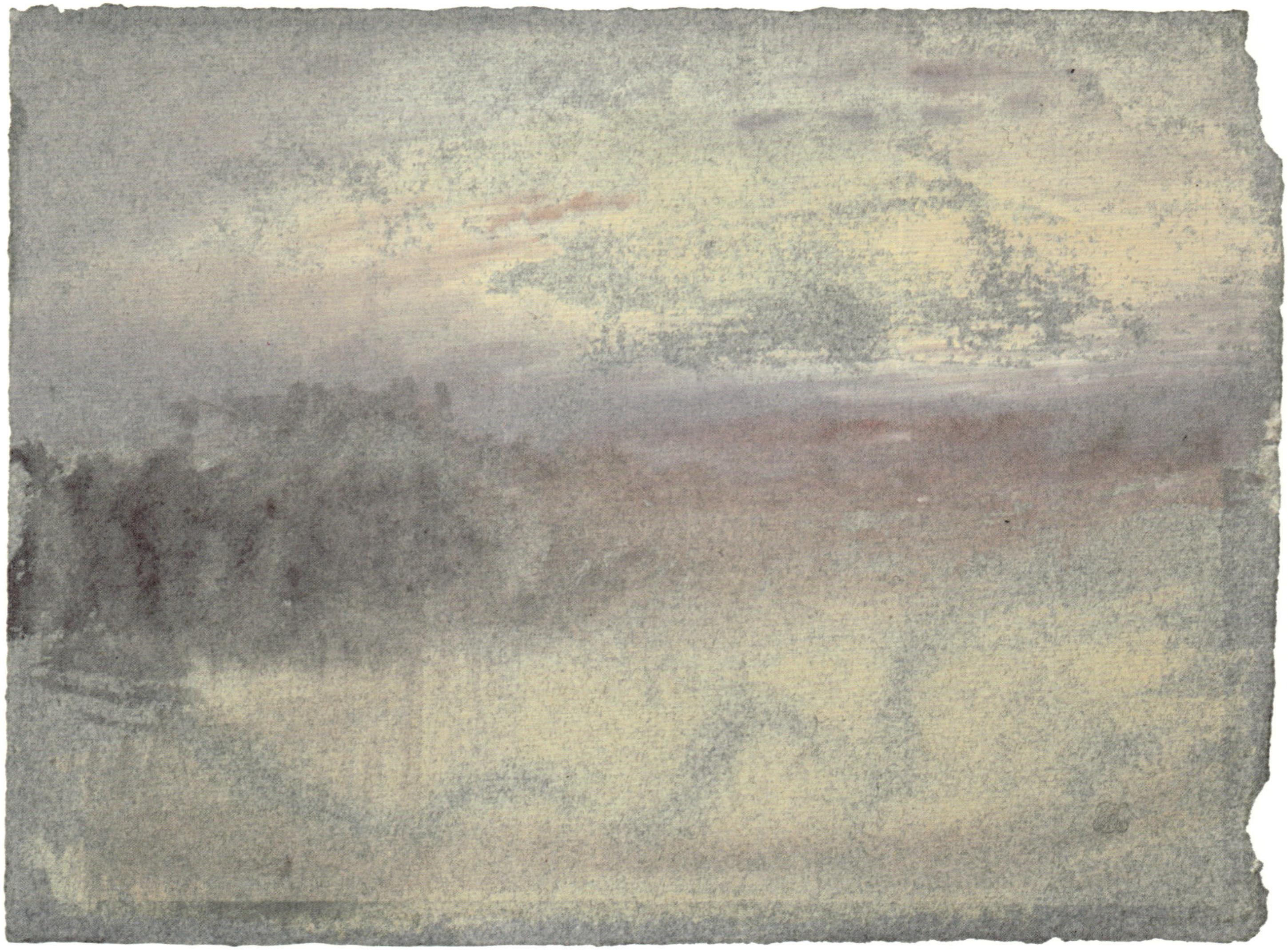

PLATE 130

A River Scene, possibly connected with Turner's drawings of the Rivers Meuse-Moselle

TB CCXLIV–10

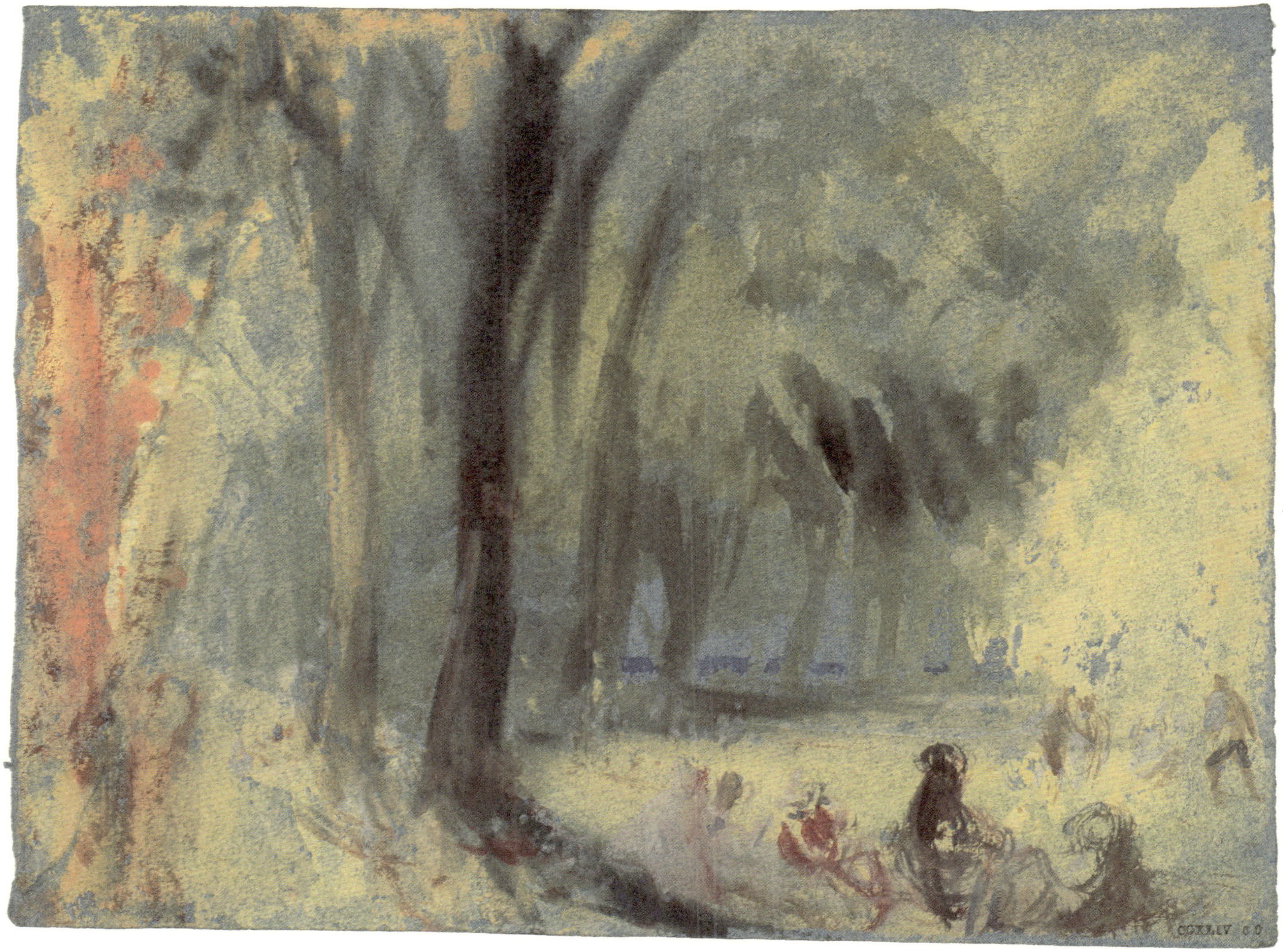

PLATE 131
A Fête-Champêtre: ?East Cowes Castle
TB CCXLIV–60

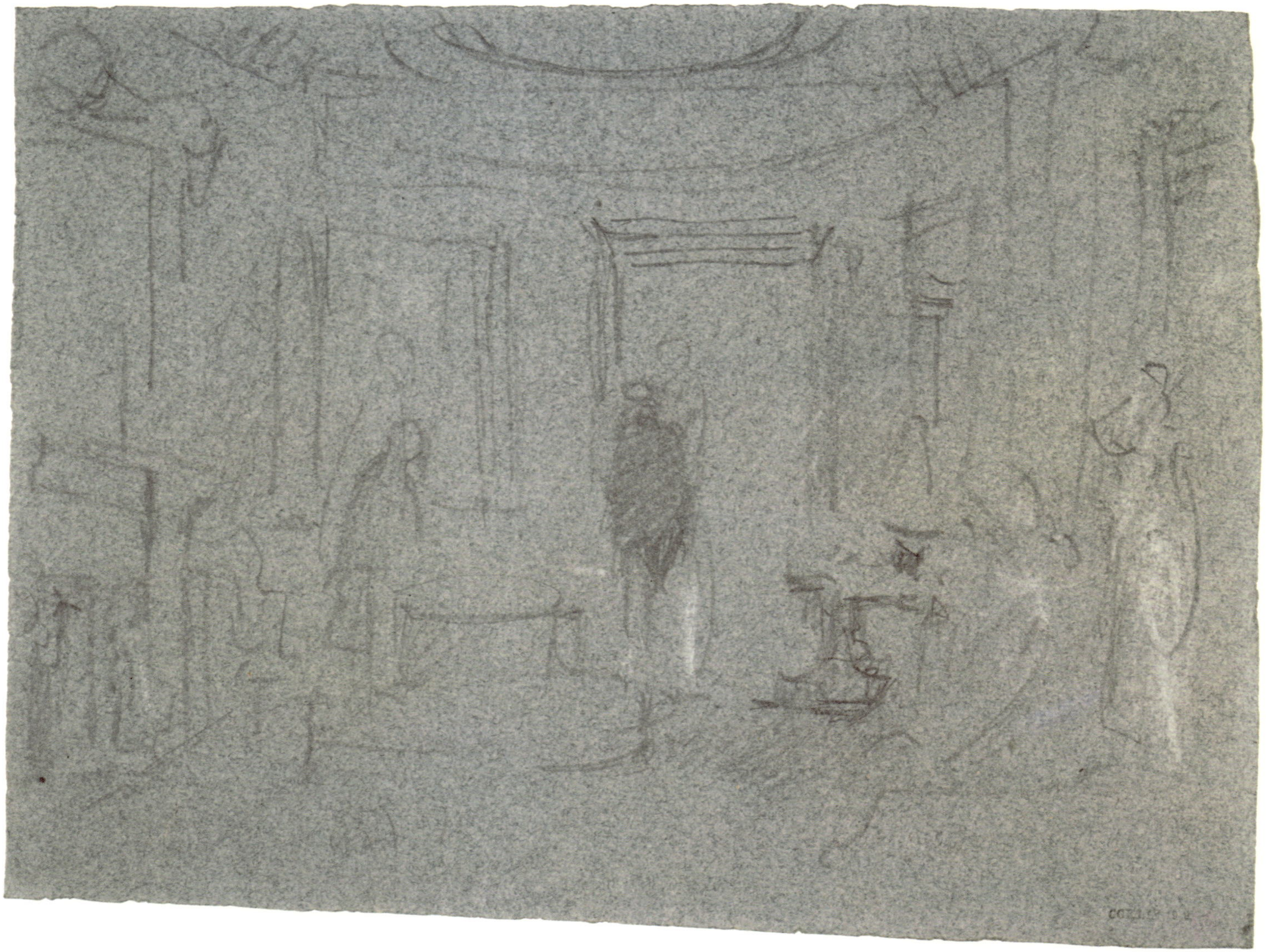

PLATE 132

East Cowes Castle: the Octagon Room

Formerly known as 'Interior, with figures'

TB CCXLIV–99 Pencil and some gouache

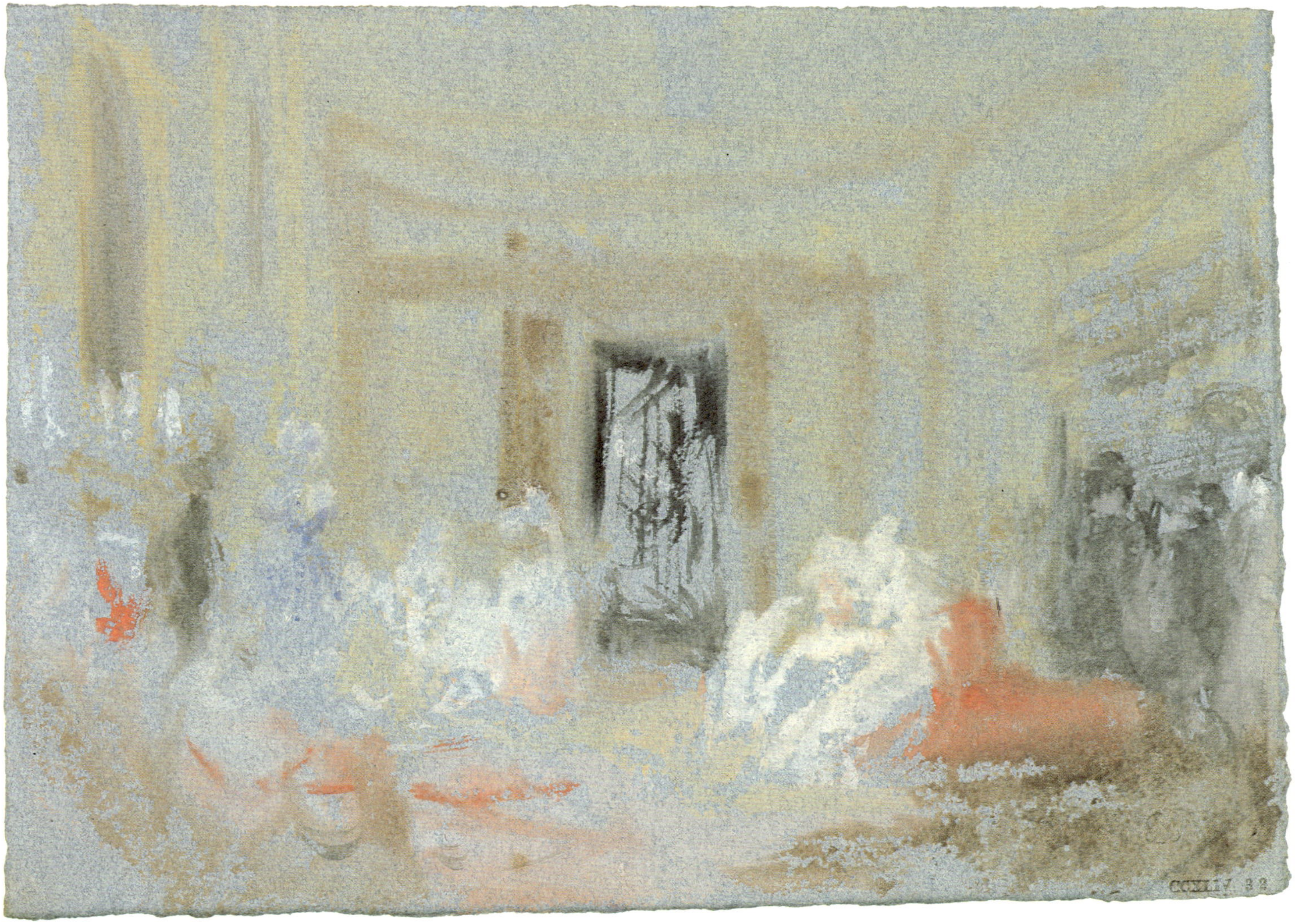

PLATE 133

East Cowes Castle: the Drawing Room

Formerly known as 'The ladies' drawing room'

TB CCXLIV–32

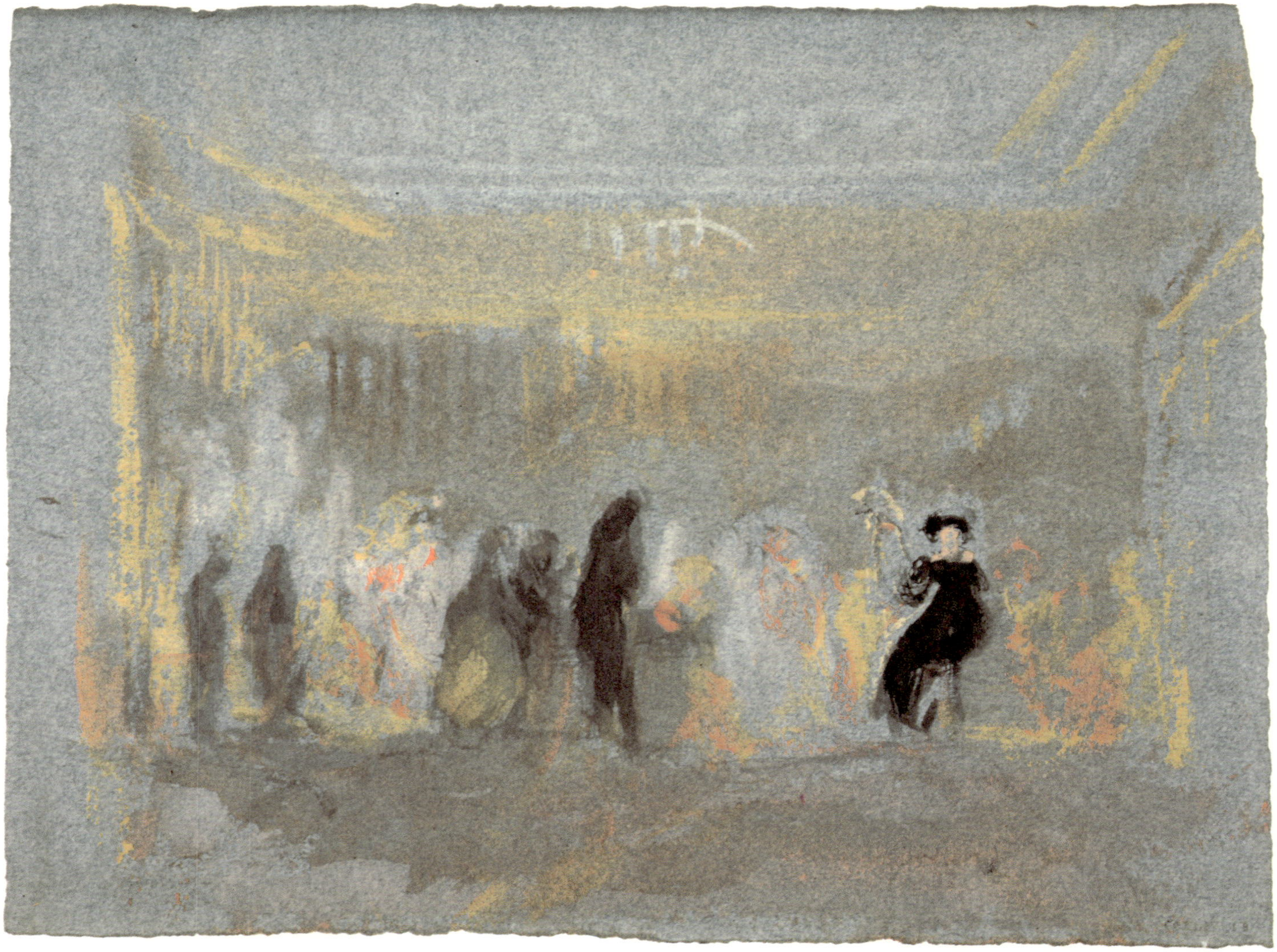

PLATE 134

? East Cowes Castle: music in the Library

TB CCXLIV–43

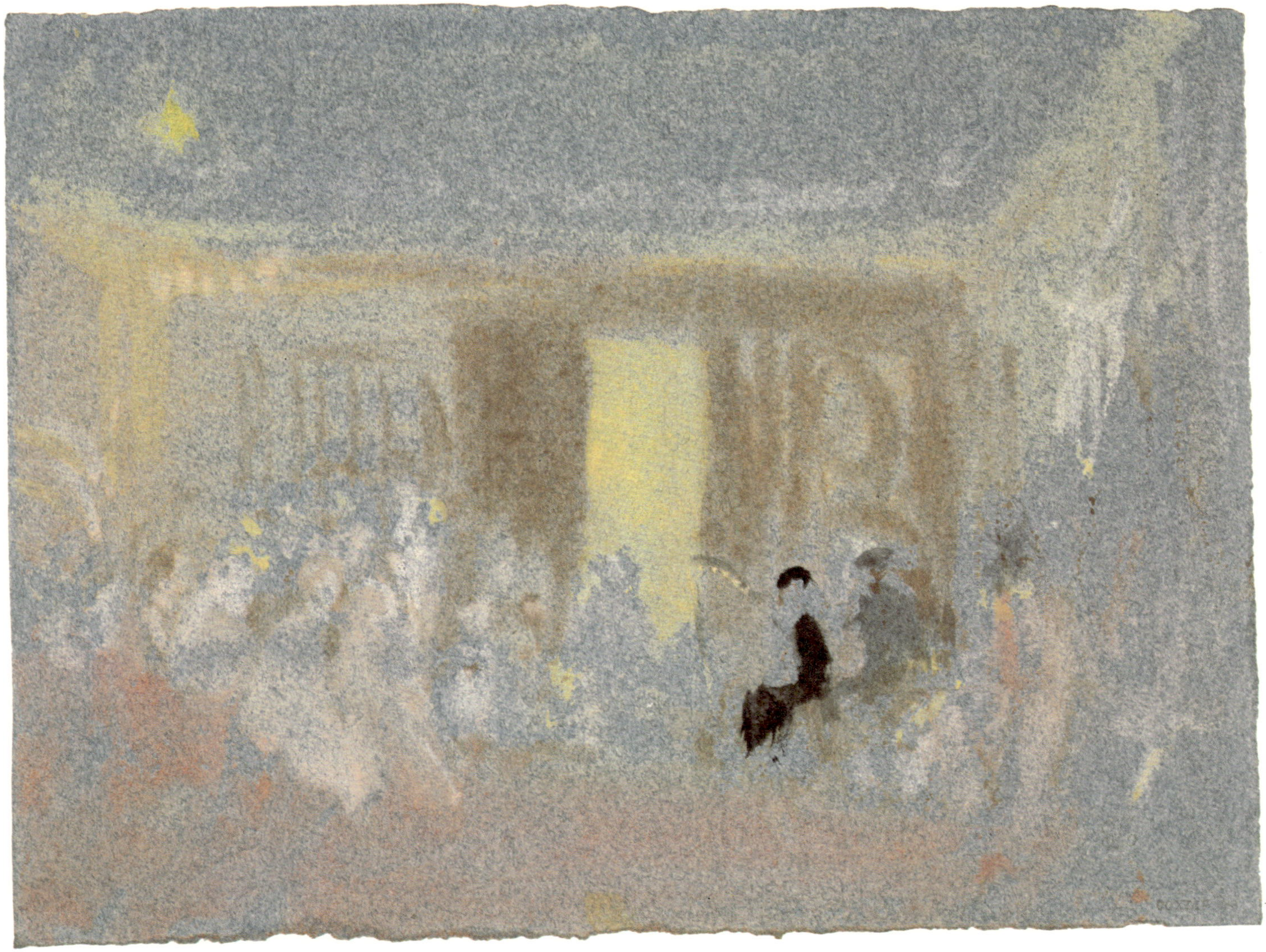

PLATE 135

? East Cowes Castle: music in the Library

TB CCXLIV–28

Bibliography

Material on Turner:

BM 1975 — *Turner in the British Museum*, exhibition catalogue, written by Andrew Wilton, 1975

BM 1977–8 — *Turner Watercolours from the British Museum*, organized by the International Exhibitions Foundation. Catalogue by Andrew Wilton.

Butlin & Joll — Martin Butlin & Evelyn Joll, *The Paintings of J.M.W. Turner*, revised edition, 1984

Clark 1949, 1970 — Kenneth Clark, 'Turner at Petworth', *The Ambassador*, Vol. 8, August 1949, pp. 75–90; reprinted in the catalogue *Turner at Petworth* for the exhibition at Petworth House, June–August 1970

Falk 1938 — Bernard Falk, *Turner the Painter: His Hidden Life. A frank and revealing biography*, 1938, pp. 89–99

Finberg 1909 — A.J. Finberg, *A Complete Inventory of the Drawings of the Turner Bequest: with which are included the Twenty-Three Drawings Bequeathed by Mr. Henry Vaughan*, 2 vols, 1909

Finberg 1910 — A.J. Finberg, *Turner's Sketches and Drawings*, 1910, pp. 126–28

Finberg 1924 — A.J. Finberg, *The History of Turner's 'Liber Studiorum'*, 1924

Finberg 1969 — A.J. Finberg, *The Life of J.M.W. Turner*, revised edition, 1969

Gage 1969 — John Gage, *Colour in Turner: Poetry and Truth*, 1969

Gage 1980 — John Gage, ed., *The Collected Correspondence of J.M.W. Turner*

Gage 1987 — John Gage, *J.M.W. Turner: 'A Wonderful Range of Mind'*, 1987

Herrmann 1986 — Luke Herrmann, *Turner, Paintings, Watercolours, Prints and Drawings*, 1975; 2nd ed. 1986

Hussey 1925 — Christopher Hussey, 'Turner at Petworth', *Country Life*, 19 December 1925, pp. 974–78

Joll 1977 — Evelyn Joll, 'Painter and Patron: Turner and the Third Earl of Egremont', *Apollo*, Vol. CV, no. 183, May 1977, pp. 374–78; reprinted by the National Trust in *The Picture Collection at Petworth House*

Lindsay 1966 — Jack Lindsay, *J.M.W. Turner: his Life and Work: a Critical Biography*, 1966

Nicholson 1980 — Kathleen Nicholson, 'Turner's "Apullia in Search of Appullus" and the Dialectics of Landscape Tradition', *Burlington Magazine*, Vol. CXX, 1980, pp. 679–84

RA 1974–5 — *J.M.W. Turner*, bicentenary exhibition organised jointly by the Royal Academy and the Tate Gallery, 1974–5

Rawlinson 1878 — W.G. Rawlinson, *Turner's Liber Studiorum*, 1878

Reid 1987 — Sarah A. Reid, ' "A Vaulted Hall", *c.* 1835 by J.M.W. Turner: its setting identified', *Burlington Magazine*, Vol. CXXIX, June 1987, pp. 393–94

Ruskin 1903–12 — E.T. Cook and Alexander Wedderburn (ed.), *The Works of John Ruskin*, Library Edition, 1903–12

Thornbury 1862 — Walter Thornbury, *The Life of J.M.W. Turner, R.A. founded on letters and papers furnished by his friends and fellow Academicians*, 1st ed. 1862, 2 volumes: Volume 2, pp. 1–15. 2nd ed., 1897, pp. 198–204

Wilkinson 1974 — Gerald Wilkinson, *The Sketches of Turner, R.A. 1802–20: Genius of the Romantic*, 1974

Wilkinson 1975 — Gerald Wilkinson, *Turner's Colour Sketches, 1820–1834*, 975

Wilton 1979 — Andrew Wilton, *The Life and Work of J.M.W. Turner*, 1979

Wilton 1987 — Andrew Wilton, *Turner in his time*, 1987

Youngblood *Turner Studies* 1983 — Patrick Youngblood, ' "That House of Art": Turner at Petworth', *Turner Studies*, Vol. 2, No. 2, pp. 16–33

Youngblood *Burlington* 1983 — Patrick Youngblood, 'Three mis-identified works by J.M.W. Turner', *Burlington Magazine*, Vol. cxxv, 1983, pp. 615–19

Material on Petworth and Sussex:

Arnold 1864 — Rev. T.H. Arnold, *Petworth: a sketch of its History and Antiquities with notices of objects of archaeological interest in its vicinity*, 1864

Bishop 1896 — J.G. Bishop, 'The Brighton Chain Pier', supplement to *The Brighton Herald*, 21 November 1896

Blunt 1980 — Anthony Blunt, 'Petworth Re-hung: the Restoration and Re-hanging of the Petworth Collection 1952–3', *National Trust Studies*, 1980, pp. 119–32

Cassell 1866 — *Cassell's Topographical Guides, with Map and illustrations. Sussex: its History, Antiquities, and Topography*, 1866

Church Guide — *The Church of St. Mary, Our Lady of Pity, at Petworth. A Short Guide for Visitors*, *c.* 1935

Cobbett 1830 — William Cobbett, *Rural Rides*, 1830

Collins Baker 1920 — C.H. Collins Baker, *A Catalogue of the Petworth Collection of Pictures in the Possession of Lord Leconfield*, 1920

Creevey 1948 — John Gore, ed., *Thomas Creevey*, 1948

Dallaway 1815 — James Dallaway, *A History of the Western Division of the County of Sussex*, 1815

Dallaway 1819 — James Dallaway, *A History of the County of Sussex including the Rape of Arundel and Bramber*, 1819, Vol. II.

Dallaway 1832 — James Dallaway, *Parochial Topography of the Rape of Arundel in the Western Division of the County of Sussex*, new edition, ed. Edmund Cartwright, 1832

Lady Egremont 1985 — Lady Egremont, *Petworth, West Sussex* in the National Trust *Parks and Gardens* series, 1985

Lady Egremont 1988 — Lady Egremont, *Guide to the Petworth bedrooms*, 1988

Egremont 1985 — Max Egremont, 'The Third Earl of Egremont and his Friends', *Apollo*, Vol. 122, October 1985, pp. 280–87

Excursions 1822 — *Excursions in the County of Sussex: comprising topographical delineations; together with Descriptions of the Residences of the Nobility and Gentry, Remains of Antiquity, and other interesting objects of curiosity*, 1822

Goodsall 1963 — R.H. Goodsall, *The Arun and Western Rother*, 1963

Gore 1977 — St John Gore, 'Three Centuries of Discrimination', *Apollo*, Vol. cv, no. 183, May 1977, pp. 346–57; reprinted by the National Trust in *The Picture Collection at Petworth House*

Greville 1888 — H. Reeve, ed., *The Greville Memoirs*, 1888

Gundry 1981 — Doris Gundry, *Petworth: Today and Yesterday*, 1981

Heneghan 1958 — F.D. Heneghan, *The Chichester Canal*, Chichester Papers, No. 11, 1958

Horsfield 1835 — Thomas Walker Horsfield, *The History, Antiquities and Topography of the County of Sussex*, 1835

Hussey 1925 — Christopher Hussey, 'Petworth House, I', Country Life, Vol. LVIII, 28 November 1925, pp. 818–26

Christopher Hussey, 'Petworth House, II', *Country Life*, Vol. LVIII, 5 December 1925, pp. 862–71

Christopher Hussey, 'Petworth House, III', *Country Life*, Vol. LVIII, 12 December 1925, pp. 928–35

Christopher Hussey, 'Petworth House, IV', *Country Life*, Vol. LVIII, 19 December 1925, pp. 966–73

Christopher Hussey, 'Furniture at Petworth, *Country Life*, Vol. LIX, 13 February 1926, pp. 247–50

Jackson-Stops 1973 — Gervase Jackson-Stops, 'Petworth and the Proud Duke', *Country Life*, Vol. CLIII, 28 June 1973, pp. 1870–74

Jackson-Stops 1975 — Gervase Jackson-Stops, 'Wilderness to Pleasure Ground. A new threat to Petworth Park, Sussex', *Country Life*, Vol. CLVII, 26 June 1975, pp. 1686–87

Jackson-Stops 1977 (1) — Gervase Jackson-Stops, 'The Building of Petworth', *Apollo*, Vol. CV, no. 183, May 1977, pp. 324–33

Jackson Stops 1977 (2) — 'Furniture at Petworth', *Apollo*, Vol. CV, no. 183, May 1977, pp. 358–66

Jackson Stops 1980 — Gervase Jackson Stops, *A Guide to Additional Rooms shown on Connoisseur's Days*, 1980

Jerrome, 1976 — P. A. Jerrome, ed., *Tales of Old Petworth*, 1976

Kenworthy-Browne 1973 — John Kenworthy-Browne, 'Lord Egremont and his Sculptors. The Collection at Petworth House, Sussex', *Country Life*, 7 June 1973, pp. 1640–43

Kenworthy-Browne 1977 — John Kenworthy-Browne, 'The Third Earl of Egremont and Neo-Classical Sculpture', *Apollo*, Vol. CV, no. 183, May 1977, pp. 367–73; reprinted by the National Trust in *The Sculpture Collection at Petworth House*

Leconfield 1938 — Constance Leconfield, *Random Papers*, 1938

Lower 1865 — Mark Anthony Lower, *The Worthies of Sussex: Biographical sketches of the most eminent natives or inhabitants of the county, from the Earliest period to the present times; with incidental notices, illustrative of Sussex History*, 1865

Marshall 1795 — William Marshall, *The Rural Economy of the Southern Counties; comprising Kent; Surrey; Sussex; the Isle of Wight; the Chalk Hills of Wiltshire; Hampshire etc. and including the culture and management of Hops, in the districts of Maidstone, Canterbury and Farnham*, 1795

Maude — Alan H. Maude, *The Story of Petworth Parish Church. An Illustrated Guide*

Murray 1877 — *A Handbook for Travellers in Sussex*, 1877

Nairn & Pevsner 1970 — Ian Nairn and Nikolaus Pevsner, *The Buildings of England: Sussex*, 1970

National Trust Guide — *Petworth House, West Sussex*, written by Robin Fedden, Gervase Jackson-Stops, 1978, and revised by Christopher H. Beharrel, 1984

Neale 1821 — J. P. Neale, *Views of the Seats of Noblemen and Gentlemen, in England, Wales, Scotland and Ireland* (no. 47, Petworth House, Sussex), Vol. IV, 1821

Peel 1966 — Hilary M. Peel, 'A forgotten Sussex Waterway', *Sussex Life*, April 1966

Petworth Guide — Leslie Pike, *Petworth, Rural District, Sussex: The Official Guide*, 1958

Petworth House Archives — Francis W. Steer, Noel H. Osborne and Timothy McCann (ed), *The Petworth House Archives*, 2 volumes, 1968, 1979

Phillips 1835 — H. W. Phillips, MS Catalogue of Pictures in Petworth House, 1835, National Art Library, Victoria and Albert Museum, call no. 86.FF.67.

Povey 1928 — Kenneth Povey, 'The Rise of Thomas Sockett', *Sussex County Magazine*, Vol. II, 1928, pp. 38–40

Simes 1830 — S. Simes. *Description of the Brighthelmston Suspension Chain Pier, with a Narrative of its erection, of its opening, of the Tremendous Storm of 1824; and an account of the Presentation of the Splendid Vase to Capt. Brown*, 1830

Simond 1815 — Louis Simond, *A Journal of a Tour and Residence in Great Britain, During the Years 1810 and 1811 by a French Traveller: with Remarks on the Country, its Arts, Literature, and Politics, and on the Manners and Customs of its Inhabitants*, 1815

Sockett 1833 — Rev. Thomas Sockett, *Emigration. A Letter to a Member of Parliament, containing a statement of the method pursued by the Petworth Committee,*

	in sending out emigrants to Upper Canada, in the years 1832 and 1833. And a plan upon which the sums required for Defraying the Expense of Emigration may be raised, 1833
Sockett 1856	Rev. Thomas Sockett, *Catalogue of Pictures in Petworth House Collection*, 1856
Stroud 1977	Dorothy Stroud, 'The Gardens and Park', *Apollo*, Vol. CV, no. 183, May 1977, pp. 334–39
Sutton 1977	Denis Sutton, 'The Magic of Tradition', *Apollo*, Vol. CV, no. 183, May 1977, pp. 320–23
Vermeule 1977	Cornelius Vermeule, 'The Ancient Marbles of Petworth', *Apollo*, Vol. CV, no. 183, May 1977; reprinted by the National Trust in *The Sculpture Collection at Petworth House*
Victoria History 1907	William Page, ed., *Victoria History of the County of Sussex*, Vol. 2, 1907
Vine 1965	P. A. L. Vine, *London's Lost Route to the Sea: An historical account of the inland navigations which linked the Thames to the English Channel*, 1965
Walker 1953	Richard Walker, 'The Third Earl of Egremont, Patron of the Arts', *Apollo*, Vol. LVII, no. 335, January 1953, pp. 11–13
Walpole 1784	Horace Walpole, *Essay on Modern Gardening*, 1784
Wyndham 1950	H. A. Wyndham, *A Family History 1688–1837. The Wyndhams of Somerset, Sussex and Wiltshire*, 1950
Wyndham 1915	M. Wyndham, *Catalogue of the Collection of Greek and Roman Antiquities in the Possession of Lord Leconfield*, 1915
Young 1771	Arthur Young, *A Six Weeks Tour of Sussex*, 1771
Young 1808	Rev. Arthur Young, *A General View of the Agriculture of the County of Sussex, Drawn up for the Board of Agriculture, and Internal Improvement*, 1808

Material on other artists

Beckett	R.B.Beckett, ed., *John Constable's Correspondence*, 1962–8
Boyce 1980	Virginia Surtees, ed., *The Diaries of George Price Boyce, 1851–1875*, 1980
Hamlyn 1984	Robin Hamlyn, catalogue entry on C. R. Leslie's painting, 'The Carved Room, Petworth', in *The Tate Gallery: Illustrated Catalogue of Acquisitions 1982–4*, 1984, pp. 42–45
Haydon 1963	Willard Bissell Pope, ed., *The Diary of Benjamin Robert Haydon, Volume III, 1825–1832; Volume IV, 1832–1840*, 1963
Leslie 1951	C. R. Leslie, *Memoirs of Constable*, 1951
Leslie 1978	C. R. Leslie, *Autobiographical Recollections, edited with a prefatory essay on Leslie as an artist, and selections from his correspondence, by Tom Taylor*, with a new introduction by Robin Hamlyn, 1978
Reynolds 1984	Graham Reynolds, *The Later Paintings and Drawings of John Constable*, 1984

Concordance

TB NUMBER	ACCESSION NUMBER	PLATE OR FIGURE
XXIII–E	D00379	fig. 127
XXVIII–I	D00694	fig. 129
XXX–94	D00759	fig. 110
XC–29	D05531	fig. 17
XCVII–81 verso	D06161	fig. 104
CIX–4	D07515	figs. 3 and 132
CIX–5	D07516	fig. 24
CXII–5	D07761	fig. 122
CXLII–15	D10668	fig. 64
CXLII–16	D10669	fig. 65
CLXXIX–26	D14972	fig. 86
CCVIII–F	D18139	fig. 116
CCXI–42	D18591	fig. 111
CCXIII–17v/18	D18736/7	fig. 131
CCXIII–19	D18739	fig. 123
CCXIII–20	D18741	fig. 107
CCXX–X	D20231	plate 94
CCXXVII(a)–5	D20808	fig. 60
CCXXVII(a)–48	D20851	fig. 59
CCXL–7	D22333	fig. 85
CCXLIII–1	D22577	fig. 136
CCXLIII–76v/77	D22655/6	fig. 74
CCXLIII–77v/78	D22657/8	fig. 71
CCXLIV–1	D22663	plate 117
CCXLIV–2	D22664	plate 70
CCXLIV–3	D22665	plate 90
CCXLIV–3 verso	D41414	plate 80
CCXLIV–4	D22666	plate 124
CCXLIV–5	D22667	plate 120
CCXLIV–6	D22668	plate 119
CCXLIV–7	D22669	plate 73
CCXLIV–8	D22670	plate 123
CCXLIV–9	D22671	plate 84
CCXLIV–10	D22672	plate 130
CCXLIV–11	D22673	plate 74
CCXLIV–12	D22674	plate 95
CCXLIV–13	D22675	plate 43
CCXLIV–14	D22676	plate 35
CCXLIV–15	D22677	plate 57
CCXLIV–16	D22678	plate 8
CCXLIV–16 verso	D40549	fig. 139
CCXLIV–17	D22679	plate 53
CCXLIV–18	D22680	plate 76
CCXLIV–19	D22681	plate 41
CCXLIV–20	D22682	plate 50
CCXLIV–21	D22683	plate 42
CCXLIV–22	D22684	plate 14
CCXLIV–23	D22685	plate 51
CCXLIV–24	D22686	plate 10
CCXLIV–25	D22687	plate 44
CCXLIV–26	D22688	plate 25
CCXLIV–27	D22689	plate 5
CCXLIV–28	D22690	plate 135
CCXLIV–29	D22691	plate 48
CCXLIV–30	D22692	plate 37
CCXLIV–31	D22693	plate 13
CCXLIV–32	D22694	plate 133
CCXLIV–33	D22695	plate 22

TB NUMBER	ACCESSION NUMBER	PLATE OR FIGURE
CCXLIV–34	D22696	plate 38
CCXLIV–35	D22697	plate 112
CCXLIV–36	D22698	plate 39
CCXLIV–37	D22699	plate 9
CCXLIV–38	D22700	plate 31
CCXLIV–39	D22701	plate 18 and fig. 67
CCXLIV–40	D22702	plate 23
CCXLIV–41	D22703	plate 29
CCXLIV–42	D22704	plate 52
CCXLIV–43	D22705	plate 134
CCXLIV–44	D22706	plate 33
CCXLIV–45	D22707	plate 81
CCXLIV–46	D22708	plate 40
CCXLIV–47	D22709	plate 34
CCXLIV–48	D22710	plate 56
CCXLIV–49	D22711	plate 96
CCXLIV–50	D22712	plate 118
CCXLIV–51	D22713	plate 28
CCXLIV–52	D22714	plate 104
CCXLIV–53	D22715	plate 99
CCXLIV–54	D22716	plate 79
CCXLIV–54 verso	D41416	fig. 108
CCXLIV–55	D22717	plate 100
CCXLIV–56	D22718	plate 101
CCXLIV–57	D22719	plate 78
CCXLIV–58	D22720	plate 97
CCXLIV–59	D22721	plate 98
CCXLIV–60	D22722	plate 131
CCXLIV–61	D22723	plate 116
CCXLIV–62	D22724	plate 108
CCXLIV–63	D22725	plate 105
CCXLIV–64	D22726	plate 109
CCXLIV–65	D22727	plate 106
CCXLIV–66	D22728	plate 107
CCXLIV–67	D22729	plate 111
CCXLIV–68	D22730	plate 110
CCXLIV–69	D22731	plate 64
CCXLIV–70	D22732	plate 63
CCXLIV–71	D22733	plate 113
CCXLIV–72	D22734	plate 54
CCXLIV–73	D22735	plate 1
CCXLIV–74	D22736	plate 59
CCXLIV–75	D22737	plate 55
CCXLIV–76	D22738	plate 58
CCXLIV–77	D22739	plate 60
CCXLIV–78	D22740	plate 21
CCXLIV–79	D22741	plate 62
CCXLIV–80	D22742	plate 26
CCXLIV–81	D22743	plate 27
CCXLIV–82	D22744	plate 4
CCXLIV–83	D22745	plate 61
CCXLIV–84	D22746	plate 24
CCXLIV–84 verso	D41419	plate 102
CCXLIV–85	D22747	plate 68
CCXLIV–86	D22748	plate 17
CCXLIV–87	D22749	plate 16
CCXLIV–88	D22750	plate 115
CCXLIV–89	D22741	plate 32
CCXLIV–90	D22752	plate 19
CCXLIV–91	D22753	plate 114
CCXLIV–92	D22754	plate 12
CCXLIV–93	D22755	plate 30
CCXLIV–94	D22756	plate 7
CCXLIV–95	D22757	plate 45
CCXLIV–96	D22758	plate 11
CCXLIV–97	D22759	plate 86
CCXLIV–98	D22760	plate 88
CCXLIV–99	D22761	plate 132

TB NUMBER	ACCESSION NUMBER	PLATE OR FIGURE
CCXLIV–99 verso	D41420	fig. 61
CCXLIV–100	D22762	plate 36
CCXLIV–101	D22763	plate 15
CCXLIV–102	D22764	plate 49
CCXLIV–103	D22765	plate 46
CCXLIV–104	D22766	plate 69
CCXLIV–105	D22767	plate 77
CCXLIV–106	D22768	plate 125
CCXLIV–107	D22769	plate 87
CCXLIV–108	D22770	plate 2
CCXLIV–109	D22771	plate 6
CCXLIV–110	D22772	plate 126
CCXLIV–111	D22773	plate 127
CCXLIV–112	D22774	plate 66
CCXLIV–113	D22775	plate 82
CCXLIV–114	D22776	plate 83
CCXLIV–115	D22777	plate 65
CCXLIV–116	D22778	plate 3

TB NUMBER	ACCESSION NUMBER	PLATE OR FIGURE
CCXLV–24 verso/25	D22825/6	fig. 119
CCXLV–54 verso	D22872	fig. 68
CCLIV–24	D23927	fig. 88
CCLIX–5	D24570	plate 67
CCLIX–41	D24606	plate 122
CCLIX–47	D24612	plate 85
CCLIX–121	D24686	fig. 62
CCLIX–153	D24718	plate 103
CCLIX–234	D24799	plate 93
CCLIX–250	D24815	plate 128
CCLIX–263a	D24828	plate 47
CCLIX–271	D24836	plate 129
CCLXIII–304	D25427	fig. 137
CCXCII–58/59	D29007/D29009	plate 92
CCCXLI–225	D33935	fig. 72
CCCXLI–380	D34102	fig. 73
CCCXLIV–350	D34832	fig. 87
CCCLXIV–392	D36259	fig. 66

General Index

Index of Works by Turner Illustrated or Referred to in the Text

Paintings